bug *con* *rep*

Thanh Phan

Conventional Wisdom

❑ *First Law of Debugging:* It ain't what you don't know that hurts you—it's what you do know that just ain't so. In other words, when you're sure of everything but your program still doesn't work, one of the things you're sure of is wrong.

❑ *Second Law of Debugging:* Testing can only show the presence of bugs. It says nothing about their absence.

❑ Debug the code—not the comments.

❑ *First Rule of Program Development:* A program that does only 80% of the job but works is better than one that does 100% but doesn't.

❑ *Second Rule of Program Development:* The first 80% of a program takes 80% of development time. The last 20% of development takes the other 80% of time.

❑ The sooner you start to code, the longer the program will take to finish.

❑ *Law of Least Astonishment:* The most obvious interpretation should be correct.

❑ *KISS:* Keep it simple, stupid.

❑ Crayons are more useful than keyboards for understanding pointers—draw pictures before you code.

❑ First make it work. Then you can worry about making it fast.

❑ *Brooks' Law.* Adding manpower to a late software project only makes it later.

❑ *Law of Conservation of Program Size:* If you make your code shorter, make your comments longer.

❑ The user is part of every system. When the user fails, the system has failed.

The Usual Suspects

❑ Before you Value :=Value + *anything*, make sure that Value actually *has* a value.

❑ That value parameter should have been a variable parameter.

❑ That variable parameter should have been a value parameter.

❑ read skips white space before reading numbers, but not after. eof won't be TRUE if there are trailing blanks or end-of-lines.

❑ Have an extraneous space? Get rid of the end-of-line. Need an extra `Enter` ? Look for a misplaced readln. Program hanging? Make sure you get past eoln.

❑ Did you accidentally reinitialize the counter within the loop?

❑ To catch bugs in boolean expressions, do go/no-go tests. Don't just make sure it *does* work as is—make sure it doesn't work if < becomes <=.

❑ The loop ended because it reached its bound—not because it reached the goal you had in mind.

❑ If a function that has a variable parameter doesn't have a bug yet, it will soon.

❑ The bound condition while (i <= MAX) and (A[i] <> Sought) will crash when the loop gets to A[MAX + 1].

❑ The bound condition while (Node <> nil) and (Node ↑.Value <> Sought) will crash as it attempts to inspect a nonexistent Value field.

❑ reset puts you back at the beginning of the file; rewrite erases it. Did you reset or rewrite from within a loop?

❑ If you print to an arbitrarily large number of decimal places, be prepared for most of the digits to be arbitrarily random.

for my grandparents,
Molly and Sam Brecher

OH! PASCAL!

OH! PASCAL!

Third Edition

DOUG COOPER

W. W. Norton & Company
New York and London

Acknowledgements

Cover art: Joel Shapiro, *Untitled*. 1980–1981, bronze, 52 7/8 × 64 × 45 1/2 inches (134.3cm × 162.6cm × 115.6cm). Collection of the Whitney Museum of American Art. Purchase, with funds from the Painting and Sculpture Committee 83.5.

Read Me First: Courtesy Jane Scherr; chaos by D. Cooper. **Read Me Second**: Nancy Graves, *Diagonal Sequence of Limb Movements in a Newt*, 1971, collection of the artist. **Ch. 1**: *Arakawa, A+B+C*, 1972. Silk screen on paper, 100.2 cm × 70 cm. Courtesy Ronald Feldman Fine Arts, New York. **Ch. 2**: Photograph by Christopher Fitzgerald. **Ch. 3**: © Paul Miller, all rights reserved. **Ch. 4**: *Endless Dialogue — Part 5* (1977), detail. Laura Grisi. Courtesy Leo Castelli Gallery. **Ch. 5**: Paul Gauguin, *Where Do We Come From? What Are We? Where Are We Going?* Tompkins collection. Courtesy Museum of Fine Arts, Boston. **Ch. 6**: Courtesy Jane Scherr. **Ch. 7**: Peter Monsees/The Record. **Ch. 8**: Courtesy Biblioteque Nationale. **Ch. 9**: Photo by Mike Adaskaveg. **Ch. 10**: Courtesy Library of Congress. **Ch. 11**: Courtesy Michael Bryant. **Ch. 12**: Draft board notice courtesy Kristin Cooper. **Ch. 13**: Reuters/Bettmann. **Ch. 14**: *Dressed for Ball*, 1988, Copyright William Wegman. Courtesy Pace/MacGill Gallery, New York. **Ch. 15**: Copyright Press Features Syndicate. **Ch. 16**: From THE CAT IN THE HAT COMES BACK by Dr. Seuss. Copyright © 1958 by Theodor S. Geisel and Audry S. Geisel. Copyright renewed 1986 by Theodor S. Geisel and Audrey S. Geisel. Reprinted by permission of Random House, Inc. **App. A**: *Jackson Pollack's Mother*. Benno Friedman/PushPin Studios.

Difference Engine: Science Museum, London. **Tuna Helper Creamy Noodles box**: Used with the permission of General Mills, Inc. **NeXT Computer advertisement**: Courtesy NeXT computer. **California Lottery tickets**: Courtesy California Lottery. **Sprint bill**: Courtesy Sprint. **Squares, Cubes, and Roots table**: Reprinted with permission from *CRC Standard Mathematical Tables*, 10th printing, May 1963, © 1959. Copyright CRC Press, Inc. Boca Raton, FL. **Rhind Papyrus**: © British Museum. **Babylonian Tablet (Plimpton 322)**: Courtesy George Arthur Plimpton Collection, Rare Book and Manuscript Library, Columbia University. **Crate and Barrel advertisement**: Courtesy Crate and Barrel. **Spaghettio's label**: Courtesy Campbell Soup Company. **The Jewish Calendar 1993**: Courtesy Israel Museum and Hugh Lauter Levin Associates. **Font box**: Courtesy *Font and Function* magazine. **Wheel of Fortune**: Courtesy Califon Productions, Inc. **Love Connection**: Courtesy Eric Leiber Productions.

Guess what, Kristin!: Illustration adapted from *Decline and Fall of the American Programmer*, by Ed Yourdon, © 1992, p. 79, by permission of Prentice Hall, Englewood Cliffs, New Jersey.

ISBN 0-393-96398-5 w/PC Disk
ISBN 0-393-96399-3 w/Mac Disk

W.W. Norton & Company, Inc., 500 Fifth Avenue, New York, NY 10110

W.W. Norton & Company Ltd., 10 Coptic Street, London, WC1A 1PU

Printing   1 2 3 4 5 6 7 8 9 0

Table of Contents

---

* Sections marked with an asterisk may be omitted or returned to.

Preface

Welcome to the third edition of *Oh! Pascal!* Like its predecessors, *Oh! Pascal!* is an introduction to problem solving and programming. It requires absolutely no background in computing and remains, I hope, interesting enough to be read before the lecture instead of just before the exam. I had a lot of fun putting *Oh! Pascal!* together, and I think that you'll like working with it over the next few months.

When I lecture, I encourage any student who isn't so confident to make a smart friend and to stick by her side for the term. After all, that's how I survived *my* first programming class. When I write, I try to be that friend, and to anticipate and answer questions as they arise. On paper, as in lecture, I rely on clear explanations, non-technical examples, and extensive review to make all students active participants in the class. And, when in doubt, I've added an extra example or *Self-Check Question* to make sure that nobody gets lost.

The third edition of *Oh! Pascal!* is also available for Turbo Pascal. It uses that language's programming environment and debugger extensively and includes a collection of long graphics projects and a great deal of code on diskette. Whichever you use, please enjoy!

Audience

Oh! Pascal! is intended for a mixed audience of general-education programming students and potential CS majors. Keeping them together works to everybody's benefit—the course is more interesting for the instructor, group projects (which I strongly recommend) make better programmers out of the majors, and dealing with some of the issues of writing relatively large hunks of code makes better future managers out of the non-programmers. They'll have to work together tomorrow, so why not get them started today?

Like most introductory textbooks, *Oh! Pascal!* contains far more material than any student or teacher can possibly cover in a single term, so many sections are marked as optional. Runners among you have probably seen race course maps that show a side view of elevation changes along with the traditional overhead view of the course itself. This course map for *Oh! Pascal!* reflects relative chapter lengths, and will help you establish a rhythm for the term:

Course Map for Oh! Pascal!

The major uphills all involve basic skills development: subprograms, loops, arrays, and pointers. The valleys provide a breather and give the student a chance to work on longer programming assignments, and to digest the harder issues of planning and design.

Many students who own computers must still toil on lab VMS or UNIX Pascal compilers. Thanks to the generosity of Willett Kempton and Visible Software, this book's diskette includes a command-line Standard Pascal interpreter, along with all programs from the text. Students who work at home can transfer Pascal programs to the lab and be confident that they'll compile properly (which isn't always the case with microcomputer Pascals). Visible's *Dr. Pascal* programming environment, which shows programs as they run, is available at reduced cost to students who use the bound-in coupon.

Changes from the Second Edition

We're all familiar with parents who, in trying to protect the kids from needless scrapes and spills, manage instead to keep them from having any fun whatsoever. I think the same thing has been happening to introductory programming textbooks. They've become so chock-full of rules and checklists that the fun and excitement are being left out. And I don't think students develop a better sense of 'programming maturity,' or write better programs, as a result.

Nobody wants to return to the bad old days when learning programming consisted of memorizing language syntax. But it *is* possible to teach style, planning, and design without weighing the course down with formalisms that confuse, rather than enlighten. Here are some of the tools this book uses to enliven the presentation and get students excited and involved:

— *Illustrations* have been rethought and redrawn from scratch; it's crazy for computer screens to have better graphics than books do. This is the third step of a binary search:

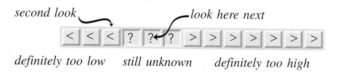

— *Pictures* abound—to make a lesson memorable, tie it to the real world. How would you spot the Fedex charges on my MasterCard bill?

we're surrounded by programming problems!

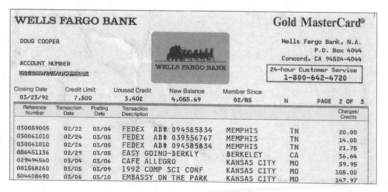

— *Test beds* use a realistic (although nonexistent) programming environment to walk students through hard ideas like parameters:

A is an alias, but B isn't

```
┌─────────────── PARAMBED.PAS ───────────┐  ┌──────── Variables ────────┐
│program ParamBed (input, output);       │  │ First: 4                  │
│  {A test bed for parameters.}          │  │ Second: 2                 │
│var First, Second, Third:  integer;     │  │ Third: 3                  │
│procedure CallMe ( var A:  integer;  {var}│  │ A: 4                      │
│                       B:  integer;  {val}│  │ B: 5                      │
│                   var C:  integer); {var}│  │ C: 3                      │
│                                        │  └───────────────────────────┘
│  begin                                 │
│    A := 4;                             │  ┌──── Uncompleted Calls ────┐
│    B := 5;    {This assignment is local.}│ CALLME(4,5,3)              │
│    C := 6;                             │  │ PARAMBED                  │
│    writeln (A:8, B:8, C:8);            │  └───────────────────────────┘
│  end;                                  │
│begin                                   │
│  First := 1;                           │
│  Second := 2;                          │  ┌──── Input & Output ───────┐
│  Third := 3;                           │  │                           │
│  writeln (First:8, Second:8, Third:8); │  │    1      2      3         │
│  CallMe (First, Second, Third);        │  └───────────────────────────┘
│  writeln (First:8, Second:8, Third:8)  │
│end. {ParamBed}                         │
└────────────────────────────────────────┘
```

Most chapters have been internally reorganized in a way that makes for easier use and review:

— *Strictly Pascal* covers syntax rules and the basic usage examples.

— *Standard Practices* discuss non-language-specific programming techniques; e.g. reasoning about loop bounds or surveying typical array applications.

new chapter organization for easier use

— *Extended Examples* are longer programs that can often be used as the basis of programming assignments.

— *Program Engineering Notes* offer advice, review, and exercises.

— Occasional *Beyond the Standard* sections bring up common extensions to Standard Pascal.

— Periodic *But First, the Issues* sections go into some of the ideas that have influenced language design and programming methodology.

Most of the book has been rewritten, and there are many new examples. Teachers who have used *Oh! Pascal!* already will find a variety of changes:

— In keeping with Elmore Leonard's wonderful advice for writing mystery novels, I've tried to leave out all the parts that people skip. Now it is easier to go further, particularly beyond arrays and records, in the first course.

— The **case** statement and enumerated ordinal types have been delayed and deemphasized.

— *Modification problems* accompany every example program and help students gain confidence in their abilities early on.

new emphasis in the
Third Edition

— *Abstraction* and the separation of *what?* from *how?* are emphasized throughout. Programming data abstractions begins in earnest with arrays.

— The discussion of *software engineering* has been greatly expanded. The limits of certainty in software development prompt a section on *professional ethics* and the responsibilities of software professionals.

— *Loop specification*—separating the loop's *goal* (what we want to accomplish) from its *bound* (why the loop terminates)—has an entirely new presentation. The method is applied to recursion as well.

— Reasoning about program *state* and the use of *postconditions* in commenting is emphasized.

— *Sorting* and *searching* have been given a chapter of their own: *An Excursion into Algorithms.*

— The exercises have been almost entirely rewritten, and there's a wider variety of both topics and difficulty. Please don't jump to the conclusion that the book is hard because I've put a few tougher exercises in, though!

— Standalone appendices discuss topics that are beyond the course, but well within the interest and abilities of many students: pseudorandom number generation, cursor addressing, and the problems of real representation and its implications for arithmetic algorithms.

— *Recursion* gets an entire chapter. However, individual sections can be taken out-of-order following loops, arrays, and/or pointers.

As usual, typesetting the manuscript has let me keep page breaks in midprogram to an absolute minimum. All code was tested from the textbook source using the Dr. Pascal compiler; additional test compilations were passed using Sun Pascal (thanks, John David Stone of Grinnell College) and VAX Pascal (thanks, George Harrison of Norfolk State University).

Tools

This book couldn't have been produced without computers. In thanks to people who *a)* lent, gave, or sold me things either in advance or at reduced cost or *b)* simply produced terrific products, here's what I used. I've added a few additional notes on the process for all you budding authors out there, and included phone numbers for some of the smaller companies.

The text was written with many UNIX tools. I stick with troff (actually Elan Computer Group's eroff, (415) 964-2200) because keeping the book in ASCII makes it easy to use sed, awk, and grep to manipulate example programs for testing and to insert output. ispell (Willisson, Buehring) did spell checking, and Sun's PageView did on-screen PostScript previewing.

All hand-drawn illustrations come from CorelDraw, which is incredibly good even though it runs under Windows. The generic programming environment screen captures originated as Turbo Pascal 6.0 screens, grabbed with EP-Screen (from Legend Communications, (800) 668-7077), a DOS TSR that saves the screen in PostScript. A UNIX shell script then automatically reti-tled the windows, changed the color map for better grayscale printing, and added a custom background.

I did preview scans with a Logitech Scanman 256 hand scanner and final versions with the MicroTek 600Z flatbed color scanner (thanks, Pam D'Amico!). Ofoto software from Light Source, (800) 231-7226, was especially useful for dealing with moiré problems that develop from scanning printed material. Television screens were captured with Hauppauge's Win/TV board. Bitmap images were improved with Image Alchemy (from Handmade Software Inc., (408) 358-1292), which runs on the Sun, and Aldus PhotoStyler 1.1a on the PC.

Raw PostScript procedures produced effects like the KEY graphics and the shaded brackets around special sections. A modest amount of postprocessing on the final PostScript files made everything—EPS files from CorelDraw and EPScreen, TIFF files from the scanner, and PostScript from eroff—fit together. Jef Poskanser's PBMPlus and Sam Leffler's libtiff bitmap tools (both freeware) were great for TIFF to EPS conversions, and for print-time tone adjustments on the duotones.

I try to use the best available tool, regardless of what platform it's on. PostScript and good networking have made this workable. I maintain a single common NFS file system on the Sun and use PC-NFS (from Sun) and GatorShare (from Cayman) to manage the PC and Mac files, respectively.

The huge scanned image files would have been impossible to deal with without a GatorBox from Cayman Systems; it connects LocalTalk and Ethernet networks and translates between AppleTalk, EtherTalk, and TCP/IP. Being able to run an Apple LaserWriter IIg at near-rated speed regardless of the contents of a page has made my life much easier. As you can see below, though, sometimes a mechanical switch is still the easiest way to share an expensive peripheral between different computers.

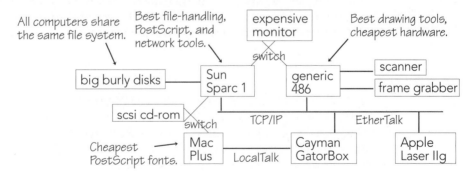

Acknowledgments

First and foremost, I'd like to thank John David Stone of Grinnell College, Iowa. His readings of the manuscript were exceptionally careful, and his comments were invariably accompanied by the details of what I should have written in the first place. I'm sure that he now regrets having rejected my payment scheme ($1.00 for each error found, less $2.00 for each bug missed).

Additional suggestions from George Harrison of Norfolk State University, Virginia, and Roland Jackson of Tuskegee University, Alabama, made their way into the text as well. Thanks also to Dean Lass, Wesleyan University, Connecticut, and David Phillips, University of Pennsylvania for their encouraging comments in preliminary reviews.

At W.W. Norton, my appreciation goes to Deborah Malmud for negotiating a multitude of permissions; to my editor, the indefatigable Jim Jordan, for working through yet another computer book, to Editorial Assistant Jessica Avery for tea and sympathy, and to Roy Tedoff for his forbearance. Copyediting was done by Elizabeth Ahl of SBI in Morristown, New Jersey, and final film was run at Tulip Graphics in Berkeley, CA.

Finally, thanks to my wife Kristin for her draft notice (see Chapter 12), her debugging, and her love.

Naturally, I'm responsible for any bugs that remain. Please e-mail anything you spot to me at:

cooper2@garnet.berkeley.edu

please register this book

I'd appreciate it if instructors who use this text will also take a moment to 'register' the adoption with me at the same e-mail address, so that I can bounce back bug fixes as they appear. Your comments would also be gratefully appreciated.

Thank you for buying this hand-made product.

Small irregularities and variations from piece to piece are a natural consequence of hand work. They are your guarantee of genuine individual production.

To the Student

Hello, and thanks for buying this text (even though you probably had no choice!). I've worked awfully hard to make *Oh! Pascal!* as good a book as possible, and I hope you'll feel that you get your money's worth.

There's a saying that there are only three kinds of people in the world: those who can do math, and those who can't. If you're in the latter group, you're probably worried about this course. You shouldn't be, since it's likely that typing will be more important than algebra. And, oddly enough, it turns out that examples that involve numbers are usually easier than word-oriented problems would be. So please, if you come across to a program that happens to involve math, don't panic. Mathematics will *never* turn out to be the hard part of a programming example.

don't worry so much

If programming comes easily to you, do me a favor: help somebody else. Introductory CS classes are hard to teach and they're usually dreadfully understaffed, so give your teacher and your classmates a hand. Believe me; it will make the course much more rewarding for you, and who knows—you might find yourself writing a textbook some day.

help somebody else

If programming is hard, here's some advice. It's no secret that, for whatever reason, some readers are going to be better at this course than others. The awful truth, though, is that students who seem to get it right off usually read ahead—before class—and increase their lead. If you're in the other group, it's essential for you to do two things:

— First, skim—no matter how briefly—the first section or two of each chapter before its contents are discussed in class.

read ahead

— Second, run *and change* at least one of the example programs when you read the chapter for real.

Not every example is going to make sense to everyone; some of you will think the book goes too slowly, while others will have trouble keeping up. But skimming the chapter and trying out a few programs ahead of time will help ensure that you have the vocabulary you'll need to ask questions, and to understand the answers.

Finally, if you think that something could and should have been presented more effectively, please let me know. You'll find a reader comment card near the end of the book. I hope you'll take a moment now and then to jot me a note as you read the text, then mail it to me at the end of the term. After all, it's not how much I know when I write the book—it's how much *you* know when you're done with it.

give me a piece of your mind

Although computer hardware makes a good photograph, it doesn't tell the whole story.
Old Faithful, hard at work on look and feel. (p. *xxviii*)

First

A Look at Hardware and Software

Why Study Programming?
Graphical User Interfaces and Programming Environments
Some Hardware Terminology ✦ *The Machine Layer*
The System Layer ✦ *The Applications Layer*
Programming Languages ✦ *Standards and Extensions*
The Field of Computer Science

ONCE UPON A TIME, IT WAS POSSIBLE to figure out what something did by inspecting it. That's because the final product usually relied on the everyday properties of the wood, metal, or fabric that it was built out of. A catapult, a loom, a printing press—it didn't matter, because there was a visible connection between the parts of a machine and what the machine did. It was, as Hugh Kenner puts it, the age of transparent technology, when machines were visual guides to their own working.*

Even the first computers gave up their secrets to plain view. You might not understand how the gears are linked together in Charles Babbage's 1822 *Difference Engine*, above, but it doesn't defy comprehension. In Kenner's words,

---

* Taken from Kenner's wonderful book *The Mechanic Muse*, Oxford University Press, 1987 — the only book in the world that uses a Pascal program to help explicate Samuel Beckett.

'the mind of the machine could be observed in its focus on a point of exquisite concentration.' You *could* eventually figure it out.

The age of electricity put an end to that era. Could you hope to discern by inspection the purpose of a toaster or an electric light bulb? The crucial ingredient—the flow of electricity—is invisible. And even if it could be seen, who would anticipate that the same flow of electrons that browned your toast would, if packed in an equally invisible vacuum, supply light instead of heat?

By the time we arrive at the computer age, the prospect of gaining understanding by casual inspection is hopeless. Is it useful to be able to peer inside a computer casing and identify this chip or that slot? Well, perhaps, in the sense that you'll make a better impression at a used car lot if you kick a jalopy's tires instead of its headlights. But to really get an idea of what's going on in a computer, it might be better to look at it the same way I do: ignore what it's built *from*, and learn to see what it's built *for*.

Let's take a look at computer systems. I'll start with a few comments on programming, then we'll look at the *user interface*—what you see when you sit down. We'll take a peek at the invisible layers of hardware and software that make computers useful and close with a brief look at Pascal's place in the big scheme of things.

Why Study Programming?

A few years ago this question would have seemed almost absurd. Why study programming? Why, because the future belongs to computers! You'd better know how to make them work if you don't want to be left in the dust!

Today, the question has become more reasonable. Only a tiny fraction of the people who own computers actually do any programming. For most people, using a computer means knowing how to point and click with a mouse. For the most part, computer users don't *make* the computer do anything. Instead, they choose between alternatives that a program somebody else wrote gives them.

Nevertheless, it's still a good idea to know something about how computers are programmed, and to get some hands-on experience for yourself. Here are some of the main reasons:

— *You can't develop intuition until you have some experience.*

Understanding almost any kind of business or management nowadays requires a feel for the inherent capabilities and limitations of computers. No matter where you look, computers are 'in the loop' of making decisions and getting things done. Computers might represent only a small fraction of total company expenditures, but when the computers stop working, everything else grinds to a halt too.

Try to imagine for a moment that your ability to shop for clothes or food was based entirely on advertising. How well do you think you'd do without enough real-world experience to weigh the claims of New! Improved! Lasts Forever!? That's the spot you're probably in with computers right now.

to gain experience

Now, anticipate some of the decisions you may be making a few years down the road. How long will it take to get a piece of software to work? How reliable is a program likely to be? How plausible are the predictions it makes? How long is it going to last? What performance improvements will running it on a faster computer yield?

Studying programming will help you to understand the baseline rules by which all programs must operate. It gives you a set of first principles for weighing claims about software and for deciding what's plausible and what's not.

> I can *tell* you endless tales of the complexity of software and the difficulty of ferreting out every last bug. But until you have the firsthand experience of struggling with a 500- or 1,000-line program, you don't have any idea of what 'Boss, I'll have those bugs gone by next Tuesday' really means.

to learn methods

— *Programmers use a different approach to problem solving, and understanding it will help you use computers more effectively.*

Programmers use *algorithms* to lay out the steps a computer will take on the way to solving a problem. Now, the notion of an algorithm is hardly unique to computer science, since anybody who's written a recipe has been thinking algorithmically. But if you look at a recipe, like this one from the back of the Tuna Helper Creamy Noodles package, you'll notice something odd: the directions seem to have been extended each time a new problem came up.

a primitive algorithm

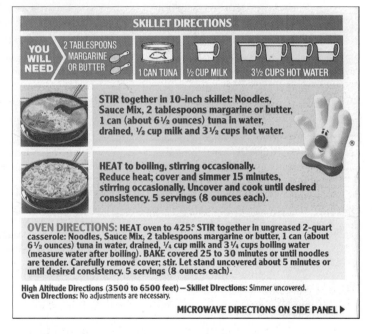

The programmer's addition to algorithmic design comes in the way individual steps are designed—as *procedures* that take *parameters*. A procedure is a general-purpose problem-solving step; its parameters customize the procedure to solve a specific instance of the problem. Rather than having a new set of instructions for each of a half-dozen cooking methods, why not recognize that common steps vary only in specific details?

the key idea: procedures with parameters

```
Mix (Servings);
Bake (Altitude, OvenType);
```

The programmer's approach makes sense when you realize that software plays under a different set of rules than ordinary construction materials. Suppose that once a part was built, it cost almost nothing to replicate? Suppose that once a step was taken, it cost almost nothing to repeat? Suppose that once information was stored, it cost almost nothing to inspect? You'd find that building to maximize the potential for reuse makes an awful lot of sense.

> I can describe the best way to use a computer to solve a problem. But it won't *really* stick until you've had to pull the all-nighter that better planning might have avoided.

to learn tools   — *Although the applications that computers are put to grow daily, the underlying tools of programming don't change very quickly.*

The face that computers present to the user has changed dramatically in the past ten years. Aside from Steve Jobs' necktie, the NeXT machine below is about as far from the traditional IBM character display as you can get.

But the languages they're programmed with—the commands that build computer displays and solve problems—have changed very slowly. Whether the information is coming in via keyboard or mouse click, program and programmers are still making decisions in the same basic way:

if LeftKeyPressed **then begin** . . .

> Is studying human anatomy the same as studying chimpanzee anatomy? Not quite. But a good understanding of where things came from helps you understand where they are now . . . and where they're going.

to make a contribution

— Although cutting-edge work in many fields involves computers, it's usually hard to find computer scientists with expertise outside their own field.

There's an enormous demand in both industry and academia for people with advanced degrees in Computer Science. While the situation has eased somewhat, it used to be common to read that this or that company had enough openings to hire *every* new PhD holder in the entire country! As a result, there hasn't been much need for computer scientists to make new homes—to sell themselves and their abilities outside their own specialties.

One consequence has been that expertise in computer applications has tended to move into other fields by osmosis, rather than by direct injection. A somewhat ironic situation develops: even though advances are being prompted by the application of computers, the methods used to program and manage those computers are outdated and suboptimal. The problem isn't a lack of efficiency. Instead, it's an excess of needless effort—a lack of the *elegance* that comes from knowing something about the classic problems and solutions of computer science.

Even if your chosen field isn't computer science, you may be able to make a significant contribution by becoming its unofficial 'computer scientist in residence.' With luck, you'll be able to bring to bear a sense of elegance in problem solving—not just know-how, but also know-why and know-when.

> Will you win the Nobel Prize for Literature at the same time as you win the Turing Award in Computer Science? Not likely! But you can help both fields by knowing something about each.

Graphical User Interfaces and Programming Environments

Let's look at a few pictures that may whet your appetite for sitting down to program. A computer's *look and feel* is provided by its *user interface*— how the person communicates with it. In the old days, every computer's look and feel was identical and horrible. The original user interface was a *punched card* that could be read by machine. Output was supplied by a *line printer*, a high-speed printing device that could print a full line at a time.

VDT's are video display terminals

Teletype machines, or *TTY*s came next; they were the predecessors of electric typewriters. They, in turn, were rendered obsolete in the 1970's by *video display terminals*, also known as *VDT*s or *glass TTY*s. Although VDT's are obviously more flexible than teletypes were (you can write anywhere on the visible 'page' of a VDT), they worked on the same basic idea: displaying fixed-size characters. Many offices and computer laboratories that use centralized computers still rely on VDT technology.

bitmapped displays

Bitmapped displays, which became widely available in the mid 1980's, provide the current face of computing. When it is blank, a bitmapped display screen looks like an ordinary VDT, or is perhaps a little larger. But when it's lit, the difference is obvious: the computer can turn each *pixel* (picture element), or point on the display, on and off. The VDT is limited to showing characters, but the bitmapped display can show any graphic image an artist can dream up.

With pictures at the programmer's disposal, it hasn't taken long for *graphical* user interfaces to take center stage. They generally rely on using a *mouse* as a pointing device for choosing. Pointing to and clicking on one of the *icons*, or small pictures, in one of the *windows*, or small screens, starts a program. For example, here's how the Microsoft Windows graphical user interface looks:

the Windows user interface

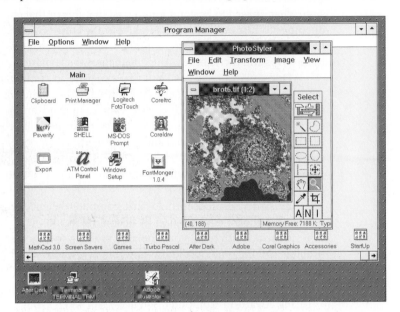

Graphical user interfaces have become the delivery vehicle for something new—a *programming environment* of tools that help the programmer. For example, here's a picture of a programming session taken on a Macintosh computer running the THINK Pascal environment. One window shows the program, another holds output, a third lets us look at the values stored in program *variables*.

the THINK Pascal user interface

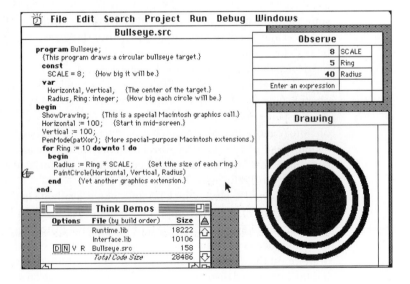

Now, we tend to think that technology runs the show. But good ideas can transcend and transform hardware. The system below (it shows a Turbo Pascal session running on a DOS computer) was taken on an old-style character terminal. The overlapping special-purpose *windows* give me the look and feel of a much more expensive system.

the Turbo Pascal 6.0
user interface

```
 ≡  File  Edit  Search  Run  Compile  Debug  Options  Window  Help
                    ── CONFOUND.PAS ──
program Confound;
  {Comments?  Nope-that would be ═[ ]══════════ Watches ══════════3=[ ]═
                                    Confound.A: 1
var A, B, C, D:  integer;           Confound.B: 2
                                    Confound.C: 3
procedure Confuse (C,A:  integer    Confound.D: 6
  var D:  integer;                  Confuse.A: 5
  begin                             Confuse.B: 6
    A := 5;                         Confuse.C: 7
    B := 6;                         Confuse.D: 8
    C := 7;
    D := 8;
    write (A : 5);    write (B : 5);
    write (C : 5);    writeln (D : 5)
  end;   {Confuse}
begin
  A := 1;
       Turbo Pascal  Version 6.0  Copyright (c) 1983,90 Borlan
              1       2        3       4
              5       6
 F1 Help  F7 Trace  F8 Step  ◄┘ Edit  Ins Add  Del Delete  F10 Menu
```

Programming environments have made learning to program much easier. Back in the days of punched cards and line printers, testing a program was an overnight affair. You'd drop off your program at the computer center, then come back the next day to find out if it had run. In contrast, a system like Dr. Pascal, shown below, literally opens a window into the program as it executes—even on old-style character terminals:

the Dr. Pascal user
interface

```
■:Freeze ■:Less delay ■:More delay
Confound->Confuse
 ┌ Confound ─────────────────────────
     D := 4;                          A=███1  B=███2  C=███3  D=███6
     write (A : 10);
     write (B : 10);
     write (C : 10);
     write (D : 10);
     writeln;
     Confuse (B, A, D);
 ┌ Confuse ──────────────────────────
     begin                            ( C=███7  A=███5  B=███6 ) D=███8
       A := 5;
       B := 6;
       C := 7;
       D := 8;
       write (A : 10);
       write (B : 10);


              1         2        3       4
              5         6
```

Dr. Pascal is a good learning environment because it runs Standard Pascal and is consistent across platforms; you'll see the same user interface on DOS, Apple, and VAX computers, even though their hardware is very different. The disk that comes with this book includes a demonstration of the environment in operation, as well as a standalone, command-line version of their interpreter (a program that lets you run programs).*

Some Hardware Terminology

Now, when you first inspect a computer it's only natural to focus on its physical components, or *hardware*. Every computer has, more or less, the same parts:

— A *central processing unit*, or *CPU*, that performs calculations. Its speed is measured in *MIPS*, or millions of instructions per second. A desktop computer is likely to range from .5 to 5 MIPS, while the most powerful general-purpose computers range well into the hundreds of MIPS.

— *Random access memory*, or *RAM*, that holds programs while they're being run. Its size is given in *megabytes*, or millions of *bytes* (which I'll define in a moment). A desktop computer is liable to have just a few megabytes of RAM, while more powerful computers may have dozens or even (when they have special applications) hundreds of megs.

basic hardware

— A *hard disk* that permanently stores information. Disk capacity is also given in megabytes; it's accurate to think of each byte as being equivalent to a single stored character. A desktop computer might have somewhere between 10 and 100 megabytes of hard disk storage, or the ability to store between ten and one hundred million characters. For comparison, this book has about 1.5 million characters.

— Drives for *removable media*, like floppy diskettes and tapes, that make it easy to transfer information (including programs) from one computer to another. Desktop computers generally work with removable diskettes that hold from .3 to nearly 1.5 megabytes.

— Different kinds of *input* devices, like a keyboard and/or a mouse, and *output* devices, like a printer and a monitor.

Knowing all these numbers is, somehow, comforting. But although computer hardware makes a good photograph (like the one of my desk at the start of this chapter), it doesn't tell the whole story. That's why I'm leaving out the nearly mandatory textbook photo of a computer's innards.

basic software

A computer's real power depends on its *software*, or programs. If I could somehow X-ray each machine to make its software visible, you'd see the MS-DOS operating system and a couple hundred other programs on the computer I use for programming and making pictures, the UNIX operating systems and a couple *thousand* other programs on the computer I use to write and to preview

---

* Incidentally, Visible Software has no business relationship with me or W.W. Norton. They were nice enough to *a*) prepare the command-line interpreter and *b*) let us give it away. We're more than happy to recommend their Dr. Pascal environment, since it's a great tool for doing exercises in this course.

output, and just one program—a processor for a language called PostScript—on the printer. (As it happens, the printer uses the same CPU as many Apple Macintosh computers.)

When I look at a computer system, I usually makes sense of the many kinds of hardware and software by splitting them into *layers.* Here's a software 'picture:'

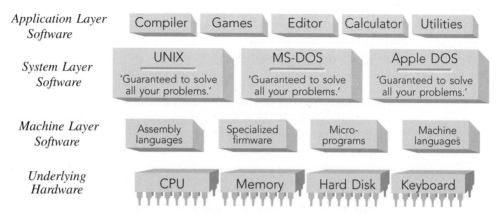

I've obviously taken some artistic license by showing every piece of hardware as a *chip*—a little plastic package that hides an integrated circuit (like the CPU) and has tiny wires sticking out of it. However, that's basically the way that I think about hardware. As long as the wires can be plugged in properly, I can use software to make a system work. I might have to worry about the physical connections *between* parts, but not about the inner workings *of* parts.

Hardware is the bedrock of every computer system. Its strength ultimately determines what can be built above. But hardware, like bedrock, is hidden beneath layer upon layer of software. This layering turns out to be a great scheme because it lets us ignore what we can't see. As long as the top layer meets our needs, we usually don't have to worry about what it conceals.

This book ignores hardware and most of the layers of software as well. But because we're all sometimes like the Princess—no matter how many layers shield us from the pea, it can still make us miserable—let's take a brief look down below.

The Machine Layer

Software at the bottom level—the *machine layer*—is closely tied to specific hardware. It takes two basic forms:

— *Machine language* instructions are built into the computer, just like the + and − keys are built into hand calculators. Machine language is a *binary* code of zeros and ones. It's sometimes called the *first generation* computer language.

— *Assembly language* instructions use brief English-like *mnemonics* that carry out slightly more complicated operations, and are much easier to remember. Assembly language is sometimes called the *second generation* computer language.

In early computers, there was a clear distinction between machine and assembly languages. In fact, you had to run a special program, called an *assembler*, to translate assembly language into machine language.

Nowadays the distinction is becoming blurred by computers whose machine language, for all practical purposes, actually *is* an assembly language. This magic is accomplished by hiding small translation programs in the CPU itself. In effect, requesting an assembly language command tells the CPU to run a *microcoded* program—a machine language program that is built into the CPU. Such programs are sometimes called *firmware*. They're not built out of hardware, but they are permanently loaded into the computer soon after it's manufactured.

firmware and microcode
are embedded in
hardware

This system is convenient for the people who design and manufacture CPU's. Suppose that a CPU is redesigned. It's easier to rewrite just one program and change the way that microcode *emulates* or carries out an assembly language command, than it is to throw away all existing assembly language programs.

If you reflect for a moment, you'll see why I say that software comes in layers. From above, the machine layer is usually *defined* as the collection of assembly language commands that all 'higher'-level software will use to operate the computer. Programmers can work to this definition even before the hardware is ready. From below, machine layer software is *implemented*, or made to work, by hidden, extremely CPU-specific machine languages that are permanently loaded into the CPU as part of the final manufacturing process.

layers separate what?
from how?

> We'll find that this separation of *what it does* from *how it does it* is one of the recurring themes of working with software.

The System Layer

The software you use at the machine layer isn't really a consumer decision. For all intents and purposes, assembly language is built into the computer. But although machine layer software can control everything the computer does, few people want to spend time giving machine layer instructions. Instead, we rely on a second layer of software, called the *system layer*, to take care of details for us.

The system layer's main feature is a constantly running program called the *operating system*. It's the first program that's installed on a computer, and it usually starts automatically whenever the computer is turned on. The operating system keeps track of the computer's resources—terminals, printers, storage devices, access to memory and the CPU, and so on. As far as we're concerned, the operating system controls the computer. Its jobs can include:

— 'Listening' to a keyboard or mouse for input and 'talking' to the screen or to a printer.

— Interpreting the meaning of commands as they're typed or letting the user know that it can't figure them out.

— Making stored programs available to the user and letting her install new ones.

— Storing information in *files* and letting users inspect or change files.

— Controlling access to the computer, especially on multi-user systems, by requiring login names and passwords.

— Automatically splitting the CPU's attention between different jobs, say, so that the computer doesn't grind to a halt every time a file gets printed.

— Communicating with other computers via electronic *network* connections.

Operating systems vary in subtle and not so subtle ways. One system might be limited to a single user, while another allows *timesharing*, so that many users can share a single computer. One operating system could be oriented toward keyboard input, while another relies more heavily on a *graphical interface*, which is a fancy way of saying that you use a mouse more often than you type.

There are many different operating systems, and you're liable to come into contact with more than one as you continue to use computers. Three of the most common are UNIX, MS-DOS, and the Macintosh System and Finder.

UNIX

Among computer scientists and Computer Science departments, UNIX is the most widely used system. That's partly because UNIX is designed to let many users, or many jobs from one user, run at once. It's also because several hundred programs, for every conceivable purpose, are invariably installed as part of the UNIX system. It's also because the original code of the programs (including the operating system itself) is usually available, and can be studied or customized.

MS-DOS

MS-DOS is probably the most widely used system in the consumer world. It's a very small system, meant for single users on 'personal' computers, that comes with almost no software beyond the bare minimum required to get started. In many ways, MS-DOS is a poor imitation of UNIX. Its advantage is that it will run on very small, cheap computers; its disadvantage is that it doesn't run any better on machines that have greater capabilities (although the latest versions are taking steps in the right direction).

Apple Macintosh operating systems

The Apple Macintosh operating systems fall roughly in the middle. A great deal of software is built into the system, and it's very much oriented toward the sort of graphical interface that used to be reserved for high-priced research computers. But as usual, there's a tradeoff involved: we get the benefit of Apple software at the cost of having to buy Apple equipment.

There are other systems, of course. I'll mention just one: VMS is the 'vanilla' operating system of Digital Equipment Corporation computers, and is very widely used on college campuses. But the other three are the most likely candidates if you ever buy your own computer.

Good ideas fly from system to system with dizzying speed. For example, Microsoft's Windows bills itself as an operating system, but it's really just a fancy *front end*—another way to say user interface—to MS-DOS. Microsoft and Apple are locked in massive legal combat over who 'owns' basic ideas like overlapping, resizable windows and pull-down menus—ideas that were first put into practice at places like Xerox's Palo Alto Research Center years ago.

'vanilla' means 'standard, but not exciting'

You will find, if you ever have occasion to buy software, that your choice of operating system is the most significant determinant of what you can buy. The software shelf is often marked with the name of an operating system, rather than with a particular manufacturer's CPU or hardware. That's because as programs become increasingly sophisticated, they rely on the standards imposed by an operating system, rather than dealing with the hardware directly.

The Applications Layer

But I'm drifting into the outermost software layer—the *applications layer*. Application programs are run to do specific jobs—calculate taxes, play *Leisure Suit Larry*, build a spreadsheet for financial scheming, or even prepare new programs to run as applications. Application programs are like kitchen appliances. Some appliances, like the can opener, do just one job, but do it extremely well. Others, like food processors, attempt to be all things to all cuisines.

tools vs. systems

Application programs, too, can be either special-purpose tools or all-encompassing systems. For example, when I wrote this book, I used entirely separate programs to create the original text, check spelling, format pages, draw, print each chapter, and so on. However, if I wanted to, I could have used a 'food processor'—a full-fledged book composition system that has all the tools built into one humungous program—instead.

a consumer's world view

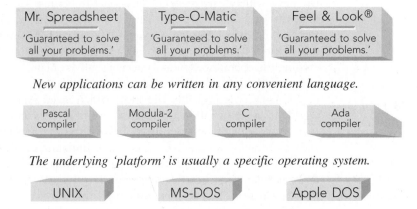

New applications can be written in any convenient language.

The underlying 'platform' is usually a specific operating system.

In general, you can choose between special-purpose tools and general purpose environments. For every company that sells a text editor or formatter, there's another company hawking a 'word processor' that claims to do both. But as always, there's a tradeoff. All-purpose environments are usually easiest to get up and running, since all the pieces have already been fit together. On the other hand, they're not adaptable; it's hard, if not impossible, to replace just one part of the system with an improved program.

Many (but not all) Pascal systems have a foot in each camp. At heart, just one program—the *compiler*, which translates English programs into an *executable* form the computer can run—is essential. You can run the compiler as an ordinary command if you just want to compile an existing program. However, the compiler can also be run as part of a programming environment that includes an editor, a debugger, and other tools you may become familiar with.

Programming Languages

There's a story about an untutored country bumpkin who listened to some big city know-it-alls as they talked about the stars. She was impressed by the number of stars they claimed existed and by their estimates of distance. What totally amazed her, though, was how the devil they had managed to figure out the stars' *names!*

People often approach programming languages in the same way—as though they were deciphered, rather than invented. In fact, a language is usually conceived when a programmer becomes frustrated with whatever language she's currently working with. Instead of saying everything in this or that machine layer language, she reasons, why not write one last program (a compiler) that will translate what I have to say (my *source*) into the machine layer language (my *target*) for me?

Thus are programming languages born. I've already described assembly languages. They are *low-level* or *operation* languages that are closely tied to particular computer instruction sets. Low-level *first* or *second generation* languages are invaluable in two circumstances:

first and second generation languages

— when a program must use a piece of hardware that can be controlled by only very low-level instructions;

— when a program has to make the best possible use of low-level instructions in order to run very quickly.

Video games are usually programmed in low-level languages for precisely these two reasons: they use special hardware (like trackballs or fancy screens), and they have to blaze along.

Programming languages like Pascal can be described as *high-level*, or *implementation*, languages. To a degree, these *third-generation* languages resemble spoken languages, but with severely limited vocabularies. What's important is that they express programming ideas in human-oriented terms, rather than in ways that are convenient for translation into assembly language. Most programs, including operating systems, application programs, and even higher-level languages are coded in third-generation languages. High-level languages are general purpose in two different ways:

— *They can be used to solve any kind of problem*. It might be more or less convenient to use one language instead of another, just as it could be inconvenient to do chemistry homework with a statistics calculator. Nevertheless, there is a great deal of overlap between high-level language applications.

high-level languages

— *They can run on any kind of computer*. Again, some features might be relatively ineffective on some kinds of hardware. But in general, high-level languages don't require special-purpose machines to run.

Pascal belongs to the family of *imperative* programming languages. 'Imperative' means 'expressing a command,' which pretty accurately describes what the statements of an imperative programming language do. You've probably heard of some other members of the same family—BASIC, FORTRAN, C, Ada, and Modula-2 are probably the best known. Pascal was designed by a Swiss computer scientist named Niklaus Wirth in 1971.

The languages Niklaus Wirth develops tend toward simplicity. Wirth believes that it's important for a programmer to understand the entire language well and that this is impossible when a language becomes too big. He also prefers to incorporate the lessons of each language in a new language, rather than in an 'improved,' but more complicated, version of an old one. He's reluctant to add a new feature without removing an existing one.

There are languages that are even more high-level than Pascal and its cohorts, but they return to being rather specialized. They are called fourth-generation *application languages.* Each is meant to help solve just one kind of problem, but to do it very well. For example, PostScript is a page-description language I used to help typeset this book. In effect, PostScript lets me program a book in terms of the curves and shading that every word, letter, and illustration consists of. Within this specialized realm, PostScript is immensely powerful; outside of it, the language is unbelievably tedious to program in.

Database languages control storage and retrieval of large amounts of information. They're another common fourth-generation application. They're meant to let us use information without worrying about how it's going to be stored or found again. They may rely on special-purpose hardware that lets many people use the system at once, without interfering with each other's actions.

fourth-generation languages

In the final analysis, of course, the choice of programming language to study is up to you. Computer Science departments usually teach a third-generation language like Pascal in their introductory courses to strike a balance: the language reflects enough of the underlying machine layer to give students a feel for some of the potential and limitations of computing, but it hides the gruesome details of low-level programming. Pascal provides a particularly good vehicle, because its techniques are easily carried over to other programming languages.

Standards and Extensions

One last mystery remains: just what is Standard Pascal, and how does it differ from any other Pascal? It's confusing, but true, that there's more than one version of Pascal. Almost every hardware manufacturer offers its own officially endorsed Pascal compiler. And, if hardware is widely used, other software companies will develop and sell Pascal compilers for it too. Multiply the number of computer hardware companies by four or five, and you'll have an idea of the number of Pascals in the world.

Fortunately, most Pascals are quite similar, especially from the viewpoint of a beginning programmer. Just about all of them are *supersets* of Standard Pascal, the formal international Pascal specification. This means that almost any compiler will process Standard Pascal programs correctly.

Standard Pascal is portable

> Another way of putting this is to say that Standard Pascal programs are *portable.* A source program written in Standard Pascal can be compiled on almost any kind of computer.

Pascal compilers usually can't make sense of each other's programs unless they're written in strict adherence to the standard. That's because almost every compiler adds a series of *extensions* to the standard language:

— *Convenience* extensions add features that could probably be written using Standard Pascal. For example, most Pascals have *string* extensions that let programs read and write words as easily as they can numbers.

kinds of Pascal extensions

— *Hardware* extensions take advantage of computer features that weren't common when Standard Pascal was first defined. For example, most PC and Macintosh Pascals have extensions for graphics programming. These extensions are similar in function when they exist, but they may be absent entirely.

— *Software* extensions connect Pascal programs to the computers they run on. They usually offer tie-ins to the computer's *operating system*—the mechanisms it uses to control programs and access to files of information. These extensions are usually present, but differ between Pascal implementations.

— *Evolutionary* extensions make changes in language design. Frequently, such alterations originate in other languages. If they're successful, Pascal vendors expropriate the new ideas and try to patch them into the existing language. Extensions like this vary widely between Pascal systems, and often lead to new languages.

Some of the most popular versions of Pascal are:

— *Turbo Pascal*, from Borland International, dominates the IBM PC-compatible market.

— *THINK Pascal*, from Symantec Corporation, dominates the Macintosh market.

a few Pascal systems

— *VAX Pascal*, from the Digital Equipment Corporation, dominates on VAX computers that use the VMS operating system.

— *Berkeley Pascal*, developed at U.C. Berkeley, is generally found on VAX computers that use Berkeley UNIX (or Ultrix, DEC's repackaging of the same).

— *Dr. Pascal*, from Visible Software is available for PC, Mac, and VMS systems. It hews very closely to the international Pascal standard. They also have an Extended Pascal compiler (see below).

There is an 'official' follow-up to Standard Pascal called *Extended Pascal*. It includes many real-world extensions to Pascal and tries to incorporate ideas that have been explored in other post-Pascal languages. In this text I'll refer to it when I want to describe a common solution to a problem that's been found in the design of Standard Pascal.

The Field of Computer Science

So far I've concentrated on describing computers and programs—the tools of the trade. But this can be a little misleading, as though I were to describe the science of chemistry entirely in terms of test tubes and Bunsen burners.

As an academic discipline, Computer Science goes far beyond developing better and faster spreadsheets. If we were to divide up the courses on the roster into distinct areas, here are most of the basic topics and questions we'd find:

— *Algorithms and data structures.* What steps do we take to solve problems, and how do we store the information they involve?

— *Programming languages.* How do we encode algorithms and data structures?

— *Computer architecture.* How do we design and build the physical computers? How can hardware design support software applications?

specialties within Computer Science

— *Operating systems.* How do we manage the connection between hardware and software?

— *Software engineering.* What systematic methods are there for writing large, reliable, software systems?

— *Symbolic and numerical computation and modeling.* How do we build accurate mathematical models of real-world events?

— *Databases.* How do we store and retrieve large amounts of information?

— *Artificial intelligence.* How can we encode the ability to make decisions— to apply stored knowledge in new, unanticipated ways?

— *Robotics.* How can we use hardware or software to operate mechanical devices that must make decisions?

Other individual topics might appear almost anywhere, depending on the interests and talents of the local faculty. For example, understanding and designing computer *networks* involves studying the operating systems that manage the network, the physical architecture and implementation of the network, mathematical predictions of the network's loads and performance, etc.

Hardware   Software   Theory

most areas overlap

Architecture   Languages   Algorithms

Software Engineering

Operating Systems

Symbolic/Numerical Computation

Databases

Artificial Intelligence

Robotics

Although most professionals would describe themselves as being in one of the major areas of hardware, software, or theory, computer scientists must often be generalists, rather than specialists. There's a considerable amount of overlap, and progress in one area often helps work in another.

So what's the most important thing to know about computers? *How to use them!* Turn the page, and let's get on with our main topic: writing programs and solving problems with Pascal.

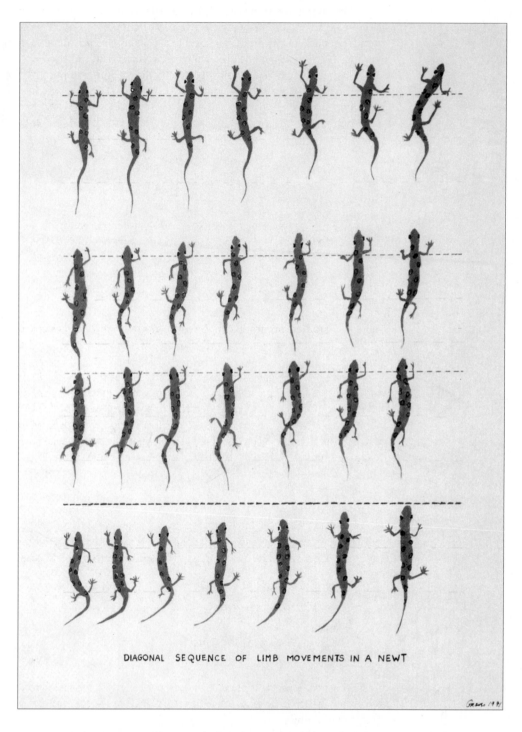

DIAGONAL SEQUENCE OF LIMB MOVEMENTS IN A NEWT

After all, complicated tasks usually do inherently require complex algorithms, and this implies a myriad of details. And the details are the jungle in which the devil hides. The only salvation lies in structure. — N. Wirth   Above, a newt solves the crawling problem. (p. xliv)

Second

Studying a Program

Hello, World ❖ *Reserved Words and Identifiers*
Comments ❖ *The Statement Part* ❖ *Syntax Charts and Style*
Program Planning and Design ❖ *How to Run Programs*
A Generic Demonstration Environment
Beyond the Standard ❖ *Chapter Notes*

Have you studied programming before? Then try to make your mind totally blank. Haven't ever seen a computer, perhaps? Great—you're already prepared!

In this preliminary section you'll get a taste of what you'll be studying for the next term. We'll go over a one-line program in detail—in *great* detail—and get an idea of what's going to be involved in studying Pascal. I'll show you most of the tools this text is going to use and get in a few words about what we in the trade grandly refer to as *the issues*—the ideas that underlie the facts. You'll learn just enough to be able to dig in properly when we get to Chapter 1.

Hello, World!

ALTHOUGH IT'S JUST A FEW LINES LONG, program FirstRun, below, contains the essence of a thousand other programs. It's about as short and sweet as a piece of code can be, and I'm sure that you can already figure out what it does.

```
program FirstRun (output);
    {This is our first example program.}
begin
    writeln ('Hello. I love you.')
end.
```

As with every program printed in this book, the *source code* (what you see above) of FirstRun is available on diskette. You'll be able to run it and to see exactly what it produces.

I haven't supplied the source code just to tantalize you, though. It's also there for you to *modify*—to add to, change, and improve. Although there's a time and place for testing your expertise at writing programs from scratch, you'll learn more by experimenting than by memorizing.

Let's go through FirstRun one line at a time. The heart of every program generally holds at least one *procedure call*. Procedure calls do things; this particular call prints a message for the program user. It's one of the dozen or so *standard procedures* that are built into every Pascal system.

```
writeln ('Hello. I love you.')
```

If we look at the procedure call carefully, we can break it into two parts. The procedure's *name*, shaded here:

the procedure call

```
writeln ('Hello. I love you.')
```

specifies the exact procedure that we want to call. writeln (most people just say 'write line') is the procedure we use to print a *string*—the sequence of characters between quote marks—followed by a carriage return.

The procedure call also includes an *argument* that goes between parentheses. This argument is a string:

its argument

```
writeln ('Hello. I love you.')
```

If we want, we can change the argument and print something else. Here are two different strings (sequences of characters between quotes) as arguments. Can you see what else I've added, and can you guess why?

```
writeln ('Hello. I love you.');
writeln ('Do I know you, or just your type?')
```

The question tests insight as well as eyesight—I've added a single semicolon to the end first procedure call. It's needed to separate one call from the next.

A procedure call, with its argument, is the basic tool of programming. Procedures are as important to the programmer as sentences with subjects and verbs are to a writer, or functions to a mathematician. Why?

the Big Idea

> A procedure solves a general problem. Since its argument can change from call to call, one general method can be applied to different specific tasks.

writeln solves part of the problem of sending program *output* to a program user—it lets us print a string. Soon, we'll see other procedures that take care of *input* and get information from a program user.

Let's stand back a bit to notice something important. For all practical purposes, a Pascal program is just a delivery system for procedure calls, some of which came standard with the system and some of which are new because they were written by the programmer. Conceptually, I like to split programs into two parts:

```
program FirstRun;
```
This is where new procedures are written.
```
begin
```
This is where both standard and new procedures are used.
```
end.
```

a simple program
outline

For the next few weeks, you'll be learning the details of Pascal. But in the months and years that follow, *programming* will come to mean *writing and learning about procedures.*

Reserved Words and Identifiers

Let's get back to the *syntax*, or word-by-word construction rules, of our first Pascal program. The first line of FirstRun was:

> **program** FirstRun (output);

the program heading

A program *heading* names the program. As you can see, I've printed the words **program** and FirstRun in two different typefaces. I do so to help distinguish between *reserved words* and *identifiers:*

— **program** is a *reserved word*—one of the thirty-six words that are unchangeable in the Pascal language.

— FirstRun is an *identifier*—a word that *I* chose to use as a name. Reserved words can't be used as identifiers.

identifiers defined

What's an *identifier?* In Pascal it's defined as a letter followed by any series of letters or digits. Identifiers *can't* start with numbers, contain punctuation, or spell out reserved words. This makes Smithereens, UB40, and InXS all legal identifiers, while begin, R.E.M, and 2CoolFoolz aren't. Pascal doesn't distinguish between upper-case and lower-case letters, by the way, so sally, SALLY, and sAllLy are all the same.

The program heading ends with an instruction to the computer. It must know in advance if it will get information from us—*input*—or deliver results to us—*output.* This particular program only has output, so its heading ends with:

> **program** FirstRun (output) ;

If the program had input too, its heading would be:

> **program** AddMe (input, output) ;
> {*We'll write this program in a few pages.*}

Comments

Program FirstRun's heading is followed by a *comment:*

> **program** FirstRun;
> {*This is our first example program.*}

comments

Comments are explanatory notes. A comment can say anything that can be put between *comment brackets* like these: { }:

> {   *The content of the comment*   }

There's no standard way to comment away sections of code that contain comments, but that's a common extension. I'll say more in a few pages, in the *Beyond the Standard* section.

> As far as program operation is concerned, comments are unnecessary—the computer ignores everything that's put between comment brackets. But in practice, comments should be used in *every—EVERY*—program you write.

the KISS philosophy

Most programmers follow a philosophy called KISS: 'Keep it simple, stupid!' After all, you never know who'll be reading your programs—the grader, your teacher, your boss. Comments help these easily confused people understand your programs, so use them. More seriously, I find that comments help me understand even my own code a few weeks after the fact, and I think that you'll have the same experience with yours.

The Statement Part

As our program continues, we come to its *statement part*.

the statement part

```
program FirstRun (output);

    {This is our first example program.}

begin
    writeln ('Hello. I love you.')     {This call is a statement.}
end.
```

```
Hello. I love you.
```

To help you picture our programs in action, I'll show their output, as I have above, with arrows that separate code from results. Output is always printed this way because it looks a little like the print you'll see on your screen.

A procedure call is a single statement. A program can contain more than one statement, as long as a semicolon—Pascal's *statement separator*—appears between any two statements:

a modified program

```
program Second (output);

    {This is our first modification.}

begin
    writeln ('Hello. I love you.');
        {A semicolon separates statements.}
    writeln ('Do I know you, or just your type?')
end.
```

```
Hello. I love you.
Do I know you, or just your type?
```

Take a moment to notice a subtle feature of program Second: writing it took almost no mental effort! That's because I just copied FirstRun and made a few small changes.

<table>
<tr><td>some sage advice</td><td>Whenever you can, program by modifying existing programs. That, in a nutshell, is how to get through the first half of this course.</td></tr>
</table>

The secret to getting through the second half is to write programs that are easy to modify and reuse, but let's not get ahead of ourselves.

Congratulations on making it this far! Although program FirstRun wasn't too exciting, what we've just managed to do certainly is. A language that perhaps ten minutes ago was barely conceivable (and totally incomprehensible) is starting to mean something. *We're* in charge now! A certain amount of mystery—and maybe a little magic as well—has left our lives forever.

Syntax Charts and Style

If you've been paying attention, you should already be worried about all the syntax rules you'll have to remember. I can make life a bit easier by supplying *syntax charts*, which are informal pictures that describe Pascal syntax. The syntax of an identifier is:

identifier

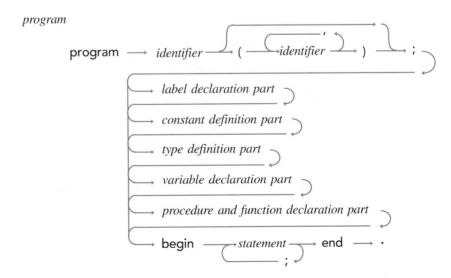

As long as you start on the left and follow the arrows, you'll have an identifier that satisfies Pascal's rules: it must start with a letter, and can contain as many additional letters or digits as you want. The shortest possible path yields a one-letter name. Note that the underscore character _ isn't legal in a Standard Pascal identifier, but it is a common extension in many Pascal systems.

A Pascal program as a whole gets a syntax chart too. It's a bit counterintuitive, but one of the most useful skills a computer scientist can have is the ability to ignore the parts she doesn't understand (yet!). If you ignore the five 'parts' in the middle, you'll see that it traces the syntax of programs FirstRun and Second.

program

> The *Pascal Pages* appendix summarizes all syntax charts and includes brief examples and explanations of all Pascal features.

But programming isn't just syntax, because the computer is only half of the equation when it comes to understanding programs. *The programmer is just as important.* Humans find that a consistent *style* of indentation and naming makes code much easier to understand. For example, since Pascal programs are *free format*—exact positioning and indentation don't matter—this minimally named and spaced program is legal:

```
program X(output);begin writeln('Hello. I love you.')end.
```

But it's a lousy style example. It's hard to follow, and is even harder to fix if there's a problem.

the golden rule of style

> Programs should be as easy for humans to read and understand as they are for computers to execute. When you write code, try to follow the format of the examples in this book. Above all, be consistent.

Program Planning and Design

Printing wisecracks isn't much of a problem. But when we start to deal with harder problems, you'll want more than yuks. Instead, you'll want a *program*—something that can be run, admired, and perhaps improved and extended later.

I malign BASIC

But programs don't just happen. You may be surprised to hear this news (especially if you've taken a course in BASIC) but most programming is *not* a matter of sitting back and giving commands to an obedient computer. Instead, it's planning and organizing:

— Developing an *algorithm*, or sequence of steps required to solve a problem.

— Planning procedures that *implement*—carry out—the algorithm's steps.

— *Parameterizing* the procedures to make them as general as possible.

— *Coding* and *commenting* the procedures.

— *Testing* the final program.

If we had only simple goals, then a simple methodology—sit at the terminal and code—and a simple language—like good old BASIC—would suffice. But we are ambitious! We want to be able to solve problems that are too big to carry around in our own modest heads. Our salvation, as Pascal's creator Niklaus Wirth points out, is found in organization:

'details are the jungle'

> After all, complicated tasks usually do inherently require complex algorithms, and this implies a myriad of details. And the details are the jungle in which the devil hides. The only salvation lies in structure.*

* Niklaus Wirth, *Programming in Modula-2*, Fourth Edition, Springer-Verlag, 1988, p. 87.

Wirth emphasizes structure as the road to *abstraction*: planning in terms of high-level descriptions instead of low-level details. It's a lesson we'll be going over again and again. Some of the phrases that have been used over the years to describe the process of program planning are:

— Breaking a program down into procedures that carry out particular tasks is sometimes called *procedural abstraction*.

some useful buzzwords

— Stating a big goal first, then restating it in terms of smaller subgoals is called *top-down design*.

— Restating the outline of a single procedure in more and more precise, code-like terms is called *stepwise refinement*.

The key idea is *design*: programs are designed to have desirable characteristics—to be easy to write, understand, and change—as well as to find answers.

> Design procedures before you write statements and think in English before you code in Pascal. The sooner you start to code, the longer it will take to finish.

This focus on design, rather than coding, is what leads to my emphasis on modifying programs instead of writing them from scratch. If you've spent a lifetime writing English and History papers (as I'm sure you have) you've probably learned to hide your sources and to make everything you produce seem unique. That's because in most fields, the real world is the same as the academic world: copying the work of others is plagiarizing, and you'd expect to be penalized for it.

But cooperation is essential in the real world of computer science. Finding an existing program that almost solves your problem, then making the few changes it requires, is the road to rewards and honors. When you must create new code, designing it so that other people can understand and reuse it is just as laudable. As students, you have to expect that you'll be tested on individual efforts. But don't ever let that make you forget that cooperation is the key to progress in software.

How to Run Programs

Programs are generally first written on paper. Actually running one on a computer is usually a three-step process:

edit

— *Open a file.* First, you have to write a program. You might copy and modify an existing program (like FirstRun), or you might have to open an empty file and start adding to it. The exact keys that control adding, deleting, searching, and so on may vary, but learning them won't tax your intelligence.

compile

— *Compile the program.* Second, the file is read by a *compiler*, which is a program that translates English-language Pascal instructions into *object code* the computer can run. If the compiler spots errors, you'll have to return *noi lại*

to step one and fix them. In some systems, you'll have to invoke an additional program called a *linker* before your object code is ready to go.

— *Execute*. Third and finally, you'll get to execute, or run, your program. Don't worry—it's practically impossible to break anything. However, you should try to make sure that the program does what you wanted—and not just what you wrote.

execute

Unfortunately, the exact rules for running programs vary from system to system, so I won't go into precise details. The operation of text editors and word processors is even less standardized, so I can't be any help there either. Indeed, you may find yourself spending most of this week learning to use one of the many *programming environments* that merge editor, compiler, and other development tools.

A Generic Demonstration Environment

In this book I'll periodically use a generic or typical environment (it's a lot like Turbo Pascal's) to show programs in operation. A programming environment generally takes over the entire screen and splits it into special purpose windows.

— An *editing* window shows the program that's running. Note that the name of the file the program is in doesn't have to be the same as the name of the program itself.

typical programming environment windows

— An *input and output* window shows all interaction with the program user.

— A *variables* window shows the values that variables (we'll get to them in Chapter 1) currently hold.

— An *uncompleted calls* window names the program and any procedure calls that are currently underway.

Here's how I'd use my generic environment to demonstrate program Second.

the program is finished

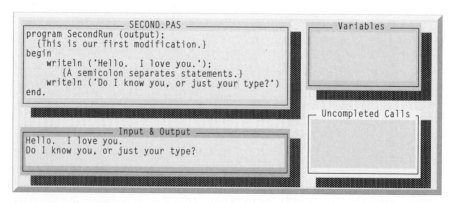

```
                    ──── SECOND.PAS ────                      ──── Variables ────
program SecondRun (output);
   {This is our first modification.}
begin
    writeln ('Hello.  I love you.');
       {A semicolon separates statements.}
    writeln ('Do I know you, or just your type?')
end.
                                                             ── Uncompleted Calls ──

                   ──── Input & Output ────
Hello.  I love you.
Do I know you, or just your type?
```

Although I won't show them, programming environments also include keys or buttons that let you step through a program one statement at a time or change values as it runs.

For example, the picture below picks up the Second program in mid-stream. Note that I've moved the windows around a bit; since screens are relatively small, most programming environments let windows overlap. The statement we're about to execute is highlighted, and the program itself is the only uncompleted call:

the program is halfway completed

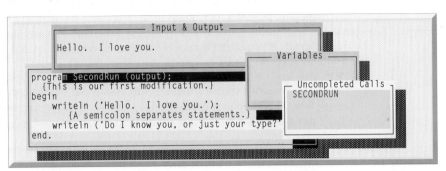

```
                    ┌────────── Input & Output ──────────┐
                    │ Hello.  I love you.                │
                    │                         ┌── Variables ──┐
  program SecondRun (output);                 │  ┌─ Uncompleted Calls ─┐
     {This is our first modification.}        │  │ SECONDRUN
  begin                                        │  │
     writeln ('Hello.  I love you.');          │  │
        {A semicolon separates statements.} ▮  │  │
     writeln ('Do I know you, or just your type?'│
  end.
```

Why bother with a made-up environment? Because learning to program often involves a little bit of experimentation. Maybe some people can just read the rules and understand everything, but I can't, and I assume that you probably can't either.

test bed programs are for experimenting

> Whenever I introduce something that's really new and different, I'll try to include a *test bed* program—a program that doesn't necessarily solve any problems, but is easy to modify and play around with.

Naturally, I'll suggest making a few changes that will help you understand the test bed program better. For example, you can try to add additional lines of output to Second. Or, you might want to see what happens if you change the first writeln procedure call to a call of the write procedure instead. You'll be able to see the results of small changes like this no matter what kind of computing environment you're working with.

Beyond the Standard

Although I'm going to refer to Standard Pascal throughout this book, it's likely that the language you'll actually use is Standard Pascal—*plus*. It will be an implementation of the Standard that will probably include many *extensions*, or additional programming features.

Are extensions a good thing? Yes and no. Here are some of the problems with the original Pascal:

shortcomings of Standard Pascal

— The Standard was defined before graphics were widely available. There's no way to write graphics programs using Standard Pascal.

— Standard Pascal can make a CPU jump through hoops, but it is weak when it comes to working with the rest of the computer system. In particular, the way that Standard Pascal deals with stored files leaves much to be desired.

— Standard Pascal doesn't supply good methods of breaking big programs into pieces that can be compiled or run separately. It won't permit some approaches to programming that make software easier to manage and reuse.

On the other hand, many computer scientists have bad memories of the pre-Pascal days, when a programming language's name might be just the first clue in a guessing game about what the language actually contained. They prefer to teach Standard Pascal even if it's a bit constrained and artificial. Here are some reasons:

— The vast majority of programming issues *can* be dealt with in Standard Pascal. A simpler language helps students focus on the *why?* of programming and program design, rather than on language syntax details.

problems with extensions

— When languages have too many features, they're hard to comprehend as a whole. If there are too many ways to do something, it's hard to develop a feel for the best way. Standard Pascal is comparatively small and can be taught in a term or two.

— It is hard for novice programmers to tell the difference between language characteristics that are due to inherent limits in programming language design and those that come from shortcomings of a particular computer or operating system. Standard Pascal avoids machine-specific features.

— Extensions are dandy if everybody has the same computing environment. But since they don't, the fact that Standard Pascal programs are *portable*—that means that they can be run on every system—helps ensure that what students learn will transfer between courses, schools, and jobs.

We've already covered enough Pascal to come across three popular extensions. Many systems will let underscores appear in identifiers, along with digits and letters:

```
{Why some systems allow underscores in identifiers.}
A_Readable_Name
AHardToReadName
```

a few typical extensions

A second common extension simplifies the program heading by making the input, output part optional:

```
{Some systems don't require program parameters.}
program Extension;
```

Making the *program parameters* optional is generally part of a larger set of extensions that make using existing files easier. This kind of extension is typically the most convenient, but also the most system-specific, of those you'll run across.

A third common extension deals with comments. In the old days, not all keyboards had the curly braces used for comments, so even Standard Pascal allows an alternative pair of brackets: (* and *). In theory, one bracket can substitute for another. But in practice, most compilers distinguish between the two forms so that this is permitted:

(∗   {*This is how to comment*} {*other comments away.*}   ∗)

This is convenient if you want to hide part of a program that contains comments itself. Programmers often do that when problems develop. It pays to simplify before you try to test or correct.

Modification Problems

The best way to become familiar with new programming ideas is to make small changes in programs that already work. These Modification Problems will accompany the example programs in the text. All of the examples are available on disk, so don't worry about typing. As a rule, if you can handle the modification, you understand the discussion.

1. Change program FirstRun so that it follows `Hello` with the name of the person sitting next to you. Use your discretion as to whether it should continue to say `I love you.`

2. If problem 1 went well, add to FirstRun a second procedure call that issues an invitation to lunch. (If problem 2 goes well, name your first child Douglas if a boy and Douglassa if a girl.)

Self-Check Questions

Self-Check Questions are just what they seem to be. On occasion, I'll sneak a new idea into a self-check just to keep you awake.

Q. Which of these are legal identifiers in Pascal? Are any legal, but inadvisable?

Start	end	3High
BEGIN	´grade´	TryAgain
NewName2	program	writeln
Yoyo	−Input	Dotted...line

A. Start, NewName2, Yoyo, and TryAgain are all reasonable names. writeln is legal but inadvisable, because it's already being used as an identifier. The others either violate syntax rules (like Dotted...line) or are reserved words that can't be redefined (like **end**).

Q. Is there anything wrong with this comment?

   { *This is a very*
     impressive, multi-line
     comment. }

A. Nothing at all—a comment can extend over several lines. Any program lines caught in the middle will be ignored, though! The following would be a mistake, because the heading is part of the comment.

   { *Here's the beginning of the comment.*
   program Mistaken (input, output);
   Here's the end of the comment. }

Chapter Notes

I CAN'T BE SURE, BUT I'LL BET THAT YOUR MOTHER wouldn't let you swallow until you'd chewed every mouthful at least twenty times. Personally, I don't want to be responsible for causing you mental indigestion, so I like to go over the high points at the end of every chapter.

debugging

Finding and fixing the bugs or mistakes that creep into programs is called *debugging*. When you start to write big programs, you'll put them on paper first—that's the first line of defense. But because it's always possible to introduce bugs (like misspellings) while typing, even the best-planned programs usually require trial runs before they're completely debugged. In fact, allowing time for debugging is an essential part of the programming process.

antibugging and defensive programming

Antibugging means writing in a manner that helps prevent bugs, or makes bugs easy to find if they do occur. It's easy to see that antibugging is a defensive strategy. As we go along in this book, we'll often find it employed as part of a general plan of defensive programming.

Bugs aren't inevitable, but they often occur in computer programs because men and women don't think in the literal way that machines operate. Beware— the computer can't always discover mistakes. People have a remarkable, automatic ability to fix mistakes that is miles beyond anything computers can do.

> *What is wrong with*
> *with this sentence?*

syntax vs. semantics

> Bugs fall into two general categories. *Syntax* bugs are 'grammatical' Pascal errors, while *semantic* bugs cause mistakes in the meaning or effect of programs.

Syntax errors are found and fixed with the least effort, because the compiler usually detects them automatically as it prepares a program for running. The underlying design of the language helps, because some syntax features are intended to provide markers and restart points the compiler can use when it tries to recover from an error.

compile-time bugs

For example, some words invariably occur in pairs—a **begin** must be matched by an **end** later in the program. A compiler that cannot find the closing **end** prints an error message to point out the problem:

```
Compiler error:   "end" expected
```

Punctuation bugs are caught in a similar manner. For instance, the semicolon is Pascal's statement separator, so the compiler expects to find a semicolon between every two statements. Compilation stops at the start of the second statement, because that's where the error became clear. The error message

```
Compiler error:   ";" expected
```

is terse, but it gets the point across.

When an **end** or semicolon is missing, not only is it easy for the compiler to spot the problem; it's also easy for us to understand the compiler's diagnosis. But that isn't always the case. Here are some common difficulties:

— The compiler may not spot the error for some time, perhaps a number of lines beyond where the problem actually occurred.

error messages can be misleading

— The compiler can misdiagnose the bug. It might accuse you of misusing a procedure when you actually misspelled a reserved word.

— Many compilers will try to *recover* from an error and keep trying to diagnose syntax problems. Unfortunately, the recovery itself might be incorrect and lead to a sheaf of spurious messages about nonexistent errors.

An ability to decipher brief, obscure error messages is one of the unadvertised skills that expert programmers have to rely on frequently! Don't be discouraged if the compiler's little missives to you seem curt and unenlightening. You'll come to understand them as time goes by. And, as you gain experience, you'll become adept at distinguishing real bugs from the imaginary ones.

runtime errors

Runtime errors are closely related to syntax bugs, but they can't be found until the program actually runs. For example, it's sometimes a mistake to use a decimal in place of a whole number. If the error appears in the text of the program, the compiler will spot it and refuse to compile the program. But if the decimal doesn't show up until a program user accidentally types it in, there's no way the compiler could have anticipated it. Instead, the program itself will spot the error and halt automatically.

> Runtime errors are usually known as *crashes*. Fortunately, this description applies to your ego—not to the computer. If you don't crash a program once in a while, you're probably not programming enough!

Semantic errors are the most difficult to deal with, because you're not always aware that there is a problem. Here are a few of the most common semantic errors:

— A program may produce an answer that's flat-out wrong.

a wrong answer

```
The sum of 3 and 5 is 9.
```

The wrong answer is easy to spot—when it's obvious. But extensive testing is often necessary to determine if a program is producing the right results.

— The right answer may appear in a way that's impossible to decipher.

an indecipherable answer

```
358
```

The output shows the correct sum of 3 and 5, but who can tell? Labeling both input and output is essential if a user who is unaware of a program's inner workings is to figure out what is going on.

— A program may produce the right answer but attach it to the wrong question.

a seemingly wrong answer

    The sum of 3 and 5 is 10.

How could this output possibly be right? Well, if we count in base 8, the numbers go . . . 6, 7, 10, 11, and so on. This kind of bug can be hard to find because both the addition *and* the output labeling are correct. It's only when they're juxtaposed that the error appears.

— A program may *hang*, or fail in a way that's invisible to the user.

a hung program

    Wait while I calculate...

Hung programs appear to be working, but they never finish. This can occur because the computer is waiting for input from the user, or because there's an *infinite loop* (we'll get to them in Chapter 6) lurking in the program. It's important to know how to kill a running program. Some of the most common kill-key combinations are:

some common kill keys

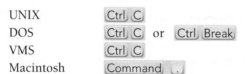

UNIX   Ctrl C
DOS   Ctrl C or Ctrl Break
VMS   Ctrl C
Macintosh   Command .

When you're dealing with Macs or PC's, it's sometimes easiest to turn the computer off and on again when it gets hung.

don't forget to test

> At first, it's tempting to think that a program is finished once it has been compiled and run. But the possibility of semantic errors is the reason that a program isn't done until it has been *tested*.

Finally, don't underestimate your own ability to debug through sheer brainpower. The key, in my experience, is to get a pencil and a program *listing*, or paper printout. Don't despair—we've all been there!

Background: Are Bugs Inevitable?

A group of programmers was presenting a report to the Emperor. "What was the greatest achievement of the year?" the Emperor asked.

The programmers spoke among themselves and then replied, "We fixed 50% more bugs this year than we fixed last year."

The Emperor looked on them in confusion. It was clear that he did not know what a 'bug' was. After conferring in low undertones with his chief minister, he turned to the programmers, his face red with anger. "You are guilty of poor quality control. Next year there will be no 'bugs'!" he demanded.

And sure enough, when the programmers presented their report to the Emperor the next year, there was no mention of bugs.

From *The Zen of Programming*, by Geoffrey James, © 1988, InfoBooks, Santa Monica, Ca. 90406

❏ comment: an explanatory note that goes between *comment delimiters*:

{*This is a comment. You'll fail if your programs don't have them.*}

❏ identifier: a name that starts with a letter, then contains letters or digits.

AnIdentifier   ThisIs12

❏ program: the package that Pascal programs come in:

program Example (output);   {*This is the heading.*}
    Definitions and declarations come first.
begin
    Procedures are called in the statement part.
end.

❏ procedure calls: invoke or run a procedure. A call typically consists of the procedure's name, followed by an argument given between parentheses:

writeln ('This is the argument.')

❏ string: a series of characters. When it's used as an argument, the string goes between quote marks:

'A string must be quoted.'

❏ Pascal uses the semicolon as a separator between procedure calls, other statements, and the different parts of a program.

❏ The thirty-six words that are part of the Pascal language proper are called *reserved words.* They can't be reused as identifiers.

❏ Good *style* helps make programs easy to read and understand. Remember to have some sympathy for humans who have to read your programs; they need it more than the computer does.

❏ Don't take *KISS* ('keep it simple, stupid!') as an insult. It's just a reminder that a program you understand perfectly today can be awfully confusing if you have to rework it a few weeks hence.

❏ Capitalization doesn't matter in Pascal programs—**program** is the same as **PrOgRaM**, and WhoKnows is the same as whoKNOWS.

❏ Most Pascal compilers permit nonstandard *extensions.* But since using extensions makes programs nonportable, you should avoid them for now.

❏ *Syntax charts* are a convenient way to show Pascal construction rules. But since they're sometimes simplified for clarity, they can't always be used as a formal reference.

❏ Syntax errors are mistakes in Pascal's grammar rules. They're usually caught by the compiler and can be corrected. Semantic errors are mistakes in meaning that can lead a program astray. They can be found only by checking your program's results.

❑   Making sure a program runs is only half the job of testing. Making sure it *works* is where the most effort must be applied.

'How am I supposed to study for exams?' is always my students' first question. Getting inside your instructor's head, which is what the 'Zen' study guide that follows each chapter is all about, is actually pretty easy. I'll always start by pointing out the Big Ideas *that sometimes get hidden by programming details. Then, since it's my experience that the best way to study for tests is to make up test questions (this is the Zen part),* Begin by Writing the Exam . . . *will get you started. More conventional warm-ups, test programs, and programming problems follow. They'll give you ample opportunity to apply what you've learned.*

══════════
Big Ideas

The Big Ideas in the introduction were:

1. *Programming is closer to construction than to writing.* What's the program for? What will it be built from? Are there the stylistic equivalents of building codes to be met? Can other people use it? You don't just write programs—you build them to last.

2. *The exact syntax of a programming language is a compromise between precision and simplicity.* When it's possible, good languages avoid imposing arbitrary rules. Requirements are presented in the most natural, intuitive manner the language designer could muster.

Imagine, if you can, that you're the instructor of your programming class. Your students have obediently read the preliminary chapter and understand program FirstRun. *It's time to write their first exam.*

══════════
Begin by Writing
the Exam . . .

1   Make up five identifiers that could be used in the question *Which of these are legal Pascal identifiers?*

2   It's picayune, but essential, to remember the exact spelling, including capitalization, of the few Pascal reserved words we've seen so far. How can you test your students? By giving them a program (it can be almost identical to FirstRun) that has mistakes. Write the problem.

3   It's always a good idea to exploit potential student panic. Therefore, don't pose the following problem: 'Copy FirstRun exactly, but have it say *Goodbye* instead of *Hello.*' Instead, tell them to write a program that prints the first line of the Gettysburg Address. How hard a problem of this sort can you pose but still answer yourself?

4   What can you do when a Pascal rule seems to be too simple to get confused about?

```
writeln ('Everything between the quotes is printed.');
```

Improvise! Ask a question like *What's the output of this:*

```
writeln ('writeln('writeln')');
```

Make up a few more questions of this variety.

5   Pascal programs are *free format,* which means that only their contents are meaningful to the computer. Layout on the page isn't relevant. Make up a trick *What's wrong with this program* question that uses the fact that Pascal programs are free format to appear incorrect.

6   For filler, ask questions like *Where is this punctuation used: . (; ˝ ?*

7   Personally, I hate to ask questions that begin *Name the 3 characteristics of . . .*—they encourage rote memorization rather than actual thinking. Instead, I'll phrase questions like this: *Describe the most important steps of developing a program.* Make up two similar questions.

8   Finally, make up three questions that require short written answers, such as *What's the difference between a reserved word and an identifier?*

Warmups and Test Programs

For me, the key to learning a new language or system is to write many short programs. Right now even a five-line test program will seem like a lot of work, but in time you'll be able to knock them out in minutes. Most important, you'll feel much better once you realize that you can figure things out by experimenting.

9   Although I try to get my programs off to a friendly (some might say *too* friendly) start, the standard first program is a bit more reserved: it prints `Hello, world!` Write it.

10   What is the shortest program you can write? It doesn't have to do anything, mind you, as long as it can be compiled and run without error.

11   In Pascal an identifier must start with a letter and can then contain letters and digits. But there's no official rule on how long an identifier can be—it varies from system to system. How would you find out your system's limit?

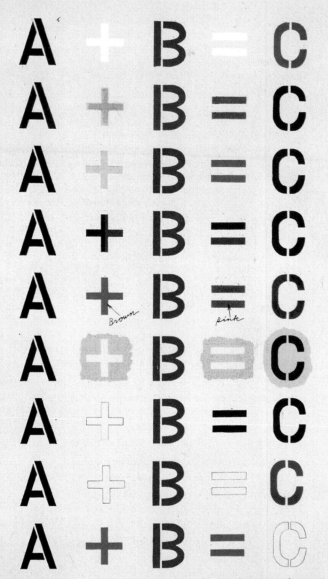

AN INVESTIGATION OF THE ELEMENTS OF REASSEMBLY AND OF THE POSSIBLE APPLICATIONS OF THESE IN ORDER TO CHANGE USAGE

TO WHAT EXTENT IS = A FUNCTION OF + ?

The range of values for each + and = is wide open as long as the above relations hold.
Other considerations are: A + + + + + B = C   A + B $\dfrac{}{}$ C
     Color, positional changes in A, B
     If + is ten years (minutes) ahead of =
     Or a shift in any other dimension

Expressions can be complicated, too. For instance, think about 1 + 1, which you probably thought was pretty simple. (p. 22)

1

Input and Output, Storage and Change

Let's get down to business. We'll start with the basics: input (getting data values), variables (storing them), output (printing them), and expressions (changing them). Chapter 1 contains a lot of information, so here are some tricks to keep you from becoming overwhelmed.

First, read the chapter twice. Start with a quick skim to see what's really important, and what's just a complicated (but small) detail. Don't try to memorize everything, because there's just too much. If you can handle the Modification Problems, you're doing fine.

Second, try to see how Pascal hangs together. Don't be afraid to question the language designer's wisdom or my method of explanation. I got *my* start in writing by complaining about the textbook *I* had to read in my first class, and maybe you will, too!

Third, accept the fact that programs are usually experiments. Expect your programs to work, but don't be put off if they don't. You'll learn just as much from your bugs as you will from getting it right. After all, how do you avoid mistakes? Experience. How do you get experience? Make mistakes.

Finally, the examples in the book are there for you to copy, borrow, alter—in short, to *steal*. Don't be bashful, because I expect you to learn by modifying—not by reinventing the wheel every time you sit down at the terminal. If you do it successfully, you'll finish this chapter able to solve some interesting problems. Almost any program from the exercises can be built by starting with one of the examples in the text. Good luck, and happy hacking!

But First, the Issues

As you learn to program, it's important not to put the cart in front of the horse. Like a cart, a programming language is just a vehicle. Its design is motivated by what it's supposed to convey or accomplish. But since it's sometimes hard to tell the cart and the horse apart, I'll periodically start out with a look at the underlying issues that have influenced Pascal's design.

The fundamental issue is *storage*. If you think about it, it's easy to see how a computer and a calculator are alike. They can both do arithmetic. Both of them can 'read' input values. And, even though the calculator's screen is very small, both of them can print output.

But there's a crucial difference. Unlike calculators, computers hold data and programs. Now, managing data storage is a job we share with the compiler. Although the exact dividing line between our work and the compiler's varies among programming languages, here are some of the issues that every language designer must wrestle with when she begins to think about data:

— *When* during program execution is the storage going to be set aside?

issue: how to store data

— *How* will it be named and referred to?

— *What* restrictions are there on the values that can be stored?

— *Where* in the program can stored values be used?

In practical Pascal terms, we're going to learn the rules of *variable declaration* (setting aside storage) and *assignment* (actually storing values).

Since using values is inseparable from storing them, we'll have to explore a second set of issues that involve representing values in expressions:

— What *operations* (beyond the obvious ones like addition and subtraction) should there be?

issue: defining operations clearly

— In what *order* should the operations be carried out?

— What *restrictions* should there be on operations? For example, we can add numbers, but should we be able to add letters, too?

After we've dealt with data it's time to think about storing programs themselves. The basic problem for the programmer is to specify the exact steps we want the program to take. For now, the only steps at our disposal are the statements and procedures that Wirth built into Pascal. However, choosing these steps was no simple matter.

Why not? Well, ask yourself how big a language should be. How many statements should it have? There's no right answer—only alternatives. A language with many special-purpose commands might permit short, precise programs. That's great. But since it will have to be larger, the language can also be harder to learn and more difficult to transfer to different computers.

issue: abstraction vs. detail

The general opinion these days is that relatively small is relatively beautiful. A well-designed language tries to allow a good blend of *abstraction*—'give me the big picture and I'll do the rest'—and detail—'you must tell me precisely what you want.' Neither extreme is safe. A program's results can be wrong if the language makes too many assumptions about what the user wants. At the same time, programmers tend to make mistakes if they must take too many low-level steps on the way to getting something simple done.

In this chapter, we'll see the results of Wirth's wrestling match in one of the toughest areas of language design—preparing the built-in procedures that are used for input and output.

The final issue we'll deal with involves *style*. Here, it's mostly up to you and me. We can't blame Wirth if nobody can read our programs. Some of the considerations we'll bear in mind are:

issue: style

— When should we use values, and when should we use names in their place?

— What names are going to be clearest?

— How should the program be laid out and commented?

Stylistic issues have an impact on language design as well. We'll see how a rather small addition to Pascal—the ability to define *constants*—can have a large impact on the appearance and readability of a program.

Things to Think About

1. When calculators were first invented, they were merely electronic versions of the old mechanical adding machines. The only service they provided was basic arithmetic. However, as time passed, calculators acquired the ability to save values (thanks to memory keys) and even to store a limited number of program steps.

At what point do you think that calculators become computers? How many storage locations does a calculator need to make the grade? How many program steps should the user be able to store? Do you think that the sort of calculator that's programmed by inserting a chip-like external module is any more or less of a computer?

2. Imagine that you are designing an electronic notepad—something that might be suitable for taking notes in class. What are some of the issues that will influence your final design? If you're having trouble getting started, think about the notepad as the character-oriented equivalent of a pocket calculator.

Values and Variables

1-1

THE FOUR SHORT PROGRAMS ON THE NEXT few pages provide a snapshot of the ground we'll be covering in Chapter 1. Here's where we stand now:

```
program Second (output);

    {This is our first modification.}

begin
    writeln ('Hello. I love you.');
    writeln ('Do I know you, or just your type?')
end.
```

```
Hello.  I love you.
Do I know you, or just your type?
```

Second is catty, but fundamentally it's dull. Fortunately, there's more than one way to use writeln, and there's more than one procedure for output.

the write procedure

```
program Chatty (output);
    {A longer program that needs semicolon statement separators.}

begin
    write ('A fine romance,  ');        {These lines are printed...}
    write ('with no kisses.  ');        {...on the same output line.}
    writeln;            {This ends the line with a carriage return.}
    writeln;            {These put two blank lines in the output.}
    writeln;
    write ('A fine romance,  ');
    writeln ('my friend, this is!')
    {writeln can be used either with or without an argument.}
end.  {Chatty}
```

```
A fine romance, with no kisses.


A fine romance, my friend, this is!
```

Do you like detective work? Well, what's the difference between write and writeln? Between reading the comments and inspecting the output you can see that write prints its argument (the thing in parentheses) without a carriage return. We need such a procedure because writeln *always* prints a carriage return, whether or not it has an argument.

write vs. writeln

There are also differences you can't necessarily discover by inspection. write must always be given an argument to print, as it has been above. write and writeln will also do some automatic formatting of numerical values. I'll get back to the details later.

But computers are more than glorified typewriters. Our next step will be to see how a program can get a value (with an *input procedure*) and store it (with a *variable*). AddMe, below, does both. Its variable, Age, holds a number; it gets the number from the program user by calling the input procedure readln.

declaring and using a variable

```
program AddMe (input, output);
    {Shows a variable declaration and input procedure call.  From page 8.}

var Age : integer;          {The variable declaration.}

begin
    write ('How old are you?   ');         {Prompt for input.}
    readln (Age);                          {Get and store the number the user types.}
    write ('In twenty years you will be  ');
    writeln (Age + 20)
end.  {AddMe}
```

```
How old are you?  21
In twenty years you will be        41
```

A fate too horrible to contemplate! I'll always use the **heavy** typeface to show values the user types in. I won't show the Enter or Return (if you're using a Mac or DEC keyboard) that must end every line of input, but you should always assume it's there.

We'll have to take one more key step to get where we're going in this chapter. Variables aren't all that useful unless we can change them. In Pascal, change means *assignment*, and a small modification of program AddMe gives us AssignMe, below:

the assignment
statement

```
program AssignMe (input, output);
    {Shows an assignment statement. Similar to page 19.}
var Age : integer;          {The variable declaration.}
begin
    write ('How old are you?   ');        {Prompt for input.}
    readln (Age);                         {Get and store the number the user types.}
    Age := Age + 20;                      {Assign a new value to Age.}
    write ('In twenty years you will be  ');
    writeln (Age)
end.  {AssignMe}
```

How old are you? **21**
In twenty years you will be   41

These four ideas—input, output, storage, and change—aren't hard. But because computer programs have to be precise and unambiguous, really understanding how they're incorporated into a programming language like Pascal is going to involve many details. We'll begin at the beginning by learning something about the vocabulary of values.

The Vocabulary of Values

If you've ever studied another language, you know that those clever foreigners have not only thought up different words for everything but also frequently insist on new sounds for the letters in the alphabet. Remembering new pronunciation is awkward at first, but after a few days it seems perfectly natural.

Programming languages also have new vocabularies, and I have to lay a little groundwork before we can go any further. We need to see just how Pascal distinguishes between different kinds of *values*—numbers, letters, and so on.

literal values

> In Pascal, every value has a particular *type*. The type names a whole category of values, while just one instance is called a *literal* value.

For example, a quoted single digit character, like '1' or '2', is a literal value of type char, but a number by itself, like 3 or 714, is a literal integer.

A basic set of *standard types*, whose names and characteristics you'll have to remember, are built into Pascal:

char   values include all of the single characters that appear on the keyboard: letters, punctuation, digits, and so on. Most Pascal implementations use the standard *ASCII* (as´-kee) set of 128 characters.

the standard types

integer   values are the whole numbers: −2,−1, 0, 1, 2, etc.

real   values are decimals and positive or negative powers of 10: 96.08, or 16.7E44, or −2.7E−03. The optional E means 'times 10 raised to the power' that follows.

boolean   (boo´-lee-an) values, sometimes called *logical* values, have just two alternatives—FALSE and TRUE. We won't use them until Chapter 5.

string extensions

What about strings (any sequence of characters between quote marks, like this: 'This is a string.')? Although there's no string type in Standard Pascal, a type STRING is a very common extension. There's usually an upper length limit and a prohibition against including carriage returns in the string.

the ordinal types

> Types char, boolean, and integer are sometimes called *ordinal* types. That just means that their values can be ordered and numbered consistently, regardless of computer system.

Type real can't be ordinal because computers vary in the way they deal with mathematical reals. In effect, one computer may have more reals between 1.0 and 2.0 than another one does, so trying to number them consistently is hopeless. There are a few rules to remember about literal values:

— A quote mark or apostrophe requires an additional single quote mark (not the double quote " key):

quoting quotes

    writeln ('You wouldn´´t, I couldn´´t, and she won´´t.');
    writeln (' The tape shows that I said: ´´But it would be wrong.´´ ')

commas are forbidden

— Commas never appear in numbers: 2001 is an integer, but 2,001 is not legal.

— real numbers must always have a digit on each side of the decimal: 0.5 is a real, but .5 isn't even a value in Pascal.

— There's an alternative way to write literal real numbers: use a *scale factor* as an exponent. The letter E means 'times 10 raised to the power' that follows, and is common in scientific notation:

using scale factors

    10.0 *is also* 1.0E1, *since it's* 1 *times* 10 *to the first power.*
    325.0 *is also* 3.25E2, *since it's* 3.25 *times* 10 *squared.*
    0.003 *is also* 3E−03, *since it's* 3 *times* 10 *to the negative third power.*

real number

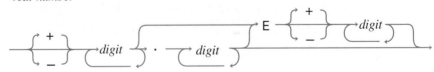

Q. What will the output of this procedure call be?

        writeln (´ ´´writeln; write (´´Printout.´´); ´);

A. The string includes everything between the single quote marks, bearing in mind that a doubled quote is printed as one quote mark. The output is:

```
´writeln; write (´Printout.´);
```

Q. What are the types of 3, ´3´, and 3E3?

A. The number 3 is a literal integer value and the digit character ´3´ is a char value that might also be used as a string. Even though it represents the whole number three thousand, 3E3 is a real because it has a scale factor.

Background: Why Won't Numbers Behave?

Even though computers can store many numbers, they usually allow only a limited number of digits for any single value. Typically, we get just five or ten digits for integer values. Add one to the largest positive number, and we *overflow* down to the smallest negative number on most computers, and crash on others.

real numbers are more complicated. There's always a tradeoff between the number of digits on the left and right of the decimal point. A number that's close to 1 can be accurate to many decimal places, but a very large number might not even be accurate to one decimal. That's why large real numbers are further apart than small ones. There just aren't enough digits to go around.

This can wreak havoc with arithmetic. Suppose that you're trying to add very small numbers to a very large one. If the big number uses most of its digits on the left of the decimal, it might not have enough left on the right to store a number that's mostly zeros. Numerical programmers must be careful to add small numbers together, then add their sum to the big value. If the small numbers are added to the big number one at a time, they may disappear entirely! The issue is discussed in more detail in Appendix C.

Variable Declarations

A variable is a temporary name for a value. 'Hold,' 'represent,' and 'store' are all equivalent ways of describing what a variable does: it keeps a value for us.

variables are type-checked

> In Pascal, every variable has to have a particular type. It can store only values that have the same type.

If we look at AddMe again, you should have a better idea of exactly what it means to say that Age is an integer variable: it means that Age has to store a whole number. Trying to store any other type of value leads to program doom.

```pascal
program AddMe (input, output);
    {Shows a variable declaration and input procedure call.}
var Age : integer;          {The variable declaration.}
begin
    write ('How old are you?    ');          {Prompt for input.}
    readln (Age);                            {Get and store the number the user types.}
    write ('In twenty years you will be   ');
    writeln (Age + 20)       {The numbers are added before they're printed.}
end. {AddMe}
```

declaring and using a variable

We'll get to the operating details of the readln procedure in a few pages.

Although some languages let you create variables on the fly just by using them, Pascal requires that all variables be *declared* at the start of the main program. In AddMe, the *variable declaration part*—the reserved word **var**, followed by individual variable declarations—is short. Here's a declaration that creates many variables. Notice that **var** may appear only once, no matter how many different kinds of variables are declared:

```pascal
program Sample (input, output);

var Counter:  integer;        {Any positive or negative whole number.}
    ShoeSize:  real;          {Any decimal value.}
    FirstInitial:  char;      {Any single character value.}
    OutToLunch:  boolean;     {Either FALSE or TRUE — we'll use this in Chapter 5.}

begin        etc.
```

sample variable declarations

> The quickest *runtime error*, or program crash, in Pascal comes if you try to give a variable of one type a value of another type. The rule can be bent—an integer value can be given to a real variable—but it can't be broken. If a program asks you to enter a number, typing a letter or word will cause it to crash, because variables are type-checked.

runtime errors cause program crashes

We can declare any number of variables, of any type, and in any order, as long as commas separate variables and semicolons separate types. This is also a legal variable declaration:

```pascal
var TimingMark:  integer;          {One integer variable.}
    GPA, BattingAverage:  real;
    Counter, Degrees:  integer;    {More integer variables.}
```

Here's the syntax chart of a variable declaration. We won't be talking about the *new type* option until we start to define our own types a half-dozen chapters from now.

variable declaration part

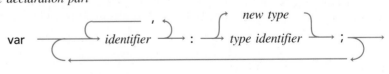

Q. Which of these is a legal variable declaration part?

    a) **var** First: integer;
            Second: char;
            Third: integer;

    b) **var** First, Third: integer;
            Second: char;

    c) **var** First, Third: integer;
        var Second: char;

A. The first two declarations are legal. Ease of understanding should be your main guideline in choosing which format to use. The third declaration is illegal because a program can't have two variable declaration parts—**var** can't be repeated.

Background: Why Have Types?

Why does Pascal use types? To protect the programmer from the computer. Since all values are held as binary numbers (sequences of zeros and ones) within the computer, it would be perfectly content to add an integer to a character or to subtract true from 45.378.

Before typing came along, errors of this sort (where a programmer forgot that she was using a variable to store characters and instead treated the stored value as a number) caused serious errors. It wasn't that the mistaken results couldn't be spotted, mind you. Rather, the source of an error was almost impossible to find—in its context, the incorrect statement seemed perfectly appropriate.

Pascal's type separation helps detect, and prevent, nonsensical activity. Most kinds of usage can be checked for type consistency at compile time, even before programs are run. To be sure, everybody complains about type checking sometimes—there are occasions when errors detected by type checks seem inconsequential (say, the difference between 1 and 1.0). But on the whole, type checking is so useful that almost every high-level language employs it.

1-2   I/O Procedures and Arguments

INPUT AND OUTPUT, OR I/O, IS ONE OF THE MORE confusing areas of most programming languages. The underlying problem is the difficulty of being relaxed and precise at the same time. Rules that make dealing with I/O of numbers easier usually make I/O of letters harder—sometimes, you just can't win.

Let's attack the gory details of the output procedures write and writeln and the input procedures read and readln. I'm going to be thorough so that you can have a comprehensive reference later. But as you read, try to avoid the thought that all programming involves as much nit-picking as this section will require.

Output Procedures

write and writeln are going to turn out to be our most frequently used procedures, so let's begin with a close look at what they do and how they differ. Recall that in a statement like this:

```
writeln ('This is a typical procedure call. ');
```

the writeln is the procedure that's being called, while the string, given between parentheses, is its argument.

— writeln adds a carriage return to its output; write doesn't.

— writeln can be called without an argument or parentheses; write must always have an argument in parentheses.

— write and writeln can be given multiple arguments separated by commas.

These three statements have just one argument per call:

```
{One argument per call is clear.}
write (10);
write ('TEN');
writeln ('10');
```

This call uses commas to separate the arguments, so it has the same effect.

```
{But multiple arguments are sometimes convenient.}
writeln (10, 'TEN', '10');
```

Now, the first time you try to print numbers you might be taken somewhat aback by their *default*, or standard, output format. Note that there's supposed to be one space after the word 'splitting,' one on either side of 'dollars,' and one before 'ways.'

default output causes problems

```
{What numerical output looks like.}
write ('Splitting ');
write (10);
write (' dollars ');     {Note that I'm trying to leave exactly one blank }
write (12);                  { where it seems necessary.}
write (' ways gives $');
writeln (10/12);
```

```
Splitting        10 dollars     12 ways gives $ 8.83333333333E-01
```

As you can see, there are extra spaces before the integer values, and many extra digits accompanying the real. The exact number of spaces and digits will vary from system to system.

numbers are formatted

> In Pascal, both integer and real values can be *formatted* for output. Formatting controls the number of blanks that precede the number and the kind of notation used to write reals.

Formatting numbers so that humans can read them is a major preoccupation of some computers. For example, here's my monthly bill for the U.C. Berkeley computer I use for electronic mail. Although I don't know anything about the program that generates the bill, I can assume that the dates and account numbers must be integers, while the amounts are real.

```
RBSBILL -O883-INVOICE                      INFORMATION SYSTEMS & TECHNOLOGY
* * * * * * * * * * * *                     UNIVERSITY OF CALIFORNIA AT BERKELEY
* MAIN ACCNT ID. - QR24    *
* * * * * * * * * * * *                     USER ACCOUNT SERVICES CUSTOMER REPORT

COOPER, DOUG
BERKELEY, CA 94707                      * * * * * * * * * * * * * * * * *
                                        *       SERVICES USED BY         *
PAGE NUMBER   -    1                    *       SUB-ACCOUNT ID.          *
REPORT DATE  - 08/31/92                 *           QR24                 *
CURRENT DATE - 09/03/92                 *                                *
                                        * * * * * * * * * * * * * * * * *


                                        QUANTITY     UNITS          TOTAL CHARGES

       SERVICES
          VAX (GARNET) DAY CONNECT          3.06 HOUR                   2.30
          VAX (GARNET) TWI. CONNECT        12.20 HOUR                   4.51
          VAX (GARNET) DAY CPU TIME         1.03 MINUTE                 8.70
          VAX (GARNET) TWI. CPU TIME        4.52 MINUTE                18.91
          VAX (GARNET) DISK STORAGE         1.74 200 BLOCKS             1.74
          VAX (GARNET) REDEYE CPU TIME      4.08 MINUTE                 8.46
          VAX (GARNET) REDEYE CONNECT      40.75 HOUR                   8.15

                    TOTAL FOR THIS SECTION. . . . . . . . . . . .      52.77
```

By default (default values are the built-in amounts) integer values are right-aligned in a *field* of blanks. The typical default field is eight or ten blanks. To specify a smaller field, follow the integer with a colon and the width you want:

writeln (10 : *width*);   {*Specifying a particular field width.*}

integer output rules

— If the *width* is greater than the number of digits in the number, blanks will precede the number.

— If the *width* is smaller than or equal to the number of digits, the whole number is printed anyway. Digits are never lost.

Since digits aren't lost, I'll usually specify a field width of 1 when I want exact spacing. The only reason for using longer fields is to make it easy to print tables of numbers like this:

printing tables

```
{Print a table of integers.}
write (234890:8);  write (77:8);  write (891:8);
writeln;
write (16:8);  write (–3394:8);  write (6:8);
writeln;
write (10:8);  write (7892349:8);  write (6832:8);
writeln;
```

```
  234890        77      891
      16     –3394        6
      10   7892349     6832
```

real values are harder. There are two ways to print real values in Pascal:

— *Fixed-point* notation is the most common way—the number is written with its decimal point fixed firmly between the ones and tenths columns.

fixed- vs. floating-point
notation

— *Floating-point* (also called *scientific*) notation puts the decimal immediately to the right of the first non-zero digit. A scale factor supplies the magnitude.

Thus, fixed-point notation never uses scale factors, while floating-point notation always does.

Pascal decides which format you want by inspecting the argument you give to write or writeln. To print a real number in fixed-point notation, you must follow the value with two additional numbers separated by colons:

writeln (10.0 : *width* : *decimal places*);

If there's just one additional argument, or if there isn't any, the number is printed in floating-point format:

writeln (10.0 : *width*);
writeln (10.0);   {*This uses the default width.*}

real output rules

— By default, reals are printed in floating-point notation. The default *width* value is typically a dozen or more place. If you provide a large *width* you'll get blanks before the number; a small value will limit the number of digits printed. Some systems require a leading blank for positive floating-point output.

— The *decimal places* value forces fixed-point notation and puts that many digits after the decimal point. It overrides the *width* value if necessary.

Suppose that Fourth equals 0.25 and Ton equals 2000.0. Then:

```
write (Fourth);      write ('   ');      writeln (Ton);
write (Fourth:4);    write ('   ');      writeln (Ton:4);
write (Fourth:6:4);  write ('   ');      writeln (Ton:6:4);
write (Fourth:1:4);  write ('   ');      writeln (Ton:1:4);
```

```
2.5000000000000000E-001      2.0000000000000001E+003
2.5E-001     2.0E+003
0.2500    2000.0000
0.2500    2000.0000
```

The decimal-places argument is useful for printing money amounts or if we merely prefer fixed-point to floating-point notation. As with integer output, I'll generally use a field width of 1 and rely on the computer to provide enough room to handle the number of decimal digits requested.

fixed-point notation

{*Note that multiple arguments are legal, but they can be confusing.*}
writeln ('Splitting ', 10 : 1, ' dollars ', 12 : 1, ' ways gives $', 10/12 : 1 : 2, '.');

```
Splitting 10 dollars 12 ways gives $0.83.
```

Q. What's the output of each of these procedure calls? Don't forget about leading (initial) blanks.

- *a*) writeln (7.0 :1 :3);
- *b*) writeln (3.0E5 :11 :5);
- *c*) writeln (16.928 :6 :2);
- *d*) write ('$'); writeln (1.599E2 :1 :2);
- *e*) writeln (3.2958777E3 :2 :8)
- *f*) write ('3*2'); write ('='); writeln (3*2 :1);

A. I've marked each blank space with an underline.

a) 7.000	*b*) 300000.00000
c) _16.93	*d*) $159.90
e) 3295.87770000	*f*) 3*2=6

Input Procedures

As Fran Lebowitz points out, the opposite of talking isn't listening—it's waiting. This is something that programs manage very well. Program BugMe, below, waits, reads, and responds.

```
program BugMe (input, output);
    {Shows a variable declaration and input procedure call.}
var IQ : integer;          {The variable declaration.}
begin
    write ('What''s your IQ?   ');        {Prompt for input.}
    readln (IQ);                           {Get and store the number the user types.}
    write ('What? I bet you can''t even count to ');
    writeln (IQ : 1)        {Print in the minimum space.}
end. {BugMe}
```

declaring and using a variable

What's your IQ? **183**
What? I bet you can't even count to 183

interactive vs. batch programs

An *interactive* program has a back-and-forth interaction with the person who's using it. Not every program is interactive. In the old days, all program input had to be prepared in advance and submitted with the program itself. The package was known as a *batch* program, a term that is still sometimes used to describe programs that can be run without any human intervention.

At any rate, an *input procedure* like readln gets the value that your program's user types and stores it in a variable. Most people pronounce it *read line*. The call:

```
readln (IQ);
```

would read whatever digit characters the user typed, calculate the integer they represented, then store the number in IQ.

> A program that expects to read a value should prompt the user to enter it. Otherwise, she has no idea that she's supposed to type one in—and a computer will *hang*, or silently wait forever.

The program user has an unstated job, too: she has to hit the `Enter` or the `Return` (on Mac or DEC keyboards) key when she's done typing. Otherwise the computer doesn't know that she's typed anything at all.

Now, if you think about it for a moment, you'll realize that the `Enter` or the `Return` key actually adds to the input the user enters. After procedure readln has gotten the value we want, it discards any additional characters, including the `Enter` or `Return` , that might remain on the input line. A second input procedure called read doesn't dump anything. Instead, it does a minimal amount of work, just reading a value for its argument and leaving any additional input untouched.

The idea of discarding lines is a bit confusing. It dates from the old days, back when both computer programs and their data were prepared on individually punched cards (sometimes called *IBM cards*), then literally stacked in a sort of input hopper controlled by the computer. Since each card was equivalent to a line of input, readln would always eject the current card and get the next one as part of its action. read, in contrast, would leave the current card in the hopper.

In general, readln does what we want, since we'll usually want to ignore the line-ending keys. Here's a summary of the differences between readln and read.

— readln automatically discards the current line of input, through and including the `Enter` or `Return` ; read doesn't.

— readln does not *require* an argument or parentheses; read does. Use readln by itself to get rid of a whole line (or the remainder of a line) of input.

— Both read and readln can be given multiple arguments, separated by commas.

This series of input procedure calls:

```
{This is a little clearer.}
read (First);
read (Second);
readln;
```

is identical to this single call:

```
{This is a bit more convenient.}
readln (First, Second);
```

Now, the precise action of both read and readln depends on the type (in the Pascal sense of the word) of the argument. The underlying theory is that when we're trying to read numbers, all white space (blanks and the like) should be skipped and ignored, but when we're dealing with characters, the lowliest blank space might be important.

argument type	*action of* read *or* readln
char	assigns the very next single input character, and only one character, to its argument. If you're at the end of the line, the argument gets a single space character assigned to it.
integer	skips any blanks, tabs, or Enter or Return keys, then reads a plus or minus sign (if there is one) and the longest series of digits it can. The ending character—the space or letter that follows the last digit—is *not* read.
real	skips any blanks, tabs, or Enter or Return keys, then tries to read a plus or minus sign (if there is one) followed by a real value. Again, the ending character—the space or letter that follows the last digit—is *not* read.

Modification Problems

1. Modify BugMe so that it asks for, but ignores, the user's name before reading the IQ.
2. Change BugMe so that it asks for the user's initials. Have it respond 'What? I bet you can't even spell . . .'

A Generic Program Crash

Can anything go wrong with input? Sure! The most common problems involve reading numbers. If your program reads a letter before it gets to a digit, the resulting runtime error will make your program blow up. But exactly what does a crash look like? I think it's time for a test bed program.

Consider program ReadTest, below. It doesn't solve any problems or attempt any useful work, but it does try to perform a few experiments in Pascal. Its variable declarations are easy to change, and its action is easy to follow.

our first crash

```
———————————— READTEST.PAS ————————————
program ReadTest (input, output);
   {A test bed for learning about read and readln.}
var First:  integer;
    Second: integer;           {It's easy to change these declarations.}
    Third:  integer;
begin
   writeln ('Ready to start testing.  What should I read?');
   read (First);                 {What would happen to the input shown}
   read (Second);                {if these were readln statements?}
   read (Third);
   writeln ('All done.  Values are');
   writeln (First : 1);          {Try minimal spacing.}
   writeln (Second : 20);        {Try a larger field.}
   writeln (Third : 0)           {See what happens!}
end.   {ReadTest}
```

```
                                      ——— Variables ———
                                       First: 10
                                       Second: 20
                                       Third: 0
```

```
———————————— Input & Output ————————————
Ready to start testing.  What should I read?
10    20    oops
Runtime error 106 at 0B2B:00B3.
```

How do we go about writing a program that will crash? Well, I could make the BugMe program crash easily enough by entering my name, say, instead of the integer IQ it requests. But as a rule, good test bed programs are easy to modify, so that I can be sure that I'm really testing what I think I'm testing. For example, I might want to run my crash test, then change its variable types and try again. That way I can be sure that the values I enter are actually causing the problems.

Can you see the problem with ReadTest? The first two integer input values were OK, but the third is just the word 'oops.' Naturally the program crashes. The error message that ReadTest shows:

error messages aren't standardized

```
Runtime error 106 at 0B2B:00B3.
```

is entirely nonstandard, by the way. This happens to be the error message that Turbo Pascal running on a DOS computer produces.

The comments suggest another alteration—changing one of the read statements to a readln. Do you think the crash will still occur if the input is the same? Notice also that I've played around with the output field widths. I understand what widths of 1 and 20 will do, but I'm not so sure about 0. There's only one way to find out—try running a test bed program.

Modification Problems

1. 'Run it up the flagpole, and see who salutes' is a well-accepted approach to business and politics. In other words, if you can't decide if an idea is good, try it out and see what happens.

It's also an excellent approach to exploring Pascal. Think first, obviously, but it never hurts to run an experiment. Write and modify a test bed program to test these propositions: *A program can ...*

a) Divide 0 by 0.
b) Add 1 to MAXINT (the largest legal integer).
c) Consist of **begin begin begin end end end.**
d) Multiply 2000000000 by 3000000000000000000000000.

Input Examples

Programming environments are great, but if you don't have one you'd better grind through some examples on paper. I'll start with simple char input.

Compare statements 1 and 8 to 3 and 9 in the chart below. Although they obtain the same values, the readlns remove the rest of the line as well. Statement 5 mimics statement 7 because it reads all input values, *including* the Enter or Return that ends the line and is read as a blank space.

Assume that we've declared these variables:

var C1, C2, C3, C4, C5, C6: char;

Assume that the sample input to each statement is: **ABCDE**

char input

	Statement	Last value read	Value about to be read
1.	read (C1);	**A**	**B**
2.	read (C1); read (C2);	**B**	**C**
3.	read (C1, C2, C3);	**C**	**D**
4.	read (C1, C2, C3, C4, C5);	**E**	*blank (the return)*
5.	read (C1, C2, C3, C4, C5, C6);	*blank*	*start of next line*
6.	read;	*illegal — there must be an argument*	
7.	readln;	*none*	*start of next line*
8.	readln (C1);	**A**	*start of next line*
9.	readln (C1, C2, C3);	**C**	*start of next line*
10.	readln (C1, C2, C3, C4, C5);	**E**	*start of next line*

leading white space defined

Numerical input is a little harder to follow, because *leading white space—* blanks, tabs, and Return, keys that come before the number—are skipped.

Assume that we've declared these variables:

var First, Second: integer;

numerical input

Assume that the input statement is: readln (First, Second);

Assume that the sample input to the statement is:

```
1.  15 182
2.  15                          182
3.  15
        182
```

All three inputs are identical, even though the amount of white space that precedes the second number is different each time.

Intermingling characters and numbers leads to the most complicated situation. The key facts to remember are that:

— Spaces are skipped before numbers—but not after.

— Any character can end a number—not just a space.

In the table below, I've shown a blank space as an underline, ´_´

Assume that we've declared these variables:

> **var** C1, C2: char;
>   N1, N2: integer;

Assume that the sample input to each statement is: **123_A45B**

		C1	C2	N1	N2	*About to be read*
1.	read (C1);	´1´				´2´, *or* **23**
2.	read (C1, N1);	´1´		23		´_´
3.	read (C1, C2, N1);	´1´	´2´	3		´_´
4.	read (N1, C1);	´_´		123		´A´
5.	read (N1, C1, C2, N2);	´_´	´A´	123	45	´B´
6.	read (N1, N2);			123		*crash!*
7.	read (N1, C1, N2);	´_´		123		*crash!*

mixed input

In examples 6 and 7, the crash occurs for the same reason: we're trying to read the letter ´**A**´ as input for the integer variable N2.

Self-Check Questions

Q. Suppose that a program contains the sequence:

> read (Number1);
> read (Char1);
> read (Char2);

If the program user types in **75 AB**, what will the values of Char1 and Char2 be?

A. Just ask yourself the usual question: according to the rules, when does the read of this particular integer stop? It stops at the space that follows the **75**. Is that space a valid char value? Of course. Thus, the value of Char1 is ´ ´ (a space), while Char2 is ´A´.

Q. Given the same input, **75 AB**, just how *do* you go about reading the values 75, ´A´, and ´B´ correctly?

A. Since there's an extra, but necessary, blank in the input, it has to be read and ignored. Either of the segments below will work, but I recommend the first—it's less confusing:

> {*First approach: use a temporary 'junk' variable.*}
> read (Number1);   {*gets the 75*}
> read (JunkCharacter);   {*gets the blank*}
> read (Char1);   {*gets the* ´A´}
> read (Char2);   {*gets the* ´B´}
>
> {*Second approach: ignore the first value read into* Char1.}
> read (Number1);   {*gets the 75*}
> read (Char1);   {*gets the blank . . .* }
> read (Char1);   { *. . . then gets the* ´A´}
> read (Char2);   {*gets the* ´B´}

Assignments and Expressions

WE'VE HAD INPUT, AND WE'VE HAD OUTPUT, BUT WE haven't really done anything yet. The *assignment* statement changes all that.

the assignment statement

```
program Multiply (input, output);
    {Shows an assignment statement.}
var First, Second, Product : integer;          {The variable declaration.}
begin
    write ('What are your favorite numbers?   ');
    read (First);                              {Get and store the numbers.}
    readln (Second);
    Product := First * Second;                 {Assign a new value to Product.}
    write ('Their product is   ');
    write (Product : 1);                       {Use minimal spacing.}
    writeln ('.  How auspicious!')
end.  {Multiply}
```

```
What are your favorite numbers?  18  37
Their product is 666.  How auspicious!
```

An *assignment statement* changes the value of a variable. It can give the variable a starting value or alter its current value. In Pascal, assignment takes the form:

variable identifier := the value represented by an expression

Don't confuse the assignment operator with an ordinary equals sign, which is used only for comparison in Pascal. The assignment statement's syntax chart is:

assignment statement

    variable identifier ⟶ **:=** ⟶ *expression*

Most people read the assignment operator as 'gets.' For example:

LuckyNumber := 7 + 5;

would be read: 'the variable LuckyNumber gets assigned the result of adding 7 and 5,' or, more succinctly, 'LuckyNumber gets 7 plus 5.'

making assignments

From the computer's point of view, assignment is a two-step process. First, it performs a calculation by *evaluating* the *expression* on the right-hand side of the statement: what does it equal? Then, the *result*, or calculated value, is given to the variable on the left-hand side.

When the expression is just a number, assignments aren't hard to understand, as in the first two statements below. Before the third assignment is carried out, the computer evaluates FirstValue and SecondValue. Result is the only variable that gets changed by the third assignment, because it's the variable on the left-hand side:

```
FirstValue := 3;
SecondValue := 5;
Result := FirstValue + SecondValue;
{Result now equals 8.}
```

Matters are slightly more confusing when the same variable appears on *both* sides of the assignment statement. For example:

```
Result := Result + 1;
{Result now equals 9.}
```

Again, you just have to ignore the left-hand side of the assignment until you're actually ready to store a value. But once you've learned to close your left eye momentarily, it won't matter how many times Result appears in the assignment:

```
Result := Result + Result + Result;
{Result now equals 27.}
```

> A variable must be *initialized*, or given a starting value, before it can appear in an expression. The variable is *undefined* until it is initialized.

```
Age := 17;        {Once Age is initialized…}
LuckyNumber := Age – 2;        {…it can appear in an expression.}
```

initializing variables

Reading new values entered by the program user is an alternative way of initializing variables. But one method or the other must be used, since an uninitialized variable is like an unmade bed. You can never be sure of what the computer put there when it started to run your program.

For example, here's what I found when I started this test bed program. You can imagine why it's called Garbage.

these values will differ from machine to machine

```
─────── GARBAGE.PAS ───────
program Garbage (input, output);
   {Shows the hazards of uninitialized variables.}
var Letter:   char;
    Number:   integer;
    Decimal:  real;
begin
    writeln (Letter);
    writeln (Number);
    writeln (Decimal)
end.   {Garbage}
```

```
─── Variables ───
Letter: 'R'
Number: 73
Decimal: 3.7909692824E-37
```

```
─────── Input & Output ───────
R
73
```

It is extremely disconcerting to find totally random values appearing in your programs, so don't forget to initialize!

Assignments must involve values and variables of appropriate types. If Age is an integer variable, and Fraction is of type real, then these are all valid assignments:

numerical assignments

{*legal assignments of* integer *to* integer *and* real *to* real}
Age := 16;   Fraction := 16.5;

But these assignments contain type clashes between Age, 16.5, and Fraction:

{*illegal assignments of* real *values to* integer *variables*}
Age := 16.5;   Age := Fraction;

The assignment of an integer to a real variable is a special case. It's allowed, even though the types are different. That's because a computer can always figure out the real equivalent of an integer value.

{*legal assignments of* integer *values to* real *variables*}
Fraction := 16;   Fraction := Age;

Assignments to char variables are also special. Since a variable's name might be just one letter long, we have a distinctive way to indicate a one-letter char value—it's enclosed within quote marks. For example:

character assignments

{*legal assignments of characters to* char *variables*}
Initial := ´E´;   SeventhDigitCharacter := ´6´;

Quote marks prevent confusion between the literal value ´E´ and a variable named E, or between the literal value ´6´ and the integer 6. Note that a char variable can only represent a single character's value—assigning ´XTC´ to a char would be an error.

Self-Check Questions

Q. Correct these assignment statements:

a) 2nd := 1st + Error;   *b)* 3+9 := Sum;
c) FirstLetter := A;   *d)* Initial := ´WS´;
e) TaxRate := 5%;   *f)* Start := Init := 0;

A. The rewritten assignments are:

a) Second := First + Error;   *b)* Sum := 3+9;
c) FirstLetter := ´A´;   *d)* A char variable holds just one letter
e) TaxRate := 0.05;   *f)* Start := 0; Init := 0;

Q. Consider each of these pairs as a separate sequence of assignments. Which pairs can be replaced by a single assignment statement? What is it?

a) IQ := SAT − 600;
    IQ := 125 + Age;
b) Quiz := 4 − Test;
    Quiz := Quiz * 3;
c) Weight := Length + 62;
    Measure := Length * Measure;
d) Margin := Margin + 6;
    Margin := 32 − Margin;

A. One statement can replace two either when the second statement makes the first one irrelevant (as in *a*) or when the second statement uses the variable assigned in the first statement (as in *b* and *d*).

a) IQ := 125 + Age;

b) Quiz := 12 – (3 * Test); *or* Quiz := (4 – Test) * 3;

c) Can't be simplified.

d) Margin := 26 – Margin;

Expressions

An expression *represents* a value. The very simplest expressions are literal values like 17 or 't'. Once a variable has been initialized, or given a starting value, it becomes an expression because now it represents a value too.

Expressions can be complicated, too. For instance, think about 1 + 1, which you probably thought was pretty simple. In fact, it has:

— an *operator*, the plus sign;

dissecting 1 + 1 — two *operands*, the 1's;

— a *result* or *value*, the answer, 2, and, finally;

— a result *type*, which is the answer's Pascal type.

Fortunately, even though I have to introduce these terms in order to write precisely, you'll use expressions in programs pretty much the same way you've always used them on paper. The main thing to remember is that no matter how simple or complicated an expression is, it always has a Pascal type, just like a variable. This makes sense, because the computer is usually going to evaluate the expression so we can assign it to a variable.

Most of the expressions we'll write for the next few chapters involve arithmetic. There are two basic kinds of arithmetic operators—those that take real operands and those that take integers. The real operators are:

real *Arithmetic Operators*

+	*addition*	1.0 + 0.03E–17
–	*subtraction*	0.03 – 6.2
*	*multiplication*	32.87 * 6.5E–02
/	*division*	5.0E20 / 2.0

real operators

The integer operators are the same except that the slash has been replaced by two special operators for division—**div**, and **mod**. They do the 'whole and remainder' division that you learned in grade school.

integer *Arithmetic Operators*

+	*addition*	3 + 2
–	*subtraction*	–7 – 1
*	*multiplication*	52 * 17
div	*'whole number' division*	10 **div** 3 (*is* 3)
mod	*'remainder' division*	10 **mod** 3 (*is* 1)

integer operators

The first of the new division operators, **div**, gives us the quotient of a division without a remainder, as though the quotient had been rounded toward div and mod

zero. **mod** (whose second operand must be positive) does just the opposite. It ignores the 'whole' part of the quotient and provides only the remainder.

9 **div** 5 *is* 1	24 **div** 9 *is* 2	−9 **div** 5 *is* −1
9 **mod** 5 *is* 4	24 **mod** 9 *is* 6	9 **mod** 24 *is* 9

Note that **div** and **mod** are reserved words that can't be redefined. They represent operations, just as + and − do.

types of operands

> The operands of **div** and **mod** are both required to be of type integer.

This rule means that some kinds of expressions aren't legal, even though they make sense to us. For example:

a few illegal expressions

Expression	*Why it's always illegal*
4.0 **div** 2.0	*Operands of* **div** *can't be* real.
1.0E+02 **mod** 50	*Operands of* **mod** *can't be* real.

> If either operand of +, −, or * is real, the entire expression is real. If the operator is /, the expression is real even if both operands are integer.

An expression's legality can depend on how it's used. These expressions can't be assigned to integer variables, because the type of each expression is real:

Expression	*Why it may be illegal*
1.0 + 1	*if one operand is* real, *the whole expression is* real
4 / 2	*if the operator is* /, *the whole expression is* real

Operator Precedence

In Pascal, as in ordinary arithmetic, we can combine small expressions into a chain of operations. As long as the rules about intermingling types are obeyed, expressions can be as complicated as you like.

However, when expressions have several operators, the problem of *operator precedence* comes up. What part of the expression will take precedence, and be evaluated first? Does 4 + 3 * 2 equal 14 (do the addition first) or 10 (do the multiplication first)?

rules for evaluating expressions

Programming languages solve this problem by fiat or decree: there is a hierarchy, or ordering, of different operations. Expressions that contain more than one operator from a given level of the hierarchy are usually evaluated from left to right. Parentheses can change the order of evaluation or make it clearer.

In Pascal, arithmetic operations have two precedence levels—addition and subtraction have less precedence than the other operations. The effect of the operations doesn't change, just the order the operations are carried out in:

operator precedence

* / **div mod**	*these operations are completed . . .*
+ −	*. . . before these operations.*

As a result:

2 * 3 + 4	*is* 10, *not* 14
9 – 4 **mod** 2	*is* 9, *not* 1
2.5 + 5.0 / 2.0	*is* 5.0, *not* 3.75

When an expression contains more than a single operator from any one level, we do the multiplications and divisions from left to right first, then perform the lower-level additions and subtractions.

5.5–3.375/1.125	*is* 5.5–3.0	*is* 2.5
5*3+14 **mod** 4	*is* 15+2	*is* 17
4.5/1.125–3.325*6.5	*is* 4.0–21.6125	*is* –17.6125
7–6*2–33 **div** 4–3	*is* 7–12–8–3	*is* –16

parentheses

Parentheses change this order of evaluation, because the part of the expression between parentheses gets evaluated before the rest of the expression does. When we *nest* parentheses—use multiple levels of parentheses—calculations are done from the inside out.

(5+3)*(8–2)	*is equivalent to*	8*6
(6 **div** 3)*(2–4)	*is the same as*	2*(–2)
2.5*(1.25+0.25)	*is*	2.5*1.5
(8 **mod** (2 * (5 – 4)))	*is*	8 **mod** 2

You can appreciate that there's usually more than one way to write an expression. You'll often feel that you're faced with a choice between relying on the operator precedence rules and using parentheses.

> Don't choose. Instead, use the combination that makes a clear, readable expression. This usually means that you should add a few parentheses even if they're not required. Write expressions that can be understood by human beings, and the computers will take care of themselves.

An expression can be confusing even though it does just what you want it to. Compare the assignment:

Income := Receipts + Tips * Share; {*A Share of what?*}

write expressions clearly

to the one below, which relies on redundant parentheses to make our intention clear:

Income := Receipts + (Tips * Share); {*A Share of Tips.*}

Self-Check Questions ─────────────────────────────

Q. Evaluate these expressions:

a) 25 **mod** 5	*b)* 25 **div** 5	*c)* 5 **mod** 5
d) 5 **div** 5	*e)* 27 **div** 18	*f)* 33 **mod** 19
g) 12.0E02 / 2.0	*h)* 1.25 * 1.0E02	*i)* 12.0E–02 / 2.0
j) 1.25 * (1.0E–02)	*k)* 5 – 9 * 3 + 2	*l)* 7 * 8 – 9 + 12 **div** 5

A. For more practice, try joining examples with parentheses.

a) 0	*b)* 5	*c)* 0
d) 1	*e)* 1	*f)* 14
g) 600.0	*h)* 125.0	*i)* 0.06
j) 0.0125	*k)* −20	*l)* 49

Constant Definitions

Let's sneak one last Pascal fact into this chapter: constants. Variables hold values that change. *Constants*, in contrast, represent values permanently. The value can't be changed during program execution—that would be more appropriate for a variable. The syntax chart of a constant definition part is:

constant definition part

Constant definitions follow the program heading but come before variable declarations. A constant's type depends on its definition. For example:

defining constants

```
const DOGname = 'Ronnie';              {a string}
      DOGage = 2;                       {type integer}
      FLATtop = '[';                    {a bunch of chars}
      CURLY = '{';
      EYES = ':';
      WINK = ';';
      NOSE = '-';
      PUGnose = '~';
      SMILE = ')';
      FROWN = '(';
      GOATEE = '>';
      CIGARETTE = PUGnose;              {renaming a constant}
```

A constant's value can't be calculated as part of its definition, nor can variables be used to supply the value. Only literal values or previously defined constants may appear. That makes these definitions illegal:

an illegal example

```
{These definitions are illegal because they require calculations.}
      DOGyears = 7 * DOGage;
      DOGiq = 5 * (DOGage / DOGyears);
```

> I capitalize the first word of constant identifiers as a matter of programming style. It makes them instantly distinguishable from variables.

Here's how I'd put together a couple of faces:

```
writeln (FLATTOP, EYES, NOSE, FROWN, CIGARETTE);
writeln (CURLY, WINK, NOSE, SMILE, GOATEE);
```

```
[ : - ( ~
{ ; - ) >
```

String constants are printed with procedure write or writeln but don't have to be put in quote marks. The identifier represents the actual string.

```
write ( 'Time for your walk,  ');        {The string goes in quotes…}
writeln ( DOGname );                     {…but the constant can't have them.}
```

```
Time for your walk, Ronnie
```

Pascal has a predefined constant that is sometimes useful. MAXINT represents the largest integer value. It varies from system to system, but here's a typical value:

```
writeln (MAXINT);
```

a predefined constant

```
32767
```

Now, suppose that we take Niklaus Wirth to task for a moment. Why did he inflict yet another language feature for us to memorize? Is there anything a defined constant can do that an ordinary variable—or even an ordinary literal value—can't accomplish? Try to answer this question and you'll begin to gain some insight into the difference between programming and memorizing (then regurgitating) syntax.

Perhaps my water bill will give you one clue. Look behind the bill, and imagine that you wrote the program that created it:

For: DOUG COOPER 61 DAYS NEXT READING 05/26/92		AMOUNT
PRIVATE RESIDENCE		
WATER CHARGES - EBMUD		
WATER SERVICE CHARGE		11.10
WATER FLOW CHARGE	20 UNITS AT 1.05	21.00
	9 UNITS AT 1.30	11.70
WATER ELEVATION CHARGE		4.35
TOTAL		48.15

What constants would you probably rely on? Here are the ones that I was able to figure out (I never got to the bottom of the service charge). The constants help *document* the program. They explain what's what in a way that plain figures—even with comments—can't.

a few water bill constants

```
const BASEunits = 20;        {More usage gets a higher charge.}
      BASErate = 1.05;       {The basic charge.}
      OVERUSErate = 1.30;    {The 'overuse' charge.}
      ELEVATIONrate = 0.15;  {The delivery surcharge per unit.}
```

Try the same exercise on my gas and electricity bill:

```
                                                              Pacific Gas and Electric Company
Questions? Call our office at:     Type of  SERVICE PERIOD Billing METER READINGS  Reading  Multiplier GAS-Therms*  Amount
2111 M L KING JR WY                Service  From    To   Days  Prior  Present  Difference        ELEC-KWH
BERKELEY     CA  94704             GAS    122  224   33   2796  2877   81 1.020        83     49.05
(510) 543-8658                     ELEC   122  224   33   5637  6682  1045     1      1045    136.70
Your Account Number                                 ENERGY COMMISSION TAX                      .21
                                                    CITY TAX 7.5%                            13.93
TJR07 38314-8             GAS MTR NO.   27241610
                         ELEC MTR NO.   419276            TOTAL CURRENT CHARGES            199.89
Rate Schedule                                            PREVIOUS BALANCE                   81.50
                                                         02/20 PAYMENT-THANK YOU           81.50-
G 1T     E  1TB
                                                         TOTAL AMOUNT NOW DUE            $199.89
ROTATING OUTAGE BLOCK 07
DOUG COOPER FEBRUARY, 1992

BASELINE QUANTITIES     GAS -     66.0 THERMS       ELECTRIC -    297.0 KWH
BASELINE USAGE          66.0 THERMS ə $0.52538       297.0 KWH ə  $0.11107
OVER BASELINE USAGE     17.0 THERMS ə  0.84556       748.0 KWH ə   0.13865
```

This time the focus is different. Here, the named constants help prevent errors.

some gas bill constants

const BASEtherms = 66.0;	{More usage gets a higher charge.}
BASEgasRate = 0.52538;	{The basic gas charge.}
OVERgasRate = 0.84556;	{The overuse gas charge.}
GASmultiplier = 1.020;	{I think this varies with the temperature.}
BASEkwh = 297.0;	{Again, more usage gets a penalty charge.}
BASEelectricRate = 0.11107;	{The basic electricity charge.}
OVERelectricRate = 0.13865;	{The overuse electricity charge.}

Suppose that the above figures appear more than once in the program. If you make an error typing in a multi-digit number, there's no safety net. The program will run, but its output will be wrong. But if you make a mistake typing in a constant name, the compiler can catch it—it's an unknown identifier.

But why wouldn't ordinary variables serve the same purpose? Well, constant definitions *localize* control, because there's only one place to change values. Variables, in contrast, could be modified anywhere within a program. This might not seem to be a big potential hazard in small programs over which you have total control, but it is an important issue when programs are long or have several programmers working on them.

Self-Check Questions

Q. Each constant can be described as a member of a particular type. Name it.

a) WIDTH = 5   b) CORRECTION = −3
c) NUMBER = ´15´   d) FACTOR = 85.0E–02
e) PRODUCT = −4 ∗ 6   f) TENspaces = ´
g) NEWsize = −CORRECTION   h) KILLcharacter = ´X´

A. The types are:

   a, b, g — *integer*
   c, f — *string*
   d — real
   e — *illegal*
   h — *char*

A Final Example

Suppose that we look at a complete example program. The problem is motivated by a minor fact I ran across one day. It seems that there is a tiny difference between International pounds, which weigh 0.45359237 kilograms, and American pounds, which are slightly heavier at 0.4535924277 kilograms. 'Does this really matter?,' you may be asking yourself! Well, perhaps it depends on your line of work:

problem: pounds to carats

A diamond dealer has gone to Amsterdam to buy a ton—2,000 pounds—of stones. She is thrilled to discover that although she buys diamonds in American pounds, her company only expects to receive International pounds, which are a shade lighter. As a little bonus, she can keep any difference! Write a program that lets her know, in carats, just how large her bonus will be. There are 5,000 carats per kilogram.

Solving the problem isn't very difficult: it just requires all the Pascal you've learned so far! Nevertheless, it won't take much of an algorithm. We'll get the information, perform a calculation, and print the results.

step-by-step to the answer

> *find out how many American pounds have to be bought;*
> *calculate the number of International pounds that have to be delivered;*
> *report the size of the difference;*

However, *implementing* the algorithm—writing it out in Pascal—requires some thought. Whether or not we consciously think about it, we're going to have to deal with some of the basic issues I brought up at the beginning of this chapter. For example, this assignment *could* be part of the solution:

```
{Some truly awful code.}
Z := (2000.0 * 0.4535924277) – (113 * 0.45359237);
```

But it's impossible to figure out. Here's a slight improvement that's still pretty inscrutable:

```
{Some merely terrible code.}
X := 2000.0 * 0.4535924277;
Y := 2000.0 * 0.45359237;
Z := X – Y;
```

Suppose that I rewrite the sequence in more self-explanatory terms:

```
{Code that's clear enough for your roommate to understand.}
KgToBuy := PoundsToBuy * USAinKg;
KgToDeliver := PoundsToBuy * INTERNATIONALinKg;
KgToKeep := KgToBuy – KgToDeliver;
```

Now the implementation makes much more sense. I've decided to do all calculations in terms of kilograms, because they're the same everywhere. The first assignment lets me know how many kilograms of diamonds I'm going to have to buy by converting American pounds into their kilogram equivalent. The second assignment makes the same calculation for delivery, and the third is pretty self-explanatory.

Without really realizing it, I've dealt with the biggest issue of programming—choosing the right level of *abstraction* versus *detail*. On one hand, I want to take things one step at a time—that's detail. But on the other, I'll try to use names in place of values whenever I can—that's abstraction. The interesting part of our final program comes before the first program **begin**, when we define constants and variables. A little effort here makes the final program easy to read and understand.

The final version of program Trader is shown below. Note the care I've taken in labeling its output, to make sure that it's meaningful to a casual program user who might be unfamiliar with scientific notation of reals.

label output clearly

> Label program output, and present it in a clear, readable manner. Don't force a program user to read a program's code to figure out what it does.

assignment statement
example program

```
program Trader (input, output);
    {Finds the carat difference between weights in International and American pounds.}
const INTERNATIONALinKg = 0.45359237;
      USAinKg = 0.4535924277;              {All constants show weight in kilos.}
      ONEcarat = 0.0002;
var PoundsToBuy, KgToBuy, KgToDeliver,
    KgToKeep, CaratsToKeep: real;
begin
    write ('How many pounds are you buying? (to nearest 0.1)    ');
    readln (PoundsToBuy);
    KgToBuy := PoundsToBuy * USAinKg;
    KgToDeliver := PoundsToBuy * INTERNATIONALinKg;
    KgToKeep := KgToBuy – KgToDeliver;
    CaratsToKeep := KgToKeep / ONEcarat;
    write ('Difference in pounds:    ');
    writeln (KgToKeep / USAinKg : 12 : 4);
    write ('Difference in carats:    ');
    writeln (CaratsToKeep : 12 : 1)
end.   {Trader}
```

```
How many pounds are you buying? (to nearest 0.1)  2000.0
Difference in pounds:        0.0003
Difference in carats:        0.6
```

To the diamond dealer's dismay, her bonus on the one-ton sale would barely suit her as an engagement ring.

It's good to be cautious when doing real arithmetic, incidentally. Computers are good with numbers, but the number of digits they use for real calculations is limited.

> write can print figures far beyond the computer's accuracy. An impressive sequence of digits can be misleading and wrong.

When I tested my first version of Trader, I found that it gave one answer on a workstation or minicomputer and another, slightly different result on a PC, because the PC allows fewer digits for storing decimals. The final version of Trader avoids the problem by restricting its result to the first non-zero digit.

Modification Problems

1. As you can see, the calls of writeln in Trader use actual numbers to specify the number of digits to print, and the size of the printing field. Define appropriate constants to take the place of the numbers.

2. Reverse the operation of Trader, so that a dealer who knows how many carats she has can find out the equivalent weights in American and International pounds.

1-4 Program Engineering Notes: Bugs and Beyond

LARGE-SCALE SOFTWARE SYSTEMS, LIKE LARGE-SCALE transportation systems, require software engineers: people who can put together enough experience, calculation, and common sense to build systems and keep them running.

Little programs take experience, calculation, and common sense, too. I might even say that we have to become *program engineers*. We have to learn skills and ideas that are language independent but are still necessary for writing clear, working programs.

Short-lived programs	Longer, shared projects	Large applications and systems
10 – 1,000 lines	*1,000 – 10,000 lines*	*10,000 lines and up*
Program Engineering	*a bit of both*	Software Engineering

Now, you don't have to be an expert to be a good engineer. Experts know facts. On one hand, they know the syntax of a programming language; on the other, they understand the details of a particular algorithm or application. However, expertise at the extremes doesn't always lead to good programming ability. A programmer has to be able to put together different talents and write programs that:

— are easy to check and test;

— can be finished or improved by somebody else if necessary;

— are completed in a reasonable amount of time;

— and, last but not least, work.

The basic guideline is simple. You already know the Golden Rule:

Every program should be as easy for a human being to read and understand as it is for a computer to execute.

write comments . . .

The first piece of advice I'll pass along under the heading of program engineering is *write comments*. Commenting is the first and best line of defense against semantic errors. How many comments? Enough so that the person sitting next to you can figure out your program.

Piece of advice number two may seem strange, but it's equally important—*Don't believe your comments*. Usually, new programmers write comments that say what they *intend* to do: *get the data, print the results*, and so on. Later, when they debug their programs, novices tend to take their comments at face value. They assume that the code that follows actually carries out the intention of the comment.

. . . but don't always
believe them

Experts, in contrast, write comments that document their accomplished *goals*: *we have data, we've printed results*, etc. When experts debug programs, they are able to look at their claims a little more suspiciously: Do we *really* have the data? Did that procedure *actually* print results? Remember—you trust your mother, but you cut the cards.

write short test programs

Tip number three is *try it!* The best way to clarify confusing points about syntax, semantics, and the details of your own Pascal system (if thinking about it gets you nowhere) is to experiment. The computer won't blow up or break down if you make a mistake, so don't worry about crashing the whole system. Soon, if you don't understand a bug or feature, you'll be able to write a six-line program that tests only the point in question. Be sure to echo or reprint any input you supply to make sure that input is really what you think it is.

The best advice of all is to ask somebody for help and to be willing to help somebody yourself. Practice in spotting and explaining bugs benefits everyone.

Mnemonics and Plain Vanilla

A considerable amount of program engineering is devoted to turning programs into what is commonly referred to as *plain vanilla*. In a way, we're constantly resisting two impulses—first, to make programs too clever, and second, to believe that they're already clear. James McKelvey puts his finger on the reason:

why resist cleverness?

> An even larger problem with unclear work is that eventually someone is going to have to read what you have written (if your work is of any consequence at all). The reader, whether teacher, colleague, or superior, must understand it. A confused reader is not likely to say, "Gosh, this is so complicated you must be a genius to understand it. How would you like a raise?" More likely, you will get a response like, "This program is so contorted and incomprehensible we'll never be able to maintain it. How good are you at filing and making coffee?" Anybody who understands enough to be reading your code in the first place is intelligent enough to appreciate a clearly written program.*

I just followed this advice in program Trader. Constants like USA and ONEcarat aren't needed to make a syntactically correct calculation. But along with meaningful variable names like KgToBuy and CaratsToKeep, they let us write program statements that are comprehensible and have a fighting chance at being correct:

---

* James McKelvey Jr., *Debugger's Handbook: TURBO Pascal*, Wadsworth Publishing Co., 1987. A very funny book with very good advice.

keeping code
comprehensible

{*from program* Trader}
KgToBuy := PoundsToBuy ∗ USAinKg;
KgToDeliver := PoundsToBuy ∗ INTERNATIONALinKg;
KgToKeep := KgToBuy − KgToDeliver;
CaratsToKeep := KgToKeep / ONEcarat;

Clear naming is simple, but it is awfully important. Names have a tremendous potential for projecting misinformation, as this selection from Abbott and Costello's famous *Who's On First?* routine shows.

(Lou Costello is considering becoming a ballplayer. Bud Abbott wants to make sure he knows what he's getting into.)

Abbott: Strange as it may seem, they give ball players nowadays very peculiar names.

Costello: Funny names?

Abbott: Nicknames, nicknames. Now, on the St. Louis team we have Who's on first, What's on second, I Don't Know is on third—

Costello: That's what I want to find out. I want you to tell me the names of the fellows on the St. Louis team.

Abbott: I'm telling you. Who's on first, What's on second, I Don't Know is on third—

Costello: You know the fellows' names?

Abbott: Yes.

Costello: Well, then who's playing first?

Abbott: Yes.

Costello: I mean the fellow's name on first base.

Abbott: Who.

Costello: The fellow playin' first base.

Abbott: Who.

Costello: The guy on first base.

Abbott: Who is on first.

Costello: Well, what are you askin' me for?

Abbott: I'm not asking you—I'm telling you. Who is on first.

Costello: I'm asking you—who's on first?

Abbott: That's the man's name.

Costello: That's who's name?

Abbott: Yes.

- - - - - -

Costello: When you pay off the first baseman every month, who gets the money?

Abbott: Every dollar of it. And why not, the man's entitled to it.

Costello: Who is?

Abbott: Yes.

Costello: So who gets it?

Abbott: Why shouldn't he? Sometimes his wife comes down and collects it.

Costello: Who's wife?

Abbott: Yes. After all, the man earns it.

Costello: Who does?

Abbott: Absolutely.

Costello: Well, all I'm trying to find out is what's the guy's name on first base?

Abbott: Oh, no, no. What is on second base.

Costello: I'm not asking you who's on second.

Abbott: Who's on first!

- - - - - -

Costello: St. Louis has a good outfield?

Abbott: Oh, absolutely.

Costello: The left fielder's name?

Abbott: Why.

Costello: I don't know, I just thought I'd ask.

Abbott: Well, I just thought I'd tell you.

Costello: Then tell me who's playing left field?

Abbott: Who's playing first.

Costello: Stay out of the infield! The left fielder's name?

Abbott: Why?

Costello: Because.

Abbott: Oh, he's center field.

Costello: Wait a minute. You got a pitcher on the team?

Abbott: Wouldn't this be a fine team *without* a pitcher?

Costello: Tell me the pitcher's name.

Abbott: Tomorrow.

- - - - - -

Costello: Now, when the guy at bat bunts the ball— me being a good catcher—I want to throw the guy out at first base, so I pick up the ball and throw it to who?

Abbott: Now, that's the first thing you've said right.

Costello: I DON'T EVEN KNOW WHAT I'M TALKING ABOUT!

Abbott: Don't get excited! Take it easy.

Costello: I throw the ball to first base, whoever it is grabs the ball, so the guy runs to second. Who picks up the ball and throws it to what. What throws it to I don't know. I don't know throws it back to tomorrow—a triple play.

Abbott: Yeah, it could be.

Costello: Another guy gets up and it's a long ball to center.

Abbott: Because.

Costello: Why? I don't know. And I don't care.

Abbott: What was that?

Costello: I said I DON'T CARE!

Abbott: Oh, that's our shortstop!

(If you don't know who Abbott and Costello are, you're not watching enough television on Saturday morning.) A program could have this kind of variable declaration:

var A, B, C, D, E, F: integer;

use meaningful names

But what's is all about? Contrast the single letters with:

var Acres, Bales, Cords, Decks, Ears, Flocks: integer;

The second list is *mnemonic* (nih-mahn´-ick). Each identifier is a memory aid that can make the variable's usage more obvious.

It's possible to argue that brief variable names are easy to remember in a short program. The problem is that as time goes on, you won't have just one short program—you'll have dozens of them. As programming assignments become more involved, you'll frequently try to incorporate previously written code in your new work. Then you'll see just how hard it is to remember what X, Y, and Z mean.

> As a rule of thumb, use names that are clear enough for your roommate, who may not be studying computer science, to understand!

Constants and Program Style

Constant definitions are a second tool of the plain programming style. Why define constants? No program needs defined constants in order to work, but

why use constants?

programs often require constants in order to be good programs. Suppose that a 2000-line program calculates property taxes like clockwork for a few years, and then—horrors!—tax reform. Must we search the entire program to update every instance of the old tax rate? Not if we had made the definition:

const TAXrate = 0.003;

for style

Changing the value of the constant TAXrate updates the whole program. Could TAXrate have been declared as a variable? Yes, but that would open the possibility of accidentally changing its value within the program. It's also misleading to call TAXrate a variable instead of a constant, because declaring something as a variable implies that its value will change or be obtained from the program's user.

as documentation

A second style motivation for constants is less obvious. Writing a program is a little like writing an instruction booklet. Just including all the facts isn't enough—they have to be presented in a manner that even a casual reader can follow. Now, comments provide running documentation that explains what's happening in a program. Defined constants go further towards making a program *self-documenting*. A statement that subtracts 5 from x doesn't say much. Better variable names and a comment make this assignment easier to understand:

Speed := Speed − 5;
  {*Find true speed by subtracting the fixed speedometer error.*}

for bug prevention

But mnemonic identifiers and a defined constant manage no-hands commenting. They document *without* additional comments and are best of all.

```
TrueSpeed := IndicatedSpeed − SPEEDOMETERerror;
```

Debugging

Antibugging is defensive programming—trying to avoid problems in the first place. Let's move on to *debugging*—finding and removing bugs that appear despite our best efforts.

A very common bug is to include a carriage return in the middle of an output statement:

an illegal example

```
writeln ('This is illegal, because carriage
                returns can''t go between the quote marks.');
{But it's perfectly all right for
 a comment to extend over two or more lines.}
```

A similarly disastrous (but easily fixed) bug comes from leaving out one of the single quotes.

Once you start to use read or readln with variables, keep three things in mind:

— First, be sure that you prompt the user to enter any data your program expects to read.

— Second, clearly specify its type, if necessary, so that a real read won't crash on integer input.

— Third, anticipate problems that might be caused by the order input arrives in. Don't forget that only numerical reads skip blanks.

It's often a good idea to use *debugging output statements* to see if you've actually read the values you expected. For example:

using writeln to debug

```
{How to confirm input.}
writeln ('Please enter your age and first initial.');
read (Number);
readln (Letter);
write (Number : 1);    {Checking the expected input.}
writeln (Letter);
```

```
Please enter your age and first initial.
23 D
23
```

What happened? As I mentioned not ten seconds ago, only numerical input skips blanks. The input **D** was discarded; Letter represents the blank that followed **23**.

I'd like you to notice a small but important point about my choice of statements: the second input uses readln instead of read.

```
writeln ('Please enter your age and first initial.');
read (Number);
readln (Letter);
{Subsequent input comes from the next line.}
```

flushing the line

> After reading what you expect and need, use readln to flush the remainder of any input line.

This practice helps prevent errors that can result if you add additional input requests later on.

Let's move on to type problems, which usually come early and often. Nobody claims that obeying picayune Pascal type restrictions is always convenient. The rules represent one of the classic tradeoffs of computer science— a little syntactic inconvenience now instead of a lot of semantic inconvenience later.

It's important to remember that operators are restricted to operands of a particular type. This expression is obviously wrong:

```
'T' + 17    {an illegal expression}
```

In general, steer clear of problems by remembering that:

— A value must be of the proper type to be assigned to a variable.

keep in mind

— **div** and **mod** must have integer operands, while / should have reals.

— If either operand in an arithmetic expression is real, or if the operator is /, the whole expression is real.

Next, *know and love your debugger*. Not every Pascal system will have a special program designed to help you find and fix bugs, but if there is one, learn it.

Of course, it's just as important to be able to be your own debugger—to be able to run programs in your own head. For example, let's look at the damage a simple spelling error can cause. Anybody who says that math is essential for success in computing doesn't know what she's talking about—typing is much more important! Can you spot the errors in this bit of code?

buggy code

```
programm Broken (input, output);
  . .
var Trial: integer;
  . .
read (Trail);
  . .
```

I don't want to shake your faith in computers, but many Pascal compilers will produce an error message that's no more correct than the bug:

```
programm Broken (input, output);
   ·.·
Compile error:   BEGIN expected.
```

That's nonsense. The problem is that **program** is spelled wrong. It's a good idea to remember that while the compiler is very good at locating syntax errors, it isn't nearly as smart about prescribing fixes. Often, we're better off when the compiler limits its comments to what it knows—or doesn't know.

```
read (Trail);
   ·.·
Compile error:   Unknown identifier.
```

This error message is correct because of a bug I bet you still haven't spotted: I declared a variable named Trial, then used a nonexistent variable named Trail in its place.

Syntax Summary

❑ types: are associated with every value, variable, and parameter in Pascal. The types we'll use most frequently are:

integer	*whole positive and negative numbers*
real	*positive and negative decimals*
char	*single character values*
boolean	*either* TRUE *or* FALSE

Most Pascal systems include a string type as an extension, but we won't rely on it.

❑ constant definition: gives a name to a value. Text constants (strings) are allowed:

```
const STOREname = 'SocksRUs';
      PAIR = 2;
      SALEStax = 0.0825;
```

❑ variable declaration: names variables and specifies their types:

```
var SomeInteger: integer;
    ACharacter: char;
    Real1, Real2, Real3: real;
```

❑ assignment statement: gives a variable its value:

```
SomeInteger := 17;
ACharacter := 'T';
Real1 := 3.0;
Real2 := 4E16;
```

❑ standard output procedures are:

write (*argument*);
>   *Print the argument in exactly the space it requires.*

write (*argument* : *minimum width*);
>   *Right-align the argument in a field of width spaces.*

write (real *argument* : *width* : *decimal places*);
>   *Print the argument in fixed-point notation.*

writeln;

writeln (*argument*);
>   *Print a carriage return; above arguments are optional.*

❏   standard input procedures are:

read (*argument*);
>   *Read a value for the argument.*

readln;

readln (*argument*);
>   *Discard the current input line, including the carriage return.*
>   *An argument is optional.*

❏   input values are read according to these rules ('blanks' includes blank spaces, tabs, and ⌞Enter⌟ or ⌞Return⌟):

char	*read the next single character*
integer	*skip blanks, then read the number*
real	*skip blanks, then read the number*

The ⌞Enter⌟ (or ⌞Return⌟ on DEC and Apple equipment) is read as a single space character.

<hr>

Remember . . .

❏   *Mnemonic* names carry meaning, so use them. As a rule, every program should be as easy for a human being to read and understand as it is for a computer to execute.

❏   *Simple* types consist of specific values, as char consists of individual characters. *Ordinal* types, like integer and char, can be ordered and numbered consistently. Type real is simple, but it isn't ordinal.

❏   A *literal* value is a written (as opposed to stored) value, like 'T' (a literal char), or 73 (a literal integer).

❏   *Expressions* represent values. They're built up from *operands* and *operators* and are *evaluated* in the process of assignment. Every value, every variable, and every argument has a specific type. Types can't be mixed; you can't add a number and a character.

❏   Operators must have operands of the proper type; an expression is real if either *a*) the operator is /, or *b*) either operand is real. **div** and **mod** must have integer operands only.

❏   strings: when typed within a program, a literal string is a sequence of characters between single quotes: 'a string'. When typed as input to a program, a string is any sequence of characters that ends with an ⌞Enter⌟ (or ⌞Return⌟ on DEC or Apple equipment).

❏   A *runtime error* causes a program *crash*. The most common runtime error is a *type clash* or mismatch during input.

❏   A variable has a value even if it hasn't been *initialized* by your program. Don't let uninitialized variables show up on the right-hand side of assignments.

❏   *Semantic* bugs cause errors in a program's results. Syntactically legal programs can produce wrong answers, so be ready to use the *debugger* to find and fix problems.

❏   real values can be input and output in either *fixed-point* or *floating-point* notation. However, the computer may print far more digits of accuracy than the stored number really has. Digits on the right may be incorrect.

❏   Pascal uses the semicolon as a separator between procedure calls, other statements, and the different parts of a program.

❏   Interactive programs communicate with the program user. If the program expects input, it must *prompt* for it; the computer won't ask questions by itself. Programs that produce results without human intervention are called *batch* programs.

Big Ideas

The Big Idea in this chapter was:

1.   *Try to learn why rules are and you'll be able to figure out* what *they are*. It takes a long, long time to memorize every detail of a programming language. But if you learn to program by writing and running programs, you'll start to see how it all fits together.

Begin by Writing the Exam . . .

It's time to return to the Zen Study Method, in which we tackle the problem of dealing with exam questions by learning to ask them.

1-1   Let's get the examination off to an easy start by making up two *Write a statement that produces this output...* questions. Naturally, the output you want printed should contain both single and double quote marks.

1-2   Recognizing the types of literal values (char, integer, and so on) is a grind, but it's a standard test question. How would you ask the question *What values can be assigned to which variables?* By starting with two columns: a list of literal values and a list of variables of different types. Try it.

1-3   *Correct this statement* is always fun. Make up five statements that are wrong because they:

  a)   incorrectly try to print a fixed-point real;

  b)   call the wrong standard procedure;

  c)   appear in the wrong place in a program.

1-4   A literal string is any sequence of characters between single quotes. Convince yourself that 3.1415 can be a string. Then, write the question *Which of these write calls isn't legal?* (If you're like me, you'll annoy your students by making them all perfectly legitimate, of course.)

1-5   Personally, I wouldn't bother my students with questions like *Prove that you have memorized every formatting option*, but you might. Make up a tedious *Produce this output* problem.

1-6   The input rules are also tedious, but they're worth making a fuss about. *Here's the input, what's the output?* is the generic name for this kind of problem. Be sure to provide sample input that causes a program crash.

1-7   Operators must have operands of the proper type. Write down a half-dozen expressions to accompany the question *Are these legal expressions in Pascal?*

1-8   When a variable appears on the right-hand side of an assignment, it must *a*) be defined, and *b*) have the proper type. Write a half-dozen assignments, then ask *Are these legal Pascal assignments?*

1-9   One set of Self-Check Questions asks you to rewrite pairs of assignment statements as single assignments. The point is that sometimes assignments are independent, sometimes they're not; sometimes merged assignments can be simplified, sometimes they can't. Write three pairs to accompany the question *Does the order of these assignments matter?*

1-10   *Evaluate these expressions.* Need I say more?

1-11   It's always fun to inflict mathematics. Find the thickest math book you can, then write the question *Which Pascal expression matches which snippet of math?*

1-12   It's tough to test a sense of style, but it can be done. Three points of attack are:

a)   *Clarify this assignment.* Write a few assignments that could be clarified by use of constants, extra parentheses, or temporary variables and extra assignments.

b)   *Simplify this sequence.* Write a series of assignments that contains a needless statement—one that is undone or ignored by later statements.

c)   *Rename these variables.* Supply an assignment (like the truly awful example I gave in the discussion of program Trader) that uses one-letter identifiers, along with a clear comment about what the statement does, and ask that it be rewritten.

1-13   Test questions don't always have to be hard. Sometimes they're there just to let your students know what you think is important. A question like *Which of these should be constants, and which variables?* serves the purpose well. Come up with the data that should accompany it.

1-14   There are roughly ten zillion problems that, like program Trader, ask you to convert between different units of measure. I'll steal the easiest one (*Write a program that converts Fahrenheit to Celsius*) myself, and ask you to make up three more *Write a program that converts . . .* problems.

1-15   In lieu of essay questions, a few basic definitions are always nice. Look for half a dozen words or phrases that you'd just as soon not see on a test and ask *What do these mean?*

Warmups and Test Programs

1-16   Can a comment contain a comment? Write a test program to find out.

1-17   Can a program use tabs for indenting? What is the tab character?

1-18   Suppose that you ruin one of your program files. Is there any way to get it back to the way it was before?

1-19   How meaningful are the decimal digits produced by write? How many can you request? Is writeln (1.0/3.0:50:50) legal?

1-20   Write the statements needed to produce the output shown below. For *d* and *e*, use an integer and real variable.

a)   ```
They can't take that away from me.
```

*b)*     ```
I said 'read my lips,' creep.
```

c)   ```
'Don't you want another chance?'
```
```

d)   ? and the Mysterians sang '96 Tears.'

e)   The price is $1.98.

1-21   I'm sure that you recall the scene, in *The Wild Ones*, in which Marlon Brando pithily answers the question *What are you against?* by asking *What do you got?* Let's break some rules just to see what happens.

a)   What happens when you type in a character for an integer variable?

b)   What happens when a procedure call has an extra (or missing) argument?

c)   What does the call writeln (); do?

1-22   Write a program that prompts its user to enter integer values for the month, day, and year. Then, print the date in *month/day/year* format. *Option*: let the separator character (the /) be supplied by the user.

Programming
Problems

1-23   Before the word 'bit' was taken over by computer scientists, a bit used to represent a Spanish *real*—better known as a piece-of-eight, or one-eighth of an old peso. In American slang, a bit is twelve and a half cents, two bits is a quarter, and so on.

In keeping with the tradition established by the early Spanish plunderers, the price of stocks is also recorded to the nearest eighth of a dollar. Write a program that prompts its user for the price of a stock, in dollars and eighths, as well as the number of shares she owns. Print the value of her holding in dollars and cents, using fixed-point notation. *Options*: prompt for today's price change as well, and print the portfolio's starting and closing values.

1-24   The ordinary *statute mile* is based on the Roman mile, which is one thousand Roman paces long. Since it is often difficult these days to find a Roman who is willing to take a thousand paces, two alternative distance measures have been developed: the *kilometer*, which is approximately one ten-thousandth of the distance between either pole and the Equator, and the *knot* or *nautical mile*, which equals one minute of arc (there are 90 degrees, with 60 minutes of arc per degree, between either pole and the Equator).

Write a program that lets you know how many kilometers are in a nautical mile, and vice versa.

1-25   Write a program that:

a)   gets two real numbers from a program user;

b)   prints their sum and product using floating-point notation;

c)   prints the sum and product in fixed-point notation.

Option: Ask the program user how many decimal places she wants the fixed-point procedure to print. Then obey her request.

1-26   The image of a program as a black box that magically computes an answer isn't far from the truth. The choice of one such box over another may depend on an issue as small as the form it requires data to be in.

Suppose that we have two representations of triangles:

1.   as three pairs of points $(X_a, Y_a, X_b, Y_b, X_c, Y_c)$ that mark the triangle's vertices;

2   as a triple (a, b, c) that represents the length of the triangle's sides.

Write and test two black boxes that calculate area. Formulas to use are:

$$area = \frac{(X_aY_b - Y_aX_b) + (X_bY_c - Y_bX_c) + (X_cY_a - Y_cX_a)}{2}$$

$$area = \sqrt{s\,(s-a)(s-b)(s-c)} \qquad \text{(Heron's formula, where s is ½ the perimeter)}$$

You will find that the *square root function*:

sqrt (*argument*)   *This function call represents a value.*

will come in handy.

Subprograms will scale; they'll let us divide the most difficult problems into manageable chunks. Moving day. (p. 43)

2

Subprograms: Reusable Solutions

Chapter 1 gave you the tools needed to write little programs. In Chapter 2, we move on to the building block of big ones—procedures. Since we're not going to be writing big programs for a while, it's perfectly reasonable to wonder why we're going to attack them now. The reason is that procedures make a key contribution to the way we think about solving problems by computer.

Subdividing a problem into parts makes it easier to solve. Writing up those partial solutions as procedures makes large programs more manageable. We can test pieces of a solution, rather than tackling the whole problem at once. And, if we're good, we'll be able to write the single steps in a way that lets them be reapplied when similar problems arise in the future. Section 2–1 gives you the hardware you'll need to build for reuse.

Section 2–2 covers the *function calls* that are built into Pascal. You'll probably be using this section for later reference, but it also gives me an opportunity to clear up a few details about how characters work. In 2–3, we'll write a few new functions and a longer example program.

I won't lie to you—many people find that procedures and parameters are confusing at first. I certainly did when I first learned to program! But the bottom line is that it's much easier to learn how to write procedures properly *before* your life (or at least your grade) depends on them. Chapter 3 will go into both design and technical details more closely.

Writing New Procedures

2-1

LET'S GET STARTED AS WE DID IN CHAPTER 1, by seeing where we're going. Here's where we stand now:

```
program Multiply (input, output);
    {Our current 'state of the art' program.}

var First, Second, Product : integer;

begin
    write ('What are your favorite numbers?   ');
    read (First);                          {Get and store the numbers.}
    readln (Second);
    Product := First * Second;             {Assign a new value to Product.}
    write ('Oh no!  Their product is ');
    write (Product : 1);                   {Use minimal spacing.}
    writeln ('.  How auspicious!')
end.   {Multiply}
```

```
What are your favorite numbers?  18  37
Oh no!  Their product is 666.  How auspicious!
```

Multiply is a neat little program, but it has an invisible problem: it won't *scale up*. If we take the same basic program but give it ninety-nine more sets of numbers to multiply, we could probably write it, and we might even be able to understand it a week later. But make the program five hundred or a thousand times longer and we wouldn't be able to do either. One statement after another is great for small programs, but it's just too complicated for the big problems we'd like to solve.

issue: scale in program design

After a chapter of hard work, we're going to be able to write the same program once more. Next time out, though, we'll be using *subprograms*—procedures and functions—to split up the jobs the program does. Subprograms will scale; they'll let us divide the most difficult problems into manageable chunks. We'll be dealing with three basic ideas:

— *Procedures* — How do we package programs so that a single procedure call can carry out many steps?

— *Parameters* — How can we make procedures use, and possibly change, their arguments?

— *Planning* — What's the long-term benefit for problem solving and program design that we can get from using procedures and parameters?

Planning will be the key. We'll see how easy it is to turn a problem restatement:

subgoals in English

> *Get the information;*
> *Make a calculation;*
> *Return the results;*

into a proposed program outline written in an informal, Pascal-like *pseudocode*:

> *GetTheInfo (First, Second);*
> *Calculate (First, Second, Product);*
> *PrintTheNews (Product);*

and then on into the completed program below. Don't panic when you read SplitUp, by the way—I'll be going over one just like it in great detail later on.

```
program SplitUp (input, output);
    {Uses procedures to get and multiply two numbers.}

var First, Second, Product: integer;

{First, new procedures are declared.}
procedure GetTheInfo (var Number1, Number2: integer);

    {Gets the user's favorite numbers.}

    begin
        write ('Give me two whole numbers to multiply.    ');
        read (Number1);
        readln (Number2)
    end;  {GetTheInfo}

procedure Calculate ( Number1, Number2: integer; var Product: integer);

    {Calculates and returns the first two arguments' product.}

    begin
        Product := Number1 * Number2
    end;  {Calculate}

procedure PrintTheNews (Answer: integer);

    {Prints its argument.}

    begin
        write ('Oh, no!  Their product is ');
        write (Answer : 1);
        writeln ('.  How auspicious!')
    end;  {PrintTheNews}

{Then, they're used in the main program.}
begin
    GetTheInfo (First, Second);            {These arguments are changed.}
    {We have our data.}
    Calculate (First, Second, Product);   {Two arguments are used, and one is changed.}
    {We've calculated a result.}
    PrintTheNews (Product)                 {These arguments are used.}
    {We've printed the output.}
end.  {SplitUp}
```

The program is essentially the same as Multiply, but our construction technique is totally different—more complicated right now, but much more straightforward in the long run. Let's dig in.

Procedures Without Parameters

A Pascal program is basically a delivery system for procedure calls. Declarations in the first half of the program create the environment in which the procedure calls will work:

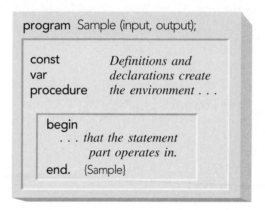

Procedures, in turn, obey the same basic construction rules as programs. They can include the same sorts of declarations and definitions and have the same kind of statement part:

procedure declaration

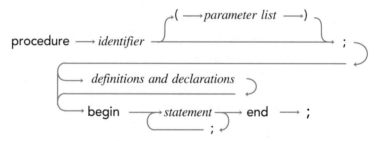

Understanding the details of the *parameter list* will take some time. Here's its syntax chart:

parameter list

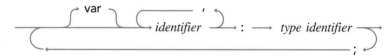

We'll begin our attack on procedures with a piece of code that prints the same thing every time (it's the intellectual equivalent of writeln). Then, we'll see how to arrange for a procedure to take arguments that can change and thus show some variety.

Consider Doggerel, below. It contains a procedure that's named Spout and is called twice:

8959 Q Pham

```
program Doggerel (output);
    {Shows the basic form of a procedure declaration.}
procedure Spout;
    {Spouts the following bit of doggerel, or bad poetry.}
    begin
        writeln ('Celery, raw, develops the jaw;');
        write ('but celery, stewed, is more quietly chewed.')
    end; {Spout}

begin      {The 'main' program, Doggerel.}
    write ('Here is a famous poem by Ogden Nash.');
    writeln;     {Call the standard procedure writeln.}
    Spout;       {Call the brand new procedure Spout.}
    writeln;
    writeln ('Did you want to hear that again?');
    Spout;
    writeln
end. {Doggerel}
```

a simple output procedure

```
Here is a famous poem by Ogden Nash.
Celery, raw, develops the jaw;
but celery, stewed, is more quietly chewed.
Did you want to hear that again?
Celery, raw, develops the jaw;
but celery, stewed, is more quietly chewed.
```

new procedures are declared

Recall that programs are split in halves. Procedure Spout is *declared* in the first half of Doggerel, before the statement part. It looks like a program, but it ends with a semicolon, rather than a period. Once it has been declared, it can be called in the statement part.

Modification Problems

1. Modify program Doggerel so that all the writeln calls are in procedure Spout.
2. Put the entire statement part of Doggerel into a procedure called Declaim, then have Doggerel call Declaim. Does it matter if the declaration of Declaim precedes or follows that of Spout? Try it both ways.

A Procedure Call Test Bed

Doggerel wasn't hard to follow. It's easy to see that the main program is temporarily suspended during each call of Spout. But I think that a test bed program will be helpful to demonstrate what happens when procedures call procedures.

declare before you call

A procedure can call any procedure that has been declared *before* it. It can't normally call procedures that are declared *after* its own declaration.

Caller, our test bed program, has three procedures: First, Second, and Third, declared in that order.

who can call whom

— We can't call any other procedures from within First.

— We can call First, but not Third, from within Second.

— We can call both First and Second from with Third.

— We can call any procedure from the main program.

At the risk of your eyesight, I've squished these screen captures so that we can see the entire sequence. Remember that the highlighted statement is *about* to be executed. Here, the program has just begun.

the program begins

Only the main program's name appears in the uncompleted calls window. After another statement, output appears as well.

about to call Third

```
─────────────── CALLER.PAS ───────────────          ┌── Uncompleted Calls ──┐
program Caller (input, output);                      │ CALLER                │
   {Show a sequence of procedure calls.}             │                       │
procedure First;       {Can't call Second or Third.} │                       │
   begin                                             │                       │
      writeln ('In procedure First.');               │                       │
   end;   {First}                                    │                       │
procedure Second;              {Can't call Third.}   └───────────────────────┘
   begin
      writeln ('Second begins...');                  ┌──── Input & Output ───┐
      First;                                          │                       │
      writeln ('Second ends.');                       │                       │
   end;   {Second}
procedure Third;     {Can call First and/or Second.}  │                       │
   begin
      writeln ('Third begins...');
      Second;                                         │ Main program begins...│
      writeln ('Third ends.');                         │                       │
   end;   {Second}
begin
   writeln ('Main program begins...');
   Third;
   writeln ('Main program ends.')
end.   {Caller}
```

When we enter Third, you see its name appear at the top of the uncompleted calls window.

inside Third

```
─────────────── CALLER.PAS ───────────────          ┌── Uncompleted Calls ──┐
program Caller (input, output);                      │ THIRD                 │
   {Show a sequence of procedure calls.}             │ CALLER                │
procedure First;       {Can't call Second or Third.} │                       │
   begin                                             │                       │
      writeln ('In procedure First.');               │                       │
   end;   {First}                                    │                       │
procedure Second;              {Can't call Third.}   └───────────────────────┘
   begin
      writeln ('Second begins...');                  ┌──── Input & Output ───┐
      First;                                          │                       │
      writeln ('Second ends.');                       │                       │
   end;   {Second}
procedure Third;     {Can call First and/or Second.}  │                       │
   begin
      writeln ('Third begins...');
      Second;                                         │ Main program begins...│
      writeln ('Third ends.');                         │                       │
   end;   {Second}
begin
   writeln ('Main program begins...');
   Third;
   writeln ('Main program ends.')
end.   {Caller}
```

I think you're getting the idea. Suppose I continue to step through the program.

about to call Second

```
 _____ CALLER.PAS _____
program Caller (input, output);
   {Show a sequence of procedure calls.}
procedure First;     {Can't call Second or Third.}
   begin
      writeln ('In procedure First.');
   end; {First}
procedure Second;           {Can't call Third.}
   begin
      writeln ('Second begins...');
      First;
      writeln ('Second ends.');
   end; {Second}
procedure Third;   {Can call First and/or Second.}
   begin
      writeln ('Third begins...');
      Second;
      writeln ('Third ends.');
   end; {Second}
begin
   writeln ('Main program begins...');
   Third;
   writeln ('Main program ends.')
end.  {Caller}
```

```
 ___ Uncompleted Calls ___
THIRD
CALLER



 ___ Input & Output ___

Main program begins...
Third begins...
```

inside Second

```
 _____ CALLER.PAS _____
program Caller (input, output);
   {Show a sequence of procedure calls.}
procedure First;     {Can't call Second or Third.}
   begin
      writeln ('In procedure First.');
   end; {First}
procedure Second;           {Can't call Third.}
   begin
      writeln ('Second begins...');
      First;
      writeln ('Second ends.');
   end; {Second}
procedure Third;   {Can call First and/or Second.}
   begin
      writeln ('Third begins...');
      Second;
      writeln ('Third ends.');
   end; {Second}
begin
   writeln ('Main program begins...');
   Third;
   writeln ('Main program ends.')
end.  {Caller}
```

```
 ___ Uncompleted Calls ___
SECOND
THIRD
CALLER


 ___ Input & Output ___

Main program begins...
Third begins...
```

about to call First

```
 _____ CALLER.PAS _____
program Caller (input, output);
   {Show a sequence of procedure calls.}
procedure First;     {Can't call Second or Third.}
   begin
      writeln ('In procedure First.');
   end; {First}
procedure Second;           {Can't call Third.}
   begin
      writeln ('Second begins...');
      First;
      writeln ('Second ends.');
   end; {Second}
procedure Third;   {Can call First and/or Second.}
   begin
      writeln ('Third begins...');
      Second;
      writeln ('Third ends.');
   end; {Second}
begin
   writeln ('Main program begins...');
   Third;
   writeln ('Main program ends.')
end.  {Caller}
```

```
 ___ Uncompleted Calls ___
SECOND
THIRD
CALLER


 ___ Input & Output ___

Main program begins...
Third begins...
Second begins...
```

inside First

```
 _____ CALLER.PAS _____
program Caller (input, output);
   {Show a sequence of procedure calls.}
procedure First;     {Can't call Second or Third.}
   begin
      writeln ('In procedure First.');
   end; {First}
procedure Second;           {Can't call Third.}
   begin
      writeln ('Second begins...');
      First;
      writeln ('Second ends.');
   end; {Second}
procedure Third;   {Can call First and/or Second.}
   begin
      writeln ('Third begins...');
      Second;
      writeln ('Third ends.');
   end; {Second}
begin
   writeln ('Main program begins...');
   Third;
   writeln ('Main program ends.')
end.  {Caller}
```

```
 ___ Uncompleted Calls ___
FIRST
SECOND
THIRD
CALLER

 ___ Input & Output ___

Main program begins...
Third begins...
Second begins...
```

The stack of uncompleted procedure calls is as high as it gets. Now we start to finish uncompleted calls.

back in Second

```
_____ CALLER.PAS _____
program Caller (input, output);
  {Show a sequence of procedure calls.}
procedure First;        {Can't call Second or Third.}
  begin
    writeln ('In procedure First.');
  end;   {First}
procedure Second;                {Can't call Third.}
  begin
    writeln ('Second begins...');
    writeln ('Second ends.');
  end;   {Second}
procedure Third;    {Can call First and/or Second.}
  begin
    writeln ('Third begins...');
    Second;
    writeln ('Third ends.');
  end;   {Second}
begin
  writeln ('Main program begins...');
  Third;
  writeln ('Main program ends.')
end.  {Caller}
```

```
┌─── Uncompleted Calls ───
│ SECOND
│ THIRD
│ CALLER

┌─── Input & Output ───

Main program begins...
Third begins...
Second begins...
In procedure First.
```

back in Third

```
_____ CALLER.PAS _____
program Caller (input, output);
  {Show a sequence of procedure calls.}
procedure First;        {Can't call Second or Third.}
  begin
    writeln ('In procedure First.');
  end;   {First}
procedure Second;                {Can't call Third.}
  begin
    writeln ('Second begins...');
    First;
    writeln ('Second ends.');
  end;   {Second}
procedure Third;    {Can call First and/or Second.}
  begin
    writeln ('Third begins...');
    Second;
    writeln ('Third ends.');
  end;   {Second}
begin
  writeln ('Main program begins...');
  Third;
  writeln ('Main program ends.')
end.  {Caller}
```

```
┌─── Uncompleted Calls ───
│ THIRD
│ CALLER

┌─── Input & Output ───

Main program begins...
Third begins...
Second begins...
In procedure First.
Second ends.
```

back in the main program

```
_____ CALLER.PAS _____
program Caller (input, output);
  {Show a sequence of procedure calls.}
procedure First;        {Can't call Second or Third.}
  begin
    writeln ('In procedure First.');
  end;   {First}
procedure Second;                {Can't call Third.}
  begin
    writeln ('Second begins...');
    First;
    writeln ('Second ends.');
  end;   {Second}
procedure Third;    {Can call First and/or Second.}
  begin
    writeln ('Third begins...');
    Second;
    writeln ('Third ends.');
  end;   {Second}
begin
  writeln ('Main program begins...');
  Third;
  writeln ('Main program ends.')
end.  {Caller}
```

```
┌─── Uncompleted Calls ───
│ CALLER

┌─── Input & Output ───

Main program begins...
Third begins...
Second begins...
In procedure First.
Second ends.
Third ends.
```

we're done

```
_____ CALLER.PAS _____
program Caller (input, output);
  {Show a sequence of procedure calls.}
procedure First;        {Can't call Second or Third.}
  begin
    writeln ('In procedure First.');
  end;   {First}
procedure Second;                {Can't call Third.}
  begin
    writeln ('Second begins...');
    First;
    writeln ('Second ends.');
  end;   {Second}
procedure Third;    {Can call First and/or Second.}
  begin
    writeln ('Third begins...');
    Second;
    writeln ('Third ends.');
  end;   {Second}
begin
  writeln ('Main program begins...');
  Third;
  writeln ('Main program ends.')
end.  {Caller}
```

```
┌─── Uncompleted Calls ───
│ CALLER

┌─── Input & Output ───

Main program begins...
Third begins...
Second begins...
In procedure First.
Second ends.
Third ends.
Main program ends.
```

debugging writelns

Whew! If you ever get confused by a series of procedure calls, remember to use the same trick I have here: a series of debugging writeln statements. They identify entry to, and exit from, every procedure and remove any doubt about where you are.

Modification Problems ───────────────────

1. As written, the main Caller program and each procedure make just one call apiece. If you add all the calls you can to each (e.g. have the main program call all three procedures) how many output lines will there be? Don't let any procedure call itself (but read the first few pages of Chapter 16 if you want to find out what would happen!).

Value Parameters

Spout is cute, but it's dull because it does the same thing each time. Spout made Doggerel easier to write, but it's so specialized that it can do only one job.

the Big Idea behind parameters

> If we're going to make a procedure general purpose, we have to be able to give it one or more arguments. That way, the procedure's action can change slightly every time it is called.

Let me pose a more general problem, then:

problem: printing two characters

> Write a procedure called PrintInitials. Make it similar to write, but have it print the words `My initials are:` followed by the two characters— its two arguments.

Solving this problem requires a new tool called a *value parameter*. A value parameter is like a variable, because it represents a value. But there are two differences:

value parameter vs. variable

— A value parameter is declared in a procedure heading—it belongs to the procedure, rather than to the program.

— A value parameter gets its value when the procedure is called—the procedure's argument supplies the parameter's value.

I've put procedure PrintInitials in program ValueArg, below. The procedure's heading includes the declaration of the value parameters First and Last.

giving arguments to a procedure

```
program ValueArg (output);
    {Shows how to arrange for a procedure to have arguments.}
procedure PrintInitials (First, Last : char);
    {Within this procedure, the names First and Last represent
      the argument values. We'll call write to print them.}
    begin
        write ('My initials are:     ');
        write (First);
        writeln (Last)
    end;   {PrintInitials}
begin
    PrintInitials ('D', 'C');    {Any two characters can be arguments.}
    PrintInitials ('Q', 'T');    {Like strings, characters are quoted.}
    PrintInitials ('&', '#')
end.   {ValueArg}
```

(output follows)

```
My initials are:   DC
My initials are:   QT
My initials are:   &#
```

When PrintInitials is first called, the literal values ´D´ and ´C´ are its arguments. Within PrintInitials, the identifiers First and Last represent these literal
values, just as variables might. The value parameters can be used in place of
the literal values when we call write. In other words, if First represents ´D´ and
Last represents ´C´, then:

> {*Within procedure* PrintInitials.}
> write (First);
> writeln (Last);
>   {*has the same effect as* . . . }
> write (´D´);
> writeln (´C´);

On each successive call, PrintInitials is given two new arguments. And, within
each PrintInitials call, First and Last represent the two new arguments, and the
call winds up printing the two new letters.

How does PrintInitials know that we want First to represent ´D´, ´Q´, and
´&´, while Last represents ´C´, ´T´, and ´#´? Because there is a *one-to-one
correspondence*, by position, between the arguments in the calls and the identifiers First and Last in the heading, or first line, of PrintInitials.

one-to-one
correspondence

procedure PrintInitials (First, Last : char);   {*A heading with parameters.*}

PrintInitials (´D´, ´C´);   {*A call with arguments.*}

Parameters are confusing, so let's step through a test bed program.
ValueBed, which you can see in the screen shot below, is almost identical to
ValueArg, but it's a little clearer when modified. In the first shot, the program is
about to begin; the line that's highlighted is the statement about to execute.

about to begin the main
program

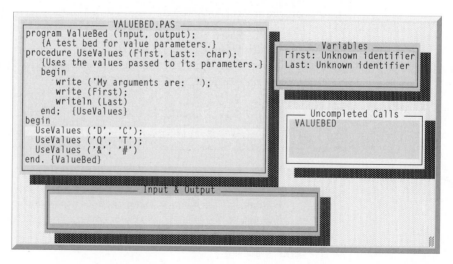

Note that both identifiers in the variables window are marked as unknown. That's because they don't exist outside of the procedure. The program itself is the only entry in the uncompleted calls window:

When we step into the procedure, two things happen. First, the uncompleted calls window gets another entry: UseValues appears, with the actual values of its arguments. Second, First and Last become defined. Naturally, they have the same values as the arguments. Here, I'm almost done with the first procedure call:

about to finish the first procedure call

```
┌─────────────── VALUEBED.PAS ───────────────┐
│program ValueBed (input, output);           │        ┌──── Variables ────┐
│   {A test bed for value parameters.}       │        │First: 'D'         │
│procedure UseValues (First, Last:  char);   │        │Last: 'C'          │
│   {Uses the values passed to its parameters.}│       └───────────────────┘
│   begin
│      write ('My arguments are:  ');
│      write (First);
│      writeln (Last)
│   end; {UseValues}                                   ┌── Uncompleted Calls ──┐
│begin                                                 │USEVALUES('D','C')     │
│   UseValues ('D', 'C');                              │VALUEBED               │
│   UseValues ('Q', 'T');                              └───────────────────────┘
│   UseValues ('&', '#')
│end. {ValueBed}
└─────────────────────────────────────────────┘

              ┌──────── Input & Output ────────┐
              │My arguments are:  D            │
              └────────────────────────────────┘
```

Back in the main program, we revert to our starting conditions. You can see from the output window that the first procedure call is completed.

back in the main program

```
┌─────────────── VALUEBED.PAS ───────────────┐
│program ValueBed (input, output);           │        ┌──── Variables ────┐
│   {A test bed for value parameters.}       │        │First: Unknown identifier│
│procedure UseValues (First, Last:  char);   │        │Last: Unknown identifier │
│   {Uses the values passed to its parameters.}│       └───────────────────┘
│   begin
│      write ('My arguments are:  ');
│      write (First);
│      writeln (Last)
│   end; {UseValues}                                   ┌── Uncompleted Calls ──┐
│begin                                                 │VALUEBED               │
│   UseValues ('D', 'C');                              └───────────────────────┘
│   UseValues ('Q', 'T');
│   UseValues ('&', '#')
│end. {ValueBed}
└─────────────────────────────────────────────┘

              ┌──────── Input & Output ────────┐
              │My arguments are:  DC           │
              └────────────────────────────────┘
```

Suppose that we jump ahead. In the final shot, below, I've just entered the third call of procedure UseValues. You can see that both the arguments and the values of the value parameters have changed once more.

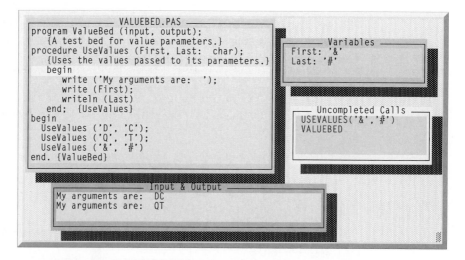

```
                      VALUEBED.PAS
program ValueBed (input, output);
    {A test bed for value parameters.}
procedure UseValues (First, Last:  char);
    {Uses the values passed to its parameters.}
    begin
        write ('My arguments are:   ');
        write (First);
        writeln (Last)
    end;  {UseValues}
begin
    UseValues ('D', 'C');
    UseValues ('Q', 'T');
    UseValues ('&', '#')
end. {ValueBed}
```

```
                   ─ Variables ──
             First: '&'
             Last: '#'
```

```
         ── Uncompleted Calls ──
         USEVALUES('&','#')
         VALUEBED
```

```
────────── Input & Output ──────────
My arguments are:  DC
My arguments are:  QT
```

back in the final
procedure call

program state

> Our generic environment shows only where we are now and not where we
> came from. Nevertheless, by inspecting the program's current *state*—the
> values of its variables and parameters and the output it has produced—it's
> easy to see where we stand in the main program.

Let's wrap up the syntax details of value parameter declarations with a
few examples. Recall that the syntax chart of the parameter list is:

parameter list

(We'll use the **var** in a moment when we get to variable parameters.) Value
parameters can have any type. A procedure that printed two numbers would
have a heading like this:

> **procedure** PrintAgeAndIQ (Age, IQ: integer);
> {*When PrintAgeAndIQ is called, its arguments must be integers.*}

declaring value
parameters

There can also be any number of value parameters:

> **procedure** PrintReadings (Out1, Out2, Out3: real);
> {*This procedure expects three real arguments when it's called.*}

A procedure might also need several value parameters of different types. Notice how semicolons are used to separate the declarations of three value parameters in the DoAll heading:

> **procedure** DoAll (Whole: integer; Decimal: real; Letter: char);
> {*This procedure expects three arguments with different types.*}

> Never forget that there is a one-to-one correspondence, *by position*, between the value parameters in a procedure heading and the arguments in a procedure call. The computer will *not* sort out mixed-up calls.

That means that in the examples below, the left-hand calls are legal (each argument is in the proper position for its value parameter), while the right-hand calls are illegal. The original DoAll heading was:

procedure DoAll (Whole: integer; Decimal: real; Letter: char);

legal and illegal calls

{*legal calls*}
DoAll (17, 6.2, ´E´);
DoAll (–6, 2.47E9, ´+´);
DoAll (0, 0.0, ´!´);

{*illegal calls*}
DoAll (´E´, 17, 6.2);
DoAll (–6, ´+´, 2.47E9);
DoAll (0.0, 0, ´!´);

Modification Problems

1. Modify either ValueArg or ValueBed so that it takes three integer arguments instead of two chars.

2. (After you've read section 2-2.) Modify ValueArg so that instead of printing its char arguments, it prints the ordinal positions of the characters (use the ord function).

3. (If you can handle problem 2.) Give the procedure a third, integer argument called Jump. Then, instead of printing the first two char arguments, print the characters that are Jump letters further along in the alphabet. In other words, if the procedure's arguments are (´A´, ´D´, 2) the program should print C F.

Self-Check Questions

Q. Suppose that these are all supposed to be calls to procedure PrintInitials, which has two char value parameters. Are any legal? What's wrong with the ones that aren't?

    a) PrintInitials (´3´, ´6´);   *b*) PrintInitials (´Z´);
    c) PrintInitials (´A´, ´B´, ´C´);   *d*) PrintInitials (72, –186);
    e) PrintInitials (´.´, ´,´);

A. Count the arguments, then check their types.

    a) Legal, since the arguments are the digit *characters*.
    b) Illegal, because there's only one argument.
    c) Illegal, because there are too many arguments.
    d) Illegal, because the arguments have the wrong types.
    e) Legal, because punctuation marks are legitimate characters.

Variable Parameters

You might not have thought about it in so many words, but it's easy to see that there's a difference in the relationships that read and write have with their arguments. Suppose that Letter is a variable of type char. Think about these two procedure calls:

```
writeln ('Type in your favorite letter.');
read (Letter);          {The read procedure changes Letter.}
writeln ('The letter you typed was:    ');
write (Letter);         {The write procedure merely uses Letter.}
```

using vs. changing an argument

As an argument to read, our variable gets changed. This makes sense because we call read only when we *want* to change a variable by reading a value for it. But as an argument to write, the variable is just used. The write procedure prints the variable's value without changing it.

> A value parameter lets a procedure use the value of an argument. A *variable parameter*, in contrast, lets a procedure permanently change an argument's value. It serves as an *alias*, or second name, for the argument.

Even though we can't see the code of the standard input and output procedure headings, it's a safe bet that write must have a value parameter. By the same token, we can reasonably guess that read has to be using a variable parameter.

Program VarArg, below, parallels the ValueArg program we wrote earlier. Instead of printing two characters as PrintInitials did, though, it reads two characters. Note that the only difference between the declaration of a value parameter and a variable parameter is that the latter must be preceded by the reserved word **var**. And, even though a variable parameter's arguments *must* be a variable, the same one-to-one correspondence between argument and parameter still applies.

a variable parameter demonstration program

```
program VarArg (input, output);
    {Demonstrates variable parameters.}

var FirstInitial, LastInitial:  char;
    {A variable parameter's argument must be a variable.}

procedure ReadInitials (var First, Last : char);
    {Within this procedure, the names First and Last represent
     the argument variables.  We'll call read to change their values.}
    begin
        read (First);        {Also changes the first argument variable.}
        readln (Last)        {Also changes the second argument.}
    end;  {ReadInitials}

begin
    write ('What are your initials?    ');
    {At this point, FirstInitial and LastInitial have no values.}
    ReadInitials (FirstInitial, LastInitial);
    {But after the call, they're both defined.}
    write ('Your initials are:    ');
    write (FirstInitial);
    writeln (LastInitial)
end. {VarArg}
```

```
What are your initials?  DC
Your initials are:  DC
```

Since First and Last are declared in the heading of ReadInitials, they're only recognized within the procedure. Since they're variable parameters, though, they act as *aliases* for their arguments.

Any change to the variable parameter also changes the variable it's an alias for. In the example above, any change to First will also change its argument, FirstInitial. If LastInitial had been the first argument instead, then First would have become an alias for LastInitial. This idea is easy to remember if you think about the traditional use of aliases: naming bank robbers. Suppose I robbed banks using the alias Pretty Boy Cooper. If I got shot, I would bleed as Pretty Boy and Doug alike.

Since they are just two names for the same thing, the variable and the variable parameter both have to be declared with the same type. In program VarArg that type was char, but it could be any type. In general:

— a value parameter's argument can be a value *or* a variable (which represents a value) because the argument is just used;

— a variable parameter's argument *must* be a variable, because it is going to be changed.

a variable parameter is an alias

value vs. variable parameters

Don't worry if value and variable parameters seem confusing at first, because just about everybody feels that way. One of the best ways to get comfortable with them is to write a program that uses both kinds. Let's do that in WiseGuy, below, so that you can see parameters in a realistic context.

picking parameters

```
program WiseGuy (input, output);
    {Demonstrates the declaration and use of variables and parameters.}
var Score: integer;
procedure GetIQ ( var IQ: integer );
    {Inside GetIQ, the variable parameter IQ renames its argument.
     It's a variable parameter because when it changes, the argument changes.}
    begin
        write ('Hi!  What''s your IQ?    ');   {Prompt for input.}
        readln (IQ);   {Read the values.}
    end;  {GetIQ}
procedure PrintValue ( First: integer );
    {Inside PrintValue, the value parameter gets its argument's current
     value.  We'll use the value, but we can't permanently change it.}
    begin
        write ('You wish!  I bet you can''t even count to  ');
        writeln (First : 1)
    end;  {PrintValue}
begin
    GetIQ (Score);   {The argument brings a value back from GetIQ.}
    PrintValue (Score)   {The argument sends a value to PrintValue.}
end.  {WiseGuy}
```

Please enter your IQ: **147**
You wish! I bet you can't even count to 147

Program WiseGuy has variables, value parameters, and variable parameters. One of its procedures, GetIQ, must use a variable parameter because it changes the values of its argument variable. The other procedure, PrintValue, uses a value parameter because it uses only its argument's value. Keep your eye on the main program variable, Score, and see if you can follow as it is passed to each procedure.

Modification Problems

1. Change program WiseGuy so that it asks for initials (i.e. reads and prints two char values instead of one integer). Have it say 'You wish! I bet you can't even spell . . .'
2. Add a procedure to program WiseGuy that gets the user's age. Then call PrintValue to make the same wisecrack about her age.

The Parameter List

How about a quick review of parameter syntax before we go on? Once again, the syntax of a parameter list is:

parameter list

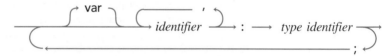

Let's look at a few sample headings. First, note that a new **var** is needed whenever there's a transition from one type to another. It isn't necessary to put different kinds of parameters on separate lines, but it can help make programs easier to debug and understand.

> **procedure** ReadAgeAndIQ (**var** Age, IQ: integer);
>   *{Two integer variable parameters.}*

> **procedure** GetDifferentStuff (**var** First: integer;
>   **var** Second: char;
>   **var** Third: real);
>   *{There must be a semicolon and a new **var** for each new type.}*

Then, be sure to understand how to intermingle value and variable parameter declarations.

some mixed headings

> **procedure** GetValues (Testee: char;
>   **var** Raw, Percent: integer);
>   *{One value and two variable parameters.}*

> **procedure** UseValues (Testee: char;
>   **var** Changed: integer;
>   Used: integer);
>   *{Two value and one variable parameters.}*

procedure ReviewResults (Testee: char;
                                                Raw: integer;
                                                var Percent: integer);
{*Similar, but the order is changed.*}

Self-Check Questions

Q. Read each of these procedure calls carefully, then guess which arguments go to value parameters and which go to variable parameters. Can't be done, you say? Sure it can!

    a) Divide (Divisor, Dividend, Quotient);
    b) ReadName (First, Last);
    c) GetCommand ('>', Command);
    d) PrintClue ('Warm!');
    e) ReadSum (17);
    f) Process (Data);

A. The rule, of course, is that if the argument is going to be changed, it should be going to a variable parameter. If it's just going to be used—or if it's a literal value—it's going to a value parameter. Here are some reasonable guesses.

    a) The names imply arguments to value, value, and variable parameters.
    b) Both variable parameters.
    c) Value parameter and variable parameter.
    d) Must be a value parameter because the argument is a value.
    e) The procedure name is misleading—it has to have a value parameter.
    f) There's no way to tell if Process uses or changes Data.

Background: Three More Questions About Parameters

Even though I encourage you to begin to program as I did—by copying and modifying—I want to explain the facts behind our programs, too. However, there are occasions that call for simplification, and the subject of parameters is one of them. But since I'm sure some of you are asking these questions, let me provide brief answers:

1. *Can a variable parameter be used without being changed?* Yes, a procedure might simply print a variable parameter's value. *However*, choosing to declare a variable parameter implies that it *will* change, and we'll follow a consistent practice.

2. *Can a value parameter be changed inside a procedure, in addition to being used?* Surprisingly, yes. *However*, the value parameter's argument, if it's a main program variable, *won't* change. Any change to the value parameter is temporary; it lasts only for the duration of the procedure call.

3. *Do variables and parameters have to have different names?* No. The compiler recognizes that a name declared in a procedure heading refers to a parameter, and not to a variable. *However*, people are confused more easily than compilers, so I make a habit of using different names for now.

As you can see, there are three big *However...*'s in the answers! Just because Pascal allows something doesn't mean that we'll want to do it; there's a reason that we do things the way we do.

A Parameter Test Bed

Are you confused? Don't worry! You'll understand parameters as you begin to put three pieces—*what?*, *how?*, and *why?*—together. Believe me, if there were a shortcut, I wouldn't keep it a secret.

Walking through another test bed program will help with the first two pieces. Program ParamBed looks at the difference between value and variable parameters. Like most test beds, it doesn't do much. Instead, it's meant to be easy to modify and run again. You'll know you're catching on when you can predict what will happen if you turn one of the value parameters into a variable parameter or vice versa.

In the first screen capture, below, I've caught ParamBed right after it has initialized and printed the values of First, Second, and Third. The highlighted statement—the call of procedure CallMe—is *about* to take place. Since we're not in the procedure yet, its parameters are all unknown identifiers.

about to make the
procedure call

```
_____ PARAMBED.PAS _____          _____ Variables _____
program ParamBed (input, output);       First: 1
  {A test bed for parameters.}          Second: 2
var First, Second, Third: integer;      Third: 3
procedure CallMe ( var A:  integer;   {var}    A: Unknown identifier
                       B:  integer;   {val}    B: Unknown identifier
                   var C:  integer);  {var}    C: Unknown identifier
  begin
    A := 4;
    B := 5;    {This assignment is local.}
    C := 6;                           _____ Uncompleted Calls _____
    writeln (A:8, B:8, C:8);          PARAMBED
  end;
begin
  First := 1;
  Second := 2;
  Third := 3;
  writeln (First:8, Second:8, Third:8);   _____ Input & Output _____
  CallMe (First, Second, Third);
  writeln (First:8, Second:8, Third:8)      1      2      3
end. {ParamBed}
```

When I step into the procedure, its parameters come to life. Note the one-to-one correspondence between the parameters and their arguments:

initial values within the
procedure

```
_____ PARAMBED.PAS _____          _____ Variables _____
program ParamBed (input, output);       First: 1
  {A test bed for parameters.}          Second: 2
var First, Second, Third: integer;      Third: 3
procedure CallMe ( var A:  integer;   {var}    A: 1
                       B:  integer;   {val}    B: 2
                   var C:  integer);  {var}    C: 3
  begin
    A := 4;
    B := 5;    {This assignment is local.}
    C := 6;                           _____ Uncompleted Calls _____
    writeln (A:8, B:8, C:8);          CALLME(1,2,3)
  end;                               PARAMBED
begin
  First := 1;
  Second := 2;
  Third := 3;
  writeln (First:8, Second:8, Third:8);   _____ Input & Output _____
  CallMe (First, Second, Third);
  writeln (First:8, Second:8, Third:8)      1      2      3
end. {ParamBed}
```

Matters get interesting after I execute the first two statements within CallMe, below. As a variable parameter, A renames First. When I assign 4 to A, the value of First changes as well. You can see the change in both the variables and the uncompleted calls windows. But since B is only a value parameter, assigning 5 to it has no effect on its argument, Second. Second's value is still 2. What do you think will happen after the highlighted assignment?

A is an alias, but B isn't

```
────────── PARAMBED.PAS ──────────
program ParamBed (input, output);
  {A test bed for parameters.}
var First, Second, Third:  integer;
procedure CallMe ( var A:  integer;   {var}
                       B:  integer;   {val}
                   var C:  integer);  {var}
  begin
    A := 4;
    B := 5;    {This assignment is local.}
    C := 6;
    writeln (A:8, B:8, C:8);
  end;
begin
  First := 1;
  Second := 2;
  Third := 3;
  writeln (First:8, Second:8, Third:8);
  CallMe (First, Second, Third);
  writeln (First:8, Second:8, Third:8)
end. {ParamBed}
```

```
──────── Variables ────────
First: 4
Second: 2
Third: 3
A: 4
B: 5
C: 3
```

```
──── Uncompleted Calls ────
CALLME(4,5,3)
PARAMBED
```

```
──── Input & Output ────
    1       2       3
```

Since C was a variable parameter, changing it altered its argument Third, too.

When we return to the main program, below, the parameters have all gone back to being unknown. You can see that the assignments to value parameters A and C had permanent effects on their arguments First and Third. Only Third is unchanged. The final line of output, not shown, will be 4 2 6.

back in the main program

```
────────── PARAMBED.PAS ──────────
program ParamBed (input, output);
  {A test bed for parameters.}
var First, Second, Third:  integer;
procedure CallMe ( var A:  integer;   {var}
                       B:  integer;   {val}
                   var C:  integer);  {var}
  begin
    A := 4;
    B := 5;    {This assignment is local.}
    C := 6;
    writeln (A:8, B:8, C:8);
  end;
begin
  First := 1;
  Second := 2;
  Third := 3;
  writeln (First:8, Second:8, Third:8);
  CallMe (First, Second, Third);
  writeln (First:8, Second:8, Third:8)
end. {ParamBed}
```

```
──────── Variables ────────
First: 4
Second: 2
Third: 6
A: Unknown identifier
B: Unknown identifier
C: Unknown identifier
```

```
──── Uncompleted Calls ────
PARAMBED
```

```
──── Input & Output ────
    1       2       3
    4       5       6
```

Local Variables

Procedures, like programs, can have their own variables. Perhaps you've seen the bumper sticker that says *Think globally, act locally?* Well, we use the same terms to describe the origin of identifiers in programs.

local vs. global

> A declaration in a procedure is described as being *local*. Main-program declarations, in contrast, are said to be *global*.

We'll make local declarations when variables aren't needed outside of the procedure. Here's an example:

echoing input in reverse

```pascal
procedure ReverseInput;
    {This intentionally simple example doesn't have parameters.}
    var NumOne, NumTwo: integer;          {Local declarations.}
    begin
        write ('Give me two numbers:  ');
        read (NumOne);
        readln (NumTwo);
        write ('In reverse order, the numbers are:');
        write (NumTwo : 5);
        writeln (NumOne : 5)
    end;  {ReverseInput}
```

NumOne and NumTwo are local variables.

— Global variables exist for the full lifetime of a program. Local variables, in contrast stick around only for the duration of a procedure call.

— Once initialized, global variables keep their values until they're explicitly changed. Local variables must be reinitialized in each procedure call.

— Local variables can reuse names that belong to global variables. Within the procedure, the local name takes *precedence*.

A short example program will make these rules seem obvious. I'm deliberately going to use the same identifier twice, just to make it easy to see that one name can have two different meanings:

reusing an identifier

```pascal
program Conflict (output);
    {A short example of precedence.}

var Name: char;

procedure Boring;
    {This procedure reuses the identifier Name.}
    var Name: char;
    begin
        Name := 'B';            {Until now, the local Name is undefined.}
        writeln (Name)          {This prints the procedure's version of Name.}
    end;  {Boring}
begin
    Name := 'A';                {Initialize the main program variable.}
    writeln (Name);
    Boring;
    writeln (Name);             {The main program variable hasn't changed.}
end.  {Conflict}
```

A
B
A

Now it's time to ask yourself the question that will see if you're catching on. What is the difference between a local variable and a value parameter?

local variables vs. value parameters

— Both of them are local. They are known only within the procedure they're declared in. However . . .

— The local variable is undefined when the procedure is entered. The value parameter, in contrast, is initialized by its argument when the procedure is called.

Self-Check Questions

Q. Name is declared as a global char variable in Conflict. Could I have made this declaration in procedure Boring?

    procedure Boring;
       var Name: integer;
       begin   *etc.*

A. Yes, even though I'm using Name as an integer variable now. Within a procedure, I can reuse a global identifier any way I want to—even to define a new, local procedure.

The Canonical Procedure Example

A *canonical* example is the standard one of its kind. For procedures, parameters, and local variables, the task is simple: write a program that reads, exchanges, and prints two values. The problem statement alone is enough to break the program into three steps:

> *Get the information;*
> *Make a calculation;*
> *Return the results*

If you think about how data are going to flow through the program, you can begin to see why this is the canonical example. If we write each step as a procedure, we're going to have to pass along information and variables as part of each call. I can outline the program in terms of mock procedure calls like this:

a program outline

> *GetTheNumbers* (*First, Second*);
> *SwapThem* (*First, Second*);
> *PrintTheResults* (*First, Second*)

The first two procedures use variable parameters, since their arguments are going to change. The third uses a value parameter, since it just prints its arguments' values.

But why is exchanging values a canonical example of local variables, too? It is because the obvious code doesn't work:

```
{The wrong way to swap values.}
First := Second;
Second := First;
```

Both variables end up equal to Second. We'll need a temporary variable to make the switch properly:

```
{The right way to swap values.}
Temporary := First;
First := Second;
Second := Temporary;
```

The temporary variable is needed only in the swap procedure, so it practically insists on being locally declared. Program Switch, below, carries out our plan.

```
program Switch (input, output);
   {Reverses two input integers.}

var First, Second:  integer;

procedure GetTheNumbers (var Primero, Segundo:  integer);
   {Reads values for the variable parameters Primero and Segundo.}
   begin
      write ('Please enter two integers:   ');
      read (Primero);
      readln (Segundo)          {Dump anything left on the input line.}
   end;  {GetTheNumbers}

procedure SwapThem (var Premier, Deuxieme:  integer);
   {Swaps the values of two variable parameters.}
   var Temporary:  integer;
   begin
      Temporary := Premier;          {Temporary is undefined until }
      Premier := Deuxieme;           { this assignment takes place.}
      Deuxieme := Temporary
   end;  {SwapThem}

procedure PrintTheResults (Primo, Secondo:  integer);
   {Prints its value parameters.}
   begin
      write ('In reversed order, the numbers are ');
      write (Primo : 1);
      write (' and ');
      writeln (Secondo : 1)
   end;  {PrintTheResults}

begin   {main program}
   GetTheNumbers (First, Second);
   SwapThem (First, Second);
   PrintTheResults (First, Second)
end.  {Switch}
```

the canonical procedure example

```
Please enter two integers:  27  -935
In reversed order, the numbers are -935 and 27
```

Be sure that you can follow the connections between arguments and parameters. GetTheNumbers has two variable parameters. It has to, because it changes the values of its arguments:

variable parameters

> **procedure** GetTheNumbers (**var** Primero, Segundo: integer);
>
> GetTheNumbers (First, Second);

SwapThem also has two variable parameters for variables it will change. In addition, SwapThem contains the local variable declaration of Temporary. Temporary isn't created until SwapThem is called, and then can be used only within the SwapThem call.

a local variable

> **procedure** SwapThem (**var** Premier, Deuxieme: integer);
> **var** Temporary: integer;
>
> SwapThem (First, Second);

Finally, PrintTheResults has two value parameters. It uses its arguments by printing their values:

value parameters

> **procedure** PrintTheResults (Primo, Secondo: integer);
>
> PrintTheResults (First, Second);

Not every program follows this three-procedure outline:

> *get the data (arguments);*
> *process it (arguments);*
> *print the results (arguments);*

but most of the programs we'll write do.

Modification Problems

1. Change Switch so that it reverses the order of four numbers instead of two.

2. The distance around a circle is about 3.1416 times its diameter. Modify Switch so that it asks for the distance between the centers of two especially unpleasant cities, as well as each city's diameter, then lets you know how big a fence is needed to enclose them both.

Self-Check Questions

Q. Why would these calls of GetTheNumbers, from program Switch, be illegal?

> {*illegal calls*}
> *a)* GetTheNumbers (First);
> *b)* GetTheNumbers (Grade, Rank, Service);

    c) GetTheNumbers (7, 59);
    d) GetTheNumbers (RealVariable, IntegerVariable);
    e) GetTheNumbers (First, Temporary);

A. You might try making up a similar exercise for the other calls.

    a) There aren't enough arguments.
    b) There are too many arguments.
    c) A variable parameter's arguments have to be variables.
    d) The arguments' types have to match the variable parameters.
    e) Temporary doesn't exist outside of SwapThem.

The Standard Functions

2-2

IF YOU PICK UP ANY POCKET CALCULATOR, YOU'LL ALMOST invariably find function keys for squares, square roots, reciprocals, and the like accompanying the arithmetic operators. Function keys save us from the death of a thousand cuts—a single keystroke takes the place of the operations of a commonly used routine.

    Instead of keys, programs use *function calls.* The assignment below is typical: sqrt's argument, given between parentheses, can be any single integer or real value. The entire call—function *and* argument—represents a real value that's assigned to Root:

        Root := sqrt(Number) ;   *{Assigns the square root of Number to Root}*

If Number is 9.0, then sqrt(Number) represents 3.0. The relevant rules and nomenclature are:

— A function *call* invokes a function, just as a procedure call invokes a procedure. sqrt(Number) is a function call.

calling and evaluating functions

— Most function calls will require an argument between parentheses. The argument can be any expression of the proper type, although *which* type is proper will vary from function to function. The sqrt function's argument (above, Number) must be of either type real or type integer.

— The function call is *evaluated*, or figured out.

— Once it has been evaluated, the function *returns* a *result*, or value. This means that every function has a type. sqrt has type real, because it returns a real value.

> A function call, complete with its argument, represents a value that can be assigned to a variable or used as an argument itself.

That means I could use sqrt as I do below, too. Let's suppose that Number equals 123.45:

```
writeln ( sqrt(Number) );               {Print the square root of Number.}
writeln ( sqrt(Number) : 5 : 2 );       {As above, but to just two decimal places}
```

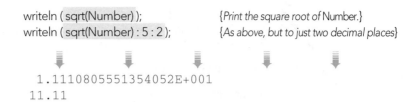

```
1.1110805551354052E+001
11.11
```

There are three points about calling functions that people sometimes find confusing. First, the type of a function's argument is quite separate from the type of its result. For instance, the argument of sqrt can be either integer or real, but its result will always be real.

the argument and function can have different types

Second, the function call doesn't change its argument. The argument's value is used—not modified. We could have used literal values instead of variables in the examples above:

functions don't change argument values

```
Root := sqrt( 31.9 );
writeln ( sqrt( 123.45 ) );
writeln ( sqrt( 123.45 ) : 5 : 2 );
```

function arguments can be literals

Finally, even though a function call looks like a procedure call, it isn't one. A procedure call takes the place of a series of statements. A function call, in contrast, takes the place of an expression. It represents a value.

functions replace expressions

Self-Check Questions

Q. What will this program segment print?

```
Side := 16.0;
sqrt (Side);
write (Side :4 :1);
```

A. It won't print anything. Instead, it will make the program it's in impossible to compile! The function call sqrt(Side) is just the representation of the value 4.0. Here's what the compiler sees:

```
Side := 16.0;
4.000000000;   {the value sqrt(16.0) represents}
writeln (Side);
```

To get the effect we want, I should have written:

```
{correct segment}
Side := 16.0;
RootOfSide := sqrt (Side);
writeln (RootOfSide);
```

Q. Suppose that I tried to fix the problem above with the code below. Will it work? Why or why not?

```
Side := 16.0;
Side := sqrt (Side);
writeln (Side);
```

A. Yes, it will work. The expression on the right-hand side of an assignment is always evaluated *before* the assignment takes place. As far as the computer is concerned, we're just making the assignment:

    Side := 4.0000000000;

Standard Functions

When Niklaus Wirth defined Standard Pascal, he intentionally limited the language to a small set of standard functions. He wanted to keep Pascal small and easy to write compilers for, yet he wanted to be certain that a few key functions would always be fast and accurate. There were also a few functions that couldn't be written using standard Pascal (say, functions whose type could vary) but which had to be provided to make the language useful.

sqr	sqrt		{*Square and square root*}
sin	cos	arctan	{*Standard trigonometric functions*}
exp	ln		{*Exponential and natural logarithms*}
abs			{*Absolute value*}
round	trunc		{*Rounding and real truncation*}
succ	pred		{*Successor and predecessor of ordinal values*}
ord			{*Ordinal (counting) position of a value*}
chr			{*Character in a given ordinal position*}
odd			{*Is an integer odd?*}
eoln	eof		{*Are we at the end of an input line or file?*}

arithmetic functions — rows: sqr/sqrt; sin/cos/arctan; exp/ln; abs; round/trunc
ordering functions — rows: succ/pred; ord; chr
boolean functions — rows: odd; eoln/eof

Let's look at the functions in more detail. The basic arithmetic functions are:

sqr(x)   The sqr function represents the square of its argument, x. The argument may be either an integer or a real; the function's result type is the same as its argument's type.

arithmetic functions

sqrt(x)   The sqrt function represents the square root of its argument, x. The argument may be either an integer or a real, but the function's result type is always real.

    sqr(3.0) *is* 9.000 . . .   sqr(3) *is* 9
    sqrt(4.0) *is* 2.000 . . .   sqrt(4) *is* 2.000 . . .

sin(x), cos(x)   These functions represent the sine and cosine of the argument, which is assumed to be a real-valued angle given in radians. They have real results.

arctan(x)   Represents the inverse tangent of its real argument as a real number of radians.

exp(x)   The exponential function represents the real value e (the base of the natural log system) raised to the real or integer power x.

ln(x)   The natural log function represents the real natural logarithm (to the base e) of its integer or real argument. In Pascal, exp and ln are commonly used to calculate powers and roots that don't involve whole-number powers (since sqr and sqrt are better for them):

$$x^n = \exp(n * \ln(x))$$
$$\underline{nth\ root\ of}\ x = x^{1/n} = \exp(1/n * \ln(x))$$

abs(x)   Returns the absolute value $|x|$ of x, which may be of either type integer or real. The function's result type is the same as its argument's type.

> abs(–10) is 10   abs(–3.5) is 3.5E00   abs(5) is 5

round(x)   Takes a real argument and returns it rounded to the nearest whole number. It always rounds away from zero for fractions including and greater than .5.

> round(1.6) is 2   round(1.5) is 2
> round(–2.4) is –2   round(–1.5) is –2

trunc(x)   Takes a real argument and cuts off any fractional part; i.e. it returns the argument rounded to the nearest whole number toward zero.

> trunc(4.8) is 4   trunc(0.22573E+02) is 22

Lest you start to think that programming is all numbers, I hasten to introduce four functions that juggle other values.

ordering functions

succ(x)   Represents the value that follows its ordinal (non-real) argument. succ has the same type as its argument.

pred(x)   Represents the value that precedes its ordinal (non-real) argument. pred has the same type as its argument.

> succ('a') is 'b'   pred(10) is 9

ord(x)   Represents the ordinal position, or place number, of a value within its entire type. In particular, if x is a char value, ord(x) can be expected to supply the position of x in the computer's character set (usually ASCII).

chr(x)   Represents the char value located in ordinal position x. The argument must be an integer within appropriate bounds. Ordinal counts start with zero for both ord and chr.

We'll take a closer look at char values in a moment. But first, a note about the last few functions.

odd(x)   This function represents the boolean value TRUE if its integer argument is an odd number and is FALSE otherwise.

We'll look at odd again in Chapter 5. The final two functions, eoln and eof, are described in detail in Chapter 7.

Self-Check Questions

Q. Write each of these as an assignment statement.

    a) Assign Answer negative 7 times the variable Result.
    b) Let Score get the absolute value of Time minus Place.
    c) Have Operation get the character that represents real division.
    d) Give Root the square root of InValue plus the real equivalent of 6.
    e) Give RightAngle half the sine of Pi squared.
    f) Assign the fourth root of 4.70237895 to Fourth.
    g) Let Fifteenth represent nine to the 15.3 power.
    h) Make LogCosine equal the logarithm of the cosine of 41.9.
    i) Have InverseSquare hold the reciprocal of 16 squared.
    j) Let Rounded be the integer nearest to a positive RealValue.
    k) Have Later represent the fourth character after Initial.

A. Like these? I can make 'em up all day.

    a) Answer := −7 * Result;
    b) Score := abs(Time − Place);
    c) Operation := ´/´;
    d) Root := sqrt(InValue) + 6.0;
    e) RightAngle := sin(sqr(Pi)) / 2.0;
    f) Fourth := sqrt (sqrt (4.70237895));
    g) Fifteenth := exp (15.3 * ln(9.0));
    h) LogCosine := ln (cos(41.9));
    i) InverseSquare := 1.0 / sqr (16);
    j) Rounded := trunc (RealValue + 0.5);
    k) Later := chr (ord(INITIAL) + 4);

Q. Write statements that would let you know:

    a) The character that follows the zero digit character.
    b) The whole part of a real variable called GPA.
    c) The place number of the letter ´A´ among the char values.
    d) 9 to the eighth power.
    e) The absolute value of Number.
    f) The value of Decimal rounded off to the nearest integer.
    g) The number that follows zero.

A. Don't overlook the distinction between digit characters (in *a*) and one-digit numbers (in *g*).

    a) writeln (succ(´0´));
    b) writeln (trunc(GPA));
    c) writeln (ord(´A´));
    d) writeln (sqr (sqr (sqr (9)));
    e) writeln (abs(Number));
    f) writeln (round(Decimal));
    g) writeln (succ(0));

A Note About Characters

Many of the programs we'll write involve char values. I've mentioned that Pascal typically uses the ASCII character set, which is a standard set of 128 characters that's used on many computers and by many programming languages.

    The ASCII set begins with 32 non-printing *control characters* that control terminals, printers, and communications in various ways. It ends with a control character as well. The ninety-five printing characters in between are shown below. You can't see it, but the very first printing character is a space:

```
! ´#$%&´()*+,-./
0123456789:;<=>?@
ABCDEFGHIJKLMNOPQRSTUVWXYZ[\]^_`
abcdefghijklmnopqrstuvwxyz{}~
```

On many computers, the ASCII set is extended by a second set of another 128 international symbols (like ¥) and graphics characters (like ⊥).

Now that you know something about ASCII, you can better understand the ordering functions described earlier. You know what ordinal numbers are—they indicate position. As far as computer scientists are concerned (and it beats me why) the ordinal numbers begin with the 'zeroth' place. Thus, ASCII 0 is the zeroth ASCII character—chr(0). As it happens the letter 'A' is the sixty-fifth ASCII character, 'B' is the sixty-sixth, and so on. Thus:

ord('A') *is* 65   chr(65) *is* 'A'

An especially useful application of the ord function arises when we want to be sure that a program is *bullet proof*, or immune to the slips that linger between brain and finger. For example, the inadvertent appearance of a letter in integer input is a common cause of program crashes.

bullet-proofing programs

To avoid the problem, the prudent programmer will read numbers as digit characters and convert them herself. That way, if a non-digit unexpectedly appears, she's able to catch it before it can cause trouble.

Let's try a one-digit example. How can we convert a digit *character* to the number it represents? Suppose that InputCharacter is a char variable that represents one of the digits '0', '1', '2', and so on through '9'. It's tempting to say that this assignment gives us the right number:

{*an incorrect assignment*}
ConvertedToInteger := ord(InputCharacter);

But a digit like '0' is nowhere near the zeroth character in the ASCII set. On the other hand, the relative positions of the digit characters are the same as the relative positions of the numbers. 2 is as far away from 5 as '2' is from '5'. This assignment does what we want:

{*the correct assignment*}
ConvertedToInteger := ord(InputCharacter) – ord('0');

**boundary-condition
testing**

A test case or two (in particular, with '0' and '9') should convince you. The trick of testing only the outside case is called *boundary-condition testing*. We assume that if an algorithm works for the highest and lowest numbers, it is well-behaved for all the in-between cases too.

Self-Check Questions

Q. If ordinal counting starts with the zeroth place and the ASCII character set has 128 characters, what is the ordinal position of the last ASCII character?

A. It's the one hundred twenty-seventh. Confusing, but true.

Q. How far away from the letter 'A' is the letter 'T'? Write an expression that tells you.

A. We subtract one letter's ordinal position from the other's:

Distance := ord('T') – ord('A');

Note that the actual values the ord calls represent are irrelevant.

Q. Quick—if ´A´ is the first letter of the alphabet, what position is ´S´ in? No fair counting, but you should assume ASCII ordering.

A. We can find the position using ord, too. We can't just subtract, though, because that would be off by one:

ord(´A´) − ord(´A´) *is* 0

However, I said that ´A´ is the first letter of the alphabet, not the zeroth. We need to correct the position by adding 1:

Position := (ord(´S´) − ord(´A´)) + 1;

Again, the actual values returned by ord are irrelevant.

2-3 Declaring New Functions*

PASCAL HAS TWO KINDS OF subprograms—procedures (which we've already used and written) and functions (which we've used, but haven't written yet). The new functions we declare will probably be a little more interesting than standard functions and library functions. We can name them as we wish, tell them what to compute, and give them as many arguments as necessary.

functions represent values

> However, all functions share one important feature: a function call represents a *value*. It must be used as part of an expression and not as a statement.

For example, consider a call of a function that implements the one formula everybody knows—that distance equals rate times time:

a function call

AmountTraveled := Distance (Speed, ElapsedTime);

Before we can use AmountTraveled, it has to be declared. As always, declarations belong in the first half of a program:

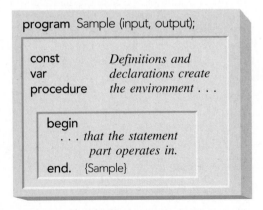

```
program Sample (input, output);

   const        Definitions and
   var          declarations create
   procedure    the environment . . .

      begin
        . . . that the statement
                part operates in.
      end.   {Sample}
```

---

* This section may be passed over for now without harm.

Syntactically, a function is identical to a procedure *except* for the heading.

function heading

function ⟶ *identifier* ⟶ (⟶ *parameter list* ⟶) : ⟶ *type identifier* ⟶ ;

You can read the declaration of Distance, below. Look for the two hall-marks of every function declaration—the specification of the function's type (real here) and the assignment of a value to the function.

its declaration

```
function Distance (Rate, Time: real) : real ;
   {Calculates Distance given Rate and Time.}
begin
   Distance := Rate * Time
end;  {Distance}
```

Now, I've managed to point out repeatedly that a function (unlike a pro-cedure) represents a value. This has two consequences:

> First, since the function represents a value, we have to specify its type. Second, the function has to contain an assignment statement that actually gives it the value and ends the function call.

function type

A function call can always represent any simple type of value, ordinal or real. The function's *result type* is specified at the end of the function heading, with a colon that is followed by the type identifier. The example function Dis-tance was of type real.

assigning the value

Having set the stage by giving the function a type, we need a way to give it a value. The statement part of a function must contain an assignment state-ment that ends the call and gives it a value. In Distance this assignment was the function's entire statement part. Functions may be very complicated, of course, but a function's last action is to give itself a value.

We'll almost invariably find that functions use one or more value param-eters to compute a value—a value that the function then represents. It is very unusual to give a function any variable parameters. The general rule is:

when function, when procedure

— If a subprogram calculates just one value in a call, write it as a function.

— If a subprogram calculates more than one value per call, write it as a reg-ular procedure that has variable parameters.

Some typical function headings are:

```
function Cube (Number: real) : real ;
function Decode (Letter: char; CodeKey: integer) : char ;
function Highest (First, Second, Third: integer) : integer ;
function NoParameters : integer ;
```

In each case the heading ends with a colon and the function's type.

As with procedure calls, there must be a one-to-one correspondence between the arguments of a function call and the value parameters of a function declaration. Thus, any given function will always be called with the same number of parameters. Try connecting them yourself:

{Function heading, which usually has value parameters}

function Yield (Investment: integer;
                       Interest: real;
                       Days: integer) : real;

parameter
correspondence

Income := Yield (1000, 0.097, 365);
{Function call, with its arguments}

Variable parameters are seldom declared in function headings because the avowed purpose of a function is to compute and return a *single* value. If a function has variable parameters, it will wind up returning more than just one value. This creates a situation that can confuse an unwary program *rewriter*. If a subprogram is supposed to calculate more than one value for the main program, then write it as a procedure.

A Few Function Examples

Let's try writing a few examples that are standard in some other computer languages and can even be found on some pocket calculators.

A reciprocal function is pretty easy (it's the fifth key on the top row, above):

function Reciprocal (Number: integer) : real ;
  {Represents the reciprocal of Number.}

reciprocals

  begin
    Reciprocal := 1.0 / Number
  end; *{Reciprocal}*

Functions Power and Root, below, are meant to let us forget, forever, exactly how to do exponentiation. Although I've written these functions to take real arguments, incidentally, many programmers will use integer arithmetic and the sqr function when whole-number powers are involved.

exponentiation

```
function Power (Base, Exponent: real) : real;
    {Raises a positive Base to the Exponent power.}
begin
    Power := exp (Exponent * ln (Base) )
end;  {Power}
```

```
function Root (Base, Exponent: real) : real;
    {Finds the non-zero Exponentth root of a positive Base.}
begin
    Root := exp (1/Exponent * ln (Base) )
end;  {Root}
```

Trigonometric functions are just as easy. You might have wondered why only three functions (sin, cos, and arctan) are standard. The answer is economy: any trigonometry or calculus text will have a table that yields all the trig relationships from just those three. For example, since tangent ϕ = (sine ϕ / cosine ϕ), it's easy to write function Tangent.

tangents

```
function Tangent (AngleInRadians: real) : real;
    {Represents the tangent of its argument.}
begin
    Tangent := sin(AngleInRadians) / cos(AngleInRadians)
end;  {Tangent}
```

Functions sin, cos, and arctan may be a bit unusual to you because they take their arguments in radians, rather than degrees. Some calculators (but not Pascal programs) have a button that switches from one form to the other. For us, there is a simple conversion formula: $180° = \pi$ radians (3.14159 radians), $360° = 2\pi$ radians, $90° = \pi/2$ radians, etc.

conversion to radians

```
function Radians (AngleInDegrees: real) : real;
    {Represents its argument in radians.}
const PI = 3.14159;
begin
    Radians := AngleInDegrees * (PI / 180)
end;  {Radians}
```

conversion to degrees

```
function Degrees (AngleInRadians: real) : real;
    {Represents its argument in degrees.}
const PI = 3.14159;
begin
    Degrees := (AngleInRadians * 180 ) / PI
end;  {Degrees}
```

Modification Problems ───────────────────────────────

1. How can you test a function? By putting it into a program that doesn't include much besides the function's definition and a call or two. Such programs are called *test harnesses* or *program shells*; I'll have more to say about them in the *Program Engineering Notes*. For now, write a test harness that lets you test functions Distance, Reciprocal, Root, and Power.

Self-Check Questions ───────────────────────────────

Q. Which of these problems should be solved with functions? Which with procedures?

   a) Exchange the value of two char variables.
   b) Find the difference between two numbers.
   c) Find the letter that's N places after Initial.
   d) Multiply Offset by 17.
   e) Multiply 33 by Distance.
   f) Print the value of an argument.
   g) Count the number of words in a string.

A. Since we'll never expect functions to change their arguments, I'd solve problems *b*, *c*, *e*, and *g* with functions. *a* and *d* are best for procedures because the arguments are changing. *f*, in contrast, doesn't return a value at all, so writing it as a function wouldn't be appropriate.

Example: the Human Light Bulb

Consider the humble electric light bulb:

The thoroughly frivolous problem I'll solve is:

problem: power consumption

If you were a light bulb, how bright would you be? Although you probably think this is an existential question, there's a formula you can use to get a pretty good estimate of how much power your body generates:

$$power\ production,\ in\ watts\ =\ (9 \times weight)^{0.751}$$

where *weight* is supplied in pounds. This formula is remarkably accurate for warm-blooded creatures, regardless of size. Write a program that lets you know about how much power it takes you to keep going.

An outline of program Wattage doesn't hold any surprises. We have to get a fact (the user's weight), perform a calculation, and print the results:

pseudocode

> *get the input;*
> *perform the calculation;*
> *print the results;*

If you're at all uncertain about parameters, it's useful to outline the program with would-be arguments in place, like this:

mock procedure calls

> *get the input (weight);* {use the weight}
> *perform the calculation (weight, result);* {use weight, change result}
> *print the results (result);* {use the result}

How can we raise a number to the 0.751 power? We've already written function Power. Why don't I just copy it to procedure Calculate in program Wattage, below?

> Any procedure or function can contain the declarations of additional local functions and procedures. Like local variables, they can only be called from within the subprogram.

Don't worry if you've never used functions like exp and ln, by the way. I've deliberately chosen a couple of functions that are probably unfamiliar so that you'll have an example of them at work.

(*program follows*)

Modification Problems

1. The light bulb package gives a value for the bulb's brightness in *lumens*. Technically, this describes the rate of flow, or flux, of luminous energy. Although the correlation between wattage and lumen output is only approximate, modify Wattage so that it lets you know how much light you'd put out.

2. Modify program Wattage so that it tells you the difference in energy production between a half-ton of mice and one half-ton moose. Assume that each mouse weighs about ⅓ ounce.

3. Since procedure Calculate changes just one variable—Watts—it could be written as a function. Turn procedure Calculate into a function that could be used as the argument to procedure PrintResults.

```pascal
program Wattage (input, output);
    {Demonstrates some fancy arithmetic.}
var Weight, Watts:  integer;
procedure GetFacts (var Weight:  integer);
    {Finds the program user's weight, in pounds.}
    begin
        write ('How much do you weigh, in pounds?    ');
        readln (Weight)
    end;  {GetFacts}
procedure Calculate (Weight:  integer;  var Watts:  integer);
    {Applies the formula for estimating power consumption.}
    {These definitions and declarations are all made locally, since they're
     only going to be used inside the procedures.}
    const MULTIPLIER = 9;
          EXPONENT = 0.751;
    var Temp:  real;
    function Power (Base, Exponent:  real) : real;
        {Raises Base to the Exponent power.}
        begin
            Power := exp (Exponent * ln (Base) )
        end;  {Power}
    begin
        Temp := MULTIPLIER * Weight;
        Temp := Power(Temp, EXPONENT);
        Watts := round(Temp)
    end;  {Calculate}
procedure PrintResults (Watts:  integer);
    {Prints the user's approximate power consumption.}
    begin
        write ('If you were a light bulb, you''d consume about  ');
        write (Watts : 1);
        writeln ('  watts.')
    end;  {PrintResults}
begin
    GetFacts (Weight);
    {We have the weight.}
    Calculate (Weight, Watts);
    {We've performed the calculation.}
    PrintResults (Watts)
    {We've printed the answer.}
end.  {Wattage}
```

```
How much do you weigh, in pounds?  172
If you were a light bulb, you'd consume about 249 watts.
```

Program Engineering Notes: Nailing Parameters

2-4

THE SYNTAX OF VALUE AND VARIABLE PARAMETERS may be confusing, but they have a simple goal—to distinguish between 'in' arguments and 'out' arguments. Pascal could have been designed with a syntax that used **INVALUE** and **OUTVARIABLE** parameters, but it wasn't, so that's that.

> Learn parameters now while programs are short and simple, and they'll help you later when your code gets more complicated.

At first, you may find it is easiest to learn to use parameters the same way that you learn to conjugate verbs in a foreign language—by rote, rather than by logic. The two most common syntax errors are:

— mismatching the type of a parameter and the type of its argument, and

— forgetting that the argument of a variable parameter must be a variable.

count the arguments

Counting winds up being as important as spelling. When you write a procedure call, be careful to have the right number of arguments! To learn to avoid these problems, I suggest that you go back into the chapter and deliberately introduce errors of this sort into sample programs. Ask a classmate if she can spot the bugs; then ask her to do the same for you.

Now, some parameter errors involve syntax, while others involve semantics. The compiler will catch only the syntactic bugs. Here are a few of the error messages we can reasonably expect from a compiler:

a few realistic error messages

```
{There are too few or too many arguments.}
Compile error:
   Number of arguments disagrees with parameter list.
```

```
{A variable parameter must have a variable as its argument.}
Compile error:
   Expression given for variable parameter.
```

```
{There can't be type clashes between arguments and parameters.}
Compile error:
   Argument type doesn't match variable parameter type.
```

However, these error messages are merely wishful thinking, since the compiler can't read your mind.

these messages are impossible

```
Compile error:
   Global variable used, try a local variable instead.
Compile error:
   Variable parameter used, value parameter is better.
Compile error:
   Variable parameter was never properly initialized.
```

Something that I do when I'm debugging programs is to take a *listing* (which is a printout of the program) and a pencil, then draw lines that connect

work from a listing

the arguments in a procedure *call* to the parameters in the procedure *declaration*. Remember that arguments and parameters are associated by their positions. The compiler can't reorder a call so that it makes sense.

```
program Multiply (input, output);
   {Gets a user's initial and two numbers to multiply.}
var First, Second:  integer;
    Name:  char;
procedure GetTheInfo
            (var Who:  char;   var Number1, Number2:  integer);
   {Gets the program user's initial and favorite numbers.}
   begin
      write ('Hi!  What''s your first initial?  ');
      readln (Who);
      write (Who);
      write (', give me two whole numbers to multiply.  ');
      read (Number1);
      readln (Number2)
   end;  {GetTheInfo}
procedure PrintTheNews (Who:  char;  Answer:  integer);
   {Prints its arguments.}
   begin
      write ('Oh, no! ');
      write (Who);
      write ('   Their product is ');
      write (Answer : 1);
      writeln ('.  How auspicious!')
   end;  {PrintTheNews}
begin
   GetTheInfo (Name, First, Second);
   PrintTheNews (Name, First * Second)
end.  {Multiply}
```

connecting arguments
and parameters

Why Not Always Use Variable Parameters?

Once you really understand the technical differences between value and variable parameters, you'll start to wonder why we don't use variable parameters most of, or even all of, the time. After all, there's no law that says we have to change a variable parameter's value. We could use it just like a value parameter—to get a value into a procedure.

The reason we stick with value parameters for one-way communication has to do with safety. Consider procedure BugBait, below. Even though it only uses its argument (by printing its value), the procedure works correctly with a variable parameter—for now:

this should be a value
parameter

```
procedure BugBait ( var Weight:  real );
   {Prints a weight.}

   begin
      write ('The weight is  ');
      write (Weight : 3 : 2);
      writeln ('  pounds.')
   end; {BugBait}
```

My bait catches its bug when I ask you to modify the procedure to convert its argument into kilograms. As a conscientious, step-by-step programmer, you might do the job like this:

```
procedure BugBait (var Weight: real);
    {Prints a weight.}
    const POUNDSperKilo = 2.2;
    begin
        write ('The weight is ');
        Weight := Weight / POUNDSperKilo;
        write (Weight : 3 : 2);
        writeln (' kilograms.')
    end; {BugBait}
```

this introduces a bug

Now the procedure works, but the program that calls the procedure may fail. Why? Because BugBait has permanently changed the value of its argument. If it had correctly used a value parameter instead, there wouldn't be any problem.

> Value parameters are an important tool of *modular* program construction. They *localize* the effect of assignments and let the programmer work without having to worry about breaking the main program.

Semantic Bugs

It's time for an important point about semantic errors, which are mistakes in the meaning, rather than the syntax, of code.

syntax precedes semantics

> The fact that a program compiles, and runs, is evidence only of syntactic correctness. It says nothing about program semantics—whether or not the program does what we expect it to.

This statement seems obvious, but it does happen that, in the process of making syntactic fixes, a program's semantics can be discombobulated. It's always good to bear the ultimate question—*Is the output right?*—in mind.

By far the most common sort of program bugs come from problems with parameters. The causes of most problems are semantic errors (problems with meaning) in programs that are syntactically correct. This pitfall is so universal that program engineering guideline Number One might well be:

> Are you sure that your value parameters are value parameters and that your variable parameters are variable parameters? Accidentally defining a variable parameter as a value parameter is the most common parameter bug.

For example, consider a procedure that prompts the program user to enter arguments. In outline, the procedure is:

```
procedure PromptAndRead ( ··· );
    {How would you define the shaded identifiers?}
    begin
        write ('Please enter ');
        write ( Count );
        writeln (' numbers:    ');
        read ( First );
        readln ( Second )
    end;  {PromptAndRead}
```

Note how each of these headings screws up:

two incorrect examples

```
procedure PromptAndRead (Count, First, Second:  integer );
    {First and Second are mistakenly declared as value parameters.
    Changing them won't change the arguments they rename.}
```

```
procedure PromptAndRead ( var Count , First, Second:  integer);
    {Count is wrongly declared as a variable parameter.  We couldn't
    call the procedure with a literal Count value; e.g. PromptAndRead(2,...}
```

The correct version of the heading is:

the correct version

```
procedure PromptAndRead (Count:  integer;
                              var First, Second:  integer);
    {Count will be used, and First and Second will change.}
```

Let me ask a question about program *style*: Can a declaration be wrong even when it's right? Sure. What's wrong with this heading?

```
procedure PromptAndRead (var First:  integer;
                             Count:  integer;
                             var Second:  integer);
```

style

What's the matter? The order of the parameters doesn't make any obvious sense, which increases the odds that the procedure will be called incorrectly.

the Law of Least Astonishment

> The *Law of Least Astonishment* says that the most obvious interpretation should be correct. Make sure that your parameter lists obey it.

Parameters should be declared in an order that automatically encourages correct calls. There's a story about the programmer who wrote procedure calls like:

```
AddGin (ToVermouth, Making, Martini);
```

but I'm not going to tell it here.

Functions and Test Harnesses

Most ordinary function problems stem from confusing them with procedures. Some points to watch out for are:

— Functions have types, procedures don't.

Each function heading must end with a colon and a type identifier:

function Calculate (*parameters*) : *type identifier* ;

— Each function must include an assignment that gives the function its value.

Naturally, you have to keep an eye on type matching. If the function's result type is char, you must assign a char to it. The types of any function arguments are irrelevant:

> return the proper type

function NthLetter (Distance: integer) : char ;
    {*Returns the Nth letter following* 'a'.}
    begin
       NthLetter := chr (Distance + ord('a'))
    end; {NthLetter}

— Functions shouldn't inadvertently call themselves.

A function or procedure that calls itself is said to be *recursive*. This is perfectly legal, but the subprogram has to be written in a manner that lets the series of subprogram calls end eventually. We'll discuss recursion further in Chapter 16; until then we'll just avoid it.

— Unlike procedures, functions almost never have variable parameters.

Since the purpose of a function is to return a single value, giving it a variable parameter can be immensely confusing.

As I mentioned in passing in one of the Modification Problems, *shell* or *test harness* programs provide a useful test bed for subprograms.

> test harnesses

A program shell or test harness is written to supply the simplest environment a procedure or function call can get away with—usually just the declaration, a variable or two, and a test call.

Test harness programs are about as close as we can come to approximating the failure tests of engineering. For example, here's how Rolls Royce airplane engines used to be tested:

> The engine would be driven to full power; this would normally result in a component failure. The component would then be strengthened and the test restarted. This time another component would fail. This process was continued until no component failure occurred.*

Test harnesses give you a chance to test new code in an uncluttered arena. You can assure yourself that a subprogram works before subjecting it to the pressure of having to cooperate with the rest of your main program. At

---

* Darrel Ince, *Software Development: Fashioning the Baroque*, Oxford University Press, 1988, p. 44.

first, it's hard to shake the feeling that writing a harness involves oodles of extra work. But, with practice, you'll get the time needed to type up a shell like this down to less than a minute:

```
program Test (input, output);
     {A test bed for procedure DryRun.}

var as necessary

procedure DryRun with its parameters, etc.
   begin
        whatever DryRun does
   end;  {DryRun}

begin
     Give DryRun a workout
end.   {Test}
```

Have fun turning up the throttle on your code!

Syntax Summary

❑ procedure declaration: similar to a program, but there can be *parameters*, between parentheses, in the heading:

```
procedure Sample (parameter list);
     definitions and declarations
begin
     procedure calls and other statements
end;    {Finish with a semicolon, not a period.}
```

❑ function: a subprogram that calculates and represents a value.

```
function Sample ( parameter list ) : integer;
     Definitions and declarations if necessary,
     begin
          statements that calculate the function's value, followed by:
          Sample := a value
     end;    {Finish with a semicolon.}
```

❑ value parameter declarations: have syntax similar to variable declarations, but go in the parameter list:

```
procedure Sample (Number:  integer;
                   Letter1, Letter2:  char;
                   Score:  real);
```

Each value parameter takes the value of its argument at the time the procedure is called. Value parameters are employed when a value must be *used* (e.g. printed) by a procedure.

❑ variable parameter declarations: also go in the parameter list. Unlike value parameter declarations, variable parameter declarations must include the word **var** for each new type of variable parameter:

procedure Sample (**var** Value: integer;
var Ch1, Ch2: char;
var Percentage: real);

A variable parameter renames a variable supplied in a procedure call. Variable parameters are used when the variable is going to be *changed* (e.g. by having a value typed in for it) in a procedure. Changing the variable parameter *inside* the procedure permanently changes the argument *outside* the procedure.

❏ local variable: is declared in a procedure or function. Syntactically, local and global declarations are identical, but local variables don't exist outside the subprogram. Local declarations may reuse previously taken global identifiers.

❏ standard functions: are built into Pascal. They include:

sqr	sqrt		{*Square and square root*}
sin	cos	arctan	{*Standard trigonometric functions*}
exp	ln		{*Exponential and natural logarithms*}
abs			{*Absolute value*}
round	trunc		{*real rounding and truncation*}
succ	pred		{*Successor and predecessor of ordinal values*}
ord			{*Ordinal (counting) position of a value*}
chr			{*Character in a given ordinal position*}
odd			{*Is an integer odd?*}
eoln	eof		{*Are we at the end of an input line or file?*}

Remember . . .

❏ Planning and organizing is the key to successful programming. Set a specific goal for each procedure you write. Lay out your program in *pseudocode* procedure calls, complete with arguments, before you write it in Pascal.

❏ Local variables are uninitialized each and every time a procedure or function is called. Value parameters, in contrast, are initialized as part of the subprogram call.

❏ Function calls are expressions; they represent values. The *result*, or value, of a function call could, for instance, be assigned to a variable or passed to a value parameter. A function call may *not* take the place of a statement or be passed to a variable parameter.

❏ Since functions are used to represent values, they're rarely given variable parameters (which would imply changing arguments). Instead, they're almost always given value parameters.

❏ There is always a one-to-one correspondence, by position, between the parameters declared in a procedure heading and the arguments supplied in a procedure call. The argument of a variable parameter *must* be a variable or parameter; it can't be a literal value.

❏ When an argument is going to be changed by a procedure, pass it to a variable parameter. When it's just going to be used, pass it to a value parameter.

❏ A program's *state* is reflected by the values of its variables and parameters. Remember that variable parameters change main-program state, but local variables and value parameters don't.

❑   *Semantic* bugs cause errors in a program's results. Syntactically legal programs can produce wrong answers, so be ready to provide test data that check your program.

❑   A Pascal compiler can use *any* character set in practically any order. Most, but not all, compilers use the ASCII set.

❑   Although watching a computer screen is almost as much fun as watching television, you'll debug more effectively if you work from a *listing*, or hard copy, of the program.

❑   The *Law of Least Astonishment* says that the most obvious interpretation should be the correct one. Obey it.

❑   *Program shells* and *test harnesses* are used to test individual procedures or functions. The shell or harness provides the simplest possible environment for exercising the subprogram.

═══════════

Big Ideas

The Big Ideas in this chapter were:

1. *Procedures and parameters are programming's main contribution to problem solving.* The idea of packaging a specialized solution step with hooks—parameters—that make it general purpose is enormously powerful. Learning to set up solutions as single steps with changing parameters is the most valuable thing you'll learn in a programming course.

2. *Every complicated program has a simple, straightforward program buried inside of it.* Most programs take just three steps: get data, do something with them, then print the results. Programs differ in the details of what happens inside procedures, rather than in their basic approach to problem solving.

3. *Program by modifying, not by working from scratch.* If possible, change an existing program by changing one of its procedures; if you can, change an existing procedure by modifying one of its parameters.

Begin by Writing the Exam . . .

2-1   How can you tell if people are getting the basic idea of grouping statements into procedures? One way is to require them to write a program that has lots of repetitious output. If they've caught on, they'll write the repeated parts as procedures, since it's faster to *call* a procedure several times than it is to write out what it does again and again. Come up with a *Write a program that prints this . . .* problem. Hint: listen to a Top-40 radio station if you need some repetitious output.

2-2   In lieu of essay questions, a few basic definitions are always nice. Look for half a dozen words or phrases that you'd just as soon not see on a test and ask *What do these mean?*

2-3   Parameters, like angry civets, are best dealt with one at a time. Start with value parameters by considering procedure PrintInitials, from program ValueArg. Although that procedure printed the values of its two char arguments, you might just as easily ask for a procedure that prints three integers, or five reals, or a few of each. Make up three questions of this sort.

2-4   Procedure GetIQ, from program WiseGuy, reads a value for one integer variable. As above, we might just as easily read five chars, or a real and two integers. Make up two questions that begin: *Write a procedure that reads values for . . .*

2-5   *Modify this program* is a great exam question, because you can test hard ideas without making students spend a lot of time writing. For instance, program Multiply was hardwired to do multiplication. If you were so inclined, you could ask that it be modified to do division (easy), or put the division in a procedure (a bit harder), or multiply and divide with procedures (harder still). Make up two *Modify this program* questions.

2-6   I'm also a big fan of *Rewrite a* this *as a* that questions. For example, I might supply a procedure that modifies a single variable parameter, and ask that it be rewritten as a function. Make up three of this kind.

2-7   Students can be led to believe that the computer understands the names they use, and will reorder the parameter lists of procedure calls to match the parameter lists of procedure declarations. Write a few incorrect headings that thus mislead and pose the problem *Fix these headings.*

2-8   When is a procedure correct, but wrong? When its syntax is correct but its semantics are not. Here is the prototype of a question that is syntactically correct and compiles just fine. However, it is semantically incorrect, because it doesn't do what the user really wants:

```
{This procedure compiles perfectly.  What's wrong with it?}

procedure ReadAge (Age:  integer);
    {Get the user's age for use in the main program.}
    begin
        write ('How old are you?    ');
        readln (Age)
    end;
```

Procedure ReadAge mistakenly uses a value parameter instead of a variable parameter. Write three similar questions that confuse the usage of value and variable parameters.

2-9   *Global/local? Argument/parameter?* Find three more word pairs that would be suitable for *What's the difference?* questions.

2-10   The test question I'm most proud of accompanies a short program and is called *Here's the output, what was the input?* After all, it's no harder to grade than *Here's the input, what's the output?,* but it's *so* much harder to do! Seriously, anybody can plug and chug through *what's the output?* eventually, but doing *what's the input?* really requires understanding. Modify a program like ParamBed so that it has input; then ask *Here's the output, what's the input?*

Warmups and Test Programs

2-11   Procedures can contain procedures. Just for practice, write a program in which the main program gets two integer values from the program user. Then, use them as arguments to a procedure that contains and calls two internal procedures and gives one of its arguments to each. Have the innermost procedure print its argument.

2-12   Characters in the ASCII character set are numbered, starting with 0. If you know a character's number, you can use the chr function (as the argument of a call of write) to print it. What happens when you print character −1?

2-13   The constant MAXINT represents the largest legal integer value. Exactly what is it? What's the smallest negative integer?

2-14   What happens when you try to print the number that follows the largest integer? The number after that? The number that precedes the smallest one?

2-15   Can you step outside the boundaries of integer during the course of an arithmetic operation? In other words, can you print the final value of an expression that adds 5 to the maximum integer, then subtracts 6 from the result?

2-16   The ordinal position of a positive integer is the integer itself. What's the ordinal position of a negative number?

2-17   Can a constant definition require a calculation? Can it involve a function call?

2-18   Suppose we've written procedures to solve these problems. Which ones will require at least one local variable?

a)   Swapping the values of two variables.

b)   Doubling the value of an integer.

c) Reading four characters and returning just the fourth one to the main program.

d) Printing a real argument along with its square root.

2-19 Write a procedure that returns its three integer variable parameters as positive numbers.

2-20 Write a procedure that reads two letters and sends them to the main program as capital letters.

2-21 Write the procedure that's called like this:

    PrintCharacterBefore (Character);

2-22 Write the procedure that's called like this:

    PrintNthLetterAfter (Letter, N);

2-23 Now, improve the procedure above so that the letter after 'Z' is 'A'. Hint: **mod** will come in handy.

2-24 Write a function that represents a) pounds as kilograms, b) degrees Fahrenheit as degrees centigrade, c) dollars as Italian lire, d) hours as minutes, e) its real argument as the next higher integer.

2-25 *Officer: Did you know that you were going 75 miles per hour?*
Offender: Well, I wasn't planning on being out that long.
The last time I got a speeding ticket I was informed that the fine was $75 plus $5 for each mile over the limit. Write a procedure or function that takes a limit and an actual speed and returns a fine.

2-26 Mathematicians are always searching for new ways to be mean. Three of my favorites are:

a) The *arithmetic mean* of two numbers is their sum divided by two.

b) The *geometric mean* of two numbers is the square root of their product.

c) The *harmonic mean* of two numbers is the arithmetic mean of their reciprocals.

Write the three functions, then write a test harness to try them out. Does it matter if you write the functions inside a procedure?

2-27 What is the Law of Least Astonishment?

2-28 Suppose that procedure Order is meant to put its three char arguments into alphabetical order (I said suppose it, not write it). Design a way to test Order. What test data will you use?

2-29 It's time to explore error messages. What happens if you write a function but forget to assign it a value? If you declare a function that has no parameters, but you give it parentheses anyway? If you misuse the function by confusing its type in an assignment?

Programming Problems

2-30 Have you ever had time on your hands? Was it a mess? Write a program that adds and subtracts time. It should ask the user for two input values—a time (like 3:57) and a duration (such as 1:05)—then print the sum (here, 5:02) and difference (2:52). If you want practice writing functions, you might want to add Hour and Minute functions that return the 'whole' hour portion and 'fractional' minute portion that result from adding minute values.

2-31 What stops people from ordering goods by telephone, then giving totally fictitious credit card numbers? Well, the thought of San Quentin must have some deterrent effect, but preventive measures are usually built into the cards themselves.

For example, one simple check would be to add the digits of a number, then tack on a zero or one, as required, to make their sum an even number. Thus, 52771 would be a legal number, since its digits sum to 22. In contrast, 49930 isn't legal, because 25 is odd.

Write a program that computes a *check character* according to the following rules:

a) Start with a ten-digit number, e.g. 1122334455.

b) Add the five pairs it contains, e.g. 11 plus 22 and so on.

c) Take the sum **mod** 26.

a) Return, as the check character, the letter in that position in the alphabet. You should assume that 0 represents ´A´.

Don't forget to test your program!

2-32 Product expiration dates are often encoded to discourage consumers from complaining. One common technique is to use letters rather than numbers in showing dates. Suppose that the White Bread Mfg. Co. encodes the months as the letters ´A´ through ´L´, each digit of the day's date as the letters ´Q´ through ´Z´, and the year as a single letter ´Z´ through ´A´, where ´Z´ equals 1993, ´Y´ equals 1994, and so on down to ´A´.

Write a program that reads an encoded date, then prints the decoded version. Be sure to use separate procedures for input, output, and calculation.

2-33 A traveling salesperson travels between five cities. Suppose that the *x, y* coordinates of each city are supplied as input to a program. What is the total distance the salesperson travels? What is the direct distance between the first and last cities on her route?

2-34 Even if you can't remember the names of the planets (I vaguely recall something about mother and jelly sandwiches) there's an easy way to remember how far from the Sun they are. It's *Bode's Law*, ascribed to J.E. Bode (1747-1826). It isn't really a law; rather, it's an empirically derived rule that describes the distances from most of the bodies in the solar system to the Sun pretty accurately. It is:

$$\text{Distance of } n\text{th planet} = (4 + 3 \times 2^{n-2}) / 10 \text{ astronomical units}$$

with the exception that Mercury has no $3 \times 2^{n-2}$ term. An astronomical unit is the distance between the Earth and the Sun, or about 93,000,000 miles. How well does Bode's Law predict the actual distances (shown below in astronomical units)? How do you account for a certain missing planet (at *n*=5)?

Mercury	0.39	Mars	1.52	Uranus	19.18
Venus	0.72	Jupiter	5.20	Neptune	30.07
Earth	1.0	Saturn	9.54	Pluto	39.67

2-35 Three professors of Classics were arguing over their coffee—or, more precisely, about their coffee. Apparently, three temperatures were available: boiling, 50°, and room temperature (which happens to be 20°). The professors all agreed that the room temperature cup wouldn't cool any further, but they disagreed about how long it would take the other cups to cool one degree apiece.

'It makes no difference—a degree's a degree,' claimed the professor of Greek, who had many degrees herself. 'Stuff and nonsense,' retorted her colleague, the Latin specialist. 'The boiling one is twice as hot, so it cools twice as quickly.' 'Hold your tongue,' snapped the third professor. 'What's important is the difference from room temperature—the hot one will shed one degree 8/3 times faster.'

The engineering student who was serving coffee (and failing all three Classics courses) knew that the real answer was proportional to the black body (coffee, in this case) temperature[4], less the room temperature[4], with all temperatures in degrees Kelvin (Celsius plus 273), of each cup. Having grown to appreciate the Socratic method, though, she didn't speak up.

Well, how much faster *does* the hotter cup cool off 1 degree? In other words (ignoring convection and conduction), solve:

$$\frac{hot\ coffee_{kelvin}^{4} - room\ temperature_{kelvin}^{4}}{warm\ coffee_{kelvin}^{4} - room\ temperature_{kelvin}^{4}}$$

2-36   A physics professor who hoped to teach her students creative methods of problem solving gave each a barometer, and the task of measuring the height of an office building. Most of the students came up with clever, innovative approaches: dropping the barometer from the top of the building and timing its fall, boiling the barometer at the top of the building and checking the water temperature, selling the barometer to the building superintendent in exchange for a glimpse at the blueprints, and so on.

Naturally, there's a dullard in every crowd. One student actually checked the pressure at ground level (30.28 inches of mercury) and on the roof (30.16 inches), then wrote a program that applied the formula:

$$height\ in\ feet\ =\ 25,000\ \ln \frac{ground\ pressure}{roof\ pressure}$$

How tall is the building? Write a general purpose program to find the answer for any two pressures.

2-37   Ten seconds remain on the Super Bowl clock when a horrible accident befalls a broadcaster stationed high overhead in the Goodyear blimp. Just as play begins, the broadcaster drops his hairpiece. Suppose that the game is being played at Mile-High Stadium in Denver, so air resistance is negligible. If the blimp is hovering at 1,350 feet over the line of scrimmage and the descent time is given by:

$$time\ =\ \sqrt{\frac{twice\ the\ height}{32.174ft/sec^2}}$$

is it possible that the hairpiece will be mistaken for a penalty flag before the game ends?

2-38   Tracks and roadways are *banked*, or tilted, to help vehicles negotiate curves at high speeds. You can see banked curves at highway exits, on bicycle racing tracks, and at Roller Derby rinks. Sometimes (on bicycle tracks, for instance) the banking is so steep that the rider seems to be as threatened by sliding off the track as by flying off it.

However, when the roadbed is properly banked, a driver is in no danger of skidding—as long as she travels neither much faster nor slower than the posted speed. The proper angle of banking for a given radius and velocity is given by:

$$\tan\theta\ =\ \frac{velocity^2}{radius}\ \times 32\,feet/sec^2$$

For instance, if a road is posted for 40 MPH, a 400-foot curve should be banked at a 16-degree angle. Write a program that asks a user for a radius and speed, then prints the proper banking radius.

2-39   An average person's surface area, in square meters, can be roughly calculated with:

$$7.184^{-3} \times Weight^{0.452} \times Height^{0.725}$$

where the weight is given in kilograms, and height is supplied in centimeters.

Use this formula to write a program that will help you solve one of the great problems of our day: *How thick is a layer of suntan lotion?* In case you don't have one around to check, an average tube of suntan lotion holds about fifty milliliters. You'll have to estimate how long it lasts by yourself.

2-40   A standard first application of procedures is to print the word MISSISSIPPI in block letters (e.g. drawn entirely with asterisks). It rapidly becomes obvious that writing just four procedures—PrintM, PrintI, PrintS, and PrintP—is much easier than writing the dozens of writes that would otherwise be required.

Make your first contribution to computer science by coming up with a new word for this example. Then write a program that prints the word using one procedure for each letter. If you have no shame, you can fall back on old reliable MISSISSIPPI.

2-41   California summer campers often take long bus rides. To occupy the campers' short attention spans, camp counselors encourage the singing of endless songs. Although the timeless classic '99 Bottles of Beer on the Wall' has been deemed to be politically incorrect (for its glorification of macho beer-swilling rituals), its replacement is not difficult to learn:

> *99 bottles of Perrier on the wall,*
> *99 bottles of Perrier.*
> *If you should drop a bottle of Perrier,*
> *You might get hit in the derriere.*
> *(and have only 98 bottles of Perrier)*

Write a program that contains a procedure that prints one verse of the song. It should require one value parameter—the number of bottles that currently remain on the wall. *Option*: let a second parameter provide a substitute name for *Perrier*.

2-42 Write a program that gets a single-digit integer from its user. Then pass the digit to a procedure that multiplies the digit by 9*12345679 (note that 8 is missing). What's the output?

2-43 Write a program that contains separate procedures to:

a) get two real numbers from a program user;

b) print their sum and product using floating-point notation;

c) print the sum and product in fixed-point notation.

Option: Ask the program user how many decimal places she wants the fixed-point procedure to print. Then use the variable that holds her response as a third parameter to the procedure.

Divide each of the difficulties under study into as many parts as is possible or are required to solve them best. Some programming advice from René Descartes. (p. 94)

3

Program Design

* Optional sections.

The competent programmer is fully aware of the strictly limited size of his own skull; therefore he approaches the programming task in full humility, and among other things he avoids clever tricks like the plague.

E.W. Dijkstra, *The Humble Programmer*,
1972 ACM Turing Award Lecture.

For most of the history of computer science, programmers have been realizing that they're not quite as smart as they'd like to be. Software is tough for many reasons. To begin with, programs can't be proofread like plain English prose. There is not a person alive whose eyes don't begin to glaze over after reading a few thousand lines of dense code.

Software can also be incredibly fragile. Everyday construction of physical things is able to rely on redundancy: the strong components can help the weaker ones. A bridge or building isn't likely to fall down because of a single loosened bolt. But a single line of faulty code can undermine the whole works.

Finally, despite its fragility, software is quite difficult to test to the breaking point. It isn't difficult to examine a weak link, even if it's written in a computer code. But finding the link, or anticipating the circumstances under which it might fail, is extremely hard.

Chapter 3 starts with a look at the big picture and a realistic, therefore glum, view of the state of software engineering. I'll briefly describe a project (the Boeing 777's flight control system) that tried to avoid needless risks by having critical software written in *three* different programming languages. Section 3-2 focuses on the design strategies we'll be using in Pascal. Section 3-3 returns to details and wraps up the discussion of procedures and functions.

Planning and Design

3-1

PEOPLE USUALLY APPROACH PROGRAMMING languages with the expectation that everything they learn will be a command of one sort or another. It comes as a surprise that a good deal of Pascal is devoted to methods of organizing programs, rather than doing things. It may come as an even greater surprise to find out that a good deal of *programming* revolves around planning how programs will be put together.

If we restrict ourselves to simple tasks, then a simple methodology (sit at the terminal and start coding) is sufficient. That works fine for tiny jobs—making a few mathematical calculations, say, or exchanging prepackaged chitchat with the program user. But our goals are loftier. If we're going to solve big problems, then we have be able to organize our thoughts well enough to write big programs.

The search for organization is nothing new. Three hundred and fifty years ago René Descartes, in his *Discourse On Method*, laid down four rules 'for rightly conducting one's reason and for seeking truth in the sciences.'

1. Never accept as true anything that is not self-evidently so.

2. Divide each of the difficulties under study into as many parts as is possible or are required to solve them best.

Descartes´ method for science

3. Conduct thoughts in an orderly fashion, commencing with the simplest and easiest-to-know items, then rising by degrees to the most composite things.

4. Make enumerations so complete and reviews so general that you can be sure of having omitted nothing.

Descartes was remarkably prescient: long before electricity was discovered, he managed to set out the approach we take to writing programs today! However, his prescriptions have been hard to follow. Programming, unfortunately, is a rather unscientific business, and one programmer's idea of orderly thinking may be her neighbor's definition of *cruft* (an unpleasant substance that is found between the lines of poorly written programs).

Now, textbooks are usually filled with clear, unequivocal statements of fact—they're meant to convince students that any problem can be solved if you study the proper methods. It's hard to say 'I don't know' in front of a class, and it isn't any easier to show doubt or uncertainty in print. Nevertheless, you will better understand the importance of careful, step-by-step planning and design if you have a realistic feel for the limitations that stymie even the best professional programmers.

Three Curves

Let's begin with a brief look at software engineering. Like economics—the so-called 'dismal science'—software engineering is an imprecise field. It's often better at describing present problems of producing software than it is at prescribing future cures.

As a result, everybody who studies the software side of computer science inevitably becomes acquainted with three simple charts.

The numbers we might attach to these charts aren't important; the shape of and long-term trend implied by each curve is. With the simplicity of a Picasso drawing, the three curves paint an immediately recognizable picture of software today.

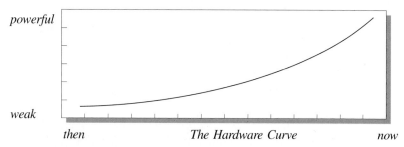

powerful

weak

then   The Hardware Curve   *now*

The first chart is a rising curve that shows the ever-increasing power of computer hardware. The hardware curve is the public image of computing. Computer hardware has been following an essentially unchecked rise for four decades. Machines are faster, cheaper, and smaller than ever, and the trend shows no signs of stopping.

The second curve is a line that also rises, but at a slow, seemingly constant increment. It represents improvements in software:

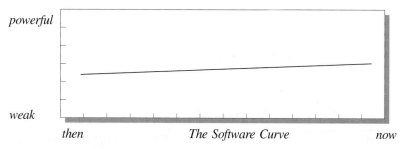

powerful

weak

then   The Software Curve   *now*

software improves, but slowly

Software, unfortunately, doesn't keep up with hardware. The productivity of individual programmers rises, but slowly. The projects they complete do more and do it better, but the improvement is incremental. I have as much computing power on my desk as an entire Computer Science Department stored in several large rooms ten years ago, but my software tools have improved only marginally. I have one hundred times as much hardware power, but only two or three times better software.

The third curve is unusual: it falls, then rises again. It represents the effect of putting more people to work on a software project.

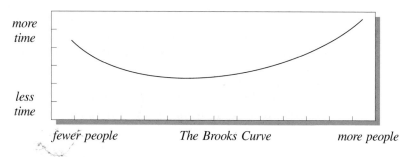

more time

less time

fewer people   The Brooks Curve   *more people*

Brooks' Law

If individual programmers can't keep up with hardware, will using *more* programmers solve problems faster? To some extent, but not entirely. Unfortunately, software development isn't like chopping wood or hauling water. It's a complex task that requires much communication among its participants. Extra help is useful at first, but it conspires rather rapidly to slow work down instead of speeding it up. According to *Brooks' Law*, named for the man who first described this phenomenon:

> *Adding manpower to a late software project only makes it later.*

I'll talk more about Fred Brooks when we discuss software engineering at length in Chapter 12.

The Silver Bullets

Although they hadn't all appeared on paper by then, the three curves we've just seen were first mentally juxtaposed in the late 1960's. What they implied was disheartening; the term *software crisis* was coined to describe the situation. I won't bore you by reciting statistics about symptoms of the crisis: software that didn't work, cost too much, or was never finished.

That's because figures would obscure the fact that the crisis was misnamed. A crisis, after all, can be passed; the patient can be cured. But software development seems to be stuck in a permanent state of affliction. It's been reported that the error rate of typical *successful* software is over four bugs per 1,000 lines of code. A study of code from NASA's space shuttle claims only 0.1 errors per 1,000 lines, but at a production cost of some $1,000 *per line* of debugged code.*

The phrase *silver bullet* (as originated by the Lone Ranger) has become a popular term of description for would-be cures. In recent years, there has been a plethora of candidates, including:

— improved training of programmers,

— reliance on formalized software design methods,

a few silver bullets

— new methods for managing programmers,

— more powerful computers, coupled with *computer aided software engineering* tools,

— a commitment to reusing existing software,

— development of better programming languages, and

— formal, mathematically based approaches to making programs reliable.

> But once again, the details of each method are less important than the overall shape of the curve. All of these methods have helped, but none of them has fixed a problem whose basic cause is the sheer complexity of software.

---

* The first figure is from N. Gross in *Business Week*, 2/11/91. Shuttle statistics are from E.J. Joyce in *Datamation*, 1989, 35(4), pp. 53-56.

Perhaps the best illustration I can give comes from a talk given at the 1991 conference of ACM SIGSOFT, the Association for Computing Machinery's Special Interest Group on Software Engineering. The speaker was Jim McWha, the chief engineer of the flight control system for Boeing Aircraft's next-generation aircraft, the Boeing 777.

Now, an aircraft is an immensely complex piece of engineering. If you've ever seen a picture of an aircraft assembly line, you'll be struck by the huge scale of the enterprise. Aircraft are assembled in enormous hangers; at any one time there will be a row of partially completed planes. Since workers travel down the line repeating essentially the same job, they become more skilled over time. They are able to check their work not only from detailed plans, but also by referring back to a plane that's a bit further along the road to completion. Every weld and wire is surveyed by independent inspectors, who check for both proper location and quality.

building airplanes: work together to avoid errors

But according to McWha, the 777's software construction must use an entirely different approach. The 777 relies on computers to an unusual extent. It is almost exclusively *fly-by-wire*, which is to say that it uses electrical signals to control the plane. Computers keep the plane flying within an envelope of specified tolerances, although they can be overridden by the pilot.

As with most aircraft systems, the 777 has a great deal of redundancy; there are three primary flight control computers. Furthermore, each computer has three computation 'lanes,' or program systems. The interesting thing about the 777's computers is that:

building software: work separately to avoid errors

— each lane's software was written by an independent programming team,

— each lane's software is written in a different language (the Ada, C, and PL/M programming languages were used), and

— before taking action in flight, the computers take a majority vote.

Obviously, Boeing attempted to use the best software engineering strategies available for design, production, and testing of the 777's software. Nevertheless, they recognized that the state of the art is limited. What might the source of a problem be? Well, it could come from almost anywhere:

— The system design might be flawed from the start, so that correctly coded software fails in practice.

where failure starts

— There may be programming bugs that were not revealed during software testing.

— There may be defects in the compiler or CPU, so that correct algorithms, written in proper code, still don't work as they should.

— Preconditions in the test environment might be different from starting conditions when the program actually runs.

— One small piece of the program might have been modified, then successfully tested in isolation, without revealing a bug in its interaction with the rest of the software.

— Part of the software may be used in a way that wasn't originally intended; e.g. a mathematical routine may be expected to deliver more accurate results than it was originally designed to.

— Program inputs may be wrong.

There is a debate within the field as to what we should call program flaws. According to Edsgar Dijkstra, winner of the most prestigious honors in computer science, the term 'bug' should be banished; an error is an error, and should be known as such. On the other hand, most software engineers believe that persistent bugs are simply a characteristic of software. They can't be avoided any more than physical structural materials like glass or steel can be absolutely free of defects.

Boeing certainly believes that, and has tried to ensure that software can be reliable without necessarily being bug-free. Boeing's approach is more formally known as *n-version programming*. It captures in a nutshell both the problems and the solutions of software engineering:

— It uses the best methods known. They may not fix all problems, but they are a step in the right direction.

— It recognizes that our ability to confirm the correctness of those methods is probably flawed.

— Finally, it attempts to minimize *by design* any necessity for the software to be absolutely perfect.

A bridge isn't built to be just strong enough to carry its expected load. Rather, it's sturdy enough to carry a load that is far more than reasonable, under conditions—winds, flood, structural failure—that are far less than perfect. Applying the same lesson to software isn't easy, but it's the only path we have.

Professional Ethics*

In the computer business, the appearance of the word *ethics* usually suggests that a lecture on the wrong-headedness of copying software or unleashing computer viruses is on the way. Yes, they are bad, but as I'm sure you already know that I'd rather not preach to the choir. A narrow focus on honesty and what you *shouldn't* do misses the point, anyway. It's as though a civil engineering text were to restrict its consideration of ethics to advising students not to take lumber home from the building site.

Instead, I'll focus on the importance of ethics to you as potential *professionals*—people who benefit from the reputations of and respect accorded to their peers. As you begin to understand the inherent complexity of software, you will also come to appreciate that more than coding ability separates professional programmers from non-programmers.

> Put plainly and simply, programmers understand that even when it works, software has limitations. And, like any engineer whose work may permanently affect a user's life or livelihood, the software engineer should use that understanding for the benefit of people further on down the line.

---

* This section is optional.

As a professional, the software engineer has a responsibility to people who directly, or indirectly, rely on software. How can a programmer work in an ethical, responsible manner? Often it is as easy as knowing—and asking—the proper questions:

— *Has the software been tested?* This seems obvious, but it isn't. The testing effort almost always benefits from an extra bit of insight and another 'But have you tried . . . ?'

— *Are the software's operating limitations clearly spelled out?* For example, it may not always be obvious that a program's results depend on the reliability of its input. That's why good programs will *sanity-check* input to make sure that it is plausible.

— *Have the bounds of software accuracy been made clear?* People tend to believe computer output. That's all right when a program is reporting on inventory or making political predictions, but it may be misplaced when when a program is recommending prison sentences or making medical diagnoses. It's the programmer's job to make sure that output is qualified when appropriate.

— *Have the risks of malfunction been considered and addressed?* No matter how unlikely it may seem, errors do occur. If the consequences of a computer error are serious, it may be necessary to require additional confirmation (like a computer operator's OK) before taking action.

— *Is there a potential for hidden abuse?* A medical billing program may produce invoices correctly and efficiently. But it might store records in a manner that compromises the privacy of patients. Somebody has to raise the issue before the product is delivered.

— *Have alternative approaches that achieve the same goals, but at lower risk, been considered?* For example, in the case of medical billing, is there a way to keep patients' names separate from their health records? Can access to sensitive information be not only restricted, but recorded as well?

Your actions as a professional can also have a great influence on your working environment. For example, Ed Yourdon's excellent book *Decline and Fall of the American Programmer* (Yourdon Press/Prentice-Hall, 1992) discusses efforts by the Software Engineering Institute to categorize the way that companies approach software development. The SEI describes five levels of management: initial (1), repeatable (2), defined (3), managed (4), and optimized (5). Its surveys indicate that 81% of U.S. sites are at level 1, about 12% are at level 2, and the remaining few percent are at level 3.*

management in the software industry

The SEI management levels could be applied to almost any business. They imply that managment techniques can be understood and improved. At first, managment is ad hoc—at best, it works from day to day. But over time the specifics of effective managment can be recognized and improved.

Yourdon argues that in the software industry, attitudes toward obtaining quality software, rather than the use of specific methodologies, tend to characterize each management level. For example, here's an illustration adapted from his description of a typical level 1 interaction:

---

* Figures come from J. Bannert in *IEEE Software*, 11/91.

His point is that all sides are at fault: the big boss for making a request that is obviously unrealistic, the manager for attempting to enforce it, Kristin for agreeing to it, and probably the customer for proposing it. Can a human run a three-minute mile? Well, although I couldn't swear that it is impossible, it's awfully unlikely.

> Acting as though achieving impossible results is simply a matter of dedication and effort is wrong. As a professional, you have a duty to provide a degree of reality checking—to help those without technical expertise understand that there are limits to technology, and that time and care may be required to achieve even the results that can be reasonably expected.

Going out on a limb is one thing—people and companies do it all the time. It's simply in the nature of humans to set goals that are ambitious, and perhaps can't be met. Everybody has the right to try, and to fail. The failure may be obvious—you knock the bar down as you attempt a high jump. Or, it may be revealed during testing—the umbrella leaks.

What's problematic about software, though, is that failure isn't necessarily evident. Adequate testing may not be possible, or what seems like sufficient testing might not be. Even the people who design a software system might not know the best way to ferret out hidden bugs. The 'unprofessional' says:

> 'We tried out the code and it worked. Besides, the legal department wrote up a terrific disclaimer in case we missed anything.'

The professional takes an active role in building reasonable expectations for her product.

building reasonable expectations

> 'We went to our users and found out what kind of demands they'd make on the software. Then we tried out the code and it worked. Next we tried to make it fail, and we couldn't. Finally, we did our best to educate our users and give them a feel for our system's limitations.'

In doing so, she helps create a more satisfying place to work and helps make sure that her job will still be there a few years down the road.

Subprograms and Abstraction

3-2

LANGUAGE DESIGNERS ARE KEENLY AWARE OF the difficulty of programming on a strictly scientific basis. Modern programming language designs try to let mechanics come to the rescue when science falls short. Languages like Pascal aren't powerful in the sense that difficult operations are built into the language.

the designer's goal: let structure help 'science'

> Instead, Pascal is strong because of its facilities for controlling the internal packaging and structure of programs. We actually can divide our difficulties into parts and reduce them to Descartes' 'easy-to-know items.'

As we saw in Chapter 2, subprograms are the main structuring tools. Over the years, subprograms have served three main purposes:

— Subprograms replicate code. Detailed code can be written once, then invoked repeatedly just by using the subprogram's name.

how subprograms structure programs

— Subprograms provide an organizing principle, along functional lines, for program code. Here, 'functional' means 'by purpose or application.'

— Subprograms can precisely specify the subactions of a program. The final program can actually be described, before coding, as a well-defined collection of specific procedures and functions.

Other languages go even further than Standard Pascal by providing a way to package procedures into reusable *libraries* or *units*. I bring up this idea because most commercially available Pascal systems, as well as the official Extended Pascal language, actually provide them.

— Libraries let procedures be removed from a program and collected in a separate place. There's a way to *import* the library of procedures and reuse the code it contains.

how libraries structure programs

— Libraries hide details. They let us use procedures and functions without having to deal with the details of their algorithms or implementation (coding).

— Libraries separate usage from implementation. This helps make their contents portable; the details of a particular procedure's coding may vary from system to system, but its usage can stay constant.

abstraction: what? vs. how?

> Alone or in libraries, subprograms encourage *abstraction* in programming. We separate application from implementation—*what* gets done is removed from *how* it gets done.

Stepwise Refinement

Thinking about *what?* before *how?* turns out to be a great strategy for solving problems as well. So far, we've relied on an intuitive notion of planning and tried to write programs in terms of procedures and functions that have had limited, specific goals.

But as programming problems become more complex, good intentions won't always be enough. A methodology called *stepwise refinement* becomes useful for deciding just what our limited and specific goals are going to be. The basic idea of stepwise refinement is to restate problems (and then parts of problems) repeatedly, in more and more detailed terms. Each restatement is a refinement; each step takes us down to a greater level of detail. For example:

Outline of a Problem

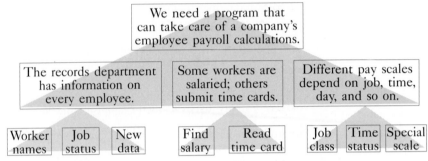

As you can see, we move from the general to the specific. Obviously, we try to stop before we get *too* specific. The stepwise refinement of a problem should get us to the point of procedures and functions, rather than to the level of individual Pascal statements.

Now, the interesting thing about using stepwise refinement to restate problems is that it practically gives us an outline for designing programs:

Outline of a Program

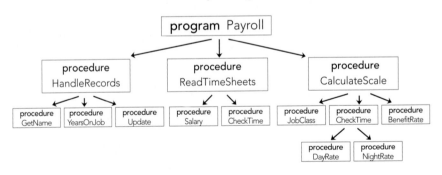

---

functional
decomposition

This approach can be described as *functional decomposition*, which means that the program is broken down along functional, *how-does-this-bring-us-closer-to-the-solution?* lines. It's best applied in programs that are heavy on algorithms and operations.

There are several reasons why stepwise refinement and functional decomposition are useful. Most obvious is that we try to conquer problems by dividing them. A formidable programming problem may turn out to be a combination of easily solved subproblems—in like a lion and out like four or five lambs.

But even if a crucial procedure is beyond our abilities at present, we can still work on the program because we've made independent subdivisions in the problem. As a result, the final program is modular. It's composed of separate pieces that can be written and tested by themselves and then eventually merged together.

When the separate pieces are ultimately joined, procedures and functions help make programs easier to understand. As we've seen, even relatively simple programs are usually broken into sequences of procedure calls like this:

```
begin
    GetInput (arguments ... );
    ProcessData (arguments ... );
    PrintResults (arguments ... )
end.
```

transparency

because procedure calls make the program's inner operations *transparent*. We know *what* the program does, but we can ignore *how* it does it. The detailed code of the procedure doesn't obscure our view of the program; it's invisible unless we go looking for it.

thinking in English

Stepwise refinement also lets a programmer plan most of a program without actually writing in Pascal. It's easier to think in English than in any sort of computerese, and tackling a problem from the top puts off the nitty-gritty of encoding for as long as possible. Outlining a program in terms of its procedures (and procedures and functions *within* procedures) provides a transitional phase between words and code.

finding the seams

In real-life programming projects, the ability to find the seams of a problem or program is the earmark of a good programming manager. If several people are to work on a single program effectively, each must have a clearly outlined task. Each individual has to know exactly how her piece of the program interacts with the whole. Stepwise refinement and goal-oriented design slice up a problem in a natural, intuitive manner. The plan for breaking down a problem goes hand-in-hand with the guide for building a program.

Stepwise Refinement of a Problem

1. State the problem simply, decomposing it into its logical subproblems.

2. If you can immediately figure out how to encode all of the subproblems, you're done. These will be the major procedures of your program. If the subproblems are too complex ...

3. Refine the subproblems into smaller, more basic subproblems. Their solutions are written as procedures or functions within procedures.

Program Planning and Design

1. Write the statement part of the main program first. In a program of any size, this will consist mainly of procedure calls. Each procedure should solve one part of the original problem.

2. The main program's statement part should be simple enough for a non-programmer to read and understand, yet detailed enough to give a programmer an idea of how the program works.

3. If a procedure is particularly complicated, or does more than one job, it should probably be broken down into subprocedures.

length of subprograms Remember that a procedure isn't a rug for sweeping code under! One page (or screenful) of code is enough for any human to try to read and understand. If the procedure is longer, *try to break it down.*

Goal-Oriented and Object-Oriented Design

Stepwise refinement is a *goal-oriented* approach to programming. We keep our eye firmly fixed on the ultimate goal (or on stepping stones to it) as we plan each step. In a word, goal-oriented programming focuses on program *action*.

But the goal-oriented approach isn't our only choice. We can subdivide a program on a radically different basis by temporarily ignoring the demands laid out by a problem statement. Instead, we can focus on how the program will deal with information, and break it down along lines of *data* instead of actions. This is the basis of *object-oriented* design—building data handling tools before worrying about problem solving statements.

It's easy to contrast the two. For example, the goal-oriented approach to writing a program that manages a public library might focus on the library's *users*, and on the tasks they set:

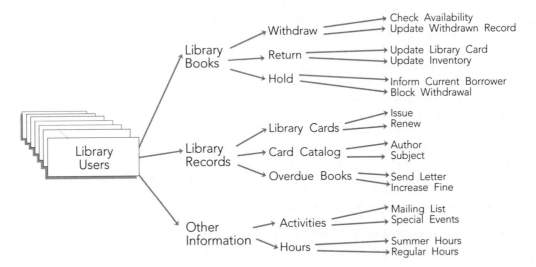

As you can see, the procedures we plan are dominated by an *algorithm*, or sequence of steps toward a solution. You can almost imagine that they were laid out by following in the footsteps of a librarian or library patron.

But what if we were to follow a *book* instead? From a book's point of view, the workings of a library are rather different:

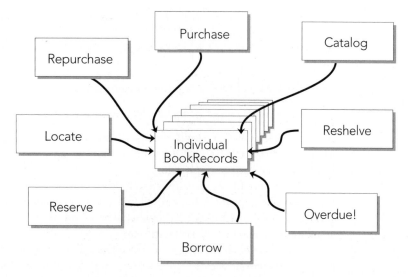

emphasizing program
data

Now, the procedures we plan are all specific operations on data. As we learn about more sophisticated means of variable creation and data storage, we'll find that writing data-handling procedures and functions first, even if they don't solve any particular problem now, makes it easier to deal with program goals later on.

Top-Down and Bottom-Up Design

Few building contractors start work on a house by attaching a knocker to the front door. It might seem like an obvious thing to do; after all, the front door is your first point of contact with a dwelling. But it doesn't make much sense. Who wants to build a bit of door, then a piece of wall, followed by a stretch of floor and foundation? How can you arrange for building materials or schedule workers under such conditions? Planning ahead to complete parts of the house in some kind of order is the only way to preserve your sanity.

the front door approach

Newcomers to software construction, on the other hand, do often take the front door approach. They begin with the first action a program takes, then try to muddle through to the last. A program that's short enough to keep in your head (the program equivalent of a birdhouse) will turn out all right. But big programs suffer when the foundation isn't laid before the rafters.

> Stepwise refinement is a *top-down* approach to program design; it always proceeds from the more complex to the less so.

Top-down design methods provide a useful way of dealing with the inherent complexity of programs. In effect, top-down design says that keeping an eye on a program's overall goal will help keep the smaller pieces on track.

top-down debugging

Top-down design applies to debugging as well. It's expensive and difficult to recover from design errors late in the game. As you become more familiar with parameters, you'll see how important it is to pay attention to the interconnections between procedures early on. Is the program's basic design workable, or do tasks have to be rearranged? A top-down approach tests major connections first, even before procedures are fully operative.

However, top-down design has a shortcoming—it doesn't always lead one to search for existing solutions in new problems. That's why a *bottom-up* approach to design has a place as well. Bottom-up design looks for known answers:

the bottom-up approach

— Do existing tools solve part of my problem?

— Can an existing program be adapted to do the job?

It is said that when your only tool is a hammer, everything looks like a nail. That's the down side to working from the bottom up—too narrow a focus can limit your problem solving ability.

But it's not always a bad idea to let the solutions that are available influence your perception of what a problem entails. Sometimes a difficult problem turns out to be a badly stated problem. The solution lies in rephrasing it in a standard form that's dealt with more easily.

There are also advantages to bottom-up debugging—thoroughly testing a standalone *module* before integrating it into the rest of a program. During top-down testing there's a tendency to focus only on the services you know a procedure or function will *have* to provide. That may be fine for your program, but it isn't really complete enough to reassure somebody else who'd like to employ the same code. Testing the subprogram on its own, without preconceptions of what it will be used for, results in more reliable code.

In the long run, learning how to merge the two styles marks your transition from amateur to professional programmer. The amateur's focus is individualistic; she starts each program with a blank sheet of paper and her own skills. But professionals focus on *cooperation*—designing programs that can use *and reuse* the code of colleagues whenever possible.

Subprogram Nitty-Gritty

3-3

IT'S TIME TO DELVE INTO THE DETAILS THAT GOVERN the construction and use of subprograms. You'll find that many details won't necessarily be important to you now, so you may wish to read this section quickly for its basic ideas and refer back later if you have to.

Before we start, let's make a deal. If you'll agree to follow the basic form of programs in this book, to use plenty of procedures and clear identifiers, and to give some thought to each choice between using value parameters, variable parameters, and variables, I'll agree not to torment you with horribly complicated examples of procedures within functions within procedures, and constants, variables and subprograms all named X, Y, and Z.

let's make a deal

> As you read, remember that our goal is to write programs that make obvious sense, rather than the kind that are obscurely correct.

As you know, a program has two distinct levels or environments:

separate environments...

— The main program contains *global* declarations of variables that persist for an entire program run.

— Every subprogram can contain *local* declarations of variables that are used only within the subprogram and don't exist between calls.

But the environments can communicate. A flow of data from procedure to procedure is supported by parameters:

...that can communicate

— Value parameters give names, meaningful within the subprogram, to values that are passed to the subprogram when it is called.

— Variable parameters provide temporary *aliases*, or renamings, of variables that are passed to the subprogram when it's called.

Value parameters let data flow into a subprogram; variable parameters let data flow both into and out of a subprogram.

Subprograms can include *local* declarations and definitions that customize the subprogram's internal environment. These include definitions of constants and declarations of variables and additional subprograms.

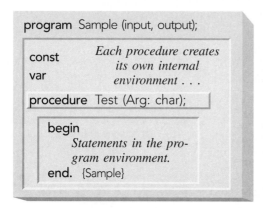
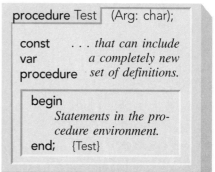

Note that the parameter list is part of the subprogram's local environment. Identifiers created there can't be referred to from the main program, nor reused within the subprogram itself.

Scope of Identifiers

Once we allow a program to establish identifiers in different locations, three problems arise:

forward reference

1. *When* will an identifier be recognized (the *forward reference* problem)? Can an identifier be used before it is declared? No (with certain exceptions).

scope

2. *Where* will identifiers be recognized (the *scope* problem)? Can an identifier defined in one procedure be recognized in another? No.

name precedence

3. *How* will we decide what to do when two identifiers are the same (the *precedence* problem)? Can an identifier from the main program be 'taken over' by a like-named local variable? Yes.

> The basic rules of the road are: first, an identifier must be declared or de-
> fined before it is used; and second, a procedure's local identifiers and
> parameters are known only within that procedure.

Here's a definition that runs afoul of the forward reference rule, since it's used before it's defined:

define before you use

```
{an incorrect example}
const NAME = FAMILYname;   {FAMILYname hasn't been defined yet.}
      FAMILYname = 'Cooper';
```

To be correct, the definitions must be reordered:

```
const FAMILYname = 'Cooper';   {a correct version}
      NAME = FAMILYname;
```

scope

Scope and name precedence are a bit more involved. Formally, the word scope describes the realm of meaning of an identifier that names a constant, variable, or subprogram. The scope of an identifier is the portion of a program—called a *block*—in which it's recognized as representing a particular value or action.

block structure

As the illustration below shows, the main program itself is the largest block. That's why a main program constant, say, will be recognized within procedures that were declared after the constant was defined—they're all within its scope.

Identifiers de- *fined in block:*	*Are recognized* *in blocks:*
A(B,C)	A,B,C,D,E,F
B(D)	B,D
D	D
C(E,F)	C,E,F
E	E
F	F

What about the name of a procedure? Where is it known? Well, the procedure's name lies outside the procedure's block, while its parameters, local variables, and so on are inside the new block. Thus, the procedure's name has the same scope as, say, a main program constant: once it has been defined, it can be used. In the illustration, procedure C can call procedure B, but not vice versa.

What about value and variable parameters? As I mentioned a moment ago, they belong to the procedure; they are local. A program that calls the procedure can't refer to its parameters, because they're part of the subprogram block. And, because a subprogram's parameter declarations and variable declarations are at the same level, the same identifier can't be used twice.

parameters are local identifiers

What about the contents of a subprogram? Local definitions and declarations are strictly part of the subprogram's own block.

> A later procedure can call an earlier procedure. However, it can't refer to anything declared *within* the earlier procedure.

Even though C can call B, C cannot refer to any of B's contents: it can't call D. Similarly, C can call procedure E or F, since they're both in C's block. F can call E, since it was declared earlier in the same block. However, E can't call F, and B and D can't call any of them.

Self-Check Questions

Q. The following procedure declaration contains an error that should be easy to spot. What is it?

```
procedure Wrong (A: integer; var B: integer);
    const A = 100;
    var B: real;      etc.
```

A. Example Wrong ignores the fact that parameter declarations share the scope of local constant and variable declarations. Procedure Wrong tries to use two identifiers (A and B) in equally local places. Whether the parameters and local variables are of identical or different types is irrelevant. It's as incorrect a pair of declarations as this would be:

```
var A: integer; A: real;
```

Precedence and Side-Effects

Now, one consequence of the scope rule is that local identifiers may be declared within the scope of identical, but non-local, identifiers. When this happens, the most local definition or declaration has precedence over an identical, but relatively global, definition.

It is also legal, but always confusing, to declare variables that have the same names as built-in procedures or functions. In general, we'll avoid doing so.

Finally, suppose there isn't any ambiguity in definitions. Can an identifier defined in the main program be used in a procedure or function? The answer is yes. Typically, we will take advantage of this on only two occasions:

taking advantage of scope

1. When a subprogram uses a main program constant (this is one reason that constant identifiers are usually capitalized—so that they immediately stand out to the program reader).

2. When one procedure calls another; for example, when a procedure that processes data calls an earlier-defined procedure or function that gets each item.

A more interesting question is whether or not we can make an assignment directly to a global variable from within a subprogram.

> Technically, nothing in Pascal prohibits making a direct assignment to a global variable from within a procedure or function. However, this sort of assignment is known as a *side-effect*. It is strongly discouraged; side-effects lead to some of the most difficult-to-find bugs in programming.

side-effects

If I catch you making an assignment to a global variable from within a procedure or function, I will personally attempt to persuade your instructor to fail you immediately. *Don't do it.*

Self-Check Questions

Q. What will the output of this program be?

```pascal
program Confound (input, output);
     {Comments? Nope—that would be telling.}
var A, B, C, D: integer;
procedure Confuse (C,A: integer; var B: integer);
     var D: integer;
     begin
          A := 5;  B := 6;  C := 7;  D := 8;
          write (A : 10);   write (B : 10);
          write (C : 10);   write (D : 10)
     end;  {Confuse}
begin
     A := 1;  B := 2;  C := 3;  D := 4;
     write (A : 10);   write (B : 10);
     write (C : 10);   write (D : 10);
     writeln;
     Confuse (B, A, D);
     writeln;
     write (A : 10);   write (B : 10);
     write (C : 10);   write (D : 10);
     writeln
end.   {Confound}
```

A. This intentionally muddled program deliberately tries to confuse value parameters, variable parameters, and local variables. Its output is:

```
        1              2              3              4
        5              6              7              8
        1              2              3              6
```

Forward Declarations*

subprogram scope

As noted above, procedure and function identifiers follow the rules of scope. Once a procedure or function has been declared, its name has meaning in other parts of the program, including the main program's statement part, the statement parts of other subprograms, and the statement part of the procedure or function itself.

Usually we'll invoke procedures or functions from the main program or from subprograms declared later on. A third case, in which a subprogram calls itself (or two subprograms call each other), won't concern us until we explore recursion in Chapter 16.

In general, subprograms are declared in an order that makes sense to the program reader, subject to the regulation *define before you use.* However, there are times when this rule seems to paint the programmer into a corner. Consider this situation:

procedures calling procedures

```
program Main (input, output);
global declarations
procedure Late ( parameters )
    declarations and statements;
    cannot call procedure Early
end;  {Late}
procedure Early ( parameters )
    declarations and statements;
    can call procedure Late
end;  {Early}
begin
    main program statements;
    can call either Late or Early
end.   {Main}
```

When a program is first compiled, the Pascal compiler works its way through the code from start to finish. As it goes along, it builds a table of known identifiers. If the compiler encounters an identifier that isn't on the list, it assumes that an error has been made. It has no way of knowing that the identifier will eventually be defined.

In the example above, procedure Early can call procedure Late, because when Early is compiled, the name and contents of Late are known. Either procedure can be called from the main program, of course. However, procedure Late can't call Early—yet.

forward declarations

> A **forward** declaration is Pascal's mechanism for letting a procedure or function name be used before it is defined.

To make a forward declaration, follow the subprogram's heading, complete with parameter list or type, by the word **forward**. When you complete the declaration later, do not repeat the parameter list:

---

* This section can be delayed until the discussion of recursion in Chapter 16.

```
program Main (input, output);
global declarations
procedure Early ( parameters ); forward;
procedure Late ( parameters );
    declarations and statements
    can call Early
end;  {Late}
procedure Early;    {omit the parameter list}
    declarations and statements
    can call Late
end;  {Early}
begin
    main program statements;
    can call either Late or Early
end.  {Main}
```

Now, Early can call Late, and Late can call Early. Naturally, they both can still be called in the main program.

Program Engineering Notes: House of Style

3-4

THERE'S A SAYING AMONG AMATEUR TELESCOPE makers that the fastest way to grind a five-inch mirror is to grind a four-inch mirror first. Learn skills with the smaller, easier version, then move up to the real test.

Doug's House of Programming Style, on the next page, works on one of the harder areas of program design: deciding when and how to use procedures. I've written up the same programming example in four different ways. Why? Because one of the hardest thing for new programmers to understand is that a piece of code might not be any good, even if it works perfectly.

All four incarnations of Switch do the same thing:

what Switch does

> ask the user to enter two values;
> swap them;
> print the reversed values;

As you can see from my comments, there are definitely wrong styles, but there isn't a single exact right way. Two things are forbidden:

— *Side-effects.* Although it is legal Pascal, referring to a global variable from within a procedure is absolutely prohibited programming style. It leads to bugs that are nearly impossible to locate.

what's forbidden

— *No procedures.* I can't say precisely what your limit will be—one screenful, a page, or thereabouts—but all but the shortest programs must rely on subprograms. Obviously, I'm stretching the point in Switch, since it's so short, but the basic rule holds.

```
program Switch1 (input, output);
    {Reverses two input integers.}
var First, Second, Temporary: integer;
begin
    write ('Please enter two integers:   ');
    read (First);
    readln (Second);
    Temporary := First;
    First := Second;
    Second := Temporary;
    write ('Reversed, the numbers are ');
    write (First);
    write (' and ');
    writeln (Second)
end.  {Switch1}


program Switch2 (input, output);
    {Reverses two input integers.}
var First, Second, Temporary: integer;
procedure GetTheNumbers;
    {Reads values for Primero and Segundo.}
    begin
        write ('Please enter two integers:   ');
        read (First);
        readln (Second)
    end;  {GetTheNumbers}
procedure SwapThem;
    {Swaps the values of two variables.}
    begin
        Temporary := First;
        First := Second;
        Second := Temporary
    end;  {SwapThem}
procedure PrintTheResults;
    {Prints two variables.}
    begin
        write ('Reversed, the numbers are ');
        write (First);
        write (' and ');
        writeln (Second)
    end;  {PrintTheResults}
begin  {main program}
    GetTheNumbers;
    SwapThem;
    PrintTheResults
end.  {Switch2}
```

```
program Switch3 (input, output);
    {Reverses two input integers.}
var First, Second: integer;
procedure GetTheNumbers (var Primero, Segundo: integer);
    {Reads values for the variable parameters Primero and Segundo.}
    begin
        write ('Please enter two integers:   ');
        read (Primero);
        readln (Segundo)
    end;  {GetTheNumbers}
procedure SwapThem (var Premier, Deuxieme: integer);
    {Swaps the values of two variable parameters.}
    var Temporary: integer;
    begin
        Temporary := Premier;
        Premier := Deuxieme;
        Deuxieme := Temporary
    end;  {SwapThem}
procedure PrintTheResults (Primo, Secondo: integer);
    {Prints its value parameters.}
    begin
        write ('In reversed order, the numbers are ');
        write (Primo);
        write (' and ');
        writeln (Secondo)
    end;  {PrintTheResults}
begin  {main program}
    GetTheNumbers (First, Second);
    SwapThem (First, Second);
    PrintTheResults (First, Second)
end.  {Switch3}


program Switch4 (input, output);
    {Reverses two input integers.}
procedure GetTheNumbers (var Primero, Segundo: integer);
    {Reads values for the variable parameters Primero and Segundo.}
    begin
        write ('Please enter two integers:   ');
        read (Primero);
        readln (Segundo)
    end;  {GetTheNumbers}
procedure SwapThem (var Premier, Deuxieme: integer);
    {Swaps the values of two variable parameters.}
    var Temporary: integer;
    begin
        Temporary := Premier;
        Premier := Deuxieme;
        Deuxieme := Temporary
    end;  {SwapThem}
procedure PrintTheResults (Primo, Secondo: integer);
    {Prints its value parameters.}
    begin
        write ('In reversed order, the numbers are ');
        write (Primo);
        write (' and ');
        writeln (Secondo)
    end;  {PrintTheResults}
procedure MakeTheSwitch;
    {Call the other procedures.}
    var First, Second: integer;
    begin
        GetTheNumbers (First, Second);
        SwapThem (First, Second);
        PrintTheResults (First, Second)
    end;  {MakeTheSwitch}
begin  {main program}
    MakeTheSwitch
end.  {Switch4}
```

Welcome to Doug's House of Style! What's the difference?

— Switch1 has no procedures—not a big deal in a small program, but disaster when programs get long.

— Switch2 has procedures, but it uses only global variables—unacceptable.

— Switch3 uses global and local variables and parameters correctly.

— Switch4 demonstrates good understanding of scope—everything is as 'local' as possible. But it's not the style I prefer myself—it's a bit too rigid for me.

I'd give a C to version 1, flunk version 2, and give an A to versions 3 and 4.

Recommendations, in turn, can't be absolute. If you compare Switch3 to Switch4, you'll see the only difference between them is that Switch4 has an extra layer of procedure call. In this particular set of circumstances, I think that the new procedure, MakeTheSwitch, is unnecessary. It makes the program longer, but it doesn't make the code any clearer or easier to follow.

Nevertheless, if I were grading the program as a teacher or manager I'd probably give it high marks. Today it's a little 'busy.' But tomorrow, if I have to incorporate the same algorithm into a more complicated program, Switch4 will be easier to reuse.

Syntax Summary

❏   forward declaration: makes a subprogram's name and parameter list known, so that it can be called before it has been fully declared.

> **procedure** Early (*parameter list*); **forward**;
> ⋱   *Other procedure and function declarations.*
>   *They may include calls of* Early.
>
> **procedure** Early;   {*Don't repeat the parameter list.*}
> ⋱   *Complete the declaration.*

Forward declarations won't be required until you write recursive programs.

Remember . . .

❏   Even when it works, software has limitations. Software professionals should help design software to make it reliable. However, they should also help plan for the nearly inevitable shortcomings that may become visible only after extended use.

❏   *Abstraction* is the separation of application from implementation. It lets you concentrate on *what?* before dealing with *how?*, and it permits changes in *how?* when necessary.

❏   *Functional decomposition* separates by purpose or application. It's the basic guide for designing subprograms.

❏   *Stepwise refinement* is solving problems by working from the general to the specific—restating problems, and then parts of problems, in increasing detail.

❏   *Goal-oriented* design focuses on a program's algorithm—what steps are taken on the way to solving a problem. *Object-oriented* design, in contrast, concentrates on building tools for handling data first.

❏   *Scope* describes the range of a program in which an identifier can be recognized. In Pascal, identifiers are known in the *blocks* they're defined in. Within a block, an identifier must be defined before it can be referred to.

❏   Blocks can enclose blocks. Identifiers created in an enclosed block can reuse names, since the most local use takes *precedence* over relatively global applications.

❏   In some circumstance, two subprograms must call each other. Since this runs afoul of the 'define before you use' rule, a *forward declaration* must be employed to let the compiler know we're going to define the undeclared name.

❏   A *side-effect* is an assignment to a relatively global variable from within a subprogram. Side-effects lead to hard-to-find bugs, so use variable parameters instead.

Big Ideas

The Big Ideas in this chapter were:

1. *Software is harder to improve than hardware.* Technical difficulties of speeding up hardware may not be immediately solvable, but they're well-understood. Software, in contrast, is still poorly understood, partly because failure, and the reasons for it, aren't always obvious.

2. *No matter how easy programming in Pascal is, planning in English is easier.* But because statements can be packaged into subprograms that are called by name, we can use the same terms to describe steps in an algorithm and procedure calls in a program. Abstraction bridges the gap between high-level problem-solving steps and low-level computer statements.

3. Scope rules keep programs flexible by avoiding restrictions on using and reusing identifiers. At first the scope rules seem like a new set of details to be memorized. In the long run, though, you'll see that they let you avoid remembering details.

You deserve a break today. If you can manage the exercises from Chapter 2, consider yourself on top of things. Instead of doing homework, why not go write a few programs?

Pascal has other loops that repeat statements, but only the **for** *loop is able to generate data.* Above, *Endless Dialogue – Part 5* (1977) Detail, Laura Grisi. Courtesy Leo Castelli Gallery. (p. 125)

4

Looping and Control: the **for** Statement

For better or worse, the first three chapters held pretty concentrated doses of facts, details, and drill. But with the basic groundwork behind us, we'll start to zoom. From here on out, every chapter introduces a new statement or two.

Since most of the statements we'll learn about actually appear in many programming languages, perhaps with slight syntactic differences, I've organized subsequent chapters to help you get an idea of what's specific to Pascal, and what is a useful programming practice in just about any language. The first section, *Strictly Pascal*, concentrates on the new statement's syntax. Then, *Standard Practices and Examples* describes programming and problem-solving techniques that use the new statement but are not really language specific.

Is this the only way to teach a programming language? Of course not. Pascal has but a half-dozen statements, and I could easily outline their operation in a single chapter. But I've always found that there's a kind of 'programming sophistication' that comes with understanding how each new statement fits into the big picture. Some of the programming techniques we'll return to in nearly every chapter include:

— How to plan and pseudocode programs before tackling the code.

— When to use existing code as the starting point for modifying or expanding.

— Why a program is useless if its output is misleading or unreadable.

Have fun with **for**, then plan to spend a few days seeing **for** loops all around you.

But First, the Issues

Now that the basic rules of program structure are behind us, it's time to get down to the business of actions. The next four chapters introduce Pascal's *control statements*—the statements that choose and repeat the actions a program can take.

The fundamental issue is managing the *flow of control* through a program. So far we've written only straight-line or sequential programs; they began with the first **begin** and continued, one line at a time, until the final **end**. Aside from an occasional detour through a procedure call, there hasn't been any difference between the printed text of a program and its appearance to the computer when it runs. The physical program (what we see) and the logical program (what we get) have been the same.

But control statements give a program more than one *control path*. Statements can be skipped or repeated in patterns that can't always be known until the program runs. Our familiar straight-line control gets two companions:

issue: flow of control

— *Branches* permit choice. The control path forks; it can decide between alternatives.

— *Loops* allow repetition. The control path retraces its steps and takes the same actions again.

Technically, two new statements are enough. A famous 1966 paper by Böhm and Jacopini showed that every *flow chart* (a graphical way of showing a program's actions) could be redrawn with just two kinds of arrows—one for branching, and one for looping.* But most languages allow additional variations to let specific programming goals be attained more easily. Pascal has two branching statements and three loops.

At first, syntax will seem to be the main consideration in learning new statements. That's almost unavoidable; I'll always deal with syntax first so that the first part of each chapter will be useful as a reference later on.

But when programs become more powerful, they become less predictable. As the distance between physical and logical programs grows, it gets more difficult to predict exactly what a program is going to do and to anticipate how small changes will affect it.

> This leads to one of the paradoxes of learning to program: how can a statement with syntax easy enough to learn in a minute or two lead to bugs that are so difficult to figure out?

The way statements are constructed provides one line of defense. When it was designed in the late 1970's, Pascal was famous as a *structured* programming language. Each statement has an obvious beginning and end; more formally:

issue: structure

— there's just one *entry point* that begins the statement, and

— there's just one *exit point* that marks the statement's close.

---

* C. Böhm and G. Jacopini, *Flow Diagrams, Turing Machines, and Languages with Only Two Formation Rules, Communications of the ACM*, Volume 9, No. 5, (May, 1966), pp. 366-371.

This seems obvious now, but only fifteen years abo it was part of a revolution in programming language design.

Learning to reason about program construction is a second line of defense. Now, naturally you think about what you're doing—you'd better! But reasoning and analysis go further. The issue is coming to understand what statements *mean* as well as what they *do*. Sure, the statement you just wrote works. But will it always work? Which prior statements does it rely on? If it's changed, will the next statement still function properly? More formally:

issue: reasoning and analysis

— What *preconditions* does the statement depend on?

— What *postconditions* does the statement result in?

Keeping each statement's preconditions and postconditions straight seems like a manageable proposition. But it isn't. No matter how smart you are, there's just too much going on in most programs to keep every detail in your head at once. Successful programmers focus on the essential and set the less relevant aside—easy to say, but hard to learn. That's why we'll go over each statement through a kind of apprenticeship, surveying dozens of small applications. Here's what you'll get as a result:

— An automatic facility with language-specific idioms (such as Pascal's usage of read and readln). Some idioms are syntactic, some are semantic; all of them detract from our overall goal of using computers to solve problems, but all must be known cold.

issue: art vs. science

— An introduction to the mini-algorithms (like using a temporary variable to swap two values) that harder problems rely on. Every statement has its own collection of techniques.

— A sense of 'programming maturity.' Like the equally desirable (and mysterious) mathematical maturity, it will help you understand what must be explained when you code, and what can be assumed—what must be eyed suspiciously and what can be relied on almost without question.

In a sense, we're going through a methodical introduction to the cliches of programming. Although cliches make for poor literature, they improve programs immensely.

> This brings us to a second paradox of programming: coding could hardly be more individual a task, yet your code must be a team player.

We don't really want to have to spend time figuring out what a piece of code does. Instead, we'd like to fit well-understood pieces together. Not only will the pieces work better, but the flow of control from one piece to the next will be easier to follow.

Things to Think About

1. An ordinary pocket calculator is, in a way, like a computer that allows only straight-line, calculation-to-calculation, flow of control. But suppose that you want to design a programmable calculator? Since you can knowingly refer to Böhm and Jacopini, you know that only a few new keys are going to be needed.

But are ⌈Branch⌉ and ⌈Loop⌉ keys enough? How will branching decisions be made? How can you specify the number of times a loop should repeat? How will you mark the number of 'statements' or calculations that should be skipped or repeated?

Try designing a programmable calculator keyboard. To make life easier, assume that the calculator's display is several lines high. Although you can look at a real-life programmable calculator for ideas, don't jump to the conclusion that that's the best model to follow.

Strictly Pascal

4-1

THE **FOR** STATEMENT MAKES THINGS HAPPEN—again and again and again. Here's an example:

for statement demonstration

```pascal
program ForTrial (output);
   {Prints a popular California bottled-water drinking song.}

var Count: integer;          {Count serves as the counter variable.}

procedure Verse (Current: integer);
   {Prints the Currentth verse of a song.}
   begin
      write (Current : 1);
      write (´ salmon fillets on the lawn,  ´);
      write (Current : 1);
      writeln (´ salmon fillets.´);
      writeln (´If one of those salmon should happen to spawn,´);
      write (Current + 1 : 1);
      writeln (´ salmon fillets on the lawn.´)
   end;  {Verse}

begin
   for Count := 1 to 100 do begin
      Verse (Count);
      writeln
   end
end.   {ForTrial}
```

```
1 salmon fillets on the lawn, 1 salmon fillets.
If one of those salmon should happen to spawn,
2 salmon fillets on the lawn.

2 salmon fillets on the lawn, 2 salmon fillets.
If one of those salmon should happen to spawn,
3 salmon fillets on the lawn.
```
        · ·   *many tedious lines of output follow, until . . .*
```
100 salmon fillets on the lawn, 100 salmon fillets.
If one of those salmon should happen to spawn,
101 salmon fillets on the lawn.
```

Whew! Program ForTrial contains a single, highly productive **for** statement. If we were to 'unfold' the statement—replace it with the statements it invokes—we'd see this sequence of calls instead:

'unfolding' the **for**

Verse (1);   writeln;
Verse (2);   writeln;

. . .

Verse (100);   writeln

for is a loop

> Statements that make actions repeat are called *loops*. A **for** loop can repeat any number of statements between the **begin** and **end** of a *compound statement*.

compound statements

A compound statement is just a bracket that groups separate actions. The **for** loop isn't required to control a compound statement—one or more statements between a **begin** and an **end**—but in my examples it almost invariably does. It makes it easier to add extra statements to the loop later on. I can outline the sort of **for** loop we'll generally see as:

for *counter variable* := *initial value* to *limit* do begin
    sequence of statements
end

If **downto** appears in place of **to**, the loop counts down instead of up. The **for** loop and compound statement's syntax charts are:

for statement

for ⟶ *counter variable* ⟶ := ⟶ *expression* ⟨ to / downto ⟩ *expression* ⟶ **do** ⟶ *statement*

compound statement

begin ⟶ *statement* ⟶ ; ⟶ **end**

Let's look at a collection of **for** loop rules:

real counters are forbidden

1. The counter variable, initial value, and limit must have the same ordinal (counting) type. real is forbidden.

The types have to be the same because the counter variable will take on every value from the initial value through the final value.

the counter is local

2. If the **for** statement appears in a procedure, its counter should be a local variable.

Only main-program **for** loops should use main-program variables.

bounds are evaluated on entry

3.   The expressions that give the counter variable's initial value and the limit are evaluated when the statement is first entered.

As a result, the number of repetitions can't be changed by the **for** loop's action. Assignments to variables that serve as the initial value and limit will not affect the counter variable or its limits.

no assigning to the counter

4.   It's an error to make an assignment to the counter variable from within the loop's action.

The counter variable, like any other variable, represents a value within the action of the **for** statement. But though it may be *used* within the **for** loop's action, it should not be *changed* there.

the counter is undefined on exit

5.   The value of the counter variable is undefined on exit from the **for** statement.

In effect, the variable is in the pristine condition it held when it was first declared. It must be reinitialized before being used in an expression.

> Many Pascal compilers do not enforce rules 2, 4, and 5. Non-local counter variables *may* be used; the counter variable *can* be assigned to; the counter variable *will* retain its last value. However, relying on these loopholes will almost invariably lead to bugs.

Modification Problems

1. Write a short-trip version of ForTrial. In other words, have it count up by twos or threes instead of one salmon at a time.

2. Like this sentence, the first few line of ForTrial's output is sadly ungrammatical. Modify the program so that the first lines of output refer to just one salmon fillet.

3. Make up an alphabet-oriented version of ForTrial, then modify the program appropriately.

Self-Check Questions

Q. The first lines of some **for** statements are shown below. What sequence of values does each loop generate? Assume that each of these assignments have been made beforehand: Letter := ´J´; Number :=7 ; Jump :=2 ; and Bound :=–3.

>   *a)* **for** Counter := 1 **to** Number **do** ...
>   *b)* **for** Index := 1 **downto** Number **do** ...
>   *c)* **for** Marker := Bound **to** Number **do** ...
>   *d)* **for** LetCount := Jump **to** Bound **do** ...
>   *e)* **for** Ch1 := ´D´ **downto** ´A´ **do** ...
>   *f)* **for** Ch2 := ´T´ **to** ´T´ **do** ...
>   *g)* **for** Ch3 := ´A´ **to** Letter **do** ...

A. In each instance, 'through' means 'through and including.'

a) The numbers 1 through 7.
b) No output—the initial value is less than the limit.
c) The numbers –3 through 7.
d) No output—the initial value is greater than the limit.
e) The characters ´D´, ´C´, ´B´, and ´A´.
f) The character ´T´.
g) The letters ´A´ through ´J´.

A Few Examples

Let's try a few examples. With all the chatter about salmon fillets deleted, Program ForTrial's goal was to generate the numbers 1 through 100. However, we can 'count' by characters just as easily. Here, I assume that CharCounter is a char-valued variable and use it to generate the lower-case letters:

generating chars

```
for  CharCounter := ´a´ to ´z´ do begin
        write (CharCounter)
end;
```

```
abcdefghijklmnopqrstuvwxyz
```

Generating values that are more than one step apart takes just a tiny bit of cleverness. For example, an auxiliary variable like Counter, below, helps generate numbers, by tens, from ten to fifty:

generating every tenth number

```
for  LoopCount := 1 to 5 do begin
        Counter := 10 * LoopCount;
        write (´   Loop:  ´);
        write (Counter : 1)
end;
```

```
Loop: 10   Loop: 20   Loop: 30   Loop: 40   Loop: 50
```

Counting backward is easy with **downto**—even if the counter variable has type char! For example, we can generate the capital letters in reverse with:

generating chars in reverse

```
for  CharCounter := ´Z´ downto ´A´ do begin
        write (CharCounter)
end;
```

```
ZYXWVUTSRQPONMLKJIHGFEDCBA
```

> Forward or backward, if the initial value and limit are equal, the **for** loop's action takes place just once.

Naturally, if the initial value is greater than the limit (or vice versa if **downto** is used) the loop's action is skipped entirely.

A test bed program may come in handy when the counter variable's initial or final value is itself a variable. That often happens when a loop contains a loop, as in program ForBed, below.

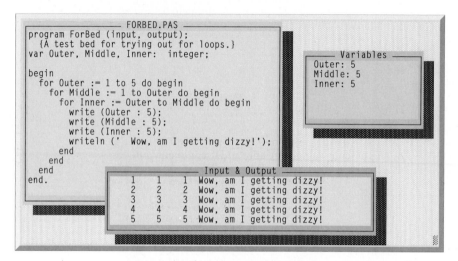

```
                  FORBED.PAS
program ForBed (input, output);
   {A test bed for trying out for loops.}
var Outer, Middle, Inner:  integer;

begin
   for Outer := 1 to 5 do begin
      for Middle := 1 to Outer do begin
         for Inner := Outer to Middle do begin
            write (Outer : 5);
            write (Middle : 5);
            write (Inner : 5);
            writeln ('  Wow, am I getting dizzy!');
         end
      end
   end
end.
```

```
                  Variables
                  Outer: 5
                  Middle: 5
                  Inner: 5
```

```
                  Input & Output
       1    1    1  Wow, am I getting dizzy!
       2    2    2  Wow, am I getting dizzy!
       3    3    3  Wow, am I getting dizzy!
       4    4    4  Wow, am I getting dizzy!
       5    5    5  Wow, am I getting dizzy!
```

I've shown all of ForBed's unexpectedly simple output. However, you might want to try reversing the innermost loop, so that it runs from Middle to Outer. Can you predict what will happen? Don't worry if you can't; we'll talk more about loop *nesting* in a few pages.

Self-Check Questions

Q. Consider these two program segments. What differences would there be in their output if the shaded **begin**s and **end**s were removed?

```
{First segment.}
for CharCounter := ´a´ to ´z´ do  begin
    write (CharCounter)
end;
```

```
{Second segment.}
for  LoopCount := 1 to 5 do  begin
    Counter := 10 * LoopCount;
    write (´   Loop:  ´);
    write (Counter : 1)
end;
```

A. The **begin** and **end** of a compound statement makes a sequence of statements seem to be a single action. Since the first compound statement controls just one action, the first **for** loop's action is the same with or without the compound statement. It prints:

```
abcdefghijklmnopqrstuvwxyz
```

The second segment, in contrast, uses a compound statement to group several actions. If we remove the **begin** and **end**, only the assignment statement will be repeated five times. The segment's output would be:

```
Loop:  50
```

Standard Practices and Examples

4-2

I LIKE TO START WITH THE PREMISE that **for** is meant to harness information, rather than actions. Pascal has other loops that repeat statements, but only the **for** loop generates *data*. The counter variable can have any ordinal (counting) type, including integer and char. Then, within the loop, we can always inspect (but not change) the counter variable's value. You'll see how useful this is as we consider some typical applications:

— Generating a particular sequence of values—the alphabet, a series of fractions, the counting numbers, etc.

for as a data generator

— Obtaining a sequence of input values from the program user—numbers to add or use in doing calculations.

— Modeling dynamical, 'feedback' systems by returning to particular data items—one or two variables—again and again.

— Generating patterns that are based on counts. For instance, a checkerboard is an eight by eight pattern of squares, while a right triangle can be drawn with a sequence of steadily lengthening rows.

— Creating tables of values; for example, combining a sequence generator with a pattern maker to produce a table of squares and cubes.

Pseudocode

Let's begin with a story about the eighteenth century mathematician Carl Gauss, whose teacher one day required his class to add a long sequence of consecutive numbers.

problem: adding
consecutive numbers

> Shortly after his seventh birthday Gauss entered his first school, a squalid relic of the Middle Ages run by a vile brute, one Büttner, whose idea of teaching the hundred or so boys in his charge was to thrash them into such a state of terrified stupidity that they forgot their own names. More of the good old days for which sentimental reactionaries long! It was in this hell-hole that Gauss found his fortune.*

> To make a long story short, Büttner had barely finished stating the problem when Gauss piped up with the answer. His insight was that the first and last numbers in any long sequence (say, 1 and 100) have the same sum as their neighbors (2 and 99) and so on (3+98, 4+97, . . .), with 50 such pairs in all. As a result, the entire sum of 1 through *n* can be expressed as the sum (n+1), times the (n/2) pairs. This is the kind of elegant solution we all wish *we'd* thought up!

---

* E.T. Bell, *Men Of Mathematics*, Simon and Schuster, 1937, p. 221.

But suppose that young Gauss had been corrupted by access to a computer. His train of thought might have run along very different lines: why not keep a running sum of the numbers generated by a **for** loop? Try to control the overwhelming temptation to start writing code! Instead, let's just describe what we want in pseudocode—a dialect of English that looks a lot like Pascal.

series-summing pseudocode

> **for** *every number from* 1 *through* 100
>   *add the number to a running sum;*

The variable that holds the *running sum* is usually called an *accumulator*, because it accumulates values. There's one important fact to remember about accumulators—they must be initialized. Returning to the pseudocode:

Gauss in pseudocode

> *initialize a* Sum *variable to* 0;
> **for** *every number from* 1 *through* 100
>   *add the number to* Sum;
> *print the final value of* Sum;

when to pseudocode

> Should you floss all of your teeth? No—just the ones that you want to keep. Should you pseudocode every one of your programs? Nope—only the ones that you want to run.

But there's one more issue to consider before we tackle the final program: is the pseudocode the best *design* for the program? No. As I've laid it out so far, Gauss is too specialized, because it adds just one sequence of numbers. But by writing a procedure that takes an argument—how high do we want to go?—we can make part of the program reusable. The final program is:

Gauss in Pascal

```
program Gauss (output);
    {Adds the sequence of numbers 1 through 100.}
var Sum: integer;
procedure Add (var Sum: integer; Limit: integer);
    {Adds the sequence 1 through Limit to Sum.}
    var Count: integer;   {The counter variable must be local.}
    begin
        for Count := 1 to Limit do begin
            Sum := Sum + Count
        end;
        {Sum represents the added sequence.}
    end; {Add}
begin
    Sum := 0;
    Add (Sum, 100);
    write ('The sum of 1 . . . 100 is:  ');
    writeln (Sum : 1)
end.  {Gauss}
```

```
The sum of 1 . . . 100 is: 5050
```

Modification Problems ─────────────────────────────

1. Modify Gauss so that procedure Add takes the lower bound of the sequence as an argument, too. If you feel up to it, rewrite Add as a function.

2. Gauss is *hardwired*, which means that the calculation it makes is built into the program. Modify Gauss so that it gets the lower and upper bounds from the program user.

3. Here's a wild claim for you: the sum of the first *n* odd numbers equals *n* squared. Alter Gauss to find out if it's true.

Nesting and Riddles

Putting statements *within* statements is a common and necessary practice. A loop statement may contain other loops, just as it contains assignments or procedure calls.

> Statements inside a loop are said to be *nested*. Nested loops are found wherever one loop includes another.

To help keep programs readable, inner loops are indented more than outer loops; the effect in a deeply nested program is of the paired wings of a flying bird. The more deeply nested a program is, the more important it is to follow two guidelines: indent inner loops evenly and comment each **end**.

indent and comment inner loops

For example, suppose that we want to give ourselves three cheers. The simplest solution would be:

```
for Cheer := 1 to 3 do begin
    writeln ('Hip, Hip, Hooray!')
end
```

However, I can use a **for** loop for each cheer, too:

the inner loop is nested

```
for Cheer := 1 to 3 do begin   {the outer loop}
    for Hip := 1 to 2 do begin   {the inner loop}
        write ('Hip, ')
    end; {inner loop}
    writeln ('Hooray!')
end   {outer loop}
```

```
Hip, Hip, Hooray!
Hip, Hip, Hooray!
Hip, Hip, Hooray!
```

When loops are nested, it's useful to distinguish between the number of times the inner loop is *reached* and the number of times it is *entered*. How many times will the inner loop execute, and how many times will the statements *inside* the inner loop execute?

— An inner loop is *reached* once for each turn of the outer loop.

— The inner loop is *entered*, and its contents executed, once for each turn of the outer loop *times* each turn of the inner loop.

Thus, the inner loop above is reached just three times, but its contents are executed 3∗2 or six times.

We can have a little fun with nested loops by trying a few *programming riddles.* Aside from providing a little mental entertainment, they should be entirely useless. Riddles that have **for** loop solutions typically involve sequences and patterns. The more nesting they require, the better.

For example, suppose that you want to print every three-letter combination of the letters ´a´, ´b´, and ´c´. How many combinations are there, and how can you use nested **for** loops to print them?

Answering the first question will help us solve the second. How many combinations are there? Well, there are three possibilities for the first letter, along with three for the second, and three more for the third. The number of combinations, 3×3×3, is twenty-seven.

Suppose I say essentially the same thing, but use pseudocode this time:

> **for** *each of the possible first letters* **do**
>   **for** *each of the possible second letters* **do**
>   **for** *each of the possible third letters* **do**
>   *print all three letters*

The final Pascal code practically writes itself:

```
for Ch1 := ´a´ to ´c´ do begin
    for Ch2 := ´a´ to ´c´ do begin
        for Ch3 := ´a´ to ´c´ do begin
            write (Ch1);  write (Ch2);  writeln (Ch3)
        end   {inner loop}
    end   {middle loop}
end   {outer loop}
```

Ready for a real-life example? How would you go about generating all the letters and numbers on a series of license plates that goes from 000AAA through 999ZZZ? My old one was clearly stamped pretty late in the game.

Easy! Just take the last example a few steps further. Notice that in the code segment below I *a*) haven't bothered with the **begin** and **end** of compound statements, and *b*) have used the multiple argument form of writeln. Why? Because doing it this way seemed to make my code clearer. Here are the first few lines of the solution.

printing license plates

```
for Ch1 := '0' to '9' do
   for Ch2 := '0' to '9' do
      for Ch3 := '0' to '9' do
         for Ch4 := 'A' to 'Z' do
            for Ch5 := 'A' to 'Z' do
               for Ch6 := 'A' to 'Z' do
                  writeln (Ch1, Ch2, Ch3, Ch4, Ch5, Ch6)
```

```
000AAA
000AAB
000AAC          etc.
```

Now, programming riddles usually rely on one fundamental technique—basing the initial value, limit, or increment of an *inner* loop on the value of the counter variable in an *outer* loop. For example, what is the effect of this program segment?

a little problem

```
for OuterChar := 'a' to 'e' do begin
   for InnerChar := 'a' to OuterChar do begin
      write (InnerChar)
   end   {inner loop}
end   {outer loop}
```

I can help you analyze the segment by 'unfolding' part of the inner loop. I'll replace the limit with the actual value that OuterChar represents each time the inner loop is reached:

unfolding the inner loop

```
for InnerChar := 'a' to 'a' do ...
for InnerChar := 'a' to 'b' do ...
for InnerChar := 'a' to 'c' do ...
for InnerChar := 'a' to 'd' do ...
for InnerChar := 'a' to 'e' do ...
```

The segment prints `aababcabcdabcde`. And if the segment above printed OuterChar instead of InnerChar what would its output be? I'll leave that for you.

Let's try one last riddle: Generate the sequence 1/2, 1/3, 1/4, 1/5, 2/3, 2/4, 2/5, 3/4, 3/5, 4/5. Hidden inside the problem is a simpler one: generate the sequence 1/2, 1/3, 1/4 ... 1/*n*.

Of course, that one is too easy for you! In pseudocode it's nothing more than:

```
for Denominator := 2 to LIMIT do
   print 1 / Denominator
```

But the sequence we want varies the numerator as well:

> **for** *each numerator from* 1 *through* 4 **do**
>   *generate denominators and print the whole works*

Suppose that LIMIT equals 5. Then:

generating the fractions

```
for Top := 1 to LIMIT – 1 do begin
    for Bottom := Top + 1 to LIMIT do begin
        write (Top : 3);
        write ('/');
        write (Bottom : 1)
    end   {Bottom}
end;  {Top}
writeln
```

1/2   1/3   1/4   1/5   2/3   2/4   2/5   3/4   3/5   4/5

Self-Check Questions

Q. Four dipsomaniacs were sharing a fifth of hundred-proof (50% alcohol) gin. Regrettably, the first one regurgitated two-thirds of her share and was unable to become inebriated. What quantity of alcohol did she manage to imbibe? In other words, how much is half of a third of a quarter of a fifth?

A. Note that Result must be initialized to 1.0, rather than 0.0.

```
Result := 1.0;
for Denominator := 2 to 5 do begin
    Result := Result / Denominator
end;
writeln (Result : 1 : 5)
```

0.00833

Q. All right, let's try another one. Suppose that you wanted to print the pattern of numbers shown below. How would you do it?

```
 1    2    3    4
 5    6    7    8
 9   10   11   12
13   14   15   16
```

A. It requires nested **for** loops, of course. The pattern is created with:

```
for Out := 0 to 3 do begin
    for Put := 1 to 4 do begin
        write (( (Out*4) + Put) : 4)
    end;
    writeln
end
```

Problem: Multiplication Tables

One of the advantages of the computer age (and I'll include the age of calculators in that) is that it's no longer necessary to buy lengthy books of tables like this (taken from the C.R.C. Standard Mathematical Tables):

Squares, Cubes and Roots

Roots of numbers other than those given directly may be found by the following relations: $\sqrt{100n} = 10\sqrt{n}$; $\sqrt{1000n} = 10\sqrt{10n}$; $\sqrt{\frac{1}{10}n} = \frac{1}{10}\sqrt{10n}$; $\sqrt{\frac{1}{100}n} = \frac{1}{10}\sqrt{n}$; $\sqrt{\frac{1}{1000}n} = \frac{1}{100}\sqrt{10n}$; $\sqrt[3]{1000n} = 10\sqrt[3]{n}$; $\sqrt[3]{10,000n} = 10\sqrt[3]{10n}$; $\sqrt[3]{100,000n} = 10\sqrt[3]{100n}$; $\sqrt[3]{\frac{1}{10}n} = \frac{1}{10}\sqrt[3]{100n}$; $\sqrt[3]{\frac{1}{100}n} = \frac{1}{10}\sqrt[3]{10n}$; $\sqrt[3]{\frac{1}{1000}n} = \frac{1}{10}\sqrt[3]{n}$.

n	n^2	$\sqrt{n}$	$\sqrt{10n}$	n^3	$\sqrt[3]{n}$	$\sqrt[3]{10n}$	$\sqrt[3]{100n}$
1	1	1.000 000	3.162 278	1	1.000 000	2.154 435	4.641 589
2	4	1.414 214	4.472 136	8	1.259 921	2.714 418	5.848 035
3	9	1.732 051	5.477 226	27	1.442 250	3.107 233	6.694 330
4	16	2.000 000	6.324 555	64	1.587 401	3.419 952	7.368 063
5	25	2.236 068	7.071 068	125	1.709 976	3.684 031	7.937 005
6	36	2.449 490	7.745 967	216	1.817 121	3.914 868	8.434 327
7	49	2.645 751	8.366 600	343	1.912 931	4.121 285	8.879 040
8	64	2.828 427	8.944 272	512	2.000 000	4.308 869	9.283 178
9	81	3.000 000	9.486 833	729	2.080 084	4.481 405	9.654 894

I won't make you print a table of roots and squares! Instead, let's start with something a bit easier:

problem: multiplication tables

Write a program that prints a 'times' table. Have it show all multiples, from $1 \times N$ to $N \times N$, of any number.

It's probably been some time since you've had to rely on such a table for help with multiplication. A pseudocode procedure call shows that there's just one parameter for the problem as stated:

pseudocode goal

print a times table (N);

But to be perfectly frank, the pseudocoded call isn't a whole lot of help. Suppose that I restate the pseudocode in a way that's a bit more useful:

first pseudocode

get N, the Limit;
print every product from 1 × 1 *to* Limit × Limit;

Print every multiple might be clear English, but it's far too vague to be the basis of Pascal code. A refinement of the pseudocode is needed:

a refinement

get the Limit;
for *every number from* 1 *to* Limit
    print all multiples of that number;

Now, what should the output look like? Why not just copy a grade-school math book? In a simple picture, the rows and columns go from 1 to N, while row/column intersections hold the current row/column product.

```
1   2   3   4   5   6
2   4   6   8  10  12
3   6   9  12  15  18
4   8  12  16  20  24      etc.
```

Where will the rows and columns—the program's data—come from? We can use **for** loops to generate them internally. In fact, we can also use the counter variables to label the rows and columns:

labeling the rows and columns

```
 |  1|  2|  3|  4|  5|  6|
 ---------------------
1|  1   2   3   4   5   6
2|  2   4   6   8  10  12
3|  3   6   9  12  15  18
4|  4   8  12  16  20  24     etc.
```

Each row and column is numbered. Wouldn't it be nice to suppress some of the output, so that duplicates wouldn't print at all?

simplifying the table

```
 |  1|  2|  3|  4|  5|  6|
 ---------------------
1|  1
2|  2   4
3|  3   6   9
4|  4   8  12  16              etc.
```

> In fact, that's the whole point of this exercise. Multiplying numbers by computer is easy, but making sense of computer output is hard.

Let's return to our pseudocode. A third refinement adds the last feature I suggested above. Can you see how it's done? Notice, incidentally, that as pseudocode becomes more complicated I'll occasionally use **end**s to keep my intentions clear.

yet another refinement

> *get the* Limit;
> *label the columns;*
> **for** *every* Row *from* 1 *to* Limit
>   *label the current row;*
>   **for** *every* Column *from* 1 *to the current* Row *value*
>   *print the value* Column *times* Row;
>   **end** *the current row*　　　{*Here, the pseudocoded* **end***s* }
> **end** *the whole series of rows*　　{ *help keep the plan clear.*}

Calculating columns only to the current Row value gets rid of the duplicates.

The completed program ShowTime is shown below. As with Gauss, dividing the program into procedures was a conscious design decision. As effective as pseudocode is at giving us insight into the problem, it can't magically split a program into bite-sized chunks. Note too that ShowTime's comments are different from its pseudocode. Pseudocode helped us write the program, but comments help us understand and correct it.

```
program ShowTime (input, output);
   {Prints a multiplication table of Limit values.}
var Limit: integer;
procedure LabelTable (Limit: integer);
   {Draw the top two lines that label the table.}
   var Column: integer;
   begin
      write ('        ');   {Leading spaces at the top.}
      for Column := 1 to Limit do begin
         write (Column : 1);
         write ('|  ')   {Print the bar and space.}
      end; {end}
      writeln;
      {The columns have been labeled.}
      write ('----');   {Leading dashes on the second line.}
      for Column := 1 to Limit do begin
         write ('---')
      end; {end}
      writeln;
      {The dashed line is done.}
   end; {LabelTable}
procedure DrawTable (Limit: integer);
   {Print the times table.}
   var Row, Column: integer;
   begin
      for Row := 1 to Limit do begin
         write (Row : 1);   {Label every row.}
         write ('|  ');
         {Going to Limit instead of Row would print duplicates.}
         for Column := 1 to Row do begin
            write (Row*Column : 3)
         end; {the inner for}
         writeln
         {Each row has been printed.}
      end  {the outer for loop}
   end; {DrawTable}
begin
   write ('Enter the upper limit for this times table:   ');
   readln (Limit);
   {Limit has been initialized.}
   LabelTable (Limit);
   {The chart is labeled.}
   DrawTable (Limit)
   {The chart is done.}
end.   {ShowTime}
```

multiplication table
program

(*output follows*)

```
Enter the upper limit for this times table:   9
      1| 2| 3| 4| 5| 6| 7| 8| 9|
   -------------------------------
   1|    1
   2|    2  4
   3|    3  6  9
   4|    4  8 12 16
   5|    5 10 15 20 25
   6|    6 12 18 24 30 36
   7|    7 14 21 28 35 42 49
   8|    8 16 24 32 40 48 56 64
   9|    9 18 27 36 45 54 63 72 81
```

Modification Problems

1. Change ShowTime so that instead of printing numbers on and *below* the center diagonal, it prints numbers only *above* the diagonal.

2. ShowTime works fine for an upper limit of 9, but what happens to its columns when we start to multiply two-digit numbers? Test ShowTime and fix the problem.

3. Modify the table-printing procedure from ShowTime so that it takes two arguments. In other words, don't require a 'square' table.

Problem: Income Projection

The nested **for** loop often appears when a calculation must itself be repeated. Let's look at a problem that will appeal to all students who are planning careers in business: making income projections.

problem: income projection

An editorial assistant who is learning just what publishers mean by 'voracious reading' asks for an increase in her $18,000 salary. Her sadistic boss makes the following offer:

Plan A: a 10% raise each year, commencing immediately, along with an immediate $1,500 bonus that won't be counted in base pay.

Plan B: a raise of 1/12 of 10% each and every month, with no bonus.

Which deal is better? She has ten minutes to decide.

According to my sources, incidentally, these figures are too high. Unfortunately, I don't think that you would find an accurate example to be credible.

Note that the more frequent raises of Plan *B* will work like compound interest, and lead to somewhat higher yearly raises. All the same, the $1,500 bonus of Plan *A* is nothing to be sneezed at. We can anticipate that, over time, one deal will replace the other as the best offer.

What will the program's output be? A novice coder might be tempted to calculate and print only the exact date on which the better early deal becomes the long-run loser. But the program engineer's approach is more sophisticated.

people read output

> From the viewpoint of human decision making, limiting output to a single figure can be misleading. Factors that have not been explicitly mentioned in a problem statement may turn out to be influential when a final decision has to be made. Programs should supply *information*, not just answers.

In the case of this particular problem, the worse long-run choice might be favorable if the employee needs quick money and the long-run cost isn't too great. Since 'too great' is one of those concepts that's hard to program, projecting the actual figures involved over some period will be the best approach.

Let's turn to pseudocode. We want to produce a table that let's us make an intelligent comparison. Two kinds of calculations will be involved—those of Plan *A* and those of Plan *B*. Our first goal pseudocode will be a bit different:

goal pseudocode

> *initialize variables as necessary;*
> **for** *some reasonable number of years*
>   *label the table;*
>   *do Plan A (this year's A income, running total A income);*
>   *do Plan B (this year's B income, running total B income);*

Instead of highlighting the goal-oriented steps, I want to draw your attention to the background material. By now, we're getting smart enough to anticipate having to do some program initialization, along with some labeling of output. The pseudocode of *do Plan A* is pretty straightforward:

Plan *A* refinement

> CurrentPayA := *a 10% increase;*
> TotalPayA := *increased by* CurrentPayA;

Plan *B* is a little harder to calculate:

Plan *B* refinement

> **for** *each month of the current year*
>   CurrentPayB := *one twelfth of a 10% increase;*
> TotalPayB := *increased by* CurrentPayB;

The final version of program Project is shown on the next page; its output appears below. Note that we're using the **for** loop counter variables in the most limited way possible: they don't generate data, and they're not part of any calculation. Instead, the loops let us revisit and linger over particular variables, adjusting and readjusting their values as we make our income projections.

		A: Yearly	A: Total	B: Yearly	B: Total
Year	1	19800.00	21300.00	19884.84	19884.84
Year	2	21780.00	43080.00	21967.04	41851.87
Year	3	23958.00	67038.00	24267.27	66119.15
Year	4	26353.80	93391.80	26808.37	92927.52
Year	5	28989.18	122380.98	29615.56	122543.08
Year	6	31888.10	154269.08	32716.70	155259.78
Year	7	35076.91	189345.99	36142.56	191402.34
Year	8	38584.60	227930.58	39927.16	231329.50
Year	9	42443.06	270373.64	44108.06	275437.56
Year	10	46687.36	317061.01	48726.75	324164.31

this is the program output

(*program follows*)

income projection program

```pascal
program Project (input, output);
   {Develops an income projection for two alternative salary offers.}

const YEARS = 10;          {We'll run this projection for ten years.}

var Year: integer;
    CurrentA, CurrentB,       {The current yearly pay rates.}
    TotalA, TotalB: real;     {The running totals for each plan.}

procedure PlanA (var Current, Total: real);
   {Calculates the 10% yearly raise of Plan A.}

   begin
      Current := 1.1 * Current;
      Total := Total + Current
   end; {PlanA}

procedure PlanB (var Current, Total: real);
   {Calculates the monthly pay raises of Plan B.}

   var Month: integer;

   begin
      for Month := 1 to 12 do begin
         Current := Current + ((0.10/12.0) * Current)
      end;
      Total := Total + Current
   end; {PlanB}

begin
   CurrentA := 18000.00;
   CurrentB := 18000.00;
   TotalA := 1500.00;          {Plan A starts with the $1,500 bonus.}
   TotalB := 0.00;
   {All variables have been initialized.}
   writeln ('      A: Yearly  A: Total  B: Yearly   B: Total');
   {The output table has been labeled.}
   for Year := 1 to YEARS do begin
      write ('Year  ');
      write (Year : 2);
      PlanA (CurrentA, TotalA);
      write (CurrentA : 12 : 2);
      write (TotalA : 12 : 2);
      {We've calculated and printed a year according to Plan A.}
      PlanB (CurrentB, TotalB);
      write (CurrentB : 12 : 2);
      writeln (TotalB : 12 : 2)
      {We've calculated and printed a year according to Plan B.}
   end
end.   {Project}
```

Modification Problems

1. Suppose that our editorial assistant were to make a counteroffer—a bonus of $750, with a daily raise of 1/365 of 10%. Under what circumstances should her editor accept?

2. Procedure PlanB contains a calculation that's usually regarded as a no-no. It's the division within the loop. Since the answer is always the same (0.10/12.0) is a constant,

why bother to calculate it again and again? Modify the code to remove the constant from the loop.

3. Plans *A* and *B* are equivalent to compound interest—additional increases come on top of raises already received. However, many companies give yearly bonuses that are not included so that they won't have to raise base pay—they're like simple interest. Add a PlanC procedure to Project that analyzes the effect of a yearly bonus of $10,000.

Background: Do Computers Supply Answers?

A programmer went to a business meeting. The first speaker threw a slide upon the overhead projector, displaying many columns of figures. 'This spreadsheet shows,' he said, 'that we will make a great deal of money.'

The programmer asked: 'What assumptions did you use when you prepared the spreadsheet?'

The speaker scratched his head. 'I produced this slide on the computer.'

The programmer gritted his teeth. 'Have you never heard the saying "'Garbage In, Garbage Out'"?'

The speaker threw his head back and laughed. 'You misquote it. The correct saying is "Garbage In, Gospel Out"!'

From *Computer Parables*, by Geoffrey James, © 1989, InfoBooks, Santa Monica, Ca. 90406

Program Engineering Notes: Learning Doubt

4-3

THE LONG-TERM GOAL OF THIS COURSE may be to teach you faith in computers, but our immediate goal is to learn how to doubt software. One of the hardest aspects of program engineering is to recognize that intentions are not always accomplishments. What a loop is meant to accomplish and what it actually does are often quite different.

Confirmation Commenting

Debug the code, not the comments. A simple rule describes the program engineer's main weapon: doubt. What a program was supposed to do is not nearly as important as what it actually did.

For example, consider this program segment. Try to find the bug before you go past the example:

the averaging loop bug

```
{Calculate the average of HowMany input values.}
writeln ('How many numbers are there?');
readln (HowMany);    {Find out how many numbers there are.}
writeln ('OK, type in the numbers.');
for Count := 1 to HowMany do begin
    Total := 0;    {Initialize the running total.}
    read (Number);    {Get the next number.}
    Total := Total + Number    {Add it to the running sum.}
end;
write ('The average was:    ');
writeln ( (Total / HowMany) : 2 : 5)
```

Where's the bug? The first Total assignment is in the wrong place. Total should be initialized to zero before the loop begins, rather than once each iteration.

The 'loop average' bug is exceptionally educational because it boldly ignores the first two rules of programming:

— *Plan ahead.* Use pseudocode to outline code before you write it.

— *Code from comments.* As you write code, stick to the plan.

By itself, planning ahead isn't enough. The pseudocode below is reasonable, but it won't always prevent the bug:

planning alone doesn't prevent bugs

> *initialize as necessary;*
> *sum the input values;*
> *calculate and print the average;*

Speaking realistically, programmers often gloss over the initialization step when they're planning. They make a mental note to add the appropriate statement later, then never get around to it.

commenting alone doesn't prevent bugs

Nor has coding from comments worked as an error-prevention tool in the buggy segment above. It has *lots* of comments! In a literal sense, the comment *initialize the running total* isn't incorrect—Total is being initialized. Unfortunately, the comment is correct only when it causes us to read the statement out of context.

How can we avoid such problems? By erecting a third safety barrier.

— *Confirm the outcome.* Confirm what you think your code has done.

> A *confirmation comment* follows a code segment. By summarizing what we've done, it sets the stage for the program's next actions.

confirmation comments

Confirmation comments don't have to detail everything we've done; regular commenting still helps to explain a tricky piece of code. However, confirmation comments do describe the current program *state*—the facts that *must* be true if the rest of the program is going to work properly. Let's take another look at the code segment, with confirmation commenting in place of our previous 'intention' comments:

the bug is still here

```
writeln ('How many numbers are there?');
readln (HowMany);
     {We know how many numbers to read.}
writeln ('OK, type in the numbers.');
for Count := 1 to HowMany do begin
     Total := 0;
     read (Number);
     Total := Total + Number
end;
     {Total represents the sum of HowMany values.
     HowMany represents the number of values read.}
write ('The average was:     ');
writeln ((Total / HowMany) : 2 : 5)
     {We've printed the average.}
```

The confirmation comment makes the error—the assignment to Total—stick out like a sore thumb. The comments don't describe everything the program does, but they do explicitly set out the facts that the rest of the program relies on.

Confirmation commenting won't prevent bugs either, of course! Nevertheless, it helps to mirror the process an expert programmer goes through in checking her work—she checks what she's done, rather than what she intended to do.

> *The First Law of Debugging*
> It ain't what you don't know that hurts you. It's what you *do* know that just ain't so.

Bugs

Let's turn to a review of potential **for** statement bugs that have a syntactic flavor. First and foremost, don't forget that the statements the loop repeats should be put within the **begin** and **end** of a compound statement. Can you see what this segment does wrong?

a missing compound statement

```
{Give three cheers.}
for Count := 1 to 3 do
    write ('Hip hip  ');
        writeln ('Hooray!');
writeln ('Congratulations!')
```

```
Hip hip Hip hip Hip hip Hooray!
Congratulations!
```

Rather than giving three cheers, it seems to be sighing with relief after conquering the hiccups. Indenting the second writeln means nothing to the **for** statement, which controls just one action. We tell the compiler to treat the two output statements as a single action by turning them into a compound statement.

```
for Count := 1 to 3 do begin
    write ('Hip hip  ');
    writeln ('Hooray!')
end;
writeln ('Congratulations!')
```

```
Hip hip Hooray!
Hip hip Hooray!
Hip hip Hooray!
Congratulations!
```

use compound statements

As a general rule, use compound statements even if they enclose just one action. Put the framework in place to help avoid bugs if you add to your code later.

A second general rule is to view all three of the identifiers and values that appear in the **for** statement as parameters that are *used* but not *changed*. Thus, in the statement:

for Count := Low **to** High **do begin** . . .

all three identifiers—Count, Low, and High—can be inspected. This is correct:

the control values can be inspected

```
for Count := Low to High do begin
    writeln (Count);
    writeln (Low);
    writeln (High)
end
```

On the other hand, attempting to make changes is either illegal or fruitless. The illegal kind are tricky, because a Pascal compiler won't necessarily detect them. For example, a good Pascal compiler won't compile the code below. But even though both statements in the loop are illegal (because the counter variable can only be changed before or after—and never within—the **for** statement) the program they're in will still run on most systems:

the control variable bug

```
for Count := Low to High do begin
    read (Count);          {Illegal attempts at input and assignment.}
    Count := Count + 1
end
```

You must treat the counter variable as though it is *read-only*. It can be inspected, but it shouldn't be changed.

A final **for** statement bug is subtle. What's wrong with this sequence?

the undefined control variable bug

```
readln (Finish);
for Count := 1 to Finish do begin
    whatever the loop does
end;
write ('Number of repetitions was:    ');
writeln (Count)
```

The problem is that a **for** statement's counter variable is undefined *by definition* when the loop ends. It may have a value—in fact, it certainly has a value—but exactly what that value is isn't specified by the Pascal standard.

Syntax Summary

❑   compound statement: a sequence of statements grouped between a **begin** and an **end**.

```
begin
    writeln ('For syntactic purposes, these two statements are ');
    writeln ('treated like a single statement.')
end
```

Although statements like **for** can control individual (rather than compound) statements, I'll almost invariably use compound statements to avoid inadvertently omitting actions.

❑ **for** statement: causes a *counter variable* to assume a predetermined sequence of values; also, lets an action be repeated for a predetermined number of times. If **downto** replaces **to**, below, counting is reversed.

> **for** *counter variable* := *initial value* **to** *limit* **do begin**
>   *sequence of statements*
> **end**;

❑ The initial value and limit must have the counter variable's type and can't be real.

❑ The counter variable should be a local variable.

❑ The initial value and limit are determined when the loop is first entered.

❑ It's an error to make an assignment to the counter variable from within the loop.

❑ The counter variable is undefined on exit from the statement.

❑ nested statement: an 'inner' statement that takes place within the body of an 'outer' statement.

Remember . . .

❑ **for** loops control the availability of data. They can generate a sequence of data values internally (via the counter variable), or by returning to particular variables again and again, or they can count values entered by the program user.

❑ Compound statements tell the compiler to treat a sequence of distinct actions as a single statement. Make a habit of using compound statements even if they enclose just one action, and you'll avoid bugs if you add to your code later.

❑ *Visual commenting* by consistently indenting nested statements is essential for keeping complex programs comprehensible. Commenting **end**s helps as well. Overall, a program's physical appearance should reflect its structure in Pascal.

❑ *Confirmation comments* follow program actions. They describe what we believe we've accomplished, and document changes in program state.

❑ Pseudocode is a pidgin Pascal that's used for program planning. Although pseudocode doesn't obey Pascal's syntax rules, it illustrates the flow of information through a program, and the final code's basic construction.

❑ An *accumulator* is a variable that keeps a running sum. Remember to initialize it.

❑ Programs should provide information, not just answers. Why? Because answers can be wrong (they might only reflect the programmer's misunderstanding of the problem) even when the information they're based on is right.

When possible, supply enough program output to let the reader draw her own conclusions.

❏ Label program output so that it makes sense in addition to being right.

❏ The First Law of Debugging: 'It ain't what you don't know that hurts you. It's what you do know that just ain't so.'

Big Ideas

The two Big Ideas in this chapter are:

1. *Most programs process a sequence or stream of data values.* Therefore, most programming languages include a statement that can generate basic streams of values—counting numbers, letters, odd numbers, and the like. *Most programs repeat actions.* Therefore, most programming languages include a statement that will repeat an action for a fixed number of times. In Pascal, the **for** statement serves both purposes.

2. *You have to outline programs before you write them.* Pseudocode is a reasonable middle ground between the vagueness and imprecision of English and the excessive precision of actual Pascal code. English is too informal to let you know what kind of problems you'll face when coding time comes around. In contrast, Pascal is too rigid to let you sketch out alternative ideas.

Begin by Writing the Exam . . .

4-1 The first Self-Check Questions asked you what sequences various **for** loops produced. Write half a dozen more. Make them hard by:

    a) using char counters,
    b) decrementing rather than incrementing the counter,
    c) having a negative initial value,
    d) using bounds that cause the statement to be skipped, or
    e) including syntax errors.

4-2 Nesting is inherently confusing. Therefore, one basic **for** loop test question is a variation on the following:

```
for Outer := A to B do begin
    for Inner := C to D do begin
        something that involves Outer or Inner
    end
end
```

Make up a few questions of this ilk. Make them harder by using the tricks suggested above, as well as by replacing C or D with an expression that contains Outer.

4-3 We can use a counter variable to generate just about any regular sequence. For example, assume that Counter goes from 1 through N by ones. It's easy to recognize the sequences that these generate:

    1/Counter *generates* 1/1, 1/2, 1/3, 1/4 ⋯ 1/N
    Counter–1/Counter *generates* 0/1, 1/2, 2/3, 3/4 ⋯ N–1/N
    Counter∗Counter *generates* 1, 4, 9, 16 ⋯ N^2

Use the Zen Study Method to create a few *Write a loop that creates this sequence* problems. Use the lazy (i.e. my) method by first modifying the operation on Counter, then figuring out what sequence is created.

4-4   Table-making is a standard **for** loop application. Make up two questions for each of these kinds of tables:

     a) Conversion tables, like Fahrenheit to Centigrade.
     b) Arithmetic tables, of sines, square roots, and so on.
     c) Comparison tables, like the output of the income-projection program.

4-5   *Here's the input, what's the output?* The basic question is built around a loop like:

```
Total := 0;
for Count := 1 to 5 do begin
    read (Value);
    Total := Total + Value
end;
write (Total);
```

Write three *Here's the input, what's the output* questions that are complicated by *a)* reading the final value as part of program input, *b)* changing the final value within the loop, *c)* having an extra input statement within the loop, or *d)* adding the counter variable to the running total.

4-6   Supply a short program and *What's the output?* can always be ground out eventually, but *Here's the output, what was the input?* questions are my own personal favorite. Start with a loop that reads a 'count' value, then reads and prints that many input numbers. Make the output harder to reverse by performing an arithmetic operation on the number before you print it, or by using the previous input number as part of the arithmetic computation. Make up three such problems.

4-7   The basic outline of a program that uses a **for** statement to get data from the program user is:

     for *all available data*
       get a value;
       process the value;
     print the results

Some of the processes such a program might carry out include adding the input values or finding their average. Think of three other processes that might rely on the same basic program shell.

Warmups and Test Programs

4-8   Is **begin begin begin begin begin end end end end end** a legal compound statement? How about **begin begin begin begin begin** ; ; ; **end end; end end end**? Just how far can you take this line of inquiry?

4-9   Write a procedure that prints all the even numbers between 3 and 43.

4-10   Write a procedure that prints every third capital letter, starting with ´C´.

4-11   Write a program that prints all numbers divisible by 5 from 50 down to zero.

4-12   Write a procedure that is passed two parameters—a character and a length—then prints a line of that many characters.

4-13   Write a program that reads eleven numbers and prints the difference between each successive pair. Thus, only ten numbers appear as output.

4-14   Write a procedure that averages a sequence of real numbers. The length of the sequence should be passed as a value parameter, while the answer should be returned with a variable parameter.

4-15   Error messages are often hard to understand or even misleading. It can be very useful to make errors intentionally, just to see if the compiler makes a helpful diagnosis. So, try the forbidden! Write test programs that:

   a)   attempt to change the value of the counter variable;

   b)   use a counter variable of type real;

   c)   use a global counter variable for a **for** loop that's inside a procedure.

4-16   Are there any limits on the size of the initial or final values?

4-17   How many of the ASCII characters do interesting things? Write a program that attempts to print each character. To keep them from whizzing by, print each character's ordinal position, and ask the program user to hit a key (just read and ignore the character) after each output statement. If you're lucky, you may get to explore the existential question 'How can I debug a program that locks my keyboard?'

4-18   Two bottles hold exactly one liter of soda each, although one container holds Coke and the other Pepsi. Suppose that you pour precisely one tenth of the Coke into the Pepsi, and then pour one tenth of a liter of the disgusting mixture that results back into the Coke. Repeat the process exactly ten times, then answer this question: is there more Coke in the Pepsi, or Pepsi in the Coke?

Programming Problems

4-19   Calculating a *weighted average* is like calculating an ordinary average, except that some values are given greater weight, or importance. As you know, weighted averages are very important in college; after all, examinations are given primarily in order to prepare you to take more examinations. Thus, it is essential that each test count more heavily in the final reckoning than its predecessor did.

Suppose that a set of course exams carries the following weights: 10%, 25%, 30%, 35%. Write a program that reads in ten sets of exam grades, then prints each student's weighted average and the overall unweighted average *on each test* for the entire set.

4-20   Imagine, if you can, a set of Chinese boxes that are neatly nested one inside the next. The smallest box, which measures one inch on a side, fits inside a box with two-inch sides, which is inside a box with three-inch sides, and so on.

Next, imagine that you unpack the boxes and place them in a row. Thus, the length of the row is one inch, plus two inches, plus three inches, etc. Draw a square whose sides equal the length of this row.

Finally, take a great imaginary leap. Suppose that you cut each box into six pieces, and lay them flat. Will they cover the square? If you can solve this in your head, you're done. If not, write a program that solves the problem for any number (say, up to ten or fifteen) of Chinese boxes.

4-21   A chain letter is the surest route to popularity with friends, neighbors, and the Federal Postal Inspector. In effect, *n* people sign the letter; then each one must send the letter to *n* more people. Calculate, and print a table of, the number of letters that will be generated in ten generations of a letter with one, four, seven, and ten signers.

4-22   In the year 1202, a man named Leonardo of Pisa described a sequence that begins 0, 1, 1, 2 and continues indefinitely: each new number is the sum of the prior two numbers. Leonardo is better known as *Fibonacci* (from *Filius Bonaccii*, or son of Bonaccio), and his numbers are now called the *Fibonacci sequence*. The sequence has been studied for hundreds of years; there's even a journal (the *Fibonacci Quarterly*) devoted to articles on it.

Write a procedure that generates values in the Fibonacci sequence. Then, use it to answer these questions:

a)   What is the largest Fibonacci number you can generate on your system?

b)   Fibonacci devised his sequence to describe the growth of a rabbit population. If rabbits never die and each pair produces a new pair monthly (starting at the age of one month), you will indeed find you have one pair, then two, then three, then five, etc. How many rabbits will there be in a year?

c)   The ratio between successive Fibonacci numbers comes closer and closer to the *golden ratio*. What is it?

d)   Write a subprogram that takes the golden ratio you just calculated, raises it to the *n*th power, then divides by the square root of five. Round the result, and print it. How does this result compare, for increasing values of *n*, to the *n*th Fibonacci number?

4-23   As everybody knows, Californians hew to intellectual pursuits. Their allegedly excessive interest in suntanning is a vile slander. In fact, they lie in the sun only to free their minds for their first love, conversation.

Recently, however, concern has been growing about the possible hazardous effects of oversunning. There are really two issues of risk: daily exposure and cumulative exposure. Although suntanning progressively reduces the danger of burning, the hazardous effects of exposure to the sun's rays accumulate day after day.

Write a program that a Californian might use to keep track of her daily tanning time, as well as the total time she's spent in the sun. Have it print a table that is based on the assumption that she starts out with fifteen minutes in the sun and increases her time in the sun by one minute each day. Its output should begin:

```
Day         Time    Total Time
 1           15           15
 2           16           31
 3           17           48
 . . .
```

Options: Let the user choose the total number of days, change the first day's time, or increase each day's increment. Convert the cumulative total to hours and minutes.

4-24   Although the list is diminishing, there are still a few things that cannot be done with a hand-held electronic stopwatch. For example, suppose that a race requires four laps of a track. A stopwatch is capable of recording and reporting on the time of each lap, called a *split*, as well as the total elapsed time to and through that lap, called the *cumulative time*.

However, a stopwatch cannot tell us the relative difference, in percentage terms, between one lap and the next. Nor can it tell us the difference between the current lap's split and the average split run in the race so far. Finally, a stopwatch is utterly incapable of projecting, at each stage of the race, what the final time will be.

Write a program that takes care of these tasks and proves the eminent superiority of an $80,000 computer over a $19.95 wristwatch. The user must supply the number of splits that will be entered. You must choose a format for time entries. *Options: a*) Whatever the input format is, print times both in seconds and in minutes and seconds; *b*) get a goal time along with the number of splits, and calculate the current deviation from an absolutely evenly paced race; *c*) properly handle special-case races that don't have uniform splits (e.g. the 3 and 3/4 lap 1500 meter race).

Think of the Gauguin painting Where do we come from? What are we? Where are we going? *These are the questions to ask when you debug* boolean *expressions.* (p. 177)

5

Making Choices: the **if** and **case** Statements

* Optional sections.

Winnie-the-Pooh, you may recall, had a little trouble making up his mind. If 'honey or condensed milk with your bread?' was the question, then an emphatic 'Yes!' was the answer ('and then, so as not to seem greedy, he added "But don't bother about the bread, please." '). Pooh would have been a terrible programmer.

Chapter 5 introduces the basis of all computer choice: the *boolean expression*. There are just two boolean (boo´-lee-an) values—TRUE and FALSE—but we can use them to state just about any question and answer (except those that involve honey and bears). Are two numbers equal? Is one greater? Is it less? The answer is always yes or no—or, in boolean terms, TRUE or FALSE.

Barbers, so they say, are paid less for their ability to cut hair than for their skill at *not* cutting. Now that you've had some fun employing **for** loops to burn up impressive amounts of CPU time, try using **if** and **case** statements, and boolean expressions, to learn the barber's restraint.

Strictly Pascal

5-1

LET'S BEGIN WITH PROGRAM Shopper, which will let you know if you're the kind of person advertisers care about:

the if statement in action

```pascal
program Shopper (input, output);
    {Provides a guide for shopping in today's increasingly complex world.}
var Age: integer;
begin
    write ('How old are you?    ');
    readln (Age);
    if (Age < 18) or (Age > 34) then begin
        writeln ('Uh oh ... you´´re not in prime consumption years. ');
        writeln ('Better stay home and watch MTV. ');
    end
    else begin
        writeln ('Go shop until you drop. ')
    end;
    writeln
end.   {Shopper}
```

```
How old are you?   17
Uh oh ... you're not in prime consumption years.
Better stay home and watch MTV.
```

Shopper illustrates this chapter's two main concerns. The shaded portion is, of course, an **if** statement. The **if** lets us pass over and ignore the parts of a program that we don't want to use or explicitly select those parts that we do. In the example, we select an output statement (Uh oh . . .) if the value of Age falls within certain bounds, and pick the alternative otherwise.

Shopper also demonstrates the construction of boolean expressions. This little segment:

a boolean expression

> (Age < 18) **or** (Age > 34)

actually contains two kinds of expressions. First, there are *relations* between integer values—the comparisons between Age and 18, and between Age and 34—that are either true or false. Second, the **or** operator creates an expression by joining the relations. If either one of them is true, then the entire segment has the boolean value TRUE. We'll look at boolean values in detail in a bit.

The **if** statement makes two kinds of choices: *yes/no* and *either/or*. Its syntax chart is:

if statement

if ⟶ *boolean expression* ⟶ **then** ⟶ *statement* ⟶

└⟶ **else** ⟶ *statement* ⟶

In the basic *yes/no* choice, an action is taken if the boolean expression is TRUE or is skipped entirely if it's FALSE. Technically, the **begin** and **end** of a compound statement are required only if the *sequence of statements* consists of two or more statements, but I'll almost always use them.

a yes/no choice

```
if boolean expression then begin
        sequence of statements
end
```

Adding an **else** part allows an automatic *either/or* choice. If the statement's boolean expression is FALSE, the **then** action is skipped, and the **else** action is taken instead. As above, I'll almost always use the **begin** and **end** of a compound statement.

an either/or choice

```
if boolean expression
    then begin
        sequence of
        statements
    end     {no semicolon}
else begin
        alternative sequence
        of statements
    end;     {semicolon is ok}
```

no semicolon before else

If you read the above example carefully, you'll notice that the **end** of the **then** part isn't followed by a semicolon. A semicolon can *never* precede an **else**, because it makes the compiler think that it's about to read an **else** *statement*— which doesn't exist— rather than an **else** *part*, which does.

Finally, an **else** part is always the alternative of the most recent **then** it can legally be tied to. You should always indent deeply enough to make this connection clear to a human who is reading the program. For example:

```
if (Age < 18)
    then writeln ('Too young to spend serious amounts of money.')
    else if (Age > 34)
        then writeln ('Too old to know what to buy.')
        else writeln ('Just right for a journey to consumer Nirvana.')
```

Indenting is essential when there are subtler ties. For example, the inner if, below, doesn't have an **else** part. The **else** is tied to the first **then**:

```
if (Age < 18)
    then begin
        if (Age < 10) then writeln ('Too young to watch MTV.')
    end
    {Since that if is completely within the compound statement, it has no else.}
    else writeln ('Old enough to vote (18 or over).');
{No action is specified for values of Age from 10 through 17.}
```

Naturally, a nested if can have only one **else** part. The second **else**, below, is tied to the outer **then**:

```
if (Age < 18)
   then if (Age < 10)
           then writeln ('Too young to care about MTV (under 10).')
           else writeln ('Too young to consume meaningfully (10 .. 17).')
         {Since that if is complete, the next else belongs to the outer statement.}
   else writeln ('Old enough to worry about money (18 or over).');
```

You may anticipate that when there are a lot of alternatives, a series of **if** statements can become confusing. Fortunately, Pascal has another statement for choice: **case**. We'll look at it at the end of this section.

Modification Problems

1. Can you modify Shopper (by changing the boolean condition) so that its advice is reversed?

2. It is a well known fact that with enough money, one can temporarily overcome the bonds of age. Modify Shopper so that an over-the-hill (but not an underage) program user can qualify for shopper status. You'll have to set the minimum necessary income yourself.

The Relational Operators

the boolean constants

Using the **if** statement effectively requires a crystal clear understanding of boolean expressions. To begin with, there are only two values: FALSE and TRUE, in that order. The standard function odd(x) also represents a boolean value—FALSE if its integer argument x is even, and TRUE if it's odd.

We can create longer boolean expressions with the *relational* operators.

relational operators

Math	Pascal	English
=	=	*equal to*
<	<	*less than*
≤	<=	*less than or equal to*
>	>	*greater than*
≥	>=	*greater than or equal to*
≠	<>	*not equal to*
∈	in	*set membership*

The last operator, **in**, comes from Pascal's **set** type. I'll get to it in a few pages.

booleans are assertions

You've probably seen these relations described as inequalities in high school algebra. Programming languages use the fact that inequalities always make an assertion, or claim, that has to be either true or false. This makes them boolean-valued expressions. For example, these are either TRUE or FALSE:

LowerLimit > 5   ApplicantsAge <= 65

They assert that a variable named LowerLimit is greater than 5 and that ApplicantsAge is less than or equal to 65. Since character sets are ordered, the following boolean expressions, which confirm or deny the alphabetical ordering or equality of char and string values, are as plausible as their numerical counterparts:

Finished = 'Y'   'X' <> chr(63)   Name = 'Nadine'

relational operands

> In stating relations, it's essential that both operands—the values that are being compared—have appropriately comparable types.

Strings of the same length can be compared to each other, and real values can be compared to integer values. You should be aware, though, that the vagaries of computer arithmetic can make comparisons unreliable if they depend on precise real representations. As an extreme example, the real value 3.0*(10.0/3.0) might equal 9.99999999 . . . instead of 10.0. See Appendix C for additional discussion of real arithmetic.

Since every relational operator expects two operands, and every two operands expect just one operator, some common mathematical notation can't be used in writing programs. In particular, multiple inequalities like $5 < X < 10$ have no meaning in Pascal. We'll see how to express such relations properly next (this particular example is correctly written as $(5<X)$ **and** $(X<10)$).

The boolean Operators and, or, and not

A 'word-symbol' is a word that is used as an operator, as **div** and **mod** are. The boolean operators are all word-symbols. Just as **div** takes integer operands to form an integer-valued expression, the boolean operators use boolean operands to create boolean-valued expressions. **and** joins two conditions.

the and operator

> If we have two boolean values, Maybe and Perhaps, the expression:
>
> (Maybe **and** Perhaps)
>
> is evaluated as TRUE if both Maybe and Perhaps are TRUE. If either or both of them are FALSE, the entire expression is FALSE.

and is frequently used to help set lower and upper boundaries on a value, as in this **if** statement:

```
if (Value>=5) and (Value<=10) then begin
    writeln ('The value is between 5 and 10, inclusive.')
end
```

and can also be part of an assignment to a boolean variable:

```
var Capital: boolean;
    ...
Capital := (Letter>='A') and (Letter<='Z');
```

The second operator, **or**, yields a result of TRUE if one or the other (or both) of its operands has the value TRUE. The English sentence *If I do well on the midterm or ace the final then I'll pass*, is a perfect example of 'oring' two boolean values, because I'll flunk only if both chances are blown:

if *(I do well on the midterm)* **or** *(I ace the final)* **then** *I'll pass*

*the **or** operator*

> The **or** operator is less restrictive than **and** is. The expression:
>
> > (Maybe **or** Perhaps)
>
> is TRUE if either Maybe or Perhaps, or both of them, are TRUE. It's only FALSE if Maybe and Perhaps are both FALSE.

For example, this program segment:

> if (PurchasePrice<=BankBalance) **or** CreditIsGood **then**
> > writeln ('Who should I make the check out to?');   *etc.*

lets a check be written if there's enough money in the bank to cover the purchase (PurchasePrice<=BankBalance) or if the value of the boolean variable CreditIsGood is TRUE. It's all right for both conditions to be TRUE, too.

The last boolean operator, **not**, reverses a boolean condition.

*the **not** operator*

> The **not** operator's result is the opposite of its operand. Thus,
>
> > (**not** Condition)
>
> represents TRUE if Condition is FALSE, and FALSE otherwise.

For example:

> if **not** odd(InputValue) **then begin**
> > write (InputValue);
> > writeln (' can''t be a prime number unless it equals 2.')
>
> **end**

Self-Check Questions

Q. Write each of these English statements as a boolean expression. Naturally, you'll have to make up some variable names as you go along.

> *a)* I have more than enough money.
> *b)* A equals 6, but B equals neither A nor 7.
> *c)* 18 ≤ my last date ≤ 34
> *d)* My age isn't *between* 20 and 30.
> *e)* My IQ is not an odd number.
> *f)* My middle initial is either '7' or 'B', and I have fewer than five pimples.
> *g)* A letter isn't a capital.

A. There are, of course, many ways to express the same conditions:

> *a)* Money > Enough
> *b)* (A = 6) **and** (B <> A) **and** (B <> 7)
> *c)* (MyLastDate >= 18) **and** (MyLastDate <= 34)
> *d)* (Age <= 20) **or** (Age >= 30)
> *e)* **not** odd(IQ)
> *f)* ((Initial = '7') **or** (Initial = 'B')) **and** (Pimples < 5)
> *g)* (Letter < 'A') **or** (Letter > 'Z')

The in Operator

One final word-symbol can be used to state relations. Technically in is a **set** operator (discussed in Chapter 14), but there's a shorthand form that is quite convenient now.

the in operator

> If Value is any ordinal (non-real) value, the expression:
>
> Value **in** [*a set of values*]
>
> is TRUE if it's in the set and is FALSE otherwise. All values in the expression can be either literal values or variables, but they all must have the same Pascal type.

The set of values is just a list, separated by commas. Note that char values must go in quotes, as usual:

defining a set

          [0, 3, 5, 7, 9]   *A set of* integer *values.*
          [´a´, ´e´, ´i´, ´o´, ´u´]   *A set of* char *values.*

When values are *contiguous*, or sequential, they need not all be listed. A pair of dots ' .. ' is used to mean through and including:

contiguous values

          [0 .. 9]   *The* integer *values* 0 *through* 9.
          [´0´ .. ´9´]   *The* char *values* ´0´ *through* ´9´.
          [´a´ .. ´z´, ´A´ .. ´Z´]   *Lower- and upper-case letters* (contiguous in ASCII).

The **in** operator can be used instead of a series of **and**s.

          writeln (´Enter "Y" or "N".´);
          readln (Entry);
          if Entry in [´y´, ´Y´, ´n´, ´N´] then begin
               writeln (´That was a legal entry.´);   *etc.*

Note that to get the opposite of the expression above, the whole thing must go between parentheses:

reversing the expression

          writeln (´Enter anything but "Y" or "N".´);
          readln (Entry);
          if not (Entry in [´y´, ´Y´, ´n´, ´N´]) then begin
               writeln (´That was a legal entry.´);   *etc.*

Self-Check Questions

Q. Could this expression be legal? Why not?

          InputValue **in** [−3 .. 3, ´a´ .. ´c´]

A. It can't be legal, because the members of a set must all have the same Pascal type. The set above fails because it has both integer and char values.

Evaluating boolean Expressions

Assignments to boolean variables are pretty much like any other assignments. However, the constants TRUE and FALSE appear only occasionally. For example, assume that Willy and Nilly are boolean variables. If you look carefully at the assignments below, you'll see that they're identical.

these are the same

```
Willy := Nilly ;        {is the same as...}
Willy := ( Nilly = TRUE );
```

The first assignment has the same effect as the second because Nilly has the same value as Nilly = TRUE.

As you've seen in the examples, I'll generally use parentheses within boolean expressions. As a basic rule, equalities and inequalities must be enclosed in parentheses when **not**, **and**, or **or** appears in an expression. Parentheses *must* be used in these examples because of the operator precedence rules:

parentheses are needed here

```
not (Key='T')
(Voltage=110) and (Amperage<10)
(Limit<5) or (Basis>=10)
(Temperature>80) and Sunny
```

Why is operator precedence an issue? Because all of the boolean operators have higher precedence than the relational operators, so A>B **or** C>D is misinterpreted by the computer as A> (B **or** C) >D, which is meaningless (unless they're all boolean values, in which case the expression is merely indecipherable!).

Parentheses may also be required to circumvent the regular precedence of the boolean operators.

boolean precedence

> The order of precedence in the boolean operator hierarchy is **not**, **and**, and then **or**. **not** has the most precedence, while **or** has the least. Among terms of equal precedence, evaluation goes from left to right.

Suppose we want an action to take place if Maybe and Perhaps are both FALSE. This statement:

```
if not Maybe and not Perhaps then    etc.
```

does the job. These expressions:

```
not Maybe and Perhaps
not Maybe or Perhaps
```

always use parentheses

might sound good in English, but their effect in Pascal is unexpected: only Maybe is being **not**ed. In fact, I'll give the unusual advice that you forget about the relative boolean operator precedences entirely. When **not**, **and**, and the others appear in boolean expressions, it's good programming practice to use parentheses as internal documentation, even if they don't affect the expressions' value. This expression uses the smallest legal number of parentheses— zero:

if not Hot and Humid or Raining then   *etc.*

But this version is self-documenting and unambiguous:

if ((not Hot) and Humid) or Raining then   *etc.*

One final detail is that in Standard Pascal boolean expressions are always *fully evaluated.* This means that the whole expression is evaluated even if the first term or two settles the issue of its truth or falsehood.

full evaluation

Why worry about full evaluation? Because carrying out an operation can sometimes cause a runtime error and program crash, especially when division is involved.

{*Crashes if* Denominator *equals zero.*}
if (Numerator / Denominator) > Fraction then *etc.*

It might seem that the statement below avoids the problem, since it checks Denominator first. But it doesn't, because the expression is fully evaluated regardless:

{*Also crashes if* Denominator *equals zero.*}
if (Denominator <> 0.0)
        and ((Numerator / Denominator) > Fraction) then *etc.*

Sidestepping the crash requires two statements:

avoiding division by zero

{*Avoids the crash by avoiding the division.*}
if (Denominator <> 0.0) then
        if (Numerator / Denominator) > Fraction then *etc.*

The Program Engineering notes contain additional hints on using *identities* and *truth tables* to simplify complicated boolean expressions.

Self-Check Questions ───

Q. Assume that First, Second, Third, and Last are all boolean values. Which of these expressions state the same condition?

    a) not First and not Last
    b) First <> Last
    c) (First or Second) and Third
    d) First = Last
    e) not First or not Last
    f) (Third or First) and (Second or Third)
    g) not (Last or First)
    h) not (Last and First)
    i) (First and not Last) or (Last and not First)
    j) (First and Second) or Third
    k) (First and Last) or (not Last and not First)
    l) (Third and First) or (Second and Third)

A. Note that even when two expressions mean the same thing, one may be a whole lot clearer than the other. The answers are $a = g, b = i, c = l, d = k, e = h, f = j.$

The **case** Statement

Using the **if** statement to choose among a multitude of alternatives can be inconvenient: a lengthy series of **then**s and **else**s can be confusing. Pascal has an alternative statement called **case**. As always, an example:

case demonstration program

```
program Gradient (input, output);
    {Makes an appropriate comment about a user's grade.}

var Score: integer;

begin
    write ('What grade did you get?    ');
    readln (Score);
    case Score of
        0: ; {This empty statement is a null action.}
        10: begin writeln ('You are a True Programming God!');
                writeln ('Prepare to embrace your destiny.')
            end;
        7, 8, 9: writeln ('Good!');
        5, 6: writeln ('Barely Passing!');
        2, 3, 4: writeln ('Flunking!');
        1: begin writeln ('Your grade is in the forbidden zone.');
                writeln ('You had better come to office hours.')
            end
    end {the case statement}
end.   {Gradient}
```

```
What grade did you get?  10
You are a True Programming God!
Prepare to embrace your destiny.
```

The syntax chart of a **case** statement is:

case statement

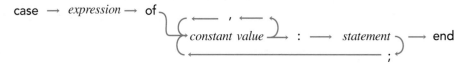

case expressions and labels

The case expression—above, Score—can have any ordinal type, which means that real (and string, if available) are prohibited. The case expression is followed by a list of potential values (the case label list) and the proper sequence of statements to take for each one.

Like Score, the case expression is frequently a variable identifier. But it may be any sort of expression, as long as it, and the case labels, could legally appear in a boolean expression together. After all, the compiler will have to compare the **case** expression to the labels to decide what to do. The label values, in turn, must be actual constant values (like 4 or 'D') or expressions that the compiler can figure out without executing the program. Thus, referring to variables is forbidden.

labels are constant expressions

empty statements

Suppose that a case label isn't supposed to have any action, as when Score equals 0. A lone semicolon shows that nothing should take place. By tradition, this 'nothing' is called an *empty statement*.

grouping actions

If any action takes more than one statement (as the 10 action does), the statements go between the **begin** and **end** of a compound statement. As always, I'll indent to show the grouping of actions, but the compiler respects only the **begin** and **end**.

As long as no constant appears more than once (since a call for two different actions would be illegal) the order labels are specified in doesn't matter.

> In Standard Pascal, it's an error—the program could even crash—if the case expression's actual value doesn't appear in the list of action choices.

If I type 15 or −3 as the input to Gradient, it may blow up. But in practice, most compilers will let the value 'fall through' without harm.

If you'd rather not take the chance, use an **if** statement and the **in** operator to 'guard' the **case** statement:

guarding a **case**
statement

```
if Score in [ 0 .. 10 ] then begin
    case Score of
        ·..
    end  {the case statement}
end  {the if statement}
```

I feel compelled to apologize for the stilted phrasing the **case** statement requires, by the way. A more natural effect could have been achieved with, say:

```
{This is NOT legal Pascal in any system.}
when expression equals
    value1 do action1;
    value2 do action2;   etc.
end
```

The form Wirth used is traditional, but it isn't cast in stone. When you design your own programming languages, you'll get to use any words you want!

Modification Problems

1. Modify Gradient so that it's more in line with current educational theory; i.e. accompany the flunking message with additional lines of output that make your parents' sole responsibility for this clear. (In other words, add at least one additional statement to each action.)

2. Suppose that you wanted one message for grades below 0, individual messages for grades between 1 and 10, and a different message for grades greater than 10. Can you figure out how to modify Gradient to do the job?

Self-Check Questions

Q. Which of these values could appear as a **case** statement label? Assume that Hour is a variable, but that all capitalized identifiers (other than procedure calls) are constants.

a) 7	*b)* Hour	*c)* RATE
d) RATE / 2.0	*e)* '0'	*f)* −3
g) 0+1	*h)* orD('T')	*i)* TRUE
j) 5.0	*k)* 'Initials'	

A. The basic rule is that labels can't require program execution to be evaluated, and that they can't be real. Thus, *b* is out (if Hour is a variable), as are *d* (which must have a real result), *j*, and the string *k*. The others are legal. In particular, note that the boolean constants may appear as labels.

Beyond the Standard: **otherwise**, **and_then**, and More*

Standard Pascal has a minimal definition of both the **case** statement and boolean expressions. We can get them to do whatever we want, but a few more built-in features would be convenient.

The **case** statement is notable for two features that it does *not* have in Standard Pascal, but which are available in most real-world Pascal systems.

two common extensions: contiguous values, alternative actions

— In Standard Pascal, each value of the case expression has to be listed. In Extended Pascal, a contiguous sequence can be shown using two periods:

> {*In Extended Pascal . . .*}
> 5,6 *is the same as* 5 .. 6
> 'a', 'b', 'c' *is the same as* 'a' .. 'c'

— In Standard Pascal, it's an error if the case expression has a value that isn't accounted for by one of the alternatives. In Extended Pascal, an **otherwise** clause works like an **else** part to show alternative actions.

This statement could be replaced with an **if**, but it's hardly likely to be as clear:

categorizing characters

```
{Counting character types, using the extended syntax.}
case Letter of
    'a'..'z':  LowerCase := LowerCase + 1;
    'A'..'Z':  Capital := Capital + 1;
    '0'..'9':  Digit := Digit + 1;
    '.', ',', ';', ':', '?', '!':  Punctuation := Punctuation + 1;
    ' ':  Space := Space + 1;
    otherwise Special := Special + 1
end
```

> Don't forget that using ranges for contiguous values, and the **otherwise** part, are both extensions to Standard Pascal. I've described them because they make good sense. Nevertheless, your system might not allow them.

The Standard Pascal rule that requires us to assume that boolean expressions are going to be fully evaluated is also frequently modified. Recall the problem: an expression like this causes a crash if Denominator equals zero.

---

* This section is optional, of course.

{*Crashes if Denominator equals zero.*}
if (Denominator <> 0.0)
    and ((Numerator / Denominator) > Fraction) **then** *etc.*

There are two different approaches to ending evaluation as soon as the first test fails:

— Explicitly state that evaluation of boolean expressions will stop as soon as the whole expression is known to be TRUE or FALSE.

— Provide new boolean operators that can interrupt evaluation.

The first approach, which doesn't require any language changes, is followed by Turbo Pascal. The second, which adds new operators to the language, is part of the Extended Pascal definition and can be found in (for example) VAX Pascal. The new operators are:

and_then is like **and**, but evaluation continues only if the left-hand operand is TRUE.

or_else is like **or**, but evaluation continues only if the left-hand operand is FALSE.

two Extended Pascal operators

the xor extension

Finally, you may run across an additional boolean operator called **xor**. Recall that **or** is TRUE if either or both of its operands are TRUE. **xor** is TRUE if one and only one operand is TRUE.

Now, all three of these extended operators can be mimicked in Standard Pascal. For instance, A <> B is the same thing as A **xor** B. It's reasonable to ask why some implementations of Pascal add them, while others don't. The answer is that the desire for clarity—wanting the plain English reading of code to indicate what it's going to do—can justify almost any addition to a programming language.

creeping featurism

But at the same time the desire to keep a language small and simple helps keep *creeping featurism*, or the endless addition of conveniences, in check. Not every language designer or implementor will see things the same way, so variations are inevitable.

Standard Practices and Examples

5-2

IN CHAPTER 4 I SUGGESTED THAT YOU view the **for** statement as a means of controlling or generating data, and not simply as a mechanical repeater of actions.

It's useful to look at the **if** and **case** statements in the same light—by considering their effect on values as well as statements. The **if** and **case** statements use a variety of techniques to control data:

— *Selecting* a particular value or kind of value from a flow of data—a dollar sign, say, or numbers that can be divided by 42.

case and if for controlling data

— *Selectively updating* counters or other variables—counting the number of consonants versus vowels or storing the smallest value seen so far.

— *Routing* data to the right part of a program—for instance, making procedure calls and passing along arguments in response to interactive user commands.

— *Error-checking* data—making sure that they fit within certain boundaries and fixing, replacing, or rejecting values that don't.

Keep this alternative view in mind as we see the statements in all their basic forms: using **if** to make yes/no decisions and either/or choices and using **case** to make complicated, multiple-alternative selections.

Problem: Sharing Toys

Our first problem poses a series of yes/no choices.

Ruth and Jim are modern parents who are determined to turn their home into Mr. Rogers' Neighborhood. To teach their Kristin and Heather to share, only toys that can be divided equally (marbles, toy soldiers, and the like) are allowed in the house.

problem: dividing toys

The problem is that Kristin and Heather have friends. Young Aphrodite from around the corner could show up, or Peace, Love, and their obnoxious little brother Happiness from next door, or they all might descend at once. Write a program that Jim and Ruth can use to find out if a particular toy that has many pieces might not be evenly divisible among some combination of kids.

For once I've managed to pose a problem that's going to seem much simpler if I phrase it mathematically! How many combinations of kids are there? There will be either two, three, five, or six. How can we decide if n can be evenly divided two, three, five, or six times? With the **mod** operator. There's no remainder from, say, a two-way division if n **mod** 2 equals zero. We can use the same approach to check out three-, five-, and six-way divisions.

Suppose that we pseudocode the steps of a program:

pseudocoding the program

> *get the number;*
> **if** 2 *evenly divides the number, say so;*
> **if** 3 *evenly divides the number, say so;*
> **if** 5 *evenly divides the number, say so;*
> **if** 6 *evenly divides the number, say so;*

It's important to recognize that these statements are independent. The fact that 2 evenly divides a number doesn't disqualify 3 from working just as well. Similarly, even though any number divisible by 6 can also be divided by 2 and 3, we *still* have to check 2 and 3 separately. Each **if** is considered in turn, regardless of what went before, or what will follow.

The completed program is shown below. As you read it, try to think up some test data that will reveal any shortcomings in MrRogers.

a yes/no example program

```
program MrRogers (input, output);
    {Determines if an input number can be divided by 2, 3, 5, and/or 6.}
var TheNumber: integer;
begin
    write ('How many toy pieces are there, Jim & Ruth?    ');
    readln (TheNumber);
    write ('Socially acceptable combinations are:  ');
    if (TheNumber mod 2) = 0 then begin write (2 :2) end;
    if (TheNumber mod 3) = 0 then begin write (3 :2) end;
    if (TheNumber mod 5) = 0 then begin write (5 :2) end;
    if (TheNumber mod 6) = 0 then begin write (6 :2) end;
    writeln
end.   {MrRogers}
```

```
How many toy pieces are there, Jim & Ruth?  18
Socially acceptable combinations are:  2 3 6
```

Modification Problems

1. Suppose that Jim and Ruth decide to become their children's best friends by including themselves in all games. What additional numbers have to be checked? Modify MrRogers to handle them.

2. The most obvious shortcoming of MrRogers is its lack of meaningful output if a number isn't divisible by any of the trials. Rewrite MrRogers so that it makes a special announcement if a toy is totally unacceptable.

3. MrRogers gets its data externally, from Jim or Ruth. Modify it to generate data internally (the integers 1 through 25 are sufficient) and print a table of its results.

Self-Check Questions

Q. The fact that **if** statements are independent doesn't mean that they can't affect each other. For example, consider the two pairs of **if** statements below. Rewrite each pair as a *single* **if** statement without an **else** part. Simplify the final assignments if you can.

    a) **if** (Time >= 5) **then begin** Time := Time ∗ 4 **end**;
           if (Time >= 20) **then begin** Time := Time **div** 2 **end**;

    b) **if** (Age > 9) **then begin** Age := 7 + (3 ∗ Age) **end**;
           if (Age > 36) **then begin** Age := 5 − (Age **div** 3) **end**;

A. Tricky, huh? A test case or two will show you that if the first statement's condition is met, the second one will also be met. If the first statement is skipped, so is the second.

    a) **if** Time >= 5 **then begin** Time := 2 ∗ Time **end**;
    b) **if** Age > 9 **then begin** Age := 3 − Age **end**;

Problem: Self-Describing Letters

Even if you hate numbers you can still love words. After the next example, you may wish to declare a temporary truce with the digits. The problem is:

> The word 'abode' is interesting because its first two letters, 'ab,' and its last two letters, 'de,' occupy the same position in the word as they do in the alphabet. The word 'cache' is in the same league, because two letters (the third and fifth) are in identical word/alphabetical ordering position.

> Write a program that reads a word and lets you know which letters are *self-describing*—i.e. which ones are in their alphabetical positions. For instance, if the program's input is **cache**, its output should be ✳✳c✳e.

problem: self-describing letters

A good first step in any pseudocode is to think of, then outline, the solution's ultimate *goal*—its central procedure or function call, complete with parameters.

goal pseudocode

> *{What I'd ultimately like to know is . . .}*
> *do they match? (current position, current letter)*

To me, refining this particular problem calls for a function. If we know a letter and its position, they either match—and the function can return TRUE— or they don't, and the function can return the value FALSE. If I had such a function, I could use it in an **if** statement:

expanding the pseudocode

> **if** *they match (current position, current letter)* **then**
>   *make the happy announcement*

Indeed, if I had such an **if** statement, I could use it in a loop that got the letters:

putting the pseudocode in context

> *find out the word's length;*
> *prompt the user for the word;*
> **for** *each letter in the word* **do begin**
>   *read a letter;*
>   **if** *they match (current position, current letter)* **then begin**
>   *make the happy announcement*
>   **end** *{of the* **if***}*
>   *{We have identified a self-describing letter.}*
> **end** *{of the* **for***}*

The mock function call has let us do remarkably well! As is usually the case, starting with a clear statement of our goal pointed the way to a program.

use boolean functions

> boolean functions expand our informal programming vocabulary. By making the flow of a program plain, they let Pascal retain some of the clarity of pseudocode. Use mock function calls as a design tool in pseudocoding, and program with them whenever complex boolean conditions have to be stated.

How can we implement the function? Well, it returns the result of a comparison that's either TRUE or FALSE:

TheyMatch := (*the current position in the word*) =
(*the relative position of the letter in the alphabet*)

function pseudocode

Try to figure out how it's done before you read program Describe, below.

letter-position checker

```
program Describe (input, output);
    {Finds out how long a word is. Then, reads the word and reports on
     any letters whose alphabetical value equals their position in the word.}
var Length,                    {of the word that's being checked}
    Position: integer;         {in the word as we read it}
    Current: char;
    function TheyMatch (Place: integer;
                        Letter: char) : boolean;
    {TRUE if Letter is in alphabetical position Place.}
    var PositionInAlphabet: integer;
    begin
        PositionInAlphabet := 1 + ( ord (Letter) − ord ('a') );
        TheyMatch := PositionInAlphabet = Place
    end;  {TheyMatch}
begin
    write ('How many letters are in your word?    ');
    read (Length);
    {We know how much input data there will be.}
    readln;
    {We've gotten rid of extra characters (like the carriage return).}
    write ('Ok, type in the word.    ');
    for Position := 1 to Length do begin
        read (Current);
        if  TheyMatch (Position, Current)
            then begin write (Current) end
            else begin write ('*') end    {if}
        {We've indicated if the letter described its alphabetical position.}
    end;  {for}
    writeln
end.  {Describe}
```

```
How many letters are in your word?  10
Ok, type in the word.  leadership
***de**hi*
```

Modification Problems

1. Give Describe the ability to check more than one word. Test cases you might want to try include **predefinition**, **academician**, and **archetypical**.

2. Turn Describe into program NonDescriptive—a program that finds input *digits* that *aren't* in the positions they describe. Thus, the input **132476** would produce as output *32*7*.

Problem: The Numbers Game

In their endless attempt to separate the citizenry from their cash, many states have legalized some forms of gambling in recent years. Lotteries have proven to be immensely popular. They're typically based on a traditional game known simply as 'the numbers.'

how the numbers racket works

In the basic, illegal numbers game, every player picks a number of one to three digits. The winning number is decided by chance. Typically, it will be a figure that *a*) is easily available every day, and *b*) can't be rigged by the contest promoter. The last three digits of the total amount of money bet that day at a local racetrack usually fit the bill. Bets of any amount (even as small as a dime or quarter) are accepted, and the payoff is typically 600 to 1—well below the 999 to 1 odds against winning.

The legal state version suffers from several handicaps. First, it pays less—as little as 500 to 1. Second, there is usually a minimum $1 bet. Finally, it's less convenient, since few states are willing to employ numbers runners to prowl the streets collecting bets! To make up for these shortcomings, state numbers games allow more complicated bets and payoffs. For example, here's California's numbers game, Daily 3:

Playstyle	Description of Win	If your # is	Winning Number is	Payout	Odds
Straight	Match exact order	529	529	$500	1 in 1,000
Box	Match any order (3 different numbers)	529	529,592,952, 925,259,295	$80	1 in 167
	Match any order (1 Duplicate number)	599	599,959,995	$160	1 in 333
Straight /Box $1 Split Between Both Playstyles	Straight (exact order) or Box (any order) (3 different numbers)	529	529 or 592,952,925 259,295	$290 or $40	1 in 1,000 or 1 in 167
	Straight (exact order) or Box (any order) (1 Duplicate number)	599	599 or 959,995	$330 or $80	1 in 1,000 or 1 in 333

Naturally, we're going to write a program that recognizes a winning number. I'll attack the simple style of betting (either straight or box) and leave the combination bet (straight/box) for you. A first pseudocode outline is:

first pseudocode

> *get the bet number;*
> *get the winning number;*
> **if** *the bet is a winner*
>   **then** *announce the payoff*
>   **else** *offer condolences*

If only matches, described as the *straight* play style, above, were allowed, spotting a winning number would be easy:

{Reading the values as integers.}
read (BetNumber);
readln (WinningNumber);
if BetNumber = WinningNumber **then begin**   *etc.*

But the requirement that we match digits in any order makes it easier to think about them individually. We could use **div** and **mod** to get each digit, or just read both numbers as separate characters. That lets us make comparisons like:

{Are the numbers identical?}
(Bet1 = Win1) **and** (Bet2 = Win2) **and** (Bet3 = Win3)

{Are any digits the same?}
(Bet1 = Bet2) **or** (Bet2 = Bet3) **or** (Bet1 = Bet3)

{Are the digits the same, but in different order?}
((Bet1 = Win1) **and** (Bet2 = Win3) **and** (Bet3 = Win2)) **or**
   ((Bet1 = Win2) **and** (Bet2 = Win1) **and** (Bet3 = Win3)) **or**
   ⋱
      ((Bet1 = Win3) **and** (Bet2 = Win2) **and** (Bet3 = Win1))

comparing the bet to the winner

Let's turn to the pseudocode again. First, we'll get our terminology straight:

— A *straight* is a digit-for-digit match between the bet and the winner.

— A *box* is an out-of-order match, with all three digits different.

— A *duplicate box* is an out-of-order match of numbers that have duplicated digits.

This time I'll try to track all three different alternatives: a straight match, an out-of-order match, and a duplicate number out-of-order match.

second pseudocode

get the bet number;
get the winning number;
if *they're the same*
   then *announce a match*
      else if *there's an out-of-order match*
         then if *all three digits are different*
            then *announce a box*
            else *announce a duplicate box*

How would you fit a 'Sorry, you lose!' message in this pseudocode?

Clear formatting is crucial in this program. Although syntax determines semantics—spacing and indentation are for the benefit of human program readers, not the computer—it's the programmer's duty to make her code readable. Format statements in a way that makes the alternative nature of the actions easy to see.

A corollary requirement arises when you test the final program. Your test data, if they're any good, will be required to test every possible control path. You're trying to find out two separate things:

developing test data   — Does the code produce the correct output for a given input?

— Does the code contain alternatives that don't make sense because they can't be reached?

As in the previous example, the final code is much easier to follow if we rely on boolean functions to make the tests. Although the program is longer, it's easier to write and test. I wrote three functions to help out:

Identical (A1, A2, A3, B1, B2, B3) *is* TRUE *if the two triples are identical.*

more boolean functions   AllPairs (A1, A2, A3, B1, B2, B3) *is* TRUE *if the first triple matches the*
second triple in any non-identical order.

AllUnique (A1, A2, A3) *is* TRUE *if the three values are all different.*

The final Daily program, below, includes code that calculates winnings as well.

```
program Daily (input, output);
    {Decides if a number will win a California lottery game.}

var Bet1, Bet2, Bet3,            {The digits you bet.}
    Win1, Win2, Win3:  char;     {The digits that won.}
    BetAmount:  real;

procedure ReadDigits (var Ch1, Ch2, Ch3:  char);
    {Reads three digit characters.}
    begin
        read (Ch1);
        read (Ch2);
        read (Ch3);
        readln;
    end;  {ReadDigits}

function Identical (A1, A2, A3, B1, B2, B3:  char) : boolean;
    {TRUE if the first three characters match the last three identically.}
    begin
        Identical := (A1 = B1) and (A2 = B2) and (A3 = B3)
    end;  {Identical}

function AllPairs (A1, A2, A3, B1, B2, B3:  char) : boolean;
    {TRUE if the first three characters match the last three in non-identical order.}
    begin
        AllPairs := ((A1 = B1) and (A2 = B3) and (A3 = B2)) or
                    ((A1 = B2) and (A2 = B1) and (A3 = B3)) or
                    ((A1 = B2) and (A2 = B3) and (A3 = B1)) or
                    ((A1 = B3) and (A2 = B1) and (A3 = B2)) or
                    ((A1 = B3) and (A2 = B2) and (A3 = B1))
    end;  {AllPairs}

function AllUnique (A1, A2, A3:  char) : boolean;
    {TRUE if all three characters are different.}
    begin
        AllUnique := (A1 <> A2) and (A1 <> A3) and (A2 <> A3)
    end;  {AllUnique}
```

numbers game program (margin note beside var/procedure block)

```
begin
    write ('How much did you bet?    ');
    readln (BetAmount);
    write ('Please enter the three digits you bet:    ');
    ReadDigits (Bet1, Bet2, Bet3);
    write ('Please enter the three winning digits:    ');
    ReadDigits (Win1, Win2, Win3);
    if Identical (Bet1, Bet2, Bet3, Win1, Win2, Win3) then begin
            write ('Congratulations on your match!  You win $');
            writeln (BetAmount * 500.0 : 1 : 2)
        end else begin        {no straight, but maybe a box}
            if AllPairs (Bet1, Bet2, Bet3, Win1, Win2, Win3) then begin
                    if AllUnique (Bet1, Bet2, Bet3) then begin
                            write ('Congratulations on your box!  You win $');
                            writeln (BetAmount * 80.0 : 1 : 2)
                        end else begin        {box with duplicates}
                            write ('Congrats on your duplicate box!  You win $');
                            writeln (BetAmount * 160.0 : 1 : 2)
                        end    {box with duplicates}
                    end    {all unique}
                else begin        {Identical and AllPairs were both FALSE.}
                    writeln ('You lose! ');
                end    {there was a box}
        end    {maybe a box}
end.    {Daily}
```

How much did you bet? **10.00**
Please enter the three digits you bet: **417**
Please enter the three winning digits: **741**
Congratulations on your box. You win $800.00

Modification Problems

1. Alter Daily so that it works with numbers rather than digit characters. While you're at it, be sure to make certain the user enters three-digit numbers.

2. Every Pascal system will have a function that generates random numbers. Use yours to test Daily. How much poorer are you after 10,000 $1 bets?

3. Extend Daily so that it permits and checks winnings for the second form of bet. Note that the odds are the same; the wager is treated as though 50¢ went to a straight bet and 50¢ went to a box bet.

Self-Check Questions

Q. Rewrite this pair of **if** statements as an **if** statement with an **else** part.

```
if (Time < 37) then begin Time := Time div 4 end;
if (Time > 36) then begin Time := 3 * Time end;
```

A. Here, a careful inspection reveals that if the first statement is entered, the second will be skipped. The rewritten pair is:

```
if (Time < 37)
    then begin Time := Time div 4 end
    else begin Time := 3 * Time end
```

Problem: Making Change with Style

Choices are so fundamental in programming that they are liable to show up in every possible permutation of nesting and sequence. Let's work a final problem that requires all three of the decisions—yes/no, either/or, and straight alternatives—we've been investigating. I'm sure you've seen the sort of receipt that brings this problem to mind.

```
ALBANY AM/PM        5222955
ALBANY, CA.         02035
CHIPS       .   .   .   .   .   .   $    0.75
#  5    12.710GAL UNL  @$ 1.259  $   16.00
             SUBTOTAL           $   16.75
             TAX ON $   0.75    $    0.06
             AMOUNT DUE          $   16.81
             REC'D $  20.00 CHNGE $    3.19
CASH RECEIPT                           T1
TRANS #  00554       10-15-92 09:11PM
    THANK YOU ,HAVE A NICE DAY
```

problem: making change

Write a change-making program. It should accept as input a price and amount of money tendered, then print the minimum number and type of coins required for change.

Who hasn't made change? First, you count out the dollars, then the half-dollars, and so on through the pennies. Aside from the detail of correctly ordering the coins, the change-making algorithm of program Coins isn't going to be a great advance in either computer science or mathematics. Nevertheless, a pseudocode outline makes it clear that **if** and **case** statements will be employed extensively and that no simple rule can govern their appearance:

pseudocode

> *find out the price and amount tendered;*
> *decide if there's enough money;*
> **if** *there's no change*
>   **then** *say thanks*
>   **else**
>   **if** *there are dollars in the change, return them;*
>   **if** *there are half-dollars in the change, return them;*
>   ⋱
>   **if** *there are pennies in the change, return them;*

where *return them* implies a procedure call that contains a sequence like:

print the number of coins;
case Coin **of**
    dollar: *print the word 'dollar'*
    half dollar: *print the words 'fifty-cent piece'*
    ⋰
    penny: *print the word 'cent'*
end;
deal with the possibility of a plural;

a coding detail

Let's move on to the question of style. In *The Psychology of Computer Programming*, Gerald Weinberg warns that reading programs is a dying art. 'Just as television has turned the heads of the young from the old-fashioned joys of book reading,' he says, 'so have terminals and generally improved turnaround made the reading of programs the mark of a hopelessly old-fashioned programmer.'*

Unfortunately, writing programs, like writing literature, can sometimes be learned only by reading. A list of prescriptions for 'literate' programs I could set down might impress me and your teacher, but it's not nearly as helpful as a good clear piece of code.

Why does a program need to be written with style? Because programming is hard. Doing an arithmetic calculation for change is easy, but that's not our problem. Instead, we face the challenge of imitating the fine steps a human change-maker takes almost automatically. A real-life clerk would inform the customer if she were shortchanged, and so should our program. A person doesn't think about pluralizing words, but we have to teach the computer to say the names of coins and to add an 's' when it's needed for a plural. A human wouldn't bother announcing the coins that she *wasn't* returning as change, and neither should Coins.

How can style be incorporated into a program? Coins should also be as well-written as possible, following the program engineering guidelines that apply to every program:

— Its output should be clear.

— It should be *robust*—able to deal with unexpected situations, like being shortchanged.

— It should be self-documenting where possible, but comments should be added to clarify less-than-obvious features.

engineering program Coins

— It should take advantage of procedures to minimize the length and complexity of its code.

— Indenting should be regular enough to help the eye automatically bracket the extent of nested statements.

It must also use statements—even the humble **if** statement—correctly. As you read the code of the following program, Coins, try to identify the different **if** applications, as well as their relation to each other.

---

* Gerald Weinberg, *The Psychology of Computer Programming*, Van Nostrand Reinhold 1971, p. 6.

For example, does the order of statements, or parts of statements, ever matter? The **if** statements in the main program of Coins are basically independent of each other. Since the statements are not nested, each statement's boolean expression is evaluated regardless of the previous statement's effect. Nevertheless, the statements must be correctly ordered, so that larger coins will be removed before smaller ones.

In contrast, the decisions in procedure GetChange rely on a **case** statement. Since the tests are alternatives, and only one can be passed, their order doesn't really matter in this application. Once one of the conditions is met, the remaining tests will be skipped.

Try to subject Coins to a critical reading. What could you have done differently, and better? Is its division into procedures and functions clear, or would you have drawn the lines elsewhere? Are its names self-explanatory? Does it make good use of constants? Do its comments help you make the changes suggested in the Modification Problems?

Appraise the program. What are its shortcomings? Does it always work? Is it robust? Does it check for, and recover from, errors as well as it might? Could its output or interaction with the user be more attractive?

> Reading another person's program can be a difficult job. However, it can give you an insight into programming that can't be taught in class.

Learn to criticize your own programs by practicing on mine.

change-making program

```
program Coins (input, output);
    {Computes minimum coinage for making change.}
const DOLLAR = 100;
      HALF = 50;
      QUARTER = 25;
      DIME = 10;
      NICKEL = 5;
      PENNY = 1;
var Price, Given: real;  {Input real dollar amounts…}
    Change: integer;  {…but use integer pennies internally.}
    ChangeIsDue: boolean;
function ConvertToPennies (Price, Given: real) : integer;
    {Returns Price–Given expressed as a whole number of pennies.}
    begin
        ConvertToPennies := round (100.0 * ( Price – Given) )
    end;  {ConvertToPennies}
```

(*program continues*)

```
procedure GetChange (Coin: integer; var Change: integer);
    {Prints number of coins. Reduces Change by that many Coins.}
    var Pieces: integer;
    begin
        Pieces := Change div Coin;
        Change := Change − (Pieces ∗ Coin);
        {We know how many coins to give, and what's still left over.}
        write (Pieces : 1);
        case Coin of   {Picks the proper action.}
            DOLLAR: write (´ dollar´);
            HALF: write (´ fifty-cent piece´);
            QUARTER: write (´ quarter´);
            DIME: write (´ dime´);
            NICKEL: write (´ nickel´);
            PENNY: write (´ cent´)
        end;  {case}
        if Pieces>1 then begin              {Takes care of multiple coins.}
            write (´s´)
        end;  {if}
        writeln
    end;  {GetChange}
begin  {Coins}
    write (´What´´s the price?    ´);
    readln (Price);
    write (´How much did you get?    ´);
    readln (Given);
    {We may, or may not, be given more than is actually due.}
    ChangeIsDue := (Price > Given);
    Change := abs (ConvertToPennies (Price, Given) );
    {Potential change is dealt with as integer pennies.}
    if Change = 0
        then begin writeln (´Thanks!´) end
        else begin
            if ChangeIsDue
                then begin write (´Too little!  You´´re short by  ´) end
                else begin write (´Your change is exactly  ´)
            end; {ChangeIsDue if}
            if Change>=100 then begin GetChange (DOLLAR,Change) end;
            {Remaining Change is less than one DOLLAR. The calls below are similar.}
            if Change>=50 then begin GetChange (HALF,Change) end;
            if Change>=25 then begin GetChange (QUARTER,Change) end;
            if Change>=10 then begin GetChange (DIME,Change) end;
            if Change>=5 then begin GetChange (NICKEL,Change) end;
            if Change>=1 then begin GetChange (PENNY,Change) end
        end  {Change=0 else part}
end.  {Coins}
```

(*output follows*)

```
What's the price?  11.98
How much did you get?  3.79
Too little!  You're short by 8 dollars
1 dime
1 nickel
4 cents
```

Modification Problems

1. Modify Coins to make change in Italian lire. The basic banknote is the 1,000 lire bill, while coin denominations are 50, 100, 200, and 500 lire. What will you do about missing small change? Note: the singular of *lire* is *lira*.

2. Write a procedure MakeChange that contains all of the GetChange calls in Coins. Will the program require other changes in support of this modification?

5-3 Program Engineering: Over-Engineering Software

THINK ABOUT A PROGRAM THAT FINDS SQUARE roots. Under normal circumstances, it should do just three things—get a value, call sqrt, and print a result. Strictly speaking, the program's job is to do something *to* its data.

However, we can rely on the **if** statement to gain knowledge about program data, even when this isn't an explicitly stated part of the job of turning raw data into information and results. We have to do this before we can calculate a square root; we have to be sure that the program user gave us a positive number. Taking this step makes the program more *robust*—less likely to crash or, worse yet, produce incorrect results.

> Second-guessing the quality of program data is one of the key arts of program engineering. It's not that incorrect or improper data are hard to find. It is easy enough to spot negative numbers or non-alphabetic input characters. Rather, it is hard to remember to be suspicious.

Gerald Weinberg tells a droll story about the importance of suspicion. He was writing an inventory program on an old-fashioned system that could read only alphabetics and numerics—letters and digits.

> When questioning the client in our very first meeting, I asked, 'Are there any special characters?'
>
> 'No,' he replied, 'none whatsoever.'
>
> 'Good,' I said, 'but I have to be sure. Are you certain that there are no special characters?'
>
> 'I'm quite certain. I know the data very well, and there are no special characters.'
>
> On that assurance we went ahead with designing and programming the application, only to discover on our first production run that the system was hanging up on cards like this: THREADED BOLT-1/2" #7

About sixty-five percent of the cards contained special characters, but when I confronted the client with this figure, he appeared genuinely puzzled. 'But there are no special characters,' he pleaded.

'Oh, no,' I said triumphantly, 'then what about this dash, slash, quote, and number sign?'

'Those? What's so special about those? They're in almost all the cards!'*

As we've seen before, bugs tend to enter at precisely the moment we start to believe that what we intended to do is what we've actually done. But the fact that a program is utterly dependent on its data doesn't mean that a programmer has to give up all control as well. She always has the opportunity to inspect data as they arrive and to decide on an appropriate course of action—including halting the program.

What can you do once you find flawed data? Here are three possibilities:

responses to flawed data

1. Note the error and proceed, possibly to an alternative process.

2. Fix the faulty data, or give the program user a chance to reenter them.

3. Announce the problem and quit.

We might use the first alternative in a square-root program, which requires positive input. In pseudocode, what we would do is:

1: take an alternative
path

if *the number isn't negative*
   then *calculate its square root*
   else *tell the user the facts of life as they relate to square roots*

However, we could also follow the second alternative, perhaps like this:

2: fix the problem

if *the number is negative* **then**
      writeln ('Negative input value. Error? Making it positive . . .');
      Number := abs(Number);
   calculate the square root;

In Chapter 6 we'll see how conditional loops can give the user a second chance to enter input.

The third option is to quit. Now, this is sometimes difficult do in Standard Pascal, because it implies that we'll need another layer of nested **if** statements each time we choose not to drop out:

nesting can be unwieldy

if *we fail the first error check*
   then *print an error message*
   else begin
         start doing stuff;
         if *we fail the second error check*
            then *print an error message*
            else begin
                  start doing stuff;
                  if *we fail the third error check   etc.*

---

* Gerald Weinberg, *Rethinking Systems Analysis and Design,* Little, Brown and Company, 1982, p. 67.

Or, we must set a boolean *flag* variable—an ordinary variable that's used to remember a condition—and check it before doing anything:

> if *we fail an error check* then NoErrors := FALSE;
> if NoErrors then *do some stuff*;
> if *we fail another error check* then NoErrors := FALSE;
> if NoErrors then *do some more stuff*;   *etc.*

As a practical matter, both alternatives can lead to complicated code.

HALT is nonstandard

> Extended Pascal, like most real-world Pascal systems, provides a HALT procedure. This nonstandard extension immediately stops program execution.

It's used like this:

3: terminate program execution

> if *the number isn't negative*
>   then *calculate the square root*
>   else begin
>   writeln ('Negative input. Halting program. ');
>   HALT   {*This is Extended Pascal, not Standard Pascal.*}
>   end

If it's available, HALT is invoked only in exceptional circumstances, when it becomes impossible for a program to continue correctly. Since the program stops immediately, it's usually a good idea to precede the HALT with a brief explanation of why the program is stopping.

Sanity Checking

Is crash-avoidance the only reason to stop a program? No. Input that wouldn't cause a moment of anguish for a running program can still bring great distress to the program's creator or user. It's the programmer's job to make sure that input makes sense. This is called *sanity checking*—asking if the input is plausible.

For example, here are some values that could be sanity checked. In each case, input errors probably won't cause a program crash. Instead, they'll lead to a correct calculation based on preposterous 'facts' or output that is so overwhelmingly voluminous that it's useless.

— A program calculates property taxes. What are reasonable bounds on property values?

when to sanity check

— A program calculates grade point averages. How many courses might one student plausibly have taken?

— A program prepares a table of mortgage payments. What are reasonable bounds on the length or size of the mortgage, or on interest rates?

> Don't forget that the computer has no mind to lose! Sanity checking is for the user's benefit—not the machine's.

Deciding if an input value is reasonable isn't always an easy task. One way to make the job less burdensome is to ask the program user for help.

asking for confirmation

```
write ('Course load of ');
write (Units : 1)
writeln (' units per term seems a mite high.');
writeln ('Would you like a chance to correct your entry?');
```

```
Course load of 297 units per term seems a mite high.
Would you like a chance to correct your entry?
```

I'll be talking about using looping statements under similar circumstances in the next chapter.

Boundary, Impossible, and Unavoidable-Condition Bugs

Let's turn to some of the specific bugs that accompany the **if** statement. In general, problems tend to arise when conditions that are easily stated in English must be translated into the much less forgiving world of boolean expressions.

Three kinds of errors are easy enough to check, even though they're not so easy to avoid entirely. A *boundary error*, in a boolean expression, is a bug that hinges right on the turning point between TRUE and FALSE. The expression is usually right, except for the close calls. An *impossible condition*, as the name implies, is an expression that can't be TRUE. An *unavoidable condition*, in contrast, can't be FALSE.

Although their effects can be very different, the causes of these bugs can usually be traced to a single misplaced or misused symbol. Problems may be entirely accidental—a < slips in in place of a >—or they may reflect a flawed understanding of the difference between **and** and **or**. In any case, the moral for debugging is:

> Make a go/no-go test of each **if** statement. Be sure that the condition can be met, as well as failed. Take particular care to check the turning-point cases.

For example, consider the statements below.

impossible vs.
unavoidable conditions

```
if (Age < 18) and (Age > 34) then . . .
    {Impossible condition—how can Age meet both criteria?}
if (Age > 18) or (Age < 34) then . . .
    {Unavoidable condition—Age can't help meeting one criterion.}
```

In each case, the boolean operator is used incorrectly.

Boundary condition problems are usually due to a lack of care in choosing between < and <=, or > and >=. Very often, such problems appear when a statement is rewritten in order to reverse a condition. For example, this statement correctly specifies the range 18 through 34, including the ends:

```
if (Age >= 18) and (Age <= 34) then . . .
```

This rewritten version, in contrast, introduces a problem:

if (Age < 18) **or** (Age >= 34) **then** . . .
    {*Boundary condition bug—34 is unintentionally excluded.*}

As with the other problems, a little bench testing goes a long way. Here, the boundaries are the critical values around the test of Age—probably 17, 18, and 19, and 33, 34, and 35.

remember to initialize variables

Sooner or later you will probably become convinced that your system's **if** statement is broken. When that happens, use debugging writelns to check the values in boolean expressions *before* you evaluate them.

{*boolean expressions can be printed.*}
writeln (1 = 5);

FALSE

It often turns out, in programming as in life, that one of the things you're absolutely positively sure of is wrong. Frequently, the statement is failing because a variable wasn't properly initialized.

Unsafe Modifications and the Flow of Control

If you spend much time around computer programmers, you're sure to see a *flow chart* sooner or later. Flow charts were once the main tool of program design. They tried to show on paper the flow of control from statement to statement within a program. Here, different kinds of boxes represent different statements and decisions:

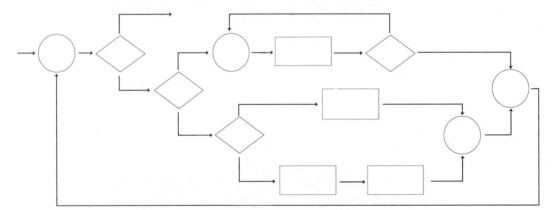

Flow charts have fallen out of favor because they are overly simplistic. A flow chart can trace an accurate path through a program, but it sometimes obscures the way in which statements depend on each other. After all, every statement has the potential of altering the environment shared by *all* statements: an assignment in line 3 might be directly tied to a choice made in line 400. Unfortunately, a flow chart that tried to show all such relationships would be impossible to decipher.

Statements depend on one another, sometimes in subtle ways. That's natural. Problems develop when you modify code: bugs appear as the result of a forgotten interaction. For example, here's a relatively obvious example. It derives from the mistaken assumption that two if statements with opposite conditions are always the same as one if with an **else** part. In other words, even though this segment:

```
if Count < 0 then Rearrange (Count);
if Count >= 0 then Modify (Count);
```

appearances can be deceiving

appears to be identical to this one on paper, they may be different in practice:

```
if Count < 0
    then Rearrange (Count)
    else Modify (Count);
```

What's the difference? The bug results from focusing on the boolean conditions, while forgetting about what the program does. Suppose that Rearrange modifies Count's value, making it greater than zero. In the first pair of statements, Rearrange is sometimes called, but Modify is *always* called. In the second statement, only one procedure is called—never both—no matter what Rearrange does to its argument.

local changes can have non-local effects

Thus, changes won't always limit themselves to the local effects you had in mind. Instead, every programmer has the experience of making a change, having the modified code work successfully—and then discovering that she has broken her program somewhere else!

It's no surprise (at least not for me) to find that a new program feature doesn't work. That's part of programming. What is unexpected, though, is to find that the price of making one feature work is that an unrelated—and untouched—program segment no longer operates. Here are a few of the questions you should learn to ask before you poke and pry:

— Do boolean expressions farther on down the line rely on this variable's value?

— Will removing a control path (e.g. removing a seemingly unnecessary **else** part) leave a needed variable uninitialized?

— Will making a change here cause your program to enter a previously unexplored control path later?

> Think of the Gauguin painting *Where do we come from? What are we? Where are we going?* These are the questions to ask when debugging or modification involves boolean expressions.

Two Annoying Semicolon Bugs

Misplaced semicolons cause two common if statement bugs. The first is hard to find because it is legal Pascal code:

semicolon after **then** bug

```
{This segment includes an empty statement.}
if Novice then ;
    GiveInstructions;
PlayTheGame;
```

Because of the semicolon at the end of the first line of code, the **if** statement controls a perfectly legal empty statement. If Novice is TRUE, the empty statement 'executes,' otherwise it is skipped. The bug's symptom is that instructions are given every single time.

An extra semicolon between the **then** and **else** parts of an **if** statement also leads to an error, but the compiler will catch it. Unfortunately, the compiler won't always recognize the exact cause, so it pays to understand the root of the problem.

semicolon before **else** bug

```
{This statement includes an extra semicolon.}
if NewHighScore
    then RecordUserInitials;
    else AskForMoreMoney;
```

Recall that the semicolon is technically a statement separator. Here's how the compiler reads the code above:

```
if NewHighScore
    then RecordUserInitials;
{At this point, the entire if statement is finished.}
else
AskForMoreMoney
```

From the compiler's point of view, the **if** statement is ancient history. The **else** appears to be a misplaced reserved word.

> The rule is simple: if you want your code to work, never put a semicolon after a **then** or before an **else**.

Simplifying boolean Evaluation

Sometimes boolean operator precedence makes an expression long enough to be unwieldy or confusing. The expression can usually be rewritten by following the *distributive* laws, as shown below. Assume that p, q, and r are boolean-valued expressions or variables:

distributive laws

$$(p \text{ or } r) \text{ and } (q \text{ or } r) = (p \text{ and } q) \text{ or } r$$
$$(p \text{ and } r) \text{ or } (q \text{ and } r) = (p \text{ or } q) \text{ and } r$$

De Morgan's laws

A similar set of relations is known as *De Morgan's* laws:

$$(\text{not } p) \text{ and } (\text{not } q) = \text{not } (p \text{ or } q)$$
$$(\text{not } p) \text{ or } (\text{not } q) = \text{not } (p \text{ and } q)$$

The effect of the boolean operators can also be summarized in this *truth table*:

not TRUE *is* FALSE
not FALSE *is* TRUE

truth tables

TRUE **and** TRUE *is* TRUE	TRUE **or** TRUE *is* TRUE
TRUE **and** FALSE *is* FALSE	TRUE **or** FALSE *is* TRUE
FALSE **and** TRUE *is* FALSE	FALSE **or** TRUE *is* TRUE
FALSE **and** FALSE *is* FALSE	FALSE **or** FALSE *is* FALSE

Syntax Summary

❏   **if** statement: examines program data to decide what to do. Two basic forms are encountered: a *yes/no* choice:

> **if** *a condition is met* **then begin** *statements* **end**;

and an *either/or* choice:

> **if** *a condition is met*
>   **then begin** *statements* **end**
>   **else begin** *alternative statements* **end**

There should never be a semicolon before the **else** part.

❏   **case** statement: makes a choice between two or more alternatives, based on the value of a *case expression*. The case expression cannot be either real or string, while the *case labels* that govern the choice can't be variables. The compiler must be able to figure out their values without actually running the program.

```
case Expression of
    CONST1: action;
    CONST2, CONST4: action;        {a list of labels}
    CONST3, CONST5, CONST6: action        {a list of labels}
end
```

❏   **empty statement**: a non-action indicated by a semicolon. For example: **then** ; shows an **if** statement controlling an empty statement. Empty statements are properly used to indicate non-actions for specific **case** labels and are probably being used in error otherwise.

❏   **relational operators**: compare two values of the same simple type:

Math	Pascal	English
=	=	*equal to*
<	<	*less than*
≤	<=	*less than or equal to*
>	>	*greater than*
≥	>=	*greater than or equal to*
≠	<>	*not equal to*
∈	in	*set membership*

❏   boolean operators: build expressions from boolean-valued operands.

not A	*the opposite of its operand*
A and B	TRUE *if, and only if, both operands are* TRUE
A or B	TRUE *if either operand is* TRUE

❏   in operator: tests for set membership. Both operands (Value and the values in the list) must have ordinal types that can be legally compared.

Value in [*a list of values*]

Two dots '. .' can be used to indicate a range of contiguous values.

❏   operator precedence: relations—equalities and inequalities—have the lowest precedence, so as a rule relations are put in parentheses in boolean expressions. The exact precedence levels are:

not	*most precedence*
and	
or	
<, >, <=, >=, =, <> in	*least precedence*

❏   The constants of type boolean are FALSE, TRUE, in that order.

❏   An **else** part of an **if** statement always belongs to the nearest prior **then** it can be legally tied to. If the nearest **then** part is 'hidden' within a compound statement, it can't have an **else** part.

❏   To write portable Standard Pascal programs, treat boolean expressions as though they are always fully evaluated. If it's important for evaluation to stop, split the expression between two nested **if** statements.

❏   Go/no-go testing is the best way to check boolean expressions. Beware of impossible conditions (that can't be met) and unavoidable conditions (which always are).

❏   An **if** statement's actions affect the overall program state. When you modify program code, be aware of changes that are being made in the overall flow of control.

❏   Robustness—for now, the ability to withstand errors that can be anticipated—is a desirable program quality. **if** statements should be used, when possible, to do sanity checking on the reasonableness of program values.

❏   When possible, programs should detect and try to do something about flawed data. Always inform the user, fix the data when possible, and stop program execution when necessary.

❏   Programs are meant to be read, as well as run. Use indenting and layout that clearly displays the grouping of statements. Using boolean functions to replace complicated expressions is another way to make code more readable.

❏   De Morgan's laws and the distributive laws can, and should, be used to simplify complicated boolean expressions.

The Big Ideas in this chapter are:

1. *Decisions are made by comparing values.* No matter how complicated a choice may be, it generally starts with a comparison of two letters or numbers. The basic comparisons are made with relations; the boolean operators are needed to let decisions be more complex.

2. *Making a decision implies that part of a program might be skipped.* Normally, data pass from statement to statement. The **if** and **case** statements let program actions be skipped; the flow of program data can be diverted.

3. *Computers may be built from silicon and steel, but programs are made of egg-shells.* When software works, it seems to be invulnerable, but the tiniest crack can lead to total collapse. Robust programs can have a margin of safety for error, but you have to put it there.

5-1   The first point of attack on Chapter 5 is the boolean expression. Make up a few questions that ask you to:

a)   *Evaluate this relation*, sticking to the relational operators.

b)   *Evaluate this expression*, using the boolean operators.

5-2   *Write this condition as a* boolean *expression* comes next. For example, 'I've studied for at least three hours' might be Studied >= 3. Make up a half-dozen phrases of this sort.

5-3   boolean expressions can always be written in a variety of ways. For example, it was easy for me to turn this expression:

> First <> Last   {*Assume that* First *and* Last *have boolean values.*}

into this one, which has exactly the same value:

> (First **and not** LAST) **or** (Last **and not** First)

Write, and then rewrite in a more complicated manner, a half-dozen boolean expressions. Then mix them up, and ask the question *Which pairs of expressions are the same?*

5-4   Look at the warmup exercises and you'll see that it's easy to invent boolean functions like Positive, IsADigit, and so on. Make up five *Write a* boolean *function that . . .* questions.

5-5   *'Rewrite a* this *as a* that' is the classic form of attack on a programming statement. For example, I might ask you to rewrite this:

```
if (A >= 3) and (B < 6)
    then begin write ('Hello!') end
    else begin write ('Goodbye!') end
end
```

as two separate **if** statements. Make up three questions of this type—going from a single statement to a sequence of statements.

5-6   Now, try the same problem in reverse. See if you can come up with a short sequence of **if** statements that can be replaced by a **case** statement. You'll find that this isn't quite as easy as it seems.

5-7   The **for/if** and **for/case** combinations are frequently used to acquire knowledge about a stream of data that originates outside a program. Suppose that you can rely on an input sequence of fifty char values. Make up three questions that have you inspect them:

a)   as independent values; for instance, how many A's were there?

b)   as paired values; for instance, how may A's are followed by B?

c)   as sequences of values; for instance, how many words ended with ED?

5-8   As above, but look at a stream of integers. What is the second largest value? How about the smallest difference between successive values? How about the average of the positive and negative numbers? Three more questions, please.

5-9   Numbers often have peculiar properties based on their digits. For example, there are four-digit numbers with the following property: each is a perfect square, the first and second pairs of digits are both odd, and the sum of the two pairs of digits is also a perfect square. Make up two questions that would require a programmer to find numbers that have some such crazy property.

5-10   Anybody can read the book and start programming. But only students who have done their programming homework can answer *Find the bug* questions. In other words, it's easier to know what's right than it is to find out what's wrong. For instance, *Find the bug*:

```
{Inspects fifty characters, counts those that aren't 'T' or '5'}
Count := 0;
for i := 1 to 50 do begin
    read (Ch);
    if (Ch <> 'T') or (Ch <> '5') then begin
        Count := Count + 1
    end
end
```

The **or** should be an **and**.

Make up three or four buggy program segments. In case you haven't been doing *your* homework, some sneaky bugs you can throw in might include *a)* using uninitialized variables, *b)* initializing a variable inside the loop rather than before it, *c)* using the wrong boolean operator (as above), and *d)* including a boundary error by using the wrong relational operator.

5-11   The **case** statement is prone to causing syntax problems at first. Take a legal example from the text, then create a few *Where's the bug?* problems by introducing syntax bugs. Rely on *a)* missing semicolons; *b)* an illegal expression in the list of labels; *c)* a label with the wrong type; *d)* a label that appears more than once.

5-12   When can a series of **if** statements with **else** parts be replaced by a **case** statement, and vice versa? Describe four problems (e.g. scoring exams, recording income) and ask which statement is most appropriate to use.

5-13   An alternative way to approach the same problem is to ask that an **if** be rewritten as a **case**, if possible. Write three **if** statements for rewriting as **case** statements. Naturally, at least one of them should be impossible to rewrite.

Warmups and Test Programs

5-14   I stated De Morgan's laws and the distributive laws as gospel, but you never know—I might have made a mistake. Knock out a program that tests them. Can you manage to reproduce the truth tables at the same time?

5-15   Being able to decipher error messages associated with **if** statement syntax errors is an especially useful talent. What is the effect of a missing **end**? An extra **end** within the statement? An **ifelse** (yes, that's right) part? An out-of-order **else** part?

5-16   Writing incorrect programs is so much fun that I'll suggest a few more. What happens when you try to compile programs that include:

a)   the expression A < B **or** C > D?

b)   the expression 1 **and** 2?

c)   the expression 'a' <> 7?

5-17   Write a function Even that returns TRUE if its integer argument is an even number, and FALSE otherwise.

5-18   Write a function called Divisible that returns TRUE if its first integer argument is evenly divisible by its second.

5-19   Write a function Positive that returns FALSE if its real argument is a negative number.

5-20   Write a function IsADigit that tells you if its char argument is a digit character.

5-21   Write a function WithinLimits that returns TRUE if its first char argument is in the range given by its second and third char arguments.

5-22   Suppose that you want an action to take place if two conditions are both TRUE or both FALSE, but not otherwise. Write a boolean function that tests this condition.

5-23   Write a procedure that lets you know if a sequence of N input values is all (take your pick) positive, odd, or increasing.

5-24   Why must relations be put in parentheses when they're part of longer boolean expressions? Do you have any relations you like to see in parentheses?

5-25   Compare these two program segments. Is there any difference between them? Explain.

```
if (a <= b) and (a <= c)                     Smallest := a;
    then begin Smallest := a end             if b < Smallest then begin
    else begin if (b <= a) and (b <= c)          Smallest := b
        then begin Smallest := b end         end;
        else begin Smallest := c end         if c < Smallest then begin
end                                              Smallest := c
                                             end;
```

5-26   Consider this program segment:

```
First := 1;
for Last := 7 downto First do begin
    for LetterNumber := First to Last do begin
        Print (LetterNumber)
    end
end
```

Its output is:

```
whereas  wherea  where  wher  whe  we  w
```

Write procedure Print (which should, of course, contain a **case**).

5-27   One cause of bugs associated with boolean expressions is the unexpected appearance of outcomes that were not explicitly ruled out. Here are a few everyday questions whose answers are similarly unexpected:

a)   Two coins add up to thirty cents, yet one of them isn't a nickel. How can this be?

b)   Some months have 30 days, and some have 31. How many months have 28 days?

c)   Two people played seven games of chess, yet they each won the same number of games. What happened?

d)   A boy broke his collarbone playing football. When he arrived at the hospital, his coach told the nurse 'My son is injured.' However, when the doctor set the bone, the boy complained 'Ouch, Dad! That hurts!' If the doctor isn't also the football coach, can everybody be telling the truth?

Programming Problems

5-28   My local sporting goods store periodically makes the following offer: *Buy five items, and the sixth one is free!* Which is the free item? Is it the last one over the counter? The smallest? The lightest? No, of course not. It's the cheapest one, naturally.

Write a program that the store's electronic cash register might rely on. Have it read all six prices, find the lowest one, and print a total cost. Local tax is 6.5%, incidentally.

5-29   Genius, according to Thomas Edison, is 2% inspiration and 98% perspiration. Nowadays, of course, perspiration is usually socially inappropriate, except for men and horses. Alternatives—sweating, glowing, and dripping—exist, and it is important to know when to use them, regardless of the consequences to genius.

According to my social secretary, the rules are:

Temperature	Cooling Mechanism
over 100°	Dripping
91° to 100°	Sweating
81° to 90°	Perspiring
71° to 80°	Glowing
70° or below	Gleaming

Write a program that can read a temperature, and let you know what to do.

5-30   For many years, power companies gave bulk discounts to their largest consumers. In effect, those companies that were most effective at squandering energy were given incentives to continue doing so.

Recently, matters have changed somewhat. For example, my own power bill last month set two levels of use:

Baseline Quantities	Gas — 31.0 Therms	Electric — 238.7 KWhrs
Baseline Price	$0.50403 / Therm	$0.10294 / KWhr
Over Baseline Price	$0.82421 / Therm	$0.13682 / KWhr

Write a program that takes four meter readings (starting and ending reading for both gas and electric meters) and calculates charges to the nearest cent.

5-31   A well-known author of computer science textbooks proposed the following grading policy in his course:

Homework 1 through 5	5% each
Midterm 1	15%
Midterm 2	25%
Final Exam	35%

His students pleaded for the following changes:

—   Throw out the lowest homework grade.

—   Throw out the lower of the first two test grades.

—   Count only half of the final exam grade if it was lower than the average of the two midterm scores. Make up the difference by increasing the influence of the average of the first two exams.

—   Let a homework score of 20 or less be replaced by a special project grade. However, don't permit more than two homeworks to be replaced like this, even if more special projects are done.

The well-known author agreed to institute these changes, but only if his students would write a program that could do the grading. Unfortunately, they could not, so he returned to his previous policy of passing only students who could prove that they had bought extra copies of his textbook for their relatives.

Can you handle the problem? Assume that the first line of grade data contains only the number of grades. Then, each successive line has the homework grades, followed by the exam grades. As noted, any homework score of 20 or below is followed by a project score, although only the first two special project scores are counted. Assume that all grades are on a scale of 0 to 100. Finally, in addition to printing each student's average grade, also print the average score on each of the exams.

5-32   To truly hip skiers, only one word has meaning: vertical. Fortunately, it is fairly easy for a skier to figure out how many vertical feet she has managed to ski in a day. Since, for all practical purposes, you can only ski downhill, all she has to do is to find the difference between the starting and finishing elevation of each run.

Runners who hope to be truly hip, however, face a much more difficult task. A run may begin and end at the same elevation, but have a considerable amount of up and down in between. The only way to calculate total vertical is to go along the trail with a topographical map and add up all the increasing elevation changes.

For example, a typical run might be described in terms of these ten elevation figures:

| 500 | 530 | 550 | 550 | 575 | 540 | 500 | 480 | 465 | 500 |

The total change going up is $30 + 20 + 25 + 35$, or 110 feet.

Write a program that will read a fixed number of elevations, and let you know how much vertical was covered—going up!

5-33   I'm sure that *Home on the Range College* ('where seldom is heard a discouraging word') was your first choice of schools. But since you didn't get in, you probably have to calculate your grade-point average once in a while.

Write a program that calculates a grade-point average. Assume that an A is worth 4.0, B is 3.0, and so on. Grades may be modified by + or − (worth plus or minus 0.3), except that A+ is still only 4.0. Out of respect for the students' self-esteem, F− counts as 0.0. To make the program a bit harder, assume that grades are separated by one *or more* blank spaces.

5-34   A number's divisors are the numbers that divide it evenly. For example, the divisors of 12 are 1, 2, 3, 4, 6, and 12. If a number is another number's divisor, an integer division doesn't leave any remainder—A is a divisor of B if A **mod** B equals 0.

It's easy enough to write a boolean-valued function that lets you know if a number is another number's divisor. Then, you can find a number's divisors through brute force: just test every value between 1 and the number.

a)   Write a program that finds and prints a number's divisors.

b)   Modify it to print a table of divisors for all numbers below 1003.

c)   Modify that to find out what number below 100 has the largest number of divisors.

5-35   Yes, another question about divisors. We live in times that are reluctant to make value judgments; nevertheless, consider these traditional descriptions of a number, and the sum of its divisors (excluding the number itself):

—   *Perfect* numbers equal the sum of their divisors (less themselves). 6 is perfect because it equals $1 + 2 + 3$.

—   *Abundant* numbers have divisors that add up to *more* than the number.

—   *Deficient* numbers have divisors that don't add up to the number itself.

Write a program that answers these questions:

a)   Which three numbers below 1000 are perfect?

b)   What odd number below 1000 is abundant? What seven odd numbers below 5,000?

c)   What are the relative proportions of deficient, abundant, and perfect numbers?

5-36   Like divisors, digits are easy to come by. Taking a three-digit number **mod** 10 gives you the 'ones' digit, while taking it **div** 100 provides the 'hundreds' digit. Getting the middle digit requires a combination of the two methods.

As it happens, I know of a few numbers that have a peculiar relationship with their digits:

a)   Which three-digit numbers are equal to the sum of each digit raised to the third power (as, for instance, 153 equals $1^3 + 5^3 + 3^3$)?

b)   Which three-digit numbers are equal to the sum of each digit, factorial? (N factorial means $1 \times 2 \times \cdots N$.)

5-37   The word 'begin' is moderately interesting because its letters are strictly increasing—no letter alphabetically equals, or is less than, the letter before it. 'coop' also increases, but not strictly, since some of its letters are duplicated.

Write a program that can rely on, say, ten letters of input. Announce whether the letters are the same, increase, increase strictly, or decrease.

5-38   A *toggle switch* is just a two-position switch. Toggling usually refers to either/or switching, rather than on/off switching. For instance, a walkie-talkie might use a toggle switch to flip between sending and receiving. Naturally, you can build toggle switches into programs as well. For example, a program that reads and echoes characters might use the appearance of an exclamation point as a toggle—from that point on, letters should be echoed as capitals. A second appearance of the exclamation point switches back, so that letters echo in lower case.

> *Input:* **Here is ! a test ! of MY system.**
> *Output:* here is A TEST of my system.

The toggle switch itself can be implemented as a boolean variable. The **not** operator can be used to flip its current value.

Write a program that reads fifty values and implements one of these toggles:

a)   Switch between printing only odd and only even numbers, toggling at each zero.

b)   Toggle between echoing characters in upper and lower case, switching at each period, question mark, or exclamation point. (Assume all input is lower-case.)

c)   Read numbers, and switch between printing them as positive or negative. Start by printing odd numbers as negatives and evens as positives, and toggle at zero.

5-39   Write a program whose input is a date supplied as a month, day, and year, e.g. **7/29/53**.

a)   Print the day's number within the year, i.e. if the date supplied is **2/3/85**, the output should be be 34. Don't forget that a leap year occurs every fourth year except if the year is divisible by 100, but not 400.

b)   Read a second date, and then calculate and print the number of days from one to the next (that is, including one but not the other).

5-40   Write a program that reads an integer value, then prints the 'word' equivalent. For example, for input **23567**, output should be:

> Twenty three thousand five hundred sixty seven

5-41   Write a little stack calculator. In stack notation, input is given as:

> *x y operation*

where *x* and *y* are values, and *operation*, for our purposes, will be a single character. The more familiar order of evaluation is, of course:

> *x operation y*

Your calculator should accept two numbers and an operand, e.g.:

> **2.34 5.92** *   or   **-1.03 16 /**

and perform the correct operation. Have your calculator correctly handle +, −, *, and /. If you like, give the calculator an integer mode that permits the operations **D** and **M** (for **div** and **mod**).

5-42 Suppose that our universe contained just four fruits—say, lemons, oranges, watermelons, and bananas. Although fruit salad would be rather dull, we would find that just two different questions—Is it round? Is it yellow?—could be used to determine a fruit uniquely.

However, not all questions have just two answers. Consider the questions that might describe an animal:

> *diet = carnivorous, vegetarian, omnivorous*
> *size = humungous, regular, tiny*
> *hair = long, short, none*

and so on. We will find that twenty-seven different animals can be uniquely identified through just three different questions. Write a program that does so. Please send your answer to the author.

5-43 The word *therein* is interesting because at least eleven words can be 'cut' from it without rearranging any letters—*the, here, in*, and so on.

Suppose we label the letters from 1 through 7. It turns out that a triply nested **for** loop (calling on a **case** statement for actual printing) can be used to generate every possible subsequence of the letters in the word. How? What are the words?

A loop does not end because it has achieved its goal. Instead, it ends because the loop has reached its bound. Above, why the computer scientist never got out of the shower. (p. 200)

6

Conditional Loops: while and repeat

* Optional sections.

Can you do something hard, like finding every three-digit number that equals the square of the sum of its digits? Sure—you have the **for** loop and the **if** statement. But can you do something easy, like counting the number of letters in a word? No way—you don't have a loop that stops when it reaches a blank. The **while** and **repeat** statements come to the rescue.

Loops are so important that I'll present two classes of applications: text processing examples that involve words and 'number-crunching' examples that involve math. Since text examples get in-depth coverage, I've devoted all of Chapter 7 to them. Section 6–3 is optional and takes care of the mathematical kind. Whichever path you choose, our focus will be on *design* and on reasoning about loops before they're written.

These chapters are among the most fun in the entire book (along with the array chapter), because you'll learn how to do things that would be pretty impossible without a computer. How long is an average word? Are there more odd or even numbers in the first 10,000 digits of π? Just how many sentences *are* there in *Bartleby, the Scrivener*? I bet you didn't even know you cared about questions like these! Well, maybe you don't—but after a week you'll be making them up too.

Sections 16–1 and 16–2, which discuss recursive procedures and functions, may be read after this chapter.

Strictly Pascal

6-1

IS THERE A READER AMONG US WHO has not seen the TV show *Love Connection?* A contestant chooses one of three potential dates, then the two of them report on the encounter. Occasionally it works out, but the studio audience seems to enjoy the disasters much more. Afterward, the audience casts a strictly advisory ballot on whom the contestant should have chosen. If the date was a nightmare, the contestant gets a second chance with the audience's pick.

From the computer scientist's perspective this is the most interesting part of the show. I can't show the votes clicking in, and each candidate's percentage changing as they do, but here's what's left when the dust settles:

the moment of truth arrives

How does the Love Connection computer do it? The math is easy:

{*Calculating the percentages.*}
(*each prospect's votes / all the votes*) ∗ 100 = *that prospect's percentage*

If we can manage to loop until all of the votes are counted, we can duplicate the Love Connection display. Naturally, we'll use a **while** loop. Its syntax chart is:

while statement

> **while** ⟶ *boolean expression* ⟶ **do** ⟶ *statement* ⟶

As in the past, I'll always use the **begin** and **end** of a compound statement, even though they're not needed when the **while** loop only controls a single action.

while syntax

> **while** *a* boolean *condition is* TRUE **do begin**
> *a sequence of statements*
> **end**

A pseudocode solution to the central part of our problem is:

processing the votes

> **while** *votes are still arriving*
> *count a vote;*
> *print the current percentage totals;*
> *get the next vote*

It isn't hard to follow in the completed program, below.

```pascal
program LoveCon (input, output);
   {Reports on the percentage of votes cast for each of three potential dates.}
var Vote, Total, Ones, Twos, Threes:  integer;
procedure Report (Total, One, Two, Three:  integer);
   {Prints the actual percentages.}
   begin
      write (trunc ( (One/Total) * 100) : 5 );        write ('%');
      write (trunc ( (Two/Total) * 100) : 5);         write ('%');
      write (trunc ( (Three/Total) * 100) : 5);       write ('%');
      writeln
   end; {Report}
begin
   writeln ('Please enter votes: 1, 2, or 3.  Any other number quits.');
   Total := 0;
   Ones := 0;          {Initialize the counters.}
   Twos := 0;
   Threes := 0;
   read (Vote);          {Get the first vote.}
   writeln ('    One    Two    Three');          {Label the output.}
   while Vote in [ 1 .. 3 ] do begin
      Total := Total + 1;                          {Count the total.}
      case Vote of                                 {Count each vote.}
         1: Ones := Ones + 1;
         2: Twos := Twos + 1;
         3: Threes := Threes + 1;
      end; {case}
      Report (Total, Ones, Twos, Threes);          {Report on the situation.}
      read (Vote)                                  {Get the next vote.}
   end; {while}
   writeln ('May all your dates be love connections!')
end. {LoveCon}
```

```
Please enter votes:  1,  2,  or  3.   Any  other  number  quits.
2   1   2   1   3   2   2   1   2   0
   One    Two    Three
   0%    100%    0%
  50%     50%    0%
  33%     66%    0%
  50%     50%    0%
  39%     39%   19%
  33%     50%   16%
  28%     57%   14%
  37%     50%   12%
  33%     55%   11%
May  all  your  dates  be  love  connections!
```

priming the pump

The **while** loop makes an entry test—in this case, it checks the value of Vote. To ensure that the test can be made, we prime the pump by reading the first Vote value before the loop. If the first vote isn't in the legal range of votes, the loop's action never gets carried out at all.

I usually insist on using compound statements in **while** loops because it's easy for an errant semicolon to cause problems. Consider the program segment below. If the user's first number is negative, the loop gets stuck at the shaded line. It's endlessly executing an empty statement.

a bug that causes an infinite loop

```
{An empty statement bug.}
writeln ('Enter a positive number.');
readln (Number);
while (Number <= 0) do ;    {This semicolon shouldn't be here.}
    readln (Number);
writeln ('Thank you.');
```

You'll know that a program is stuck in an *infinite* loop if it *a)* prints the same thing endlessly, *b)* appears to do nothing (also endlessly), or *c)* suddenly dies with a runtime error message along the lines of `Runtime Error: Statement Limit Exceeded`. The problem is easy to diagnose: throw in a debugging writeln that prints 'In the loop,' and see if it appears a zillion times. It's a good idea to find out what your system's kill key is first, just in case.

Modification Problems

1. Modify LoveCon so that it announces the total number of votes cast, and the votes given to each candidate, when it's done.

2. Suppose we help Chuck guard against voter fraud by building in an upper limit on the number of votes that can be cast. Add a LIMIT constant to the program, then add it to the **while** loop check. Pick any audience size you think is reasonable.

3. It's always a good idea to prepare for disaster under controlled conditions. Intentionally modify LoveCon so that it contains an infinite loop, then make sure you know how to halt the program.

The **repeat** Statement

Pascal has another loop statement: **repeat**. It's used like this:

repeat syntax

> **repeat**
>   *a sequence of statements*
> **until** *a* boolean *condition is* TRUE

Note that the **begin** and **end** of a compound statement aren't needed with **repeat**, since the words **repeat** and **until** enclose its statements quite nicely. The statement's syntax chart is:

repeat statement

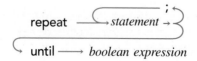

How about a quick **repeat** problem? Suppose that you've been cleaning out your kitchen cupboards and have found a cache of birthday candles. Great! but if you start to use them up each year, how long will the supply last? In outline, the solution is:

problem: the birthday cake

> *find out the current age;*
> *find out how many candles there are;*
> **repeat**
> > *add* 1 *to the age;*
> > *subtract the proper number of candles*
>
> **until** *there won't be enough for the cake;*
> *print a 'buy more candles' notice for the final age;*

In Pascal, the completed program is:

a repeat example

```
program Candles (input, output);
    {Determines how long a supply of birthday candles will last.}

var Candles, Birthday:  integer;

begin
    write ('How old are you now?    ');
    readln (Birthday);
    write ('How many candles do you have?    ');
    readln (Candles);
    {We have the starting information.}
    repeat
        Birthday := Birthday + 1;
        Candles := Candles – Birthday
    until Candles < 0;
    {There aren't enough candles for the next birthday cake.}
    write ('You''ll have to buy more candles before you turn   ');
    writeln (Birthday : 1)
end.  {Candles}
```

```
How old are you now?  17
How many candles do you have?  872
You'll have to buy more candles when you turn 45
```

while and **repeat** are very similar. Their only semantic difference is that the **repeat** action always takes place at least once. The **while** action, in contrast, may be skipped entirely.

the condition must change

> Every loop must eventually *terminate*, or end. To make sure that this happens, it must be possible to meet the boolean condition that controls the loop. Almost inevitably this means that a variable whose value changes *within* the loop helps state the boolean condition.

Loops that don't obey this basic law will either fail to terminate (they'll be infinite loops), or they'll always terminate on or before the first trip through (and not really be loops at all).

Modification Problems

1. Modify Candles so that it lets you know how many candles, if any, are left over.
2. Improve Candles so that it adds one candle to the cake each year for good luck.
3. Suppose that a thrifty party-goer saves candle stubs and fashions them into new candles. Modify Candles so that it can handle this form of recycling. Let the user specify the number of stubs it takes to make a whole candle.

Another Canonical Example

How many sides does a circle have? If your answer was two—inside and outside—you're on the right track for thinking about loops.

A program that reads and averages numbers is the canonical loop example. It's the one that every student sees, because it manages to pack so many loop programming issues into such a simple problem. RealAvg contains a loop with three 'sides': before, during, and after. This particular loop's *bound* condition—the reason it ends—is that it has read a negative number. In pseudocode, the program's action is:

averaging pseudocode

> *prompt the user for input;*
> *initialize variables as necessary;*
> **while** *there are more values available*
>   *read a value;*
>   *add it to a running total;*
> **if** *no values were entered*
>   **then** *print an error message*
>   **else** *print the average*

The final code of program RealAvg is on the next page. Its output is:

```
Give me some numbers to average.
End the list with a negative number.
23.9  85.68  227.0E02  0.00863  75.0 -1.0
The average of 5 values is 4576.918
```

```
program RealAvg (input, output);
    {Averages a series of numbers.}
var Value, Total: real;
    Counter: integer;
begin
    writeln ('Give me some numbers to average.');
    writeln ('End the list with a negative number.');
    Total := 0.0;          {initialize an accumulator}
    Counter := 0;          {initialize a counter}
    read (Value);          {get the first value to see if we've reached the bound yet}
    {Before: Should we enter the loop?}
    while (Value >= 0.0) do begin
        {During: Do we take the right steps within the loop?}
        Total := Total + Value;            {increase the accumulator}
        Counter := Counter + 1;            {increment the counter}
        read (Value)                       {approach the loop's bound}
    end; {while}
    {After: What do we really know after the loop is done?}
    {The loop's postcondition — what we know — is that Value is negative. If
     Count is non-zero, then it holds the number of values, and Total is their sum.}
    if Counter = 0
        then begin writeln ('There weren''t any data entered.') end
        else begin write ('The average of ');
                    write (Counter : 1);
                    write (' values is ');
                    writeln (Total/(Counter) : 1 : 3)
             end {if}
end.    {RealAvg}
```

average until sentinel program

Let's look at RealAvg carefully. As I said, every loop has three sides: before, during, and after. The initializing statements, including the first read of Value, cover the bases before the loop is entered. Indeed, if the first number we read is negative, we won't enter the loop at all.

Within the loop, we can safely make additions to Total and Counter because they were initialized before the loop. Since Value continues as the variable that sets the condition for leaving the loop, it's the most important variable. It must have the opportunity to change on each *iteration*, or repetition, of the loop.

updating the bound condition

```
{From RealAvg}
Total := 0.0;
Counter := 0;
read (Value)
while  (Value >= 0.0) do begin
    Total := Total + Value;
    Counter := Counter + 1;
    read (Value)
end;
```

The loop's 'after' part poses the most subtle challenge. Let me ask a question that will seem naive, if not downright dumb. Why do we leave the loop? Is it because we know the average of the input numbers? No! Is it because we are ready to compute the average—to divide the sum by the count? Again, an emphatic no! Instead, we leave the loop *because we have read a negative number.*

pre- and postconditions

> A loop's *postcondition* describes our state of knowledge about program data after the loop. The postcondition should focus on facts that are relevant as the *precondition* of the next program segment.

We can't reach any other sure conclusions—not even if there *were* any input values—without making additional checks. That's why the loop's postcondition—what we know after the loop—is so important. It is the next statement's precondition, since it has to answer any questions the next statement will ask in order to work properly.

a look after the loop

```
{The loop's postcondition — what we know — is that Value is negative. If
  Count is non-zero, then it holds the number of values, and Total is their sum.}
if Counter = 0
    then begin  write ('There weren''t any data entered.') end
    else begin  write ('The average of  ');
                write (Counter);
                write ('  values is  ');
                writeln (Total/(Counter) : 1 : 3)
end  {if}
```

> Most loop bugs derive from a postcondition that doesn't follow from the loop's bound. When you program, check one against the other. Does the postcondition accurately restate the bound condition? Does the bound condition lead to the postcondition you want? Always look after you loop.

graceful degradation

Reread RealAvg, and notice that it prints an explicit message if the data list is empty. This attention to detail could be quite important in a larger program, where an incorrect or unsupplied value could lead to wrong results, or even an inexplicable program crash. Explicit built-in error messages help a program to *degrade gracefully,* rather than failing catastrophically or invisibly.

Can you hazard a guess, incidentally, as to why program RealAvg uses a **while** statement rather than a **repeat**? Well, a **repeat** statement is always entered at least once. However, there is a circumstance under which the loop shouldn't be entered: suppose that there aren't any numbers to add. That would make the very first number the negative end marker. If we entered the loop, we'd add the negative number to Total, which would be a mistake.

Finally, here's how I'd write a test bed program for loops. Although it has all the basic ingredients of RealAvg, program LoopBed, below, doesn't do anything useful. It does give me an open window on a loop that's easy to modify: change it to a **while**, look for a particular Current value without adding it to the total, read characters instead of numbers, etc.

```
┌──────────────────── LOOPBED.PAS ────────────────────┐
│program LoopBed (input, output);                      │
│  {A test bed program for loops.}                     │
│var Count, Total, Limit:  integer;                    │
│    Current:  integer;        {Make this easy to change.}│
│begin                                                 │
│    writeln ('Enter number of numbers, followed by numbers.');│
│    Total := 0;                                        │
│    Count := 0;                          ┌─── Variables ───┐│
│    read (Limit);                        │ Count: 2        ││
│    repeat                               │ Total: 3        ││
│      read (Current);                    │ Limit: 5        ││
│      Total := Total + Current;          │ Current: 3      ││
│      Count := Count + 1;                └─────────────────┘│
│    until (Count = Limit) or (Current = 5);           │
│    writeln (Count);                                   │
│    writeln (Total)                                    │
│end.  {LoopBed}        ┌──────────── Input & Output ────────────┐│
│                       │Enter number of numbers, followed by numbers.││
│                       │ 5  1  2  3  4  5  6  7                 ││
│                       └────────────────────────────────────────┘│
└──────────────────────────────────────────────────────┘
```

about to add 3 to the total

Modification Problems

1. Modify RealAvg so that besides spotting a negative number, it will also stop if *a*) the input values total more than 100.0, *b*) five values have been read, or *c*) both of the above.

Self-Check Questions

Q. RealAvg checked the value of Counter to decide if any numbers had been entered for averaging. Could it have checked the value of Total instead?

A. Sure—but what it found out might be wrong. Suppose that the program was calculating the average temperature of a chilly icebox and that every value entered was 0.0. The `There weren't any data entered` message would be wrong, because there would be an actual average of zero.

Q. What's wrong with these bound conditions? Why are they probably in error?

      a)   **while** TRUE **do** . . .
      b)   **while** FALSE **do** . . .
      c)   **while** abs(Counter)<0 **do** . . .
      d)   **while** (Value>10) **and** (Value<=5) **do** . . .
      e)   **while** (Value<=10) **or** (Value>=11) **do** . . .

A. Try a go/no-go test—all the conditions are either unavoidable or impossible. Statements *a* and *e* can't help being TRUE, while *b*, *c*, and *d* are invariably FALSE. Since there's no way any of them can be modified, the TRUE loops will exit immediately, and the FALSE loops will repeat forever.

eof and eoln, Briefly

a plea for help

Standard Pascal has two built-in functions that are useful when loops read numbers. I'll just give you a quick introduction here, since we're going to be using them extensively in Chapter 7. I'm counting on your professor to help me out if you're going to be expected to use them now.

two standard boolean
functions

— eoln, the standard end-of-line function, is TRUE when you're about to read the ⎡Enter⎤ (or ⎡Return⎤ if you're using a Mac or DEC keyboard) at the end of a typed line and is FALSE otherwise.

— eof, the end-of-file function, is TRUE when you're about to read a special, unreadable marker that appears at the end of a file and is FALSE otherwise.

The meaning of end-of-line is a little more obvious than end-of-file. End-of-line is a control character that's generated whenever you hit the ⎡Enter⎤ or ⎡Return⎤ key. When you type it, it jumps to the next line, but if you read it, you'll get a space:

the end-of-line is read as a space

```
{Echo a single line.}
while not eoln do begin
    read (Ch);
    write (Ch)
end;
{Since eoln is true, we're about to read the end-of-line.}
read (Ch);    {The end-of-line should be read as a blank.}
if Ch = ´ ´
    then writeln (´<end-of-line>´);
    else writeln (´The end-of-line was not read as a space.´);
```

```
First line.
Second line.
First line.<end-of-line>
```

The next character read will be the **S** that begins **Second line.**

The end-of-file character is also unreadable; in fact, your program will crash if you try to read it. In effect (what I'm about to say isn't literally true), it is automatically placed at the end of every file stored on the computer, and can also be generated from the keyboard if you know the right control key. We'll be going over the details in the next chapter.

Why bring up eoln and eof now? It's because they have to be used in a certain way when you're reading lines or files of numbers. Put these two facts in your mind and you may see why.

— When read is used to read a numerical value, it skips blanks, tabs, and end-of-lines, then reads a number. read stops reading at the last digit.

— Both eoln and eof are TRUE only when the very next character is the appropriate control character and are FALSE otherwise.

read skips blanks and empty lines only *before* a number, not after. Consequently, eoln will be FALSE if there's a space or two after a number, even if there aren't any more numbers on the line. Similarly, eof will be FALSE if there are one or more blank lines at the end of a file, even if there aren't any more numbers to be found.

I won't bother going over all the problems this can cause, or all the things you shouldn't do. Instead, I'll give you a simple rule to follow:

When you read a line of numbers one at a time with read, make sure that the last number actually ends the line. When you read a file of numbers, read just one number per line with readln.

reading a line of
numbers

```
{Using eoln to read one line of numbers.}
writeln ('Give me a few numbers, then hit "Enter" ');
Sum := 0;
while not eoln do begin
    read (Number);
    Sum := Sum + Number
end;
readln;          {In case the next read wants a new input line.}
write ('Their sum is ');
writeln (Sum : 1);
```

Assume that I press Enter to end my input, below:

```
Give me few numbers, then hit "Enter"
1 3 5 7 9
Their sum is 25
```

Were I reading a file's worth—and remember, I'm not going to go over file details until Chapter 7—I'd ask for just one number per line and use readln:

reading a file of
numbers

```
{Using eof to read a file of numbers.}
writeln ('About to read and add a file of numbers. ');
Sum := 0;
while not eof do begin
    readln (Number);
    Sum := Sum + Number
end;
write ('Their sum is ');
writeln (Sum : 1);
```

```
About to read and add a file of numbers.
1
3
5
7
9
Their sum is 25
```

Here, readln works because it gets rid of any extraneous characters that might follow the numbers, along with the end-of-line itself.

Standard Practices: Loop Specification

6-2

IT ISN'T HARD TO WRITE A LOOP THAT will compile. However, it's always a good idea to lay out the loop's semantics—what it will do—in advance. For the purpose of planning, we can break every loop into three distinct parts:

— A *goal* that states the overall purpose of the loop.

— A *bound* that gives the reason the loop will end.

— A *plan* that describes the action the loop is going to take.

In other words, the goal is what we hope to accomplish, the bound is our exit condition, and the plan explains how we'll approach the goal and bound.

Now it's time for an insight that is so obvious it's often overlooked.

bounds, not goals, end loops

> *A loop does not end because it has achieved its goal.* It ends because the loop has reached its *bound*.

The loop's goal describes the happy state of events we hope to attain. However, the bound condition supplies the strongest statement we can make with certainty when the loop is done. If the loop's plan was a good one—and program data were what they were supposed to be—we'll reach the bound just as we achieve our goal. But if we reach the goal before the bound, or hit the bound before the goal, we're courting errors.

A *loop specification* is a pseudocode description of a loop's goal, bound, and plan. For example, the specification of the loop in our example program RealAvg might have been:

loop specification

Goal: To know the sum, and number, of a series of input numbers.
Bound: We've read a negative number.
Plan: Read a number.
  Add it to a running sum.
  Add one to a counter.

Note that the loop's goal and bound are quite distinct. I could set other goals with the same bound: find the numbers' product, or convert the numbers into base 9. I might also apply other bounds to the same goal: stop adding once the sum exceeds 500, or after we've read twenty numbers.

Stating the goal and bound separately help us to design the loop's plan. Most successful plans follow one simple rule: think about the bound first.

designing a loop plan

> Take the smallest step necessary to approach the bound. Frequently this step must be taken before the loop, as well as within the loop. Then, and only if necessary, add additional steps that help reach the loop's goal.

The plan's first step, *read a number*, brings us toward the bound. It's taken before the loop, then again before each repetition:

```
read (Value);
while (Value >= 0) do begin
    Total := Total + Value;
    Counter := Counter + 1;
    read (Value)
end
```

Second and third goal-oriented steps—*add it to a running sum* and *add one to a counter*—help meet the goal of this particular loop. In pseudocode, the example program's main loop is:

a pseudocoded loop

initialize a counter;
initialize an accumulator to hold the running sum;
approach the bound—read a number;
while *we haven't reached the bound* **do begin**
    approach the goal—add the number to the running sum;
    approach the goal—add one to the counter;
    approach the bound—read a number
end *of the loop*
{*Postcondition: the last number read was a negative number*}

I've added a postcondition to the pseudocode. It may start to sound as repetitious as a **while** loop, but ...

comment cautiously

> The postcondition that follows the loop is based on the exit condition. It is the only statement we can make with certainty. Any additional claims have to be carefully checked against the action of the loop.

Self-Check Questions

Q. Come up with a bound and plan for each of these goals:

a) *Goal: Skip fifty input characters.*
b) *Goal: Find the position of the letter F in input that includes an F.*
c) *Goal: Divide 35 by 6 using subtraction.*
d) *Goal: Count the number of F's in an input word.*
e) *Goal: Print an* integer *in reverse.*

A. Try drafting the pseudocode that applies to each of these loop specifications.

a) *Bound: A counter equals 50.*
   Plan: Add 1 to a counter that started at 0.
       Read a value.

b) *Bound: Reading the letter F.*
   Plan: Read a value.
       Add one to a position counter.

c) *Bound: The remainder is less than 6.*
   Plan: Subtract 6 from the current remainder.
       Add 1 to the quotient.

d) *Bound: Reading a space character.*
   Plan: Read a character.
       Add 1 to a counter if the character is an F.

> e) *Bound: The number has been reduced to zero.*
>   *Plan: Print the one's digit by printing the number* **mod** *10.*
>   *'Strip off the one's digit by recalculating the number* **div** *10.*

Loops and Their Bounds

Most of the attention we pay to loops involves bounds. Why would we want a loop to stop?

sentinel bounds

— A *sentinel* or marker value—usually, a number or character that marked the end of a certain kind of input—was encountered. For example, a blank space is a sentinel that marks the end of a word, while 0 or –99 might mark the end of positive integer input.

count bounds

— A *count* was attained—the loop's action was repeated enough times. You can recognize that the **for** statement is a special-purpose loop that's been customized for count bounds. However, **while** and **repeat** loops are needed when the count won't necessarily increase on every trip though the loop, e.g. when we count certain kinds of input, rather than every input value.

limit bounds

— A *limit* was reached—one more iteration wouldn't get us closer to the loop's goal and might have even led to error. Limits can be given as exact figures (reducing a number to zero), as boundaries (exceeding an upper size limit), or in relative terms (the difference between two successive calculations is less than 0.000001 percent).

data bounds

— The *data* were used up, or we reached an imaginary border within the data. Data bounds will be more common in later chapters, when we write programs that actively subdivide stored information into known and unknown parts. However, text processing provides a major application that's also pursued in depth in Chapter 7.

For example, suppose that our goal is to add numbers. Our bound can vary, depending on the task at hand. It's a:

one goal, different bounds

sentinel, if we add numbers until we spot a negative one;

count, if we add just ten numbers;

limit, if we add numbers until the total exceeds 500;

data bound, if we add numbers until there are no more.

Now, the bounds I've described are terms of convenience. Nobody's going to test you on them, and you don't have to try to fit programming problems into one category or another.

Nevertheless, categories are useful because they help point out an important fact of program engineering: that loops often have *multiple bounds*, or more than one reason for terminating. Loops often have:

goal-oriented vs. error-avoiding bounds

— an *intentional* bound that is tied to achieving the loop's goal;

— one or more *necessary* bounds that guarantee loop termination and are needed to prevent errors.

> When you establish a loop's bound condition, always ask: *Does this bound alone guarantee that the loop will end?* If the answer is no, add necessary bounds.

For example:

— We may be looking for a sentinel value but be aware that it might not appear at all.

when necessary bounds are needed

— We may be repeating a computation that approaches a 'correct answer' or 'good enough' limit, but gets there so slowly that we want to put an upper count bound on the number of repetitions allowed.

— We may not be sure that a correct answer exists or that our method of seeking it is correct and wish to set a bound on the amount of time we spend trying to find it.

— We may not be sure of the reliability of our data and wish to provide a fail-safe exit condition if they don't meet our expectations.

Usually, we'll find that buggy situations arise when the intentional bound is in one category, while the necessary bound is in another. Use the sentinel, limit, count, and data categories as a checklist for avoiding potential errors.

Self-Check Questions

Q. The **while** loops below all lack boolean conditions, but that doesn't mean that they don't have bounds. Read each segment's postcondition, then write an appropriate entry/exit condition for the **while**.

```
CharCount := 0;                                      {Segment A.}
read (Letter);
while . . .
    CharCount := CharCount + 1;
    read (Letter);
end
{CharCount represents the number of letters that came before a SENTINEL.}

Guesses := 1;                                        {Segment B.}
read (NewGuess);
while . . .
    Guesses := Guesses +1;
    read (NewGuess);
end
{NewGuess equals Answer, or five guesses were taken.}
```

```
Tries := 5;                                    {Segment C.}
read (NewTry);
while . . .
    Tries := Tries −1;
    read (NewTry);
end
{NewTry equals Answer, or five guesses were taken.}
```

A. It's important to read the initializing statement that precedes the loop, since it can affect the exact wording of the exit condition.

> *A)* **while** (Letter <> SENTINEL) **do begin**
> *B)* **while** (NewGuess <> Answer) **and** (Guesses < 5) **do begin**
> *C)* **while** (NewTry <> Answer) **and** (Tries > 1) **do begin**

Sentinel Bounds

Let's turn to specific examples of the different bounds, starting with sentinel bounds. Some typical applications that involve sentinels are:

— Finding the position of a particular value, or ignoring input until a particular value appears. The value itself serves as the sentinel.

where sentinels appear

— Doing calculations on a series of numbers. The sentinel follows the last 'legitimate' value in the series.

— Prompting a program user to provide a value that falls within a limited range or group of allowable entries ('Y' or 'N', say, or a positive number). The correct value need not be any one particular value, but nevertheless it serves as the sentinel.

In general (and experience will teach you this much better than memorizing), loops that obey sentinel boundaries are set up like this:

a typical sentinel-bound loop

> *approach the bound—get a value;*
> **while** *the sentinel hasn't been seen* **do begin**
>   *approach the goal—do normal processing (if any) with the value;*
>   *approach the bound—get a value*
> **end**

For example:

problem: sentence length

One definition of 'sentence' you won't learn in Composition 101 is 'a series of letters, spaces, and punctuation marks that ends with a period, question mark, or exclamation point.' Write a procedure that counts the number of characters in such a sentence.

A sentinel marks the end of input. However, it can have three different values: period, question mark, or exclamation point. I can outline the loop required by the sentence length counting problem as:

loop specification

Goal: Count the characters that precede a sentinel.
Bound: We've read the sentinel.
Plan: Read a character (approach the bound).
   Add 1 to a counter that began at 0 (approach the goal).

Note that it would be awkward to write this loop as a **repeat** statement. If I did, I'd probably end up adding the sentinel to the count of characters.

A pseudocode expansion of the specification is accompanied by a confirmation comment—the loop's postcondition:

pseudocode

initialize a counter variable to 0;
read a character;
while *it isn't one of the sentinel characters* **do begin**
    add 1 to the counter;
    read a character
end *of the loop*
{*Postcondition: The counter represents the number of non-sentinel characters read.*}

The final code of the procedure is:

letter counting procedure

```
procedure ChCount (var Count: integer);
    {Counts the number of letters in a sentence that ends with ., ?, or !.}

    var Ch: char;

    begin
        Count := 0;
        read (Ch);  {Approach the bound.}
        while (Ch<>'.') and (Ch<>'?') and (Ch<>'!') do begin
            Count := Count + 1;  {If we're in the loop, increment the count.}
            read (Ch)  {Approach the bound again.}
        end
        {Postcondition: Count represents the number of non-sentinel characters read.}
    end;  {ChCount}
```

Modification Problems ──────────────────────

1. Suppose that a number is a sequence of digit characters that ends with a space. Turn ChCount into DigitCount. However, to make life harder, let the characters '.', 'E', '+', and '−' appear in a number without being counted as digits.

2. What if I define a 'word' as a sequence of characters that ends with a space? Modify ChCount so that it counts the number of words in a sentence. Don't forget to think about how you'll deal with a one-word sentence.

3. Rewrite SkipToNumber (below) so that it uses a **while** loop, then redo ChCount so that it uses **repeat**.

4. Put procedure SkipToNumber (below) inside a loop that finds the sum of the first five numbers embedded in the text described below.

Self-Check Questions ──────────────────────

Q. Dollar amounts appear in text that is interesting, but extraneous to our immediate interests. A line of input might begin:

> Allocated to payoffs: $100000.00 for favors . . .

Dollar signs appear only before dollar amounts. Write a procedure that skips past the irrelevant characters, then reads and returns the number.

A. Since dollar signs precede only numbers, they're ideal sentinels. Note that a single step, read (OneCharacter), moves us closer to the loop's bound (reading a dollar sign) as well as to its goal (finding a dollar amount).

```
procedure SkipToNumber (var TheNumber: real);
    {Returns the real value that follows a dollar sign.}
    var OneCharacter: char;
    begin
        repeat
            read (OneCharacter);
        until OneCharacter = '$';
        {Postcondition: OneCharacter equals '$', so we're about to read a number.}
        read (TheNumber);
    end; {SkipToNumber}
```

Count Bounds

Loops with count bounds are our second category. Applications that call for count bounds include:

— Counting repetitions of an action. We're already intimately familiar with this application, thanks to our experience with the **for** statement.

where count bounds are used

— Counting data items—some number of input values. Again, this is precisely the sort of application we've employed **for** loops in.

— Counting events—input of vowels or correct answers—rather than iterations. We are concerned with the results of a loop's plan, rather than how long it takes to achieve them.

— Providing an upper limit on iteration. The count serves as a necessary bound that can guarantee the termination of a runaway loop or merely limit the number of incorrect answers in a guessing game.

In general (although once again, experience will be the best teacher), loops that only have count bounds follow this basic pattern. The key statements initialize and increment the counter:

a typical count bound loop

```
initialize a counter;
repeat
    take an action;
    if it's appropriate, increment (add one to) the count;
until the count is reached or exceeded, as appropriate
```

> Always check count bound loops for off-by-one errors. Should the count be equaled or exceeded? Ask 'would it work if the bound were 1?'

when to use **for**

Of course, **repeat** and **while** won't replace **for**. The **for** loop initializes and updates the counter. It 'counts' by non-numeric types. Best of all, it cannot fall victim to either premature or laggardly exit.

However, the count that controls a loop won't always be tied to the number of actions the loop repeats; we may be interested in counting results, instead. Whereas a **for** loop is condemned to repeat a fixed number of times, **repeat** and **while** statements can rely on count bounds to repeat only as often as is necessary or practical—usually, until there have been a certain number of successes or failures at some task. For example:

problem: the computer tutor

Computer-aided instruction has been the educational panacea of the future for some time now. Write a program that drills its user in multiplication and won't quit until she gets three correct answers.

Although such a program requires some additional input and output, we can focus on the central *drill the user* loop.

loop specification

Goal: Quiz a user on her favorite multiplication table.
Bound: She got three questions right.
Plan: Ask the question.
        Get the answer.
        Increase the Correct *count if the answer was right.*
        Prepare the next question.

Note that most of the plan is dedicated to taking one step toward the bound. Only the last step, *prepare the next question*, is goal-related. In a sense, we reach the loop's goal—quizzing the user, in the process of trying to attain the bound—getting those three wrong answers. I'll pseudocode the specification as:

pseudocode

initialize the Correct *count;*
find out what multiplication table to test;
find out how high to start;
repeat
    ask the question;
    read the answer;
    if *the answer was right increase* Correct *by one;*
    get ready to test the next product
until Correct *equals the bound*

As usual, it's important to keep your eye on the bound. We don't leave the loop because the user got three answers right. Instead, we leave it because a variable named Correct equals three. It's essential that the actual code back up our understanding of the exit condition. The final program is shown below.

a count-bounded loop
program

```
program Tutor (input, output);
    {Mercilessly drills the user in multiplication.}
const EXITlimit = 3;
var Multiplier, Multiplicand,        {Drills the Multiplier times table,}
    Answer, Correct:  integer;       {from Multiplier * Multiplicand on up.}
begin
    write ('Time to multiply.  What''s a number you hate?  ');
    readln (Multiplier);
    write ('How high should I start the drill?  ');
    readln (Multiplicand);
    Correct := 0;
    repeat
        write ('What is  ');  write (Multiplier : 1);
        write (' times  ');  write (Multiplicand : 1);  write ('?  ');
        readln (Answer);
        if Answer = (Multiplier * Multiplicand) then begin
                Correct := Correct + 1;
                write ('Right!!!      ')
            end
            else begin
                write ('Wrong!!!      ')
        end; {if}
        Multiplicand := Multiplicand + 1
    until Correct = EXITlimit;
    {Postcondition:  The user made ERRORlimit mistakes.}
    writeln ('I hope you appreciate the beauty of math now.')
end.   {Tutor}
```

```
Time to multiply.   What's a number you hate? 3
How high should I start the drill? 7
What is 3 times 7? 21
Right!!!    What is 3 times 8? 25
Wrong!!!    What is 3 times 9? 27
Right!!!    What is 3 times 10? 29
Wrong!!!    What is 3 times 11? 32
Wrong!!!    What is 3 times 12? 36
Right!!!    I hope you appreciate the beauty of math now.
```

Modification Problems

1. Give Tutor the additional code it needs to be at least modestly helpful to its user. For instance, add a procedure that helps the user when she enters the wrong answer!

2. Suppose that I initialized Correct to 1. Modify Tutor so that it still works.

Limit Bounds

Let's turn to limit bounds. They are appropriate for:

— Loops that methodically reduce a number to zero or to less than some known value. For instance, algorithms for **div** and **mod** rely on repeated subtraction; eventually, we can tell that an additional subtraction would be useless or cause an error.

limit bound applications

— *Successive approximation* methods. Here, each time a calculation is performed the result is compared to a previous calculation. The bound is reached when two successive calculations yield approximately equal results.

— *Bisection* methods that calculate mathematical approximations. The limit is set by approaching to within some tiny amount of an answer that is known to be correct.

— *Non-convergence* tests, which must often be applied to the iterative methods described above to ensure that calculations have not gone astray (producing meaningless results) or have grown uncontrollably (and threaten the legal limits of real or integer).

I won't beat around the bush: loops that rely on limit bounds tend to involve numbers (so skip this example if you reach *your* limit). The problem I'll pose is:

The equation $y^2 - y = x$ isn't terribly exciting. Were we all unimaginative English majors, I'd probably solve it with the quadratic formula. Whole-number solutions are easy to find; for instance, $5^2 - 5 = 20$.

problem: pervasive roots

However, as proto-computer scientists, I'm sure you'll appreciate the opportunity to see and solve the same equation like this:

$$y = \sqrt{x + \sqrt{x + \sqrt{x + \sqrt{x + \sqrt{x + \cdots}}}}}$$

Rather astonishingly (to me, at least), the long sequence of added square roots (and roots of roots) of 20 also converges to 5—the two equations really are equivalent. Write a program that calculates a so-called *pervasive root* to the limit of your computer's accuracy.

Aren't computers wonderful! Now, not all solutions will converge on a whole number, but computer arithmetic ultimately provides a limiting factor. Although we intend to add an infinite sequence, eventually the root of a root of a root, etc., becomes too small to influence the computer's real representation of the sum.

elegance vs. brute force

The quadratic formula and the pervasive root represent, in a way, the two approaches open to the programmer. The formula is elegant and mathematical; its answer is the result of computation, rather than calculation. The pervasive root, in contrast, suggests *brute force*—calculating and recalculating square roots until we exhaust ourselves or the computer.

Let's use the brute-force approach, persisting until we reach the limit of computer accuracy. At the same time, we'll keep track of the number of steps that were required to reach that limit. Our bound, in this case, will be that two successive sums seem to be equal.

limits on real comparison

> Two real values that appear to be equal may not actually be equal. Comparisons between reals are used to demonstrate the limits of real accuracy, rather than the accuracy of real calculations.

In other words, adding yet another tiny decimal value to a real won't appear to change the real's value. This fact has caused nasty headaches for numerical programming over the years. Fortunately, we're not concerned with finding the *right* answer. Instead, we want an answer that will meet our bound:

loop specification

Goal: Count steps needed to approximate an infinite series of calculations.
Bound: The difference between successive calculations is undetectable.
Plan: Save the previous calculation.
      Find the square root of (the number + the previous calculation).
      Increment a step counter that began at 1.

In the pseudocode below, notice that the pervasive root is calculated from the inside out.

pseudocode

initialize a counter to 0;
calculate the innermost root;
repeat
    calculate the addition of another term;
    increment the counter
until *it 'equals' the prior calculation;*
print the results

In effect, the calculation is:

$$\text{Last} = \sqrt{\text{Current} + \cdots + \sqrt{\text{Current} + \sqrt{\text{Number}}}}$$

The completed version of program Pervade is shown below. Later in this chapter I'll show a much more common approach to doing real comparison—comparing the difference of two numbers to a very tiny constant.

limit-bounded loop
example

```
program Pervade (input, output);
    {Computes a pervasive square root to the limit of real accuracy.}
var Number, Current, Last: real;
    Count: integer;
begin
    write ('Enter a number.     ');
    readln (Number);
    Count := 0;
    Current := sqrt(Number);
    repeat    {until two approximations are indistinguishable}
        Last := Current;
        Current := sqrt(Number + Last);
        Count := Count + 1
    until Current = Last;
    {Postcondition: We've reached the limit of real representation.}
    write ('The root took ');
    write (Count : 1);
    write (' steps to converge on ');
    writeln (Current : 3 : 10);
end.    {Pervade}
```

```
Enter a number.  20.0
The root took 15 steps to converge on 5.0000000000
```

Self-Check Questions

Q. Write a Pascal code segment that implements this loop specification. What do you think the loop's goal is? You can assume that Number starts out with some positive value.

> *Goal: For me to know, and you to find out.*
> *Bound:* Number *equals* 0.
> *Plan: Print the value* (Number **mod** 10).
> *Divide* Number *by* 10 *using* **div**.

A. In Pascal, the specification is:

```
repeat
    write (Number mod 10);
    Number := Number div 10
until Number = 0
```

The loop's goal is to print the digits of Number in reverse. I can use a **repeat** loop because at least one digit always gets printed.

Q. That was so much fun we'll do it again. What does this do, and how does it do it?

> *Goal: Those who know don't tell, and those who tell don't know.*
> *Bound:* Number *equals* 0.
> *Plan: Add* 1 *to a counter that began at* 0.
> *Divide* Number *by* 10 *using* **div**.

A. The goal is given away by the variable identifiers:

```
Digits := 0;
while Number <> 0 do begin
   Number := Number div 10;
   Digits := Digits + 1
end
```

The segment counts the digits in Number. It assumes that Number is non-zero.

Data Bounds

The fourth kind of loop bound is called for when an explicit sentinel, count, or calculated limit can't be relied on to provide an exit condition. Instead, we leave a loop because we've run out of data to examine. In fact, the plan of a data-bound loop is generally devoted to arriving at this exhausted state as rapidly as possible!

In a sense, the obvious data bound arises when we're reading values until the built-in eof function is TRUE. Since we can't actually read the end-of-file, we're not looking for a sentinel *per se*. But much more interesting data bounds appear in such applications as:

— Searching through organized collections of values. The position (e.g. in the middle) of data items helps to delimit the boundaries of a search.

where data bounds appear

— Reorganizing stored data according to bounds that aren't fixed but are associated with particular values.

— Working with *streams*, or sequences of values (usually characters), whose end isn't marked by a sentinel. We'll discuss these ideas further in Chapter 7.

binary search

Let me describe an algorithm called *binary search* that will give you a feel for what a data bound consists of. Suppose that you want to find a name in a telephone book. I'll simplify matters by limiting the search to masseurs in the 15th Arrondissement of Paris:

At first, the range of possible positions includes the whole list of names, from Jean-Pierre Abric through Pierre Zuani. But instead of starting with the first name, and patiently working your way to the last, why not follow this algorithm instead:

1. Look at the value that falls right in the middle of the boundaries; i.e. we might pick Annick Le Verre-Ronne from the top of the third column.

divide and conquer

2. It might be the value you want. If it isn't, though, you've found a new lower bound (if it's less, alphabetically, than the name you want) or a new upper bound (if it's greater, alphabetically, than the name you want) for continuing the search.

3. Start all over again at step 1 *unless* the lower and upper bounds have met, which means that there are no data left to split.

Binary search is a *divide-and-conquer* technique. Each time we inspect a name, we learn something about the data: we learn that half of them are irrelevant because they're too big or too small. We conquer the data by making their unknown portion smaller and smaller. With binary search and ordered data, we can find one value out of thirty *million* by inspecting, at most, twenty-five names.

The remainder of this chapter is devoted to numerical examples. Chapter 7, however, deals exclusively with *text*, or letters and words, which you might find more copacetic. (If you don't know what copacetic means perhaps you should stay with 6-3.)

Extended Examples: Mathematical Processing*

6-3

LET'S TURN OUR ATTENTION TO A FEW MATHEMATICALLY oriented programs. The first two examples, Euclid's algorithm and Newton's method, involve methods of calculation that predate computers by thousands of years. Nevertheless, they are so effective that they are among the most frequently programmed mathematical algorithms. The third, approximating π, uses brute-force methods that would never have been practical without computers.

Mathematical processing, like text processing, tends to follow typical models. All of our examples have limit bounds, and all but the first involve approximations. That's what calculation is like with real numbers; the only way to get exact figures is to be very clever about fudging and rounding! We'll try two different approaches to approximation:

two limits on approximation

— Using Newton's method to calculate square roots will bring us closer and closer to an exact answer; we'll quit when 'closer' gets arbitrarily tiny.

— Approximating π will focus on getting closer to an exact answer than an existing approximation; we'll quit when we're good and ready.

Appendix C takes a more detailed look at real storage and talks about a few of the issues involved in programming numerical algorithms.

---

* This section may be skipped by the faint of heart. But you'll be sorry.

Example: Euclid's Algorithm

Our first example implements an algorithm that is attributed to Euclid (about 330–270 B.C.E.). Although he's best known for his contribution to geometry (and for his crack—'There is no royal road to geometry'—that even kings have to study), Euclid also formalized a method for finding two numbers' greatest common divisor. It has come to be known universally as *Euclid's Algorithm*.

Euclid's algorithm is based on a fact, followed by a clever insight. The fact is that if a number divides both *Bigger* and *Smaller*, it also divides *Bigger–Smaller*. Why? Well, let's call the divisor *x*. Then:

the fact

  Bigger equals some number *A* times *x*, and
  Smaller equals some number *B* times *x*, so
  Bigger–Smaller equals *A–B* times *x*.

which brings us back to where we started from—saying that if a number divides *Bigger* and *Smaller*, it also divides *Bigger–Smaller*.

Enough for the fact; let's get to Euclid's clever insight. Take a moment to match wits with a guy who probably lived in a mud hut. You want to find the greatest common divisor (GCD) of two numbers. You know that the smaller number, and the numbers' difference, share the same GCD. Can you figure out a method of finding the GCD?

the insight

Give up? The insight is that we can replace *Bigger* and *Smaller* with *Smaller* and the *Bigger–Smaller* difference over and over again. It is a step that can be repeated; it's an algorithm. How many times should the algorithm be repeated? Until the *Smaller* value equals zero. When it does, the *Bigger* value will equal the greatest common divisor, and we'll have the answer.

Let me plug in some numbers and grind through an example. Say the GCD is *x*, the bigger number starts as 9*x*, and the smaller number begins as 7*x*. Then:

Euclid's algorithm in action

Bigger	Smaller	Bigger – Smaller
9x	7x	9x − 7x = 2x
7x	2x	7x − 2x = 5x
5x	2x	5x − 2x = 3x
3x	2x	3x − 2x = x
2x	x	2x − x = x
x	x	x − x = 0
x	0	Bigger has been reduced to x—the greatest common divisor

Now, although you may have never thought of it in this way, the **mod** operator carries out precisely this kind of subtraction, but much more quickly. Note that the result of each **mod** operation will always be smaller than the prior 'smaller' number, which makes it easy to keep *Bigger* and *Smaller* straight:

Euclid's algorithm using mod

Bigger	Smaller	Bigger **mod** Smaller
9x	7x	9x **mod** 7x = 2x
7x	2x	7x **mod** 2x = x
2x	x	2x **mod** x = 0
x	0	Bigger has been reduced to x—the GCD

Rephrasing Euclid's algorithm as a loop specification gives us:

loop specification

> *Goal: Find the greatest common divisor of two numbers.*
> *Bound: One number has been reduced to zero.*
> *Plan: Take the larger number **mod** the smaller.*
>   *Save the new larger and smaller values.*

Should we implement the algorithm as a procedure or as a function? Since it returns a single value and doesn't modify its arguments, most people calculate GCD with a function. A pseudocode restatement of the specification is:

function pseudocode

```
repeat
    take Larger mod Smaller;
    save the result and the smaller number;
until Smaller is zero;
GCD := the value of Larger
```

Finally, we have the Euclid's algorithm function itself:

Euclid's algorithm function

```
function GCD (Larger, Smaller: integer) : integer;
    {Employs Euclid's algorithm to return the GCD of two numbers.}
    var Remainder: integer;
    begin
        repeat    {until each instance of the GCD is removed from Smaller}
            Remainder := Larger mod Smaller;
            Larger := Smaller;
            Smaller := Remainder
        until Smaller = 0;
        {Larger represents the greatest common divisor.}
        GCD := Larger
    end; {GCD}
```

Modification Problems

1. As written, GCD has a teeny-weeny little problem. Try using a Smaller argument of 0, then fix the bug.

2. Rewrite GCD as a procedure that returns the number of iterations it took to find a GCD. Then, see how big a number you can get.

3. The chance that two numbers taken at random share a common divisor greater than 1 is $\pi^2/6$. Or is it? Put GCD in a program that tests this conjecture by calculating the GCD of every pair of numbers from 1,1 to *n*,*n*.

Example: Newton's Method

Our second historical example is a method of calculating square roots. It dates from the Hammurabi dynasty (ca. 1800–1600 B.C.E.) in the Old Babylonian era.

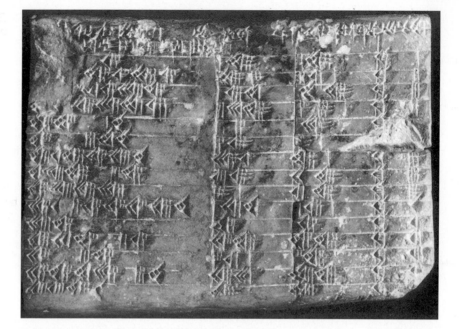

Although the method is often attributed to Isaac Newton (hence its name) it was fully described on clay tablets, in lovely base-60 cuneiform, more than three millennia before Newton arrived. The algorithm is:

Take a guess (besides zero) at the number's square root. The assignment:

calculating square roots

```
Guess := ((Number / Guess) + Guess) / 2;
```

gives a new Guess value that is closer than the original to being correct, no matter how wild the original guess was.

> Newton's method is typical of iterative approaches to numerical approximation. The accuracy of the result is limited only by our patience or by the number of places a computer provides for storing digits. There is no fundamental limit to the method itself.

A Pascal loop, however, must have a bound. In this case, the bound is provided by a mathematical limit: we continue to approximate the root until the difference between two subsequent approximations is quite small. In mathematical terms we'd say that the difference approaches ε, or *epsilon*, which is Greek for *itsy-bitsy*. A specification of the loop is:

approaching ε

> *Goal: Approximate a square root.*
> *Bound: The difference between subsequent guesses is < EPSILON.*
> *Plan: Take a new guess.*
>   *Save the old guess.*

We can describe the EPSILON in two ways: either as an *absolute* or as a *relative* value. In other words, the difference might be a small number (an absolute error), or it might be a small percentage of the numbers that are being compared (a relative error). Suppose I use an absolute EPSILON value of 1.0E–09, and let you modify it into the relative version later. We can pseudocode a Newton's method function as:

Initialize an NewGuess *value;*
repeat
    Make OldGuess *the current* OldGuess
    Calculate a new value for NewGuess
until NewGuess *is within* EPSILON *of* OldGuess;
Newton := *the most recent* NewGuess

Newton's method pseudocode

The final function is shown below. I tried calculating the square root of 2 with OldGuess initialized to 1.414222—the Babylonians' best recorded estimate—and got to within 0.0000000001 of the correct root in just one iteration!

Newton's method procedure

```
function Newton (Number: real) : real;
    {Use Newton's method to approximate a square root.}
    const EPSILON = 1.0E–09;
    var OldGuess, NewGuess: real;
    begin
        NewGuess := 1.0;  {Take a lousy first guess.}
        repeat
            OldGuess := NewGuess;
            NewGuess := ((Number / OldGuess) + OldGuess) / 2.0
        until abs (NewGuess – OldGuess) < EPSILON;
        {The difference between approximations is less than EPSILON.}
        Newton := NewGuess
    end;  {Newton}
```

Modification Problems

1. Improve the first guess by making it vary with Newton's argument.

2. The absolute EPSILON value Newton uses can make the function fail if we're trying to find the square root of a number that is very large, or is close to zero. Change the loop's exit condition so that it looks for a relative difference between guesses. In other words, look for an EPSILON*th* difference, rather than a difference of EPSILON.

Example: Approximating π

Let's consider a final example of settling for an answer that is 'good enough'—finding a rational approximation to π.

The search for whole numbers that, when divided, equal π has provided mathematical employment for centuries. Famous approximations include 19/6 (the Ahmes Papyrus, circa 1650 B.C.E.), 25/8 (a Babylonian guess), $223/71 < \pi < 220/70$ (Archimedes, around 150 B.C.E.), and 377/120 (Ptolemy of Alexandria, early first century).

The most remarkable approximation comes from Tsu Ch'ung-chih (in the fifth century). His value—355/113, approximately equal to 3.1415929—was not improved on for a thousand years.

Such searches are ultimately in vain, as π is irrational and can't be expressed as the quotient of two integers. However, I can pose this problem:

problem: rationally approximating π

On the assumption that you already know the value of π to an arbitrary number of decimal places, write a program that finds the shortest rational fraction that is closer to π than Tsu's approximation.

As we've seen, the customary way to state a 'good enough' limit is to say that:

abs (π – *our approximation*) < EPSILON

EPSILON, as usual, represents a very small number. How small? For our purposes, the difference between π and Tsu's approximation is small enough:

choosing EPSILON

const EPSILON = abs (π – 355/113);

A brute force approach to working up an approximation isn't very hard. Take any fraction. If it's too large, incrementing the denominator makes it a bit smaller, while increasing the numerator will make it a tad larger. I can outline the loop specification as:

loop specification

Goal: Find a better rational approximation to π than Tsu's.
Bound: The approximation is closer to π than 355/113 is.
Plan: Make the current approximation slightly larger or smaller.

A first refinement, below, is typical of numerical approximation loops. If our first guess is close enough, we can exit. If not, we have to recalculate:

make an initial approximation;
while *the approximation isn't close enough* **do begin**
    try to get closer

first pseudocode

end
print the answer

The *initial approximation* can be any positive fraction. The *try to get closer* step is taken care of by adding one to the numerator or denominator.

initialize a Numerator *and a* Denominator;
calculate the approximation, Numerator/Denominator;
while *the approximation isn't close enough* **do begin**
    if *the approximation is too small*
        then *increase* Numerator *by one*
        else *increase* Denominator *by one*
    recalculate the approximation

second pseudocode

end
print the answer

The completed program is shown below. Its result is indeed a millionth or two closer to π, even though it may take a little while to appear on your screen.

pi approximation program

```
program PiApprox (input, output);
    {Finds a rational approximation to PI that's closer than 355/113.}
const PI = 3.14159265358979;          {From Al-Kashi.}
var Numerator, Denominator: integer;
    Approximation: real; {Will hold Numerator/Denominator.}
    TSU, EPSILON: real;  {I'll use these like constants to help set the bound.}
begin
    writeln ('The next closer approximation to pi than 355/113 is');
    Numerator := 1;  {Let's start with a terrible guess.}
    Denominator := 1;
    Approximation := Numerator / Denominator;
    TSU := 355.000000000000/113.000000000000;  {From Tsu Ch'ung-chih.}
    EPSILON := abs(PI–TSU);
    while abs (Approximation–PI) >= EPSILON do begin
        if Approximation < PI
            then begin  Numerator := Numerator + 1 end
            else begin  Denominator := Denominator + 1 end;
        Approximation := Numerator / Denominator
    end  {while};
    {Numerator/Denominator is closer to PI than TSU is.}
    write (Numerator : 1);
    write ('/');
    write (Denominator : 1);
    write (' = ');
    writeln (Approximation : 20 : 18)
end.  {PiApprox}
```

(*output follows*)

⬇   ⬇   ⬇   ⬇   ⬇

```
The next closer approximation to pi than 355/113 is
52163/16604 = 3.141592387376536120
```

Before we congratulate ourselves on our calculative prowess too strenuously, I might point out that the accuracy of this answer was easily surpassed in the early fifteenth century by Al-Kashi in Tamerlane's (of Mongol hordes fame) capital city of Samarkand. I used his best result as my reference value for π in program PiApprox, calculated on a PC.

Modification Problems ─────────────────────────────────

1. Remove the assignment to Approximation from PiApprox. Are other changes required? What about making the assignment the first action the loop takes?
2. It takes some time for PiApprox to come up with its approximation. Meanwhile, your computer appears to be stone cold dead. Modify PiApprox so that it periodically does something to let you know it's still alive and running, e.g. print a period every thousand trips through the loop.

Program Engineering Notes: Let's Get Robust

6-4

THE ABILITY TO RECOVER FROM FAILURE, even in part, is a key part of good program engineering. What does a robust program—one that's able to recover—do when it encounters incorrect input? It tries either to undo the error or to recognize that it is in a state of error and act accordingly. In contrast, a non-robust program may crash or produce incorrect output *without informing its user*.

But it is not always necessary to give up when confronted with problems. We can always use the **while** or **repeat** statement to try again:

a moderately informative loop

```
repeat
    writeln ('Pick a number between 1 and 10.');
    readln (Number);
until  (Number >= 1) and (Number <= 10)
{Number is in the range 1 .. 10.}
```

For an improved example, consider procedure GetInput, below. It increases a program's robustness by letting the user correct improperly entered data. We don't know when an appropriate value will be entered or what its exact value is. We *do* know, though, that the exit condition can conceivably be met and that the crucial variable, Value, is reinitialized on each iteration.

```
procedure GetInput (var Value: integer;
                         Lower, Upper: integer );
    {Gets and returns a Value between Lower and Upper, inclusive.}
    begin
        repeat   {until Value is in the proper range}
            readln (Value);
            if Value < Lower
                then writeln ('That''s too small.  Try again.')
                else if Value > Upper
                    then writeln ('That''s too large.  Try again.')
        until  (Value>=Lower) and (Value<=Upper)
    end;  {GetInput}
```

*input error check
procedure*

improving robustness

Interactive programs should include such error-checking and mistake-correcting loops whenever possible. Nothing is more infuriating than a computer program that *can't* let a user change input she knows is wrong—or *won't* let her know what is right. Try not to forget that interactive programs must always tell the user what she can do.

> A well-designed program *a)* never leaves the user at a loss for options to follow and *b)* tries to anticipate potential miscommunication. Programs are extensions of their programmers; as such they should work *with* their users, rather than one for the other.

For example, the *What's your answer* loop, below, has a problem that is subtle on paper, but is glaringly obvious in actual practice. Can you guess what it is?

*a moderately robust
loop*

```
writeln ('What is your answer − − yes or no?');
repeat
    write ('Enter "Y" or "N"    ');
    readln (Answer)
until  (Answer = 'Y') or (Answer = 'N');
{Answer indicates yes or no.}
```

Well, imagine that you're responding to the prompt:

```
What is your answer - - yes or no?
Enter "Y" or "N"   y
Enter "Y" or "N"   n
Enter "Y" or "N"   i hate this program!
Enter "Y" or "N"
```

The program expects the user to type in a capital letter. This is really a shortcoming in the program, and not in the user. It isn't hard to fix:

an improved loop

```
repeat
    write ('Enter "Y" or "N"    ');
    readln (Answer);
until  Answer in [ 'y', 'Y', 'n', 'N' ]
```

repeat vs. while

When should you **repeat**, and when should you **while**? The issue isn't really a matter of choice between right and wrong. Instead, each statement has its own benefits and its own inherent risks. The basic rule of thumb is:

— If the action will take place at least once, a **repeat** is appropriate.

— If the action might not take place at all, use a **while** statement.

In effect, the **while** statement sets up an *entry* condition. If it isn't met, the **while** is skipped entirely. If it is met, the entry condition becomes an *exit* condition the next time around. The **repeat** statement, in contrast, starts out with its exit condition plainly stated.

On occasion, the fact that an exit condition (say, Ch = SENTINEL) can't be turned into an entry condition just by reversing it (to Ch <> SENTINEL) leads to unexpected grief. For example, suppose that we want to read characters while we search for a particular sentinel value. As a **repeat** statement our code is:

*using **repeat***

```
repeat
    read (OneCharacter)
until OneCharacter = SENTINEL
```

Rewriting the segment as a **while** statement requires a bit of thought, though. We'd like to say:

```
while OneCharacter <> SENTINEL do begin
    read (OneCharacter)
end
```

but that won't work. Why not? Because OneCharacter isn't defined until we read a character. Writing the loop correctly requires that OneCharacter be initialized before the loop:

*using **while***

```
read (OneCharacter);
while OneCharacter <> SENTINEL do begin
    read (OneCharacter)
end
```

If I pose a problem that is a bit more difficult, you can see why the loops are not interchangeable alternatives. Suppose that instead of just spotting a sentinel, we read and add numbers that precede it. This **repeat** statement seems easy, but it's incorrect:

*a summing **repeat**, with bug*

```
Sum := 0;
repeat
    read (Number);
    Sum := Sum + Number        {Are you sure?}
until Number = ENDmarker
```

Can you see what the problem is? We can't avoid adding the sentinel to the sum. The **repeat** statement, which *always* takes the action, isn't suitable.

while, in contrast, provides a correct solution. As before, though, we have to be sure that the variables that make up the boolean expression are defined before the statement:

```
Sum := 0;
read (Number);
while Number <> ENDmarker do begin
    read (Number);
    Sum := Sum + Number
end
```

Loop Boundary Errors

You may recall the discussion of boundary errors in boolean expressions in Chapter 5. They were bugs that hinged right on the turning point between TRUE and FALSE.

Because loops rely on boolean expressions they also fall prey to boundary errors, and can go on just a bit too long or end just a bit too quickly. A *termination checklist* is one way to avoid problems:

> The common loop bound conditions—sentinel, count, limit, and data—provide a convenient checklist to help assure us that a loop will terminate.

I put loop bound conditions into categories mainly for this reason. But I'll also point out that there are two ways to use a termination checklist. The novice looks at what she *wants* to do:

1. *Sentinel:* Is there a sentinel? Is it the only one? Have you considered the possibility that the sentinel won't show up?

2. *Count:* Is there an upper limit on iterations? Should there be one? Are you counting the right thing? Can a partial result blow up before you reach the limit?

3. *Limit:* How long can calculations go on? Are additional iterations always meaningful, or can you get 'close enough?' Are you looking for a limit beyond your machine's accuracy? Is a fail-safe count bound needed?

4. *Data:* Is the loop limited by the availability of raw data? Should an additional check for end-of-file be added?

But the expert programmer follows up with these questions, which are aimed at what she's *not* looking for, rather than what she *is* seeking:

1. *Sentinel:* Should you be watching for a 'just in case' sentinel? For example, will the appearance of a sentinel like the carriage return indicate that something has screwed up?

2. *Count:* Is a count bound on total number of iterations going to be a necessary precaution in a limit-bound loop?

3.   *Limit:* Will a seemingly innocuous bit of arithmetic push the limits of computer accuracy? Might a partial result blow up (e.g. go beyond the legal limit for integer)?

4.   *Data:* Can you run out of data unexpectedly? Is a check for the end of input going to be needed?

Next, think back to the first law of debugging: *It ain't what you don't know that hurts you; it's what you do know that ain't so.* A loop has three sides—before, after, and during—and you have to remember to question what you think you know at all three. After all, it's no shame to get confused, but it is foolish to think that it can't happen to you.

When I debug my students' code, I use a debugger or start adding writeln's right away. It's not so much that I doubt *them*; rather, I doubt my own ability to overcome my own mindset about what is and what isn't.

Checking the values that establish a loop's exit condition is particularly important. Try to keep the basic law of debugging in mind: *If you're sure about everything but your program still doesn't work, then one of the things you're sure of is false.* I usually make bugs by doing something dumb in a boolean expression; e.g. the variable I was sure had to be between twenty and thirty was never initialized.

You'll find additional comments on loop debugging in Chapter 7.

Syntax Summary

❑   while statement: allows a sequence of statements to be repeated:

> while *a bound has not been reached* do begin
>   *sequence of statements;*
> end

❑   repeat statement: like while, but will always execute at least once:

> repeat
>   *sequence of statements;*
> until *a bound has been reached*

❑   eoln: a boolean function that is TRUE if the last ordinary value on a line has been read and FALSE otherwise.

❑   eof: a boolean function that is TRUE if the last ordinary value in a file has been read and FALSE otherwise.

Remember . . .

❑   A loop's entry or exit condition must be attainable. This implies that part of the condition must be changed on each trip through the loop.

❑   A *loop specification* is a semi-formal loop outline. It splits a loop's description into three parts: the *goal*, or overall purpose of the loop; the *bound*, which gives the reason the loop will end; and the *plan*, which describes the actions the loop will take.

❑   Loop bound conditions can be put into distinct categories, but only for convenience. Most loop bounds involve counts, sentinels, limits, or data. These terms are intended only to provide a checklist for typical loop designs.

❏   An *intentional* bound is the reason we want a loop to end. However, since good intentions aren't always enough to guarantee loop termination, additional *necessary* bounds may be needed as well.

❏   A loop does *not* end because it has achieved its goal. It ends *only* when it reaches its bound. When a loop has multiple bounds, it must be followed by a check to determine which bound caused the loop to terminate.

❏   A loop's *postcondition* is a confirmation comment that describes a program's state on loop exit. It describes the loop's intended goal, of course, but it must also point out any possible deviations from that goal. It acts as the *precondition* of the next program statement.

❏   A loop's *boundary conditions* are the circumstances of its first and last iterations. The most common loop errors (in particular, *off-by-one* errors) occur there.

❏   A computer's representation of a real value is often a very close approximation, rather than an exact equivalent. Comparing real values says more about the limits of real storage than about the correctness of calculations. To be safe, compare the difference between two values to a small predefined constant.

❏   *Graceful degradation* is one form of program robustness. If a program cannot recover from an error, it should still give the user an idea of what has caused the problem. Under no circumstances should a program fail abruptly or produce incorrect results.

❏   When possible, use loops to give interactive-program users the opportunity to confirm and correct their input.

❏   The Basic Law of Debugging: 'When you're sure of everything but your program still doesn't work, then one of the things you're sure of is wrong.' Take the time to question what you know.

❏   Number reading and processing loops will generally use readln and read just one value per input line. That way, a check for eof won't be FALSE if only trailing blanks remain on a line.

Big Ideas

The Big Ideas in this chapter are:

1.   *Loops do many things, but they follow a few basic patterns.* If you can recognize the pattern before you begin to program, you'll have an idea of how to plan and what bugs to watch out for.

2.   *A loop's goal is not its bound, and its bound is not its goal.* The fact that a loop has terminated doesn't necessarily mean that it accomplished what you had in mind. Always keep a clear distinction between what a loop does and why it ends.

Begin by Writing the Exam . . .

6-1   Difficulty in stating conditions makes for excellent test questions. Write a series of **while** loop entry conditions that include impossible conditions (that can't be met) and unavoidable conditions (that will always be met), along with a few plausible conditions (that can be met correctly). The question, of course, will be *Which of these conditions are in error? Why?*

6-2   *Find the bug* questions are enjoyable to put on tests because they reward students who have done their homework—after all, they're the ones who have probably seen the bugs already. Take a half-dozen pieces of code from the text and introduce the most devious bugs you can. Hints:

a)   slightly change a **while** loop's entry condition;

b)   slightly change a **repeat** loop's exit condition;

c)   remove a statement from within the loop;

d)   if there is an initializing statement before the loop, change any zero to one or vice versa;

d)   put the initializing statement inside the loop instead of before it.

6-3   Which of these are equivalent?

```
repeat
    action
until not A or not B;

action;
while A and B do begin
    action
end;

action;
while A or B do begin
    action
end;
```

Make up three more questions of this ilk. Make them harder by replacing *action* with code that actually does something.

6-4   Stripped of its camouflage, the basic sentinel loop question is *Write a loop that spots the first...* A sentinel like *the first zero* or *the end of the line* is fine and dandy, but it isn't arbitrarily complicated, the way test questions are supposed to be. Think up a half-dozen sentinels that go from hard to harder (usually because they require your program to remember more and more current input states). Tricks to employ include requiring multiple sentinels (spot A or B or C), conditional sentinels (spot A followed by B), and compound sentinels (spot A followed by B, or C followed by D or E).

6-5   Pick a looping program or procedure (like RealAvg or ChCount), then make up three sets of test data. Naturally, two sets should fail to check boundary conditions. Ask the Zen Essay Question *Which set of data should you use to test this program, and why?*

6-6   *Rewrite this segment using that statement* is a particularly effective test question when loops are involved. The syntax of the **while** and **repeat** statements can hardly be accused of posing much difficulty. But using them correctly requires a real understanding of the segment's semantics and intent.

Pick a few **while** or **repeat** statements from the text, and present them as *Rewrite this using the other* (or *Rewrite using a* **for** *statement if possible*) problems. Can you come up with any general rules for making the transformations?

6-7   Time for *Here's the input, what's the output?* and *Here's the output, what's the input?* What might your example segment do? How about capitalizing lower-case words, or doubling odd numbers, or counting words that begin with a capital letter, or only echoing increasing values in an input sequence of random numbers? As always, you will find that the interesting part is choosing the segments that *can* be run in reverse.

6-8   How about a few vocabulary questions? What is a *sentinel*? What's a *boundary error*? Come up with three more.

Warmups and
Test Problems

6-9   Write a loop that reads numbers and prints every number that equals its own position in the list. For example, 3 equals its own position in the list 2   9   3   6   1.

6-10   Come up with a loop that reads numbers, then prints the largest and smallest values along with their positions within the list.

6-11   Write a loop that finds the first power of two that is equal to or greater than a number entered by a program user. Be sure that it will work correctly if the user enters zero.

6-12   Write a loop that reads and echoes input integers until the difference between any two successive numbers is greater than or equal to ten.

6-13   Imagine that you have a can of whipped cream. Every second the nozzle stays open, 2% of the remaining cream squirts out. How long, to the nearest second, will it take to empty half the can?

6-14   Write a loop that reads a sequence of real values, and finds the number of values in the longest *decreasing* sequence. For example, in the sequence:

$$1.0 \quad 4.0 \quad 3.0 \quad 2.0 \quad 9.0 \quad 10.0 \quad 8.0 \quad 6.0 \quad 2.0 \quad 5.0$$

the longest decreasing sequence (10.0 through 2.0) has four values.

6-15   Straighten out a paper clip, and ask yourself this question: Suppose you cut the clip in two, then bend one part into a circle, and the other into a square. How long should each portion be to yield figures with equal areas?

6-16   Write a procedure that finds the least common multiple of three numbers.

6-17   Suppose that you have a file of prime numbers. Write a procedure that can use the file to find the smallest sequence of *n* consecutive *non*-primes.

6-18   Write a program that reads and echoes numbers according to this rule: echo only odd numbers or even numbers, starting with even and switching whenever you read a zero.

Programming
Problems

6-19   An addict who likes cigarettes very much is willing to go to great lengths to continue her habit. She's even willing to roll new cigarettes from butts and newspaper. Suppose that she starts out with a carton (ten packs of twenty) of the filthy things. Assuming that she rolls a new cigarette from every three butts, how many smokes will she have in all? Will any butts be left over?

6-20   One plus two is three. One plus two plus three is six. One plus two plus three plus four is ten. If we keep this up long enough, we'll find that the sum of the numbers 1 through *n* is a perfect square. Find the first three numbers for which this is true.

6-21   Did I ever mention that even most mathematical programming is really text processing? Well, where do numbers come from? Do you think that it's easy to read a real? Write a procedure that could replace read. You can warm up for this by figuring out how to read an integer one digit character at a time. Don't forget about the sign.

6-22   The January 1984 issue of *Scientific American* contains an article on an interesting sequence of numbers known as a *hailstone* series. The series is formed like this:

a)   Pick a number.

b)   If it's odd, triple the number and add one.

c)   If it's even, divide the number by two.

Can you imagine why the sequence is likened to a hailstone? Although numbers bob up and down, eventually they reach a repeating 'ground' state: 4 2 1 4 2 1 . . . This has been shown for every number up to about 1.2E12.

Write a program that gets a starting number, then answer these two questions:

a)   How many steps does it take to get to the repeating 'ground' state?

b)   What is the largest number the sequence reaches along the way?

If you're a go-getter, generate a few numbers for inspection automatically. Which sequences, beginning at 100, have the greatest maximum value? Which are the longest?

6-23   A biologist doing research into pheromones, or chemical attractants, decides to drive a few of her bugs crazy. She places four bugs in the corners of a square test area, then douses each with a chemical that is sure to attract its right-hand neighbor. Driven by genetics, each bug starts walking counterclockwise toward its neighbor.

    Now, each bug walks at the same speed. Before moving one of its little bug feet, the bug may change direction slightly so that it is heading directly toward its quarry. Write a program that answers these questions: Where do the bugs meet? How far has each bug walked, measured along its curved path, when they all finally collide?

6-24   *Buffon's Needle* is a famous method, first presented by the Comte de Buffon in 1777, for estimating the value π. A needle of length l is dropped onto a wooden floor whose boards are exactly d apart. If the probability of the needle landing partially on a crack is called P, then $P = 2l/\pi d$, or π approaches $2l/Pd$ as the number of trials increases.

    In 1812, Laplace extended Buffon's method to allow a grid of intersecting parallel lines. If the lines in one direction are a apart, and are b apart in the other, and the needle's length l is less than a or b, then:

$$P = \frac{2l(a+b)-l^2}{\pi ab}, \quad or \quad \pi = \frac{2l(a+b)-l^2}{Pab}$$

    Write a program that simulates the dropping of the needle using Buffon's or Laplace's method. How many trials are needed to approximate π to within five decimal places? Does the length of the needle affect the speed at which either approach approximates π?

6-25   Two alternative methods of computing π are:

$$\frac{\pi}{4} = 1 - \frac{1}{3} + \frac{1}{5} - \frac{1}{7} + \cdots \quad \text{(from Leibnitz)}$$

$$\frac{\pi}{4} = \frac{2}{3} \times \frac{4}{3} \times \frac{4}{5} \times \frac{6}{5} \times \frac{6}{7} \times \frac{8}{7} \times \cdots \quad \text{(from Wallis)}$$

Which method—the sum of the series or the product of the series (or dropping needles)—approaches π most rapidly?

Additional loop problems follow Chapter 7.

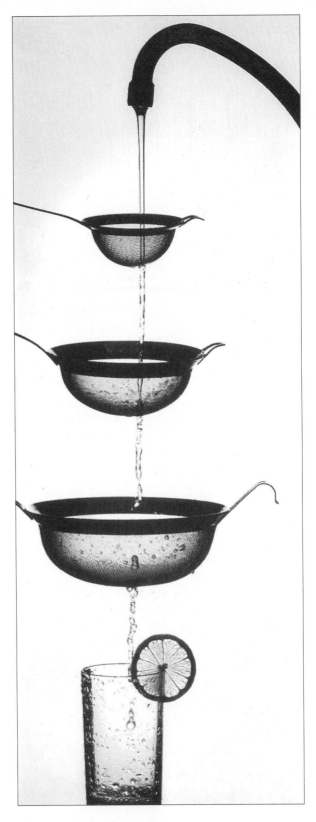

It's easy to view text processors as filters that change, use, or learn about the stream of values as it flows through the program. (p. 240)

7

Text Processing: a Detour

This chapter is about the letters and words that form text. We're going to pursue the theme of text as a *stream* of words and sentences; not as fixed jots and dots on a page, but as a column of characters that marches inexorably through our loops. Our programs will serve as *filters* through which every character must attempt to squeeze: some will survive, some may be altered, and others may disappear entirely.

Text processing filters are generally cut from two patterns: either they do something *to* the text, or they learn something *about* the text. But whichever pattern they follow, the beauty of filter programs is that they can usually be strung together (with the assistance of the operating system, which can make one program's output be another's input) to accomplish tasks that might not have even been considered when the filters were written.

It's easy to study the textbook examples of text processing. But as a practical matter, working with files is going to take some investigation of your own computer system as well. The *Beyond the Standard* section describes some typical extensions. You may find that a brief detour ahead to the start of Chapter 13, *The* file *Type*, is useful too.

Strictly Pascal

7-1

LET'S BEGIN WITH A BUG. PROGRAM EchoBug, below, reads and *echoes*, or immediately reprints, characters. Its bug is that it doesn't understand Pascal's notion of a line. EchoBug reads an [Enter] (or [Return] if you're using a Mac or DEC keyboard), but it echoes only a single space. I didn't type EchoBug's input directly; if I had, input and output would have been intermingled and confusing. Instead, I made EchoBug read from a file by *redirecting* its input. Later in this chapter, I'll show you how.

line-unaware text-echoing program

```
program EchoBug (input, output);
     {Reads and echoes text input, but mishandles the end-of-line.}
var Ch: char;
begin
     writeln ('Type in a few lines for me to echo.');
     while not eof do begin      {eof means end-of-file. It's unpronounceable.}
          read (Ch);                  {Read one character.}
          write (Ch)                  {Print the character.}
     end {while}
end.   {EchoBug}
```

Type in a few lines for me to echo.
Those who know don't tell,
and those who tell don't know.
Those who know don't tell, and those who tell don't know.

EchoBug tries to process a *file*. I can outline the main loop specification as:

echoing text incorrectly

> *Goal: Echo text.*
> *Bound: There's no more input.*
> *Plan: Read a character.*
>   *Print the character.*

Now, computer systems in general, and Pascal in particular, make a few simplifying assumptions about files. In Pascal, they revolve around two boolean functions that have unpronounceable names: eof (for *end of file*) and eoln (for *end of line*), both mentioned in the last chapter. Most people just spell the names out. Suppose that we grit our teeth and take all the medicine at once:

eof and eoln

— A *text file* is a sequence of characters that's broken into lines.

— Every line ends with an end-of-line character, and every file ends with an end-of-file character.* There's always an end-of-line before the end-of-file.

— Calling writeln is the only guaranteed way to produce the end-of-line character. There's no way (and no need) to produce the end-of-file character in Standard Pascal.

---

* This statement isn't literally true, since the operating system may use other tricks to mark the line and file ends. However, because we never look at the actual characters—we use eof and eoln to 'sense' if they're there, instead—it is a useful simplification to pretend that they exist.

when are eof and eoln TRUE?

— The boolean function eoln is TRUE when we're about to read the end-of-line and is FALSE otherwise.

— The boolean function eof is TRUE when we're about to read the end-of-file and is FALSE otherwise.

the end-of-line is read as a blank space

— If eoln is TRUE, then:

read (Ch);	*gives you a single space character and puts you at the start of the next line.*
readln (Ch);	*gives you a single space character, skips the next line, then puts you at the start of the line after that.*
readln;	*puts you at the start of the next line*

to crash, read when eof is TRUE

— If eof is TRUE, then

read (Ch);	*causes a program crash.*
readln (Ch);	*causes a program crash.*
readln;	*causes a program crash.*

This may seem like a lot of detail, but we're going to rely on the same characteristic program form again and again. It won't be hard to remember.

Echoing text correctly requires a check for the end-of-line. If you spot one, call readln (to get rid of the end-of-line), then writeln (since that's the only way to create a new end-of-line). Although our goal—echoing text, and bound—running out of data, remain the same, our plan is a bit more sophisticated:

echoing text correctly

> *Goal: Echo text.*
> *Bound: There's no more input.*
> *Plan: Check to see if we're at the end of a line*
>   **if** *we are* **then** *do line-end processing*
>   **else** *read and echo a single character*

The complete, correct program is:

line-aware text-echoing program

```
program EchoText (input, output);
    {Reads and echoes text input while preserving line structure.}
var Ch: char;
begin
    writeln ('Type in a few lines for me to echo. ');
    while not eof do begin
        if eoln then begin         {Deal with the end-of-line.}
            readln;                {Dump the remainder of the line.}
            writeln                {Print a carriage return.}
        end else begin             {Deal with an ordinary character.}
            read (Ch);
            write (Ch)
        end {if}
    end {while}
end.   {EchoText}
```

(*output follows*)

```
Type in a few lines for me to echo.
Those who know don't tell,
and those who tell don't know.
Those who know don't tell,
and those who tell don't know.
```

I've left one important detail out of both example programs. It's obvious that the [Enter] (or [Return] on Mac and DEC systems) key supplies the end-of-line when we're typing from the keyboard. But how do we name the end-of-file? The answer is totally dependent on your computer and its operating system. Here are the most common values:

UNIX	[Ctrl] [D]
DOS	[Ctrl] [Z]
VMS	[Ctrl] [Z]
Macintosh	[Enter]

The Macintosh [Enter] key is found on the numeric keypad. The [Return] key produces an end-of-line.

Modification Problems

1. Even though EchoBug doesn't echo the end-of-line properly, it still manages to look at each character. Modify it so that it counts and reports on the number of characters it reads.
2. Modify EchoText so that it counts the number of lines of input it has seen.
3. Modify EchoText so that it echoes only odd-numbered lines of input.

Self-Check Questions

Q. What does this program segment do?

```
while not eoln do begin
    read (Ch)
end;
read (Ch)
```

A. It mimics the operation of a single readln call. First, it reads (and ignores) characters until eoln is TRUE. At this point, it has reached, but hasn't read, the end of the line. Then, it reads (and ignores) one more character: the end-of-line.

Q. What is the value of Ch after the last read, above?

A. When eoln is TRUE, the next character is *always* read as a single space. Ch equals ' ', and we're about to read the first character on the next line (if there is one).

Background: The Perils of Compatibility

We usually think of *compatibility*, or the ability of different products to work together, as a good thing. *Upward compatibility*, or the ability of older versions of an item to work in harmony with newer versions, is equally desirable.

However, the wish for compatibility can make matters worse when there have been significant changes in technology or applications. It can force new technology and applications to conform to old standards.

When Pascal was first defined, almost all input and output was managed through *punched cards*, known popularly as *IBM cards*. The eoln and eof functions made perfect sense, since there weren't any special characters to read. After all, each card was a line of input, so there was no need for a special end-of-line character. The end of input was marked by a special end-of-data card, again removing any need for an end-of-file character.

Punched cards were replaced by keyboards and stored files in the early 1980's, when the first international Pascal standard was developed. It would have been convenient to pick control characters or other special keys to serve as the end-of-line and end-of-file. Unfortunately, relying on special keys would make new Pascal programs incompatible with old ones. Standard Pascal kept eoln and eof because they could work with all systems.

A Harder Example

Let's take the basic EchoText program and turn it into something a little more useful:

problem: counting lines and characters

> Write a program that counts the number of lines and characters in a text sample. Do *not* count the end-of-line as a character.

The central loop specification is nearly identical to the text echoing program's:

> *Goal: Echo text.*
> *Bound: There's no more input.*
> *Plan: Check to see if we're at the end of a line*
>   **if** *we are* **then** *count and dump a line*
>   **else** *count and dump a character*

A pseudocode outline of the whole program adds some familiar steps: initializing counter variables, and reporting on their contents.

pseudocode

> *initialize* LineCount *and* CharCount *variables to* 0;
> **while not** eof **do begin**
>   **if** eoln *is* TRUE
>   **then** *add one to the* LineCount;
>   *call* readln *to discard the end-of-line*;
>   **else** *add one to the* CharCount;
>   *read and ignore a character*;
>   **end** *of the loop*;
> *report on the results*

> Using **while not** eof . . . as a bound is nearly universal in text processing loops. It may be the loop's intentional bound—we want to exit because we've run out of data, or it may be a necessary bound—we *have* to exit because we've run out of input—but it almost always appears.

The completed program is shown below; thank Dorothy Parker for the input.

character and line
counting program

```pascal
program Counter (input, output);
    {Counts the number of characters and lines in input text.}
var Ch:  char;
    CharCount, LineCount:  integer;
begin
    CharCount := 0;
    LineCount := 0;
    writeln ('Give me a few lines of input to count.');
    while not eof do begin
        if eoln then begin
                LineCount := LineCount + 1;
                readln
        end else begin
                CharCount := CharCount + 1;
                read (Ch)
        end;  {if}
    end;  {while}
    write (CharCount : 1);  write (' characters read, ');
    write (LineCount : 1);  writeln (' lines read.')
end.  {Counter}
```

```
Give me a few lines of input to count.
Although I work, and seldom cease,
At Dumas pere and Dumas fils.
Alas, I cannot make me care
For Dumas fils and Dumas pere.
120 characters read, 4 lines read.
```

Modification Problems

1. Improve Counter so that it counts sentences as well as lines.
2. Convert Counter into a program that capitalizes and prints its input.
3. Change Counter into a program that tells you only the number of lines that are *a*) shorter than ten characters and *b*) longer than twenty.

Beyond the Standard: Redirecting I/O*

When a program has just a few lines of input and output, it's easy to sit at a desk and pound keys. But if either input or output is more voluminous, there's a better way. It's called *redirection*. By redirecting input, output, or both, we can fool programs into thinking that they're still dealing with the keyboard and screen, while in actuality they're getting input from, and/or sending output to, stored files.

   Now, we've been talking about files all along, even though imagining that a terminal is a file obviously requires a certain willingness to suspend one's

---

* This section is optional.

disbelief. A keyboard is only full of information to the same extent that a ball-point pen is, while a screen says no more than a blank sheet of paper.

But pretending that files and keyboards are the same turns out to be worthwhile. Our life as programmers is infinitely simpler if we can write the same exact program no matter where its input comes from or where its output goes. All we need is a way to switch between different sources of input or destinations for output without changing the program.

Unfortunately for us, Standard Pascal doesn't supply the tools we need to carry through on the game. In Standard Pascal, you have to know the actual name of any permanent file a program is going to use *before* you write the program. Clearly, this is unrealistic: just imagine writing with a text editor that only lets you use file names from a pre-existing list!

input, output, and files

But since the need is so clearly apparent, nearly every real-world Pascal system will provide some mechanism for *redirecting* input and output. Redirecting input means 'changing the place that input comes from,' while redirecting output means 'changing the place that output goes.'

standard input and
output defined

> The *standard input file* is the keyboard. The *standard output file* is the monitor.

There are two basic approaches to redirecting input and output:

— Rely on the operating system to fool the program. This is easy for UNIX and DOS, hard but doable for VMS, and impossible on the Macintosh.

— Supply Pascal extensions that let the program fool the operating system.

Let's take a quick survey of these alternatives. Be sure to find out about your own system, because the rest of this chapter is going to assume that you have some means of reading input from, or writing output to, a permanent disk file.

operating system
redirection

DOS and UNIX systems use the **<** and **>** signs to mean 'input comes from' and 'output goes to.' Suppose that **MyProg** is the name of an executable Pascal program, which is to say that the Pascal version has been compiled and saved. If typing **MyCode** by itself runs the program using the keyboard and monitor, then this version redirects I/O:

DOS, UNIX

```
MyCode < InFile > OutFile
```

When program **MyCode** runs, its input will come from **InFile**, and its output will go to **OutFile**. Both **< InFile** and **> OutFile** are optional.

VMS requires more elaborate advance preparation. A small operating system program must be run before you execute your own Pascal program.

The second approach, fooling the operating system by extending Pascal, is completely nonstandard. The basic issue is simple: we want to associate a Pascal *file variable*, like input or output, with the name of a permanent file. Moreover, we want that association to stick for the rest of the program, so that read and write calls (as well as eof and eoln) will do the right thing.

redirection within the
program

Although the name of the procedure will vary among Pascal implementations, it obviously needs two pieces of information to work: which file (input or output) do we want to redirect and what file name (usually supplied as a string, between single quotation marks) do we want to use in its place? Here are some typical solutions. They're all built around the Standard Pascal procedures reset and rewrite. I haven't introduced these procedures, incidentally, because we won't use them in their standard form until Chapter 13.

some typical extensions

```
{VAX Pascal}
Open (input, 'actual_name', old);
reset (input);
Open (output, 'actual_name', new);
rewrite (output);
{Turbo Pascal}
SYSTEM.Assign (input, 'actual_name');
reset (input);
SYSTEM.Assign (output, 'actual_name');
rewrite (output);
{Think Pascal and Berkeley Pascal}
reset (input, 'actual_name');
rewrite (output, 'actual_name');
```

It's a safe assumption that any system that provides these file extensions will also supply a string type that makes them easy to use. After the proper calls, read, readln, eof, and eoln will automatically refer to the permanent file that's providing input, while write and writeln will add to the permanent file that's holding output. We'll talk more about standard and nonstandard uses of reset and rewrite when we discuss files in Chapter 13.

The File Window*

No matter how well you code, there will be tasks that seem to be well-nigh impossible to accomplish. For example, we know that when we're reading integer input, both read and readln will skip blanks and other white space, then read a number that ends with any non-digit.

non-digits can follow. . .

```
{Leading blanks are skipped, and ending non-digits are OK.}
read (Number);
writeln (Number : 1);
```

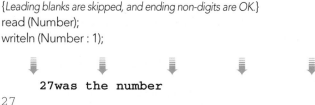

```
27was the number
```
27

But what if I reverse the problem and ask you to skip non-digits first? The regular input procedures won't work.

. . . but they can´t lead

```
{Leading non-digits will cause a crash.}
read (Number);
writeln (Number : 1);
```

```
was the number27
Runtime error . . .        etc.
```

---

* The file window is an optional detail at this point.

A call that expects to read a number will cause a program crash if it reads non-digits (or non-blanks) instead. The *file window* is Pascal's solution.

> The *file window* is a built-in variable that represents the value that we're about to read. The standard input file window's name is input ↑. On your keyboard, use the circumflex, ˆ, rather than an up-arrow.

I use the up-arrow because it's easier to read.

What's the file window's type? That depends on the type of the file. Technically, input and output are *textfiles*, which means that they're files of characters. That gives input ↑ type char as well.

The file window is handy when we want to know what's coming, but don't want to disturb it. Let's use it to solve the number-reading problem. In pseudocode, our job is:

reading numbers robustly

> *find the start of the number;*
> *read the number;*

Since we may have to skip non-digits, *find the start of the number* is going to take a loop.

non-digit skipping specification

> *Goal: Skip leading non-digits.*
> *Bound: We're about to read a digit.*
> *Plan: Read a single character.*

A practical solution is actually a bit more complicated, since legal integer values can be preceded by a plus or minus sign. I'll leave that for you in the Modification Problems.

The final procedure is shown below. It relies on the fact that the digit characters are ordered ′0′ through ′9′.

bullet-proof positive integer input

```
procedure ReadInteger (var Number: integer);
    {A robust form of read for positive integer input.}
    var Ch: char;    {For the junk characters, if any.}
    begin
        while not (input ↑ in [ ′0′ .. ′9′ ]) do begin
            read (Ch)
        end;
        {Postcondition: the next character is a digit.}
        read (Number);
    end; {ReadInteger}
```

Modification Problems ——————————————————————————

1. Suppose that there aren't any numbers. Just how robust is ReadInteger then? Improve the procedure by checking for the end-of-file.

2. In Pascal, an integer may be preceded by a plus or a minus sign. Modify ReadInteger so that it handles signs properly. Be sure that you can handle +-+-10.

Standard Practices: Streams and Filters

7-2

PROGRAMS THAT PROCESS TEXT are often called *filters*. That's because we can think of the sequence of characters that text consists of as forming a *stream* of values. The stream might be temporarily frozen into a file, or it might be trickling out of your keyboard one character at a time. In either case, it's easy to view text processors as filters that change, use, or learn about the stream of values as it flows through the program.

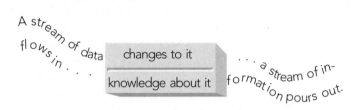

> A program's *input stream* is its input—usually the characters we type into a keyboard. A program's *output stream* is the output it produces and typically sends to a terminal screen.

standard input and output

I've already mentioned that the keyboard and screen are usually referred to as the *standard* or *default* input and output streams, and that just about every Pascal system will give you a way to *redirect* them to specific files. Redirecting input lets you process data that are currently stored in a file, while redirecting output lets you send your program's results to a file.

But regardless of the stream's origin or destination, it will pass through our program. That's why the term filter is so descriptive. I'll be talking about two kinds of filters: *process* filters and *stream* filters.

A process filter does something to the stream of data:

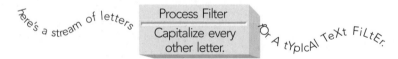

Text-handling problems that process filters typically solve include:

— Copying files or searching for a particular value in a stream of data.

some process filters

— Capitalizing letters, transforming all letters to lower-case, or changing the order of values in a stream.

— *Stream editing*, or carrying out a stored sequence of editing commands on a stored file.

— Translating data from one form (say, binary) to another (like decimal).

In each case, the process filter applies some basic rule—the process—to the values in the stream. The simplest process filter does very little indeed—it just reads and echoes a sample of text without changing its line structure.

State filters, in contrast, produce information by learning something *about* the data stream.

Computer scientists talk about the state of data as a shorthand way of saying 'What do these data mean? What is their status? What do we know about them besides their values?' For instance, the characters on this page have individual values, but they also occupy distinct and meaningful states: as words, as white space,* as illustrations, and so on.

also marginal notes

A *state transition* is a change from one state to another. The goal of most state filters is to spot or establish state transitions. Some of the problems we can solve by writing state filter programs include:

— Counting the number of words in the input stream (by counting in-a-word/not-in-a-word state transitions).

state transitions

— Printing one word or sentence per output line (by adding a carriage return whenever the in-a-word or in-a-sentence state changes).

— Compressing blanks in input (by turning off echoing of characters whenever we're in a blank-spaces state).

— Suppressing extraneous blanks at the beginning (*leading blanks*) or end (*trailing blanks*) of lines of text (by recognizing distinct before-the-line, during-the-line, and after-the-line states).

> Distinguishing between process and state filters is useful only if it suggests a method of problem solving—not for its own sake.

Perhaps you can modify an existing process filter or rephrase a complicated problem as a simpler state filter. As with loop bounds, you won't get tested on petty differences. You will find for yourself, though, that seeing the similarities between programs helps make your life that much easier.

Self-Check Questions

Q. Suppose that the process at the heart of a procedure that reads and echoes text *without* regard for line structure is this shaded pair of statements:

```
while not eof do begin
    read (Ch);
    write (Ch)    {We'll ignore line structure here.}
end
```

Write the central process statement or statements for each of these alternative goals:

---

* Footnotes, too, of course.

a) Print every input letter as the one before it.
b) Replace each '&' with two carriage returns.
c) Get rid of all the carriage returns.
d) Print every dollar sign twice.

A. It's not hard once you get the hang of it:

a) read (Ch);
    write (chr(ord(Ch) – 1))

b) read (Ch);
    if Ch = '&' then begin
                 writeln;
                 writeln
             end
    else begin write (Ch) end

c) if eoln
        then begin readln end
        else begin
            read (Ch);
            write (Ch)
        end

d) read (Ch);
    write (Ch);
    if Ch = '$' then begin
        write (Ch)
    end

A Process Filter: Searching for Letters

As the Self-Check question above makes clear, the basic **while not** eof **do** . . . loop is easily adapted to a variety of ends. One of the most common text-filtering problems is *searching*—sifting through a text stream for a particular value. Suppose that I ask the question simply:

problem: finding the letter s

Write a program that finds the letter 's' in a sample of input and lets you know its position.

If you think about it, this is really a sentinel bound problem. We want to find a value that equals the sentinel 's'. On the face of it there's no difficulty: we just read characters until the sentinel shows up. But is the sentinel bound effective enough to *guarantee* termination? No. Suppose there isn't an 's' in input. Even though it's one of the most common letters in English, it doesn't have to appear.

necessary bounds guarantee termination

Like most search loops, our search for an 's' requires a necessary bound—a bound that makes the loop stop if its intentional bound can't be met.

A variety of candidates might serve as the necessary bound. When should we call off the search? After some number of characters? At the end of the line? When there's no more input? It doesn't matter—as long as the necessary bound can *guarantee* that the loop will terminate. Thus, the specification of a typical searching loop is:

loop specification for a
text search

> *Goal: Find a sentinel.*
> *Intentional bound: The sentinel was found.*
> *Necessary bound: Data was somehow exhausted.*
> *Plan: Read a single value.*

I can describe our search loop for an ´s´ a bit more precisely.

loop specification

> *Goal: Find the position of the first ´s´ in input.*
> *Intentional bound: We read an ´s´.*
> *Necessary bound: We ran out of input.*
> *Plan: Read a character.*
>   *Add 1 to a position counter that began at 0.*

Pseudocode adds a few details. Notice that I have to initialize the character-holding variable, Letter, since it helps state the **while**'s exit condition. The ASCII *nul* character, chr(0), is frequently used to initialize char variables, in same way that the number 0 might serve to initialize integer variables.

ASCII nul

Read the loop's confirmation comment—its postcondition—carefully.

pseudocode

> *initialize the position counter to 0;*
> *initialize* Letter *to anything but the* SENTINEL
> **while not** eof **and** (Letter <> SENTINEL) **do begin**
>   *read a character;*
>   *add 1 to the position counter*
> **end** *of the loop;*
> {*We found the sentinel or ran out of input. If the sentinel was found, we know its position.*}
> *print the position of the ´s´ if one appeared*

bounds, not goals, end
loops

> Loops end because they reach their bounds, not because they achieve their goals. When there are multiple bounds, *look after you loop* to decide exactly what caused termination.

A postcondition comment should help a program reader confirm her mental picture of what has happened. A postcondition that merely parrots the **while** statement doesn't say enough; she can read the bounds for herself. However, a postcondition that jumps to a conclusion about why the loop ended is even worse. We *hope* that we found the sentinel's position, but there's always the possibility that that's not why we left the loop. The comment that I've used leaves no doubt that an extra check has to be made.

The final program is shown below. Although I'm showing its input, I'll assume that input has been redirected from a file.

(*program follows*)

a search with multiple bounds

```
program FindS (input, output);
    {Reports the position of the first 's' it reads.}
const SENTINEL = 's';
        NULL = 0;    {the ASCII nul character's position}
var Position: integer;
    Letter: char;
begin
    Position := 0;
    Letter := chr (NULL);
    write ('All set to look for an  ');
    writeln (SENTINEL);
    while not eof and (Letter <> SENTINEL) do begin
        read (Letter);
        Position := Position + 1
    end;
    {Postcondition:  if the sentinel was found, it's at Position.}
    {Question:  are the end-of-lines added to the count?}
    if Letter = SENTINEL then begin
        write ('The sentinel was found in position  ');
        writeln (Position : 1)
    end
    else begin writeln ('No sentinel was found.') end;
end.    {FindS}
```

```
All set to look for an s
Mary had a tiny lamb with fleece a pale white hue,
And everywhere that Mary went the lamb kept her in view.
To academe he went with her, illegal and quite rare.
It made the children laugh and play to view a lamb in there.
No sentinel was found.
```

Modification Problems

1. Modify FindS so that it reports both the sentinel's line number and its position within the line.

2. Put the sentinel-searching code of FindS into a procedure that has two parameters—the value of the sentinel and the position it's found in. What value might you give to the position parameter if the sentinel wasn't found?

3. Modify FindS so that it looks for, and prints the position of, any 'i' before an 'e' that follows a 'c'.

4. The poem above is a *lipogram*—a composition that omits one letter—written by A. Ross Eckler. Can you rewrite it so that some other letter (say, 'e') is missing?

A State Filter: Counting Words

Looking for changes in state is an approach to problem solving that finds many applications in text processing. Recall that state filters use or act on information about the input stream. Counting words provides a good example:

problem: counting words

We can define *words* as sequences of characters that are separated by *white space*—blanks, tabs, and control characters. Write a program that counts the number of words in a stream of text. There may be extra white space between any two words or at the beginning or end of the stream of characters.

The fact that there can be extra blanks prevents the kind of quick and easy solution that I prefer—count spaces, and add 1.

Suppose that I rephrase the problem like this: look for, and count, state *transitions*—changes from one state to another. As we read through the input stream one character at a time, we always know at least two facts about the data: either we're in a word, or we're not in a word. Those are our two states. It doesn't matter how long the word is or how many blanks there are. If we can count state transitions, we can count words.

state transitions

Now, the smallest step a word counter can take toward the loop bound is trying to read a single character. This single step is also big enough to let us know if a state transition has occurred, since it just takes one character to enter or leave a word. A loop specification is:

loop specification

> *Goal: Count the number of words.*
> *Bound: We ran out of data.*
> *Plan: Read a single character.*
> > *If a transition occurred, update the current state*
> > *and add* 1 *to the count of words.*

Rephrasing the problem of counting words as one of spotting state transitions is the kind of elegant solution that makes life difficult for the people who give you examinations. You are going to become very good at solving problems once you're able to recognize an underlying 'sameness,' and can see that one solution can be applied to a variety of seemingly different problems:

some equivalent problems

> *Spot transitions from in-a-word to not-in-a-word, then*
> > *Count words* (increment a count after each transition)
> > *Compress blanks* (print a single space after each transition)
> > *Print one word per line* (print a carriage return after each transition)

I'll add states to our bag of tricks with two boolean variables. Note that the last character read and the last character processed will usually be two different values.

InAWord *will be* TRUE *if the last character processed wasn't white space.*

ItWasBlank *will be* TRUE *if the last character read was white space.*

A brief pseudocode is:

first pseudocode

> **while** *there are more data*
> > *get a value;*
> > *update the current state;*
> > *act on a state change;*

Naturally, there are many details to fill in:

second pseudocode

> *initialize a state variable* InAWord *to* FALSE;
> *initialize a counter variable to* 0;
> **while not** eof **do begin**
>   *read a character;*
>   **if** *it was a blank*
>   **then** *set* ItWasBlank *to* TRUE
>   **else** *set* ItWasBlank *to* FALSE;
>   *set* InAWord *to* TRUE;
>   **if** ItWasBlank **and** *we were* InAWord *the state changed so*
>   **then** *set* InAWord *back to* FALSE;
>   *count the word*
> **end** *the loop;*
> *report on the results;*

In the final code, below, note the method I've used to define white space. Since the end-of-line is read as a single space, I don't bother with checks for eoln. And, because the space character is the very first printing character in ASCII (i.e. it follows the control characters), every character whose ordinal position is less than or equal to ord(´ ´) can be considered to be a blank. However, since we can compare characters as readily as numbers:

$$ord(Ch) <= ord(´ \ ´) \qquad \textit{is the same as} \qquad Ch <= ´ \ ´$$

I use the simpler, right-hand version. Pay particular attention to the shaded lines of Words, because we'll be returning to them in a moment.

word counting program

```
program Words (input, output);
    {A state filter that counts words that are separated by one or more blanks.}
var InAWord, ItWasBlank: boolean;
    Count: integer;
    Ch: char;
begin
    writeln ('Say something poetic so I can count words.');
    Count := 0;
    InAWord := FALSE;
    while not eof do begin
        read (Ch);
        if Ch <= ´ ´
            then ItWasBlank := TRUE
            else begin    {Ch was a character.}
                ItWasBlank := FALSE;
                InAWord := TRUE
            end;
        if ItWasBlank and InAWord then begin    {A word just ended.}
            InAWord := FALSE;
            Count := Count + 1
        end {if}
    end; {while}
    write ('The number of words was:    ');
    writeln (Count : 1)
end.    {Words}
```

```
Say something poetic so I can count words.
The forehead of Shelley was cluttered with curls,
And Keats never was a descendent of Earls,
And Byron walked out with a number of girls.
The number of words was:  25
```

Modification Problems

1. Modify Words so that it makes explicit tests for the space, tab, carriage return, and line feed characters.

2. Change Words into CountSentences. In particular, deal with the problem of mistakenly counting '...' as three sentences.

3. Extend Words so that it finds out the average number of words per sentence in its input. Then get the average length of each word, too. Make sure the count is right if the last line doesn't end with a carriage return.

Variations on a State

Let's take another look at the central part of program Words.

a state filter boilerplate

```
InAWord := FALSE;
while not eof do begin
    read (Ch);
    if Ch <= ' '
        then ItWasBlank := TRUE
        else begin    {Ch was a character.}
            ItWasBlank := FALSE;
            InAWord := TRUE
                                          {The it-was-a-letter empty space.}
        end; {if}
    if ItWasBlank and InAWord then begin
        InAWord := FALSE;
                                          {The a-word-just-ended empty space.}
    end {if}
end; {while}
```

Why the shaded empty spaces? Because they're ours to fill in with whatever code strikes our fancy. As the comments show, they hold valuable state information. Suppose that I want to compress white space, so that no more than one blank separates any two words:

compressing white
space

```
InAWord := FALSE;
while not eof do begin
    read (Ch);
    if Ch <= ´ ´
        then ItWasBlank := TRUE
        else begin    {Ch was a character.}
            ItWasBlank := FALSE;
            InAWord := TRUE
            write (Ch)          {Print Ch if it-was-a-letter.}
        end;
    if ItWasBlank and InAWord then begin
        InAWord := FALSE;
        write (´ ´)             {Print a space if a-word-just-ended.}
    end
end; {while}
writeln
```

```
Here     is
    a short
test.
Here is a short test.
```

Note that we get *exactly* what we asked for—a single space separates each and every word. How can we preserve the line structure? Well, if there's no extraneous white space after the last word on a line, it takes this additional line:

compress white space,
but preserve lines

```
InAWord := FALSE;
while not eof do begin
    read (Ch);
    if Ch <= ´ ´
        then ItWasBlank := TRUE
        else begin    {Ch was a character.}
            ItWasBlank := FALSE;
            InAWord := TRUE
            write (Ch);
            if eoln then writeln  {Spot the line end if it-was-a-letter.}
        end;
    if ItWasBlank and InAWord then begin
        InAWord := FALSE;
        write (´ ´)          {Print one space if a-word-just-ended.}
    end
end; {while}
```

```
Here      is
    a short
test.
Here is
a short
test.
```

Suppose that I want to compress blanks, but print only one word per output line. That means that whenever *a-word-just-ended*, it must be time to print a carriage return. Ordinary blanks never get printed at all.

compress blanks, print
one per line

```
InAWord := FALSE;
while not eof do begin
    read (Ch);
    if Ch <= ´ ´
        then ItWasBlank := TRUE
        else begin      {Ch was a character.}
            ItWasBlank := FALSE;
            InAWord := TRUE
            write (Ch)             {Print it if it-was-a-letter.}
        end;
    if ItWasBlank and InAWord then begin
        InAWord := FALSE;
        writeln                    {Print a return if it-was-a-space.}
    end
end; {while}
```

```
Here       is
     a short
test.
Here
is
a
short
test.
```

This tiny little stretch of code turns out to be amazingly versatile, doesn't it? What's even better is that making a minute change in the rule we follow for establishing the state we're in leads us to a new collection of programs. Suppose that I pose a new problem that I thought up in the shower. Can you guess what it's going to be?

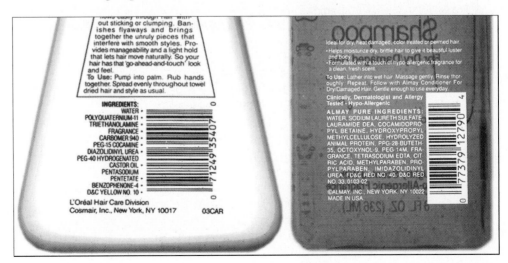

problem: corrupted data

While waiting for my shower to finish (remember, I'm a computer scientist!), I made the mistake of reading a few ingredient lists. Let's leave aside such questions as *just what is Octoxynol-9?* and *who is the alluring Peg-15?* Instead, how would you write a program that reads the ingredients, but echoes only numbers, one per line?

I call this the 'corrupted data' problem because that's what it is in more serious applications: a file of numerical data has somehow acquired extraneous non-digit characters. In Pascal, it's a runtime error if the upcoming character is anything but a digit when you're reading integer or real values.

```
write ('Give me your favorite number.    ');
read (AnInteger);
```

```
Give me your favorite number.    Plan9 from Outer Space
Runtime error ...    etc.
```

We have to clean up the data before we can use them. Unfortunately, the simple solution—echoing only digit characters—won't separate whole numbers, one per line.

In state terms, the problem is almost exactly like that of printing one word per line. The only difference is that instead of wanting to suppress blanks, we now want to suppress non-digits. The underlying pseudocode is:

pseudocode

while *there are more data*
   get a value;
   update the current state;
   act on a state change;

The solution, which barely differs from program Words, is shown below.

clean up numbers
program

```
program Numbers (input, output);
   {Prints only whole numbers, one per line.}
var Ch: char;
   NonDigit, InANumber: boolean;
begin
   writeln ('Type in the list of ingredients.');
   while not eof do begin
      read (Ch);
      if not (Ch in [ '0' .. '9' ])
         then NonDigit := TRUE
         else begin    {Ch was a digit.}
            NonDigit := FALSE;
            InANumber := TRUE;
            write (Ch)
         end;
      if NonDigit and InANumber then begin    {The state has changed.}
         InANumber := FALSE;
         writeln
      end {if}
   end {while}
end. {Numbers}
```

```
Type in the list of ingredients.
Polyquaternium-11, Carbomer-940, Peg-15...     first label continues
Ppg-28-Buteth-35, Octoxynol-9, Peg-14M...     second label continues
11
940
15
40
4
  · · ·    output continues
40
33
0103
02
```

Modification Problems

1. Fix Numbers so that it won't print any leading zeros (like those in 0103 and 02).

2. Modify either Words or Numbers so that it reads a Pascal program, then prints it exactly as it was *except* without comments.

3. Modify Words so that it reads names in *first name, last name* format, then prints them in *last name, first initial* format. Naturally, there may be any number of blanks before either of the input words.

4. Numbers works fine for positive integer values, but what about real? This is a rather more difficult problem, but I have great faith in your ability to make it so.

Program Engineering Notes: KISS

7-3

In my experience, relatively few of the really tough programming errors have to do with a loop's action. One can make mistakes, of course, but the sneaky bugs hide at the loop's *boundary conditions*—the circumstances of its first and last iterations. For example:

Exit and entry condition bugs: Is the loop's exit or entry condition doing what you intended it to do? Have you accidentally phrased an *unavoidable* condition that will always be met on the first trip through the loop, or an *impossible* condition that can never be met? Does the loop's exit condition guarantee that the loop will terminate? What if you run out of data, or don't arrive at an answer, or look for a sentinel that doesn't exist?

boundary condition problems

Off-by-one bugs: Is it possible for the loop to take place one time too often? One time too few? Should a < be a <=, or vice versa?

Synchronization bugs: Is the exact moment of exit properly synchronized with the loop's action? Is it possible that one last variable should have been updated before the loop was finished? Or that one last iteration of the loop was counted incorrectly?

> The KISS philosophy—*keep it simple, stupid!*—is excruciatingly important in loop programming. Always take the simplest possible step that approaches the loop bound; never add goal-oriented actions that might cause you to miss the bound.

Suppose, for instance, that we want to print every other character, starting with the first, on each line of input. For example, if a loop is bounded by the end of an input line, reading just one character—or even *no* characters—may reach the bound. This loop can't tell if it's at the end of the line when it starts:

buggy character skipping

```
repeat
     read (Ch);          {Print this one.}
     write (Ch);
     read (Ch)           {Skip this one.}
until eoln;
```

However, simply rewriting it as a **while** loop doesn't solve the underlying problem, which is that you can't read two characters and expect to avoid trouble.

more buggy character skipping

```
while not eoln do begin
     read (Ch);          {Print this one.}
     write (Ch);
     read (Ch)           {Skip this one.}
end
```

eoln becomes TRUE as soon as we've read the last regular character on the line. Unfortunately, it becomes FALSE after we read the carriage return. If an input line has an odd number of characters, we'll miss the end of the line entirely. One correct version is:

correct character skipping

```
while not eoln do begin
     read (Ch);          {Print this one.}
     write (Ch);
     if not eoln then begin
        read (Ch)        {Skip this one.}
     end  {if}
end; {while}
```

The difficulty of synchronizing input and activity can cause a perplexing bug that is difficult to diagnose. At some point, an off-by-one error enters a text processing loop and won't go away. The program user knows that something is out of synch because the program requires an extra `Enter` or `Return` every now and then. But aside from this quirk, everything seems to work properly.

the problem

Here's what's probably happening. Some commands given by the user may be just one character (or one line) long. Suppose that after reading and identifying the command, the programmer calls a procedure that obeys it. Then, she calls readln to get rid of the end-of-line, so that subsequent input will start on a fresh line. So far, so good.

But suppose that a single command is more complicated and requires multiple characters (or lines) of input. The procedure that obeys the command might do additional reading on its own. That's fine. But if the procedure *contains* the cleanup readln, problems result. Note that this isn't at all uncommon, by the way, since the more complicated procedure might have been written and tested in a driver program that required the internal readln.

the diagnosis

Whatever the cause, the program ends up with two readlns: one in the procedure and one back in the main program. Each one is supposed to flush the remnants of the current command line, usually in preparation for issuing a prompt for a new command. Unfortunately, the bug doesn't appear until the program user thinks the computer has mysteriously hung and impatiently hits the ⎡Enter⎤ key a few times.

the cure

Synchronization bugs that involve input are hard to find because they appear to be where they ain't—as part of the next command, rather than as a remnant of the previous one. Command processing is a difficult situation because there's no 'right' place for the readln to appear. The best way to avoid such problems is to work for consistency where possible, and to document exceptions when that's impossible.

Syntax Summary

❏   eof: is TRUE when we're about to read the end-of-file marker. This marker is always present at the end of a permanently stored file and can be entered from the keyboard using a control key that varies from system to system.

❏   eoln: is TRUE when we're about to read the end-of-line marker.

❏   input↑: the file window provides a look ahead at the value that's about to be read. Since input consists of character values, input↑ has type char.

Remember . . .

❏   Whatever the action of a text processing loop is, it almost invariably requires a check for eof to guarantee that the loop will terminate.

❏   The *standard input file* is the keyboard, while the *standard output file* is the monitor. If input or output is *redirected* (usually at the operating system level) a program can treat stored disk files as the source of input or the place for output to go.

❏   A *stream* of data is a sequence of values. The *standard input* stream usually comes from the keyboard (but it can also come from a file or other input device). The *standard output* stream is usually directed to the terminal screen, but it too can be redirected (perhaps to a printer or file).

❏   Text-processing programs are often called *filters*, because a stream of data flows through the program for modification or analysis.

❏   Filters that change the stream's contents can be described as *process filters*, which implies that some process is invoked on each item in the stream.

❏   Filters that analyze a stream's contents can be called *state filters*, which implies that they learn about the stream by looking for *state transitions*, or changes in the contents' meaning.

❏   The KISS philosophy is extremely important in loop programming. A loop action that tries to accomplish too much runs the risk of missing the bound.

Big Ideas

The Big Idea in this chapter is:

1. *Thinking in terms of filters makes programs easier to write and reuse.* A filter does just one thing but it does it very well. Write special-purpose tools rather than general-purpose systems.

Begin by Writing
the Exam . . .

7-1   The basic read and echo code is simply:

```
while not eof do begin
    read (Item);
    write (Item)
end;
```

Make up three *Write a program that . . .* problems that are really just outlandishly complicated variations of this basic loop. For example, you might require the program to print a carriage return only before printing a dollar sign, a question mark whenever you reach the end of an *input* line, and a plus sign at the end of every *output* line.

7-2   Let's try the same kind of variation with state filters. Recall that the basic state filter counted words by keeping an eye out for *in a word/not in a word* transitions. Use the Zen Study Method by thinking up three more counting problems that can be solved by spotting and counting state transitions.

7-3   If you can spot question marks, you can count questions; if you can spot dollar signs, you can add dollar amounts. Come up with two more tasks that require you to *see* something before you *do* something.

7-4   Time for *Here's the input, what's the output?* These questions can usually be compli-cated by doing something unexpected: skipping the first or last character on each line.

7-5   Naturally, *Here's the output, what's the input?* can't be far behind. How about capi-talizing lower-case words, or doubling odd numbers, or counting words that begin with a capital letter, or only echoing increasing values in an input sequence of random numbers? As always, you will find that the interesting part is choosing the segments that *can* be run in reverse.

7-6   It's important to understand the sequence of steps involved in opening, reading from, writing to, and closing files. The typical Zen study question, *Where's the bug?*, will try to do something very simple—say, copy one file to another—but manage to screw things up somehow. Write it.

Warmups and
Test Problems

7-7   Rewrite this segment without the first **if** statement:

```
if not eoln then begin
    repeat
        read (Ch)
        write (Ch);
    until eoln
end
```

7-8   Write a loop that reads a file of numbers and stores only the odd numbers in a file named odd.out.

7-9   Write a procedure that reads and echoes characters, with the following proviso: turn echoing *on* whenever an ´A´ is read, and turn it *off* whenever a ´T´ appears.

7-10   Write a procedure that reads and echoes text, preserving line structure, but prints only every other sentence starting with the first.

7-11   Write a procedure that connects pairs of lines whenever the first ends with an ampersand (&).

7-12   As above, except join only odd-numbered lines to even-numbered lines.

7-13   Write an encryption program. It should read characters, and replace each letter with a letter from the opposite end of the alphabet; e.g. replace 'a' with 'z,' 'b' with 'y,' and so on.

7-14   Write a decryption program that assumes that every *n*th input character is garbage and shouldn't be printed. The value of *n* is obtained by adding 2 to the remainder of dividing the length of the previous line by 3. Assume that the first line has no junk characters.

7-15   Write a program that counts completely blank input lines.

7-16   Write a program that reads and echoes a file. However, instead of printing words, just print the length of each word. Maintain the line structure of the original file.

7-17   Write a procedure (and a program to test it, of course) that asks the user for go-ahead permission:

```
Proceed? [Y/N]?
```

The procedure should repeat the prompt until a legal lower- or upper-case response is entered, and return the user's choice.

7-18   As above, but add a 'default' parameter—the value returned if the user hits Enter only—to the procedure.

Programming Problems

7-19   Ifay ouyay ancay eadray histay, ouyay ancay robablypay igurefay outay hatway hetay roblempay isay.

7-20   Write a short program that performs the following short analysis of its input:

a)   Print every letter that appears twice in a row.

b)   Print every three-letter sequence that's in alphabetical order.

Some sample input for you is:

```
Miss Metteer, displaying calmness, deftly made crabcakes from
excess cottonseed.  A studious bookkeeper under a canopy, she
laughingly hijacked the corrupted terra cotta, too.
```

7-21   A *gerund* is the 'ing' form of a verb: *Seeing is deceiving, but eating is believing* contains four gerunds. Write a program that can translate the infinitive form of a verb (the 'to be' form) into the gerund form. Hint: you'll find that the last two letters of a verb usually tell you how the gerund is formed.

7-22   Think of a letter between ´A´ and ´Z´. With a little help (you have to tell me if my guess was too low or too high), I can figure out which letter it was in no more than five guesses. Your job is to *a)* figure out how I do it and *b)* write a program that uses your method.

Then, write a program that picks the letter and lets a player guess. As above, the program should announce if a guess is high or low and allow no more than five guesses.

7-23   Suppose that a file contains the names of various sports:

```
Basketball
Weightlifting
Running
```

and so on. Write a program that reads and echoes the file one line at a time, preceding each output line with the words Bo Knows. Options (if your system supports a string type and string handling subprograms) *a)* if the input line is **Diddley** have the output line begin Bo Don't Know; *b)* as above, but if the input line is **Programming**, just print No.

7-24   'Massaging the data,' when applied to the results of scientific tests, usually means 'fudging the answers.' Programs, however, frequently require that data be massaged into shape for processing. For example, some of the changes that might be needed are:

a) Rewrite a file of integers in real format; e.g. turn 1 into 1.0.

b) Turn lower-case letters into capitals.

c) Find, and get rid of, extraneous blank lines.

d) Make sure that alphanumerics (letters and digits) are the only characters in a file. (Spaces and carriage returns are usually acceptable exceptions.)

Can you manage to make all of these checks in a single trip through a file?

7-25 A *pretty printer* is a program that turns raggedy old piles of code into shiny new masterpieces. In other words, a pretty printer applies a consistent and readable standard for line breaks, indenting, and so on to programs. Pretty printing can't make a program work, but it can help you discover what's wrong with one.

Like so many programs, pretty printers can be as complicated as you'd like. Here are some features that a simple pretty printer might include:

a) Have all indenting be a multiple of five spaces.

b) Put each comment on a line by itself.

c) Don't let multiple blank spaces appear within a line.

d) Don't allow multiple blank lines.

e) Limit the length of any line, and indent by some fixed amount if you're forced onto a second line.

f) Number each program line.

Write a pretty printer that enforces these rules.

7-26 A *text formatter* is a program that applies various rules for indenting, line length, page length, and so on to text. Formatters can become arbitrarily ('unbelievably' might be a better word) complicated, but at heart they just read and echo characters.

Write a text formatter that follows these rules (using values for *a*, *b*, and so on entered by the program user):

a) Print exactly *a* lines per page.

b) Space *b* lines between each line of output.

c) Print *c* words on each line.

d) Doublespace between sentences.

e) Capitalize the first word of each sentence.

Add three more options to the list.

Relying on runtime crashes to do error checking is like using telephone poles (instead of brakes) to stop your car. Still . . . Above, a boundary error. (p. 276)

8

Creating Values: Enumerations and Subranges

Chapter 8 wraps up the simple value types. We'll start out with extensions—ways that we can define new types and values. After all, when he designed Pascal, Wirth could easily guess that you might find it useful to have a type integer with values 1, 2, 3 and so on. But it would have been rather extraordinary for him to have built type FlavorTYPE with values chocolate, vanilla, and strawberry into Pascal. Instead, we can *enumerate*, or define, new types ourselves.

Next, we'll turn to type *subranges*. If enumeration giveth, then subranging taketh away. A subrange is part of the full range of a type. It is a safety device—giving a variable a subrange type, rather than the entire type, limits it to representing a restricted sequence of values.

Section 8–2 deals with the details. We'll look at various rules that control the construction of assignments and expressions. Finally, the Program Engineering Notes discuss variations in programming style that result from relying on enumerated types to hold state information.

But First, the Issues

In his book *1, 2, 3 ... Infinity* George Gamow imagines a primitive counting contest. 'How high can you go?' is the question. The winner gets to three—beyond that, 'many' is good enough.*

Before you snicker, take a moment to realize that you're in the same position. How many data types are there? For our purposes, a few simple types—real, char, and so on—have been enough. But I'd look foolish if I said that's all there were.

issue: type identity

Thinking about data storage has gone through several distinct phases. At first, all that really mattered was that values could be stored and retrieved. The idea of associating particular *names* with individual storage locations and *types* with the values stored there was a turning point in sophistication. Names and types make the computer manage data *for us*. They force the machine to keep storage straight, so that values are always retrieved according to the interpretation used to store them. In Chapter 8, we'll see how to add new simple types to Pascal.

The second era introduced *structured types*. The *array* came first: it could hold any number of values. Now, array-like storage was always there, because computer memory is basically nothing more than a long series of storage locations. But before structured types were through out, you had to manage that storage yourself. The programmer had to write, and remember, the arithmetic formulas that determined what went where.

issue: structure

But when structured types began to be built into programming languages, we managed to shift work to the computer again. Suppose that a group of values with different types have a common purpose. The canonical example is the employee record, since a single record contains data—a name, age, pay rate—of every type imaginable. We *could* store them using a collection of individual variables or a group of the abovementioned arrays, each dedicated to holding values of one type. But think of all the bookkeeping we'd have to do and all the chances for mistakes that would occur.

Structured types make the machine do our bookkeeping. For example, Pascal's *array* type (Chapter 9) holds any number of rows, or rows *and* columns, or rows *and* columns *and* aisles for as many dimensions as you can imagine of values of one type. Pascal's *record* type (we'll meet it in Chapter 11) can hold individually named values of more than one type.

Now, a simple type like char or real is characterized by the sort of operations we can perform on its values. A structured type like an array or record is characterized by the way it manages storage for us—what requirements it imposes, and what it does in return. Our introduction to each type will deal with the same basic set of issues:

— What is the syntax of the type definition?

issue: structured type mechanics

— How is type checking imposed and maintained?

— What sort of initialization does the type require?

— How do we inspect individual *components*, or stored values?

---

* George Gamow, *1, 2, 3 ... Infinity*, first published in 1947 and now available from Dover Publications.

— How can we change the components' values?

— How do we visit all of its components?

— What are the type's classic applications?

As usual, this list seems weighted toward syntax, and in fact, every chapter begins with the syntax details to make reference easier later on. But you'll find that studying the new type's standard applications will occupy most of your time.

But I digress. As convenient as the structured data types are, they limit us to structures conceived by the language designer. Suppose that there were a way to describe new types in the same terms as those that are built in—in terms of what we could do with them? Suppose that we could define new types according to the *primitive* operations we'd like to permit? Suppose that we could describe them as *abstractions*, separating the *what?* we want from each type from the *how?* the computer must go about to give it to us?

issue: abstraction

These 'supposes' bring us to the third era: the time of *data abstraction* and the *abstract data type* that results. I can boil the structured type mechanics I just listed down to three just basic categories:

— There must be *constructors* that store values.

what makes an abstract
data type

— There must be *observers* that inspect what's stored.

— There must be *iterators* that travel through the structure.

The notion that we can write procedures and functions that define a type has had an enormous impact on program (and programming language) design in the past decade. In a way, the book on problem solving has been rewritten. Although most examples are the same, we approach their solutions seeking the same benefits from data abstraction that we've gotten from procedural abstraction:

— Code that's easier to write and test.

— Solutions that can be reused in new programs.

As you might expect, there's a collection of 'standard' abstract data types that aren't built into Pascal, but are part of every programmer's repertoire. We'll meet a few (*stacks* and *queues*) in Chapter 15. You'll encounter the others in your next Computer Science course.

Things to Think About ───────────────────────────────

1. Suppose that you're designing an electronic datebook. Many of the values it will use, like times and dates, are similar to arithmetic types built into Pascal. However, they have specific limits on legal values and obey their own peculiar rules of arithmetic.

What additions to Pascal would make it easy to write a datebook program? What might the mechanics of a built-in Time or Date type be? How many distinct types do you think there should be? How will you define their values? What operations (don't forget about input and output) should be allowed? What should happen in case of errors?

Creating New Values

8-1

IN EARLY COMPUTER LANGUAGES, EVERYTHING—commands, identifiers, values and all—had to be expressed in zeros and ones. As languages improved, the vocabulary of description expanded. Nevertheless, a fairly limited set of basic measures (usually equivalents of real, integer, and char) had to be employed to describe every value imaginable.

But the real world is filled with a number of things that already have perfectly good names. This month might be January or July; my favorite music might be rap, rock, reggae, ragtime, or retch (e.g. Barry Manilow). In Pascal, such groups of named values can be the basis of an *enumerated type* that's defined by the user. For example:

```
program Menu (input, output);
    {Demonstrates an enumerated type definition.}
type FruitTYPE = (apple, grapefruit, orange, prune);
     VegetableTYPE = (cabbage, leeks, beets, okra);
var Appetizer, Dessert:  FruitTYPE;
    Entree:  VegetableTYPE;
begin   etc.
```

The first few lines of program Menu introduce two new types, FruitTYPE and VegetableTYPE. They are defined in the shaded *type definition part*, which *enumerated type syntax* always begins with reserved word **type**. Each *type identifier* is followed by an equals sign and lists the type's value identifiers, or *constants*, within parentheses and separated by commas. In chart form:

enumerated type definition

$$type\ identifier \longrightarrow = (\overset{\frown}{\underset{\longrightarrow}{}} constant\ identifier \overset{'}{\underset{\longrightarrow}{}}) \longrightarrow ;$$

The definitions and declarations from Menu allow assignments like:

defining enumerations

Appetizer := apple;	{Appetizer *gets the value* apple.}
Dessert := Appetizer;	{Dessert *is* apple *too.*}
Entree := leeks;	{Entree *is* leeks.}
Entree := cabbage;	{*Change* Entree *to* cabbage.}

Appetizer or Dessert could not be assigned values of type Vegetable, since that would cause a type clash. However, values or variables that have the same type can be compared:

```
case Appetizer of
    grapefruit:  writeln ('A grapefruit a day makes your thighs go away.');
    orange:  writeln ('An orange each day will put scurvy at bay.');
    prune:  writeln ('A prune every day keeps your colon ok.');
    apple:  writeln ('I couldn''t think of any more rhymes.')
end
```

There are three things to remember when you use enumerations. First of all, no value can belong to more than one type, because being in two types would make type membership ambiguous. For example, consider some of the hazards associated with defining a type that names the days. Here's my calendar, which is complicated by carrying the names of Jewish months as well:

SUNDAY	MONDAY	TUESDAY	WEDNESDAY	THURSDAY	FRIDAY	SATURDAY
	DECEMBER	FEBRUARY	1	2	3	4 _Parashat Va-Era_
			New Year's Day TEVET 25	TEVET 26	TEVET 27	_Shabbat Mevarekhim_ TEVET 28
5	6	7	8	9	10	11 _Parashat Bo_
TEVET 29	_Rosh Ḥodesh_ SHEVAT 1	SHEVAT 2	SHEVAT 3	SHEVAT 4	SHEVAT 5	SHEVAT 6

ambiguous type membership is illegal

The definition below is illegal because the position of Friday, as well as its type, is unclear. Is it the last value of type WEEKday, or the first value of WEEKend?

type WEEKday = (Monday, Tuesday, Wednesday, Thursday, Friday);
WEEKend = (Friday, Saturday, Sunday); {*Illegal definition.*}

Second, in Standard Pascal enumerated type values can't be input or output. The constants of an enumerated type don't have any *external character representation*. This is a fancy way of saying that they cannot be read with **read** nor printed using **write**. Although many real-world Pascal systems *do* extend the language by permitting enumerated type I/O, this particular feature is notorious as a cause of portability problems. Later, we'll use a **case** statement to take care of input and output at least on a small scale in Standard Pascal.

no external character representation

Finally, the same scope rules apply to type and constant identifiers as apply to variable and subprogram identifiers. Once a type has been defined, its name and the names of its constants are known in all subprograms—unless they are locally redefined. However, the identifiers of types (and their constants) are usually preserved globally. Since they are often used for communication between different parts of a program, they're seldom redefined.

scope of enumerated types

Self-Check Questions ————

Q. Is this the beginning of a valid statement? Assume the definitions of program Menu.

if Appetizer <> Entree **then begin**   *etc.*

A. No, because comparing values of different types causes a type clash. We can no more compare apple and leeks (even for inequality) than we could ´S´ and TRUE.

Q. Is this a valid type declaration? Why or why not?

type LETTERS = (´A´, ´B´, ´C´, ´D´, ´E´, ´F´);

A. It's illegal. ´A´, ´B´, etc., are not identifiers—they're constant values of type char. The definition doesn't conform to Pascal syntax. We *could* use A, B, C, etc., as identifiers, but only if we omitted the quote marks.

Ordinal Procedures and Functions

Enumerated types *are* ordinal types. In other words, functions and procedures that work with ordinal types like integer and char apply to enumerated types as well. Remember that counting always begins with zero, not one. Monday has ordinal position 0 in type WEEKday, defined above. The standard functions are:

ordinal type functions

ord(val) If val is a value of any ordinal type, ord(val) represents the value's ordinal (counting) position within the type. Numbering begins with zero.

chr(pos) Represents the value, of type char, that occupies ordinal position pos.

pred(val) Represents the predecessor of its ordinal-type argument val.

succ(val) Represents the successor of its ordinal-type argument val.

You should always bear in mind the danger of going past the end of a type's legal values. Suppose that all the days are defined as a single type, so that OddDays can represent the values Monday through Sunday. Can you see what's wrong with this attempt to *do something* every other day?

a buggy example

```
OddDays := Monday;
while OddDays <= Sunday do begin
    do something;
    OddDays := succ(succ(OddDays))        {something's fishy}
end
```

The problem is that the loop tries to increment OddDays beyond its last legal value, Sunday. What do you think will happen then? The program will crash.

Faking Enumerated Type I/O

Everybody who starts to program with enumerated types immediately runs into the same problem: they can't be written or read with ordinary I/O procedures. Here's a typical problem:

problem: enumerated type I/O

Jolt Cola ('all the sugar and twice the caffeine') sponsors an award for high-quality software and is the primary food of many programmers. However, it is not capable of sustaining human life indefinitely. Suppose that you now believe that you will survive this course and have become concerned with nutrition. Enumerate a type that names the essential information on a nutritional information label, then write TypeOut and TypeIn procedures that allow output and input of the values.

For example, consider the nutritional information on the label of the official food of *Oh! Pascal!*

Let's make NutriTYPE our underlying type definition:

type NutriTYPE = (protein, vitaminA, vitaminC, thiamine,
                                        riboflavin, niacin, calcium, iron);

var Category: NutriTYPE;

Recall that the enumerated types have no external character representation. Even though we think of them as strings—character sequences—the compiler is not concerned about their apparent English values. A statement like write (Category) won't compile, because Category isn't a string. But consider this alternative approach:

printing enumerated values procedure

```
procedure TypeOut ( Value:  NutriTYPE );
    {Prints the string that corresponds to a Value of NutriTYPE.}
  begin
    case Value of
        protein:  write ('protein');
        vitaminA:  write ('vitamin A');
        vitaminC:  write ('vitamin C');
        thiamine:  write ('thiamine');
        riboflavin:  write ('riboflavin');
        niacin:  write ('niacin');
        calcium:  write ('calcium');
        iron:  write ('iron')
    end
  end;  {TypeOut}
```

Pascal provides the tools we'll need to carry out a translation. Output is taken care of by using a **case** statement to choose the proper argument for write. Note that the alternatives I supply are intended to cover all the bases.

Input of enumerated type values is less convenient than output. Suppose that we agree to rely on a common extension for a moment: a type STRING that can represent a series of characters and can be input and output using ordinary I/O procedures.*

imagine that we have a STRING type

The few lines of code below show an appealing, but illegal, example. They assume that TheString has been declared as a string-type variable.

an illegal try

```
{Strings can't be case constants.}
case TheString of
    'protein': Category := protein;
    'vitamin A': Category := vitaminA;
    'vitamin C': Category := vitaminC;
             etc.
```

Unfortunately, even when they're allowed as a standard type extension, strings can't be used as **case** labels.

Instead, we have to rely on the **if** statement and use it to compare strings. In this situation, I use a final **else** part, because the string that was entered might be entirely wrong.

non-standard input of enumerated values

```
procedure TypeIn (var Category: NutriTYPE);
    {Read a string and assign the proper value to Category.}
    var Name: STRING;    {NOTE: this type is not Standard Pascal.}
    begin
        readln (Name);   {NOTE: string input is not Standard Pascal.}
        if Name = 'protein'    {NOTE: comparing unequal lengths isn't Standard Pascal.}
            then Category := protein
            else if Name = 'vitamin A'
                then Category := vitaminA
            else if Name = 'vitamin C'
                then Category := vitaminC
            else if Name = 'thiamine'
                then Category := thiamine
            else if Name = 'riboflavin'
                then Category := riboflavin
            else if Name = 'niacin'
                then Category := niacin
            else if Name = 'calcium'
                then Category := calcium
            else if Name = 'iron'
                then Category := iron
            else write ('ERROR –– Category is undefined.')
    end; {TypeIn}
```

---

* If we don't make this agreement, we'll have to use arrays—which aren't covered until the next chapter—to read and write strings in Standard Pascal.

Modification Problems

1. Write a program harness to test the TypeIn and TypeOut procedures. Add your favorite vitamin to the NutriTYPE definition.

Subrange Types

All ordinal types allow the definition of named *subrange types*. A subrange definition gives a type identifier to a particular segment of any ordinal or enumerated type, which becomes known as the *underlying* type.

type DayTYPE = (Monday, Tuesday, Wednesday,
Thursday, Friday, Saturday, Sunday);

WEEKday = Monday .. Friday;   {*Subrange of* DayTYPE.}
WEEKend = Saturday .. Sunday;   {*Subrange of* DayTYPE.}
CAPITALletters = ´A´ .. ´Z´;   {*Subrange of* char.}
HOURSinADay = 0 .. 24;   {*Subrange of* integer.}

var CardNight, SickDay: WEEKday;
SailingDay, GameDay: WEEKend;
HoursWorked: HOURSinADay;
FirstInitial, MiddleInitial: CAPITALletters;

The syntax chart of a subrange definition is:

subrange type definition

type identifier $\longrightarrow$ = $\longrightarrow$ *lower bound* $\longrightarrow$ .. $\longrightarrow$ *upper bound* $\longrightarrow$;

limits of subranges

In the example above, a DayTYPE variable might represent any of the days, but CardNight can have a value only in the WEEKday subrange. Similarly, HoursWorked can represent only a value from 0 through 24—the values included in the subrange HOURSinADay. Note that WEEKday and WEEKend have the same underlying type—DayTYPE. Any assignments from the wrong subrange, not to mention the wrong underlying type, will cause a program crash.

There is also a shorthand way to define subranges. The range of values a variable can represent may be specified when a variable is declared, but not when a parameter is declared:

shorthand subrange declarations

type DayTYPE = (Monday, Tuesday, Wednesday,
Thursday, Friday, Saturday, Sunday);

var CardNight, SickDay: Monday .. Friday;
SailingDay, GameDay: Saturday .. Sunday;
HoursWorked: 0 .. 24;
FirstInitial, MiddleInitial: ´A´ .. ´Z´;

The variables declared with this shorthand are like the variables in our last declaration and represent the same limited range of values.

Is there any reason to define a subrange as a distinctly named type? Yes—we may have to use it to make declarations.

subrange parameters,
function types

> When a value parameter, variable parameter, or function is declared, its type must have a name. The shorthand way to specify subranges can't be used.

The shorthand form can't provide the types of parameters. This is illegal:

an illegal try

procedure MakeLowerCase (Letter: ´a´ .. ´z´);

Function NextWork, below, returns a value of the subrange type WEEK-day defined earlier. Since its value parameter is of type DayTYPE, its argument can be any value or variable whose underlying type is also DayTYPE, e.g. even a WEEKend-type variable. The function's result has subrange type WEEKday.

a subrange-type function

```
function NextWork (Today:  DayTYPE) : WEEKday;
    {Represents the first working day to follow Today.}
    const FIRSTworkDay = Monday;
          LASTworkDay = Friday;
    begin
        if (Today>=FIRSTworkDay) and (Today<LASTworkDay) then begin
            Today := succ(Today);    {Increment Today.}
            NextWork := Today
        end
        else begin  NextWork := FIRSTworkDay  end
        {The assigned values have to be in the WEEKday subrange.}
    end; {NextWork}
```

Modification Problems

1. Change NextWork into a procedure that returns the next school month. Naturally, you'll have to define a MonthTYPE to back it up.

Self-Check Questions

Q. Which of these definitions are legal? If not, why not?

    a) SmallRealTYPE = 1.0 .. 5.0;
    b) VOWELrange = ´a´, ´e´, ´i´, ´o´, ´u´;
    c) VowelTYPE = (´a´, ´e´, ´i´, ´o´, ´u´);
    d) DayNumbersTYPE = (1, 2, 3, 4, 5, 6, 7);

A. Unfortunately, not a single example is legal. *a* can't use real for a subrange. *b* can't declare a subrange of non-contiguous values. *c* can't have a new type that uses values already taken by char. Finally, *d* suffers from the same problem as *c*, although it could have been legally declared as a 1 .. 7 subrange.

Naming Values, Attributes, and States

Why complicate Pascal with enumerated types? They're appealing because they enhance program readability. Just as an individual constant definition relieves the program reader of remembering whether FLUNKING equals ´D´, ´E´, or ´F´, an enumerated type definition can name the values of any arbitrary group of values, expressions, or conditions.

enumerated types increase abstraction

> In a word, the benefit of enumerated types is abstraction. Enumerated types let us deal with the *values*, *expressions*, and *states* that appear in a program in practical, human-oriented terms, rather than concrete, numerical, computer-directed ones.

Enumerating types to name elementary values is the most obvious application. For instance, the days of the week can be named:

```
type DayTYPE = (Monday, Tuesday, Wednesday,
                                Thursday, Friday, Saturday, Sunday);
var AllDays, WorkDays: DayTYPE;
```

abstracting values

then used later on:

```
for WorkDays := Monday to Friday do begin
     . .          etc.
```

We can enumerate planets, colors, chess pieces, and the like just as easily. Although we could have used numbers—after all, we often refer to the months of the year with numbers—the association of numbers and values is often arbitrary and error-prone. Is day 1 Sunday, Monday, or Tuesday? Meaningful names avoid the possibility of errors.

Enumerated values can also name *attributes*. Attributes are properties or characteristics of expressions that are distinct from literal values. For example, a boolean expression might have the literal value TRUE, but it could also carry some meaning: what is the significance of a TRUE expression?

abstracting expressions

Consider the type definitions below. RelationTYPE describes a comparison between two values. CharGroupTYPE, in turn, might categorize a single character:

```
type RelationTYPE = (LessThan, EqualTo, GreaterThan);
     CharGroupTYPE = (Letter, Digit, Punctuation, Spacer, Control);
```

In each case, the enumerated values name the attributes of an expression. The literal value of A = B might be TRUE, but we think of it in a different way—one value is EqualTo another. Function Compare, below, returns the attribute that describes a comparison between its arguments. It's easy to imagine how it might improve the readability of program code.

function Compare (A, B: char) : RelationTYPE;
  {*Represents the relative alphabetical ordering of* A *and* B.}
  begin
   if A = B
    then Compare := EqualTo
    else if A < B
     then Compare := LessThan
     else Compare := GreaterThan
  end; {Compare}

naming an A, B comparison

Finally, enumerated types are indispensable for recording and remembering the state of a process or computation:

— A search might be ongoing, successful, or failed.

abstracting states

— A mathematical algorithm might 'raise' an error because of overflow, underflow, or loss of precision.

— We might leave a loop in a known but non-unique state—any of several potential bound conditions could have terminated it.

I'll return to an example of such state variables later.

Modification Problems

1. Add a fourth value to RelationTYPE called Undefined. Extend compare so that it returns Undefined if either one of its arguments isn't a letter.
2. Put the RelationTYPE definition and procedure compare into a program. Use them to let you know if characters in an input sequence always get bigger.

Self-Check Questions

Q. Suppose that program input is a series of numbers in numerical order. We wish to find a particular sentinel value. Define a type whose values indicate the status of the search. Then, declare a function that gets passed the sentinel and current input value, and returns the status of the search.

A. Note the obvious similarity to procedure compare, above.

type StatusTYPE = (Continuing, Found, Failed);

function SearchState (SENTINEL, Current: integer) : StatusTYPE;
  {*Returns the state of the program's search for* SENTINEL.}
  begin
   if Current < SENTINEL
    then SearchState := Continuing
    else if Current > SENTINEL
     then SearchState := Failed
     else SearchState := Found
  end; {SearchState}

Type Compatibility Rules

8-2

JOIN ME NOW AS WE GRIND THROUGH a few observations about types. Try to strike a general understanding as you read. Don't despair—most of these details are here for the sake of future reference, rather than out of any present necessity.

> Type separation is intended to ensure that values are never stored or retrieved incorrectly. The rules *reflect* problems of storing values with a computer; they don't *cause* them.

I think you'll understand the compatibility rules best if you learn to ask three questions:

— *Can a variable of one type be the argument of a variable parameter of a second type?* Only if the types are *identical* can one take the place of the other.

— *Can a value of one type be compared to, or used in some other expression with, a value of a second type?* Only if their types are *expression compatible* will the comparison or expression make sense.

— *Can a value of one type be assigned to a variable of a second type?* Only if their types are *assignment compatible* will it make sense to assign one the other's value.

Now let's turn the answers around:

the identical type rule

Identical types are required for a variable parameter and its argument variable. Identical means literally what it says—both variables must have been declared with the exact same type name. (Technically it's possible to make one name equivalent to another, but we won't ever do that.)

the expression-compatible type rule

Expression-compatible types can appear in an expression together. To be expression compatible, the expressions must have the same underlying type, but one or both can be subranges. real and integer types are also expression compatible (1 + 1.5 makes sense). Even mutually exclusive subranges (say, 'A' .. 'C' and 'X' .. 'Z') are expression compatible, because they can still be sensibly compared.

the assignment-compatible type rule

Assignment-compatible types can be assigned to each other. To be assignment compatible, the variable in question must be able to represent the value in question. For instance, any pairs of numbers that are expression compatible won't be assignment compatible. We can compare the integer value 1 to the real value 0.5, but we can't assign 0.5 to an integer variable.

A Few Examples

Note that even the relatively lax rule of assignment compatibility doesn't always mean that an assignment is going to be legal. That depends on the actual values involved. For example:

```
type LOWrange =  1 .. 5;
     MIDrange = 1 .. 10;
     HIGHrange =  6 .. 20;

var LowValue:  LOWrange;
    MidValue:  MIDrange;
    HighValue:  HIGHrange;
    AnyValue:  integer;
```

LowValue, MidValue, HighValue, and AnyValue are clearly not of identical types, because they're all declared with different type identifiers. All four variables, however, are assignment compatible. This may or may not mean that assignments are actually legal. These assignments:

legal assignments

```
{legal assignments}
MidValue := LowValue;
AnyValue := MidValue;
```

will always be OK because the actual value of LowValue falls within the subrange of MidValue, and the actual value of MidValue always falls into range of AnyValue.

However, this won't always be the case. These assignments:

possibly legal
assignments

```
{potentially legal assignments}
LowValue := MidValue;
MidValue := HighValue;
HighValue := AnyValue;
```

may or may not be valid, depending on the values of MidValue, HighValue, and AnyValue when the assignment actually takes place. If values are in the wrong subrange, a type clash will occur.

As I mentioned earlier, variable parameters and the variables that are their arguments must have identical types. This makes sense because a variable parameter merely renames its argument. But since value parameters treat their arguments as values, they need not have identical types—assignment compatibility is enough. Again, this makes sense because the argument is just used to initialize the value parameter. A runtime error occurs only for an out-of-range argument.

Self-Check Questions

Q. Suppose that we make the definitions and declarations shown below:

```
type LowTYPE = 1 .. 7;
     MidTYPE = 5 .. 10;
     HighTYPE = 11 .. 20;
     BroadTYPE = 1 .. 20;

var LowValue:  LowTYPE;
    MidValue:  MidTYPE;
    HighValue:  HighTYPE;
    BroadValue:  BroadTYPE;
```

Which of these assignment are always in error, sometimes in error, or never in error?

    a) LowValue := 2 * MidValue;
    b) MidValue := LowValue;
    c) BroadValue := HighValue;
    d) HighValue := BroadValue;
    e) MidValue := 3 * HighValue;

A. *a* and *e* are always going to be in error. *b* and *d* will sometimes be correct and some-times wrong, while only *c* is always going to be a legal assignment. For extra practice, you might want to try making up some procedure calls that incorporate the same sorts of errors.

Program Engineering Notes: Saving States

8-3

ENUMERATED TYPES AND **CASE** STATEMENTS MIGHT seem to be an unlikely pair. However, they prove to be an effective combination for keeping track of, and acting on, constantly changing program states.

State is usually misunderstood as referring to the condition of a program, as in 'My program is in a dismal state.' But it really means *knowledge* about *data*. As we know, a program turns data into information:

The simplest programs have just one focal point: they do something to data values (add them or double them), or they learn something about data (are they all positive?). But more complex programs—the kind we'll be writing—usually have to do both. What we do will often depend on what we know, and that will change during program execution. And, when *determine the current state* becomes confused with *act on the current state*, problems result.

> Look before you leap. Be sure that you know the current state before com-mitting yourself to a particular action.

For example, let's look at a concrete instance of loop design. Suppose that we want to read and somehow process numbers until we spot a sentinel or out-of-bounds value or run out of input.

    repeat
        read a value
    until *we reach the bound condition;*
    decide which bound condition we reached

Here's a complicated bound condition—the solution we're most familiar with. The shaded section is devoted to establishing our state after the loop.

```
{Read until sentinel, out of range, or no more data.}
repeat
    read (Value)
until eof or (Value > UPPER) or
    (Value < LOWER) or (Value = SENTINEL);
{Now, decide why we left the loop.}
```

establishing the state
after the loop

```
if Value > UPPER
        then 'value too big' message and action
    else if Value < LOWER
        then 'value too small' message and action
    else if Value = SENTINEL
        then 'found the sentinel' message and action
    else it must be eof so
        ran out of data message and action
```

As long as we have data to begin with, there is nothing incorrect about this approach. However, we are in an awkward position between the **repeat** and the **if** statement check that follows it: we don't know our state.

Now consider an alternative approach. It begins with the definition of an enumerated type:

a state type

```
type ExitTYPE = (searching, under, over, found, missing);
var State: ExitTYPE;
```

Then, the loop is written in a way that establishes state *before* any action, including leaving the loop, is taken. Line-for-line, we use essentially the same code as we did before. But in the reordered code we know our state at all times:

```
repeat
    if eof
        then State := missing
        else begin
            read (Value);
            if Value > UPPER
                then State := over
            else if Value < LOWER
                then State := under
            else if Value = SENTINEL
                then State := found
            else State := searching
        end  {if eof else part}
until State <> searching
{Now, take the appropriate post-loop action.}
case State of
    found: 'found the sentinel' message and action;
    over: 'value too big' message and action;
    under: 'value too small' message and action;
    missing: 'value missing' message and action
end
```

establishing state within
the loop

The code is a bit longer, but it's simpler. We can tell what's going on.

Why Use Subranges?

Although they may not lead to the largest number of bugs in Pascal programs, the subrange types present the greatest confusion. It is important not to put the cart before the horse, though. As I pointed out, the rules reflect some realities of computing; they don't cause them.

— First, type separation is intended to make sure that values are never stored or retrieved incorrectly.

— Second, although the type of a variable is known at compile time, the type of an expression *once you allow subranges* might not be known until runtime.

— Third, at the machine level, different machine-language commands may be used to carry out the same operations—for example, the exact addition command used depends on the type of its operands.

In effect, types attach an invisible set of rules to every value and variable. They make sure we never add apples and oranges.

Why make the effort of learning to deal with subranges? They're desirable for three reasons—self-documentation, program efficiency, and antibugging.

for self-documentation

1. Self-documentation. Knowing the range of values that a variable is going to represent, and saying so at the time of variable declaration, helps demonstrate that you have a firm grasp of what your program does.

It also helps another person who may be working on your program get an idea of appropriate values within a program. The declaration:

```
KilnTemperature: integer;
```

says nothing, whereas this is informative:

```
KilnTemperature: 400 .. 1200;          {or, better yet . . .}
KilnTemperature: 400 .. MAXtemperature;          {or, still better . . .}
KilnTemperature: TempRangeTYPE;
```

for efficiency

2. Program efficiency. A variable declared to represent only a limited range of values can be dealt with (by the compiler) in a more economical manner than a variable that can represent *any* value of its type.

This is really the least important reason. Under certain circumstances, though, a program may require so many variables that limiting the storage they require is a valid programming consideration.

for antibugging

3. Antibugging. Restricting the values that a variable may represent to a range of values we know it *should* have extends the protection. We help assure ourselves (and the computer) that any operations we'll try to carry out will make sense.

Real life often places limits on the values that a variable can reasonably represent. A payroll program may 'work', but allow 37 deductions or −2. A checker-playing program might spend a considerable amount of time looking for the ninth row of a checkerboard. A computer croupier could spin a computer roulette wheel and decide the ball has landed on number 39—which doesn't exist.

These are all obviously bugs that should, and could, be spotted or prevented by the programmer. The most annoying aspect of bugs, though, is that you don't see them until it's too late. When a program announces that the sum of two and two is five, the programmer knows that something has gone wrong and takes another look at her code. The results of a more complex program, however, are more likely to be taken for granted—even if some input datum or partial result hidden within the program is totally absurd.

the moral

> Subrange types provide a constant check on variables and assure us that they have values appropriate to their application. They help prevent a very dangerous kind of program—one which appears to be reliable, but is not.

Using subranges doesn't absolve the programmer of responsibility for error checking and keeping track of data within a program. The subrange philosophy is rather nihilistic—if a variable takes on an inappropriate value, the program stops! Relying on runtime crashes to do error checking is like using telephone poles (instead of brakes) to stop your car. Still, strong type checking makes Pascal sympathetic to a programmer's woes; data inevitably get screwed up for reasons beyond the control of programmer, program user, or computer. Subrange types won't make programs work, but they will make it easier to debug programs and to keep them running.

Syntax Summary

❑ enumerated type: a type declaration that names, and provides the constants of, a sequence of values.

> **type** MotownTYPE = (Temptations, Smokey, Marvin, Supremes);
>   NoWaveTYPE = (Prince, RickeyLee, Elvis);

❑ subrange type: a type declaration that names a subsequence of an existing *underlying type*.

> **type** LowerTYPE = ´a´ .. ´z´;
>   SMALLnumbers = 1 .. 10;

❑ ordinal functions: are built into Pascal. The standard functions include:

ord(value)	*ordinal (counting) position of* value *in its type*
chr(position)	*value of type* char *in ordinal position* position
pred(value)	*value that precedes its ordinal argument* value
succ(value)	*value that follows its ordinal argument* value

Remember . . .

❑ The constants of enumerated types must be distinct. Two enumerated types can't share values, although subranges of a single underlying type can.

❑ Enumerated type constants are ordered by their definitions. Their ordinal numbering always starts with zero.

❑ The constants of an enumerated type can't be input or output because they have no external character representation. They must be translated to and from strings.

❑ Two variables have the same, identical type only if they're declared with the same type identifier. A variable parameter and its argument must have identical types. Assignments between variables of identical types will always be valid.

❑ Two values are expression compatible only if it makes sense to compare them (e.g. a < b) or to use them both in an expression (e.g. A + B).

❑ A value and a variable are assignment compatible if it makes sense to assign the value to the variable (or an argument to a value parameter).

❑ Subrange types are useful because they help make programs self-documenting and enforce automatic runtime checks on program values.

Big Ideas

The Big Ideas in this chapter are:

1. *Type membership is meant to ensure that values will always be stored and retrieved correctly.* Enumerated and subrange types are natural extensions to the built-in standard types, because they increase the programmer's vocabulary without endangering the correctness of programs.

2. *The type of variables can be determined at compile time, but expressions are not evaluated until runtime.* The compatibility rules reflect this fact; they don't cause it.

Begin by Writing the Exam . . .

8-1   The syntax of enumerations and subranges is entirely arbitrary and sometimes confusing. Write a half-dozen definitions that ask the question *Enumeration, subrange, or incorrect?* Some of the syntactic details you can confuse include *a*) using brackets instead of parentheses; *b*) using a non-contiguous subrange of values (e.g. the vowels); *c*) including the same constant in more than one type definition.

8-2   Ask three prose questions that require the definition of new types (e.g. the months) and subranges (particular seasons).

8-3   A multiple-choice question that's easy to pose (and grade) is put together by declaring a few variables, then listing a series of values and expressions. Which values can be assigned to which variables? The legal values fall within appropriate subranges, while illegal values have the wrong type, or are outside of a particular subrange. Write the question.

8-4   Asking whether a procedure call has legal arguments is more complicated than checking assignments. Recall that variable parameters must have the same types as their arguments, while value parameters only have to be assignment compatible. Write three headings with at least two parameters each, then make up a half-dozen legal and illegal calls.

8-5   Can you read a value that has an enumerated ordinal type? Can you print it? If I'm asking the question then the answer must be 'no,' of course. Try to plant the illegal operation in a code segment, then ask *Where's the bug?*

8-6   Writing conversion programs is a standard problem for enumerated types and **case** statements. For example, converting to and from foreign currencies requires enumerating a type (for the currency names), writing input and output procedures (to get and print the names), as well as a **case** statement that chooses the right conversion formula. Make up two conversion program questions and draft (but don't write) their solutions.

Warmups and
Test Programs

8-7   Is there a limit on the length of new type names? On the length of the constants of enumerated types? Does your system allow any non-standard characters (like underlines) to appear in identifiers?

8-8   What is an ordinal type? What simple type isn't an ordinal type? What does it mean to say that a type is enumerable?

8-9   Suppose that we make this type definition:

> **type** NicknameTYPE = (Boss, BigBopper, Killer, MainMan);

Write a procedure that takes a parameter of type NicknameTYPE and prints its value.

Programming
Problems

8-10   'Take care of the spares, and the strikes will take care of themselves' might not improve your bowling ability, but it's the only advice I know. But if you're having trouble keeping score, you can always write a program. In brief, the rules are:

A game consists of ten *frames*.

A *strike* is scored if all the pins are knocked down by the first ball rolled in a frame. A strike ends the frame.

A *spare* is scored if any pins that remain after the first ball are felled on a second attempt.

If neither a strike nor a spare was scored, add the number of pins knocked down to the score.

If a strike was scored, increase the total by ten plus the number of pins toppled on the next two balls.

If a spare was scored, increase the total by ten plus the number of pins knocked down on the next single ball.

If a spare or strike is scored in the last frame, give the bowler one or two extra balls.

Why bring this up now? Because if you think about it, you'll see that scoring depends on knowing the bowler's current state—her position in the frame and possibly the results from prior frames.

Write a program that keeps bowling scores. To make life easy for yourself, allow only a single bowler.

8-11   Two biology students are carrying out important scientific research on fleas. One student's job is to motivate the flea to jump (through use of a little electric flea prod), while the other student keeps tabs on its travel. The second student, unable to bear the sight of the suffering flea, resolves to write a program that will take over her job.

Write a program that tracks the flea as it hops around. Start at the origin $x, y = (0,0)$ and print the current position after each hop. Each input should consist of a distance, and a direction. For example, input **2.3 nw** would mean 'move 2.3 units northwest.' Legal directions should be:

```
n   nw   w   sw   s   se   e   ne
```

8-12   A mischievous bartender likes to fool her more tipsy customers by pouring drinks containing two different liquors, in equal quantities, into the serving glass.

Write a program that asks for two liquors from the list below, then prints the alcoholic content of the mixed drink. Assume that:

beer	4% alcohol
ale	7% alcohol
wine	12% alcohol
bourbon	40% alcohol
scotch	60% alcohol
rum	77% alcohol

The bartender is not exactly sober herself, so allow for the possibility that the two liquors are the same.

8-13   Consider the scene in a closed room, secret design session for the new model of a big-name Detroit automobile. All around the conference table are engineers and executives trying to strike a balance between greed (which leads them to build the cheapest car possible) and fear (which pulls in the other direction toward more reliable machines).

Now, the relation between the mean time between failures (MTBF) of a system and its subsystems can be described as:

$$\frac{1}{MTBF_{Total}} = \frac{1}{MTBF_{Sub1}} + \frac{1}{MTBF_{Sub2}} + \cdots + \frac{1}{MTBF_{Subn}}$$

and is correct if the failure of any subsystem dooms the entire car.

Suppose that the costs and MTBF's of various subsystems are:

Subsystem		MTBF	Manufacturing Cost
brakes	disc	4 years	$15.00
	drum	5 years	$25.00
engine	Wankel	3 years	$1,067.00
	conventional	6 years	$1,850.00
suspension	air	9 years	$430.00
	oil	7 years	$320.00
electrical	computer	2 years	$130.00
	standard	4 years	$40.00

Write a program that models each combination of subsystems (a quadruply nested **for** loop will do nicely), and answers these questions:

a)   Which system is the cheapest?

b)   Which has the longest mean time between failures?

c)   Which system has the lowest cost per failure-free year?

Hint: Since an enumerated type value can't be printed directly, use a **case** statement to print its character equivalent.

The most common labor of all is visiting each array component. This is sometimes called traversing *the array.* (p. 300)

9

The **array** Type

Arrays bring to data what loops bring to action—power. We can hardly imagine programming without loops; a few reserved words multiply our efforts beyond comprehension. The array is an equally powerful programming device for handling data. Ultimately, we'll be limited only by our own ingenuity when it comes to devising new schemes for storing and using information.

This chapter is longer than most—not harder, just longer—so a brief guide is in order. We'll start with some pictures of what arrays might look like if we could build them with wood instead of type declarations. Arrays encourage *visual thinking*—if you can mentally picture a structure of data, you can probably build it out of an array. After we go over the syntactic details, section 9–2 covers typical loop/array interaction. You might want to return here if you have trouble with the exercises.

Section 9–3 moves into what will be a recurring theme of the rest of this book: *data abstraction.* Although we'll be looking at characteristic applications of each type, our real concern lies in learning how to design and work with new types before we resolve their implementation details. The classic array applications of sorting and searching are reserved for Chapter 10.

Section 16–3 discusses recursive array programming and may follow this chapter.

Strictly Pascal

9-1

BEFORE WE SEE WHERE WE'RE GOING, let's start with an example that shows where we're coming from. Program Average reads, averages, and prints the average of a series of input numbers. It has nothing new:

ordinary averaging program

```
program Average (input, output);
    {Averages a series of numbers.}
var Average: real;
    Counter, Value, Total: integer;
begin
    writeln ('Give me a line of numbers to average. ');
    Total := 0;          {initialize an accumulator}
    Counter := 0;        {initialize a counter}
    while not eoln do begin
        Counter := Counter + 1;        {increment the counter}
        read (Value);                  {approach the loop's bound}
        Total := Total + Value         {increase the accumulator}
    end; {while}
    readln;
    Average := Total / Counter;        {Assume there's always input.}
    write ('The average was ');
    writeln (Average : 1 : 2)
end.    {Average}
```

```
Give me a line of numbers to average.
35 84 51 26 93 77 47
The average was 59.00
```

Average has a simple stream view of its input. Once a value goes past, it's gone, because we have just one storage location—Value—for the incoming data.

But suppose that we want to read and average the input stream, and echo *only* the values that exceed the average. There are two approaches to a solution:

echoing above-average values

— Read the input stream twice, averaging the first time, and printing large values the second time. This would be a file-oriented solution.

— Read and store the input values, averaging them as they're stored. Then echo only the larger ones. This solution will use an *array*.

visualizing the data

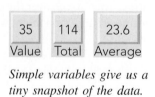

35	114	23.6
Value	Total	Average

Simple variables give us a tiny snapshot of the data.

Store 35 84 51 26 93 77 47 52 67 9 1 3 6
      [1] [2] [3] [4] [5] [6] [7] [8] [9] [10] [11] [12] [13]

An array lets us reinspect any part of the data stream.

Like any addition to Pascal, arrays will require a certain amount of syntax followed by a collection of new programming techniques. But even before we get to all that, it's easy to see how the definition of StoreTYPE, in program ArrayAvg, below, builds an array.

what to look for

— What's the variable's type? StoreTYPE. What's its name? Store.

— What kind of values can it hold? integers.

— How many integer values can it hold? Any number between 1 and LIMIT.

— How do we refer to the individual values? As Store [1] through Store [LIMIT]. Or, if we want, we can use a variable to name the value: Store [Current].

using arrays to echo larger than average numbers

```
program ArrayAvg (input, output);
    {Prints only the numbers that exceed the average.}
const LIMIT = 50;              {How many numbers can we hold?}
type StoreTYPE = array [1 .. LIMIT] of integer;
var Average: real;
    Counter, Value, Total, Current: integer;
    Store: StoreTYPE;          {This array variable holds all the numbers.}
begin
    writeln ('Give me a line of numbers to average.');
    Total := 0;           {initialize an accumulator}
    Counter := 0;         {initialize a counter}
    while not eoln do begin
        Counter := Counter + 1;        {increment the counter}
        read (Value);                  {approach the loop's bound}
        Total := Total + Value;        {increase the accumulator}
        Store [Counter] := Value       {save the number}
    end; {while}
    {Postcondition: Store [1] through Store [Counter] holds the numbers.}
    readln;
    Average := Total / Counter;        {Assume there's always input.}
    write ('The average was ');
    writeln (Average : 4 : 2);
    write ('Above average numbers were:    ');
    for Current := 1 to Counter do begin       {For each stored value . . . }
        if Store [Current] > Average then begin  { . . . if it's bigger than average . . . }
            write (Store [Current] : 4)          { . . . print the number.}
        end   {if}
    end;  {for}
    writeln
end.  {ArrayAvg}
```

```
Give me a line of numbers to average.
35 84 51 26 93 77 47
The average was 69.28
Above average numbers were     84  93  77
```

Here's another example that's easy to understand, even without knowing all the array definition details. Program Reversal, below, uses an array to hold a line of input. It reads the letters one at a time, then prints the line in reverse. Note that I'm being a little more careful this time, by making sure that there's room to store each value. In pseudocode, we:

> prompt for a line of input;
> **while** *there are still letters available* **and** *there's still room to store another*
>   *read a letter into the current* Last *array component;*
>   *increase* Last *by* 1;
> **for** *each component from* Last *down to* 1
>   *print the letter stored there*

I rely on an array because *a*) it can hold as many characters as I need, and *b*) it will let me inspect them in any order I desire. The program is:

```
program Reversal (input, output);
    {Reads a line of input, then prints it in reverse.}
const LIMIT = 80;
type ArrayTYPE = array [1 .. LIMIT] of char;
var Last,           {the current sentence length}
    Current: integer;        {the for loop's counter variable}
    Hold: ArrayTYPE;          {the array variable}
begin
    writeln ('Type in a sentence that''s up to 80 letters long. ');
    Last := 0;
    while not eoln and (Last < LIMIT) do begin
        Last := Last + 1;
        read ( Hold [Last] )
    end;
    {Postcondition: Hold[1] through Hold[Last] holds the sentence.}
    readln;
    for Current := Last downto 1 do begin
        write (Hold [ Current ]);
    end;
    writeln
    {We've printed them in reverse order.}
end.  {Reversal}
```

```
Type in a sentence that's up to 80 letters long.
evil star war nuts
stun raw rats live
```

Because it can hold distinct values, the array is known as a *structured* type. It will radically alter the scale of what we can accomplish with programs. The definition:

```
type BigTYPE = array [1..100] of integer;
```

creates a type name, BigTYPE, that can be used to declare a variable that holds a hundred integers—the array's *components*. An extra zero in the right place:

type VeryBigTYPE = **array** [1..1000] **of** integer;

makes VeryBigTYPE—a structure of one thousand components.

You can picture a BigTYPE or VeryBigTYPE variable as a very long row of distinct integer values. When the row just extends in one direction, it's called a *one-dimensional* array. But if we want, we can create a structure with more than one row of components. Here is a *two-dimensional* array definition:

a two-dimensional array

type HugeTYPE = **array** [1..1000, 1..1000] **of** integer;

HugeTYPE is two-dimensional because it has rows *and* columns, as though it were a giant checkerboard. In all, it has one thousand rows of one thousand components each—a total of one *million* components!

Modification Problems

1. Feel up to modifying ArrayAvg already? Have it read and store real values instead of integers.
2. That was probably too easy. Change ArrayAvg so that it prints the stored values that are less than, or equal to, the average—and print them in reverse order.
3. Modify ArrayAvg so that it prints three lines of output: values that are less than average, values that are greater, and those that equal the average if it is rounded.
4. Modify Reversal so that it prints its output one word per line. Assume that a single blank separates each word. Suppose that more than one blank can come between words? Can you make Reversal handle that as well?

What Arrays Can Do

Let's take a quick look at what arrays let us do. We've already seen that arrays can hold lots of data easily. Better yet, we don't have to name the components individually. Each component's position has a *subscript* to uniquely identify it.

Since we can select components at will, the array is a *random-access* structure. When we're processing data, an array's values don't have to be stored or retrieved in any particular order.

subscripts, not names

35	84	51
Item1	Item2	Item3

Simple variables must be named and declared one at a time.

ItemList 35 84 51 26 93 77 47 52 67 9 1 3 6
[1] [2] [3] [4] [5] [6] [7] [8] [9] [10] [11] [12]

Array components can be named and declared wholesale.

Because an array has a beginning and an end, the *order* in which we store values contains information too:

storing in order

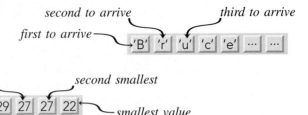

If we want, we can treat the subscripts that name each component as a *coordinate* system. Every component of a one-dimensional array has one coordinate, those in two-dimensional arrays have two, and so on:

by numerical coordinates

Columns

Rows

	1	2	3	4	5	6	7	8	9
1	1,1	1,2	1,3	1,4	1,5	1,6	1,7	1,8	1,9
2	2,1	2,2	2,3	2,4	2,5	2,6	2,7	2,8	2,9
3	3,1	3,2	3,3	3,4	3,5	3,6	3,7	3,8	3,9
4	4,1	4,2	4,3	4,4	4,5	4,6	4,7	4,8	4,9

The row, column coordinates act as subscripts for the array components.

Why limit coordinate subscripts to numerical values? We can use the new values of enumerated types instead. For example, a two-dimensional array might use the days of the week to subscript one dimension and the hours of the day to subscript the other:

by non-numerical coordinates

	mon	tue	wed	thu	fri	sat	sun
AM	free	goof off	free	ski	free	rest a bit	work hard
PM	free	free	sail	kick back	free	free	free

A typical work schedule for California writers.

If an array's subscripts are the values of an enumerated type, we can describe a component in terms of its *characteristics*:

by characteristic

	hairy	clever	slow	bare	quick
little	rat	bat	cod	ant	cat
midsize	ewe	fox	pig	eel	doe
large	gnu	ape	cow	?	nag

What kind of animal is large and bare?

We can also work the other way around: if we find a component that is interesting, we can use its position to find its *attributes*:

by attribute

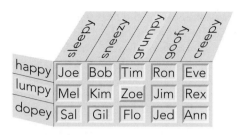

What sort of person is Zoe?

An array might also be used to associate pairs of values that are related to each other, but possibly have different types or uses. The array acts as a function, storing the correspondence between the values of two different groups:

to associate values

A few useful words in case you ever find seven Italian snakes under your chair.

Sound exciting? It is! But before we can start to program, we have to get acquainted with basic array syntax and usage.

Array Definitions

Type definitions in general tell the compiler how to set aside storage for variables. The definition of an array type, in particular, describes three things:

1. The type of the array's components, or stored values. Components can be simple (like char or real), or they can have structured types themselves.

components, subscripts, size

2. The *subscripts* that will name and number the individual components. All of the subscripts aren't given—just the lower and upper *bounds* of each dimension. Subscripts can have any ordinal type; they can't be real.

3. The size of the array—how many components it holds—as determined by its bounds and the number of dimensions it has.

The reserved word **type** always starts a definition part. The syntax chart of an array type definition is:

array type definition

$$identifier \longrightarrow = \underset{\smile}{\overset{\frown}{\text{packed}}} \text{array} \quad [\underset{\smile}{\overset{\frown}{\underset{,}{bound \;..\; bound}}}^{\text{ordinal type identifier}}] \text{ of } \underset{identifier}{\overset{component}{\longrightarrow type \longrightarrow}} ;$$

The array's dimensions can be given in two different ways. Usually, we'll supply the first and last value of each dimension, the bounds, as though we were defining a subrange. However, the name of a 'small' ordinal type like boolean or char, or of an enumerated or subrange type can be used instead. If a name is given, the compiler looks up the first and last values of that type and sets the array bounds with them. Some typical definitions are:

specifying the dimensions

type
    TideLevelTYPE = **array** [0..11] **of** real;
        {*one dimension, twelve components*}
    LowerCaseCountTYPE = **array** [´a´..´z´] **of** integer;
        {*one dimension, twenty-six components*}
    BoardTYPE = **array** [1..8, 1..8] **of** boolean;
        {*two dimensions, sixty-four components*}
    CodeTableTYPE = **array** [´a´..´z´, boolean] **of** char;
        {*two dimensions, fifty-two components*}
    TolerancesTYPE = **array** [´A´..´C´, 1..3, –2..0] **of** real;
        {*three dimensions, twenty-seven components*}
    CharCountTYPE = **array** [char] **of** integer;
        {*one dimension, as many components as there are char values*}

In the CodeTableTYPE definition, the second, boolean, dimension is automatically replaced by FALSE..TRUE. The CharCountTYPE definition, the char dimension is automatically replaced by the first and last values in the ASCII character set. Arrays that are subscripted by char are usually defined like this so that a one-dimensional array will be able to index non-contiguous stretches of characters, e.g. the letters and the digits.

The values of each dimension provide subscripts. Later, after we declare variables, we'll put the subscripts in square brackets to name array components individually:

— Each variable of TideLevelTYPE holds a dozen real values, subscripted [0], [1], [2], through [11].

what subscripts do

— Variables of LowerCaseCountTYPE and CharCountTYPE identify their integer components by letter subscripts: [´a´], [´b´], [´c´], and so on.

— TolerancesTYPE variables require three coordinates to identify each component: [´A´,1,–2] locates the first, [´A´,1,–1] the second, [´A´,1,0] the third, and so on through [´C´,3,0].

> If values are given to set array bounds in a type definition, they must be constants—not variables—because the size of an array has to be known at compile time.

restrictions on bounds

This means that bound values have to be type names, constants, or literal values. They can't be supplied with variable identifiers or by expressions that can't be calculated without actually running the program.

Q. What is the size of each of these arrays? Are any definitions illegal?

    a) **type** StorageTYPE = **array** [1..5, 1..10] **of** char;
    b) **type** MeasureTYPE = **array** [–5..5] **of** real;
    c) **type** TruthTYPE = **array** [boolean] **of** integer;
    d) **type** ScienceTYPE = **array** [1.0 .. 5.0] **of** real;
    e) **type** DigitTYPE = **array** ['1', '2', '3'] **of** char;
    f) **type** GraphTYPE = **array** ['0'..'9', 0..9] **of** integer;

A. The answers are:

    a) 50 values of type char.
    b) 11 (don't forget the 0th value) of type real.
    c) 2 integer values, subscripted FALSE, TRUE.
    d) Illegal—the dimensions can't be given with real.
    e) Illegal—the dimension has to be a range, not just values.
    f) 100 values of type integer (each dimension has ten values).

Assignment

Once we define array types we can declare array variables. Let's start with the one-dimensional array defined below. LowerCaseCountTYPE has integer components and uses the lower-case char values as subscripts.

    type LowerCaseCountTYPE = **array** ['a'..'z'] **of** integer;
    var Paper, News: LowerCaseCountTYPE;

> There are two ways to make assignments to array variables: all at once, or one component at a time.

assigning to arrays

When two variables have the exact same type (as Paper and News do, above), we can assign one's value to the other. Naturally, the variable on the right-hand side of the assignment had better be initialized first itself.

assigning to components

To refer to an individual component, put its subscript between square brackets. Even though bounds have to be given with constants, subscripts can include variables or arithmetic expressions. These are all legal assignments to the arrays we just declared:

using subscripts

    Paper['a'] := 5;
    News['a'] := Paper['a'];
    Paper['b'] := Paper['a'];
    News['a'] := News['a'] + 1;
    News[chr(98)] := News[chr (ORD ('z') –25)];
    Paper := News;   {*an array-to-array assignment*}

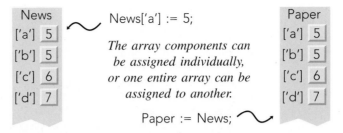

News['a'] := 5;

The array components can be assigned individually, or one entire array can be assigned to another.

Paper := News;

News and Paper were easy to deal with because they had just one subscript apiece. But suppose that an array has two or more dimensions? No problem—the array variable will just have two or more subscripts:

{We change this component's value.}
ThreeDimensions[Sub1, Sub2, Sub3] := TwoDimensions[Pos1, Pos2];
{We inspect this component's value.}

It *is* important to remember that no matter how long and complicated subscripts might make an identifier, they're just pieces of a name. A component named ThreeDimensions[Sub1, Sub2, Sub3] is certainly more complicated than a simple variable called Ch or Count, but the component might be identical to the variable in type and value. Similarly, TwoDimensions[Pos1, Pos2] might seem to be more complex than, say, 16, but it could easily represent that very integer.

Now, finally, the rules. The three important things to remember about the values you use as subscripts are:

1.   Every subscript's value must have the proper type. If an array has, say, integer-valued bounds, subscript values always have to be integer as well.

subscript rules
2.   Every subscript has to be within the proper subrange. If an array's bounds are ['a'..'d'], then ['A'] and ['e'] are illegal subscripts. They'd cause a *subscript range* error and program crash.

3.   If an array uses more than one subscript, the subscripts have to be in the proper order. At best, misordered subscripts will cause compile-time or runtime crashes. At worst, the misordered subscripts may still have proper types and ranges, and cause bugs that are extremely difficult to find.

Self-Check Questions

Q. Suppose that I make these definitions and declarations. Which of the subsequent statements are legal? Why not?

```
type TenTYPE = array [1..10] of integer;
     FiveTYPE = array [1..5] of char;
var TenArray: TenTYPE;
    FiveArray: FiveTYPE;
    Letter: char;
       ⋱
a) TenArray := 10;
b) FiveArray [6] := 'a';
c) read (TenArray[1]);
```

d) TenArray [TenArray[1]] := 3;
e) Letter := FiveArray;
f) Letter := FiveArray [´a´];

A. Not too many are legal, I'm afraid.

a) Illegal—we can't assign a single integer value to the whole array.
b) Illegal—FiveArray's highest subscript is 5.
c) Legal.
d) Legal if TenArray[1] holds a value in the range 1..10.
e) Illegal—we can't assign an array to a single character.
f) Illegal—FiveArray is subscripted by numbers, not letters.

A Few Test Beds

Just in case you're having trouble getting a mental picture of array manipulation, let's pause for a few test bed programs. Now, more than ever, you'll find it helpful to go into 'professor mode.' Suppose that you were making up an exam. What questions would you ask? The three basic exam problems are:

— *Initialize* an array in some weird way.

three basic questions

— *Rearrange* an array's contents in some even weirder way.

— *Find* something within an array.

The most common complication is to involve some sort of interaction between arrays—initialize one to another's current contents, say, or see if a short array's contents are hidden within a longer one. But simply initializing an array is a good way to get started. Program OneDBed, below, works with one-dimensional arrays. It defines two array types, ShortTYPE and LongTYPE. OneDBed initializes one array variable to a single value and the other to a simple sequence.

As you can see, my generic programming environment shows array components simply by listing them. When I took this screen shot, I was about to initialize the fifth component of Long. Note that components five through ten are filled with junk values that just happened to be lying around in memory.

initializing one-dimensional arrays

```
────────── ONEDBED.PAS ──────────
program OneDBed (input, output);
  {A test bed program for one-dimensional arrays.}

type ShortTYPE = array [1..5] of integer;
     LongTYPE = array [1..10] of integer;
                                      ────── Variables ──────
var Short:  ShortTYPE;          Short: (0,0,0,0,0)
    Long:   LongTYPE;           Long: (1,2,3,4,-26023,1193,22819,16003,84,29962)
    Current:  integer;          Current: 5

begin
   for Current := 1 to 5 do begin
      Short [Current] := 0
   end;   {Short is initialized.}
   for Current := 1 to 10 do begin
      Long [Current] := Current
   end;   {Long is initialized.}
end.   {OneDBed}
```

The next screen shot shows how I'd modify OneDBed to practice calculating subscripts. Now, Short is initialized backward (yes, I *could* have used a **downto** loop but that would be too simple!). Long, in turn, gets two copies of the contents of Short. Note that I've used defined constants for setting the array bounds, since that makes the subscript calculations easier to follow. We're about to make the final two assignments below:

more complicated one-dimensional array manipulation

```
────────────────── ONEDMOD.PAS ──────────────────
program OneDMod (input, output);
  {A more complicated modification of OneDBed.}
const SHORTmax = 5;
      LONGmax = 10;

type ShortTYPE = array [1..SHORTmax] of integer;
     LongTYPE = array [1..LONGmax] of integer;
                                        ┌──────── Variables ────────
var Short:  ShortTYPE;                  │ Short: (5,4,3,2,1)
    Long:   LongTYPE;                   │ Long:  (5,4,3,2,193,5,4,3,2,12296)
    Current: integer;                   │ Current: 5

begin
   for Current := 1 to SHORTmax do begin
      Short [(SHORTmax - Current) + 1] := Current
   end;   {Short holds numbers in reverse.}
   for Current := 1 to LONGmax div 2 do begin
      Long [Current] := Short [Current];
      Long [Current+(LONGmax div 2)] := Short [Current]
   end;   {Long has the reversed numbers twice.}
end.   {OneDMod}
```

A third test bed explores a two-dimensional array. GridTYPE is a simple 4 ×4 array of integer components. I've declared a few grids, then initialized them in three different ways, first numbering components row by row and column by column, and then storing the product of the subscripts. Reading the variables window is hard enough—each row's values are shown in a separate set of brackets—so I've let this program run all the way through:

initializing two-dimensional arrays

```
────────────────── TWODBED.PAS ──────────────────
program TwoDBed (input, output);
  {A test bed for two-dimensional arrays.}
const MAX = 4;

type GridTYPE = array [1..MAX, 1..MAX] of integer;

var Grid1, Grid2, Grid3:  GridTYPE;
    i, j:  integer;

begin
   for i := 1 to MAX do begin
      for j := 1 to MAX do begin
         Grid1 [i,j] := j + ((i-1) * MAX);   {Row by row.}
         Grid2 [j,i] := j + ((i-1) * MAX);   {Column by column.}
         Grid3 [i,j] := i * j
      end;
   end;                         ┌──────────── Variables ────────────
end.   {TwoDBed}                │ Grid1: ((1,2,3,4),(5,6,7,8),(9,10,11,12),(13,14,15,16))
                                │ Grid2: ((1,5,9,13),(2,6,10,14),(3,7,11,15),(4,8,12,16))
                                │ Grid3: ((1,2,3,4),(2,4,6,8),(3,6,9,12),(4,8,12,16))
```

You can appreciate that programming environments are incredibly useful when stored data get complicated. If you don't have one, you'll have to write a Dump procedure (see this chapter's *Program Engineering Notes* for more details) like the one below to get the same kind of picture.

printing a GridTYPE
variable's contents

```
procedure Dump (Data: GridTYPE);
    {Imitates a programming environment's 'variables' window.}
    var Row, Column: integer;
    begin
        write ('Contents:  (');
        for Row := 1 to MAX do begin
            write ('(');          {One row's opening parenthesis.}
            for Column := 1 to MAX do begin
                write (Data [ Row, Column ] : 1 );
                if (Column < MAX) then begin write (',') end
                    {Only print commas between values.}
            end;  {Column for}
            write (')');          {One row's closing parenthesis.}
        end;  {Row for}
        if (Row < MAX) then begin write (',') end;
        {Only print commas between rows.}
        writeln (')')
    end; {Dump}
```

```
Contents:  ((1,1,1,1)(2,2,2,2)(3,3,3,3)(4,4,4,4))
```

Modification Problems

1. Add a procedure like Dump to either of the test bed programs.

2. Modify program OneDBed so that it reads initializing values from the keyboard rather than generating them internally. There should be exactly one line of input per array. Then, change both arrays' component types to char. Does the program still work properly? Fix it.

3. Change OneDBed so that after reading and storing values, it lets you know if any stored value equals the subscript of the component it's stored in. For example, if Long[3] equals 3, the program should announce that fact.

4. Add a short (MAX components) one-dimensional array to TwoDBed. Then, add code that searches one of the two-dimensional arrays for a row whose stored values match those in the two-dimensional array. If that's too easy, try to find a column that matches in reverse.

String Types

When Pascal was first defined, it didn't include a built-in type for storing *strings*, or sequences of characters. Although Standard Pascal has a limited version of strings, most real-world Pascals include additional extensions. Let's see what Standard Pascal allows and also what common extensions are likely to provide.

In Standard Pascal, a string type is an array that obeys three rules:

— It must hold char values.

what makes a string

— It must be a **packed array**, rather than a plain **array**.

— Its lower subscript must be 1.

For example:

```
type ShortSTRING = packed array [1 .. 5] of char;
     LongSTRING = packed array [1 .. 80] of char;

var Noun, Verb:  ShortSTRING;
    Line1, Line2:  LongSTRING;
```

In Standard Pascal, strings get certain privileges that ordinary arrays don't:

— Strings can be compared alphabetically. Other arrays can't be compared.

what strings get to do

— Strings can be output in their entirety using write or writeln. Other arrays must be dumped item-by-item.

— Strings can have text constants assigned to them, as well as other string variables. Other arrays can have arrays assigned to them, but the arrays must have been previously initialized.

In Standard Pascal, a string must be read one component at a time. But just about every real-world Pascal implementation lets you read strings using read (white space ends the string) or readln (the end-of-line ends the string).

Similarly, Standard Pascal requires that any text constant assigned to a string variable have the exact same number of characters as the string can hold. However, almost every Pascal implementation permits *shorter* constants to be assigned. They will automatically *pad*, or extend, the constants with blanks or null characters.

How about a few examples? These are all legal Standard Pascal:

using Standard Pascal

```
Noun := 'Hello';        {Assigning a text constant.}
Verb := Noun;           {Assigning one string to another.}
if Verb >= 'Hello' then    etc.        {Comparing strings.}
writeln (Verb);         {Printing the whole string array.}
```

The next lines rely on very common extensions:

using Pascal extensions

```
if Noun <> 'Goodbye' then    etc.    {Lengths aren't equal.}
Line1 := 'Not quite eighty characters.'
                    {The string will be padded (filled) with blanks or nulls.}
readln (Line2);        {A whole line will be read and stored.}
```

Reading a string in Standard Pascal is tedious, but not difficult. Although we have to get the characters one at a time, we can read them directly into the array. Suppose it's called Word. Then:

string reading pseudocode

```
while we're still reading do begin
      read (Word [Current]);
      increment the counter
end of the loop
```

Don't go past the end! When loading an array, always be careful to distinguish between the *intentional* bound condition—why you want to stop—and a *necessary* bound that may be needed to guarantee termination.

Suppose that we let blanks or other white space end the string. We want to stop when we see white space, but we may have to stop when the string array is full:

string reading specification

> *Goal: Read a string.*
> *Intentional bound: Reaching white space.*
> *Necessary bound: The array is full.*
> *Plan: Get the next character.*

In situations like this, it's convenient to use the file window as a 'lookahead' variable:

> **while** (input ↑ > ´ ´)   {*the intentional bound*}
>   **and** (Current <= LIMIT) **do**   *etc.*   {*the necessary bound*}

A complete program that reads and echoes a string using only Standard Pascal is:

string reading program

```
program StringIn (input, output);
    {Demonstrates Standard Pascal string input.}
const LIMIT = 15;    {The maximum string length.}
    BLANK = ´               ´;    {Fifteen blanks.}
type StringTYPE = packed array [1 .. LIMIT] of char;
var Element: StringTYPE;
    Current: integer;
begin
    Element := BLANK;    {Initialize the string array.}
    Current := 0;
    writeln ('Please type in the name of your favorite element. ');
    while (input ↑ > ´ ´) and (Current <= LIMIT) do begin
        Current := Current + 1;
        read (Element [Current] )
    end;
    write ('Few elements are as laid back as ');
    writeln (Element)
end.   {StringIn}
```

```
Please type in the name of your favorite element.
californium
Few elements are as laid back as californium
```

Note that I was careful to make the array long enough to hold any element (even the sneaky rare earth elements like Praseodymium, number 59). I also began by initializing Element to all blanks. This precaution ensured that Element was fully defined even though my particular favorite is only seven characters long.

Modification Problems

1. Modify StringIn so that it is able to read, and echo, two separate strings. Note that you'll have to be able to skip white space that comes *before* each string to manage this.

2. Once you can read two strings, you can compare them. Improve StringIn so that it re-gurgitates its input strings in alphabetical order.

3. StringIn has a bug (or at least a non-feature) that doesn't appear in its sample output. Hint: try to print something immediately after the string-variable output. Fix the bug by a) using non-printing null characters (chr(0)) instead of blanks to fill out the string or b) writing a new WriteString procedure.

Arrays of Arrays

It frequently turns out that an array's components are also arrays. An array of arrays is a lot like an array that's defined with more than one dimension in the first place, but it can be a bit more flexible.

For example, suppose that an array's components are strings. If I make this definition:

arrays of arrays

```
type StringTYPE = packed array [1..80] of char;
     ManyLinesTYPE = array [1..20] of StringTYPE;

var OneLine:  StringTYPE;
    List:  ManyLinesTYPE;
```

we can make the assignments below.

variations on array assignment

```
OneLine [1] := 'a';        {since components of this string have type char}
List [1] := OneLine;       {since List components and OneLine both have StringTYPE.}
List [2][0] := 'b';        {since the smallest component of List is a char}
List [3,0] := 'c';         {this is a legal shorthand for a pair of brackets}
```

The shorthand of the last assignment is legal, and we'll always use it. Multiple subscripts can be put between a single pair of brackets.

We might even take advantage of the array-to-array assignment to initialize the entire list:

initializing arrays

```
{Initialize a single line to all blanks.}
for Count := 1 to 80 do begin
    OneLine[Count] := ' '        {Fill the string with blank characters.}
end;
{Initialize the entire list of lines to blanks.}
for Count := 1 to 20 do begin
    List[Count] := OneLine       {Fill the list with blank lines.}
end
```

Arrays of strings are common, but we can easily move up to more dimensions. For example, suppose that we define a type that holds a checkerboard. I can go on to declare an array of checkerboards, too:

```
type PieceTYPE = (red, black, empty);
     BoardTYPE = array [ 1 .. 8, 1 .. 8 ] of PieceTYPE;
     ManyBoardsTYPE = array [ 1 .. 25 ] of BoardTYPE;

var OneBoard:  BoardTYPE;
    ManyBoards:  ManyBoardsTYPE;
```

As before, I have a choice about which components I refer to. Note that I'll always use just one pair of brackets, since it's a legal shorthand in Standard Pascal:

assigning to arrays of arrays

```
OneBoard [ 1,1 ] := red;            {assign to one square}
ManyBoards [ 1 ] := OneBoard;       {save the whole board}
ManyBoards [ 1, 2, 2 ] := red;      {assign to another square in that board}
ManyBoards [ 2 ] := ManyBoards [ 1 ];   {copy the first board}
```

why define an array of arrays

> To the computer, the storage of a multi-dimensional array is indistinguishable from that of an array of arrays: they both take the same amount of space and hold the same values. The practical Pascal reason for giving arrays components that are also arrays is that we get to use the components as arguments to subprograms.

Suppose that you're storing a month's worth of temperature readings taken once each hour. The definition:

type ReadingTYPE = **array** [1 .. 31, 1 .. 24] **of** real;

creates a 31 day × 24 hour array and is certainly suitable for *holding* the data.

passing the whole array

```
{The parameter must be the entire two-dimensional array.}
GetAllTheInfo (var AllData: ReadingTYPE);
```

However, it may turn out that *obtaining* the data is most easily managed one day at a time. Even though this definition sets aside the same amount of memory for storage, it can be used differently:

type OneDayTYPE = **array** [1 .. 24] **of** real;
    OneMonthTYPE = **array** [1 .. 31] **of** OneDayTYPE;

Any one-dimensional 'slice' can be used; it's a variable in its own right.

passing one slice

```
{The parameter can be a single 'slice' of the array.}
GetOneDaysInfo (var SomeData: OneDayTYPE);
```

As we'll soon see, the advantage is *not* that more or less work will be done if the argument is large or small. Rather, it's a conceptual matter: is it easier for us to think of components as individual reals or as a day's worth of readings?

As long as we're on the subject of arrays as parameters, I'd better mention an issue of concern in some special circumstances. You know that a value parameter is a local copy of its argument. If the argument is a large array, it is conceivable that the time required to copy the array, or the memory used by the value parameter, could impose a significant burden on program operation.

variable parameters for large arguments

In this special case, it may be permissible to pass an array to a variable parameter even if the array is meant only to be used—and not altered—within the procedure. Variable parameters take less time and space because they merely rename their arguments. No matter how big the array is, only one small variable (in effect, it holds the array's name) will be created and initialized.

Frankly, I'm being more than a little cautious with this advice. That's because the time required for copying is usually very small, while the danger of accidentally changing the array's contents is large. Nevertheless, this trick must be used on some computers that have limited room for program variables.

Conformant Array Parameters*

One of the articles of faith that Pascal programmers rely on is that every type must be fully defined before it can be used. Every variable, parameter, and value must have a specific type. When an array variable is defined in a program, its size, and the type of its components must both be known before the program is even run.

But programmers frequently want to write general purpose procedures or functions that work just as well whether their array arguments have ten components or ten thousand. We'll be willing to restrict the arrays to holding one kind of component—all integer or real—but not to just one length.

dynamic arrays

> Arrays whose contents stay the same, but whose length may vary, are commonly known as *dynamic* arrays.

Although Wirth's original Pascal didn't permit dynamic arrays, the demand for them was so great that they were added—with different names and syntax—to both Standard and Extended Pascal.

Version	Treatment of dynamic arrays
Standard Pascal Level 0	not allowed
Standard Pascal Level 1	allowed as *conformant array parameters*
Extended Pascal	allowed as *schemata*

Most Pascal systems allow conformant arrays, so let's take a brief look at them. A *conformant array parameter* is defined in the procedure or function heading. It can be either a value parameter or a variable parameter. For example:

```
{Conformant is a conformant array parameter.}
procedure Heading ( Conformant: array [ Lower .. Upper : integer ] of char );
```

bound identifiers

The shaded portion takes the place of a type identifier. Lower and Upper are called *bound identifiers*. They are read-only variables (you can't change them) that represent the lower and upper bounds of the array that's going to be used as an argument. Notice that as usual, there's a distinction between the type of the bound identifiers (here, integer) and that of the conformant array's components (here, char). Its subscripts are going to be numbers, but it stores characters.

How about an example? Here's a procedure that multiplies each component of its conformant array parameter by a second argument, Times. Notice that we're using a variable conformant array parameter this time, because we want the changed values to persist after the procedure is done.

---

* This section is optional.

using a conformant
array parameter

```
procedure Multiply ( var Info:  array [First .. Last : integer ] of real;
                           Times: real );
{Multiply every component of Info by Times.}
   var i:  integer;    {This counter variable has the same type as the bounds.}
   begin
      for i := First to Last do begin
         Info [ i ] := Info [ i ] * Times
      end
   end;  {Multiply}
```

If I had made these definitions and declarations:

```
type ShortTYPE = array [ 1 .. 2 ] of real;
     LongTYPE = array [ −1000 .. 1000 ] of real;

var Short:  ShortTYPE;
    Long:  LongTYPE;
    Multiplier:  real;
```

then both of these calls would be legal:

```
Multiply (Short, Multiplier);
Multiply (Long, Multiplier);
```

Modification Problems ──────────────────────────────

1. Change Multiply so that it takes an array of char values as its argument, then capitalizes every letter it contains.

2. Modify Multiply so that it takes three arrays of integer values as its arguments. Then multiply corresponding components of the first two arrays, and store the product in the third array; e.g. Third [i] :=First [i] * Second [i].

Self-Check Questions ──────────────────────────────

Q. What does function WhoKnows, below, do?

```
function WhoKnows (var Data: array [ Lower .. Upper:  integer ] of integer) : real;
   var i, Sum:  integer;
   begin
      Sum := 0;
      for i := Lower to Upper do begin
         Sum := Sum + Data [ i ]
      end;
      WhoKnows := Sum / ( (Upper − Lower) + 1 )
   end;  {WhoKnows}
```

A. WhoKnows calculates and returns the real average of the integer values stored in Data.

Standard Practices: Basic Array Loop Bounds

9-2

I SEEM TO RECALL PROMISING YOU THAT ARRAYS would let you soar with the eagles. First, though, let's plod with the pigeons for a bit and refresh the loop reasoning skills that almost all array applications will require. I assure you that learning to solve these basic examples will prepare you for the innumerable variations that life (and the exercises) will throw your way. We'll look at the four basic categories of loops:

— Count-bounded loops are used mainly to *traverse* (travel through) an entire array.

— Sentinel bounds are needed for array *searching*.

— Data bounds are useful in *divide and conquer* methods that work by subdividing arrays.

— Limit bounds are required by many kinds of *simulations* and mathematical problems. I'll describe an application but won't do any coding.

Suppose that I create a couple of simple arrays to work with. Sequence, of type ListTYPE, will be a one-dimensional array of integer values. Table, of type MatrixTYPE, is a two-dimensional array of char values.

our practice arrays

```
const MAXrow = 5;
      MAXcol = 10;
type  ListTYPE = array [1..10] of integer;
      MatrixTYPE = array [1..MAXrow, 1..MAXcol] of char;
var   Sequence:  ListTYPE;
      Table:  MatrixTYPE;
```

Notice, incidentally, how the constants MAXrow and MAXcol help define MatrixTYPE. Although the practice of using defined constants instead of actual numbers isn't universal, we'll see below that it is helpful when array inspection loops are nested.

Count Bounds

The most common labor of all is visiting each array component. This is sometimes called *traversing* the array: the bound is set by the number of components. Arrays have to be traversed to:

arrays and count
boundaries

— initialize the array or modify every stored value;

— print the array's contents or retrieve them for some other purpose;

— find the largest or smallest stored value or count the number of components that share some characteristic;

— shift the location of a sequence of components within the array;

— do vector and matrix arithmetic.

The loop specification that underlies most array traversals is:

*a general loop
specification

> *Goal: Do something to or with the array's components.*
> *Bound: We've reached the end of the array.*
> *Plan: Add one to a counter.*
> > *Do something to or with the current component.*

for is usually the loop of choice. The basic array traversal pseudocode is:

one-dimensional
pseudocode

> **for** *each component or column in the array*
> > *inspect or process the current component;*
> *report on the results;*

For example, we can add the contents of Sequence, a one-dimensional array of integers, with:

adding components

```
Sum := 0;
for Subscript := 1 to 10 do begin
    Sum := Sum + Sequence[Subscript]
end;
write ('The sum of the components is:    ');
writeln (Sum : 1);
```

What do you think the next snippet of code does?

comparing components
to subscripts

```
Count := 0;
for Subscript := 1 to 10 do begin
    if Sequence[Subscript] = Subscript then begin Count := Count + 1 end
end;
{What does Count represent now?}
```

It counts components whose subscripts and stored values are the same.

Now, every component actually has two pieces of information associated with it: both the stored value and the stored value's location. If we want to find the largest stored value, we may also want to know where that value was:

saving the subscript

```
{Find the largest stored value and its position.}
BigPos := 1;
for Subscript := 2 to 10 do begin
    if Sequence[Subscript] > Sequence[BigPos] then begin
        BigPos := Subscript
    end
end;
write ('The biggest value,  ;
write (Sequence[BigPos] : 1);
write (', was in component   ');
writeln (BigPos : 1);
```

In this case the subscript was merely a number. However, if it were a value of an enumerated type, it would tell us something about the characteristics of the number we'd found.

Traveling through a two-dimensional array takes a nested loop. Think of the problem as repeating the shaded *column-by-column* pseudocode once for each row:

two-dimensional
pseudocode

> **for** *each row in the array*
>   **for** *each component (or column) in that row*
>   *inspect or process the current component;*
> *report on the results;*

For example, suppose that a two-dimensional array, Table, holds letters. How can we print the subscripts of every ´X´ stored in the array? Expanding and slightly modifying the outline above gives us the code shown below.

a row-first search

```
{Search the entire array for every hidden ´X´.}
writeln (´The value ´X´ is stored in components:    ´);
for Row := 1 to MAXrow do begin
    for Column := 1 to MAXcol do begin
        if Table[Row, Column] = ´X´ then begin
            write (Row : 1);
            write (´,´)
            writeln (Column : 1)                    {Print the coordinates.}
        end  {if statement}
    end  {inner for}
end;  {outer for}
```

> It's important to keep the subscripts straight. Table is a two-dimensional array that has a [MAXrow, MAXcol] component. However, it doesn't have a [MAXcol, MAXrow] component: [5, 10] exists, but [10, 5] doesn't.

use self-documenting
subscripts

It is very easy to make errors of this sort if you follow the near-universal practice of using the convenient, but meaningless, names i and j as subscripts. Using mnemonic, self-documenting subscripts like Row and Column takes a few extra keystrokes, but it saves trouble in the long run.

Self-Check Questions

Q. Pascal stores two-dimensional arrays in *row-major order*—a fancy way to say that the first subscript names the row, while the second subscript identifies a column in a row. So, what does this segment of code do? Notice that the loop bounds, MAXcol and MAX-row, seem to be reversed.

```
for col := 1 to MAXcol do begin
    for row := 1 to MAXrow do begin
        inspect Table[row,col]
    end  {inner, row-by-row for}
end;  {outer, column-by-column, for}
report on the results
```

A. The code traverses a two-dimensional array column-by-column, rather than row-by-row. I've reversed the regular loop order so that row, the row counter, changes more rapidly than col, the column counter.

Q. A checkerboard can be seen as an eight-by-eight array. However, only every other square is colored, starting with a colored square on the top left-hand border. Write a loop that traverses a checkerboard but stops only on the colored squares.

A. Since we want to visit each row, the outer *row-by-row* code is a typical **for** loop. The inner, *column-by-column* code changes in a clever way, since we want to alternate between starting with the first and second square of each row.

```
for row := 1 to 8 do begin   {visit each row}
    if odd(row) then Start := 1 else Start := 2;   {choose odd or even}
    for col := 0 to 3 do begin
        visit Board[row, Start + (2*Col)]
    end   {column-by-column for}
end   {row-by-row for}
```

Sentinel Bounds

Sentinel bounds are the second staple of array processing. Although we start out by traversing an array, we're liable to cut the trip short, so **for** loops won't do. Typical sentinel problems include:

arrays and sentinel boundaries

— finding the location of a particular stored value;

— processing words or sentences stored in an array (spaces or punctuation marks act as sentinels);

— locating a subsequence with a particular characteristic (e.g. it is ascending or descending).

a warning

We will usually find that when we're searching an array for a sentinel, a count bound will be needed as well. If the sentinel isn't found, we have to guarantee loop exit lest we sail past the end of the array.

For example, suppose we want to find the first number greater than 0 in the one-dimensional Sequence array (which was defined as an **array** [1..10] **of** integer). The simple solution is to inspect components, one by one, until we see one that fits the bill:

a simple one-dimensional search

```
{Find the first number greater than 0.}
Current := 1;   {Initialize the subscript counter.}
while Sequence[Current]<=0 do begin
    Current := Current + 1   {Move to the next component.}
end   {Postcondition — Sequence[Current]>0 — we think!}
```

Stating a postcondition doesn't guarantee that a program will survive to reach it. If no stored value is greater than 0, we'll run past the end of the array. The *range error* this causes will crash the program.

To avoid range errors, a loop specification typically has a necessary bound that guarantees termination (the count) in addition to the intentional bound that helps get us to our goal (the sentinel). But if we do add a second possibility for exit, we can't be sure why we left the loop. In pseudocode:

pseudocode

initialize the subscript counter;
while *we haven't reached the sentinel*
      and *we haven't hit the end of the array*
   add 1 *to the subscript counter*
end *of the loop;*
decide why we left the loop

The Pascal version, below, has a postcondition and post-loop check we'll see again and again:

a safer one-dimensional search

```
Current := 1;  {the subscript also acts as a counter}
while (Sequence[Current]<=0) and (Current<10) do begin
    Current := Current + 1
end;
{Postcondition: If Sequence[Current] isn't greater than zero, no component is.}
if Sequence[Current] <= 0
    then begin writeln ('No value exceeded zero.') end
    else begin writeln ('Found it!') end
```

Now, suppose that we're searching for a sentinel—say, an ´X´—in a two-dimensional array of char. Will anything change? Yes. We can use a problem solving method called *case analysis*—just a common-sense look at the alternatives that might arise—to help us move through the array. A specification of the array-searching loop is:

loop specification

Goal: Find the position of the letter ´X´.
Intentional bound: Spotting the sentinel.
Necessary bound: Reaching the last component of the array.
Plan: Advance to the next component.

The case analysis helps decide what *advance to the next component* means. This wasn't really a problem for a one-dimensional array search, because *advance to the next component* always meant *add one to the subscript*. But the 'next' component in a two-dimensional array is sometimes on the next row:

advancing to the next component

initialize the subscript counters;
while *we haven't found the sentinel* **and**
     we haven't reached the end of the array **do begin**
  if *we haven't reached the last column in the current row*
    then *advance to the next component in this row*
    else *advance to the first component in the next row*
end *of the loop;*
decide why we left the loop

The program segment below implements the loop pseudocode. The exit condition parallels the bound of the one-dimensional array search but is necessarily more complicated. Nevertheless, the loop postcondition—and the requirement for a post-loop check—remain the same.

safely searching a two-
dimensional array

```
{Search the two-dimensional Table array for the first 'X'.}
Col := 1;
Row := 1;        {Prepare to inspect the first component.}
while (Table[Row, Col] <> 'X') and
         ( (Col < MAXcol) or (Row < MAXrow) ) do begin
    if Col < MAXcol
        then begin Col := Col + 1 end
        else begin Row := Row + 1;
                       Col:= 1
        end  {if}
end; {while}
{Postcondition: If Table[Row, Col] isn't an 'X', no component is.}
if Table[Row, Col] <> 'X'
        then begin writeln ('No value equaled "X".') end
        else begin writeln ('Found it!') end
end
```

Modification Problems

1. Suppose that Table were an array of integer values. Modify the code segment above so that it locates the component that equals the product of its subscripts.

Self-Check Questions

Q. This program segment is intended to search a Sequence array (that is, an **array** [1..10] **of** integer) and let us know if it holds a 3. Assuming that Found is a boolean variable, what's wrong with the code? It isn't a syntax problem.

```
for Current := 1 to 10 do begin
    Found := (Sequence[Current] = 3)
end;
if Found then begin write ('Found it.') end
```

A. In effect, Found acts like a switch. To spot the bug, imagine that there isn't a 3 in Sequence[10]. Found will become FALSE even if there's a 3 elsewhere in the array. If, for some reason, we want to use a **for** statement to find a sentinel, we have to invent a one-way switch that can be turned on, but not off.

```
Found := FALSE;
for Current := 1 to 10 do begin
    if Sequence[Current] = 3 then begin  Found := TRUE
    end
end;
if Found then begin write ('Found it.') end;
```

Data Bounds

Data bounds appear frequently in array programming. They're exceptionally useful for *divide-and-conquer* problem-solving methods that:

arrays and data
boundaries

— describe sections of the array in terms of relative borders, rather than by fixed subscripts or stored data values;

— divide a large array into smaller pieces that can be dealt with separately;

— place barriers between the potentially 'useful' information stored in an array, and a steadily shrinking or growing 'irrelevant' portion;

— gradually shrink the unexplored portion of an array until it either holds the solution we're looking for or is empty.

auxiliary subscripts are
pointers

> Data bounds are generally set with auxiliary subscript variables that serve as *pointers* to the portion of an array that we're interested in. They limit the problem's *solution space* by minimizing the array's unknown area.

I'll use subscript pointers and data bounds to solve a variation of the *saddleback search* problem, which was first presented by David Gries who attributes it to a U.C. Berkeley undergraduate.

Suppose that a two-dimensional array holds char values that increase along each row and down each column, as they do here:

problem: saddleback
search

```
B  C  D  F  H  L  N  R
C  D  E  G  I  M  O  S
D  E  F  H  J  N  P  T          The letters get higher as you
F  G  H  J  L  P  R  V          move down or to the right.
H  I  J  L  N  R  T  X
L  M  N  P  R  S  V  Y
N  O  P  R  T  X  Y  Z
```

Devise an algorithm for counting the number of times a particular letter appears. For example, 'L' appears four times, and 'N' appears five.

The hammer and tongs approach slogs through the entire array. I'll call it Table and assume that MAXrow and MAXcol are arbitrarily large:

searching the whole
array

> {*Counting the* Ns *in a* MAXrow *by* MAXcol *array.*}
> *initialize* Count *to* 0;
> **for** i := 1 **to** MAXrow **do**
>   **for** j := 1 **to** MAXcol **do**
>   **if** Table[i,j] *equals* Letter **then** *add* 1 *to* Count

But an *exhaustive search* like this is needlessly tiring. It doesn't take advantage of an important piece of information supplied with the problem—that the stored values increase along each row and down each column.

Instead of mechanically searching the entire array, we can develop a case analysis that minimizes the number of components that have to be inspected. Look at the array and pick a component at random. No matter which component you choose, letters that are down or to the right are always larger.

developing a case
analysis

Suppose that we start searching from the upper-right corner—in the last column of the first row. The value this component holds will either be too big, too small, or just right. If it's too big, a smaller value will be found in one of the columns to the left on the same row. If it's too small, a bigger value will be on the next row down, but in the same column. Finally, if the component happens to equal the letter we want, the next potential candidate will be one column to the left and one row down.

Why don't I repeat what I just said in pseudocode?

inspecting one component

if Table[Row, Col] > Letter
    then *decrease* Col *by* 1 *to go back one column*
    else if Table[Row, Col] < Letter
        then *increase* Row *by* 1 *to go down one row*
        else Table[Row, Col] *equals* Letter *so*
            count another appearance of Letter;
            decrease Col *by* 1;
            increase Row *by* 1

Try it out. Remarkably, as long as we start from the upper-right corner, at component Table[1, MAXcol], the rules always work.

Now, whenever we move to the left, we can ignore values in *every* column to the right. Similarly, when we move down, we can ignore all other values in *every* row that is above our current position. If you take a pencil and shade the areas that are discounted at each step of the way, you'll see that a larger and larger area can be ignored, while a smaller and smaller rectangle—the remaining solution space—is left to be searched.

How do we decide when to stop searching? Since our plan for spotting the number we want has the very desirable effect of reducing the size of the area that must still be searched, we can easily establish a data bound for the loop. In effect, we cross the border and exit when the 'unknown' area has been reduced to zero. A loop specification that incorporates this data bound is:

loop specification

Goal: Count the number of stored Letters.
Bound: Crossing row MAXrow or column 0.
Plan: Count a Letter *if we've reached one.*
      Move on to the next row and/or the previous column.

The final search is precisely the pseudocoded case analysis given above.

the saddleback search

```
read (Letter);          {What are we looking for?}
Count := 0;             {How many have we seen?}
Row := 1;
Col := MAXcol;
repeat    {until we cross the bottom or left-hand bound of the array}
    if Table[Row, Col] > Letter           {It's greater than Letter,}
        then Col := Col − 1               {so go back one column.}
        else if Table[Row, Col] < Letter  {It's less than Letter,}
            then Row := Row + 1           {so go down one row.}
            else begin Count := Count + 1;  {It equals Letter,}
                    Col := Col − 1;       {so go back and down.}
                    Row := Row + 1
            end  {last else}
until (Row > MAXrow) or (Col < 1);
write ('Number of appearances was:   ');
writeln (Count : 1)
```

Modification Problems

1. The example array held letters. But if you can figure out how to create an array that holds the sums of prime numbers, you can do some interesting things. Let each i,j component hold the sum of the ith and jth prime numbers, where both counts run 1, 2, 3, 5, 7, 11, 13, 17, 23, 29. Write a procedure that initializes the table.

2. Once you know how to build the table, use the saddleback algorithm to test Goldbach's conjecture, made in 1742 and never disproved, that every even number six or greater is the sum of at least one pair of primes.

3. A theorem from the mathematician Fermat says that any prime number that leaves a remainder of 1 when divided by 4 is the sum of two squares (e.g. $13 = 2^2 + 3^2$, $41 = 4^2 + 5^2$), and no other two squares. Try to disprove it.

4. Vinogradov's *three primes* theorem shows that every sufficiently large odd number is the sum of three primes. Can you build a three-dimensional table of the sums of primes? If so, just how large seems to be sufficient?

Limit Bounds

Finally, we arrive at limit bounds. When arrays are used to simulate or model real-world processes, an entire arrayful of data will often be subjected to some action again and again. For example, each component might be averaged with the values of its nearest neighbors. As with mathematical limits, we can reach a point of diminishing returns—a point at which one more trip through the array might not improve its contents.

Limit bounds are used to spot that point. Some typical applications are:

— Modeling *diffusion* or *flow*; for instance, tracking the spread of pollution through an environment, or of heat through a conductive surface.

arrays and limit bounds

— Modeling population *growth*; simulating conditions that might lead to eventual survival or extinction.

— Modeling *cycles*; trying to detect rhythmic patterns that change, but are stable (like the cyclic, yet predictable, population of locusts).

Problems like this are a little beyond us because they have three equally difficult parts: figuring out what starting data are, figuring out what to do with them, and figuring out how to recognize that we've done enough!

One classic that's pretty straightforward, though, is modeling heat flow across a metal surface. We assume that one or more spots are inexhaustible heat sources, while other areas (perhaps the edges) are insatiable heat consumers. An array holds the starting temperatures at regular intervals across the metal surface.

modeling heat flow

The surface's temperature will, naturally, reflect a flow from hot to cold areas. We can simulate the process by averaging adjacent array components— really just a counting bound, since we visit each component in turn—until the change between one sweep and the next is very small. For all practical purposes, the array's contents have managed to find a state of equilibrium. In pseudocode:

repeat {*until the temperature is relatively stable*}
　repeat {*reset each component's temperature*}
　　average a component with its neighbors
　until *we're at the last component — the count bound*
until *there wasn't much change — the limit bound*

a limit bound
application

You'll get a chance to write a program like this in the exercises.

Extended Examples: Data Abstraction

9-3

THERE IS AN ENDLESS SUPPLY OF programming problems that involve arrays. I've tried to provide a selection that is entertaining as well as educational. The first example works with palindromes—words or phrases that (like *a Toyota*) read the same forward and backward. Our focus will be on manipulating one-dimensional arrays.

Afterward, you'll have a reasonable supply of technique under your belt, so I'll switch the focus to programming methodology. We'll concentrate on *data abstraction* and an *object-oriented*, or 'data first,' approach to solving a few problems.

Since courses vary in the extent to which they delve into array searching and sorting, I've reserved that discussion for Chapter 10. You'll also find a problem there (the *Dutch National Flag*) that somehow seems to use every algorithm you've learned.

Example: Identifying Palindromes

Let's begin with the problem of identifying palindromes.

problem: spotting
palindromes

Palindromes are words or phrases that read the same forward and backward. According to the rules of the game, capitalization, punctuation, and spaces are ignored. Write a program that reads a phrase and confirms or denies its palindromicity.

These are all palindromes:

a few palindromes

Go hang a salami. I'm a lasagna hog.
Dennis and Edna sinned.
Satan, oscillate my metallic sonatas.
Sore was I ere I saw Eros.

Checking palindromes is an interesting problem because of the way its solution relies on data bounds. Suppose that I say that a phrase is a palindrome if:

how to identify a
palindrome

— its first and last letters are the same;

— the remaining phrase, without the first and last letters, is also a palindrome.

I put the definition in these terms to invite an algorithm that uses subscript pointers to mark the first and last letters of the steadily shrinking *remaining phrase*. Get two pencils, and cross out the first and last letters of one of the phrases above. Eventually you'll run out of letters—it's a palindrome—or arrive at a mismatch—it isn't.

Now, suppose that the phrase is held in an array. Our pointers start out at the beginning and end, so we can compare the first and last letters. Each time we have a match, we can move the pointers closer together by one component each. If there's ever a mismatch between the current 'first' and 'last' components, the phrase is automatically disqualified; it's not a palindrome. But as long as letters keep matching, we can continue to move the pointers and shrink the unexplored portion of the phrase.

The heart of our palindrome verifier involves a loop that I'll specify as:

> *Goal: Decide if an array contains a palindrome.*
> *Bound: The unknown portion of the array is empty* **or**
>   *two components are different.*
> *Plan: Shorten the array by one component at each end.*

If we rely on the specification, we'll have to include the all-important *look after the loop*:

> *get the lower-case, spaceless, depunctuated phrase;*
> *initialize pointers to the first and last components;*
> **while** *the unknown portion of the array isn't empty*
>   **and** *the first/last pair still match* **do begin**
>   *move the pointers at each end one component closer*
> **end** *of the loop;*
> *decide if the phrase was a palindrome*

How can we tell when *the unknown portion of the array is empty?* Well, suppose that First and Last mark the array ends. It's easy to move them a step closer together:

> First := First + 1;
> Last := Last − 1

But when is the unknown part of the array empty? It's safe to say that while:

> (First + 1) < Last

the unknown can still be shrunk a little further (try it out). Later, I'll write this up as function Palindrome. It will be TRUE if the phrase is one.

With the central part of our program in hand, let's get the phrase in the first place. It is easy enough to read it one letter at a time into an array of char:

> Last := 0;
> **while not** eoln **do begin**
>   *increment* Last;
>   read (Phrase [Last])
> **end** *of the loop*

But can we carry out the algorithm the pseudocode describes? No, because we haven't gotten rid of lower-case letters, spaces, and punctuation. I *could* filter out the problem letters as I read, but there is a harder, less efficient, more educational approach. Why not read the phrase as above, then go through it, capitalizing as necessary? If we come across a blank or punctuation mark, we can shift the remainder of the string one component to the left. Here, we're on the way to setting up the phrase: 'No, Hal, I led Delilah on.'

'N' '0' 'H' 'A' 'L' 'I' 'L' 'e' 'd' ' ' 'D' 'e' 'l' 'i' 'l' 'a' 'h' ' ' 'o' 'n' '.'

The first seven characters have already been dealt with.

In outline, the plan for cleaning up the array is:

specification

Goal: Remove embedded spaces and punctuation from Phrase.
Bound: We've reached the Last *character in* Phrase.
Plan: Inspect the Current*th character.*
    if *it was a letter*
      then *capitalize it*
      else *slide every remaining character one position to the left;*
          reduce Last *by* 1
    Increase Current *by* 1.

Here's a pseudocode outline for reading, then cleaning up, the phrase. I'll eventually turn it into procedures ReadThePhrase and FixThePhrase.

how to prepare the phrase

```
{Read the phrase, then get rid of lower-case, spaces, and punctuation.}
Last := 0;
while not eoln do begin
     increment Last;
     read (Phrase [Last])
end;
{Postcondition:  there were Last characters in the phrase.}
Current := 1;
while Current <= Last do begin
     {Precondition:  Phrase[Current] .. Phrase[Last] is unknown.}
     if Phrase[Current] is a letter
          then capitalize it
               increment Current
          else slide every remaining component to the left by one;
               decrease Last by 1
end of the loop
{Postcondition:  Phrase[1] .. Phrase[Last] are capitalized letters.}
```

Once again I'm using subscripts as pointers to the start and finish of the 'still unknown' part of the string. I'm going to leave the *slide every component to the left by one* part for you.

    Suppose that I jump ahead to the main program. Given the three subprograms we've already outlined, I can show it as:

final pseudocode

> *give the user instructions;*
> **repeat**
>   ReadThePhrase (Phrase, Length);
>   FixThePhrase (Phrase, Length);
>   **if** Palindrome (Phrase, Length)
>   **then** *make a positive announcement*
>   **else** *make a negative announcement*
> **until** *it's time to quit*

Why don't you try to figure out an easy way to quit before you read program TestPals, below? As you read procedure Palindrome, incidentally, be sure that you understand why a phrase is a palindrome if, and only if, Phrase[First] equals Phrase[Last].

palindrome check program

```
program TestPals (input, output);
    {Decides if the user has typed in a palindrome.}

const MAX = 80;    {Longest allowed input string.}

type StringTYPE = packed array [ 1 .. MAX ] of char;

var Phrase: StringTYPE;
    Length: integer;

procedure ReadThePhrase (var Phrase: StringTYPE; var Last: integer);
    {Reads the phrase and returns its length.}

    begin
        Last := 0;
        while not eoln and (Last < MAX) do begin
            Last := Last + 1;
            read (Phrase [Last] )
        end;
        {Postcondition: Phrase[1] .. Phrase[Last] holds the phrase.}
        readln
        {Get rid of the end-of-line.}
    end; {ReadThePhrase}

function Palindrome (Phrase: StringTYPE; Last: integer) : boolean;
    {Returns TRUE if Phrase holds a palindrome.  Does NOT error-check blank lines.}

    var First: integer;

    begin
        First := 1;
        while ( (First + 1) < Last) and
                    (Phrase[First] = Phrase[Last]) do begin
            Last := Last – 1;          {Move the subscripts closer together.}
            First := First + 1
        end;
        {Postcondition:  We've inspected the whole phrase or found a mismatch.}
        Palindrome := Phrase[First] = Phrase[Last]
    end;  {Palindrome}
```

```
procedure FixThePhrase (var Scrunch: StringTYPE; var Last: integer);
    {Capitalizes the phrase, removes spaces and punctuation.}
    var Current, i: integer;
    begin
        Current := 1;
        while Current <= Last do begin
            {Precondition: Scrunch[Current] .. Scrunch[Last] is unknown.}
            if Scrunch[Current] in [ ´a´ .. ´z´ ] then begin
                Scrunch[Current] :=
                        chr(ord(Scrunch[Current] ) – ord(´a´) + ord(´A´));
            end;
            if Scrunch[Current] in [ ´A´ .. ´Z´ ] then begin
                Current := Current + 1
                {The stored phrase is one letter longer.}
            end
            else begin for i := Current + 1 to Last do begin
                        Scrunch [i–1] := Scrunch[ i ]
                        end;  {for}
                        Last := Last – 1
                end   {else}
        end   {while}
        {Postcondition: Scrunch[1] .. Scrunch[Last] are capitalized letters.}
    end;  {FixThePhrase}
begin
    writeln ('Type in a palindrome for me to check ("yo" to quit).´);
    repeat
        ReadThePhrase (Phrase, Length);
        FixThePhrase (Phrase, Length);
        if Palindrome (Phrase, Length)
            then begin writeln (´It was a palindrome.´) end
            else begin writeln (´It wasn´´t a palindrome.´) end
    until (Phrase[1] in [´y´, ´Y´]) and (Phrase[2] in [´o´, ´O´])
end.   {TestPals}
```

Type in a palindrome for me to check ("yo" to quit).
Harass sensuousness, Sarah.
It was a palindrome.
Straw? No, too stupid a fad. I put soot on warts.
It was a palindrome.
yoyo
It wasn't a palindrome.

Modification Problems ———————————————————————————————————

1. TestPals doesn't do any housekeeping on the Phrase array. As a result, leftover letters from earlier palindromes may clutter it up, and make debugging more difficult. Make TestPals clean up Phrase before reusing it. While you're at it, come up with a method of quitting that *doesn't* process the sentinel.

2. Will Palindrome handle a palindrome with an odd number of letters? How about an accidental blank line? Either convince yourself that it will or fix it.

3. Use Palindrome to search through an on-line dictionary. How many palindromes can you find?

4. We can describe a sentence as being a palindrome in terms of its words. For instance, *Girl, bathing on Bikini, eyeing boy, finds boy eyeing bikini on bathing girl* reads the same forward and backward. Modify TestPals to work wordwise as well. Mail me your clever test data, please.

Data Abstraction

The problems we've solved so far have concentrated on the techniques of using arrays. But as we move on, we'll become less concerned with planning a step-by-step course of action and more concerned with deciding how to store information. Why? Because there is a close partnership between a program's algorithm and its data. As the equation that names one of Niklaus Wirth's textbooks puts it:

$$Algorithms \ + \ Data \ Structures \ = \ Programs$$

Teaching programming, which used to focus on algorithms and methods, is incomplete unless it also pays plenty of attention to the data structures that algorithms use.

structures are abstract

Now, data types are *concrete*; like statements, they're built-in features of a programming language. Data structures, in contrast, are *abstract*. Like algorithms, structures are language-independent. They can be constructed in any language, and they can be studied apart from any particular application.

making tradeoffs

A program's algorithm might be likened to its plot—what happens? Its data structures, in contrast, provide the cast of characters—who does what, and to whom? And in programs, as in literature, there can be a tradeoff between the two: a programmer who puts time into designing a good data structure may be rewarded with a less complicated algorithm. Conversely, an algorithm that has to compensate for a quick and dirty data structure may end up being unnecessarily complex and detailed.

primitives define abstractions

> Data structures are typically described in terms of their *primitive operations*. Primitives carry out basic operations, like input, output, or assignment. A data type or structure that's defined strictly in terms of its primitives, rather than by the way it's implemented, is called a *data abstraction*.

Data abstraction isn't all that different from the *procedural abstraction* we've been using all along. We haven't had any trouble with talking about imaginary pseudocode procedures as though they really existed. All we needed was to agree on what the procedures would do if we had them. Using abstractions has been quite convenient, because it has let us avoid nitty-gritty details of implementation until we were ready to deal with them.

Data abstraction gives us the same advantage. We're not tied to any particular method for storing or manipulating data. Data abstractions, like procedural abstractions, let us delay: we decide what we want to do before we choose the best way of doing it.

A data abstraction's primitives tie it to reality. We can talk about primitives all we want, but actually writing primitives will require that we know details of how a data abstraction is implemented. Some of the primitives that most data abstractions will require are:

common primitives

— An *initialization* procedure that sets up the value or structure to begin with.

— An *assignment* procedure that lets values be stored or changed.

— An *inspection* procedure that retrieves or prints the stored values.

Working with data abstractions, rather than procedural abstractions, encourages a new style of program design—object-oriented design. Recall that procedures encourage a goal-oriented approach that focuses on step-by-step progress toward a solution. The object-oriented strategy begins with data, instead. In effect, it argues that making data handling tools more sophisticated makes goals easier—much easier—to attain. We'll try this approach several times.

object-oriented implies
data first

Unfortunately, Standard Pascal is limited in its ability create data abstractions that really can stand alone, independent of any particular program's needs. We can get the idea of object-oriented design, but real object-oriented programming is beyond the capacity of the language. Other languages, like Turbo Pascal, C++, and Smalltalk, supply the syntax that's needed to package data abstractions in a way that lets other programs use and extend them. Nevertheless, we can start to attack the hard part—design—right now.

Example: Checking Magic Squares

Most textbooks start out with rather dull examples of data abstraction—fractions, say, or strings. I'll begin with something unexpected—a *magic square*.

Magic squares have been around practically forever. The 1514 engraving below, *Melancholia*, was made by Albrecht Dürer, a contemporary of Leonardo da Vinci. This four-by-four magic square appears at the upper right.

Dürer's magic square

16	3	2	13
5	10	11	8
9	6	7	12
4	15	14	1

If you look at the square carefully, you'll see that every number from 1 through 16 appears once. That's easy. What's magical is that the numbers in every row and column, and both diagonals, add up to the same number: 34.

More formally, a magic square is an $N \times N$ square of numbers that obeys these conditions:

problem: check for magic

—Every number from 1 through N^2 must appear just once.

—Every row, column, and diagonal must add up to the same total.

Write a program that lets you know if a square is magic.

As usual, there are two ways to approach the problem. The goal-oriented approach seems matter-of-fact. We start by reading the magic square's components into a two-dimensional array. As we go along, we can make sure that each number appears exactly once. If the square remains potentially magic, we can methodically go about checking the sums of its rows, columns, and diago-

goal vs. object-oriented approaches

nals.

But why can't we treat a square of numbers as a new kind of data structure? If we look at the problem from the viewpoint of our data—the object-oriented approach—the questions to ask are: 'What do we want our data to tell us? What primitive operations are we going to want?'

—   An *initialization* procedure that reads the numbers.

—   An *inspection* procedure that prints the square.

magic square primitives

— A *unique* function that's TRUE if the square holds just one instance of each number, as it should.

— *Inspection* functions that return the sum of the numbers stored in any particular row or diagonal.

> Conceiving of the number square as a data abstraction lets us plan before we code. We can decide how the program is going to work before we're committed to any particular way of storing its data.

Eventually, I'll have to get around to defining a MagicTYPE and declaring a Square variable. When I do, I'll be able to make calls like these:

calling the primitive MagicTYPE operators

Load (Square) *reads the square* :
Unique (Square) *is* TRUE *if there's one of each number;*
SumRow (Square, Row) *returns the sum of a particular* Row;
SumColumn (Square, Column) *returns the sum of a particular* Column;
SumDiagonal (Square, Diagonal) *returns the sum of a particular* Diagonal;

I won't insult your intelligence by saying that outlining primitives makes our job as easy as, say, reading and multiplying two numbers. But it does make the final design job easier. We can focus on the algorithm that solves the problem, rather than the detailed mechanics of traversing rows and columns. Here's one possible solution:

pseudocode

Load (Square);
use Unique *to check the distribution of numbers;*
get the sum of one row, column, or diagonal to use as a reference;
use SumRow *to check the rows;*
use SumColumn *to check the columns;*
use SumDiagonal *to check the diagonals;*
if *the square passes all the tests* **then** *say so*

By the same token, we'll be able to reconsider the implementation of individual primitives without worrying that we'll discombobulate the main program. As long as the primitives supply the results they advertise, how they get them is their own business.

There are not too many alternatives for a final design of the underlying data types. A square of whole numbers is going to call for an array. I'll also enumerate a type that names the two diagonals:

the underlying data type

const MAX = 4;   {*Size of the square.*}

type MagicTYPE = **array** [1 .. MAX, 1 .. MAX] **of** integer;
    DiagonalTYPE = (left, right);

Suppose that we try a more realistic look at the main program. In order for a square to be magic, it has to pass each and every test. If any test is ever failed, there's no point in carrying out more checks, since the square can't be magic. I'll use a boolean variable called StillMagic to keep track of the current state of the ongoing check. If the state is ever FALSE, I can short-circuit the remaining checks.

```
Load (Square);
if Unique (Square) it's worth checking out, so
    save a CheckSum by calling SumDiagonal (Square, left);
    StillMagic := the other diagonal equals CheckSum
    while StillMagic do check out each row and column
        StillMagic := the current row and column both equal CheckSum
        go to the next row and column
    end of the loop;
    report on the results
```

Before we move on to a completed version, let's take a moment to consider the algorithm of the Unique primitive. In words, the problem is:

An $N \times N$ array holds numbers. Write a subprogram that lets you know if every number from 1 through N^2 appears exactly once.

How would you solve the problem on paper? I'd just make a list of numbers, then go through the Square array and check off each Square [i, j] value as it appeared:

$$1 \quad 2 \quad 3✓ \quad 4 \quad 5 \quad 6✓ \quad 7✓ \quad 8 \quad 9 \quad 10 \quad 11✓ \quad 12 \ldots$$

I can manage the same thing by using a one-dimensional array of boolean values (call it Appears) as the checklist.

```
initialize the Appears array to all FALSE;
for every i,j component in the Square array do
    set Appears [ Square [ i, j ] ] to TRUE
if any FALSE value remains in Appears
    then the Unique function is FALSE
    then the Unique function is TRUE
```

I've shown a completed version of Magic below, and used Dürer's magic square as its input.

```
program Magic (input, output);
    {Reads and decides if a square is magic.}
const MAX = 4;              {Size of the square.}
      MAXsquared = 16; {The number of unique numbers it should hold.}
type MagicTYPE = array [ 1 .. MAX, 1 .. MAX ] of integer;
     DiagonalTYPE = (left, right);
var Square: MagicTYPE;
    CheckSum, Current: integer;
    StillMagic: boolean;
```

(*program continues*)

```
procedure Load (var Square: MagicTYPE);
    {Reads the magic square.}
    var Row, Column: integer;
    begin
        for Row := 1 to MAX do begin
            for Column := 1 to MAX do begin
                read (Square [ Row, Column ] );
            end;    {We've read a single row.}
            readln
        end          {We've read every row.}
    end; {Load}
function Unique (Square: MagicTYPE) : boolean;
    {TRUE if Square holds each number in the range 1 .. MAX∗MAX.}
    type CheckTYPE = array [ 1 .. MAXsquared ] of boolean;
    {I'll mark components TRUE if the number has appeared.}
    var Appears: CheckTYPE;
        Row, Column, Current: integer;
        Result: boolean;
    begin
        for Current := 1 to MAXsquared
            do begin Appears [ Current ] := FALSE end;
        {As far as we know, nothing has appeared yet.}
        for Row := 1 to MAX do begin
            for Column := 1 to MAX do begin
                Appears [ Square [ Row, Column ] ] := TRUE
            end    {When a number does appear, mark it TRUE.}
        end;
        {Postcondition: a FALSE entry means the number didn't appear.}
        Result := TRUE;   {Temporarily, at least, the square is unique.}
        for Current := 1 to sqr (MAX) do begin
            if Appears [ Current ] = FALSE
                then begin Result := FALSE end
        end; {for}
        {Postcondition: Result is TRUE if every number appeared.}
        Unique := Result
    end; {Unique}
function SumRow (Square: MagicTYPE; Row: integer) : integer;
    {Adds the values in one row.}
    var Column, Sum: integer;
    begin
        Sum := 0;
        for Column := 1 to MAX do begin
            Sum := Sum + Square [ Row, Column ]
        end;    {We've added the contents of each column in one row.}
        SumRow := Sum
    end; {SumRow}
```

(*program continues*)

```
function SumColumn (Square: MagicTYPE; Column: integer) : integer;
    {Adds the values in one column.}
    var Row, Sum: integer;
    begin
        Sum := 0;
        for Row := 1 to MAX do begin
            Sum := Sum + Square [ Row, Column ]
        end;    {We've added the contents of each row in one column.}
        SumColumn := Sum
    end; {SumColumn}

function SumDiagonal (Square: MagicTYPE; Which: DiagonalTYPE) : integer;
    {Adds the values in one diagonal.}
    var Point, Sum: integer;
    begin
        Sum := 0;
        case Which of
            left: for Point := 1 to MAX do begin
                    Sum := Sum + Square [ Point, Point ]
                end;    {We've added the upper-left to lower-right diagonal.}
            right: for Point := 1 to MAX do begin
                    Sum := Sum + Square [ Point, (MAX − Point) + 1 ]
                end    {We've added the upper-right to lower-left diagonal.}
        end;
        SumDiagonal := Sum
    end; {SumDiagonal}
begin
    write ('Reading a magic square with side  ');
    writeln (MAX : 1);
    Load (Square);
    if Unique (Square) then begin
        CheckSum := SumDiagonal (Square, left);
        StillMagic := SumDiagonal (Square, right) = CheckSum;
        Current := 0;
        while StillMagic and (Current < MAX) do begin
            Current := Current + 1;
            StillMagic := (SumRow (Square, Current) = CheckSum) and
                (SumColumn (Square, Current) = CheckSum)
        end   {the loop test}
    end; {passing the Unique test}
    if StillMagic
        then write ('Square was indeed magic, with a sum of  ')
        else write ('Square was not magic.  Left diagonal check sum was  ');
    writeln (CheckSum : 1)
end. {Magic}
```

```
Reading a magic square with side 4
16    3    2   13
 5   10   11    8
 9    6    7   12
 4   15   14    1
Square was indeed magic, with a sum of 34
```

Modification Problems

1. What data does Magic require for a complete test? Develop a set of test squares that exercises each control path. Make sure that an early failure doesn't cut the test short.

2. Magic has no error checking on its input. Where will this cause problems? Modify the program so that it tells the user what went wrong if there weren't enough values entered. If the Unique check fails, have Magic tell the user which values are missing or repeated.

3. Magic has the size of its square fixed at 4 by 4. Modify the program so that it fixes a *maximum* magic square size, but still permits smaller squares to be tested.

Example: Counting Characters

Our next design example is a program that depends on its data in an obvious way. Here's the problem:

problem: character counting

The ambition of every person of our era is to go on *Wheel of Fortune* and play for the car. In case you have been in a coma for the past decade, Vanna exposes a vowel and five other letters if they appear in a hidden phrase. The contestant gets to add three consonants and another vowel, then tries to guess the rest.

some days seem to be easier than others!

Assume that you are preparing for your appearance and would like to know which letters are most likely to appear. Count the total number of characters in a sample of input, then print a table of the relative number of appearances of lower-case letters.

The grunt work of counting and tabulating values is a typical array application. The analysis itself has other, more traditional applications:

— Decoding an encrypted message, on the assumption that its symbols will have the same letter frequencies as letters in plain text.

a few applications

— Seeing if different languages have unique letter-frequency 'signatures.' These might be used to help produce nonsense text that, despite being meaningless, can instantly be identified as being in a particular language.

— Determining if Morse code is as efficient as it might be—do common letters have brief codes and vice versa?

Let me start sketching a character-counting data structure in abstract terms by outlining its basic primitives:

> *Initialization:* Initialize *will initialize the character-count data structure;*
> *Assignment:* CountData *will add* 1 *to the count of a character appearances;*
> *Inspection:* CountWas *will let us know the count stored for any single value;*

Suppose I gave you these three procedures. Could you solve the problem of counting characters? Sure you could! A rough pseudocode might be:

first pseudocode

> *use* Initialize *to initialize variables as necessary;*
> *get and process the input data with* CountData;
> *use* CountWas *to calculate and print the program's results;*

primitives define the abstraction

> None of the primitives can be written without knowing how the underlying data structure is going to be implemented. However, they fully define the abstraction for our purposes. We don't *have* to know anything else about it.

In fact, I can take a step that's pretty amazing: I can write the headings of the primitive subprograms, as I have below. The only commitment I'm making here is that Ch is a char variable. *How* the primitives are going to work is an issue for another time; what's important now is *what* they do.

describing the data abstraction

> **type** CountTYPE *underlies the structure that holds the counts;*
> **var** CountArray: CountTYPE;
>   Ch: char;
> **procedure** Initialize (**var** CountArray: CountTYPE);
>   {*Initializes the CountTYPE structure.*}
> **procedure** CountData (**var** CountArray: CountTYPE; Ch: char);
>   {*Counts the appearance of a character.*}
> **function** CountWas (CountArray: CountTYPE; Ch: char) : integer;
>   {*Returns the number of times Ch was counted.*}

This little collection doesn't define a data *type*—you can see that I haven't even tried to describe what the CountTYPE definition is going to be. However, it does define a data *abstraction*—we know exactly how to use the structure even though we don't know what it's made of. Let me refine the first pseudocode to take advantage of the extra details:

second pseudocode

Initialize (CountArray);
initialize a Total *counter;*
while not eof **do begin**
    read Ch;
    CountData (CountArray, Ch);
    add 1 *to the* Total
end *of the loop;*
for Ch := *each of the lower-case letters* **do begin**
    print CountWas(CountArray, Ch) / Total *as a percentage*
end *of the for*

Stop for a moment to recognize how looking at data abstractions first—the object-oriented approach—differs from our old methods:

the object-oriented approach

— We began by getting an idea of what kind of information a solution to the character-counting problem would require.

— Then, we outlined some data handling tools—the primitives Initialize, CountData, and CountWas.

— Finally, we returned to the traditional goal-oriented approach and outlined a program that used the new tools.

— Our next step will be to define the underlying data type and write the bodies of the primitives.

In contrast, the old method would have had us begin by getting an idea of what steps the program would take. We might have decided exactly how data would have been stored, then outlined procedures for getting data and calculating results. We would have considered *first* what we now put off until *last*—deciding how to hold the character counts.

Implementing the Primitives

How are we going to hold character counts? Well, we could write the data abstraction primitives using twenty-six different counters—one for each letter. But from our present learned vantage point this approach is too tedious to bother with. Why declare all those different variables (and have procedure calls with twenty-six parameters), when just one array can hold all the counts at once? Consider this definition instead:

the CountTYPE definition

```
type CountTYPE = array [char] of integer;
var CountArray: CountTYPE;
```

CountArray is an array whose bounds are chr(0) and chr(127). After it has been initialized, I can add 1 to any character's count with the assignment:

```
CountArray[Ch] := CountArray[Ch] + 1;   {Increment the proper counter.}
```

When we ultimately PrintResults, we can ignore all components outside of the ´a´..´z´ sequence.

Now that we know the definition of the underlying data type, we can think about implementing the abstraction's primitives. Procedure Initialize can traverse the entire array via a **for** loop:

```
{Initialize the array.}
for Ch := chr(0) to chr(127) do begin
    initialize the current component to 0
```

back to the primitives

Procedure CountData's job was to add 1 to one character's total. As we've seen, its central assignment is:

```
CountArray[Ch] := CountArray[Ch] + 1;   {Increment the proper counter.}
```

Finally, function CountWas returns the count that's been collected for a single character. Its main statement is:

```
CountWas := CountArray[Ch]
```

Let's turn to our program. If I wanted, I could use procedural abstractions to describe what it's going to do:

```
initialize variables as necessary;
get and process the input data;
calculate and print the program's results;
```

If I did, these goal-oriented procedures would call Initialize, CountData, and CountWas just as they might call read or write. However, I think that writing them out as procedures will make our program overly complicated.

A final version of program ChCounts is shown below. Shading shows how it might be broken into goal-oriented procedures. The output is an analysis of the program text contained in my file ChCount.PAS. I also added an extra touch; can you figure out how the table of output was produced?

character counting program

```
program ChCounts (input, output);
    {Count input characters, print relative frequency of lower-case letters.}
type CountTYPE = array [char] of integer;
var CountArray: CountTYPE;        {CountArray holds the character counts.}
    Ch: char;                     {Ch holds the current input character.}
    Total,                        {Total counts the total number of letters.}
    LineCount: integer;           {LineCount helps produce neat output.}
procedure Initialize (var CountArray: CountTYPE);
    {Initializes the CountTYPE structure.}
    var Position: char;
    begin
        for Position := chr(0) to chr(127) do begin
            CountArray[Position] := 0
        end
    end;  {Initialize}
```

```pascal
procedure CountData (var CountArray: CountTYPE; Ch: char);
    {Counts the appearance of a character.}
    begin
        CountArray[Ch] := CountArray[Ch] + 1
    end;  {CountData}
function CountWas (CountArray: CountTYPE; Ch: char) : integer;
    {Returns the number of times Ch was counted.}
    begin
        CountWas := CountArray[Ch]
    end;  {CountWas}
begin
    {the initialization segment}
    writeln ('Counting letter frequencies . . .');
    Total := 0;
    Initialize (CountArray);

    {the processing segment}
    while not eof do begin
    {Count appearances of all available characters.}
        read (Ch);
        CountData (CountArray, Ch);
        Total := Total + 1
    end;  {while}
    {We know individual and overall character counts.}

    {the results segment}
    writeln ('Lower-case frequencies (among all input characters):');
    LineCount := 1;
    for Ch := 'a' to 'z' do begin  {Print the output table.}
        write (Ch);
        write ('  =  ');
        write ( 100.0 * (CountWas(CountArray, Ch)/Total):4:2);
        write ('%   ');
        if (LineCount mod 5) = 0 then begin writeln end;
        LineCount := LineCount + 1  {Newline after every fifth character.}
    end;  {for}
    writeln;
end.  {ChCounts}
```

```
Counting letter frequencies . . .
Lower-case frequencies (among all input characters):
a = 3.99%   b = 0.54%   c = 1.86%   d = 1.00%   e = 5.40%
f = 0.82%   g = 0.82%   h = 2.13%   i = 3.17%   j = 0.00%
k = 0.05%   l = 1.72%   m = 0.41%   n = 4.94%   o = 3.99%
p = 0.86%   q = 0.14%   r = 4.54%   s = 1.72%   t = 5.80%
u = 2.99%   v = 0.41%   w = 0.68%   x = 0.00%   y = 0.73%
z = 0.27%
```

Modification Problems

1. Although the output I've shown look impressive, it's impossible to tell by inspection if it's right. Produce test data for ChCounts that can be checked.

2. Reconstruct ChCounts with goal-oriented procedures. You can have them call the primitives that ChCounts uses now, or you can 'decompose' the program entirely—in effect, rewrite it from scratch.

3. As written, ChCounts must have input either typed in or redirected using an operating system extension like < data. Modify the program so that it asks the user for the name of a file to analyze. You'll probably want to make use of an extended form of the standard reset procedure.

4. Modify ChCounts so that *a*) it *folds* upper-case letters—counts them as though they were lower-case—and *b*) it only prints each letter's appearance as a proportion of all *letters*, rather than of all *characters*. Are you tempted to modify the definition of Count-TYPE? If you do, how will it affect the primitives?

Program Engineering Notes: Tools for Inspection

9-4

IMAGINE THE DIFFICULTY OF CONSTRUCTING A BUILDING from invisible bricks and mortar. Beams fly into thin air, girders sail into space, and, most likely, rubble collects at the foundation.

Building a program is not at all a dissimilar proposition. As long as unseen parts fit together, construction proceeds apace. However, when invisible components aren't where they're supposed to be, the error messages start to pile up and programming grinds to a halt. The most useful tool a program engineer can have is sight—the ability to look inside her program's components. Translated into precept form, we have a basic rule of working with structured types:

> *Build tools before you build programs.* As you define new types, write primitives that will let you look inside them.

Taking this peek may help you overcome one of the programmer's most dangerous prejudices: that an array doesn't hold anything until she's put something in it. Although some systems may automatically initialize arrays to zero (or a non-numerical equivalent), many don't. Unthinkingly relying on a stored value that just happens to be there creates intermittent bugs that are very difficult to find, because:

creating intermittent bugs

— the first program run's variables contain entirely random values, but

— the next program run's variables hold values from the first program run.

What's unexpected (and leads to hair-tearing debugging sessions) is that the *second* program run may be the one that crashes. The moral? Make sure that you initialize arrays before you use them, and look inside your arrays to make sure they're actually initialized.

Visibility is more of an issue for structured types (like arrays) than for simple types (like plain integer or char variables) because the structure itself may hold information. In simple variables, *what* is the value is the only real question. Arrays, in contrast, require answers to *where* is the value as well—what is its subscript, and how does it relate to its neighbors?

Two Tools — Load and Dump

The two most useful tools go by rather unceremonious names:

— Load initializes an array for testing.

— Dump prints the contents of an array.

Specialized load and dump procedures aren't necessary for simple variables. After all, we have assignment statements and procedures for input and output built into Pascal. But for structured variables, like arrays, they're absolutely essential. How can an array-manipulation procedure be tested if you aren't certain about the original contents of the array? And how can you be certain until you've taken a look inside?

Load procedures create a level playing field for program testing. After all, what you intend to do *with* data is only part of the programming problem.

know your test data

> *Getting there is half the fun.* Before a program can modify data it must obtain them. Before you can debug a modification procedure, you have to be able to give it data.

For example, testing the searching procedures we'll use in the next chapter requires a load procedure that can initialize an array in four different ways: to just one value, to ascending and descending sequences of values, and to a set of values I stored in a file. I certainly didn't want to enter all of these test data by hand, so I wrote a general-purpose procedure.

You probably won't need to be convinced about the usefulness of dump procedures. However, you should take a little time to write them well. Two pieces of advice are:

— *Label the output.* Print the subscripts along with the stored values.

— *Format the output.* Take an extra five seconds to make sure that subscripts aren't confused with values.

An array usually holds a large amount of information. A dump of its contents should be helpful rather than confusing. A typically unhelpful array dump is:

an unhelpful dump

```
{Print the contents of a ten-component array.}
for i := 1 to 10 do write (Data[ i ] : 1);
```

8923894280923893 2267217

Just adding labels doesn't necessarily help, either:

another useless version

```
{Print and label the contents of a ten-component array.}
for i := 1 to 10 do begin
    write (i : 1);
    write (Data[ i ] : 1)
end
```

⬇   ⬇   ⬇   ⬇   ⬇

189223389442580962307893822269721107

Instead, try adding brackets, white space, and an occasional carriage return to make output clear:

help at last

```
{Print, label, and format the contents of a ten-component array.}
for i := 1 to 10 do begin
    write ("    [");
    write (i : 1);
    write ("]:  ");
    write (Data[ i ] : 3)
    if (i mod 5) = 0 then writeln end
end
```

⬇   ⬇   ⬇   ⬇   ⬇

```
[1]:   89  [2]:   23  [3]:   89  [4]:   42  [5]: 809
[6]: 230  [7]: 893  [8]: 226  [9]: 721  [10]:    7
```

Note that load and dump procedures stand apart from the primitives that help define a data abstraction. They aren't necessarily meant to be well-refined additions to a textbook process of program development. Instead, they're the hammer and pickaxe of programming—nitty-gritty tools that do a simple job quickly.

Test Harnesses and Incremental Development

Load and Dump procedures are often built into programs and left behind in case they're needed again. It is also common practice to build certain testing tools that are thrown away.

> A *test harness* is a program shell that is used to test procedures in isolation, before they are integrated into a more complex final program.

Way back when, I described a program as a delivery system for procedure calls. A test harness is precisely that—a delivery system for procedure tests that contains:

— the type definition;

— procedures that initialize and/or inspect data structures; and

— the new procedure that is undergoing testing or modification.

The new procedure can be tested without having to deal with a main program that is more complex and finicky than the harness is. Once it works, the new procedure can be transferred to the main program.

Using test harnesses is part of a more general approach to programming called *incremental program development*. An increment is a small amount; incremental development means programming by improvement. There is one basic reason for its appeal.

incremental program development

The First Law of Program Development
A program that does only 80% of the job but works is better than a program that does 99% of the job but crashes.

As the saying goes, writing the first 80% of a program takes 80% of the time, while polishing up the last 20% takes the other 80% of the time. Part of the reason for this weird arithmetic is that as programs become more complex, changes have a tendency to introduce unexpected effects.

Incremental programming tries to isolate the effect of changes. We add new features in preference to adding new functions, and add new functions rather than writing new programs. The short-program approach of *write / compile / test* becomes:

incremental additions

> *define types / compile / fix;*
> *add load and dump procedures / compile / test;*
> *add first processing function / compile / test / fix;*
> *add features / compile / test / fix;*
> *add second processing function / compile / test / fix;*
> *keep adding features / and compiling / and testing / and fixing.*

Dealing with Data Deluge

As you have probably gathered by now, each chapter promises a simpler life as long as you learn umpteen new things to worry about. What's happening, of course, is that new material really does simplify the solution of problems—but only of problems you wouldn't have attempted otherwise. Overall, we're solving problems that are progressively more difficult and complicated.

Work with arrays is inherently more complex than work with individual variables because we have more balls in the air at once. Programming maturity means that there are a deluge of data in contrast to the few piddly drops we're used to. Here are three ideas that will help make life easier:

build scale models

1. *Build scale models.* Use defined constants to reduce the size of each array to the smallest practical size for testing your approach.

Is multiplying two 4-digit numbers any different from multiplying two 100-digit numbers? As long as the same data structure is used for both, the answer is no.

What *is* different? Testing. As difficult as it is to spot a bug in a few lines of output, it is impossible to spot a bug when output runs longer than one screen. And what about input? Do you really *want* to type in two 100-digit numbers over and over again? Worse, do you really want to check a 199- or 200-digit answer? In short, scale models reduce testing to reasonable terms.

check intermediate results

2.   *Avoid combining intermediate steps.* Try to check the results of every action.

Suppose that you are writing a text-editing program. If an array contains twenty lines of text, the command *delete lines 6 through 10* might be implemented as a single Delete command. However, I would much rather use this sequence:

> *erase the contents of 6 through 10;*
> *move lines 11 through 20 to 6 through 15;*
> *erase the contents of 16 through 20;*
> *change* TotalLength *from 20 to 15;*

checks between steps

Why? So that I can use my Dump procedure to confirm that the array's physical contents match my mental image of what has happened. Even though I 'know' that copying one line over another erases it, I would still rather take the extra step of explicitly erasing the vanishing line first. The extra step doesn't make a correct program any better, but it helps me spot the unexpected bug in my own frequently incorrect code. Perhaps I read the wrong numbers for deleting, or perhaps an earlier command has messed up the array's contents.

make data self-explanatory

3.   *Embed debugging information in data.* During testing, try to make test data self-explanatory.

This simple suggestion is particularly important for text-processing programs. There is nothing visibly wrong with the next few lines as test data:

poor test data

```
I am failing computer science.
Sunshine beckons.
Printout hits the floor.
```

However, they do not shine a spotlight on bugs. Suppose that my test command is *move line 3 to follow 1.* The output:

```
Sunshine beckons.
Printout hits the floor.
I am failing computer science.
```

is wrong. Line 1 now follows line 3, rather than vice versa.

In contrast, the test data below may be of more modest interest as haiku, but they're more useful for debugging programs. The right order is obvious:

better test data

```
1 Life to Live.
2 good 2 B true.
3 piece power bands.
```

A Collection of Subscript Bugs

Technique or no, there will still be bugs. Syntax problems are a plague at first, but you should have enough experience interpreting compile-time error messages by now to work through them. In fact, you can use the compiler to check your definitions as soon as you make them; after all, nobody ever claimed that a program had to do something. This program can be compiled in an attempt to find the bug it contains:

```
program Test (input, output);
type TwoTYPE = array [1..5], [1..10] of integer;
    {Can you see the syntax bug yet?}
var TwoArray: TwoTYPE;
begin
end.   {Test}
```

A Pascal compiler will complain that it expected to find the word **of** after the first right bracket:

```
type TwoTYPE = array [1..5],[1..10] of integer;
                           ^     Compile error:  OF expected
```

Runtime array errors generally derive from subscripts whose type is correct (so they pass the compile-time check), but whose value during program execution falls outside the legal range of the array. Suppose that you have been assured that the letter 'T' can be found in a twenty-component array. This loop searches for it:

```
i := 1;
while (TheArray[ i ] <> 'T') do begin
    i := i + 1
end;
write ('The T is in component  ');
writeln ( i : 1 )
```

All is well and good if the 'T' is really there. But if it's not, we eventually try to inspect TheArray[21]—a component that doesn't exist.

```
Runtime Error:  Subscript out of range.
```

> You trust your mother, but you still cut the cards. Always, but always, make sure that your intended loop bound will guarantee timely termination. A count bound on the subscript value is almost always appropriate.

The corrected segment below still contains a bug. To spot it, jot down the loop's postcondition:

```
i := 1;
while (TheArray[ i ] <> 'T') and (i < 20) do begin
    i := i + 1
end;
write ('The T is in component  ');
writeln ( i : 1 )
```

Despite the fact that we prepared to leave the search if the 'T' wasn't there, we blithely announce that it is in component 20 if and when we *do* bail out. The shaded line must be replaced with a post-loop check:

look after you loop

```
{Postcondition: If TheArray[ i ] doesn't hold a 'T', no component does.}
if TheArray[ i ] = 'T'
    then begin write ('The T is in component  ');
                writeln ( i : 1 )
         end
    else begin writeln ('The T wasn''t there.') end
```

Out-of-range subscripts also come up in two-dimensional arrays. If both subscripts have the same type, then misordered subscripts will pass muster at compile time. They'll even work at runtime as long as a search doesn't delve too deeply. For example, suppose that an array has five rows and ten columns. Normally, we'd refer to a component as:

misordered subscripts

```
{A correct application.}
AnArrayVariable [Row, Column] where Row ≤ 5 and Column ≤ 10
```

However, as long as the current value of Column stays at five or less, this reference is going to be correct, too:

```
{This isn't necessarily incorrect.}
AnArrayVariable [Column, Row]
```

watch subscripts, not components

This kind of bug is tough because it's intermittent; the code works until you really push the array to its limits. A useful debugging technique is to focus on the subscripts, rather than on the components.

> Fixing bugs is easy—it's finding them that's hard. Before you decide where a bug *isn't*, find out where you are.

Watching subscripts is exceptionally useful when subscripts are being calculated on the fly. Such calculations are susceptible to off-by-one errors of the simplest sort. For example, what are the components that surround SomeArray[i, j]? Are they:

are these the neighbors of i,j?

above:	$[i-1, j-1]$	$[i-1, j]$	$[i-1, j+1]$
alongside:	$[i, j-1]$		$[i, j+1]$
below:	$[i+1, j-1]$	$[i+1, j]$	$[i+1, j+1]$

Not necessarily! What if the component is on an edge of the array? Not every component *has* eight neighbors; in fact, a corner component has only three.

Testing for Semantic Bugs

You will find, as time goes on, that the kinds of bugs described above are the ones that you're happy to have, because the compiler helps you find them. Semantic bugs are harder to deal with, because you may not even be aware that they're occurring.

By definition, you are afflicted with *semantic* bugs when a program runs, but arrives at the wrong conclusion. Testing is the only way to find semantic bugs—the choice is up to you whether you run the test or a grader does! Recall that since testing can show only the presence of bugs, and remains silent about their absence, you have to be pretty aggressive in ferreting out potential errors.

Since array manipulation usually involves loops, semantic problems with arrays tend to arise from improper loop formulations. For example, off-by-one errors are common in shifting data within an array or between two arrays. Suppose that we have this array:

what we have

and want to copy the first Length components (1, 2, and 3 if Length equals 3) into the last Length components.

what we want

Here's an incorrect attempt at making the shift:

```
{An incorrect shift.}
for i := 1 to Length do begin
    AnArray [LIMIT − i] + 1 := AnArray[ i ]
end
```

Can you see the problem? Suppose that Length is 3 and LIMIT is 9. Then, we're moving components 1, 2, and 3 into components 9, 8, and 7.

what we get!

The corrected assignment would be:

```
{The corrected shift.}
for i := 1 to Length do begin
    AnArray [(LIMIT − Length) + i] := AnArray [ i ]
end
```

My advice is to remember that, first and foremost, you're writing a loop to generate subscript values. Any array manipulations that take place are, in a way, secondary applications of the stream of subscripts. Comment out the switch code, then print the numbers you generate.

testing subscript streams

```
{Testing subscripts in isolation.}
for i := 1 to Length do begin
    { AnArray [(LIMIT − Length) + i] := AnArray [ i ] }
    write ('To:  ');   write ( (LIMIT − Length) + i);
    write ('  From:  ');   writeln ( i );
end
```

```
To:  7    From:  1
To:  8    From:  2
To:  9    From:  3
```

This is a very common problem, so I'll debug a second faulty example. Suppose that we want to reverse the contents of an array, so that the last component is moved to the first and so on. This code segment is incorrect:

a faulty reversal

```
{Tries to reverse an array, but really leaves it in its starting configuration.}
for i := 1 to LIMIT do begin
    Temp := TheArray [ i ];
    TheArray[ i ] := TheArray[ (LIMIT – i) + 1 ];
    TheArray[ (LIMIT – i) + 1 ] := Temp
end
```

Why? Well, let's imagine once again that the array manipulation loop's purpose is to generate a stream of subscript values. The goal of the incorrect loop above is really:

Incorrect goal: Generate every subscript from 1 *through* LIMIT.

But what we actually want is a little bit different:

Correct goal: Generate all LIMIT **div** 2 *pairs of subscripts.*

another subscript printer

```
{Assume that LIMIT = 10}
writeln ('Generating pairs of subscripts for an array reversal:');
for i := 1 to LIMIT div 2 do begin
    write (i : 3);
    write ( (LIMIT – i) + 1 : 3);  write (',      ')
end;
```

```
Generating pairs of subscripts for an array reversal:
    1 10,       2  9,       3  8,       4  7,       5  6,
```

If we're satisfied with it, the shaded parts can come out, and the actual shift of data in the array can go in.

Syntax Summary

❏   array: a structured type that contains *components* of any one type. The type must be defined before variables can be declared:

```
const N = 50;
type AnArrayTYPE = array [1 .. N] of integer;
     TwoDimensionTYPE = array [1 .. N, 'A' .. 'Z'] of char;
var OneArray:  AnArrayTYPE;
    TwoArray:  TwoDimensionTYPE;
```

❏   string array: a one-dimensional array of char values. The lower bound must be 1, and the array must be defined as a **packed array**.

```
type StringTYPE = packed array [1 .. N] of char;
```

String arrays can be compared alphabetically, may be output in their entirety (using write or writeln), and can have text constants (character strings, given between single quote marks) assigned to them. However, Standard Pascal requires that strings be read one character at a time, like ordinary arrays.

❏   bounds: in the array type definition, they establish the array's size and the form of its subscripts.

[1..10]	*bounds given with literal values*
[LOWER .. LIMIT]	*bounds given with constants*
[char]	*bounds given by an ordinal type name*
[*bounds, bounds*]	*bounds of a multi-dimensional array*

Bounds can have enumerated types, but they may not be real.

❏   subscripts: help construct the name of an array variable by identifying a particular component. Given the declarations above:

> OneArray[1] *is an* integer *variable*
> TwoArray [1, ´A´] *is a* char *variable*

❏   components: can be of any type, including another structured type.

❏   conformant array parameter: a feature of Standard Pascal Level 1. Conformant array parameters are sized *dynamically*, so that arrays of different sizes may be used as arguments.

> **procedure** Heading (Conformant: **array** [Lower .. Upper : integer] **of** char);

Within the procedure, Lower and Upper are read-only *bound variables* that represent the array's bounds.

Remember . . .

❏   Arrays are random-access types because components can be stored or inspected in any order.

❏   The values that set array bounds can't be variables, but they can be constants. If an ordinal type name is used to set bounds, they are automatically set to the first and last value of the type.

❏   An array-to-array assignment gives values to all of an array's components at once. Such assignments can be made only between arrays that were declared with the same type identifier.

❏   In Standard Pascal, string arrays must be assigned text constants of the exact same length. However, automatically *padding* (extending) the constant with blanks is a common extension.

❏   An array component's identifier may be complicated by brackets and subscripts, but ultimately it's just the name of a variable or value. Subscripts can be expressions of any kind, but they have to be properly ordered and within the legal range of the array's bounds. If they're outside the bounds, a fatal subscript *range error* will occur.

❏   A one-dimensional array of one-dimensional arrays and a two-dimensional array can have the same number of components, but they are syntactically distinct. The first has arrays as components, the second has just simple variables.

❏   Traversing an array means visiting all its components. Remember that an array *search* for a particular component may turn into a *traversal*, so be sure to watch out for the end of the array.

❏   Auxiliary variables can be used as *pointers* to particular array components. They're useful in *divide-and-conquer* problem-solving methods that split arrays into 'interesting' and 'uninteresting' segments.

❏   *Object-oriented design* is an alternative to the *goal-oriented* design we've used thus far. It begins by asking how a program uses data, rather than starting by trying to break the problem down into goal-oriented procedures. We'll generally use object-oriented design to build the tools that make goal-oriented programming easier.

❏   A *data abstraction* outlines a type or structure in terms of the *primitive* operations it must allow, rather than the Pascal type definitions it should be based on. The primitives usually include only operations that can't be implemented without knowing details of the underlying definition.

❏   Some advice on arrays: use a Load procedure to initialize arrays for testing. When operations are complicated, take small steps and use a Dump procedure to show the array's contents frequently.

❏   Some advice on dealing with larger programs: build them in incremental stages, use *test harnesses* to try out individual procedures, test with scale models, and embed meaningful information in test data.

Big Ideas

The Big Ideas in this chapter are:

1.   *Every structured type requires rules for specifying the types, and constructing the names, of stored values.* The specific rules of each type differ, but their purpose is the same: to let values be stored and retrieved without confusing the compiler.

2.   *Arrays have as much information in their structure as they do in their stored values.* Information is built into arrays in various ways: by the kinds of subscripts we use to define them, by the components we choose to store values in, and by the position of stored values relative to each other. A well-designed program can use this built-in information to simplify other parts of its algorithm.

3.   *Data abstraction separates the use of a data-handling tool from its implementation.* A data abstraction's primitives act as a performance specification (of what the abstraction can do), and as a requirements specification (of what its eventual implementation must allow).

Begin by Writing the Exam . . .

9-1   *How many components does this array have?* Fortunately, if you can answer one such question, you can probably answer them all. Make up one inordinately complex definition, then ask how many components it contains.

9-2   I like to introduce single- and multi-dimensional arrays at the same time because I think that subscripting—not the number of them—is the hard idea. As prof, you'll have to test this theory. Make up a few *How are these structures alike?* questions, where points of similarity can be number of dimensions, type and number of stored components, and type of subscripts.

9-3   To get anywhere with arrays, you have to know how to access stored values. To test somebody's understanding of access, you have to give her the chance to answer one of these questions incorrectly:

a)   Do the subscripts have the right type?

b)   Are they in the proper range of values?

c)   Are they in the right order?

d)   Is the type of a component correct? What is it?

e)   Has a type name accidentally appeared in place of a variable identifier?

Make up a few complicated array definitions, then use them to create a series of *Is this statement legal?* questions.

9-4   Traversal is an array topic that you can and must have down cold. There are several ways to pose traversal problems:

a)   *Initialize this array*, perhaps so that its contents match its subscripts.

b)   *Print an array's contents in this pattern*, perhaps in reverse or in rows twice as long.

c)   *Move this array's contents to that array*, again, perhaps changing relative ordering or working from arrays with different dimensions.

d)   *Merge these arrays*, perhaps interleaving two short arrays into one long array.

Make up three traversal problems you might encounter on an exam.

9-5   Looking for a sentinel within an array is a pretty cut-and-dried problem. It's easy to make the same question much more difficult by looking for a sequence of values within an array. Naturally, the sought-for sequence will be held in an array as well.

The simplest version of the problem is: *Are the components in these two arrays identical?* A slightly more complicated version is *Does one array match the other array in reverse?* Come up with two more variations on the problem.

9-6   A harder version of the above problem assumes that one array is shorter than the other. Two ways of phrasing questions are *Can this short array's contents be found within this long array?* and *Can this short array's contents be found in this two-dimensional array?* Again, come up with two variations on this theme.

9-7   If a practice question has been *Do the values stored in this array increase?* as you work from left to right, it's a reasonable bet that the exam question will be *Do the values in this array decrease or stay the same?* as you travel the same route. Make up three more questions of this ilk.

9-8   Some problems can't be solved without arrays, while others needn't be solved with them. For example:

a)   Find the (alphabetically) least word in a series of words.

b)   Calculate the sum of a series of numbers.

c)   Find the second-largest number in a sequence of input numbers.

d)   Read exactly two hundred numbers and print them in decreasing order.

e)   Read exactly two hundred numbers and print the ones that fall within a specific range.

Problems *a* and *d* need arrays for solution, while the rest don't.

Make up another half-dozen questions of this sort. Try to choose examples that appear to require arrays but really don't, and vice versa.

9-9   Data type definitions are the word problems of computer science. The solutions aren't hard, necessarily, but getting to them from the problem statement can be. You'll find some in the warmups, below. For now, make up five word problems that require a type definition for solution; for instance, *Define a type that might be used to represent the results of a track meet.*

9-10   Any easy array problem can be made more difficult by the simple expedient of enclosing it within a bigger array. For example, knowing that you have mastered *Are all* *the values in this one-dimensional array identical?* the crafty instructor instead asks *Find the row of this two-dimensional array whose values are all identical*, while the truly wicked teacher asks *Find the column whose components increase in value.*

I'm sure that you can be at least as crafty, if not as truly wicked, as a prof. Dress up five one-dimensional array problems in two-dimensional clothing.

Warmups and
Test Programs

9-11   What is the largest array you can define? Can you define an **array** [integer] **of** anything? Does the type of the array's components (boolean, integer, or real) change the maximum legal array size? What if the components are structured themselves?

9-12   What error messages do you collect for:

a)   trying to inspect or assign to a component that's beyond the end of an array;

b)   misordering the subscripts of a two-dimensional array;

c)   leaving out one subscript of a two-dimensional array;

d)   trying to assign a simple value to an array variable;

e)   defining an array **fo** (yes, **fo**) char;

f)   using parentheses instead of brackets in a definition?

9-13   Define array types that would be suitable for holding:

a)   the heights and weights of one hundred elephants;

b)   fifty students' letter grades in five subjects, named as an enumerated type;

c)   a tic-tac-toe board;

d)   the number of times each capital letter is used in a text sample;

e)   a month's worth of hourly rainfall measurements, stored in a manner that makes it easy to find the measurement of a particular date and time.

9-14   Assuming that you have a suitable two-dimensional array, initialize it in these ways:

```
 1  2  3  4        1  5  9 13
 5  6  7  8        2  6 10 14
 9 10 11 12        3  7 11 15
13 14 15 16        4  8 12 16

 4  3  2  1        4  8 12 16
 8  7  6  5        3  7 11 15
12 11 10  9        2  6 10 14
16 15 14 13        1  5  9 13
```

9-15   Outline procedures that find a value in *a)* a one-dimensional array, *b)* the same array working backward, *c)* a two-dimensional array, *d)* the same array but searching by columns first, *e)* the same array but searching by columns upward first.

9-16   A spelling checker requires that you store up to one hundred 10-character words. Define a suitable type for storing them.

9-17   Write a program that interleaves two arrays, component by component, into one array that's twice as long.

9-18   Write a program that finds the *n* largest values, in order, in an array of integers. Hint: as you find and print each 'largest' value, figure out a way to get rid of it.

9-19   A *saddle point* in a two-dimensional array is a component whose stored value is simultaneously the highest its row and the lowest in its column (or vice versa). Write a program that inspects a two-dimensional array and finds any and all saddle points.

Programming Problems

9-20 The **Hum** package is a collection of programs, written by Bill Tuthill, that are useful for work in the *hum*anities. They count and rearrange text in ways that make it easier to study.

One interesting command that had never occurred to me was **wheel**. It 'rolls' through the text, printing *n* words at a time. For example, the command **wheel 3** would yield:

```
Here is a
is a three
a three word
three word example      etc.
```

Write a program that wheels through a file in groups that can range, at the user's option, from one to ten words per line.

9-21 An *anagram* is produced by rearranging the letters of one word or phrase to produce another. Write a program that determines if two sequences (of up to ten letters each) are anagrams. Test it on *cat/act*, and *scare/races/cares/acres*.

9-22 A *palindrome* is a series of letters that spell the same words both forward and backward, as Napolean's lament 'Able was I ere I saw Elba.' A *numerical palindrome* is a bit simpler—it's just a number that's the same front to back and back to front. 1234321 is a numerical palindrome, but 123431 isn't.

Numerical palindromes can usually be generated from arbitrary integers with an easy algorithm: reverse the number, then sum the original number and its reversal. It may take many such steps, but a palindrome generally results: 561+165=726, 726+627=1,353, 1,353+3,531=4,884, which is palindromic. There are some notable exceptions to this—196 is the smallest—from which a palindrome *never* seems to result, however.

Write a program that generates palindromic numbers up to fifty digits long. Announce the number of steps required, and be sure to check for, and halt before, overflow (just in case you try one of the 5,996 numbers below 100,000 that do not appear to be palindromic no matter how long you persist).

9-23 If you have access to an on-line dictionary, here are a few word problems:

a) What is the longest word? The shortest? The longest ascending (abcd) and descending (dcba) words? Which has the largest number of different letters?

b) What is the most common prefix, where the prefix is *n* letters long? The most common suffix?

c) What are the relative frequencies of single letters? Of letter pairs? Of letter triples? Can you generate words at random, giving each letter the appropriate likelihood of showing up?

d) Which words have the highest Scrabble letter values?

9-24 There are several ways to use the alphabet to encrypt a *plain-text* message:

a) A simple *substitution cipher* uses a fixed substitution alphabet:

```
Plain:   abcdefghijklmnopqrstuvwxyz
Code:    !=#$%^&*()_+<,>.?/"'~'{[}]
```

b) The *Caesar* code, named after Julius Caesar, shifts the alphabet by a fixed number of places, then uses simple substitution:

```
Plain:   abcdefghijklmnopqrstuvwxyz
Code:    DEFGHIJKLMNOPQRSTUVWXYZABC
```

c) The method of Johannes Trithemius, described in 1510, applies a different Caesar code to each letter:

```
1st Code:    ABCDEFGHIJKLMNOPQRSTUVWXYZ
2nd Code:    BCDEFGHIJKLMNOPQRSTUVWXYZA
                 . . .
26th Code:   ZABCDEFGHIJKLMNOPQRSTUVWXY
```

Each of these leads to countless variations, and each is open to attack by computer. The difficulty lies in recognizing success: how can a program distinguish a meaningful decryption from one that's nonsense?

Write an interactive tool that is able to apply different strategies for decryption. It should display a good portion of the encrypted text and immediately update the display as the user selects different methods of attack. If you're doing this as a one-person project, focus on the simple substitution cipher and include at least two features:

– Display the encrypted characters in order of frequency, and

– let the program user specify particular substitutions.

9-25   Computers are terrific at doing arithmetic. Unfortunately, the numerical data types that are built into most programming languages strictly limit the size of numbers.

However, it isn't very hard to build tools that will allow operations on numbers that are hundreds, or even thousands, of digits long. Design and implement a data abstraction that supports 100-digit whole numbers. At a minimum, you should supply primitives for input, output, and addition. Naturally, you can add additional primitives (subtraction, multiplication, and so on) if you like.

9-26   It's not hard to imagine using an array to represent a checkerboard. But can you imagine playing a game of checkers on it? Or, more to the point, can you imagine a checkerboard as a data abstraction, complete with primitive operations?

Plan and implement a set of procedures that support operations on a checkerboard variable. Include primitives for:

a)   *initialization*, to position checkers at the start of play;

b)   *inspection*, to print the current checkerboard; and

c)   *input* and *assignment*, to make moves, but only if they're legal.

Some bonus enhancements to consider are:

d)   Detect a move that causes the moved piece to become endangered.

e)   Detect a move that causes *any* piece to become endangered.

f)   Take a piece automatically.

What additional primitives will this automatic playmaking require?

9-27   DNA molecules are comprised of triples that consist of four different organic bases—adenine, cytosine, guanine, and thymine, usually abbreviated as A, C, G, and T. Although the entire molecule can be incredibly long, a single missing base can have catastrophic effects. For example, one particular rat gene associated with hereditary diabetes differs from the normal 1,000-base sequence by just one missing G residue:

normal sequence	GGA	AGC	GGA	GGC	CGC
diabetic sequence	GGA	AGC	GAG	GCC	GCT

The resulting *frame shift mutation* is apparent in the third triple.

The problem of spotting off-by-one errors of this sort has interesting applications in text processing as well; e.g. in comparing two files that differ by only one line. For now, though, just write a program that is able to find the location of a frame shift mutation in a DNA base sequence. Be sure to confirm that the molecules differ by only this one base and do not diverge entirely at the point of departure.

9-28   Many maps include a table of distances between points. The table is basically a square two-dimensional array, subscripted on each axis by a list of cities, with each component showing a distance. The distance between a city and itself, of course, is zero.

Write a program that implements a table of distances between cities. Let a program user employ it to:

a)   Find the distance between any two cities.

b)   Find the cities closest to, and furthest from, any city.

c)   Find the total distance on a trip between any sequence of cities.

d)   Find out whether or not a journey between two cities can include a detour to a third city that will not extend the total trip length by more than *x*%. The user should enter only the first and final locations.

9-29   Computer modeling can show that events that appear catastrophic at close range can be quite stable and recur naturally in long-term cycles. For example, forest fires are usually viewed as disastrous, yet periodic, naturally occurring (e.g. by lightning) fires are an essential part of healthy forest ecology.

An interesting variation on the theme involves competition between species through *infestation*. For example, the spruce budworm is an unpleasant little beastie that defoliates balsam and spruce trees. Unfortunately for the budworm, these trees are replaced by beeches, which they find indigestible. The beeches, in turn, are eventually invaded and displaced by spruces and balsams, and the cycle starts again.

A simpler model of infestation can be set up with just three rules:

a)   An infested area becomes defoliated next year.

b)   A defoliated area becomes green next year.

c)   An infested site infects its neighbors to the north, south, east, and west next year, if they are currently green.

Write a program that tracks, and displays, a sequence of generations. Assuming a green forest to begin with, use a variety of patterns to initialize the model (at the center of the forest), including:

```
i i i i            g i  g            d g d
d d d d            g d g            i  g i
```

where i means infested, g means green, and d means defoliated. Note that when a focus, or center-point, of infestation is known, intentional defoliation can be used to break the cycle. Perhaps you should try to make your program run backwards as well!

9-30   Write a program that lets two players play the game of *Nim*. One version of this game starts out with three rows of pebbles:

```
o o o o o o o
 o o o o o
  o o o
```

On each turn a player may remove one or more pebbles, but can take them only from a single row. The winner is the player who removes the last pebble. Can you use binary arithmetic to figure out a winning strategy? The secret is in the columns!

For a harder problem, expand your program to let the computer play one side. Under what conditions can it always win? Can changing the number of rows or pebbles lead to a disadvantage?

9-31   Topographical maps are easily represented with two-dimensional arrays of integer- or real-valued heights. However, the bird's-eye view they provide is sometimes difficult to appreciate after a day of lugging a 70-pound backpack.

a)   Write a program that locates *peaks*. We define a peak as any point that is higher than its eight neighbors.

b)   Write a program that locates *valleys*. A valley is any series of three points along a row or column that are lower than their twelve neighbors. (Can you deal with longer valleys as well?)

As always, the multiple bound possibilities lead to an ambiguous postcondition. Or, why you should look after you loop. (p. 345)

10

Sorting and Searching: an Excursion into Algorithms

The study of algorithms is one of the foundations of computer science, quite independent of any language they might be written down in, or even any specific purpose they might serve. And within the arena of algorithms, two particular applications stand out: searching and sorting.

Searching is looking for things. After all, what good is a computer that can hold a million pages of data if you can't find what you need? The basic problem is simple enough to state—find a value that's stored in an array. But we'll find ourselves writing five different procedures to do the job.

Sorting is arranging things. We don't just sort for the sake of sorting, of course—this is computer science, not flower arranging. Instead, an awful lot of sorting gets done today in order to make searching easier tomorrow. We'll attack the problem in three different ways and try to see why we might choose one approach over another. One more sorting algorithm (the recursive *Quick-Sort*) is discussed in 16-2.

Section 10-3 has an extended discussion of a single programming example: Dijkstra's *Dutch National Flag* problem. I've included it for readers who find the searching and sorting algorithms entertaining and want to tackle a harder problem. Finally, we'll take a look at complexity and performance—trying to figure out just how difficult a problem is or how effective an algorithm will be.

Searching

10-1

IF COUNTING THINGS IS A MAJOR THEME OF programming, then searching for them is one of the primary minor variations. Searching *algorithms* are usually described in terms of the simplest possible formulation of the problem: trying to find a word or number that's supposed to be stored in an array of words or numbers. Although the data that have to be searched might start out somewhere else (in a file, perhaps), it can usually manage to wind up in an array.

Our goal is to learn about algorithms and general-purpose implementations. Even if we're looking for a word or number, searching can really be boiled down to hunting through an array of characters for a single letter. So why complicate matters? I'll treat the subject of searching (and sorting) in terms of a simple array of letters.

introducing abstraction

I'm also going to introduce a degree of *abstraction* into the discussion. Even though we're going to look at the nuts and bolts of searching and sorting, we'd like to end up with procedures that hide the details from us. How the procedures are called will stay the same, but their algorithms and implementations are going to change. Here are the type definitions and three basic primitives we'll be using:

three primitives

```
const MAX = 10;
type PhraseTYPE = array [ 1..MAX ] of char;
procedure Initialize (var Data: PhraseTYPE);
    {Loads Data with test data.}
procedure SearchMethod (Data: PhraseTYPE;        {what we're searching}
                        Letter: char;            {what we're seeking}
                        var Position: integer);   {where it is}
    {Sets Position to the location of Letter in Data, or –1 if absent.}
procedure SortMethod (var Data: PhraseTYPE);
    {Sorts the array, if necessary. We'll be writing three versions later.}
```

SearchMethod is highlighted because we're going to write five different implementations, using five different algorithms:

alternative search implementations

Search *is the basic component-by-component search of an unordered array.*
StateSearch *is a state-oriented version of the* Search *algorithm.*
Linear *makes a component-by-component search through an ordered array.*
Quadratic *is like* Linear, *but it takes bigger jumps.*
Binary *uses a divide-and-conquer algorithm for the fastest search of all.*

In section 2 of this chapter, we'll be looking at three alternative algorithms for the *SortMethod* primitive.

Searching Unordered Arrays

The first variation of the searching problem assumes that the array—call it Data—isn't in any special order. Our task is to find the position of a particular value, say, the letter ´S´, or to report that the value wasn't found. We set the stage with:

Initialize (Data);
    {*Postcondition: Data is defined, but isn't necessarily ordered.*}
SearchMethod (Data, ´S´, Position);
    {*Postcondition: If Position isn't −1, it holds the S's position in Data.*}

the ground rules

using postconditions

> Note the use of postconditions. Each one clearly documents any assumptions that subsequent statements may rely on.

How will the search proceed? Well, we hope to find a sentinel—the stored letter ´S´. However, since the sentinel won't always be found, the sentinel alone won't guarantee loop termination. A necessary bound—we've inspected every component—has to be part of any searching loop. In outline, the search loop is:

an unordered search specification

Goal: Locate a value, or decide it isn't there.
Intentional bound: Spotting the value.
Necessary bound: We've reached the last component.
Plan: Advance to the next component.

As always, the multiple bound possibilities lead to an ambiguous postcondition. The search loop is followed by an **if** statement that decides which of the bound conditions caused the loop to terminate.

first approach to searching

```
procedure Search (Data: PhraseTYPE;
                          Letter: char; var Position: integer);
    {Search procedure for an unordered array.  Position is −1 for absent Letter.}
    var i: integer;  {the current array component}
    begin
        i := 1;  {Data's bounds are 1..MAX.}
        while (Data [ i ]<>Letter) and (i<MAX) do begin
            i := i + 1
        end; {while}
        {Postcondition:  If Data [ i ] isn't Letter, then no component is.}
        if Data [ i ] = Letter
            then begin Position := i end
            else begin Position := −1 end
    end; {Search}
```

A State-Oriented Version

I pointed out that Position's central loop leaves us in an ambiguous situation on exit. We have to check the contents of Data [i] to decide whether or not we found Letter. However, we're perfectly capable of writing the loop unambiguously, if you're willing not to be frightened by the prospect of using a *state-oriented* approach.

In the past, we've written state-oriented programs as filters that processed input data. You'll recall that a state filter spots and records or acts upon *state transitions*—changes in our knowledge about a program's data.

However, we can spot state transitions when we look at data stored in an array, too. What states can exist during an array search? How about:

— found—the sentinel bound was satisfied because the value was found.

— absent—only the necessary count bound was satisfied.

— searching—neither of the bounds has been satisfied yet.

In effect, the state values name the loop's bound conditions. The possibility of a state transition looms every time we look at a new component:

Goal: Locate a value, or decide it isn't there.
Bound: Our state is either absent or found.
Plan: Advance to the next component.
   Update the state.

I've rewritten the search code using the state-oriented approach below.

```
procedure StateSearch (Data: PhraseTYPE;
                            Letter: char; var Position: integer);
   {State-oriented search of an unordered array.  Position is –1 for absent Letter.}
   type StateTYPE = (found, absent, searching);
   var State: StateTYPE;
       i: integer;
   begin
      i := 1;  {Data's bounds are 1..MAX.}
      repeat   {until we're not searching anymore}
         if i > MAX   {Why is this state set first?}
               then State := absent
               else if Data [ i ] = Letter   {So we don't bomb out here.}
                  then State := found
                  else begin i := i + 1;
                              State := searching
                  end  {if}
      until State <> searching;
      {Postcondition:  if Letter was there, State = Found and Data [ i ] = Letter.}
      case State of
         found: Position := i;
         absent: Position := –1
      end  {case}
   end;  {StateSearch}
```

In a simple application like this, naming states is simply a curiosity—in fact, it makes the program more complicated. But loops sometimes have bounding conditions that are difficult to phrase or which may be added to as time goes on. 'State bounds' clarify reasons for loop termination and help ensure that the bound conditions are evaluated in the proper order.

Modification Problems ————————————————————

1. Write a simple version of procedure Initialize. What are suitable test data for Position and StateSearch? Remember—you're trying to make the search procedures *fail*, not show that they can work.

2. Add another possibility to the state-oriented search—that the array was never filled with data and has length 0. If that's the case, have Position return the value MAXINT.

Self-Check Questions ————————————————————

Q. In procedure StateSearch, why is the absent state the first one updated? Why wouldn't this sequence work as well?

```
repeat   {A version with a bug.}
    if Data [ i ] = Letter
            then State := found
        else if i > MAX
            then State := absent
        else begin i := i + 1;
                    State := Searching
        end {if}
until State <> searching
```

A. The rewritten version above contains a potential bug. If Letter isn't there, then we'll eventually try to inspect a component that's beyond the end of the array. The rewritten version *could* be made to work by changing the i > MAX expression to i = MAX instead.

Q. The *size* of a searching problem is usually described by the number of values that are actually inspected. This number is referred to as *n*. If *n* is big, then the search is a big problem; if *n* is small, the problem is small.

When an array isn't ordered, we might have to look at every single value to find the one we want. Another way of phrasing this is to say that *worst-case size* of the search is *n*. What are the *best-case* and *average-case* sizes of the problem—searching for a letter in an unordered array? In other words, at best, and on average, how many of the *n* components must we look at before we find the letter?

A. At best, the size of the problem is just 1. That's because the value we're seeking might be the very first one we inspect. In the average case, the letter might be anywhere. On average, though, we'll find it after looking through about half, or *n*/2, of the components.

Searching Ordered Arrays

When the values in an array aren't ordered, inspecting each component until either the proper one is found, or none are left to inspect, is the only sure strategy for finding a value.

But when the component values *are* ordered, many approaches are more effective. We can explore three of them: linear, quadratic, and binary searches. Our ground rules will be:

the ground rules

Initialize (Data);
   {Postcondition: Data is defined, but not necessarily ordered.}
Sort (Data);
   {Postcondition: Data is defined and ordered, smallest to largest.}
SearchMethod (Data, S, Position);
   {Postcondition: if Position isn't –1, it holds the S's position in Data.}

As before, we'll always return a negative Position value if the number we're searching for isn't found.

Linear Search

I'll begin with a *linear search*. Since we're looking for a sentinel, the search of an ordered array is quite similar to the search of an unordered array. But since spotting a 'larger' letter means that all the remaining letters are too large as well, our bound changes:

loop specification

Goal: Locate a value, or decide that it isn't there.
Bound: The current component equals or exceeds the sought value.
Plan: Advance to the next component.

Is there much difference between the algorithms of procedure Linear, below, and procedure Search, from a few pages back? No. There's just a tiny change in the first condition: <> becomes <.

{From procedure Search, which searches an unordered array.}
while (Data [i]<>Letter) **and** (i<MAX) **do begin**

little changes have big effects

has been changed to:

{In procedure Linear, which searches an ordered array.}
while (Data [i]<Letter) **and** (i<MAX) **do begin**

But however minuscule the change might be, it's essential to remember the key *precondition* that makes Linear work: that the array was sorted before the search began. This usually makes the linear search of a sorted array more effective than the search of an unsorted array.

advantage of Linear over Search

> A linear search through a sorted array will either find the sought value, or decide that it's not there, after looking, on average, at half the components. In contrast, an unsorted array that doesn't hold the value will always have to be searched all the way through.

Searching an unordered array can't be improved beyond Search, but Linear is just the first step in improving ordered-array searches. Note a small simplification in procedure Linear, below. Instead of declaring a local variable as the subscript counter, I'm using the variable parameter Position. Naturally, we have to be sure that Position holds the proper value when the procedure ends.

```
procedure Linear (Data: PhraseTYPE; Letter: char; var Position: integer);
   {Linear search for Letter.  Return negative Position if not found.}
   begin
      Position := 1;
      while (Data [Position]<Letter) and (Position<MAX) do begin
         Position := Position + 1
      end;
      {Postcondition:  If Data [Position] isn't Letter, then no component is.}
      if Data [Position] <> Letter then begin
         Position := -1
      end
   end;  {Linear}
```

a linear search
procedure

Modification Problems ——————————————————————————————

1. Write a state-oriented version of Linear.
2. Make Linear search from the high end of the array, instead of from the low end.

Quadratic Search

The linear search patiently trudges toward the sought value one component at a time. It's not hard to imagine that we would find the value a bit faster if we could take larger jumps:

> *take big jumps to get close to the sought value;*
> *take single steps to locate it exactly*

What's a reasonable size for the *big jumps*? Well, we'd like to strike a balance between the amount of ground covered by the big steps and the number of single steps that might be left over. On one hand, a relatively small jump size wouldn't travel through the array quickly enough. On the other, a very large jump size could, in the worst case, leave a lot of single steps left over. Here are some figures for arrays of various lengths n:

ramifications of some
jump sizes

		Maximum number of big jumps ($n = 10, 1,000, 1,000,000$)			*Maximum number of single steps* ($n = 1,000,000$)
	(1)	10	1,000	1,000,000	999,999
Jump	($n/10$)	10	10	10	99,999
size	($\log_2 n$)	3	10	20	49,999
	($sqrt\ n$)	3	32	1,000	999

Having the jump size remain constant, at 1, merely duplicates the linear search. Surprisingly, perhaps, making the jump very large—either a tenth of the total array size, or the base 2 logarithm of it—doesn't leave us in much better shape. Whatever we save by making big jumps at first is lost by the having to take many, many single steps in the final approach to the number.

However, if we make the jump size equal to the square root of the array's length, the number of big jumps and single steps will be balanced—and, when they're balanced, the very worst case won't be so bad. At worst (as well as at best *and* on average) the number of single steps will just about equal the number of big jumps. That's what happens for a million-component array in the table above. At worst, the value we're looking for is hidden in component 1,000,000. It will take us 999 big jumps, plus 999 single steps to get there—a much better performance than any of the other options in the table.

balancing jumps and steps

> The *quadratic search* algorithm—quadratic means *square*—is based on a jump size that equals the square root of the number of components to search.

I've used the state-oriented approach to write procedure Quadratic, below. Recall that the very rough outline of the search was:

> *take big jumps to get close to the sought value;*
> *take single steps to locate it exactly.*

A more detailed pseudocode outline is:

a state-oriented refinement

> *calculate the step size;*
> **repeat**
>   *update states and* Position;
> **until** State = CloseEnough;   {*end of the big jump loop*}
> {*Postcondition: if the value is there, another big step would go past it.*}
> **repeat**
>   *update states and position;*
> **until** State <> searching;   {*end of the single step loop*}
> {*Postcondition: If State = found then Data [Position] = Letter.*}
> *set* Position *to* −1 *if* State *equals* absent

Because of type mismatches, the *calculate the step size* requires that a real result be truncated (rounded down) to the nearest integer. The completed procedure appears on the next page; its modification problems are out-of-order, below.

Modification Problems ———————————————————————————

1. Build a test harness for Quadratic, then modify the procedure so that it prints the number of big and small steps it takes while searching.

2. As it's written, Quadratic's first loop doesn't distinguish between getting CloseEnough to the letter we want and actually finding it. Rewrite Quadratic so that found is one of the states that's set in the first loop.

3. As long as the size of the big jumps is fixed, we can't improve on the size (the square root of *n*) we've been using. However, you can search more quickly by changing the jump size—starting with big steps, then reducing them. Can you figure out a way of modifying Quadratic to do it? Hint: add a third loop.

```
procedure Quadratic (Data: PhraseTYPE; Letter: char; var Position: integer);
    {Quadratic search for Letter.  Return negative Position if not found.}
    type STATUS = (searching, found, absent, CloseEnough);
    var State: STATUS;
        JumpSize: integer;
begin
    JumpSize := trunc (sqrt (MAX) );
    Position := 1;
    State := searching;  {Initialize the current State.}
    repeat   {by big jumps until we're CloseEnough}
        if (Position + JumpSize) > MAX
                then State := CloseEnough
                    {Or we'd pass the end of the array.}
                else if Data [Position+JumpSize] > Letter
                    then State := CloseEnough
                        {Or we'd pass the sought value.}
                    else Position := Position + JumpSize
                        {State remains unchanged.}
    until State = CloseEnough;
    {Postcondition:  if the letter is there, Data [Position] <= Letter.}
    State := searching;  {Reset the current State.}
    repeat    {by single steps until we're not searching}
        if Position > MAX then State := absent
            else if Data [Position] > Letter then State := absent
            else if Data [Position] = Letter then State := found
            else Position := Position + 1   {State is unchanged.}
    until State <> searching;
    {End of the single step loop.
     Postcondition:  If Letter is there, State = found and Data [Position] = Letter.}
    if State = absent then begin
        Position := –1
    end
end;  {Quadratic}
```

quadratic search procedure (margin note)

Self-Check Questions

Q. You guessed it—just how good is the quadratic search algorithm in terms of *n*, the number of values there are to be searched? What's the best, worst, and average case?

A. As usual, the best case is easy to figure out—we spot the value we want on the first try. The best case is the constant 1.

The worst case starts to improve on the linear search. Although we might get lucky and catch it on a giant step, the worst case will take the maximum number (the square root of *n*) of big steps, followed by the same number of little steps. Both sequences might require one less step in order to 'max out,' but it's safe to say that the worst case of the problem is about twice the square root of *n*.

By the same reasoning, we can see that the average case equals the square root of *n*. On average there will be half that many big jumps, plus half that many single steps.

Binary Search

Our third and final method of searching an ordered array is the *binary search* algorithm. It's the fastest method we'll see. Binary search is quick because the jump size changes; it starts big, but gets smaller on each jump. The first jump is half the size of the array, the second jump is one-fourth of the array's length, the third jump is one-eighth, and so on.

Binary search is the basic *divide-and-conquer* algorithm. Here's how it works. Assuming, as usual, that the array is ordered, start by looking at the middle component. If the value it holds is too high, go to the middle of the bottom half of the array and look again. If the middle component's stored value was too low, go to the middle of the top half instead. Then, repeat this 'split the remainder' step until you find the value you want, or decide that it doesn't exist. That's just how you might find an industrial photographer named Dijkstra in the Amsterdam phone book: he's somewhere in the middle of a list bounded by Aerophoto Schiphol and Zwetsloot, Geek.

divide-and-conquer

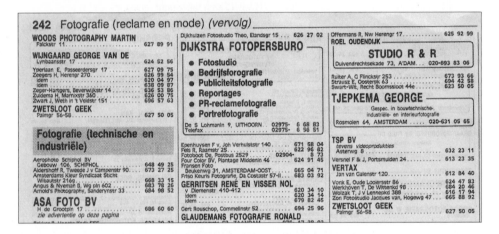

How would you characterize the bound condition of a binary search loop? Instead of thinking about jumps, imagine what happens to the boundaries of the unknown portion of the array. At first, the entire array is unknown—its boundaries are the first and last components.

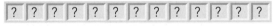

all of the stored values are unknown

After the first guess, though, we're able to set new lower and upper bounds on the unknown part that we're still concerned with:

moving the data bound

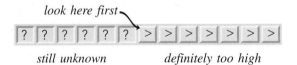

still unknown   *definitely too high*

A second look, in the middle of the unknown area, shrinks the bounds even further:

second look   *look here next*

definitely too low   still unknown   definitely too high

Eventually—in fact, pretty quickly—we'll run out of unknown data. If we happen to find the value, the loop has an ordinary sentinel bound. If we don't find it, the searching loop requires a data bound that guarantees termination—the lower and upper borders of the unknown area collide (just as they did when we checked palindromes in Chapter 9).

A loop specification for binary search would be:

loop specification

> *Goal: Locate a value, or decide it isn't there.*
> *Intentional bound: We've found the value.*
> *Necessary bound: The lower and upper bounds of our search coincide.*
> *Plan: Pick a component midway between the lower and upper bounds.*
> > *Reset the lower or upper bound, as appropriate.*

As always in the case of multiple loop bounds, we have to decide why the loop terminated. In pseudocode, a first refinement of the binary search algorithm is:

first pseudocode

> *initialize the starting upper and lower bounds to the array's end;*
> **repeat**
> > *inspect the component in the middle of the unknown area;*
> > *reset the boundaries of the unknown area*
>
> **until** *we find the value or run out of unknown data;*
> *decide why we left the loop*

How do we locate the middle component? Well, no matter what the lower and upper bounds of the unknown portion are, we can always find the middle by adding the bounds and dividing by two. After each wrong guess, the old middle becomes the new lower or upper bound. In practice, we'll add or subtract 1 each time, since we've already checked the actual middle value. A second refinement would be:

pseudocode refinement

> *initialize* Lower *and* Upper *to the lower and upper array bounds;*
> **repeat**
> > *let* Middle *equal* (Lower *plus* Upper) **div 2;**
> > **if** *the value of* Data [Middle] *is low*
> > > **then** *make* Middle *(plus* 1) *the new lower bound*
> > > **else** *make* Middle *(minus* 1) *the new upper bound*
> >
> > **until** *we find the value or run out of unknown data;*
> > *decide why we left the loop, and return an appropriate* Position

The binary search is implemented below. As in the earlier searching examples, I return a negative Position if the sought Letter isn't found. This time, though, I've dispensed with the state variable and written the searching code as tersely as possible.

binary search procedure

```
procedure Binary (Data: PhraseTYPE;
                    Letter: char; var Position: integer);
    {Binary search for Letter.  Returns Position = –1 if not found.}
    var Middle, Lower, Upper: integer;
    begin
        Lower := 1;
        Upper := MAX;
        repeat
            Middle := (Lower + Upper) div 2;
            if Letter < Data [Middle]
                then Upper := Middle – 1
                else Lower := Middle + 1
        until (Data [Middle] = Letter) or (Lower > Upper);
        {Postcondition:  If Data [Middle] isn't Letter, no component is.}
        if Data [Middle] = Letter
            then Position := Middle
            else Position := –1
end;   {Binary}
```

Modification Problems

1. Rewrite Binary as a function that returns the position of the sought value, or –1 if it's not there.

2. Off-by-one errors are common in binary search procedures. What test data would you use to find them? Embed enough debugging code in procedure Binary to let you spot and fix any reasonable problem.

Self-Check Questions

Q. As usual, what are the best, worst, and average cases in a problem of size n using procedure Binary?

A. As always, the best case takes just one step—the value we want is the first one we look at. In the worst and average cases, binary search is even better than quadratic search. Consider the worst case. Here are four different ways to state the problem (and, implicitly, the answer):

— How many times can we divide an array of length n in half before we're left with an array of length one?

— If a jump size starts at $\frac{1}{2}$ of n, then goes to $\frac{1}{4}$, $\frac{1}{8}$, and so on, how many steps will it take to work our way down to $1/n$ of n?

— Starting with one, how many times can you double a value before it's as large as n?

— To what power should you raise 2 if you want it to be as big as n?

In each case, the answer is the same—it's the logarithm, base 2, of n. This figure, written $log_2 n$, is the worst-case size of the search—the number of candidates that have to be inspected to find a match or decide it isn't there.

Finally, what's the average case? On average, we have to look at half of the potential candidates. Surprisingly, perhaps, this takes just one less step than looking at them *all*. The average search is $(log_2 n) - 1$.

Sorting

10-2

COMPUTERS END UP SPENDING A LOT of time sorting—it's been estimated that up to a quarter of the time of centralized computers is devoted to sorting things. Why? Well, as our discussion of searching makes clear, it's a whole lot easier to find a value in an array that has been sorted than to search an array that's in no special order.

why sort?

> Computers sort data for the same reason the telephone company alphabet-izes the phone book. Nobody needs to have the names in alphabetical order—it just makes it an awful lot easier to look one up. Wanting to have the names in alphabetical order is relatively unimportant; being able to look up one name very quickly is crucial.

We'll look at sorting algorithms as though we were considering alterna-tive implementations of a Sort procedure. Recall that the other primitives of the 'sorted array' data abstraction were:

the data abstraction

procedure Initialize (**var** Data: PhraseTYPE);
   {*Loads Data with test data.*}
procedure *SearchMethod* (Data: PhraseTYPE;
                           Letter: char; **var** Position: integer);
   {*We just looked at several alternatives for this one.*}
procedure *SortMethod* (**var** Data: PhraseTYPE);
   {*Sorts the array into descending numerical order.*}

The three versions of *SortMethod* we'll write are:

versions of SortMethod

   Select *is based on the selection sort algorithm.*
   Insert *is based on the insertion sort algorithm.*
   Bubble *is based on the bubble sort algorithm.*

I'll start with a look at the different algorithms, then compare them briefly. For variety, I'll assume that the order we want is always largest to smallest—the op-posite of our searching order. Finally, we'll implement the three sorting pro-cedures.

Selection Sort

The first approach, *selection sort*, works like this:

Suppose that we have an array of integer values.

| 18 | 35 | 22 | 97 | 84 | 55 | 61 | 10 | 47 |

selection sort

Search through the array, find the largest value (97), and exchange it with the value stored in the first array location (18).

| 97 | 35 | 22 | 18 | 84 | 55 | 61 | 10 | 47 |

Next, find the second-largest value in the array, and exchange it with the value stored in the second array location. This is identical to the first trip through the array, except that we don't look at the first value—we already know it's the largest.

| 97 | 84 | 22 | 18 | 35 | 55 | 61 | 10 | 47 |

Now, repeat the 'select and exchange' process, each time beginning the search one value further along the array. As we go we'll build an ordered array of values. Eventually, we'll get all the way to the end of the array—which has to be the smallest stored value—and the array will be ordered.

| 97 | 84 | 61 | 18 | 35 | 55 | 22 | 10 | 47 |

| 97 | 84 | 61 | 55 | 35 | 18 | 22 | 10 | 47 |

| 97 | 84 | 61 | 55 | 47 | 18 | 22 | 10 | 35 |

| 97 | 84 | 61 | 55 | 47 | 35 | 22 | 10 | 18 |

| 97 | 84 | 61 | 55 | 47 | 35 | 22 | 10 | 18 | *22 happens to be OK.*

| 97 | 84 | 61 | 55 | 47 | 35 | 22 | 18 | 10 |

A pseudocode expansion of the selection sort algorithm is:

selection sort
pseudocode

> **for** *every 'first' component in the array*
>   *find the largest component in the array;*
>   *exchange it with the 'first' component;*

Insertion Sort

Algorithm two, *insertion sort*, also concentrates on keeping the left side of the array sorted. However, instead of sorting the very largest values, it sorts the values seen so far, even if this means more rearranging in the long run. The algorithm is:

Start with the same set of values as last time. The leftmost value, 18, can be said to be sorted *in relation to itself*. At the same time, we might anticipate having to move the next value, 35:

| 18 | 35 | 22 | 97 | 84 | 55 | 61 | 10 | 47 |

insertion sort

Now, remove the second value, 35. To insert it in its proper place, to the left of 18, we slide the 18 over to make room. Once more, we can anticipate the move we'll have to make to locate the next value properly:

| 35 | 18 | 22 | 97 | 84 | 55 | 61 | 10 | 47 |

Now the leftmost two components are relatively sorted. We can remove the third component, 22, then slide the 18 over again to make room.

| 35 | 22 | 18 | 97 | 84 | 55 | 61 | 10 | 47 |

Continue the process. Notice that the popped-out portion is always in correct order. However, inserting a new value may—or may not, in the case of 10—require moving all or part of the popped-out portion down to make room:

| 97 | 35 | 22 | 18 | 84 | 55 | 61 | 10 | 47 |

| 97 | 84 | 35 | 22 | 18 | 55 | 61 | 10 | 47 |

| 97 | 84 | 55 | 35 | 22 | 18 | 61 | 10 | 47 |

| 97 | 84 | 61 | 55 | 35 | 22 | 18 | 10 | 47 |

| 97 | 84 | 61 | 55 | 35 | 22 | 18 | 10 | 47 | 10 *stays put for a moment.*

| 97 | 84 | 61 | 55 | 47 | 35 | 22 | 18 | 10 |

Writing out the algorithm in pseudocode results in:

insertion sort pseudocode

> **for** *every 'newest' component remaining in the array*
> *temporarily remove it;*
> *find its proper place in the sorted part of the array;*
> *slide smaller values one component to the right;*
> *insert the 'newest' component into its new position;*

a quick analysis

Let me pause for a quick comparison between selection and insertion. As I've stated the problem, we always begin with an array of mixed-up values (well, maybe it's the array that's mixed up, rather than the values). Algorithm one, selecting and repositioning values in order of their size, is a pretty effective way to reorder the array, while minimizing the number of moves that have to be made.

But suppose that the ground rules are different. If we're given an empty or partially sorted array and told to fill it *in order*, then the insertion algorithm is better. As each new value arrives, we can insert it in the place it should occupy given the values we've gotten already.

Bubble Sort

Algorithm three is called *bubble sort*. Like selection sort, it's usually applied to arrays that are already filled with values. Bubble sort usually requires fewer comparisons, but many more exchanges, than a selection sort. A bubble sort works like this:

Begin with the same array as before:

$$\boxed{18}\;\boxed{35}\;\boxed{22}\;\boxed{97}\;\boxed{84}\;\boxed{55}\;\boxed{61}\;\boxed{10}\;\boxed{47}$$

bubble sort

Compare the first two values. If the second is larger, exchange them.

$$\boxed{35}\;\boxed{18}\;\boxed{22}\;\boxed{97}\;\boxed{84}\;\boxed{55}\;\boxed{61}\;\boxed{10}\;\boxed{47}$$

Next, compare the second and third values, exchanging them if the third is larger.

$$\boxed{35}\;\boxed{22}\;\boxed{18}\;\boxed{97}\;\boxed{84}\;\boxed{55}\;\boxed{61}\;\boxed{10}\;\boxed{47}$$

Then compare (and possibly exchange) the third and fourth values, the fourth and fifth, etc., until you reach the end of the array. Note that the smallest stored value ends up stored in the last position. However, despite all the movement, the rest of the array isn't ordered.

$$\boxed{35}\;\boxed{22}\;\boxed{97}\;\boxed{84}\;\boxed{55}\;\boxed{61}\;\boxed{18}\;\boxed{47}\;\boxed{10}$$

Now, go back to the beginning of the array and start all over again. Work your way through the array comparing and exchanging values again. However, since the smallest value is already at the far right, you need not compare the final value.

$$\boxed{35}\;\boxed{97}\;\boxed{84}\;\boxed{55}\;\boxed{61}\;\boxed{22}\;\boxed{47}\;\boxed{18}\;\boxed{10}$$

Repeat the process of comparison and exchange without bothering the final *two* values.

$$\boxed{97}\;\boxed{84}\;\boxed{55}\;\boxed{61}\;\boxed{35}\;\boxed{47}\;\boxed{22}\;\boxed{18}\;\boxed{10}$$

As you can see, an ordered list is forming on the right. Continue the process of comparison and exchange, ignoring the last *three* values this time.

$$\boxed{97}\;\boxed{84}\;\boxed{55}\;\boxed{61}\;\boxed{47}\;\boxed{35}\;\boxed{22}\;\boxed{18}\;\boxed{10}$$

This array is almost ordered. It will be when we get to the point of comparing only the first two values.

In a sense, the smallest values 'bubble' to the right side of the array. A pseudocode version of the algorithm is:

bubble sort pseudocode

> **for** *every 'last' component*
> > **for** *every component from the first to the 'last'*
> > > *compare that component to each remaining component;*
> > > *exchange them if necessary;*

Three Implementations of Sort

It's time to make an important point:

> *Deciding to sort in the first place, and*
> ➡ *choosing a particular sorting algorithm, and*
> ➡ *implementing the algorithm, and*
> ➡ *defining the underlying data structure and primitives*

can each be discussed in relative independence, although not necessarily in total ignorance, of each other.

Obviously, choices at one level can affect our judgment in another. The sorting methods I've described would not be very practical if we were sorting files, rather than arrays. Nevertheless, we can work with an eye toward making effective choices at each and every stage. Each of the sorting methods I described has its own set of advantages:

— The selection sort is simple because it doesn't require any wholesale moves; only two values are exchanged on any trip through the array.

each method's advantages

— The insertion sort minimizes unnecessary travel through the array. If the values are sorted to begin with, a single trip through the array establishes that fact. In contrast, selection sort requires the same number of trips no matter how well-organized the array is.

— The bubble sort is worse than selection sort for a jumbled array and will require many more component exchanges. Unlike the insertion sort, it's utterly incapable of minimizing travel through the array. Why use it? Because it's usually the easiest one to write correctly!

As you read procedures Select, Insert, and Bubble on the next few pages, I'd like you focus on three points of comparison:

1. At best and worst, how many comparisons are made between components?

comparing the algorithms

2. Again, at best and at worst, how many times will two components' positions be changed?

3. Finally, will there be any difference between the starting and ending order of two or more components that have exactly the same value? Sorts that leave such components in order are called *stable*, while sorts that may change order are *unstable*.

To help you keep track, I've written the procedures to count the number of switches and comparisons each method requires. All output reflects the test string B D C I H F G A E, which is ugly but matches the numerical examples shown earlier.*

---

* John David Stone, whom I know for a fact speaks Latin, points out that D I F U T O R A L (pertaining to yuppies who possess two futons) has the same property.

selection sort procedure

```
procedure Select (var Data:  PhraseTYPE);
    {Uses the selection sort algorithm to order an array of characters.}
    var First, Current, Largest, Comparisons, Swaps:  integer;
        Temp:  char;
    begin
        Comparisons := 0;
        Swaps := 0;
        for First := 1 to MAX − 1 do begin
            Largest := First;
            for Current := First + 1 to MAX do begin
                {Don't bother comparing the first component to itself.}
                Comparisons := Comparisons + 1;
                if Data [Current] > Data [Largest] then begin
                    Largest := Current
                end
            end; {Current for}
            {Postcondition:  Largest subscripts the largest item from First .. MAX.}
            if Largest <> First then begin     {We have to make a swap.}
                Swaps := Swaps + 1;
                Temp := Data [Largest];
                Data [Largest] := Data [First];     {Make the swap.}
                Data [First] := Temp
            end  {if}
            {Postcondition:  1 through First subscript the array's largest values.}
        end; {First for}
        write (Comparisons : 1);  write (´ comparisons, ´);
        write (Swaps : 1);  writeln (´ swaps.´)
    end;  {Select}
```

36 comparisons, 7 swaps.

A procedure for the insertion sort algorithm is shown below. Note that I've counted each 'slide' as a swap. Since the slide takes just one assignment and a call of procedure Swap requires three, do you think this is fair?

insertion sort procedure

```
procedure Insert (var Data:  PhraseTYPE);
    {Uses the insertion sort algorithm to order an array of characters.}
    var Newest, Current, Comparisons, Swaps:  integer;
        NewItem:  char;
        Seeking:  boolean;
    begin
        Comparisons := 0;
        Swaps := 0;
```

(procedure continues)

```
for Newest := 2 to MAX do begin
    Seeking := TRUE;
    Current := Newest;
    NewItem := Data [Newest];
    while Seeking do begin
        Comparisons := Comparisons + 1;
        if (Data [Current − 1] < NewItem) then begin
            Data [Current] := Data [Current − 1];   {Slide a value to the right.}
            Swaps := Swaps + 1;
            Current := Current − 1;
            Seeking := Current > 1
        end
        else begin Seeking := FALSE end;   {if}
    end; {while}
    {Postcondition:  NewItem belongs in Data [Current].}
    Data [Current] := NewItem
end; {Newest for}
write (Comparisons : 1);  write (′ comparisons, ′);
write (Swaps : 1);  writeln (′ swaps.′)
end;  {Insert}
```

```
25 comparisons, 19 swaps.
```

Finally, the procedure for the bubble sort algorithm is:

bubble sort procedure

```
procedure Bubble (var Data:  PhraseTYPE);
    {Uses the bubble sort algorithm to order an array of characters.}
    var Last, Current, Comparisons, Swaps:  integer;
        Temp:  char;
    begin
        Comparisons := 0;
        Swaps := 0;
        for Last := MAX downto 2 do begin
            for Current := 1 to Last − 1 do begin
                Comparisons := Comparisons + 1;
                if Data [Current] < Data [Current+1] then begin
                    Swaps := Swaps + 1;
                    Temp := Data [Current];
                    Data [Current] := Data [Current + 1];
                    Data [Current + 1] := Temp
                end {if}
            end  {Current for}
            {Postcondition:  Components Last through the end of the array are ordered.}
        end; {Last for}
        write (Comparisons : 1);  write (′ comparisons, ′);
        write (Swaps : 1);  writeln (′ swaps.′)
    end;  {Bubble}
```

```
36 comparisons, 19 swaps.
```

Modification Problems

1. If you haven't already done so, write a test harness for the sorting procedures. You'll need to generate test data, of course. As I pointed out earlier, the test data should try to make the sorts *fail*, not show that they can work.

2. It's always nice to see an algorithm in action. Embed debugging code in any of the three procedures to print the contents of the array after each pass. Make sure that your output is decipherable.

3. All of the sorting code arranges values from largest to smallest. Modify it so that values are ordered from smallest to largest.

Dijkstra´s Dutch National Flag*

10-3

problem: Dutch National Flag

OUR FINAL PROBLEM HAS ACQUIRED A GREAT deal of renown because it illustrates methods that apply to much more sophisticated jobs. However, our discussion of sorting and searching has given you quite a head start. E. W. Dijkstra named his *Dutch National Flag* problem in honor of his country's flag, which has three horizontal stripes: one red, one white, and one blue. The problem is:

> Suppose that an array of length N holds three different values: red, white, and blue. Write a program that puts all the red values at the left end of the array, the blue ones at the right end, and the white values in the middle.

> The trivial solution—go through the array to count all the pebbles first—is forbidden, naturally. You've got to do it all in one pass through the array.

Solving the Dutch Flag problem relies on some techniques I touched on earlier: using subscripts as pointers, developing a case analysis to guide decision making, and exploiting data bounds to determine the right time for loop exit. You'll also note similarities to some of the code we used for sorting and searching.

But how will we get started? Suppose I employ the time-honored problem-solving method of developing a simpler example first. Indonesia's flag, a relic of its colonial past as the Dutch East Indies, has only two stripes: one red and one white. We can imagine, then, that a Flag array starts out as:

R	R	W	R	W	W	R	W	R

mixed red and white components

the ´Indonesian Flag´ problem, algorithm one

Let me suggest the following algorithm for sorting the mixed array. I'll work my way through the array from left to right. Since we only have two colors to sort out, I'll keep the red components on the left end of the array, and throw the white components to the right end. Since I'll have to remember where the last red and first white components are, I'll need a couple of auxiliary variables. As you can see below, they're used as *subscript pointers*; they separate the sorted part of the array from the unsorted unknown.

* This section is presented for your entertainment only.

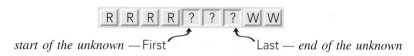

start of the unknown —First   Last — *end of the unknown*

How can I tell when the array has been unjumbled? Well, let's imagine the situation a few steps in the future. Once the array has been neatly divided into red and white, the two sorted parts will pass each other. Thus, we can use the subscript pointers as data boundaries. They let us know that the array is sorted by letting us know that the unknown portion is empty.

| R | R | R | R | R | W | W | W | W |

start of the unknown —First   Last — *end of the unknown*

algorithm one in detail

Let's walk through the algorithm in more detail. At first, our boundary pointers (call them First and Last) are situated at the Flag array's first and last components. They will always subscript the first and last unknown components. Suppose that Flag [First] is red. We leave it alone and increase First by one, heading toward Last. We might even go all the way through the array like this, if every component is red.

At the same time, the component subscripted by Last pointer might be white. In this case, we'd decrease Last by one, heading back toward First. As before, we'd travel the entire array like this were every component white.

the switch

One possibility remains. Suppose the array isn't perfectly ordered in advance and doesn't just hold components of one color. If we follow the rules suggested above, we'll eventually find that Flag [First] is white, while Flag [Last] is red. When this happens, we swap, or exchange, the two components, and advance *both* subscripts.

In case you haven't noticed, we've developed a case analysis. We have an appropriate action to take regardless of what situation is encountered. In pseudocode:

'move the bound' case analysis

> **if** *the current component* Flag [First] *is red*
>   **then** *increment (advance) the* First *pointer*
>   **else if** *the current component* Flag [Last] *is white*
>   **then** *decrement (decrease) the* Last *pointer*
>   **else begin** *swap* Flag [First] *with* Flag [Last]
>   *increment* Current;
>   *decrement* Last
> **end** *the last* **else** *part*

Now, unless the Flag array happens to be just one or two components long, this pseudocode plan is going to have to be put into a loop. What will the exit condition be? Well, there's no sentinel or mathematical limit bound, and even a count is not at all obvious.

> What is clear, though, is that the First and Last pointers, which mark the borders of the 'unknown data' area, get closer and closer together. Thus, we can use them to provide a data bound condition: we leave the loop when we run out of unknown data.

In pseudocode:

initialize First *and* Last *to the array's beginning and end;*
repeat
    carry out the case analysis described above
until First *and* Last *pass each other*
{*Postcondition: there are no more unknown components to check.*}

*two-color flag
pseudocode, algorithm
one*

An Alternative Case Analysis

That was a great algorithm, wasn't it? But it's not the only one I came up with. Before we move on to the full three-color version of the Dutch National Flag problem, let me present a different two-color solution.

Superficially, the second algorithm is like the first: it uses a case analysis, and it's inside a loop. However, both the analysis and the loop bounds are quite different. Instead of tossing the white components to the end of the array, I'll toss them to the end of the red section. I can get the effect of sliding *all* the white components to the right just by swapping a single component.

The sorted array segments are built like this. Suppose that this is our current position. I'll call the pointers RedBorder and WhiteBorder. WhiteBorder advances to the right, and it always points to an unknown.

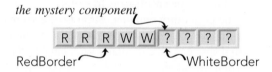

The rule we'll follow is:

> *If the next unknown component is white, advance the white border only.*
> *If it's red, swap it with the leftmost white component and advance both borders.*

Suppose the mystery component is red. The array and border pointers end up as:

the new one is red

Now imagine instead that the mystery component was white. We'd wind up with:

the new one is white

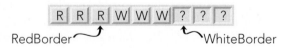

Now for a more detailed explanation. I'll begin with the RedBorder set to 0—just before the first array component—and the WhiteBorder set to 1—the first array component. For all intents and purposes, the RedBorder pointer is always one component behind the first known white value. If there aren't any red components, it doesn't even point to the array.

The WhiteBorder, in contrast, always points to the first of the remaining 'unknown' components. It is always one component *ahead* of the *last* known white value. If there aren't any white components, of course, it's one step ahead of the last red component.

Let's consider all the possibilities. Suppose that the current WhiteBorder component's value is white. Great! I can advance the white border by one and start again. If advancing takes me past the end of the array, I'm done.

But what if the WhiteBorder component is red? Now it gets tricky. I advance the RedBorder by one. This takes me one step into white territory (if there are stored white values) or to the WhiteBorder (if there are no white components). Then, I must exchange the white RedBorder component with the red WhiteBorder component, and advance the WhiteBorder component by one.

Why does the exchange and advance work? Because afterward, the starting conditions hold again: RedBorder points to the last known red component, and WhiteBorder points to the first remaining 'unknown,' if there is any.

Stated as a loop specification, the second algorithm is:

loop specification, algorithm two

Goal: Segregate an array's red *and* white *components.*
Bound: Reaching the last array component.
Plan: If the current WhiteBorder *component is* white, *then*
  advance the WhiteBorder.
 If the current component is red, *then*
  advance the RedBorder;
  swap the value at RedBorder *for the value at* WhiteBorder;
  advance the WhiteBorder.

Read the second algorithm pseudocode carefully, because it will be useful in solving the final three-color flag problem.

a two-color pseudocode, algorithm two

```
initialize RedBorder to 0;
initialize WhiteBorder to 1;
repeat
    case the current WhiteBorder component is
        white: increment WhiteBorder
        red: increment RedBorder;
             swap Flag [RedBorder] with Flag [WhiteBorder];
             increment WhiteBorder
    end  {case}
until WhiteBorder goes past the end of the array
```

What is the loop's bound condition? WhiteBorder, the white border pointer, is increased by 1 on each trip through the loop. In effect, it is a counter variable—the loop ends when inspecting the counter itself shows that we're past the end of the array.

> The second algorithm's pseudocode has one other notable feature. Since we're keeping the known red and white components on the left-hand side of the array, the right-hand end is free. This is in contrast to the first version's pseudocode, which needed the right-hand end to store red components.

Solving the Three-Color Flag Problem

Now, in algorithm two, the right end of the array spent most of its time languishing as an unknown region. However, we can make good use of it to solve the full Dutch National Flag problem. We'll use the right end of the array for storage as we did in algorithm one—but store blue components. In effect, we combine versions one and two of the two-color flag solutions.

three-color pseudocode

```
initialize RedBorder to 0;  {i.e. before the first known red}
initialize WhiteBorder to 1;  {i.e. the first of the remaining unknowns}
initialize BlueBorder to N, the array limit, plus 1;  {i.e. after the last unknown}
repeat
    case the current WhiteBorder component is
        white:  increment WhiteBorder
        red:  increment RedBorder;
                swap Flag [RedBorder] with Flag [WhiteBorder];
                increment WhiteBorder
        blue:  decrement BlueBorder;
                swap Flag [BlueBorder] with Flag [WhiteBorder]
    end  {case}
until WhiteBorder passes BlueBorder
```

Take a close look at the case analysis. Either the WhiteBorder will advance by one component to the right (if the current component is either red or white) or the BlueBorder will 'advance,' or actually decline, by one component to the left (if the current component is blue). Since the unknown area is always between the WhiteBorder and the BlueBorder, the loop's bound condition is a data boundary—the unknown area shrinks to zero when these two borders pass.

My aim in this section was to explore an algorithm for solving the Dutch National Flag problem. I'll give you a program that tests our solution *gratis*.

Dutch National Flag program

```
program Dutch (input, output);
    {A test harness for a solution to the Dutch Flag problem.}
const LIMIT = 15;        {Size of the flag.}
        DEBUGGING = TRUE;   {Controls a call of Print in FlagSort}
type ColorTYPE = (red, white, blue);
        FlagTYPE = array [1..LIMIT] of ColorTYPE;
var Flag: FlagTYPE;
procedure Initialize (var Flag:  FlagTYPE);
    {A truly simple-minded procedure that initializes the flag.}
    var i:  integer;
    begin
        for i := 1 to (LIMIT div 3) do begin
            Flag [ (3*i) − 2 ] := red;          {Alternate red, white, and blue.}
            Flag [ (3*i) − 1 ] := white;
            Flag [ (3*i) ] := blue
        end
    end;  {Initialize}
```

```
procedure PrintFlag (Flag:  FlagTYPE);
    {Displays the contents of the Flag array.}
    var Count:  integer;
    begin
        for Count := 1 to LIMIT do begin
            case Flag [Count] of
                red:  write ('R ');
                white:  write ('W ');
                blue:  write ('B ')
            end   {case}
        end;  {for}
        writeln
    end;  {PrintFlag}
procedure FlagSort (var Flag:  FlagTYPE);
    {Sorts an array of mixed red, white, and blue values.}
    var RedBorder, WhiteBorder, BlueBorder:  integer;
    procedure Swap (var First, Second:  ColorTYPE);
        {Exchanges two component values.}
        var Temp:  ColorTYPE;
        begin
            Temp := First;  First := Second;  Second := Temp
        end;  {Swap}
    begin   {FlagSort}
        RedBorder := 0;
        WhiteBorder := 1;
        BlueBorder := LIMIT + 1;
        repeat
            case Flag [WhiteBorder] of
                white:  WhiteBorder := WhiteBorder + 1;
                red:  begin RedBorder := RedBorder + 1;
                        Swap (Flag [RedBorder], Flag [WhiteBorder]);
                        WhiteBorder := WhiteBorder + 1
                    end;
                blue:  begin BlueBorder := BlueBorder – 1;
                        Swap (Flag [WhiteBorder], Flag [BlueBorder])
                    end
            end;  {case}
            if DEBUGGING then begin PrintFlag (Flag) end
        until WhiteBorder = BlueBorder
    end;  {FlagSort}
begin   {main program}
    writeln ('Initial flag is:');
    Initialize (Flag);
    PrintFlag (Flag);
    writeln;
    FlagSort (Flag);
    writeln ('Flag sort complete.')
end.  {Dutch}
```

(*output follows*)

```
        ▼          ▼          ▼          ▼          ▼
Initial flag is:
R W B R W B R W B R W B R W B

R W B R W B R W B R W B R W B
R W B R W B R W B R W B R W B
R W B R W B R W B R W B R W B
R W W R W B R W B R W B R B B
R W W R W B R W B R W B R B B
R R W W W B R W B R W B R B B
R R W W W B R W B R W B R B B
R R W W W R R W B R W B B B B
R R R W W W R W B R W B B B B
R R R R W W W W B R W B B B B
R R R R W W W W B R W B B B B
R R R R W W W W B R W B B B B
R R R R W W W W W R B B B B B
R R R R W W W W W R B B B B B
R R R R R W W W W W B B B B B
Flag sort complete.
```

Modification Problems

1. If *my* grade depended on it, I wouldn't be too happy about taking credit for the method used to initialize the flag. Come up with an initialization procedure, then describe the data you would use to test program Dutch.

2. Find a country whose flag has *four* colored stripes. Then, modify FlagSort so that it can handle the four-color flag problem.

10-4

Complexity and Performance*

I HOPE THAT THE PRECEDING SECTIONS have convinced you that there are better and worse ways to go about doing things. Let's turn to mathematics to find a more formal way to size up and compare different algorithms or problems.

We can easily count the number of statements a program executes or determine to the nearest milli- or microsecond how long it takes to run. However, neither statement counts nor actual running times are good means for comparison of algorithms. They'll vary depending on such unrelated factors as:

— what language was used to implement the algorithm and how well the program was written;

— the speed of the computer the program was run on;

— the compiler used to translate the program into executable form;

— the speed of peripheral equipment (like disk files) a program might require.

As a result, running-time measurements say more about the computer than the algorithm. They're helpful for comparisons of computers or compilers, or of different methods of coding a given algorithm.

---

* This section is optional.

Mathematical descriptions are more useful because they give us a means of comparison that isn't tied to any particular computer. Instead of describing an algorithm with the time it takes to run on a given computer, we describe it in terms of the size of the problem it solves and the inherent difficulty of that sort of problem. As we'll see, different algorithms can have similar performance for small problems, yet diverge wildly when things get difficult.

But the performance of an algorithm isn't our only concern. Even if you have the best possible algorithm, you still must ask how well *any* algorithm can ultimately perform. Performance is limited by a problem's underlying *complexity*—just how difficult is it under the best of circumstances?

performance vs. complexity

> A problem's complexity and an algorithm's performance are two sides of the same coin. A complexity measure tells us just how difficult a problem really is, while a performance measure lets us know just how well our solution works.

feasible vs. tractable

In a rough sense, because nobody calculates the actual figures, the ratio of performance to complexity can be thought of as describing a given algorithm's *efficiency*. In the long run, a paper analysis of performance can determine whether an algorithm is *feasible* (capable of being performed) or infeasible. Similarly, a complexity analysis can decide if a problem is *tractable* (capable of being solved exactly) or intractable.

Problem Size and Difficulty

The most important contribution a mathematical description makes is to let us rate performance in terms of both the problem's size and its difficulty. If we look carefully, we can always find a number that describes any problem. The number can come from almost anywhere, since there's no telling what a problem will require. It might be:

where the problem size comes from

— the number of components in an array, or

— the number of items in a file, or

— the number of pixels on a screen, or

— the amount of output the program is expected to produce.

But simply counting the items isn't enough. Once we've chosen an n to supply the size, we must allow for the prospect that even for a given n, one problem might be much more involved than another. After all, adding two fifty-digit numbers is much easier than multiplying them, even though both n's are the same. Besides size, then, we want to employ a function that can tell us something about a problem's inherent difficulty.

functions have different growth rates

> Instead of characterizing a problem in terms of a single number n, we describe it with a function, too: as the square of n, perhaps, or as n times n's logarithm. The functions share an important characteristic—as n gets bigger, they get bigger. However, they get bigger at different rates.

Now, most functions will be only approximations, and approximations can be more or less precise. A set of symbols is used to describe the kind of approximation a function makes. Their colloquial meanings are shown below. In each case, Task(n) means 'the complexity of a problem or algorithm of size n.'

various meanings of 'approximates'

form	name	meaning for very big n
Task(n) = Ω(f(n))	'omega'	f(n) is an underestimate or lower bound
Task(n) = ~(f(n))	'tilde'	f(n) is almost exactly correct
Task(n) = O(f(n))	'big O'	f(n) is an overestimate or upper bound
Task(n) = o(f(n))	'little o'	f(n) increasingly overestimates

Big O Notation

Big O notation turns out to be the most useful kind of approximation for computer science. It says that a complexity-describing function should serve as an upper bound on real-life performance. We use big O notation to say the performance of an algorithm (or the difficulty of a problem) is *on the order of* the value of function f(n). Suppose we're dealing with algorithm A and a problem of size n. Informally:

> *The complexity of A(n) is on the order of f(n) if A(n) is less than or equal to some constant times f(n)*

The constant could be five or 5,000, as long as the relation always holds true once n reaches some threshold. A more formal statement of the same definition is:

the formal definition

> A(n) is O(f(n)) *as n increases without limit if there are constants C and k such that* A(k) $\leq$ C(f(k)) *for every $n > k$*

n might have to climb for a while (all the way up to the kth value) before the relation is true. We might even have to multiply the function by a constant C to make it an accurate approximation. At a certain point, though, the actual performance or complexity measure can be bounded above by—and thus closely tied to—the value f(n).

A(n) means 'algorithm A on an n-sized problem'

Thus, big O notation lets a simply stated function f(n) serve as an approximation to the actual statement count of algorithm A(n) by promising that the actual count won't exceed the approximate count. It lets exact performance (which can be extremely difficult to figure out) be compared using easily understood mathematical functions.

How can we dismiss multiples so blithely? After all, it would seem that there is a big difference between some function f(n) and ten times that function. How can we say that an estimate is accurate when we allow so much variation in what the estimate's value is? The answer is that, in the big scheme of things, being off by a factor of ten or more isn't that significant—as long as the error is constant and doesn't increase with n.

multiplicative constants don't affect growth rate

Allowing such variations is the only way to compare algorithms that are implemented in different programming languages or on different machines. A ten-statement sequence on one computer may require dozens of statements on another, but it is the rate of growth of functions that's important—not their exact mathematical values at any given point.

This idea also keeps expectations of improved computer performance in perspective. Doubling or tripling a computer's speed sounds like a lot, but such speedups can be small in comparison to the price exacted by a high growth rate. Thus, a computer that's twice as fast won't necessarily let you solve problems that are twice as big.

Big O notation can describe both the performance of algorithms and the basic complexity of problems.

upper and lower bounds

> The worst-case performance measure of an algorithm states an upper bound—no instance of a problem, however complicated, will take more time. Similarly, the best-case complexity measure of a problem states a lower bound—no algorithm, however good, can take less time.

Let me reiterate that the crucial idea that makes big O notation so useful revolves around the ratio of growth *rates*. Compared to n, what is the growth rate of $10n$? It's identical, determined by n. What about $13n + 73$? Once again, the rates are the same—n controls them. (Note that we can ignore the additive constant 73 by slightly increasing the multiplicative constant 13; e.g. $14n \geq 13n+73$ for all $n \geq 73$.) The value of $10n$ is certainly larger than the value of n, but their growth rates march in lockstep; as n doubles, cost doubles. Moreover, *any* linear growth rate (see below), no matter how small, is greater than *any* strictly logarithmic rate, no matter how large.

rates are the key

The Basic Complexity Measures

Let's turn to functions that describe performance and complexity. The key idea behind all the functions is their rate of growth—how rapidly the functions increase as the n that describes a problem increases. There are four major groups, which I might describe as *cheap, affordable, expensive,* and *forget it!* Here's a somewhat stylized graph that will give an idea of relative growth rates:

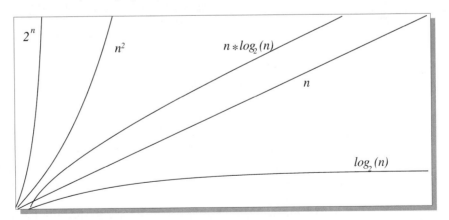

— Near-constant growth rates are so slow as to not really grow appreciably at all: call them cheap. *Logarithmic,* or $log_2(n)$, growth is typical.

— Linear growth rates increase directly with the size of the problem itself: call them affordable. n is linear, $n*log_2(n)$ takes a little longer.

basic growth rates

— Polynomial growth rates increase rapidly, but are still doable: call them expensive. n^2, perhaps with additional terms, is a polynomial rate.

— Exponential growth rates increase so rapidly that it becomes infeasible to solve substantial problems: say forget it. 2^n is an exponential growth rate.

The first group of functions has low growth rates. The cheapest have constant times; if we ignore the cost of arithmetic or I/O, the size of n doesn't matter. More expensive—but still slowly growing—functions involve logarithms of n.

near-constant times

	Size of n			
	10	100	1,000	1,000,000
$f(n) = constant$	C	C	C	C
$f(n) = log_2 (n)$	3.3	6.6	9.9	20

The second group of complexity-estimating functions has essentially linear growth rates. They are the functions that grow apace with, or slightly faster than, n, but which still don't explode as n gets very large.

near-linear times

	Size of n			
	10	100	1,000	1,000,000
$f(n) = n$	10	100	1,000	1,000,000
$f(n) = n * log_2 (n)$	33	664	9,965	20,000,000

Growth becomes expensive when powers get involved. n^2 or *quadratic* algorithms are about as high as PC's can comfortably go. Why? Well, think about a basic quadratic problem—any graphics program that involves a visit to every pixel (or point) on the screen.

quadratic growth

Length of a side:	10	100	500	1,000
Total number of pixels:	100	10,000	250,000	1,000,000

Any significant amount of calculation at each pixel rapidly ups the ante. *Exponential* algorithms (2 raised to a power of n) are so expensive that they may require special hardware that can carry out operations in parallel, or users who are willing to settle for suboptimal results.

A Case in Point: Divide-and-Conquer

An insight into complexity measure helps explain the power of *divide-and-conquer* algorithms like binary search. Such algorithms are O($log_2 n$); their running time is proportional to the logarithm, base 2, of the n that describes the problem size.

Recall that binary search works by splitting the 'still unknown' portion of an array in two. As I pointed out earlier, there are several approaches to finding out the length of the longest possible, worst-case search.

calculating a logarithm

— How many times can we divide an array of length *n* in half before we're left with an array of length one?

— If a jump size starts at ½ of *n*, then goes to ¼, ⅛, and so on, how many steps will it take to work our way down to 1/*n* of *n*?

— Starting with one, how many times can you double a value before it equals *n*?

— To what power should you raise 2 if you want it to equal *n*?

In each case, the answer is the logarithm, base 2, of *n*. Since doubling *n* increases the logarithm by just 1, growth is extremely slow. Algorithms that grow logarithmically remain feasible for an extremely long time; algorithms that grow even more slowly are as rare as hen's teeth.

What are the practical applications of studying different growth rates? Theoretical computer scientists are generally concerned with studying the complexity of *problems*. Their work often consists of:

— Increasing the theoretical lower bound on the complexity of a problem. This is very reassuring to programmers (below) who despair at their lack of progress in improving algorithms.

complexity of problems

— Determining not just the best-case complexity of a problem, but its worst and average-case complexity as well.

— Showing that a problem falls into a given complexity class (e.g. requires at least, or no more than, polynomial time) in the first place.

Despite all the precise notation we've worked with, theoreticians often work with just two words: easy and hard. 'Easy' problems, by convention, can be solved in polynomial time *or less*. 'Hard' problems, in contrast, have only non-polynomial solutions—exponential or worse.* Showing that a problem is easy is easy: if we can't prove it mathematically, we can still come up with an

easy vs. hard

easy algorithm. The method serves as evidence. On the other hand, it's hard to prove that problems are hard, since a hard algorithm might say more about our own lack of programming ability than about the problem's inherent obstinacy.

Theoreticians with an interest in programming often concern themselves with analyzing known *algorithms* or devising new ones; for instance:

— Devising algorithms that take advantage of fundamentally different computer hardware, especially hardware that supports massive numbers of parallel operations.

performance of algorithms

— Devising *probabilistic* algorithms that have extremely good average-case performance (even though their worst cases might be very bad).

— Narrowing the gap between the inherent complexity of a problem and the best currently known algorithm for solving it.

---

* So as not to strain your credulity, incidentally, I'll confess that, theory or no, an n^4 polynomial time algorithm gets awfully slow awfully soon.

Remember . . .

❑ When you search an array, always remember the possibility that what you want might not be there. Don't go past the end of the array during the search, and be sure to document the search *postconditions* carefully.

❑ A *linear* search goes through an array one component at a time. It's the least effective search method, but it can be improved by sorting the array beforehand.

❑ A *quadratic* search is similar to linear, but it takes square-root-sized jumps to get close to the sought value. The array must be sorted first.

❑ *Binary* search is the basic divide-and-conquer search algorithm. It minimizes the search space by discarding half of the unknown portion with each step. It also requires a sorted array.

❑ *Selection* sort builds a sorted array by finding, and selecting, the largest value that remains in an array. Thus, the unsorted portion of the array is traversed repeatedly, but once a value has been placed in the sorted side it never moves again.

❑ *Insertion* sort works by inserting incoming values into the appropriate place in a partially sorted array. The unsorted part of the array is inspected only once, but the sorted side must be revamped to make room for newly arriving components.

❑ *Bubble* sort works by making pairwise comparisons and exchanges. As the sorted array is built it stays in place, but there are many unnecessary exchanges.

❑ A *stable* sort leaves identical array components in the same relative order; an *unstable* sort may change their order.

❑ Programs aren't usually compared by measuring running times: the results can be skewed by extraneous factors, and running times are poor predictors of performance on different kinds of hardware. Instead, their *algorithms* are characterized by the way *performance* changes with *input size*. The *complexity* of problems can be described in the same way.

❑ *Big O* notation is a convention used to describe performance and complexity. A well-understood mathematical function serves as an upper-bound approximation of the actual value. Big O notation's main purpose is describing, in an intuitive fashion, the way that difficulty increases as problem size increases.

❑ The basic complexity measures include *constant* (no growth), *logarithmic* (very slow growth as size increases), *linear* (growth is proportional to size), *polynomial* (very fast growth as size increases), and *exponential* (explosive growth as size increases).

❑ Divide-and-conquer algorithms typically have logarithmic growth rates, which is why they're so popular. In contrast, only relatively simple polynomial algorithms are practical, regardless of how fast a computer is.

The big ideas in this chapter are:

1. *It's important to study the details of searching and sorting, but it's important to ignore them, too.* For many programs, searching and sorting are the only significant CPU 'costs,' so methods have to be chosen carefully. But from the overall viewpoint of program design, they are no more important than other basic program steps—input, output, error checking, and so on.

2. *Fundamental program improvements come from better algorithms, not from better implementations.* Sometimes it's best to stand back and ask yourself just how well a program will work under the best reasonably expected circumstances. There's no point in grinding out slight improvements in a method that will never be good enough in the final analysis. Or, as Dijkstra puts it, if one blunt axe will not sharpen a pencil, ten blunt axes will do no better.

I think that you can think up a few sorting exercises on your own. Additional problems that involve sorting accompany the next chapter's exercises.

A successful data abstraction lets you work with values without having to know anything about their underlying implementation. Zip up that potato! (p. 387)

11

The **record** Type

Scientific programming tends to revolve around real and integer. Since arrays are great at holding large numbers of anonymous integer or real values, languages like FORTRAN—which only have arrays—remain popular in engineering classes.

But non-science programming is built around collections of values that have distinct names and types. For instance, although baseball players players have numbers, they also have names, teams, positions, favorite batting and throwing hands, and exhaustive statistics that document every play they've ever made (or missed). Arrays can be convinced to hold *anything*, of course, but a lot of arm-twisting is required.

Records come to the rescue. A record uses individually named *fields*, which can have different types, to package information in a way that models the real world. In practice, programmers often define arrays of records and get the best of both worlds: large numbers of components, each capable of storing a package of disparate values.

Section 11–1 deals with the syntax and basic applications of records. As with arrays, our focus in 11–2 will shift to data abstraction—design will take precedence over technique. Finally, 11–3 has some good advice on having data make sense even if a program doesn't.

Strictly Pascal

11-1

A RECORD IS A COLLECTION OF VALUES. Of course an array is a collection of values too, but records are different:

— First, the stored values can have different types. This makes records potentially *heterogeneous*—composed of values of different kinds. Arrays, in contrast, hold values of just one type, so they're said to be *homogeneous*.

— Second, a record's stored values are called *fields* and are given identifiers. A record's fields are individually named, like ordinary variables, whereas an array's components are selected according to their subscripts.

A single record type can also be defined in a way that lets it hold two or more completely alternative sets of fields. These *variant* definitions aren't important to us now, but I'll describe their syntax later.

Record types are built by identifying the type as a record, then naming and typing the individual fields. A somewhat simplified chart (it ignores variants and describes only the fixed part) of a record type definition is:

record type (with fixed-part only)

field lists

Together, the field identifiers (and their types) create a *field list* that follows the general form of a variable declaration. The field list goes between the words **record** and **end**, which let the compiler know where a field list ends and where the next definition or other declaration begins. Fields can have any type—standard or user-defined, simple or structured. For example, consider this definition of StatTYPE:

a very basic record

```
type StatTYPE = record
                  Initial: char;          {The field list.}
                  Count: integer
                end;
var Most, Least:  StatTYPE;
```

The declaration creates two record variables, each with two fields: Most.Initial, Most.Count, Least.Initial, and Least.Count.

dot notation

> Notice the period (usually read 'dot') between the variable and the field name. It serves the same purpose for a record that square brackets serve for an array: it helps single out one component of a more complicated structure.

I can also use the StatTYPE records as components of an array:

```
type StatTYPE = record
                    Initial: char;
                    Count: integer
                end;
```

an array of records

```
     StatArrayTYPE = array [1..26] of StatTYPE;
        {Holds twenty-six of the StatTYPE records.}
var  Most, Least: StatTYPE;
     Storage: StatArrayTYPE;
```

Here's what a snapshot of the variables might look like:

Records can be individual variables, or they can serve as components of larger structures.

Storage

Storage	Initial 'w' Count 3	Initial 'o' Count 9	Initial 'r' Count 0	Initial 'd' Count 7
	[1]	[2]	[3]	[4]

The StatArrayTYPE definition and Storage variable are more sophisticated than Most and Least, but they're more typical. The twenty-six components of the Storage variable are records. Storage[1], Storage[2], and the others each have type StatTYPE, just like Most and Least. And, just as Most and Least each have two fields, so do each of the array's components: Storage[1].Initial, Storage[1].Count, and so on.

Records can appear within arrays, or a record can hold arrays. Indeed, a record's fields can have any type, simple or structured, and can even be records themselves. This hierarchy of nested definitions can go as deeply as the compiler allows. Fortunately, the identifiers used for fields have limited scope, and they don't conflict with identifiers used for variables or for the fields of other records.

limited scope of field names

Self-Check Questions

Q. Define a type that might be used to represent a deck of playing cards. Include types for the suits, one card, and the entire deck.

A. I've made individual card values 1 through 13, below. Can you think of a better way to handle card names?

```
type SuitTYPE = (heart, club, spade, diamond);
     ValueTYPE = 1..13;
     CardTYPE = record
                    Suit: SuitTYPE;
                    Value: ValueTYPE
                end;
     DeckTYPE = array [1..52] of CardTYPE;
```

Access to Fields

There are three ways to access the values stored in a record variable.

1. An individual field can be identified using the 'dot' notation.

2. The complete record can be assigned with a single statement—all the fields of one record variable can be assigned to the corresponding fields of another record with the same type in a record-to-record assignment.

3. The **with** statement lets us access individual fields without bothering with the dot notation.

I'll define a somewhat more complicated record to experiment with. It's pulled from this parking ticket; we'll store the time.

No, despite the company's name, I don't have a day job parking cars. Here's a TimeTYPE definition:

```
type HalfTYPE = (AM, PM);
     TimeTYPE = record
                    Hour: 1 .. 12;
                    Minute: 0 .. 59;
                    AMorPM: HalfTYPE
                end;
var InTime, OutTime: TimeTYPE;
```

The series of assignments to InTime, below, uses the dot notation. The record variable's identifier is followed by a period and the name of a field. Formally, the trio of variable, period, and field name is known as a *qualified identifier*—the variable name and period *qualify*, or specifically identify, a particular field.

```
InTime.Hour := 9;
InTime.Minute := 42;
InTime.AMorPM := AM;
```

qualified identifiers

I can store the same values in OutTime with this shortcut, complete-record assignment:

record-to-record assignment

```
OutTime := InTime;
```

This single assignment is equivalent to a sequence of field-by-field assignments. Every field of OutTime gets the value of its counterpart in InTime. Naturally, all of InTime's fields should be defined before making such an assignment.

> Remember that record-to-record assignments can be made only between records of an *identical* type, i.e. declared with the same type name.

Although record-to-record *assignments* can be made, record-to-record *comparisons* cannot. You can't compare two complete records to see if they're equal or not. Instead, you have to compare them field by field.

The **with** Statement

Now, suppose that we want to gain access to individual fields, but we don't want to have to go to the trouble of qualifying—preceding with a record name and period—each field name. For convenience, Pascal includes a 'statement' that lets a record be named once, then accessed directly.

with statement

with is really just a syntactic scope-establishing device (like the 'dot'), but everybody calls it a statement because that's what it looks like. The series of assignments below is equivalent to the last example assignment:

using **with**

```
with OutTime do begin
    Hour := 10;
    Minute := 9;
    AMorPM := AM;
end
```

In a sense, the fields inside the **with** above are 'attached' to OutTime. If we wanted to make assignments to another TimeTYPE variable, we'd have to use the dot notation:

```
with OutTime do begin
    Hour := 10;        {refers to OutTime.Hour}
    InTime.Hour := 9;
end
```

Frankly, this last example is something you're only likely to create by accident. I would skip using the **with** if I were making the assignments above.

Multiple arguments to **with** are useful when a record contains record-typed fields.

> with Outer, Inner **do begin**
>   Field := Value;   *{Refers to Outer.Inner.Field.}*
>   ⋰   *etc.*
> **end**

Self-Check Questions —————————————————————————

Q. Show two different ways (i.e. using dot and **with** notation) of reading a value for the Hour field and printing the value of the Minute field of InTime.

A. As long as it's properly named, a field can be inspected or passed as a parameter just like any other variable. After all, it is a variable.

>   write (InTime.Minute);
>   read (InTime.Hour);
>   *{is the same as . . . }*
>   **with** InTime **do begin**
>   write (Minute);
>   read (Hour)
>   **end**

Q. Below are a few examples that have been exaggerated to make a point (and to let me sneak in yet a few more details about records!). Which ones are legal? What are the names of the legal example's fields?

> *a)*   **type** HAVE = **record**
>   HAVE: integer
>   **end**;
>   **var** Save: HAVE;
>
> *b)*   **type** HAVE = **record**
>   Save: integer
>   **end**;
>   **var** Save: HAVE;
>
> *c)*   **type** HAVE = **record**
>   HAVE: integer
>   **end**;
>   **var** HAVE: HAVE;

A. The inside of a record creates a new scope for names, just as the inside of a subprogram does. That makes definition *a* legal—the field name is in a different scope than the record's type name. It's referred to as Save.HAVE.

Definition *b* is also ok. As in *a*, the field Save and the variable Save are in different scopes. Within the record, the field name takes precedence; outside the record, the other usage of a name holds sway. Here, the field is called Save.Save.

Finally, definition *c* is illegal because of the variable declaration. It errs because a type and a variable have the same identifier but are in the same scope. The compiler has no rule for giving one use precedence over the other, so it announces an error.

A Longer Example

TimeTYPE was a simple definition; good for examples, but not very realistic. In real life, records have two very common applications:

— They become the 'elemental' values of new data types. Values of such types might consist of more than one component—a playing card has a number and a suit—but the record inextricably joins them. In applications like this, I think of a record as creating new, indivisible, *atomic* values.

— They're used as the building blocks of databases: collections of information that have been organized to make finding things easy. In such applications, records usually show up as array components. Since an array of records is built from separately defined structures, I usually think of it as a *constructed* type.

Let's construct a relatively complicated type for practice: an address book. Here's a page from mine:

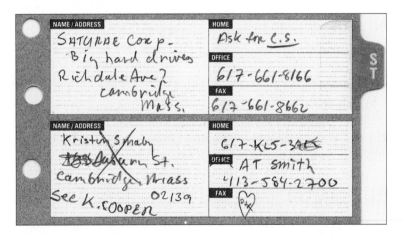

Address books can get away with rather vague categories, but we'll need to be precise when we pick fields. What information should an address book type store? Names, obviously, along with telephone numbers and addresses. We could treat all the values of one entry as though they were part of a long sequence of char values stored in an array:

| 'P' | 'r' | 'i' | 'n' | 'c' | 'e' | ' ' | '6' | '1' | '2' | '-' | '5' | '8' | '3' |

An address book *could* be an array of these arrays, but it wouldn't be very convenient to program with. A record type, with distinct fields for each entry, is much more appropriate.

a basic telephone book

```
type StringTYPE = packed array [ 1 .. 50 ] of char;
     EntryTYPE = record
                    Name, Street, Town:  StringTYPE;
                    Zipcode:  integer;
                    {telephone number fields}
                    Area, Prefix, Number:  integer
                 end;
     BookTYPE = array [1..100] of EntryTYPE;
var OneNumber:  EntryTYPE;
    PhoneBook:  BookTYPE;
```

EntryTYPE is a record that has an array-typed field. I *could* have gone even further by giving it record-typed fields as well. The version below can hold three different phone numbers:

an even more
complicated version

```
type StringTYPE = packed array [ 1 .. 50 ] of char;
     PhoneTYPE = record
                    Area, Prefix, Number:  integer
                 end;
     EntryTYPE = record
                    Name, Street, Town:  StringTYPE;
                    Zipcode:  integer;
                    Home, Office, Fax:  PhoneTYPE
                 end;
```

hierarchical vs. flat
definitions

Records defined like this are sometimes called *hierarchical* records, as opposed to *flat* definitions that have all fields at one level. For the purpose of this example, I'll use the simpler form.

Note that the Zipcode field won't necessarily work, since most microcomputer Pascal implementations limit integer values to a maximum of 32767. That's fine for Northampton, as you see below, but my Berkeley zip code, 94707, would cause problems. In practice, micros will generally provide a 'long' number type, longint, as a Pascal extension.

Making assignments to a stand-alone record like OneNumber is pretty straightforward. I'll use an old address that you can't use to hunt me down:

records as variables

```
OneNumber.Name := ´Doug Cooper´;
OneNumber.Street := ´33 Washington Avenue´;
OneNumber.Town := ´Northampton, Massachusetts´;
OneNumber.Zipcode := 01060;
OneNumber.Area := 413;
OneNumber.Prefix := 584;      and so on.
```

The assignments to the Name, Street, and Town fields all take advantage of the common extension for string assignments: that 'short' literal values can be assigned to string variables.

Since the components of PhoneBook have the same type as OneNumber, the values I assigned to OneNumber fields can be copied in a record-to-record assignment:

```
PhoneBook[1] := OneNumber;
```

Let's make every record in PhoneBook equal the first one:

initializing PhoneBook

```
for i := 2 to 100 do begin
    PhoneBook[i] := PhoneBook[1]
end
```

A series of direct assignments to the second record of the PhoneBook array is:

records as components

```
PhoneBook[2].Name := ´Prince Fan Club´;
PhoneBook[2].Street := ´City Hall´;
PhoneBook[2].Town :=  ´Minneapolis, Minnesota´;
PhoneBook[2].Zipcode := 55415;
PhoneBook[2].Area := 612;
PhoneBook[2].Prefix := 348;     and so on.
```

I might also use a **with** statement, perhaps with the ordinary I/O input procedures:

```
with PhoneBook[3] do begin
    write (´Please enter the name:    ´);
    i := 1;
    while not eoln do begin
        read (Name [ i ]);
        i := i + 1
    end;
    readln;    {Dump the carriage return.}
    write (´Please enter the zip code:    ´);
    readln (Zipcode);
        . . .
end
```

Now let's try the tough ones. How would I assign ´X´ to the third character of the Name field of the fourth record of PhoneBook? Like this:

```
PhoneBook[4].Name[3] := ´X´;
```

How about making every zip code in PhoneBook equal Bruce Springsteen's old zip code in Asbury Park?

```
for i := 1 to 100 do begin
    PhoneBook[i].Zipcode := 07712
end
```

problem: lookup

Putting information into our phone book is just half of it, of course. We can also get data out. Suppose I want to know who was at the other end of that $87 telephone call: I have the number, but need the name. Finding it requires a typical linear array search. In pseudocode:

> *get the number from the program user;*
> *look for it;*
> *print the name or a failure message*

The loop specification of *look for it* is:

loop specification

> *Goal: Find the stored name that goes with a stored number.*
> *Intentional bound: We've found a matching number.*
> *Necessary bound: We've run out of numbers to check.*
> *Plan: Increment a counter variable.*

And in Pascal we have:

looking up a name

```
procedure LookUp (PhoneBook: BookTYPE);
    {Asks for and tries to look up a particular phone number.}
    var Area, Prefix, Number, i: integer;
    begin
        write ('Enter the number in three parts: XXX XXX XXXX    ');
        read (Area);
        read (Prefix);
        readln (Number);
        i := 0;
        repeat
            i := i + 1
        until ( (Area = PhoneBook[i].Area) and (Prefix = PhoneBook[i].Prefix)
                and (Number = PhoneBook[i].Number) )
                    or (i = 100);
        {Postcondition: If the name was found, it's in the ith component.}
        write ('The mystery name was ');
        if (Area = PhoneBook[i].Area) and (Prefix = PhoneBook[i].Prefix)
                            and (Number = PhoneBook[i].Number)
            then writeln (PhoneBook[i].Name)
            else writeln ('not in your book.')
    end; {LookUp}
```

Modification Problems

1. "Enter a number in three parts"? Get serious—LookUp has a pretty terrible user interface. Write a procedure that can read a phone number entered in any reasonable format and return it separated into the area code, prefix, and number fields.

Self-Check Questions

Q. BookTYPE holds one hundred of the EntryTYPE records. This is fine for a bookish type like me, but a true party animal would have to be a little more creative. Use the definition of BookTYPE to define a structure that holds hundreds and hundreds of numbers, and that makes it easy to store entries in alphabetical order.

A. Piece of cake—we can define an array that is subscripted by the alphabet. There's a separate array of one hundred names for each letter.

```
type PartyListTYPE = array ['A'..'Z'] of BookTYPE;
```

Q. Which of these code segments actually initializes the Name field of each BookTYPE record to 'Ronnie'?

```
Current := 1;  {segment A}
repeat
    with PhoneBook[Current] do begin
        Name := 'Ronnie';
        Current := Current + 1
    end   {with}
until Current > 100

Current := 1;  {segment B}
with PhoneBook[Current] do begin
    repeat
        Name := 'Ronnie';
        Current := Current + 1
    until Current > 100
end   {with}
```

A. Segment *A* works, but segment *B* doesn't. Why not? Because the reference to PhoneBook[Current] is established when Counter equals 1. Even though Current changes *within* the **with** statement, the record assignment continues to be made to PhoneBook[1].Name.

11-2
Extended Examples: More Data Abstraction

A *DATA ABSTRACTION* DESCRIBES NEW KINDS of values in terms of the *primitive operations* they allow. This makes the description indirect: we talk about what you can do with them, rather than about how they're defined in Pascal. As a result, a successful data abstraction lets you work with values without having to know anything about their underlying implementation.

The common bond of primitives is that writing them requires knowledge of an abstraction's underlying implementation. They can't be written without knowing details like the names of specific fields. And yet, a good set of primitives ensures that we don't have to know such details to use the abstraction in an application. If an operation can't be carried out with available primitives, we assume that the operation doesn't exist for that abstraction.

For example, consider this collection of record type definitions. What primitives might you anticipate that each requires if we're going to deal with it as an abstraction?

```
{hold a fraction}
type FractionTYPE = record
                        Numerator, Denominator: integer
                    end;

{or the time}
type TimeTYPE = record
                    Hour: 0 .. 23;
                    Minute: 0 .. 59
                end;
```

{*or a date*}
type DateTYPE = **record**
       Month, Date, Year: integer;
       Time: TimeTYPE {*from above*}
     end;

{*or a Cartesian coordinate*}
type CoordinateTYPE = **record**
        X, Y: real
     end;

{*or the phrase on Wheel of Fortune*}
const PHRASE = 100; {*Maximum phrase size.*}
type LetterTYPE = **record**
       Letter: char;
       Showing: boolean
     end;
   GameTYPE = array [1..PHRASE] of LetterTYPE;

{*or a chessboard*}
type ColorTYPE = (Black, White);
   PieceTYPE = (Empty, Pawn, Knight, Bishop, Rook, Queen, King);
   SquareTYPE = **record**
      Occupied: boolean;
      Piece: PieceTYPE;
      Owner: ColorTYPE
     end;
   BoardTYPE = array [1..8, 1..8] of SquareTYPE;

Besides a type name, a few basic kinds of primitive operations will almost always be required:

— *Assignment* primitives let the abstraction hold information.

— *Inspection* primitives let us find out something about the values that are being held.

— *Operation* primitives change the stored values or alter the way they're stored.

For example, suppose I list some (but not necessarily all) of the primitive operations we'll want for TimeTYPE, as defined above.

Type name: TimeTYPE
Assignment: AssignHour, AssignMinute
Inspection: Print, ReturnHour, ReturnMinute
Operations: AddHours, SubtractHours, AddMinutes, SubtractMinutes

a name layer of primitive operations

Primitives provide a *name layer* that separates the type definition (the actual record definition) from its application (calls of the primitives). They keep the type definition that underlies a new abstraction at arm's length.

performance vs. requirements

> The name layer serves as a *performance specification* of what the data abstraction *can* do. At the same time, it is a *requirements specification* of what it *must* do. Ultimately, we'll want name layers that are tight enough to let one programmer use the new type while her partner codes it.

In contrast to more recently developed languages, Standard Pascal is weak when it comes to packaging type definitions in a way that guarantees the secrecy and security of parts, like field names, that we want to keep hidden. In more modern *object oriented* languages, data abstraction can be the law, rather than just a good idea. For now, programming in terms of primitives will help you get a better understanding of the way that new data types interact with program goals.

Example: Strings

Let's begin with an abstraction whose usage is going to be intuitive and obvious: an abstraction for strings.

problem: string abstraction

Define a type and the primitives necessary for working with strings. Provide all the tools needed to use strings without having to know details of the actual string definition.

The textbook approach at this point would begin by compiling a long list of the applications we'd like to use strings for. Then we'd try to pull out a name layer of primitives. Next we'd ask ourselves if performance considerations would require any special considerations for the underlying implementation. Finally, at long last, we'd get around to considering actual Pascal type definitions for the final string type.

But, to be honest, it takes a lot of experience to follow the textbook approach. Suppose that we cheat this time by working in reverse. Here's a type definition.

the underlying StringTYPE definition

```
const MAX = 80;        {the longest string}
type StringTYPE = record
                   Length: 0 .. MAX;
                   Data: packed array [1 .. MAX] of char
                 end;
```

We can look, but we musn't touch. Our job is to devise the primitive procedures that will:

— first, fulfill our expectations about what strings should do, and

— second, guarantee that no programmer will ever have to rely on specific details of the StringTYPE definition.

Keeping details at arm's length seems relatively unimportant now, but it becomes a fundamental issue when programs get large. Let's move along to the name layer.

Type name: StringTYPE
Assignment: ReadString, AppendString, Blank
Inspection: WriteString, Length
Operations: TruncateString, SubString, Capitalize
Comparison: Equal

I wasn't really serious about having you write a complete string-handling package, so I won't propose every last possible primitive (and we won't even write all of these). But I will attempt to startle you by suggesting a different implementation of the underlying StringTYPE:

```
{An alternative definition of the underlying type.}
const MAX = 80;          {the longest string}
type NewSTRING = array [ 0 .. MAX ] of char;
```

The first definition used a record to hold the string and defined a specific field to keep track of its length. NewSTRING, in contrast, uses a one-dimensional array to hold both the string *and* its length. It will rely on a classic hack: the ordinal value of the character stored in the zeroth component will equal the string's meaningful length. It gets a simpler definition, but working with it can be slightly more complicated.

> But as far as a program that uses strings is concerned, the relative merits of StringTYPE versus NewSTRING shouldn't matter. The fact that we rely *only* on primitives keeps us from worrying about such details.

Let's turn to the code of a few procedures we'll use later in this chapter. First, let's read a string. I'll take the easy way out here by reading a full line. But if I were a masochist, I might try to write a procedure that would skip leading white space, then read a string that ends with white space. In pseudocode:

initialize the Length;
while *there are characters on this line* **and** *room in the array*
     read a character;
     increment Length

In Pascal, the procedure is:

```
procedure ReadString (var Value:  StringTYPE);
    {Read a full line.  Returns a zero-length string if the line is empty.}
    begin
        Value.Length := 0;
        while not eoln and (Value.Length < MAX) do begin
            Value.Length := Value.Length + 1;
            read (Value.Data [ Value.Length ]);
        end;
        readln
    end; {ReadString}
```

Inspection procedures like Length are, in a sense, akin to the standard transfer functions trunc and ord. Length lets us look at a StringTYPE value in a slightly different way.

string length

```
function Length (Value: StringTYPE) : integer;
    {Represents the length of the stored string.}
    begin
        Length := Value.Length
    end; {Length}
```

Writing a string is no more difficult, in technical terms, than reading one. But suddenly we find that we must make design decisions: should there be a carriage return after the string? Well, perhaps not. After all, we can always call writeln after calling WriteString if we need a newline.

printing a string

```
procedure WriteString (Value: StringTYPE);
    {Write the string contents of Value without a newline.}
    var i: integer;
    begin
        for i := 1 to Value.Length do write (Value.Data [ i ])
    end; {WriteString}
```

String comparison also points out the necessity of thinking about the performance specification carefully. Is it plausible to believe that two strings should be equal if their only difference is that one ends with blank spaces? Yes, of course it is. What difference does an extra blank space make to a programmer whose real concern is analyzing Shakespeare? But if an Equal function insists on equal lengths as well as content, its documentation must mention that. In pseudocode:

equality testing pseudocode

> if *the strings aren't the same length*
> > then *they aren't equal*
> > else while *corresponding components are equal* and *components remain*
> > > *move on to the next component;*
> > > *decide if the strings are equal*

And in Pascal, the function is:

testing for equality

```
function Equal (Value1, Value2: StringTYPE) : boolean;
    {TRUE if the strings are equal in length and content.}
    var i: integer;
    begin
        if Value1.Length <> Value2.Length
            then begin Equal := FALSE end
            else begin
                i := 1;
                while (Value1.Data [ i ] = Value2.Data [ i ])
                        and (i < Value1.Length) do begin
                    i := i + 1
                end;
                {Postcondition: if the current components are equal, the strings are too.}
                Equal := Value1.Data [ i ] = Value2.Data [ i ]
            end
    end; {Equal}
```

Since our focus is on records and data abstraction, rather than on making arrays jump through hoops, I'll stop the exercise here. In a few pages we'll make use of the procedures we did write.

Example: Counting Strings with an Associative Array

Let's turn to a data abstraction that's more complicated, but is much more powerful. You know that an ordinary array uses plain ordinal values, which must be known when the array is defined, as subscripts. We put the subscripts to good use when we counted appearances of individual characters:

character subscripts

type CountTYPE = **array** [char] **of** integer;

But suppose that we want to count the appearance of *words*, rather than characters. We'd like to be able to make statements like:

string subscripts?

{*Initialize the cat count to 1. This is istinctly NOT legal!*}
WordCounts['cat'] := 1;

Strings can't be used as subscripts in Pascal, of course. But we need not be shy about coming up with an abstraction that can. It's known as an *associative array*.

Associative arrays use stored values as subscripts. They're incredibly handy for all kinds of real-world data processing problems. For example, consider the major and minor league career of Chico Walker, third baseman for the Chicago Cubs. Although there are only two dozen major league baseball teams, minor league teams are found practically everywhere. That makes it hard to enumerate a TeamTYPE that might be used as an array subscript.

Chico Walker's stats

Year	Club	Pct.	G	AB	R	H	2B	3B	HR	RBI	SB	BB	SO
84	Pawtucket	.263	130	499	91	131	26	5	18	51	42	80	88
85	Red Sox	.000	3	2	0	0	0	0	0	1	0	0	1
85	Iowa	.284	89	331	47	94	17	8	5	46	42	50	60
85	Cubs	.083	21	12	3	1	0	0	0	0	1	0	5
86	Iowa	.298	138	530	97	158	30	11	16	65	67	62	68
86	Cubs	.277	28	101	21	28	3	2	1	7	15	10	20
87	Cubs	.200	47	105	15	21	4	0	0	7	11	12	23
87	Iowa	.244	90	315	64	77	13	3	8	31	28	65	52
88	Edmonton	.289	79	304	58	88	17	4	7	39	25	29	47
88	Angels	.154	33	78	8	12	1	0	0	2	2	6	15
89	Syracuse	.239	123	431	61	103	11	5	12	63	37	58	61
90	Charlotte	.265	88	310	49	82	15	1	12	45	10	44	72
90	Iowa	.360	32	114	30	41	7	1	6	19	9	25	17
91	Cubs	.257	124	374	51	96	10	1	6	34	13	33	57
ML Totals		.237	285	751	106	178	18	5	8	59	45	68	133

Counting the number of teams he's played for, or deciding which team or teams he played for in any given year, is easy. But how many years did he play for the Cubs? How many in Iowa? We can't change Pascal's syntax, but we can construct a type and provide a collection of primitives that will let us make assignments that are the conceptual equivalent of:

{*What we'd like to be able to say . . .* }
read (Team);
Years [Team] := Years [Team] + 1;

I *could* use enumerated types to make a special-purpose solution to the problem. But designing an associative array as an abstract data type gives me a general-purpose tool I can use for other purposes.

Here are some entirely different problems that, at heart, could be solved using the same tool. First, my MasterCard bill. How much did I spend on overnight mail (the Fedex entries)? How much at the ASUC bookstore? How much at the annual ACM conference on Computer Science education, held in Kansas City?

WELLS FARGO BANK   Gold MasterCard®

DOUG COOPER

ACCOUNT NUMBER

Wells Fargo Bank, N.A.
P.O. Box 4044
Concord, CA 94524-4044

WELLS FARGO BANK

24-hour Customer Service
1-800-642-4720

Closing Date	Credit Limit	Unused Credit	New Balance	Member Since			
03/23/92	7,500	3,402	4,055.69	02/85	N	PAGE	2 OF 3

Reference Number	Transaction Date	Posting Date	Transaction Description			Charges/Credits
030059005	02/22	03/04	FEDEX AB# 094585834	MEMPHIS	TN	20.00
030061010	02/24	03/05	FEDEX AB# 039556767	MEMPHIS	TN	14.00
030061010	02/26	03/05	FEDEX AB# 094585834	MEMPHIS	TN	21.75
886451136	02/29	03/05	EASY GOING-BERKLY	BERKELEY	CA	36.64
029494560	03/04	03/06	CAFE ALLEGRO	KANSAS CITY	MO	59.95
081568260	03/05	03/09	1992 COMP SCI CONF	KANSAS CITY	MO	105.00
504408690	03/06	03/10	EMBASSY ON THE PARK	KANSAS CITY	MO	147.97
360597143	03/02	03/11	DELTA	BERKELEY	CA	585.00
645141522	03/09	03/11	WHOLE EARTH ACCESS(E)	BERKELEY	CA	127.74
171103407	03/09	03/12	WALDENBOOKS 011034	BERKELEY	CA	23.38
645143587	03/11	03/13	ASUC BOOKSTORE	BERKELEY	CA	59.92
645143652	03/11	03/13	ASUC BOOKSTORE	BERKELEY	CA	15.53
525933280	03/14	03/18	SBI DBA STANFORD BKSTR	STANFORD	CA	110.31
042587250	03/16	03/19	CHEVRON #96463 00964	EL CERRITO	CA	29.24
500000002	03/13	03/20	FEDEX AB# 036664565	MEMPHIS	TN	14.50

Next, part of my telephone bill. If I were trying to analyze it, I'd probably want to be able to look at both locations called *and* numbers called. How many times have I called a particular city? How long did I spend on the line to a particular number?

◆ *Sprint*

DOUG COOPER   PAGE: 2
SPRINT PLUS SERVICE   INVOICE DATE: 4/17/92
ACCOUNT ID: INVOICE NUMBER: 36042000000000
PRINTED ON RECYCLED PAPER

ITEMIZATION OF CALLS

BILLED TO NUMBER: 510 525-
SERVICE LOCATION: BERKELEY, CA

NBR	DATE	TIME	*	CALLED LOCATION		CALLED NUMBER	MINUTES	CHARGES
1	3/16/92	4:15 PM	D	CAMBRIDGE	MA	617 661-	7.0	$1.75
2	3/18/92	11:46 AM	D	PRINCETON	NJ	609 683-	1.0	.25
3	3/18/92	3:27 PM	D	PRINCETON	NJ	609 683-	53.0	13.25
4	3/18/92	4:21 PM	D	NORTH DADE	FL	305 944-	81.0	16.35
5	3/19/92	9:28 AM	D	ST PAUL	MN	612 635-	1.0	.24
6	3/19/92	9:29 AM	D	ST PAUL	MN	612 635-	1.0	.24
7	3/19/92	9:30 AM	D	MINNEAPOLS	MN	612 626-	1.0	.24
8	3/19/92	9:32 AM	D	NASHUA	NH	603 881-	27.0	6.75
9	3/19/92	9:59 AM	D	CAMBRIDGE	MA	617 661-	3.0	.75
10	3/19/92	10:03 AM	D	CAMBRIDGE	MA	617 661-	2.0	.50
11	3/19/92	10:18 AM	D	SEATTLE	WA	206 329-	1.0	.23
12	3/19/92	12:08 PM	D	SEATTLE	WA	206 329-	25.0	5.75
13	3/19/92	2:27 PM	D	MINNEAPOLS	MN	612 626-	15.0	3.69
14	3/20/92	10:03 AM	D	NEWARK	NJ	201 643-	7.0	1.75
15	3/20/92	4:44 PM	D	BROOKVILLE	PA	814 849-	92.0	15.78
16	3/22/92	9:49 AM	N	BROOKVILLE	PA	814 849-	27.0	3.66
17	3/22/92	2:39 PM	N	NORTH DADE	FL	305 944-	5.0	.67

The non-programmer sees all of these as unique problems, but I think that you can start to see their underlying similarity. Although other languages (particular the object-oriented ones) go beyond Standard Pascal in supplying the tools you'd need to code up a truly reusable, general-purpose associative array, the really hard issue is coming to understand why they're needed at all.

The Name Layer

Suppose that I present the associative array problem in its simplest form, like this:

the problem

Write a program that can read strings and count the number of times each one appears.

The solution requires a type that can hold a reasonable number of strings *and* a count for each. We'd like to be able to increase each string's count by one, and it would be nice to be able to retrieve the strings and counts as well.

Most of all, we don't want to be burdened with any bookkeeping. If we choose to increment a string's count by one, we don't want to have to find out if the string is already stored in the associative array. The increment operator should take care of that for us.

Suppose that I list a few of the names and operations we'd like to have. I'm not thinking up anything new here—just repeating what I just said in the form of one-word procedure names.

AssociativeTYPE's name layer

Type name: AssociativeTYPE
Initialize the list: Initialize
Adjust the stored count: Increment
Find a string's position, or store it: LookUp
Return a stored count: ReturnCount
Return a stored string: ReturnWord
Find the number of entries: ReturnLength

The primitives' common bond is that they depend on knowledge of the type's underlying definition. In fact, that's why they're primitives; they can't be written without knowing such details. At the same time, they help ensure that *we* don't have to know any details. As long as we meet the requirements set up by the name layer, our choice of implementation really is a choice. The actual type definition we use is a hidden detail. As long as AssociativeTYPE variables behave properly, it doesn't matter how they're put together.

String input and comparison will also require a bit of code, but it's code we're already familiar with. As long as we can read one word at a time, we'll be able to feed input to the associative array. All we need are a few primitive procedures and functions:

StringTYPE's name layer

Type name: StringTYPE
Initialize a string: Blank
Read a string: ReadWord
Print a string: WriteString
Decide if two strings match: Equal
Find out how long a string is: Length

The Code Layer: Type Definitions

Let me begin by clearing up the basic mystery of how our associative array will work. I'll keep each word, and its count, in a record. Naturally, there will be a whole array of these records. Since there's no magical way to use a string as a subscript, I'll have to slog through the array each time I want to find a stored word in order to add 1 to the count of times it has appeared. When it's time to report, I'll go through the array again, inspecting both the stored strings and the stored counts.

Experience has taught me that short type definitions are easier to create and test. I'll start out by defining a string:

storing a word

```
const MAXlength = 10;          {Keep the strings short.}
type StringTYPE = record
                Length: 0 .. MAXlength;
                Data: packed array [1 .. MAXlength] of char;
            end;
```

Next, we need a record that can hold a word along with the number of times it's been seen.

a single entry

```
{Type definition continues . . . }
{type} EntryTYPE = record
                Info: StringTYPE;
                Count: integer          {This word's frequency.}
            end;
```

The final step is to build an array of EntryTYPE records. Suppose that we let our associative array hold up to MAXdata (say, 500) words. Don't forget the requirement for the ReturnLength primitive: we'll have to know how many different words are stored at any given time. Since the two variables—the list of words and its length—are so closely tied together, I've made them fields of a single record type:

an array of entries

```
{const} MAXdata = 500;          {Number of words we can store.}
{type} AssociativeTYPE = record
                    Length: integer;   {Number of words we have seen.}
                    List: array [1 .. MAXdata] of EntryTYPE;
                end;
```

Why don't I put the three definitions together as they'll appear in the final program?

*the underlying type
definition*

```
const MAXdata = 500;          {Number of different words.}
        MAXlength = 10;          {Length of longest individual word.}
type StringTYPE = record
                Length: 0 .. MAXlength;
                Data: packed array [1 .. MAXlength] of char;
            end;
```

(*definition continues*)

```
EntryTYPE = record    {one word}
               Info: StringTYPE;
               Count: integer
         end;
```

```
AssociativeTYPE = record    {all the words}
                     Length: integer  {Number of different words.}
                     List: array [1 .. MAXdata] of EntryTYPE;
                  end;
```

The Code Layer: Primitives

Let's turn to the primitives that will bring AssociativeTYPE to life. Most of them merely inspect and return the value of a hidden field:

Initialize works by assigning AssociativeTYPE's Length field to 0;

how the primitives work

ReturnLength works by returning the same field's value;

Increment works by adding 1 to EntryTYPE's Count field;

ReturnCount works by returning EntryTYPE's Count field's value;

ReturnWord works by returning EntryTYPE's Info field's value.

LookUp is more difficult. It searches the associative array for a particular string, and adds it to the end of the array if it's not there already. Here's the call I would like to be able to make:

```
LookUp (Data,        {the associative array}
          Entry,       {the word we want to find or store}
          Position);   {where we found it or stored it}
```

LookUp gets the associative array and a string and returns the position the string occupies (if it's there already) or the position LookUp puts it in (if it wasn't there). Thus, the Data argument might or might not be changed, depending on whether the word is found. The Entry argument might be stored, but it won't be changed. Finally, the Position argument will definitely change, because it will always return a value.

Now let's see how to carry out the search itself. I'll use an old trick to make matters easier: I'll put the string we're seeking at the very end of the array before we even begin to look. That way we'll be sure to find it. In pseudocode:

LookUp pseudocode

{*What procedure LookUp does.*}
store the string at the end of the array;
go through the array until you find a match for the string;
if *it was found at the end, it must be new, so*
    then *initialize its count to* 0;
        increase Data.Length *by* 1;
    else *it was stored previously, so make the array end blank again*
{*Postcondition: we know where the string can be found.*}

The last **else** step is just housekeeping; I could have left the word there.

*first make it work —
then make it fast*

Does LookUp use the best possible algorithm? No—it's just the easiest one to code. If lookup performance becomes an issue, though, we can fix just one procedure. As long as LookUp continues to do *what* it advertises, *how* it does it is hidden from the user.

Program Appears

Let's pause to outline the final program, Appears. The problem it solves is to count the number of times each word appears in an arbitrary collection of words. It makes the count, then prints the stats:

*final program
pseudocode*

{*Start by getting the words.*}
initialize the associative array to zero entries with Initialize;
while *there are still words to read* **do**
   read a word with ReadWord;
   find its position, or store it, with LookUp;
   increase its count with Increment;
{*Report on the total number of words.*}
use ReturnLength *to report on the number of different words read;*
{*Report each word's individual appearance count.*}
for *each of the* ReturnLength *entries* **do**
   get the word from the associative array using ReturnWord;
   print the word with WriteString;
   print its count, using ReturnCount;

I tested Appears with Chico Walker's baseball data.

*associative arrays in
action*

```
program Appears (input, output);
    {Uses an associative array to count word appearances.}
const MAXdata = 500;        {Number of different words.}
      MAXlength = 10;       {Length of longest individual word.}
type StringTYPE = record
                Length: 0 .. MAXlength;
                Data: packed array [1 .. MAXlength] of char;
             end;
     EntryTYPE = record     {one word}
             Info: StringTYPE;
             Count: integer
          end;
     AssociativeTYPE = record    {all the words}
                Length: integer;  {The number of different words.}
                List: array [1 .. MAXdata] of EntryTYPE;
             end;
var AllWords: AssociativeTYPE;
    OneWord: StringTYPE;
    Position, Count: integer;
```

(*program continues*)

```
{*****************************************************************}
{I'll get the string-handling subprograms out of the way first.}
procedure ReadString (var Value:  StringTYPE);
    {Read a full line.  Returns a zero-length string if the line is empty..}
    begin
        Value.Length := 0;
        while not eoln and (Value.Length < MAXlength) do begin
            Value.Length := Value.Length + 1;
            read (Value.Data [ Value.Length ] );
        end;
        readln
    end;  {ReadString}
procedure WriteString (Value:  StringTYPE);
    {Write the string contents of Value without a newline.}
    var i:  integer;
    begin
        for i := 1 to Value.Length do write (Value.Data [ i ] )
    end;  {WriteString}
procedure Blank (var Value:  StringTYPE);
    {Store null characters in the string.}
    var i:  integer;
    begin
        Value.Length := 0;
        for i := 1 to MAXlength do Value.Data [ i ] := chr (0);
    end;  {Blank}
function Equal (Value1, Value2:  StringTYPE) : boolean;
    {TRUE if the strings are equal in length and content.}
    var i:  integer;
    begin
        if Value1.Length <> Value2.Length
            then begin Equal := FALSE end
            else begin
                i := 1;
                while (Value1.Data [ i ] = Value2.Data [ i ])
                        and (i < Value1.Length) do begin
                    i := i + 1
                end;
                {Postcondition:  if the current components are equal, the strings are too.}
                Equal := Value1.Data [ i ] = Value2.Data [ i ]
            end
    end; {Equal}
function Length (Value:  StringTYPE) : integer;
    {Represents the length of the stored string.}
    begin
        Length := Value.Length
    end;  {Length}
```

```
{***************************************************************}
{Next, we'll take care of the AssociativeTYPE primitives.}
procedure LookUp (var Data: AssociativeTYPE;      {The whole array.}
                      Entry: StringTYPE;          {What we want.}
                      var Position: integer);     {Where it will be.}
    {Looks up a string, and makes an entry for it if it's absent.}
    begin
        with Data do begin
            List[Length + 1].Info := Entry;
            {Store it at the end to make the search easy.}
            Position := 1;
            while not Equal (List[Position].Info, Entry) do begin
                Position := Position + 1
            end;
            {Postcondition: the word we want is in component Position.}
            if Position = Length + 1 then begin
                {We found it, but in the last slot, so it must be a new entry.}
                List[Position].Count := 0;      {No previous instances of this word.}
                Length := Length + 1            {Lengthen the array of words.}
            end
            else begin  {It's in component Position.}
                Blank (List [ Length + 1 ].Info);   {Remove the word we stored.}
            end   {if}
        end   {with}
    end;  {LookUp}

procedure Initialize (var Data: AssociativeTYPE);
    {Initializes the count of entries.}
    begin
        Data.Length := 0;
    end;  {Initialize}

procedure Increment (var Data: AssociativeTYPE; Position: integer);
    {Add 1 to the count associated with Entry.}
    begin
        Data.List[Position].Count := Data.List[Position].Count + 1
    end;  {Increment}

function ReturnLength (Data: AssociativeTYPE) : integer;
    {Represents the number of entries in Data}
    begin
        ReturnLength := Data.Length
    end;  {ReturnLength}

function ReturnCount (Data: AssociativeTYPE; Position: integer) : integer;
    {Represents the count associated with a particular entry.}
    begin
        ReturnCount := Data.List[Position].Count
    end;  {ReturnCount}
```

(program continues)

```
procedure ReturnWord (Data:  AssociativeTYPE;
                          Position:  integer; var AWord:  StringTYPE);
    {Returns the string stored in a particular position.}
    begin
        AWord := Data.List[Position].Info
    end;  {ReturnWord}

begin
    Initialize (AllWords);
    writeln ('Give me a file of words to count.');
    while not eof and (ReturnLength(AllWords) < MAXdata) do begin
        ReadString (OneWord);
        LookUp (AllWords, OneWord, Position);
        Increment (AllWords, Position)    {We counted a word.}
    end;
    {All the MAXlength-letter words were counted.}
    write (ReturnLength (AllWords) : 1);
    writeln (' different words read.  Number of appearances was . . . ');
    for Count := 1 to ReturnLength (AllWords) do begin
        ReturnWord (AllWords, Count, OneWord);
        WriteString (OneWord);
        writeln (ReturnCount (AllWords, Count): 3)
    end
end.  {Appears}
```

⇩   ⇩   ⇩   ⇩   ⇩

```
Give me a file of words to count.
Pawtucket
Red Sox
Iowa
Cubs
Iowa
Cubs
Cubs
Iowa
Edmonton
Angels
Syracuse
Charlotte
Iowa
Cubs
8 different words read.  Number of appearances was . . .
Pawtucket  1
Red Sox   1
Iowa   4
Cubs   4
Edmonton  1
Angels   1
Syracuse  1
Charlotte   1
```

Modification Problems

1. As written, Appears keeps separate counts for words that are really the same: 'Record' is different from 'record', and both differ from 'record,'. Modify LookUp so that it does the right thing.

2. As written, we can only count appearances of words. But suppose that each word is preceded by a number. For example:

```
$1.29     sox
$3.98     glue
$0.83     gum
$3.86     glue        etc.
```

Modify the associative array so that it is able to add and sum all the numbers associated with a particular word, instead of counting the words themselves.

3. LookUp is pathetically stupid about the way it stores words, with the result that it takes forever to find anything. Suppose that we want to retrieve the words and counts we've stored in alphabetical *or* numerical order. Take your choice of two modifications: *a*) have LookUp keep the entries stored in alphabetical order, or *b*) have LookUp keep the entries stored in numerical order.

Program Engineering Notes: Self-Describing Data

11-3

AS YOU BEGIN TO WORK WITH records you will find that:

— the amount of data programs use tends to increase overall; and

— it is very often necessary to save data between program runs.

Although the simple filters we've written in the past could be used to process reams of data, they might not actually have to hold more than a few characters' worth at a time. In contrast, programs that use more elaborate data types usually have to manage a great deal of information. Indeed, that's why we're using the fancier types in the first place.

If enough data are involved, it may turn out to be convenient to try to save data between program runs. A graphics program might save its screen, a game-playing program might save current board positions, and an address-book program would certainly save stored names and numbers.

As a result, Load and Dump procedures that read data from files and write data to files can become a program's main input and output routes. This means that we'll have to think a little more carefully about how they're put together—about what Load expects to read and what Dump is expected to put out.

Consider a basic application like maintaining an address book. You'd want to write a program to look up a particular number or address or to sort data by name or zip code. But some ordinary, everyday operations, like adding a new entry or correcting an old one, might be more easily handled with a very ordinary, everyday tool—a text editor.

Similarly, a program that keeps track of your checkbook or bank balances will certainly want to use real and integer variables. It will probably rely

write tools, not systems

on structured types like arrays and records as well. But when the program ends, there should be some way to dump all data in a form that humans can read on paper.

transfer data as text

> Programs move and transform data quickly, but not always conveniently. When it is possible, assume that data will start and finish as plain text— ordinary characters in an ordinary file. In other words, use plain text as the medium of exchange between *programs*, as well as between your program and you.

Self-Describing Data

Now, what does it mean to use plain text as a medium of exchange? Well, you have to recognize that a file of stored data has two potential users: people and programs. It has to hold information in a manner that:

— makes it easy for a human reader to understand and interpret the meaning of the stored values; and

— makes it easy for a program to load its internal data structures from the file and to dump data in the same format.

Thus, data should be labeled (for the benefit of humans), but the labels can't interfere with input and output (for the benefit of programs). The phrase *self-describing data* has been used to describe this goal.

Let's look at some examples. Suppose that a record holds a name, an age, and various other assorted data items.

a lot of stored data

```
type InfoTYPE = record
                     Name: StringTYPE;        {as defined earlier}
                     Age: integer;
                        · ·.      {other fields}
                 end;
      EntireTYPE = array [1..100] of InfoTYPE;
```

What kind of standardized formats can we establish for Load and Dump? I've tried to attach names that highlight the differences between these examples:

Example	*Format*
`Kristin`	*line-oriented*
`22`	

different data formats

  · ·. *other fields of one record*

`User's name is Kristin`	*embedded*
`She is 22 years old.`	

  · ·. *other fields of one record*

`User's Name: Kristin`	*labeled and delimited*
`Age: 22`	

  · ·. *other fields of one record*

```
Kristin   #the user's name        positional
22        #the user's age
 · · · other fields of one record
```

The first format is line-oriented; each line contains a single item of data. The second embeds each item within a prose description of its meaning. The third format uses a colon (:) as a delimiter to mark the end of a descriptive comment. Finally, the fourth format has a delimiter (the **#**) to catch your eye, but it's really positional—the first item on the line is the data value.

What are the relative advantages of each approach?

advantages and disadvantages

— The basic line-oriented format is easiest from the viewpoint of computer input and output, but it's hard for a human reader to understand what the data mean—especially if it's mistaken.

— Embedding the data in a description errs in the other extreme. Humans can read it easily, but it's difficult to write a Load routine that can extract the actual data.

— Labeled output is typical of interactive programs. A Load procedure can skip to the delimiter that marks the end of the descriptive comment. This is a little restrictive because the comment can't contain the delimiter, and because the space that follows the delimiter might be a meaningful char.

— Positional notation is probably the best method. Actual data values can lead the line, while the delimiter *follows*.

Note that these guides apply to the contents of a single record. How would you separate one record from the next? Most people use one or two completely blank lines, or have yet another delimiter that separates one record from the next, e.g.:

delimiters between entries

```
!
one record's data
!
the next record's data
!
the next record's data
$    end of input
```

The ultimate goal, as noted above, is to embed descriptions of data within the data file itself. Although *programs* that use the data may ignore the descriptions, *people* who read it will be grateful.

Record Bugs

Like arrays, records pose the immediate problem of notation. We have barely mastered square brackets when, out of the blue, we have to deal with dots as well. Is this a variable identifier?

This[That].TheOther.Something.Else[3]

Well, it might be. On the other hand, it could be bug city.

An old game that I just made up is custom-tailored to give you practice with notation. If you've been to camp, you probably know how to tell *continuation stories*. Each camper gets a minute or two to add a new chapter to a continuing, usually ever-more-grisly campfire story. Well, let's do some continuation naming. Start with an identifier:

Age

Make it one field of a record:

Facts.Age

practice with
constructed types Turn that record into one component of an array:

Camper[32].Facts.Age

Turn the array into a field:

Boys.Camper[32].Facts.Age

I think that you get the idea. For more practice, make up an arbitrarily complicated variable name, like:

Room[273].NextWeek[Monday].Schedule[3, PM] := Busy;

Then, figure out what's going on. Here, it seems that Room is an array of records. One field of each record—the NextWeek field—is also an array of records. One field of the Monday record—the Schedule field—is a two-dimensional array. By reading the assignment one step at a time (and breathing very slowly) we can conclude that on next Monday, Room 273 will not be available at 3 P.M.

Enough notation! Two other common errors in working with records are:

1. forgetting to use the **end** that marks the conclusion of a record type definition, and

2. accidentally using a type identifier in place of a variable identifier.

These are syntax bugs, so the compiler can catch them. Nevertheless, they're annoying. Leaving the **end** off a record is confusing because it may lead to a misdiagnosis of the actual error. For example:

```
type PropertyTYPE = record
                    Price: real;
                    Zoning: char;
     var ApartmentNumber: integer;
         House: PropertyTYPE;
```

a missing end

What will the compiler read? Well, it doesn't know that **var** isn't intended to be another field for PropertyTYPE. You'll get an error message that points out the futility of using a reserved word as a field identifier. Compilers freak

out because they're built that way; they usually don't look ahead and try to rees-
tablish a correct context. You, on the other hand, should look for the missing
end before you panic.

Using a type name as part of an expression is almost always a mistake.
It's obvious here because of the capitalization of type names:

> write (PropertyTYPE.Price);
>   {*This should refer to* House.Price.}

> As a rule, type identifiers *never* appear in statements. If you see a type iden-
> tifier lurking about a main program, it's up to no good.

with Bugs

The **with** statement also provokes a few perplexing situations. **with** simplifies
naming for just one record. As a result, using **with** to simplify the name of a
record that's an array component can be tricky. This sequence is wrong:

a buggy sequence

> **with** AnArray[i] **do begin**
>   **for** i := 1 **to** Last **do begin**
>   *references to the fields of the current* AnArray *component*
>   **end**
> **end**

Even though i changes inside the **for** statement, the particular record that **with**
is attached to doesn't. The order of the statements has to be reversed:

the correct version

> **for** i := 1 **to** Last **do begin**
>   **with** AnArray[i] **do begin**
>   *references to the fields of the current* AnArray *component*
>   **end**
> **end**

Syntax Summary

❏   record: a structured type whose components—the record's *fields*—can
have different types:

> **type** ExampleTYPE = **record**
>   Field1: ItsTYPE;   {*the field lists*}
>   Field2, Field3: TheirTYPE
>   **end**;
> **var** Test, Sample: ExampleTYPE;

The fields can have any type, simple or structured.

❏   dot notation: used to *qualify* a field, i.e. to construct its full identifier:

> Test.Field1 *is different from* Sample.Field1

❏   **with** statement: establishes a reference to a particular record variable so that its fields don't have to be individually qualified:

```
{Assume that Test and Sample are records.}
with Test do begin
    Field1 := whatever;  {this refers to Test.Field1}
    Sample.Field1 := whatever  {Sample still requires dot notation}
end
```

Remember . . .

❏   Assignment can be made between any two record variables as long as they have the same type. However, none of the relational operators, not even =, is defined for record types. Records must be compared one field at a time.

❏   A record definition creates a new scope for identifiers, just as a subprogram does. An identifier used as a field name doesn't conflict with an identifier used outside the record definition, e.g. in other record definitions.

❏   Records that contain records are sometimes called *hierarchical*. They set up a relationship between stored values, in contrast to *flat* records that put all fields at the same level.

❏   Within a given **with** statement, you can't switch from one record to another. In particular, when looking at records that are components of arrays, traverse the array outside the **with** statement, not inside it.

❏   A type *abstraction* consists of plain English definitions of its values and plain English explanations of the names or symbols that invoke operations on those values. Another way of phrasing this is to say that a type is defined, in abstract terms, by its *values* and its *operations* and not by its implementation.

❏   A *name layer* is a design tool for formalizing a type's abstract definition. It consists of the type's identifier and the *calling forms*—names and headings—of subprograms that will carry out its primitive operations. The name layer acts as a *performance specification* for using the type abstraction and as a *requirements specification* for implementing it.

❏   A type's *implementation*, or code layer, includes its underlying definition in Pascal and the code required to carry out operations on values of the type. It is always possible to suggest alternative implementations for any given abstraction.

❏   A *primitive* operation on a value can't be implemented effectively without knowing the value's underlying type definition. A data abstraction should have a complete set of primitives—the programmer shouldn't *have* to know type definition details.

❏   An *associative array* uses arbitrary values as subscripts. Although it isn't a built-in type in Pascal, we can define and implement the primitive operations it requires.

❏   First make it work, then make it fast.

❏   It's usually a good idea to save data as plain text. Although this makes more work for programs—they have to read and translate input and output—it makes life easier for programmers. It's easy to check plain text files, and to use ordinary text editors to create or correct them.

❑   Try to make stored data *self-describing*; where appropriate, add information for the benefit of human readers, even if a program will ignore it.

Big Ideas

The Big Ideas in this chapter are:

1. *Type design methodologies are meant to separate what a type does from how it's done in Pascal.* Data abstraction, with its clear division between name and code layers, uses a small, well-defined set of primitive operations as a performance specification for using the type and as a requirements specification for implementing it. Using the abstraction means using the primitives; implementing the abstraction means implementing the primitives.

2. *Variables of structured types will usually have constructed names.* Identifiers frequently have to be constructed using arbitrary symbols like '.', '[', and ']'. The identifier FirstName may seem more 'name-like' than List[7].First or Store.Last[3,5], but they are all variable identifiers.

3. *Most record programming is actually array-of-record programming.* The record is a syntactic mechanism that lets arrays store packages of related values that have different types. As a result, record programming is primarily concerned with type design (unlike array programming, which focuses on algorithms).

Begin by Writing the Exam . . .

11-1   Scope rules are intended to let identifiers be reused within programs, while at the same time forbidding any reuse that could lead to ambiguity. The prototype test question for exploring scope confusion is *Do any of these identifiers have to be renamed?*

```
type Atype = record
                  A: integer;
                  B: real;
              end;
     Btype = record
                  A: integer;
                  B: real;
              end;
var A: Atype;
    B: Btype;
```

This particular example is perfectly legal. Make up three variations that are not so acceptable.

11-2   Once a structured type has been defined, access to its values can be made arbitrarily difficult. The most confusing variables involve records within arrays within records, ad infinitum. Define the most hideously complex type you can think of, then ask *Which of these are legal assignments?* to it.

11-3   Initializing a single record isn't too hard. Nor is initializing an array of simple values. But suppose that you have an array of records? You might be given an array of twenty-six records, each with a single integer and char field, and be asked to initialize the records to *a)* 0 and ´A´, *b)* increasing numbers and letters, *c)* increasing numbers and decreasing letters, etc.

Make up a few mechanical questions of this sort. The two variations to make are *a)* making relatively complicated initializations of simple records and *b)* keeping the initialization simple, but giving the records a more complex internal structure.

11-4   The **with** statement issues two invitations for appearance on a quiz. First, suppose that two record variables called Left and Right have the same type. Each includes a field called Up. If you're given this code segment:

```
with Left do begin
    with Right do begin
        Up := 0
    end
end
```

questions you might pose include *a) Is this segment legal?*, *b) Which record's Up field is being assigned to?*, and *c) How would you assign to the other record's Up field within the inner statement?* Make up another question or two, then create two more potentially confusing code segments of this sort.

11-5   A word might be best suited for storage in an array, whereas a word and its frequency might work best within a record with an array field—and a hundred words and frequencies would be ideal in an array of records with array fields. Because I know that you probably watch *Jeopardy*, please make up the ten questions whose answers are:

a)   an array;

b)   a record;

c)   an array of records;

d)   a record with an array field;

e)   an array of records with array fields.

11-6   If I were writing a test, I'd love to supply a few primitive operations on a type as a specification, then ask my students to propose two alternative implementations of the underlying type definition.

Come up with three new data types (say, ColorTYPE or TimeTYPE), and name a few of the primitive operations each one requires. Then, supply two or three alternative definitions for each type. Why two or three alternatives? So that you can ask the question *Which of these definitions would* not *be suitable for the primitive operations listed above?*

11-7   Choose any three board games and ask the question *Define a type suitable for representing this board.* You can make this a little harder by asking *What are the primitive operations of this game?* as well.

11-8   Developing test data is, by now, as critical a programming skill as coding. Suppose that you are in possession of a Sort procedure and can run three tests on it. Write six possible sets of test data (an array of ten values each should suffice) for the question *Which three of these six tests should you run on* Sort?

11-9   Another test data question. A *stable* sort leaves the relative order of two equal values unchanged, while an *unstable* sort can exchange them. This isn't important when you're just sorting numbers, but it can be important if the sort key (the number you sort on) is one field of a larger record.

Suppose that you plan to sort this array:

```
type ItemTYPE = record
                    Count: integer:
                    Value: char
                end;
    SortedListTYPE = array [1..26] of ItemTYPE;
```

Write two procedures that initialize a SortedListTYPE array for testing purposes. Then, ask the question *Which of these procedures will let us know if* Sort *uses a stable or unstable sorting algorithm?*

Warmups and
Test Programs

11-10 What error messages accompany:

a)   a record that's missing its **end**?

b)   a record that uses the same field name twice?

c)   a **RECRD**?

11-11 How deeply can record definitions be nested? Does your system impose any limit?

11-12 Define an array of fifty-two records, where each record holds a number and a character. Initialize the array so that:

a)   each number field is 0 and each character field is the letter ´B´;

b)   the numbers ascend from 1 through 52, while the letters go from ´a´..´z´, ´A´..´Z´;

c)   the numbers go from 52 down to 1, while the letters go from ´a´ to ´z´ twice.

11-13 Suppose that a file contains as many as fifty lines, each of which contains a name and an age, in that order. These definitions create a structure suited for storing the names and ages:

```
type StringTYPE = packed array [1 .. MAX] of char;
     ItemTYPE = record
                    Name: StringTYPE;
                    Age: integer
                end;
     ListTYPE = array [1 .. LENGTH] of ItemTYPE;
```

Write two primitive procedures: one should read from the file to initialize the array of records, while the other should print the same information in reverse (age followed by name).

11-14 Define primitives, then a data type, suitable for representing the game of Monopoly.

11-15 Define primitives, then a data type, that could be used for finding the distance between geographic locations.

11-16 Define a data type that might be used to represent 100-digit real numbers. Don't forget about signs and exponents.

Programming
Problems

11-17 Blood pressure is given by a pair of numbers—the systolic and diastolic pressures—in millimeters of mercury. Pulse pressure, in turn, is defined as the difference between the two. Write a program that is able to:

a)   order blood pressure records by systolic, diastolic, or pulse pressures;

b)   print the *n* records with the highest pressures of a given type;

c)   print any records that appear on all three 'high-pressure' lists.

Hint: use a single sorting routine by defining a SortKey field for each record. Don't forget to number (or somehow identify) individual records.

11-18 A fraction consists of a numerator and denominator. Write a program that reads an expression that contains plus or minus signs and numerator/denominator pairs, then:

a)   orders them by denominator;

a)   adds or subtracts, as appropriate, numerators of like denominators;

a)   prints the resulting expression.

For example, the input $+\frac{2}{7}+\frac{3}{5}-\frac{1}{5}+\frac{3}{7}-\frac{1}{9}$ should yield $+\frac{2}{5}+\frac{5}{7}-\frac{1}{9}$. Try your program by adding a *Farey Series*, devised by John Farey in 1816, of reduced fractions between 0 and 1, with denominator $\leq n$. The 7 series is:

$$\frac{1}{7}+\frac{1}{6}+\frac{1}{5}+\frac{1}{4}+\frac{2}{7}+\frac{1}{3}+\frac{2}{5}+\frac{3}{7}+\frac{1}{2}+\frac{4}{7}+\frac{3}{5}+\frac{2}{3}+\frac{5}{7}+\frac{3}{4}+\frac{4}{5}+\frac{5}{6}+\frac{6}{7}$$

(An interestingly difficult problem that I will raise, but not pose, incidentally, is to write a program that produces a Farey series.)

11-19 Use the binary search method described in Chapter 10 to implement a form of reverse telephone directory—one that is ordered by telephone number, rather than by the subscriber's name. Allow these operations:

a)   Add a name, number, and address.

b)   Look up a number, and print the name and address.

c)   Delete a subscriber.

11-20 Write a program that reads twenty x, y coordinate pairs, and sorts them:

a)   In order of increasing x values.

b)   In order of decreasing y values.

c)   In order of increasing distance from 0,0.

Why might a mechanical pen plotter find this sorting useful? How difficult is it to sort the points in order of distance from an arbitrary point?

11-21 We usually think of computerized scheduling as an attempt to minimize usage of time or allocation of resources absolutely. In real life, though, such precision is impossible. Consider the problem of defining routes for garbage pickup. Two factors limit the length of each run: the garbage truck may get filled up, or it may be time to take a break. Suppose that we are given data of the following form:

```
block 1 weight 0.3 time 14
block 2 weight 0.1 time 8
         · · .
```

Each block has two figures associated with it—the weight of its garbage and the time it takes to pick it up. Naturally, blocks must be visited in order. Write a program that can be used to schedule pickups, subject to these constraints:

a)   *Garbage-constrained* routes are limited by the capacity of the truck.

b)   *Time-constrained* routes are limited by the length of a shift.

A truck is assumed to be filled (or a shift ended) on the block prior to overflow (or overtime).

Your program should read data for an arbitrary number of blocks. Then, subject to maximum garbage and time constants supplied by the user, print the blocks on each garbage-constrained or time-constrained route. If you really want to help the dispatcher, order the list of time-constrained routes according to how full the truck is, and sort the list of garbage-constrained routes according to how long they take.

11-22 Anybody who has ever gone on vacation is familiar with the problem of *bin packing*—storing objects of varying sizes into a number of containers, or bins. There are actually many ways of picturing situations that involve bin packing—filling freight cars, stocking standard lengths of pipe, scheduling television commercials, buying assorted stamps from a vending machine, and so on—but the underlying problem is always the same: we want to store fixed-size values in the smallest possible number of fixed-size bins.

Packing and unpacking bins will eventually lead to the most effective solution, but the amount of work involved rapidly makes this approach infeasible. Two rote approaches that rely on simple rules are:

a)   *First fit increasing* loads the bins starting with the smallest items first.

b)   *First fit decreasing* loads bins starting with the largest items first.

Taking for granted that loads are ordered to begin with, write a program that implements and tests each method. Assume that we have twenty or more bins of capacity 100 each, and are given the following loads:

$$
\begin{array}{cccccc}
51 & 51 & 51 & 51 & 51 & 51 \\
27 & 27 & 27 & 27 & 27 & 27 \\
26 & 26 & 26 & 26 & 26 & 26 \\
23 & 23 & 23 & 23 & 23 & 23 \\
23 & 23 & 23 & 23 & 23 & 23
\end{array}
$$

What are the contents of each bin after it is packed? Which strategy is better? Is either optimal? Can you devise a strategy for loads that arrive in random order? (It has been shown, incidentally, that first fit increasing requires no more than (17/10), plus 2, of the number of pins used in the optimum packing, while first fit decreasing requires no more than (11/9), plus 4.)

11-23   We can define the *information content* of a letter as its predictive potential for the letter that follows. Since 'q' is invariably followed by 'u,' for instance, we can say that 'q' has a high information content.

Write a program that reads the contents of a textfile, and creates a table of letter-pair frequencies. You should convert all letters to lower-case. Then, either:

a)   print the 100 most common letter pairs, in order (you'll find that keeping an array of records, where each record holds a letter pair and its count, is convenient), or

b)   print, in declining order of information content, a list of letters. For this exercise, say that a letter that can be followed by many letters has a low information content, while a letter that can be followed by few of its fellows has a high information content. (You'll find it's convenient to order 26 records, where each record holds a letter, and the number of different letters that follow.) Can you suggest a method of ordering that doesn't automatically allocate a high information content to letters that appear infrequently?

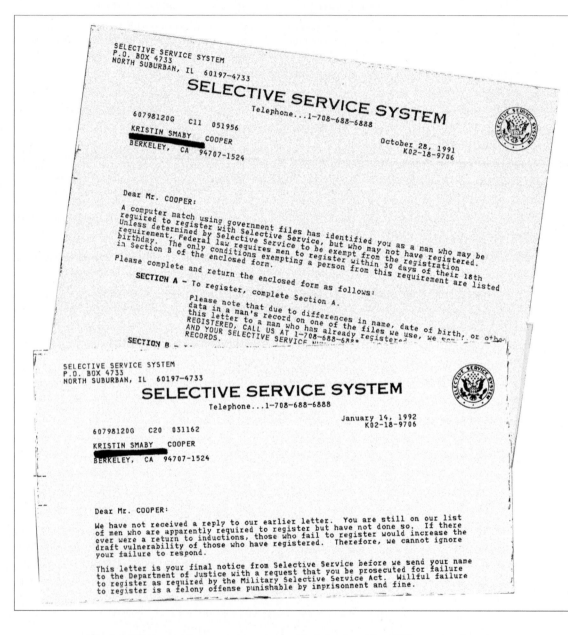

A program that controls a weapons system, on the other hand, is a different matter entirely. . . . Many computer scientists believe that there isn't any way to test such systems adequately. Above, my wife's draft notice. (p. 430)

CHAPTER

12

Software Engineering

Writing programs is usually just that—writing. But when programs become large enough to be described respectfully as *software*, we usually begin to think about programming in terms of construction. Before we get to files, pointers, and the other tools of 'big' programming, let's pause for a discussion of construction techniques.

Now, most people have an intuitive sense of the process of construction. How is a building built? Plans are prepared, a big hole is dug, a foundation laid, and so on. We can even imagine how an old building's safety might be tested. We know this sort of sequence even if we're not civil engineers because we see evidence of building construction around us all the time.

Software construction, by contrast, is invisible. Worse yet, it often runs against intuition. Software is a wonderful construction material—weightless, powerful, capable of prodigious feats. But it is a mistake not to treat code as though it were actually bricks and mortar. A software system may be weightless, but it can still cause serious damage if it collapses around your ears. Time after time, organizations that depend on software have been stunned to find just how incomplete a 'finished' software product can be.

Section 12-1 looks at programs in the small and has some suggestions for dealing with day-to-day programming issues. Section 12-2 deals with the problems of larger software systems. It describes the different stages of the software *life cycle:* analysis, specification, design, implementation, testing, and maintenance. Finally, 12-3 describes some of the formal approaches used to understand and improve program reliability.

In the Small: Defensive Programming

12-1

NOBODY INVITES ANTS TO A PICNIC, but they tend to show up anyway. So it is with program bugs. Although we try to be as careful as we can, bugs usually appear. Defensive programming prevents them from ruining the day.

By now, you should have a fairly good understanding of how to diagnose and repair compile-time bugs. They are, after all, served up to you on a silver platter: the compiler burps and presents you with its diagnosis. On occasion the diagnosis is wrong, but debugging doesn't require much detective work.

Not so with runtime (the program crashes) and semantic (it comes up with the wrong answer) errors. Not only do we often not know what or where the bugs are: it often isn't apparent that there even *are* any. Debugging turns into testing, and our work begins.

Testing vs. Debugging

Now, I've probably never explained carefully enough the difference between debugging and testing:

> *Debugging* is what *you* do before you consider a program completed. *Testing* is what a program user does as she makes your program crash.

The programmer, faced with a particularly recalcitrant program, tends to think only of getting it to compile—if it works for a particular set of data, so much the better. This is debugging. But someone who must use (or grade) your program applies stiffer criteria. It doesn't matter that the program compiles, since that's a bare-minimum expectation. Nor is the user concerned with its operation under ideal conditions. Instead, she tries to find your program's limitations—to make it produce wrong results or crash. *That's* testing.

Thus, debugging tries to get rid of known bugs, while testing is an attempt to show that more bugs still exist. It's an unfortunate fact that both methods have severe limitations. The effectiveness of debugging depends largely on the diligence and experience of the programmer.

limits of testing

> Testing can show the *presence* of bugs but can't guarantee their *absence*.

For instance, let's consider the problem of testing a random number generator that returns a real value between 0 and 1. Suppose we decide that we can check the function by seeing if its result, on average, is 0.5. Ten thousand calls are easy to arrange.

a naive test

```
Sum := 0.0;
for Count := 1 to 10000 do begin
    Sum := Sum + Random        {Assume that Random is a function.}
end;
writeln (Sum / 10000.0);
```

4.9809564916E−01

The answer is just a hair below our expectation. But just how clever have we been? For all we know, the random function has produced many 0.4's, and just enough 0.9's to raise the average nearer to 0.5 (or even thousands of 0.5's!).

problems with testing

How about inspecting the actual sequence of values, then? Well, although we might write a driver that prints the first ten or twenty numbers in the pseudo-random sequence it produces, such a small sample won't do us too much good. If we call the function repeatedly:

```
for Count := 1 to 10000 do begin
    writeln (Random)
end;
```

we're no better off. Nobody can inspect a list of ten thousand umpteen-digit real numbers and declare that they're randomly distributed.

Let's construct a test that combines our earlier tries. Suppose we modify the function call to produce a number in some reasonable integer range, say 1 through 10, then use an array to keep track of many calls.

random number generator test program

```
program TestRand (input, output);
    {Checks the distribution of the Random function's output.}

const NUMBERofTrials = 10000;

type Data = array [1..10] of integer;

var Counter, Temp: integer;
    TestBed: Data;

function Random : real;
    {Returns a real in the range 0.0 .. 0.999...}
    ⋰.          {Its code details aren't important.}

begin
    for Counter := 1 to 10 do begin
        TestBed [Counter] := 0
    end;    {The output counter is initialized.}
    for Counter := 1 to NUMBERofTrials do begin
        Temp := trunc (1 + (Random * 10)) ;   {i.e. 1 .. 10}
        TestBed [Temp] := TestBed [Temp] + 1
    end;    {We've counted appearances of 10,000 numbers.}
    writeln ('Random test distribution:');
    for Counter := 1 to 10 do begin
        write (Counter : 3);
        write ('''s')
    end;    {The heading is printed.}
    writeln;
    for Counter := 1 to 10 do begin
        write (TestBed [Counter] : 5)
    end;    {The counts are printed.}
    writeln
end. {TestRand}
```

```
Random test distribution:
  1's   2's   3's   4's   5's   6's   7's   8's   9's  10's
  952   987   941   980  1006  1036  1021  1043  1038   996
```

At this point can we safely say that Random doesn't contain any bugs? Well, not quite. Although a test has shown that none of the bugs we anticipated is present, it would be wishful thinking to hope that all bugs are absent. For instance, suppose that Random's output simply yielded a sequence close to 1, 2, 3...10 repeatedly. Our test shows a reasonable distribution of values, but says nothing about their predictability. Nevertheless, step by step, we're starting to build confidence in Random.

Stub Programming

As programs get more complicated, testing and debugging alone may not be enough to produce reliable code. Instead, we have to write programs in a manner that will help insure that errors are caught or avoided. *Stub* programming is a method that allows for error and improvement.

> A stub program is a stripped-down, skeleton version of a final program. It doesn't implement details of the algorithm or fulfill all the job requirements. However, it does contain rough versions of all subprograms and their parameter lists. Furthermore, it can be compiled and run.

A stub program helps demonstrate that a program's structure is plausible. Its procedures and functions are unsophisticated versions of their final forms, but they allow limited use of the *entire* program. For example, if we were writing a payroll program, we might begin by developing a stub program that handles a fixed group of workers who each put in 50 hours per week, receive the same rate of pay, and declare the same number of dependents. Another stub programming trick calls for generous use of comment brackets.

commenting out code

```
GetCommand (Command);
case Command of
    'A': Add;
    'D': Delete;
  { 'F': Find;
    'S': Skip;
    'T': Translate;
    'V': Verify   }
end;
```

We'd like to have our high-level procedures ready to call lower-level code, even if the more detailed subprograms haven't even been written in the abbreviated form suggested above. 'Commenting out' segments of a **case** statement does the job: The comment brackets can be moved, call by call, as the underlying procedures are actually written. In this segment, 'F', 'S', 'T', and 'V' will be written later.

> Stub programs let systems be debugged and tested *as they are built.*

Major program connections are tested first, which means that major bugs and shortcomings are detected early in the game. Furthermore, testing and debugging are distributed throughout the entire writing process. You're not forced to do all your program fixing just before the program is scheduled to be completed (which is invariably when the computer is least available). Even if a program isn't completely finished by the due date it's a preliminary *working* version—not just a useless mess of code.

How can a program be tested or debugged before it's in operating shape? The dummy modules of stub programs can support rough runs on the computer. The proposed program can also be subjected to the intense scrutiny of your programming team—usually yourself and anybody else you can collar for ten minutes—in a *walkthrough*, or guided tour, of the partially completed program. It's an explanation *and defense* of the program's algorithm and implementation. I'm sure you've found that working on a program tends to create a mind set in the programmer that renders obvious mistakes invisible. Merely explaining a program aloud can give you a totally new view of it.

walkthroughs

Effective User Interfaces

No matter how much effort you've put into a program, it has been in vain if the user can't figure out how it works. A program's *user interface* is its connection to the human; if it fails, the program has failed too. Here are some tips on how to make user interfaces that work.

Tell the user how to quit. With a dozen chapters behind you, you may have forgotten just how petrified a novice can be. She might be afraid to type anything at all, lest something break. Once your program starts, make sure that the user can figure out how to get out.

Allow plausible variations. It may seem obvious to you that **X** means quit: after all, it sounds like 'exit.' But users might expect **Q** to 'quit'—or even **q**. Unless they're being used for something else, make sure that variations are processed correctly when they make sense, even if they haven't been advertised as synonyms.

Don't leave the user at a loss for the next step. There's nothing worse than a program that starts up with a blank screen. No matter how simple a program's job is, the user might not make a connection between the program's name and what it's supposed to do.

Show as you tell—describe input as you ask for it. The classic example is a prompt for the date. `Enter today's date` will garner ten different variations, from **2-30-92** to **Wensday** (yes, Wensday) **Febuary** (yes, Febuary) **30**. Adding an actual sample to the prompt tells the user what you want. A simple prompt like `Enter today's date (MM/DD/YY)` won't prevent requests for the thirtieth of February, but it helps guide the user along the path you want her to follow. The proper response to `Proceed(Y/N)?` is hard to mistake.

a few tips for effective user interfaces

Confirm important facts. If it's worth having, it's worth giving the user the chance to confirm or change what she's added. Here, the classic example is a request for a password the user can set. Usually, a program won't echo the characters the user types, so that nobody can snoop over her shoulder. But if she inadvertently makes a typing mistake, she won't know her own password! The solution: ask for it twice, and only accept it if the versions match.

Show a default—and make it sensible if it's irrevocable. The prompt `Proceed(Y/N) Y` implies that hitting `Enter` or `Return` gets you the 'Y' alternative—it's there already. This can be a convenient shortcut when the next action is showing the next page of instructions. But it can lead to disaster if the next step is to remove all files! In general, make the obvious and likely easy and the less obvious and less likely a bit harder.

Let the user back out. The implications of a choice aren't always obvious. I'm sure that you've had the experience of making changes, then wishing you had a magical way to undo them, and put things back the way they were before! A `Cancel` button or `Escape` key is a good way to let changes be undone.

Obey the Law of Least Astonishment. Research hasn't been very successful in coming up with surefire, laboratory-tested secrets for good user interfaces. Instead, use keys or commands that are obvious when available (arrow keys for movement), mnemonic when possible (**Q** for quit), and, at the very least, do not defy credulity (the `Tab` key for fast horizontal movement). Consistency is important: there's no sense in knowingly contravening common practices. For example, DOS programs typically use `Alt` keys, rather than `Ctrl` or `Shift` keys for commands. Are they any more 'right'? Of course not. But they do meet users' expectations, so we might as well use them.

In the Large: the Life Cycle

12-2

SOFTWARE ENGINEERING IS THE SCIENCE of developing *software systems*—programs, large and small, that will be used to solve real problems. Like traditional engineering endeavors, the study of software engineering is motivated by a desire to avoid repeating mistakes—mistakes that were only belatedly seen to involve engineering at all. The opening paragraphs of a seminal text on software engineering (written not two decades ago) describe the situation:

> No scene from prehistory is quite so vivid as that of the mortal struggles of great beasts in the tar pits. In the mind's eye one sees dinosaurs, mammoths, and sabertoothed tigers struggling against the grip of the tar. The fiercer the struggle, the more entangling the tar, and no beast is so strong or so skillful but that he ultimately sinks.

the tar pit

> Large-system programming has over the past decade been such a tar pit, and many great and powerful beasts have thrashed violently in it. Most have emerged with running systems—few have met goals, schedules, budgets. Large and small, massive or wiry, team after team has become entangled in the tar. No one thing seems to cause the difficulty—any particular paw can be pulled away. But the accumulation of simultaneous and interacting factors brings slower and slower motion. Everyone seems to have been surprised by the stickiness of the problem, and it is hard to discern the nature of it. But we must try to understand it if we are to solve it.*

---

* Frederick P. Brooks, Jr., *The Mythical Man-Month*, Addison-Wesley Publishing Co., 1975.

Dozens of software systems have fallen into the tar pit Brooks describes. Sometimes the development effort is entirely unsuccessful; a satisfactory system isn't constructed. Other systems may be accepted by the end user, but be late, over budget, poorly suited to the intended application, or hamstrung by inefficient use of system resources. In either case, the programmer and user are equally dissatisfied with the end result.

Why wasn't the software problem immediately obvious? Well, until the mid-1960's, the cost of hardware greatly outweighed the cost of software, and the capacity of hardware was easily overwhelmed by the capability of software. But in the late '60's, a series of studies pointed up two unexpected facts:

— *Software was hard and expensive to produce.* People were shocked to find that the average professional programmer managed to produce, on average, only *twelve* debugged lines of code *per day*!

— *The cost of producing software was only the tip of the iceberg.* Even more astonishing was the discovery that some eighty percent of the cost of software was incurred after it was placed in service.

The concept of a *software life cycle* developed in response to these findings. We can pick out distinct phases in the life of every program:

— *Analysis* of the problem.

— *Specification* of the software's abilities.

stages in the life cycle   — *Design* of the software.

— *Implementation* or coding.

— *Testing* of the completed system.

— *Maintenance* and evolution of the system.

We'll look at each of these stages in turn. But first, I'll digress briefly to caution against a too literal reading of their descriptions.

Two Models: Waterfall and Spiral

The software life cycle I just laid out is often described as the *waterfall* model of program development. Water flows only downhill; in the waterfall model, software proceeds only forward from step to step.

As you may be able to tell, notions about the predictability of the software life cycle were strongly influenced by everyday perceptions about more ordinary kinds of construction. If plans for buildings are completed before construction starts, why shouldn't plans for software be completed as well?

theory meets practice   Unfortunately, while the waterfall model accurately describes many facts about software at various points in its lifetime, it's a misleading tool for planned software development. In practice, reassessment and revision, especially in the early stages, are almost invariably required. In other words: *Stop the life cycle, I want to get off.*

An alternative to the waterfall model, called the *spiral* model, is often used to guide project work. In a phrase, the spiral model is based on the idea that you get smarter as you go along. Planning is *never* sufficient, because you gain the knowledge needed for effective planning only through experience.

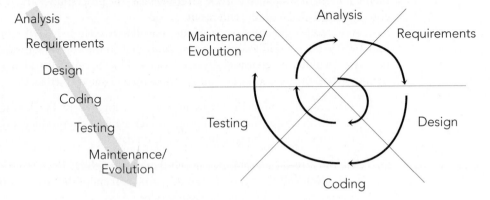

The waterfall on the left allows just one try. The spiral on the right implies that at least two trips through the entire process will be required.

Let's take a look at the traditional life cycle approach. Afterward, I'll return for a few critical comments on its shortcomings and on the limits of software engineering in general.

Analysis

Analysis of the problem is probably the most difficult step in the software life cycle. The real-life problems faced by potential computer users are at a far remove from the neatly prepared exercises presented in computer science textbooks. This is not because real-life problems are any more difficult; indeed, the reverse is quite often the case. Instead, it is because customers and programmers often speak very different languages. As a result, simple problems can be misunderstood or difficult ones understated.

Analysis tries to answer the question 'What should the software do?' in a manner that will be meaningful to the software designer. Simply saying that the software should 'keep our books,' or 'monitor our test equipment,' or 'give sample Pascal examinations' doesn't give much direction. Instead, the analyst must work with the end user to answer many questions about the system. The system is pictured both as it is now and as it may come to be:

— What will the system's input be? What output should the system produce?

— Will these requirements change? How seriously? How often?

— What sort of people will use the system? Can they be specially trained?

questions for analysis

— Will there be errors in input? In stored data? How should errors be fixed?

— What kind of equipment is available? What can be obtained?

— How fast should the system work? How reliable does it have to be?

— Will the system grow? In what directions?

software prototypes

One current area of computer science research that's intended to help with the problems of analysis is *rapid software prototyping*. The idea of building prototypes, or test models, is common to many engineering disciplines. A prototype is a scaled-down model that can be examined and tested before any commitment is made to a final design. Prototyping is especially appropriate for software systems, because it helps the user and designer communicate their understanding of what problems are and how they can be solved.

Software prototyping relies on the idea that many software components—routines for input, output, data sorting—are more or less independent of the systems they're found in. These building blocks can be joined, with a minimum of new code, to rough out a prototype of the end-user's system. This working model can be used to help give the user an idea of a computer's capabilities, as well as to give the software analyst a feel for the users' needs.

Requirements Specification

The specification of a software system's requirements is a formal statement of its capabilities, capacities, and constraints. Whereas analysis is meant to determine in general terms what the proposed system is supposed to do, the requirements specification states in detail what the finished system *will* do.

The requirements specification will be referred to throughout the entire software development process. It can act as the contract between programmer and end user, and it is often the only point of contact between the two groups. If a feature or requirement isn't specified in the requirement, it's not liable to show up in the final product. The requirements specification will also generally be the standard against which the final system is tested.

Specification of software requirements is a more difficult task than it might appear to be at first glance. Consider the variety of areas that a specification has to define:

— It must state the specific abilities of the system—the commands that will be available to the user. These are the system's *functional requirements.*

details of the specification

— It must name the assumptions that will be made about the system's input, users, response time, data—its operating environment.

— It must define the system's limitations—how many users there will be, how much data must be handled, etc.

— It must describe any special hardware requirements or any restrictions imposed by hardware limitations.

— It must specify possible modifications to the system that have to be allowed for in the system's design.

— It should describe the nature and extent of documentation that's supposed to accompany the system. A preliminary users' manual may be required, too.

The functional specification is the most visible part of a requirements document. In small systems, stating functional requirements is a pretty straightforward task. A list of allowed commands may be all that is needed. In more complex systems, though, a list of commands may not be enough—we'll need a better mechanism for describing the big picture.

A variety of schemes have been developed to help in stating specifications. Most of them are elaborate charting systems that try to fix the action of a program on paper. In general, specification systems are object-oriented. They describe a program in terms of its data—how they are stored and transferred, and what can be done with them in the process.

Once we begin to talk about data, programs can't be far away. Before we begin to code, though, it's a good idea to spend some time on design.

Design

Analysis and specification help determine *what* should be done. Design, in contrast, specifies *how* it should be done. The result of the design phase is what might be called a *software blueprint* that can be implemented with a minimum of difficulty.

software blueprint

Although it is inconceivable that one would embark on the construction of a building without a detailed plan of action in hand, software projects used to be undertaken routinely without the barest hint of advance planning. But how do we go about designing software?

There has been a continuing series of answers to this question. At first, *high-level languages*, like FORTRAN and its many successors (including Pascal) seemed to be the answer. These languages are high-level in comparison to assembly language, which is to say that they are at least somewhat like English. They allowed a departure from the machine-specific names of assembly language to the higher ground of rudimentary abstraction.

high-level languages

One feature of the first high-level languages that seemed essential was called the **goto**. It was similar to *jumps* of assembly language. But where jumps leapt here and there in computer memory, **goto**s went to different lines of a program. What a convenience! Well, at least for a little while. As great as the **goto** was for writing code, the flow of control from statement to statement was so snarled that programs were likened to spaghetti.

The second set of answers is *structured programming* and its companion, *stepwise refinement*. If high-level languages tried to make programs easier to write, structured programming aimed at making them easier to read.

structured programming

Structured programming introduced ideas that are taken for granted these days: statements with just one entry and one exit point, using pseudocode for design (rather than the flowcharts made of boxes and arrows that were generally used to outline FORTRAN programs), and relying on functions and procedures to signify, and to help simplify, the actions of the finished product. Once again, the programmer's ability to abstract increased.

But in a way, as solutions become more elegant, the problems they solve become less relevant. The very success of structured programming made the problems it solved seem too simple, hardly knotty at all. Being able to read programs was no longer the answer, because the problem had changed to *how can we avoid reading programs entirely*, which is to say, *how can we reuse code*?

code reuse

Now, compared to the hardware side of computer design, the development of software is incredibly tedious and primitive. As far as possible, computers are built from prepared components. My PC consists, more or less, of a half-dozen prefabricated circuit boards that I bought through a catalog, then snapped together. The boards, in turn, are built almost entirely from integrated circuit chips (IC's) that were probably picked out of catalogs by the board manufacturers. Even the IC's themselves were probably largely made using standard designs pulled from reference books.

Although the software equivalents of circuit boards and IC's do not exist, the idea of preparing software in a way that lets it be reused is immensely attractive. Naturally, there are problems. After the first few obvious pages (of sorting and searching routines, for example) what should be in the catalog? How will the pieces fit together? Must improved versions retain all the features of the code they replace? And, most important, just what will the code actually be made of?

Libraries of subprograms were one proposal. Although their syntax varies from one language to another, the basic idea is to separate the way code is used from the way it's implemented: subprogram headings are separated from subprogram bodies. Libraries are very effective at hiding details (such as how graphics boards work) that we really don't want to know about.

object-oriented programming

But libraries deal almost exclusively with implementing *algorithms* in isolation from *data*. Object-oriented languages merge the two: an object is a data type that specifies both data and the procedures and functions that manipulate it. Such languages often come with collections of predefined objects; their goal is to get the programmer up and running with as little effort as possible.

This is a particularly exciting time to be programming because the use of objects is not very well developed. Nobody really knows the best way to let programmers pick and choose from libraries of objects. A few years down the pike, though, tools that haven't even been developed yet will be taken for granted—perhaps some of them will be yours.

As I've pointed out, abstraction is the key idea behind all of the design schemes. We want to separate design from implementation—*what?* from *how?* Thus, regardless of the system used to design and specify code, the design phase has two goals. First, any ambiguities located in the requirements specification should be found and clarified. Second, a detailed guide should be prepared for the next step—coding.

Coding

For most of the history of computing, coding the main program has been thought of as the programmer's main activity. Surprisingly, surveys consistently show that program coding occupies only about 20% of the time and effort involved in producing software systems. Nevertheless, carefully made specifications and designs are all for naught if they are not well-implemented.

The software engineer looks at the coding phase of programming in several different ways. First, there's the code. What language, or languages, should be used? What should units, or subprogram libraries, contain? How long should subprograms be? What rules should be followed for defining identifiers? How should the code be laid out? How efficient must it be? How detailed should comments be? Are any programming tricks forbidden?

Next, there's the programming staff. How can work be divided? What are the responsibilities of individual coders? How closely should programmers be supervised? How should proposals for coding be reviewed? How much communication should there be between programmers, and how can it be arranged? How can we estimate the difficulty of specific program segments?

Finally, there are the methods used to produce the code. What electronic tools are there for coding support? How are different versions of programs maintained? How should debugging or testing code be built into the software? Will different hardware or software *programming environments* have any effect on programmer productivity?

Of all the phases of software development, coding is probably the least formalized. One reason is that the management of coding efforts has turned out to differ from other kinds of management in unexpected ways. A particularly instructive example comes from attempts to apply general notions of manpower to coding. Now, in most sorts of organized activity—stenography, or claims processing, or chopping wood—work accomplished grows in rough proportion to the amount of effort expended. As a consequence, doubling effort doubles results—or halves completion time, more or less.

the mythical man-month

The unanticipated results of applying this rule to programming gave Brooks the title of his book: *The Mythical Man-Month*. He found that most project managers treated software production just like other sorts of production. When a project fell behind schedule, they would add additional programmers. To their astonishment, they often found that adding help made matters worse! Extra programmers only made the project fall further behind schedule. Brooks characterized this experience rather cynically in Brooks' Law: *Adding manpower to a late software project makes it later*.

On close inspection we can recognize the two characteristics of software production that give the law its grain of truth. First, new staff must be trained. Even if they are expert programmers, the current project must be explained; they have to be brought up to speed in the project's goals, rules, coding strategies, etc. Second, they must communicate as they work, because a program's units can never be made entirely independent of each other. A group of n people can meet in $n!/2(n-2)!$ different pairs, which means that doubling a group from three programmers to six increases the number of two-person meetings they can hold by a factor of *five*.

Testing

The test phase of the software life cycle can involve as much time and effort as the coding phase. No matter how carefully a program is planned and coded, it will still contain bugs and imperfections. In addition, large software systems may not even be fully assembled until the test phase begins. A ship's maiden voyage is traditionally a shakedown cruise; a program's first run marks the start of the test period.

module testing

The test phase has several goals. Most obviously, we want to find bugs introduced during the coding process. The attempt to find this sort of bug relies on methodical testing of individual program modules. This is usually known as *module testing*. Standard Pascal's successors have made module testing much easier by permitting the *separate compilation* of distinct units.

Next, modules are put together to form systems or subsystems. This is sometimes called *integration testing*, because we are integrating the activity of different modules. The bugs found during integration testing are generally due to design errors, which typically involve the interface between separate modules. Code may have been implemented correctly, but programmers may have labored under false impressions of the input their particular modules could expect, or the output they were supposed to produce. If problems found in integration testing involve basic data storage methods, they can be very serious and involve a considerable amount of code rewriting.

integration testing

In the final testing step, the completed system is presented to its end users for *acceptance testing*. Well-managed software systems usually work their way into this phase slowly by *alpha* and *beta* site testing. The system is distributed to a limited number of sites for feedback and refinement before it is presented for final validation and acceptance. Unfortunately, problems that come up in acceptance testing sometimes date back to the original analysis and specifications phases. The program does what is called for in the design, but the design itself may be incomplete or incorrect from the end user's point of view.

acceptance testing

Is it possible to write software so well that it doesn't require testing? Although this was a fond hope for a number of years, the idea that programs could be proved to work as they were being written is fading fast. We'll look further at the issue of formal program *correctness* later in this chapter.

Maintenance and Evolution

Software may outlive its usefulness, but it never wears out. Once an individual or organization has put effort into learning (or adapting to) a particular software system, there is a great tendency to prefer modification of existing software over the acquisition of new software. Even armed with this understanding, it will probably come as a great surprise to find that maintenance and modification of a program can cost two to four times as much as its original coding—or up to 80% of the costs contained in the entire software life cycle.

There are a number of motivations for modifying software once it is presumed to be complete. A first category involves *correction*. Although the rate at which bugs are found declines drastically, they usually appear throughout a software system's lifetime. Occasionally, they will fall into the 'bug or feature?' column, especially when a user employs a poorly documented or unintended command.

correction

A second motivation for modification is the desire to improve the system's usefulness—*perfective* changes. Surprisingly, a successful system may require the most modifications, since it may be widely adopted in environments other than the one it was originally intended for. The addition of new features, or fine-tuning and improvement (perhaps by using new algorithms) of existing features are typical of this kind of modification and evolution.

perfection

A third category of modifications is sometimes called *adaptive* changes. These are mandated by changes in the system's operating environment. They may be caused by improvements in the hardware system or by changes in the external software the system relies on (for instance, a change in the computer's operating system).

adaptation

The understanding that maintenance accounts for such a large portion of software costs has been one of the prime motivating factors in the development of software engineering. Well-understood systems—say, automobiles—are designed with maintenance in mind. As a result, their construction is fairly modular, and points that need to be checked regularly are easily accessible.* Software is only recently developing this kind of self-awareness. Embedded debugging tools are a perfect example of built-in aids for program maintenance.

Criticism of the Life Cycle

For many years the costs associated with the software life cycle, and the necessity of planning in its terms, were part of the conventional wisdom of computer science. As you've seen, the basic premise is that if planning is good, then more planning is better—and enough planning might prevent all software bugs and flaws.

In practice, though, no amount of planning and preparation was ever enough. To begin with, software is far more complex than had been believed. When programs were huge hunks of code, it made sense to think that making programs more modular—splitting them into small sections—would make them easier to deal with. But modularity has problems all its own. More pieces mean more connections between pieces, and more chances for subtle and unanticipated interaction between components.

the more users know, the more they want

User requirements also refused to submit to the demands of planners. Obviously, preparatory design and analysis helps define the responsibilities and capabilities of software. But good analysis educates the system's potential users as well as its designers. It's an ironic observation, but as users become more aware of what is possible, their desires increase, too.

Formal specifications—software blueprints—worked against themselves as well. Certainly it makes sense to agree on a program's central data types and algorithms before sending coding teams off to work on particular slices. In theory, a strong central plan is meant to provide the skeleton that semi-independent programming teams will flesh out. But in practice, the framework was often too rigid. Rather than being a force for improvement, change became the enemy. Programmers drowned in the paperwork that was required to modify the core system.

too much planning can hurt results

Even successful planning methods could be used in a way that led to trouble. Take software prototyping: building small-scale test programs to firm up system requirements and try out approaches for satisfying them. A quick and dirty prototype does, indeed, provide an excellent means for teaching users what systems can do and helping programmers understand what users want. But when a prototype is successful, there's an overwhelming temptation to improve and upgrade it into a final product. Unfortunately, 'quick' really does mean 'dirty.' Robust software must be built that way from the beginning. To put it another way, quality can't go in after the name goes on!

In many ways, what we call 'software engineering' is not really engineering at all. Rather than engineering principles (that is, a well-organized and

---

* There are notable exceptions. Consider, for example, the Chevy Monza, which required that the engine be partly removed in order to change the spark plugs!

well-understood set of underlying rules) we have *methodologies*—a collection of programming techniques that usually work. To paraphrase Chamfort's comment on philosophy (and eighteenth century medicine), we can offer a great many drugs and a few very good remedies, but almost no cures.

If we look at our methods, it's easy to see just how deep our ignorance runs. We do not really know a 'best' size for modules; we know only that big modules are confusing. We don't have any idea how long software will last; we know only that it lasts longer than it's supposed to. We don't understand the best way to make changes or improvements in software; we know only that it's an awfully good idea to keep records that are detailed enough to let improvements be undone.

As Fred Brooks himself points out (recall that I cited his *Mythical Man-Month* at the beginning of this chapter), the very fact that his twenty-year-old book continues to be relevant is rather depressing. Yes, problems are solved, but they tend to be the surface problems. We get better at avoiding superficial programming errors, but progress in dealing with the inherent complexity of software systems is slow.

Perhaps the best thing to do is to take the advice I've given in the last few pages to heart. In a sense, *all* programming is itself a vast software project. The languages that we program in and the schemes we use to design and test our programs are, in this view, prototypes. Some may be more or less successful, but it is unrealistic to imagine that we're putting together systems that wouldn't be better off for being tossed out and rewritten from scratch at least once every decade.

How to Schedule Successfully

A manager asked a programmer how long it would take him to finish the program on which he was working.

'I will be finished tomorrow,' the programmer promptly replied.

'I think that you are being unrealistic,' said the manager. 'Truthfully, how long will it take?'

The programmer thought for a moment. 'I have some features that I wish to add. This will take at least two weeks,' he finally said.

'Even that is too much to expect,' insisted the manager. 'I will be satisfied if you simply tell me when the program is complete.'

The programmer agreed to this.

Several years later, the manager retired. On the way to his retirement lunch, he discovered the programmer asleep at his terminal. He had been programming all night.

From *The Tao of Programming*, by Geoffrey James, © 1987, InfoBooks, Santa Monica, Ca. 90406

Program Correctness*

12-3

THE STUDY OF PROGRAMMING HAS ALWAYS OCCUPIED an uneasy boundary between science and art. Somehow, it seems obvious that programming is a scientific pursuit. But although we can easily make sage observations about

---

* This section is entirely optional.

the characteristics of programs, we can seldom enunciate any underlying principles that will help us generate new ones. Where programming is concerned, computer science has had about as much relation to science as computer art has borne to art!

Nevertheless, it is only natural that, as scientists, we continue the search for a more formal basis of programming. A particularly interesting area of research is involved with attempting to define a language and method for reasoning about program *correctness*. This section introduces the notion of a program *proof* and shows how mathematical modes of thinking have some use, but also some shortcomings, when they're applied to writing programs.

What is Correctness?

How do we show that a program works? A few weeks ago we might have given the obvious reply—*run it*. By now, though, we've probably learned to be a bit more cautious. We understand that, at best, running a program (and checking its results) shows that it works for a particular set of data. Making up a broader range of test data gives us a stronger feeling that the program will always work, but even testing is usually limited to ferreting out bugs whose symptoms we can imagine in advance.

Let's look at some of the methods used to gain assurance about the correctness, or reliability, of programs. Now, it's tempting to think that we can simply prove that any program will always work, just as we might prove that a mathematical theorem is correct. However, we'll find that confidence in the correctness of programs is much like confidence in the empirical correctness of engineering methods, rather than the more abstract notions of correctness in mathematics.

What do I mean when I talk about developing confidence? Well, confidence lets us ride in airplanes and cross bridges. We can't prove that a bridge won't ever fall down once it's in place, but we can feel certain enough about it to trust the bridge with our lives. A combination of tests join to give us this confidence. The bridge may follow the same design as other structures. We can build models for aerodynamic testing in a wind tunnel and employ mathematical formulas for the design of structural members.

what is confidence?

We may even go so far as to stress randomly selected beams, cables, and the like to the point of destruction, in order to establish minimum-strength levels. Then, even before we build, we can deliberately over-engineer, by intentionally overestimating the demands that will be placed on the structure.

Program tests are merged in the same manner to give us confidence in code. Some features are trusted because they've worked in similar programs, while others are allowed because the programmer and her peers believe that they will work. Parts of a program may have to undergo exhaustive testing by being run on carefully gathered real data, while for others, artificially manufactured data is good enough. Finally, some portions of the code may be so crucial that we have to try to prove, on paper, that they will always work.

> Unfortunately, overengineering software is next to impossible. Instead of overbuilding, we're forced to 'under-rely'—to intentionally restrict the responsibility of any program.

Let's consider some of the less formal methods before we see what a program proof looks like. The first sort of testing most programs undergo can be called *bench testing*. The programmer explains her work to another programmer, or small group of programmers, in a structured walkthrough, or walking tour, of the code. This kind of examination is useful for two reasons. First, programmers less intimately involved with actual coding may spot conceptual errors that have escaped previous notice. Second, the discussion can lead to useful suggestions for tests that can be made at later stages of production.

bench testing

Static analysis of the program is a step that's usually reserved for very large systems. Static analyzers are programs that examine the source code (e.g. the Pascal version) of a program without actually running it. They're able to spot certain kinds of errors that aren't always found by the compiler. One kind of error is the use of uninitialized variables in assignments or as arguments to value parameters. A more interesting error that can be found through static analysis is the existence of unreachable code segments that won't ever be run, no matter what the program input is.

static analysis

Trace tools give us a window into program execution as the program runs. For instance, a trace tool might keep track of changes in the value of one or more variables. I'm sure that by now you've employed the debugger's watch window for just that purpose. More sophisticated trace tools are called *execution profilers*. They're able to report on almost any kind of program activity: how often procedures are called, how long a section of code takes to execute, which routines call which routines, and so on.

trace tools

Finally, *data testing* is a method we should be quite familiar with. Builders of large systems often create *data generators*—programs that automatically produce data that have a set of characteristics specified by the programmer. The output of a data generator might be sophisticated data intended to make a program follow every possible execution path, or it might simply be a long, randomly produced sequence of five-letter words. With huge amounts of test input available, it's no surprise to find programmers also creating automated tools for checking raw program output as well.

The methods I've mentioned here give only a rough overview of the kinds of tests that can be performed. To give you an idea of what a fertile field program testing is, consider a totally unexpected variation called *mutation testing*. This approach uses a set of test data that is as exhaustive as possible and has known results. Next, programs are systematically mutated by having small errors introduced: a plus sign might be changed to a minus sign, or a constant might be increased by 1. The mutated program is then run on the original test data. If it works (i.e. it has the same results as the original program), we can conclude either that there is something very wrong with our original program or that our test data is too weak to be useful. What an idea!

mutation testing

It's easy to imagine that a large program might require *all* of the different testing approaches described here to give us confidence that the program will really work. Even then, though, our faith in the program depends largely on its prospective application. We have greater faith in less important programs because we don't pay a high price for their failure. An interrupted video game may be annoying, but the manufacturer's desire to bring it to market will probably outweigh concern about some minor residual bugs. It's easy enough to refund the user's quarter if she's unlucky enough to find the bug the hard way.

limits on confidence

A program that controls a weapons system, on the other hand, is a different matter entirely. The recognition that no one test method is sufficient to guarantee that a program is correct and error-free is a cause for alarm, particularly when there is no way to undo a mistake. Many computer scientists believe that there isn't *any* way to test such systems adequately.

Program Proofs

In recognition of the limits of program testing, computer scientists have tried to develop other methods of gaining confidence in programs.

> A *program proof* is a paper analysis of a program that attempts to verify formally that the program will always produce a correct result.

In one sense, a program proof *is* like a mathematical proof. A mathematical proof tries to justify the correctness of a mathematical statement—a theorem. A program proof tries to give us the same sort of assurance about a sequence of code statements—a program.

However, there is also an important difference between the two kinds of proofs. A mathematical proof tries to show that following a certain sequence of steps will result in an irrefutable conclusion. A program proof, in contrast, tries to show that the conclusion reached by following a series of steps will always be correct. The mathematical sort of proof works well when we want to show that, in principle, an algorithm will work. However, proving an actual implementation—a completed program—requires a different sort of tack.

assertions

> The proof of a program is based on a series of *assertions* about the values of program variables and data.

An assertion is a statement that we expect to be true. Typically, we'll use boolean-valued expressions (like a<>b) to make assertions.

In general, we'll find that assertions come in pairs—there's an assertion right before a program action, then one immediately following it. We can think of the opening assertions as giving *preconditions*, while the closing assertions state *postconditions*. If you note that one statement's postcondition can be the next statement's precondition, you can begin to picture how program proofs are established. First, we make assertions about the effect of each statement:

preconditions,
postconditions

{assertion 1}	Statement1;	{assertion 2}
{assertion 2}	Statement2;	{assertion 3}
{assertion 3}	Statement3;	{assertion 4}

Then, by applying simple rules of logic, we can remove intermediate assertions:

{precondition}   Statement1;
                  Statement2;
                  Statement3;   {postcondition}

In practice, we usually work in the opposite manner, by starting with the outlying assertions and attempting to develop assertions for parts of the program, then parts of those parts, etc.

Now, it's pretty easy to see how to make some kinds of assertions. Suppose that we want to divide A by B and save the result in C. The closing assertion is a check on the operation—our assertion that the answer is correct is A=B*C. But if we want to be assured that we will survive the division we need an opening assertion as well—that B isn't 0. The sequence of assertions (in comment brackets) is:

verifying sequences

```
{ B<>0 }
C := A/B;
{ A=B*C }
```

verifying loops

Looping statements are more interesting because assertions before and after the loop aren't sufficient to make a proof. Why not? Well, if the assertions are to actually prove anything, they must also establish that we arrive at the loop's end—that the loop isn't infinite!

variant and invariant assertions

> A loop's *invariant* assertion is a statement about the loop that is true both before and after each iteration of the loop. Its companion is a *variant* assertion whose truth will change between the loop's initial and final iterations. This is sometimes called the loop's *bound function*.

These two assertions serve complementary purposes in a loop proof. The invariant assertion makes a statement about the correctness of the loop's action, which is why it must always be true. The truth of the variant assertion, in contrast, is changed by the loop's action. It helps assure us that the loop will eventually be terminated, which is why it's also known as a bound function. The invariant assertion helps make sure that the loop doesn't do the *wrong* thing, while the variant assertion ensures that it does do the *right* thing.

We've relied on these ideas many times already, but in a reversed form. Formal loop proofs focus on the loop invariant, whereas we have keyed on the loop's bound condition. I've done things this way because it's more intuitive—we can do some constructive reasoning about loop design without having to go the whole nine yards. However, both approaches ultimately make the same point about the loop's contents.

problem: proving division by subtraction

For instance, suppose that we want to do integer division by repeated subtraction. The segment below implements an algorithm most people learn in second or third grade.

```
Remainder := Dividend;
Quotient := 0;
while Remainder >= Divisor do begin
    Remainder := Remainder − Divisor;
    Quotient := Quotient + 1
end
```

developing the invariant

If this loop is correct, we should arrive at proper values for Quotient and Remainder. First, what's our invariant assertion? Well, both before and after each loop iteration there should be a special relationship between the dividend, divisor, quotient, and remainder:

$$\{\text{ Dividend} = (\text{Divisor}*\text{Quotient})+\text{Remainder }\}$$

Since Dividend isn't changed within the loop, we don't have to worry about monkey business that would require us to save Dividend's original value, which would make our invariant more complicated. While the invariant relation is true, we can be confident that our loop, at the very least, isn't doing the wrong thing.

However, the invariant relation isn't enough. Suppose that the loop's action made no assignments to either Quotient or Remainder. Although the invariant assertion would remain true, it wouldn't assure us that the loop would ever end. We need to state some sort of bound that is approached by the loop's action, but which can act as a threshold beyond which the loop won't venture.

need for a bound

The variant assertion:

$$\{\text{Remainder} >= \text{Divisor}, \textit{ and } \text{Remainder } \textit{declines}.\}$$

works for us. Its truth is potentially changed on each iteration of the loop—each time we change the value of Remainder. Eventually it becomes false; we pass the bound or threshold, and the loop is terminated. It is no accident that it forms the entry condition of the loop. Complete with assertions, the loop is:

```
Remainder := Dividend;
Quotient := 0;
{ Dividend = (Divisor*Quotient)+Remainder }
while Remainder >= Divisor do begin
    Remainder := Remainder – Divisor;
        { Remainder >= Divisor, and Remainder declines.}
    Quotient := Quotient + 1
        { Dividend = (Divisor*Quotient)+Remainder }
end
```

As usual, I've made everything look easy by coming up with the correct answer on our first try. Let's consider a false proof, though. Suppose that we had chosen as our variant assertion the relation Quotient<=Dividend. We would still make progress toward loop termination, because we increment Quotient on each pass through the loop. Since it provides an upper bound on the loop, it's reasonable to think that the assertion is a good bound function.

a false proof

Unfortunately, it's the *wrong* bound function. Before we reach the limit it sets, we'll have allowed the invariant assertion to become incorrect. Our attempted proof would fail, even though we set a threshold and approached it.

Difficulties in Proving Programs

The idea that we can prove that a program is correct is intensely appealing, since it would greatly increase our confidence in programs. True, verification seems complicated at first, but then again, so do mathematical proofs. Unfortunately, the promise of program proving has not been realized in as full a manner as was originally hoped. Let's investigate the reasons.

Two conditions have to be satisfied if we want a program proof to work. First, the action of a program statement can't undermine our assertions about what the statement will do. Although this notion seems obvious (we clearly wouldn't have a statement that directly contradicts an assertion), there are subtle difficulties that are easy to overlook. For instance, mathematical proofs don't have to worry about whether or not the axioms of mathematics will apply, but program proofs do. The machine code that takes care of computer arithmetic may never have been formally proven—and it may not always obey the rules!

correctness

Second, the assertions we make have to define the entire universe of the program. Any necessary assertions that are left out cause gaping holes in the program proof that may not be detected until the program fails. For instance, suppose that a routine should sort three variables into increasing order. It's not enough to prove that the variables are in order when the routine ends. We can't ignore the possibility that the routine might have accidentally given all the variables the *same* value.

completeness

> The need to fully satisfy these two conditions—correctness and completeness—makes program proofs very difficult to develop.

In mathematical proofs, small errors will not necessarily have a negative impact on the proof as a whole. It may be that an individual step is incorrect or misstated. However, this sort of error won't always invalidate the overall goal of the proof—a fact can be true even if our explanation of it is faulty. Mathematical proofs usually fail because of larger conceptual errors.

For programs, though, the smallest step is vitally important to the conclusion of the program proof. The tiniest untested assumption about a data value in a program can suffice to undo an elaborate program proof.

limits of proofs

> More important, though, the knowledge that such errors can occur in proofs without being detected by expert computer scientists tends to undermine our confidence in the absolute reliability of program proofs as a whole.

Like a good trial attorney, we can cause a proof to collapse simply by demonstrating a reasonable doubt about its correctness. As a result, programs are actually proved only in a limited set of cases, and then only for relatively small program segments that are written with eventual proof in mind.

Incidentally, you may be tempted to suggest that, since keeping track of small details is so important, program proving would be a perfect job for a computer. Why not write a program to automatically check the correctness of a proof?

automated verification

It's a good idea until you imagine what such a program's first job would be. Obviously we'd want to run it on itself. But what will we make of the answer? Suppose that the program announces that its own code is correct. Can we trust it? Worse yet (in a much more likely outcome) suppose that the automated verifier announces that its own code is *wrong*. Oh no! Back to the drawing board . . .

The file is the elephant of data structures. Its potential size makes it capable of prodigious feats, but we have to allow for a certain amount of lumbering and unwieldiness when we use it. (p. 438)

13

The file Type

Perhaps you're familiar with *Parkinson's Law*: 'Work expands to fill all available time.' Well, there is (or should be) a corollary for computers—something to the effect that files expand to fill all available disk space! No matter how big the disk, or how fast the CPU, files always manage to keep one step ahead.

But files are the problem child of computing in other ways, too. Files are closely tied to the computer's operating system, which leads to many awkward situations. In effect, the more flexible a language's built-in tools for file handling are, the less portable the language is going to be.

In Pascal, files come in two basic categories: textfiles (like the files we worked with in Chapter 7) and all others. We'll look at the basic file algorithms in terms of textfiles because they're easiest to deal with. Then we'll see how values of any type, from reals to records, can be stored in *binary* files using the same format the computer uses for internal storage.

Strictly Pascal

13-1

THE SYNTAX DETAILS OF USING FILES aren't hard, but they do take getting used to. Let's start by creating a file that will stick around when the program is done:

basic file output
program

```
program MakeFile ( Results, input, output);
    {Echoes program input into a permanent disk file.}

var Results: text;    {The file variable must match the heading.}
    Current: char;

begin
    writeln ('Give me some deathless prose to save.');
    rewrite (Results);          {Create an empty output file.}
    while not eof do begin           {We're using the standard input file.}
        if eoln then begin
            readln;           {Deal with the end-of-line.}
            writeln (Results)    {write and writeln can get a file name argument.}
        end else begin           {Deal with an ordinary character.}
            read (Current);
            write (Results, Current)    {If a file name is given, output goes to it.}
        end
    end;
    writeln ('All done.  File "Results" has been saved for posterity.')
end.  {MakeFile.}
```

```
Give me some deathless prose to save.
The cow is of the bovine ilk;
One end is moo, the other, milk.
All done.  File "Results" has been saved for posterity.
```

Yes, it's more Ogden Nash. A second program reads and echoes the same file.

basic file input program

```
program ReadFile ( Results, output);
    {Echoes the contents of an existing file.}

var Results: text;    {Textfiles are files of characters.}
    Current: char;

begin
    writeln ('About to echo the contents of a file named "Results".');
    reset (Results);          {Prepare to read the file.}
    while not eof (Results) do begin    {eof and eoln can take file arguments.}
        if eoln (Results) then begin          {Deal with the end-of-line.}
            readln (Results);    {Here, readln and read refer to file Results,}
            writeln           { and not to the standard keyboard input.}
        end else begin
            read (Results, Current);
            write (Current)    {write and writeln still refer to }
        end                    { the standard monitor output.}
    end;
    writeln ('All done.')
end.  {ReadFile.}
```

⬇   ⬇   ⬇   ⬇   ⬇

```
About to echo the contents of a file named "Results".
The cow is of the bovine ilk;
One end is moo, the other, milk.
All done.
```

If you can handle the basic read-and-echo code, you're going to be able to deal with files. I've highlighted every appearance of file Results; it's easy to see that if you get rid of each mention, you'll have an everyday echo-text program.

echo-text pseudocode

> *initialize as necessary;*
> **while** *data remain*
>   **if** *we're at the end of a line*
>   **then** *do end-of-line processing*
>   **else** *do single character processing;*
> *say goodbye*

A file identifier like Results will typically show up in four different places. First, it appears as a *program parameter*:

program parameters

> **program** MakeFile (Results, input, output);
>   {*Program parameters can be in any convenient order.*}

> If a file exists, or if you want it to exist, it must be supplied as a program parameter. If it isn't, the program will create a temporary file that disappears when the program is done.

Second, the file must be declared as a variable:

file variable declaration

> **var** Results: text;   {text *is the only predefined file type.*}

> A file of type text is a file of characters that's divided into lines. Textfiles are special because they can be used with readln, writeln, and eoln.

Third, a file has to be *opened*, or readied for reading or writing, before it can be used. I'll define these procedures in more detail soon:

opening the file

> reset (Data);   {*Prepare to read from file* Data.}
> rewrite (Results);   {*Prepare to write to file* Results.}

Fourth, a file name can appear as the first argument to any of the file-oriented procedures or functions.

referring to files besides
input and output

> read (Data, Item);   {*Read from* Data *instead of from input.*}
> readln (Data);   {*Read and ignore a whole line from* Data.}
> write (Results, Item)   {*Write to* Results *instead of to output.*}
> writeln (Results);   {*Add a carriage return to* Results.}
> **if** eoln (Data) **then begin**   *etc.*

Finally, there are two important restrictions on files:

> — Assignments cannot be made between file variables, even if they have the same type.
>
> — If used as arguments, files must always be variable parameters. They cannot be value parameters.

announce file usage

Although it's not a formal requirement, it is always a good idea to take one more step when you deal with files: *tell the user*. Why? Well, if you're attempting to read from a file, the user may not be aware that the file is supposed to be available until the program tells her. And, if you're sending all output to a file, the user can't even tell if the program is working at all.

Modification Problems

1. Change either MakeFile or ReadFile into a program that reads from the standard input (the keyboard) and writes to the standard output (the screen).
2. First, use an ordinary text editor to create a small file named Source. Then, modify MakeFile or ReadFile so that it reads Source and creates an identical file named Copy.

Characteristics of Files

The file is the elephant of data structures. Its potential size makes it capable of prodigious feats, but we have to allow for a certain amount of lumbering and unwieldiness when we use it. We'll see that some tasks that are relatively straightforward when expressed in English and programmed with arrays may require an elaborate minuet of file operations. Here are the important ideas:

files are program independent

— Files are controlled by the computer's operating system, and they exist independently of any individual program. However, by using the standard (and extended) file procedures, a program can temporarily take control of a file in order to read it or change it.

files are sequential

— Files store values sequentially. Files have to be read, component by component, from beginning to end. New components can be added only after the last current component. (In practice, though, most operating systems bend the rules to let programs seek a particular part of the file more quickly.)

files are unbounded

— File length is not limited. While arrays, say, are usually restricted to some fraction of the computer's memory, a file can occupy as much of a hard disk, floppy disk, or backup tape as the operating system will allow.

files are read- or write-only

— Files have a *state* that depends on whether they are being inspected (read) or generated (written). The legality of an input or output operation depends on the file's current state.

Files are not the neat abstractions that other Pascal types like integer and array are. It sounds sort of Zen, but it's a good idea to remember that files have two natures—one abstract and one concrete. Most of the time we can treat a file as a data abstraction, whose properties and values can be defined in terms of various file-handling procedures and functions.

But files are also subject to rules imposed by the operating system. For instance, the operating system will typically impose a limit on the number of files a program can work with. The operating system may also loosen the restrictions imposed by the abstraction, as a system like DOS does when it lets us jump to an arbitrary point in the file rather than slogging through one component at a time.

It would be foolish to study files as though any one operating system were the only operating system in the world. However, it would be equally foolish to ignore the fact that *every* operating system lets programmers monkey with files to some extent. I'll try to strike a balance and make sure that you leave this chapter equipped to deal with the basic file problems:

— opening two or more files simultaneously;

— joining files end to end;

what we'll learn   — comparing two or three files for common contents;

— merging two sorted files;

— creating and reading non-text *binary* files.

what we'll ignore   However, we won't be concerned with problems that are operating-system dependent and require extensions, like changing a file's read/write protection or dealing with errors that derive from the computer's file system.

File Procedures and Functions

The big practical difference between files and other variables lies in operators. Other variables use symbolic operators like := and +. Files, in contrast, must rely on procedure and function calls to get anything done. The basic calls are reset and rewrite.

the reset and rewrite procedures   — reset(*file variable*) prepares an existing file to be inspected (or read) from its beginning.

— rewrite (*file variable*) removes any contents from an existing file and prepares it to be generated (or added to) from its beginning.

> A file must be opened before it can be used. Once opened, a file is either being inspected or being generated—never both.

reset and rewrite both have classic bugs associated them. I'll try to put them both in one loop:

a couple of bugs

```
{The calls of both reset and rewrite are wrong.}
while not eof (FromFile) do begin
    reset (FromFile);
    read (FromFile, Ch);
    rewrite (ToFile);
    write (ToFile, Ch)
end
```

What will ToFile contain when the loop is done? If you can answer that question, you know the bugs. Think about it for a minute.

The answer is that the loop won't ever end (this was a trick question)! Every time we reset (FromFile), we start reading from the beginning again. We'll just get the first character over and over, because eof (FromFile) won't ever be TRUE (unless the file has just one item to begin with).

If we take out the reset call (put it before the loop, instead), the loop will eventually end, but ToFile will hold only the last character read from FromFile. Why? Because the rewrite (ToFile) call throws away any ToFile contents on each loop iteration.

get and put*

Two additional procedures, called get and put, are also defined for working with files. Understanding them requires us to step back for a moment. You may recall a past discussion of the file window, which was useful as a 'lookahead' variable for text input:

> if input ↑ = ´ ´ **then** writeln ('About to read a blank space.');

the file window

The file window actually applies to any file. If Results is a textfile that has been opened for reading, then this statement is equally correct:

> {*The file window exists for every file.*}
> if Results ↑ = ´ ´ **then** writeln ('About to read a blank space.');

The file window will come in handy when we declare *binary* files, which are files whose components have types other than text. Files can have any type of components (except for other files).

file type definition

For example, we might declare files of integers, records, or enumerations:

some non-textfile definitions

```
type  NumberFILE = file of integer;
      CardTYPE = record
                    ⋱    {Card's field definitions.}
                 end;
      CardFILE = file of CardTYPE;
      ColorTYPE = (red, green, blue);
      ColorFILE = file of ColorTYPE
var Numbers: NumberFILE;
    Cards: CardFILE;
    Colors: ColorFILE;
```

Note that a **file of** integer isn't the same thing as a text file that happens to hold digits. Were you to look at Numbers with a text editor, you'd see garbage. I'll get back to the difference between text and binary files later.

---

* We won't be using get or put until 13-3.

Although you would think that we'd have to declare additional variables of type integer, CardTYPE, and ColorTYPE in order to use these file variables, we don't; the file window is the only access variable we need. Our final file procedures make it work:

the get and put procedures

— get (*file variable*) advances the file window to the next component in the file. It works like a read call.

— put (*file variable*) appends the current value of the file window to the file. It works like a write call.

> The reset procedure performs the first get automatically.

For example, here's how we'd count the numbers of each kind of value in Colors, a ColorFILE variable.

an example of get

```
Reds := 0;
Greens := 0;
Blues := 0;
reset (Colors);          {Prepare to read the file.}
while not eof (Colors) do begin
    case Colors ↑ of          {Inspect the file window.}
        red: Reds := Reds + 1;
        green: Greens := Greens + 1;
        blue: Blues := Blues + 1
    end;  {case}
    get (Colors)          {Advance the file window.}
end   {while}
{Postcondition: Reds, Greens, and Blues reflect the number of each value in Colors.}
```

The file window can also be assigned to, which makes put useful. Here's how to store a few values in the NumberFILE variable:

put in action

```
{Store a few perfect squares in file Numbers.}
rewrite (Numbers);          {Prepare to fill the file.}
for i := 1 to 100 do begin
    Numbers ↑ := i * i;          {Modify the file window.}
    put (Numbers)          {Advance the window and modify the file.}
end;  {for}
{Postcondition: Numbers holds 100 integer values.}
```

We'll return to non-text files later in this chapter.

Self-Check Questions ————————————————————————

Q. Suppose that you are the proud possessor of a textfile named Stuff. Use reset and get to open the file and get to the beginning of its second line.

A. In effect, the loop below does the work of a readln call. Don't forget that eoln is defined only for files of type text.

```
{Find the second line of a file.}
reset (Stuff);
while not eoln (Stuff) do get (Stuff);
{Postcondition: only the end-of-line remains on this line.}
get (Stuff);
{We're about to read the first character on the second line.}
```

Beyond the Standard: Common File Extensions

In a 1975 paper that reviewed his experience with Pascal, Niklaus Wirth titled one section *An Important Concept and a Persistent Source of Problems: Files.* Probably the biggest problem appears right in the program heading:

```
program Example (Source, Sink);
     {Any permanent files must be named in the program heading.}
```

Standard Pascal requires that every permanent file be named as a program parameter. Unfortunately, this means that a Pascal program *user* can only employ file names the programmer knew about in advance. The simplest sorts of jobs—changing a file name by copying it, for instance—are impossible in Standard Pascal.

Since this kind of restriction is too horrible to contemplate, every Pascal implementation contains extended forms of the standard file procedures, as well as additional procedures. The most common extensions make program parameters optional. Here's how to redirect the standard input and output files from within a program under various Pascal systems:

some typical extensions

```
{VAX Pascal}
Open (input, 'actual_name', old);
reset (input);
Open (output, 'actual_name', new);
rewrite (output);
{Turbo Pascal}
SYSTEM.Assign (input, 'actual_name');
reset (input);
SYSTEM.Assign (output, 'actual_name');
rewrite (output);
{Think Pascal, Berkeley Pascal, and Sun Pascal.}
reset (input, 'actual_name');
rewrite (output, 'actual_name');
```

Even when extended forms are used, both procedures have a shortcoming. reset goes only to the start of a file. This can be really inconvenient when files are long and speed is important, because it means that you have to read all the way through a file, item by item, to get to a particular spot. rewrite, in turn, can only add to the end of a brand new file—there's no standard way to insert something in mid-file or to add to the end of an existing file.

reset and rewrite were defined as they are because of the way files were stored almost universally until the mid 1980's—in continuous blocks on reel-to-reel recording tape. You know the problem if you've ever played a reel-to-reel or cassette music tape: there's no shortcut to the part you want. More modern methods of file storage, like diskettes, allow a degree of random access. Diskettes are like LP records or CD's in the sense that there *are* shortcuts straight across the platter.

modern files have some degree of random access

The tape must wind from end to end, but the tone arm of a record player can jump directly to the track you want.

Being able to move from one area to another quickly allows a second advantage: the stored information need not be *contiguous*, or held in one continuous stretch. Instead, short segments can be chained together. There's a bit more overhead involved in remembering where the next piece of a file is, but the extra convenience is well worth it.

The point of this digression is that most real-world Pascal implementations have additional nonstandard file procedures. Their names will vary, so check your system before you try to use any of these:

— append (*file variable*) opens an existing file for writing without affecting any of its current contents; you can add to the file's end.

other common file extensions

— close (*file variable*) is required by some operating systems (e.g. DOS) that have limited file-handling resources. Files must be explicitly closed by the end of the program or before a newly-written file can be safely opened for reading.

— seek (*file variable, position*) jumps to a specific spot in a file that has been opened for reading.

— filepos (*file variable*) is a function that returns the current position in a file. It's generally used in conjunction with seek, above.

— truncate (*file variable*) gets rid of any file contents found beyond the current position.

Standard Practices and Examples

13-2

I KNOW THAT YOU PROBABLY DON'T WASTE TIME watching television, but if you have cable, you're probably familiar with schedule 'crawls' like this:

a screen captured from
cable TV

Who knows what the file that underlies a schedule crawl looks like? I don't. But I do know that I'd like to be able to use and change its contents in various ways:

— What's today's Cinemax schedule? What's on MTV, minute by minute?

— What's on at 5:00? When is the Brady Bunch on? How about House of Style?

doing the crawl

— Suppose that the cable company acquires a new station, e.g. the College Channel (all House of Style, all the time). How will its schedule be merged into the existing crawl?

— How can a particular show be changed?

All of these tasks are basically stream-handling problems. As far as *algorithms* are concerned, they can be solved using design tools we learned about in Chapter 7.

But as far as getting our programs to work is concerned, it will be a good idea to spend some time gaining experience with basic file techniques:

— splitting the input stream into two or more output streams;

— finding a particular component within a file;

low-level file processing

— adding components to a file;

— deleting components from a file;

— synchronizing these three operations between two or more files.

Although we'll still be doing things to and with streams of values, we'll take into account the prospect that more than one file may be open at a time.

Splitting Files

loop specification

We'll begin by taking a file apart. Here's the problem.

> A textfile contains only numbers, one per line. Read it and split its contents between two new files: one filled with odd numbers, the other with evens.

The specification of the central loop is:

> *Goal: Split a file in two.*
> *Bound: Reaching the end of the input file.*
> *Plan: Get a number.*
> > *Send it to the proper file.*

A pseudocode outline of the program adds two important steps. It prepares the input file to be read and readies the output files to be written. It also pays special attention to the problem of reading numbers from textfiles.

splitting pseudocode

> *prepare file* numbers *to be read with* reset;
> *prepare files* odds *and* evens *to be written with* rewrite;
> **while** *there are values in* numbers
> > readln (numbers, Current);
> > **if** Current *is odd*
> > > **then** *send it to* odds
> > > **else** *send it to* evens

Now, if you reread the problem statement you'll notice that I specifically mentioned that the input file holds just one number per line. This turns out to be an important detail, because it lets me use readln to get the input numbers.

> **while not** eof (numbers) **do begin**
> > readln (numbers, Current);   *etc.*
> > {*This dumps the end-of-line after reading the number.*}

> eof is TRUE only when the value about to be read is the end-of-file marker. It is FALSE if any other value—even a blank space or end-of-line—comes first.

Since every line in a textfile ends with the end-of-line, there will always be trailing blanks when we read numerical data. Had I used read instead, the program would crash after the last valid number was read. Since eof isn't TRUE yet—after all, the computer doesn't know that no more numbers follow the upcoming end-of-line—the program will try to read past the end-of-file as it looks for another number.

an incorrect alternative

> **while not** eof (numbers) **do begin**
> > read (numbers, Current);   *etc.*
> > {*This will eventually crash, since I'll try to read when nothing but white space remains in the file.*}

The completed program is shown below.

*file-handling example
program*

```
program Splitter (numbers, odds, evens, output);
    {Splits a file of numbers into separate odds and evens files.}
var numbers, odds, evens: text;    {They're all files of characters . . . }
    Current: integer;    { . . . but we can read integers as though they were typed in.}
begin
    writeln ('Splitting "numbers" . . . ');
    reset (numbers);
    {We're prepared to read from numbers.}
    rewrite (odds);
    rewrite (evens);
    {We're prepared to write to odds and evens.}
    while not eof (numbers) do begin
        readln (numbers, Current);
        if odd (Current)
            then begin writeln (odds, Current : 1) end
            else begin writeln (evens, Current : 1) end
    end; {while}
    {All the numbers have been read and echoed to new files.}
    writeln ('All finished creating files "odds" and "evens".')
end. {Splitter.}
```

```
Splitting "numbers"...
All finished creating files "odds" and "evens".
```

Modification Problems

1. How much work does Splitter do? Collect and print statistics on the number of values that go to each file?

2. Modify Splitter so that it can deal with a file that has more than one number per line. Hint: write a SeekEOF function that skips non-blanks before it returns TRUE or FALSE.

3. Using the file-handling extensions your Pascal system almost certainly provides, change Splitter so that it asks its user for the names of both input and output files.

Concatenating Files

The basic file job is called *concatenation*, which means attaching files end to end (or trunk to tail, if you prefer to stick with elephants). Here's the problem:

*problem: submitting
homework*

A computer science student turns in her homework with a customized **handin** command. It sticks an exact copy of her program, followed by the phrase Execution begins..., and then the actual output, into a file called **homework**.

Unfortunately, her program doesn't work. Since she suspects that the grader doesn't even read or run homework anyway, the student has a bright idea. Why not write her own version of **handin** and have it stick her program, along with a sample of correct output supplied by the instructor, into a file? Write a program that helps her out.

Solving the homework submission problem takes two basic skills:

— Opening files (call them `source` and `answers`) for reading and then reading from them.

— Opening a file (call it `homework`) for writing and then writing to it.

In outline, the final program will be something like this:

concatenation pseudocode

open `source` *and* `answers` *for reading;*
open `homework` *for writing;*
read and echo from `source` *to* `homework`;
add the single line `Execution begins...` *to* `homework`;
read and echo from `answers` *to* `homework`;

What is the *read-and-echo* step? It's the basic text processing loop:

Goal: Copy a file.
Bound: We've reached the end of the file.
Plan: Read from one file.
Write to the other file.

Program Handln, below, reads and writes one character at a time. Note that even though Copy reads FromFile without modifying it, FromFile, like all file parameters, must still be a variable parameter.

file concatenation program

```
program Handln (output, Source, Answers, Homework);
    {Concatenates two files.}
var Source, Answers, Homework: text;
procedure Copy (var FromFile, ToFile: text);
    {Copies FromFile to ToFile, one character at a time.}
    var Ch: char;
    begin
        while not eof (FromFile) do begin
            if eoln (FromFile) then begin
                readln (FromFile);          {Handle the end-of-line.}
                writeln (ToFile)
            end else begin
                read (FromFile, Ch);        {Handle a character.}
                write (ToFile, Ch)
            end  {if}
        end  {while}
    end;  {Copy}
begin
    writeln ('Copying "source" and "answers" to "homework"...');
    reset (Source);
    reset (Answers);
    rewrite (Homework);
    {Files are open for reading and writing.}
    Copy (Source, Homework);
    writeln (Homework, 'Execution begins...');
    Copy (Answers, Homework);
    {The files have been copied.}
    writeln ('All done.')
end.  {Handln}
```

⬇   ⬇   ⬇   ⬇   ⬇

```
Copying "source" and "answers" to "homework"...
All done.
```

Modification Problems ────────────────────────

1. Does your Pascal system have both string and file extensions? Good. Modify HandIn so that it lets the program user enter the names of the files that are to be copied. Then, have it perform the file copies one line, rather than one character, at a time.

2. Your computer has been grumpy lately, and it hasn't been copying files correctly. Modify HandIn so that after doing its copying, it compares the contents of **homework** to the original **source** and **answers** files.

3. Turn HandIn into UnHandIn. In other words, have it split a homework submission file like **homework** into two new files called **work** and **labor**. The line **Execution begins...** appears in the original and separates the two.

Self-Check Questions ────────────────────────

Q. Suppose that we wanted procedure Copy to do the work of opening the files for reading and writing. What's wrong with this code?

```
{Add FromFile to the end of ToFile.}
begin    {Copy}
    reset (FromFile);
    rewrite (ToFile);
    while not eof(FromFile) do begin       etc.
```

A. It's fine for the reset. However, every call of rewrite first *removes* the output file if it already exists. The final ToFile will hold only the last file copied.

Merging Files

File mergers, like corporate mergers, are intended to combine the contents of two separate entities. A merger can be very simple, of course; we might just add one file to the end of another. But in most cases, we're interested in merging files in a way that keeps them ordered.

Let's try a statement of the problem that's just complicated enough to demonstrate the basic file-merging algorithm:

problem: file merging

Suppose that files Main and Extra both contain numbers in numerical order. Write a program that creates a third file, called Merged, that holds, also in numerical order, all the numbers of both files.

Merging files of numbers is really the kernel of the real-world problem of merging files of records. Conceptually, there's not too much difference between inspecting the current line of a file and inspecting, say, the LastName field of the current *record* in a file. Numbers are much more convenient to practice with, though, because we can use an ordinary text editor to create test data and to inspect our results.

Mergers of two previously organized files are common in computer systems because of the practical complications of dealing with large files. In a paper-based filing system, files are usually updated immediately. New records are entered right away so that work won't pile up. Computer filing systems, in contrast, tend to delay updating of main files for several reasons:

— The entire file may have to be copied in order to insert a single new record. But if several records (in alphabetical or numerical order) are available, they can be inserted in a single pass through the main file.

— The main file may be so long that other tapes or disks have to be mounted in order to put the new record in its proper place. Since mounting and unmounting is tedious and expensive, it pays to wait and see if other records will require the same file portion.

— Managers of large databases are usually reluctant to allow changes to be made at the user's discretion. They prefer to collect all *transactions*, or requests for changes, and verify their correctness before modifying the master file.

— Finally, a certain amount of delay in inserting records actually adds to overall efficiency—the new record may have to be inspected again.

why file merging is common

For computerized filing systems, then, letting records pile up—in alphabetical order, of course—is very common. Updating a computer system every 24 hours, as Crate and Barrel advertises, below, isn't a feature. Instead, it reflects an inherent problem of files.

CRATE AND BARREL GIFT COLLECTION

Our Gift Registry is as different as our stores.

It would be easy to assume that all gift registries are pretty much the same. After all, they perform exactly the same function. But that's assuming that all stores are just like the Crate and Barrel if they happen to sell housewares. Our Gift Registry is different because it doesn't require the bride and groom to be shuffled between different floors, different sections, different people, and even different stores just to complete their registry. You can work with one of our consultants as you make your selections, no matter how long it may take, no matter how extensive your needs may be. Or if you prefer, we offer a system so simple, so complete, you can register yourself. We then enter your selections into our gift registry that is not only computerized and linked to all our stores across the country, but updated every 24 hours. As with all items purchased at Crate and Barrel, your gifts can be easily returned or exchanged. So, if you're browsing through this catalogue

---

How are ordered files merged? A direct analogy to paper files is appropriate. Imagine that you're merging the contents of two partially filled file cabinets by hand into a third empty cabinet. You open all the cabinets and get the first record from each of the full ones. The alphabetically (or numerically) 'lower' of the two records goes into the third cabinet, then you pick up another record to refill the empty hand.

developing the algorithm

The process of comparison, moving, and replacing goes on until one of the original cabinets is empty. Then, since all the records in the remaining cabinet belong at the end of the third cabinet, and are in order already, you move them to the third cabinet without making comparisons.

A Pascal algorithm is much the same. We'll have to prepare Main and Extra for reading and Merged for writing. After obtaining the first value from each of the existing files, we'll compare them, add the lower value to Merged, then get another value. Naturally, we have to repeat this process until Main or Extra is exhausted.

Now, our first filter's process, the one in program HandIn, was simply *echo*. The process this filter implements might be called *compare*. Instead of merely getting the next value from a single stream, we want to get the lower value from one of two streams. Then, we have to replace the value we took, so that we'll have a basis for comparison next time around. A loop specification is:

`compare` loop specification

Goal: Merge two ordered input streams into a single ordered output stream.
Bound: The end of the Main *or* Extra *file.*
Plan: Decide which file's current value is lower, then
  Add it to the end of the Merged *file.*
  Replace it with the next value from the same input file.

A pseudocode outline puts this central loop into an appropriate context:

file-merge refinement

prepare to read Main *and* Extra;
prepare to write Merged;
while not *the end of either of the files* **do begin**
 add the lower number to Merged;
 get the next number from that file
end *of the loop;*
add the non-empty file's remaining number to Merged

There's just one more problem to anticipate and avoid before we look at the final program. As you know, eof is TRUE when we've read the last value in a file. Unfortunately, it leaves us in an awkward position when we leave the loop. Even though one file will be empty, as in the pseudocode above, the last value we read from it might still be waiting to be inserted into Merged.

For example, imagine that Main holds the numbers 1, 2, and 3, while Extra has just 10. Consider:

read (Main, MainNumber);
read (Extra, ExtraNumber);
while not eof(Main) **and not** eof(Extra) **do begin**
 make the comparison described above
end;
flush the rest of the non-empty file

Even though Extra is empty, we still have to keep making comparisons after the loop if we want to stick ExtraNumber into the right place. Even though the file is empty, its stream of values hasn't been completely processed yet. Finishing that last little bit of processing will make for some ugly coding.

The common way around this problem is to add an additional value to the very end of every input stream—a dummy sentinel that will force the last value out of the stream. I've used this technique in the final version of program Merger, below. It assumes that both input files end with the number −1.

file merging program

```
program Merger (main, Extra, Merged, Output);
    {Merges Main and Extra into Merged, preserving ordering.
     Assumes that the files are ordered and that their last lines are marked.}

const ENDmarker = –1;

var Main, Extra, Merged: text;
    MainNumber, ExtraNumber: integer;

begin
    writeln ('Merging "Main" and "Extra" into "Merged".');
    reset (Main);
    reset (Extra);
    rewrite (Merged);
    readln (Main, MainNumber);
    readln (Extra, ExtraNumber);
    {We're ready to go.}
    while (MainNumber <> ENDmarker) and
            (ExtraNumber <> ENDmarker) do begin
        if MainNumber < ExtraNumber
            then begin writeln (Merged, MainNumber);
                        readln (Main, MainNumber)
            end  {then}
            else begin writeln (Merged, ExtraNumber);
                        readln (Extra, ExtraNumber)
            end  {else}
    end;  {while}
    {Postcondition:  One source file is 'empty,' so flush the other into Merged.}
    while MainNumber <> ENDmarker do begin
        writeln (Merged, MainNumber);
        readln (Main, MainNumber)
    end;  {the Main-flushing loop}
    {Postcondition:  All contents of Main are in Merged.}
    while ExtraNumber <> ENDmarker do begin
        writeln (Merged, ExtraNumber);
        readln (Extra, ExtraNumber)
    end;  {the Extra-flushing loop}
    {Postcondition:  All contents of Extra are in Merged.}
    writeln ('File merger complete.')
end.   {Merger}
```

Modification Problems

1. It isn't essential to use the end-marker technique; it just simplifies matters. Modify Merger so that it doesn't rely on an end marker. Instead, it should look for the ends of files Main and Extra.

2. Modify program Merger so that each pair of *identical* values from Main and Extra is put into a new file called Copies instead of going into Merged.

3. Modify program Merger so that just one copy of a repeated sequence of numbers, or of duplicate numbers from Main or Extra, is put into Merged.

4. Change Merger into a program that can read and merge alphabetically ordered files of string values.

Finding Common Entries: The Wall Street Crook

The next of the basic multiple-file problems involves finding common entries. As with file mergers, most searches for common entries arise from the rather dull consequences of the way files are used and updated. However, there is an entertaining form of the problem I'll pose for us:

problem: finding common lines

> The Securities and Exchange Commission has in its possession three files on disk. One lists all employees of firms involved in rendering financial advice to a particular company. The second has the names of all individuals who traded heavily in that company's stock. The third consists of every name found in the personal Rolodex of a recently convicted Wall Street success. Each file is in alphabetical order. Help the SEC search for illegal insider traders by writing a program that finds a name common to all three files.

Thus, we have three streams of names going in and just one stream—perhaps just one name—coming out. You can take it for granted that there actually *is* a common value to be found. Indeed, it's common to simplify problems like this by intentionally planting a string (like Dummy Name) at the end of each file.

Let's get an idea of what our program's central loop is going to do:

loop specification

> *Goal: Find a common value in three ordered input streams.*
> *Bound: The current values in all three streams are equal.*
> *Plan: Get the next value in any 'low' stream.*

The loop's bound condition is unexpectedly simple. Suppose that Name1, Name2, and Name3 represent the current value from each stream. Then:

comparing three components

> **if** (Name1=Name2) **and** (Name2=Name3) **then**
>   *all three strings have the same value;*

If both terms are TRUE, then Name1 also equals Name3.

the loop's goal

Now, if we accept the bound condition as stated above—and there's no reason not to—we agree that Name1 will have to be advanced if it's less than Name2. Name2, in turn, must advance if it's less than Name3. Finally, Name3 will move ahead if it's currently less than Name1. This prompts two interesting points:

— The steps can be considered in any order; no comparison or advance has to come before any other.

— Although advancing by just one component in a single file is a tiny step, it brings us closer to the overall goal of finding three matching components.

I can rephrase these ideas in pseudocode with:

common entry pseudocode

> **repeat**
>   **if** Name1<Name2 **then** *get the next* Name1;
>   **if** Name2<Name3 **then** *get the next* Name2;
>   **if** Name3<Name1 **then** *get the next* Name3;
> **until** (Name1=Name2) **and** (Name2=Name3)

This segment seems suspiciously short. Nevertheless, if we have faith in the exit condition and believe that the *get the next* . . . statements bring us closer to meeting it, the loop will work.

guarded statements

Before reading the finished program, you should note that the order of the statements makes no difference. Each statement is said to be *guarded*—the if check ensures that it can't be executed in error. The final program is shown below. For simplicity's sake (it lets me use type char), I'm assuming that each line of every file contains just one letter, rather than a whole name.

common line-finding program

```
program Common (output, First, Second, Third);
    {Finds a common entry in the sorted files First, Second, and Third.}
var First, Second, Third: text;
    Name1, Name2, Name3: char;
begin
    writeln ('Looking for a common line in "First", "Second", and "Third".');
    reset (First);
    reset (Second);
    reset (Third);
    readln (First, Name1);
    readln (Second, Name2);
    readln (Third, Name3);
    {We have the first value from each file.}
    repeat
        if Name1<Name2 then begin readln(First, Name1) end;
        if Name2<Name3 then begin readln(Second, Name2) end;
        if Name3<Name1 then begin readln(Third, Name3) end;
    until (Name1=Name2) and (Name2=Name3);
    {Postcondition: The current value from each file is identical.}
    write ('The common value in files First, Second, and Third is:    ');
    writeln (Name1)          {Note that we're writing to the terminal.}
end.   {Common}
```

Modification Problems

1. Create data files for Common, then test it. What happens if your test files aren't in alphabetical order? What if there isn't a common value?

2. Extend Common so that it is able to read and compare complete strings, rather than single characters.

3. Suppose that telephone numbers precede the names. Since the numbers are not likely to be in numerical order, Common won't work. Make Common remove all leading (start of line) blanks, digits, dashes, and parentheses before making comparisons.

Binary Files

13-3

ASIDE FROM TEXTFILES, FILES THAT HOLD COMPONENTS of a particular type are called *binary files* (the terms *typed* and *data* files are also often used). These files have components with simple types:

simple file types

> **type** NumberFileTYPE = **file of** integer;
>   RealFileTYPE = **file of** real;
>   CharFileTYPE = **file of** char;
>
> **var** Statistics: NumberFileTYPE;
>   Measurements: RealFileTYPE;
>   Letters: CharFileTYPE;

text is not **file of** char

Note that CharFileTYPE is not the same thing as type text, even though files of both types will hold the same values. Functions (like eoln) and procedures (like readln or writeln) that are meant for textfiles will work only with files of type text. Is this confusing? Yes. Is it hard to remember? No. When you mean to work with lines and characters, use files of type text.

Binary file components can also be structured types. For example:

structured file components

> **type** StringTYPE = **packed array** [1 .. 30] **of** char;
>   MovieDataTYPE = **record**
>   Title, Director: StringTYPE;
>   Rating: (G, PG, PG13, R, NC17, X);
>   Minutes: integer;
>   **end**;
>   DataArrayTYPE = **array** [1 .. 10, 1 .. 50] **of** integer;
>   MovieFileTYPE = **file of** MovieDataTYPE;
>   DataFileTYPE = **file of** DataArrayTYPE;
>
> **var** OneMovie: MovieDataTYPE;
>   MovieFile: MovieFileTYPE;
>   DataFile = DataFileTYPE;

In every case, the file window can be used as a variable that has the same type as the file's components. If the files have been opened properly, these are all meaningful assignments:

using the file window

> {*These are meaningful assignments to the file window.*}
> Statistics ↑ := 25;
> Letters ↑ := 'B';
> MovieFile ↑.Rating := NC17;
> DataFile ↑[1,1] := 0;

If you do have variables that have the same type as the file components, read and write can be used to read or write one component at a time:

> {*Reading and writing from binary files.*}
> read (Statistics, AnIntegerVariable);
> write (Measurements, ARealVariable);
> read (MovieFile, OneMovie);

---

read and write may be given only two arguments—a file name and a variable or value—when they're used with binary files. readln and writeln can be used only with text files.

For reference, here's how procedures get and put are related to read and write:

| what read and write do | read (F, X); | *is the equivalent of* | X := F ↑;
get (F); |
| | write (F, X); | *is the equivalent of* | F ↑ := X;
put (F); |

Example: Your Permanent Report Card

Let's try an example:

problem: text to real

As threatened, your elementary school has been keeping every grade you ever got on your permanent report card (which follows you for your entire life). Unfortunately, they've been using ordinary textfiles—which require more space for storage than a **file of** real would—to hold the numbers. To help them reclaim a little disk space, write a program that reads a textfile full of real numbers and produces a **file of** real.

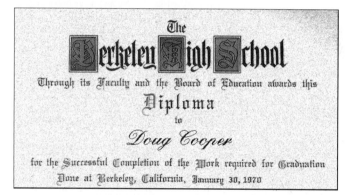

sorry, but this is the best that I could do

We'll look at some of the tradeoffs between textfiles and binary files in a couple of pages.

Changing formats is a classic filtering job. It's hardly more complicated than the basic text-processing loop. As usual, I'll simplify the problem by assuming that the file holds just one number per line.

read-and-echo specification

> *Goal: Turn a file of* text *into a file of* real.
> *Bound: We've reached the end of the input file.*
> *Plan: Read a number from the* text *file.*
>   *Write a number to the* real *file.*

Making proper declarations and keeping track of file opening and closing will occupy most of our attention.

translation pseudocode

> *prepare to read the* text *file;*
> *prepare to write the* real *file;*
> **while not** *the end of the* text *file* **do begin**
>   *read the number from the* text *file;*
>   *write the number to the* real *file;*

The final program is shown below. Note that it uses readln to get values from the textfile. As a result, only one value per line is read. Any extras get tossed away with the end-of-line.

text to real conversion

```
program RealLife (Infile, Outfile, output);
    {Reads a textfile of reals and produces a real file.}

type RealFileTYPE = file of real;

var OutFile: RealFileTYPE;
    InFile: text;
    Number: real;

begin
    write ('Translating text (InFile) into reals (OutFile)...');
    reset (InFile);
    rewrite (OutFile);
    {All our ducks are in line, and we're ready to go.}
    while not eof(InFile) do begin
        readln (InFile, Number);      {We read text . . . }
        write (OutFile, Number)       { . . . but we write real values.}
    end;
    {Postcondition: we've read InFile and filled OutFile.}
    writeln ('All done.')
end.   {RealLife}
```

```
Translating text (InFile) into reals (OutFile)...All done.
```

Modification Problems

1. How much work does RealLife do? Modify the program so that it counts the number of numbers converted. Then, write up some test data and try them out. Finally, compare the final file sizes.

2. Suppose that a textfile contains fractions, given one per line like this: 53 / 87 Modify RealLife so that it reads the fractions, then saves their real equivalents.

3. In real life, each grade would be accompanied by the name of the teacher who gave it to you. Assume that InFile has, on each line, a grade followed by a name. Define a record type with real and string fields, then read the information and assign it to the record appropriately. Build a file of records as you go.

Self-Check Questions

Q. Assuming the declarations of program RealLife, why is each statement in error?

    a)   write (OutFile, Number :10:5);
    b)   writeln (OutFile);

A. The reasons are:

    a)   formatting is allowed only for textfiles.
    d)   writeln (like readln and eoln) can only be used on textfiles.

Textfiles vs. Binary Files

Why have files with types other than text? After all, we just saw that an InFile of type text holds no more information than an OutFile that is a **file of** real. Even the information in a file of records (like the **file of** MovieDataTYPE defined at the beginning of this section) could be set up as a textfile.

The answer seems simple at first. Binary files hold data in the same format as memory does. Using the binary format usually takes much less space than storing the sequences of char digits that spell out the numbers.

binary files of numbers are short

> When there's a great deal of numerical information to be stored, binary files can be much shorter than textfiles that hold the same data.

bits and bytes

You've probably heard the terms *bit*, *byte*, and *word*. A *bit* is a binary digit—a zero or a one. A *byte*, in turn, is a group of eight bits—an eight-digit binary number. Most computer systems use one byte to represent a single character. Finally, a *word* is a few (usually two or four) bytes; the exact number varies from computer to computer.

Thus far, all of our programs' input and output has consisted of char values. Even when programs have read or printed numbers, they've worked one character—one byte—at a time. Procedures like read and write have busily translated bytes into digit characters (and then numbers) and vice versa.

Now, the translation itself isn't hard. But when numbers are long and there are a great many of them, all this translation is a waste of computer time and storage space. For example, if we use two bytes to hold the binary equivalent of an integer, we can hold numbers from −32,768 through +32,767. By reading just two bytes as an integer, we can get the same information that would require as many as six bytes worth of digit characters.

However, if most of the information consists of stored strings, the advantage is often lost. In fact, binary files may do much worse. Why? Well, a textfile holds only as many characters as you actually use, more or less. Take this list of names:

```
Job
Hud
Lew
Englebert
```

binary files of strings can be long

Saved as text, they require only as much room as there are characters, plus a little overhead for the end-of-line markers.

A binary file of records or arrays, in contrast, usually has a fixed amount of room set aside to hold each string—a fixed amount that must be able to handle the largest string anticipated. If we want to store a binary file of arrays or records, we'll need this sort of definition:

```
const LongestPossibleNAME = 10;
type StringTYPE = packed array [1 .. LongestPossibleNAME] of char;
```

A **file of** StringTYPE, or of a record that includes a StringTYPE field, stores the unused components along with the meaningful ones.

But wasting space isn't necessarily bad, particularly if it enables you to save time.

> When stored records all have the same size, most operating systems provide a way to get to a particular record very quickly.

seek is a common extension

In effect, the operating system keeps a table of locations within a file and 'knows' how to get to a particular location fast. If your Pascal system has an extended file-handling procedure called seek, it probably takes advantage of the operating system for fast file access. Even with relatively small files (say, those that fit on a diskette), it can be hundreds or thousands of times faster to seek a position directly than to read or get to it sequentially.

On the other hand, being too concerned with saving time isn't always such a good idea. Although textfiles may be slower for computers to deal with, they are much faster for human beings. Being able to inspect a data file with an ordinary text editor can be a lifesaver. The editor has built-in tools, such as the ability to search for particular strings or characters quickly and easily. It's easy to create a textfile for testing, and it's easier to fix a textfile that has been corrupted in some way.

the bottom line

> Your time is worth more than a computer's. Before you commit to using binary files, ask yourself this question: 'In the big scheme of things, is the amount of space or time I'm saving that important?' If not, stick with textfiles.

Self-Check Questions

Q. Suppose that you put a few random numbers (say, 35404, 44105, and 42529) into a binary file called Destination. What would you find if you inspected Destination with an ordinary text editor?

A. The sequence of bits in Destination can be interpreted in two ways—in word-length chunks (the way we copied them) or in byte-length units (the way an editor will show them on screen). However, the stored values are meaningful only when they're read and interpreted the way we stored them. For instance:

```
as numbers:    35404      |      44105      |      42529
as bytes:   01000101 01001100 01010110 01001001 01010011 01000001
as chars:      ´E´   |  ´L´|  ´V´   |   ´I´ |  ´S´   |   ´!´
```

As you can see, even though byte-length chunks have *some* character connotation, it's entirely meaningless. (Just kidding.)

Background: File Compression

One of the hottest personal computer products in the past few years has been *compression* software. Compression programs do just that—they make files take less space. If you have a Macintosh, you've probably seen StuffIt, while if you use a PC you've almost certainly encountered PKZip. Such programs reduce files by anywhere from 50 to 90%, depending on the files' original contents.

Compression programs rely on a few basic observations about the contents of files. If there's repetition, why not replace the repeated values with just one instance, plus a count of the number of times it should appear? If there aren't many different values, why not use a smaller number of bits to show each? Finally, if there are repeated sequences, why not build a *dictionary* of abbreviations? Compression programs may use one or all of these ideas.

Compressed text and binary data files must always be put back together exactly as they were to begin with, since nobody wants missing lines or characters. They require *lossless* compression algorithms that limit compression program performance. When pictures are compressed, though (you might have heard of *TIFF* or *GIF* files), we're usually willing to endure a tiny loss of detail in exchange for better performance. *Lossy* compression algorithms (the best-known is called *JPEG*) can reduce color pictures to 1/20 to 1/50 or less of their original size. The price is the loss of (hopefully) insignificant detail.

Program Engineering Notes

13-4

WE'VE SEEN AMPLE EVIDENCE THAT EACH type has its own quirks and tends to provoke certain errors. These mistakes usually occur in proportion to the severity of warnings against them. Mild 'Bewares!' are usually heeded, but an absolute prohibition promotes a frenzy of crashes. Three common fatal errors that involve files are:

1. Attempting to inspect or read from a file that has not been reset.

2. Trying to generate or write to a file without first calling rewrite.

3. Reading past the end of a file.

confusing reset and rewrite

The first two bugs are usually the result of oversight or of inadvertently confusing reset and rewrite. Unfortunately, some errors of omission that are obvious to us aren't caught by the compiler, since they're syntactically correct. Although this program lacks a call of rewrite(OutsideFile), it compiles (and crashes) perfectly well.

```
program DoesntRewrite (OutsideFile, output);
var OutsideFile: text;
begin
    writeln (OutsideFile, 'Hi there!')
end.
```

```
ABNORMAL TERMINATION - -
TEMP100937 NOT SET FOR WRITING
```

In some implementations, the runtime error message that's printed is of little help. In the example above, the computer printed its temporary, internal name for OutsideFile.

Attempting to read past the end of a file is another fatal mistake. The next program segment is sure to fail, given the proper test input:

```
      reset (AnyFile);
   repeat
      DoSomethingWith (AnyFile)
   until eof (AnyFile);
```

An empty input file delivers the death blow, because eof (AnyFile) is TRUE as soon as an empty file is reset.

> Check for end-of-file *before* working with any file.

A Few Non-Fatal Diagnoses

A crash may, naturally, turn out to be a preferable outcome for minimizing frustration. Suppose that you hear this complaint:

> 'My program creates a file. I'm sure of it, because I added debugging code that resets and prints the new file on the spot. But when the program is finished, the file has vanished. Help!'

Can you guess what the problem is? Here's how the guilty program begins:

```
      program Disappears (input, output);
         {NewFile never shows up.  Why?}
      var NewFile: text;
      begin
         rewrite (NewFile);
         writeln (NewFile, 'Hi there! ');          etc.
```

Yes, the file is prepared and created. Unfortunately, it's a temporary file because it doesn't appear in the heading as a program parameter. When Disappears is done, all of its temporary files vanish.

A related error that's hard to find is a misplaced reset or rewrite. Remember that reset puts us at the beginning of a file so that we can inspect it. rewrite presents us with an empty file, ready for writing. What program mistakes do you think caused these complaints?

> 'I'm not sure I'm reading the right file—I keep getting the same piece of input.'

> 'My program creates a file all right, but when I print the file it contains only the last piece of data I entered.'

Both bugs are probably the result of putting a rewrite or reset inside a loop that was supposed to write or read a file. The call should have been made just prior to entering the loop action.

Try diagnosing a problem that calls for an application of the Basic Law of Debugging: when you're sure of everything, one of the things you're sure of is wrong. I'll give you a hint: the file really *is* there:

> 'My program is supposed to read from a file. But it hangs, even though I'm sure the file is there.'

A peek at the code reveals the problem. Even though it includes a proper check for eof, the read is missing its first argument. The program is trying to read from the keyboard, rather than from DataFile.

```
while not eof (DataFile) do begin
    read (Value);          {Where is Value being read from?}
    Process (Value)
end;
```

eoln bugs

The end-of-line function has always brought grief to Pascal programmers. What's wrong with the following bit of code? It's supposed to echo the contents of Source to SavedOutput. I'll tell you that Source has no leading blanks on any line.

```
while not eof (Source) do begin
    read (Source, CurrentCharacter);
    write (SavedOutput, CurrentCharacter);
    if eoln(Source) then
        writeln (SavedOutput)
end;
```

```
This little piggie went to market;
 This little piggie stayed home.
 This little piggie had roast beef,    etc.
```

The partial contents of SavedOutput, shown above, give a broad hint: the second and third lines are indented by one space.

> The end-of-line character is a space that we're about to read when eoln becomes TRUE.

Since we forgot to get rid of the space at the end of each input line (with a readln (Source), or even an extra read (Source, CurrentCharacter)), it showed up at the beginning of the next output line.

Some of the most annoying file bugs are manifested by disappearing lines, and (for interactive programs) an inexplicable need to type extra carriage returns. I described these as *synchronization* bugs in Chapter 7. The cause is often confusion about exactly what happens at the end of a line. The code below is supposed to read and partially print an input file, echoing the initial non-blank characters on each line. Try tracing through it by hand.

synchronization bugs

```
{Print leading non-blanks—contains a bug.}
while not eof do begin
    read (CurrentCharacter);
    while CurrentCharacter <> ´ ´ do begin
        write (CurrentCharacter);
        read (CurrentCharacter)
    end;
    readln;
    writeln
end;
```

If every line begins with non-blanks, and ends with blanks, everything works fine. Suppose, though, that there are no extraneous blanks at the end of a line. When the inner loop is exited, the value of CurrentCharacter is ´ ´—it is the end-of-line character. What happens when the readln is executed? The next line is thrown away. If the program is being run interactively, the user has to enter an extra carriage return (or else there is no next line to get rid of).

> Always make sure that textfile routines can handle these three special cases:
>
> — Blanks at the beginning of a line.
>
> — Blanks at the end of a line.
>
> — Lines that are empty.

Since most line-reading bugs are related to mix-ups of read and readln, there's a real temptation to debug by trying minor variations. This is most common when good editing facilities and a lightly loaded computer are available. Why think about the right way to do something when you can make mistakes so quickly? Take it from me—it doesn't pay. You'll find yourself trading one bug for another.

Getting an initial value for eoln sometimes causes problems in interactive programs. Suppose that this is the beginning of a program.

```
begin {main program}
    while not eoln do begin
        writeln ('Please give an opinion.');
        ProcessTheInput;
            ·.    etc.
```

> In some older Pascal implementations, eoln is undefined before the start of input.

As a result, the segment above might hang (without printing the prompt) until input begins. The prompt should have been output before the check of eoln was made. This isn't a problem with programs that read from files because, in effect, all input is ready and waiting at the start of execution.

Some interactive Pascal systems that were based on the first definition of Pascal won't even allow this code:

```
begin {main program}
    writeln 'Please enter a number.');
    readln (TheNumber);
        ·.    etc.
```

This is because there's an implicit call of reset (input) at the beginning of the program. Now, reset is supposed to give the file window the first component value of the input file. However, the old Pascal standard specified that there would be no 'first value' until we entered one. As a result, the program would hang, waiting for us to enter a value—any value—so the reset could be completed. This put the programmer in a *Through the Looking Glass* position of entering the data first, and getting the prompt later. The Standard permits something that's called *lazy I/O* as a workaround to the problem. It lets the computer delay defining the file window until it's actually inspected for the first time.

The best antibugging technique is to print the file you're working on *as* you work on it. Make sure that you can explain every blank space or empty line that shows up, as well as every full line that *doesn't* appear.

Binary File Problems

non-text bugs

Non-text files cause more trouble with syntax than semantics. The file window (the file's name followed by an up-arrow or circumflex) is, in effect, the name of a variable. Unfortunately, the up-arrow makes for unusual-looking identifiers. Suppose that we have a file of records. If each record has an array field, we might see these identifiers in a program:

TheFile	*{Name of the file.}*
TheFile ↑	*{The file window—the name of one record component.}*
TheFile ↑.TheArray	*{An entire array field.}*
TheFile ↑.TheArray [10]	*{One element of the array.}*

Naturally, all assignments must involve values of an appropriate type.

TheFile	*{can't be assigned to.}*
TheFile ↑	*{may get a record of TheFile's component type.}*
TheFile ↑.TheArray	*{may get an array of TheArray's type.}*
TheFile ↑.TheArray[10]	*{may get any value of TheArray's element type.}*

procedures for textfiles
only

Furthermore, remember that some actions that are all right with textfiles will not work with files of other component types. eoln may not be given a non-textfile argument; nor may readln or writeln. Also, when procedures write and read are used in conjunction with non-textfiles, they may only be given one additional argument. As a result, only a single component may be written to, or read from, a non-textfile at any one time.

Syntax Summary

❏ *file type*: used to store any number of values of one type. Only the file type's name and the type of its components are given in a file type definition.

type Numbers = **file of** integer;

❏ text: the only predefined file type. It creates a file of char values divided into lines. The standard files input and output have type text.

var Paper: text;

❏ *file window*: used as the name of the currently accessible file component. It's the file variable's name followed by an up-arrow or circumflex:

```
        LetterFile ↑ := 'T';
        write (NumberFile ↑);
```

❑ *program parameters*: file names given in a program heading. They refer to permanent files that the program will inspect or add to. Except for the standard program parameters input and output, program parameters must be declared within the program as well:

```
    program FileParameters (input, Results, Data);
       ·.
    type DataFileTYPE = file of ... etc.
       ·.
    var Results:  text;
        Data:  DataFileTYPE;
```

❑ reset (*file variable*): prepares a file to be read, from its beginning. Performs the first get.

❑ rewrite (*file variable*): prepares a file to be generated or written. Any current file contents are lost.

❑ get (*file variable*): assigns the next component of the file to the file window. The file must be open for reading, and not at eof.

❑ put (*file variable*): appends the value of the file window to the argument file. It must be open for writing.

Remember . . .

❑ A file is a sequential access type, because file components must be inspected in sequence, starting at the file's beginning. However, most systems will provide a shortcut method for jumping to a known point in a binary file.

❑ The standard input- and output-oriented procedures and functions (read, readln, write, writeln, eof, and eoln) can all be given a file-type variable as an initial argument. The subprograms then apply to that file, rather than to the default input or output. Naturally, readln, writeln, and eoln may only be given textfiles as arguments.

❑ A file variable that doesn't appear in the program heading as a program parameter is temporary. It exists only for the duration of the program.

❑ Always, but always, check for end-of-file before you try to get data from a file.

❑ The Golden Rules of File Variables: First, assignments can't be made between file variables. Second, file variables are being either generated or inspected—never both at the same time. Third, file variables can be passed only to variable parameters—never to value parameters. File variables must be variable parameters even if the file is only going to be inspected.

❑ File redirection is useful when a program has a single input and single output stream, but file variables are necessary when there's more than one input or output at a time.

❑ Textfiles—files with type text—have special properties, mostly having to do with I/O, that are not available for **file of** char.

❏ Conceptually, files are unbounded. However, every operating system imposes some sort of restriction on maximum file length.

❏ Binary files are also known as *typed* or *data* files. Aside from storage of strings, binary files generally store values much more efficiently than textfiles do. However, they can't be inspected using ordinary editing tools.

Big Ideas

The Big Idea in this chapter is:

1. *The file is the elephant of data types—prodigious, but unwieldy.* The advantage of working with files is that they're unbounded: a file can hold any number of components. But to get this advantage for textfiles, we must generally give up random access to individual components, and the ability to make changes anywhere but the file's end.

Begin by Writing the Exam . . .

13-1 Several details of file usage are unlike other variables: a name has to be connected to the file, the file's state has to be set for reading or writing, and so on. Take two example programs from the text and, by leaving out a statement or changing an identifier, create four *Where's the bug?* questions.

13-2 Another way at looking at the question above is to tick off the steps that must be taken before a file can be used. Take a simple file-copying program, leave out a few steps, then ask yourself to *Complete this program.*

13-3 Robustness is an especially important issue for file-handling programs. Although the question *How could you improve this program?* is usually too vague to be a good test question, it's pretty reasonable when the answer is *Check for end-of-file.* Make up two improvable programs.

13-4 Time for a few essay questions? Well, maybe we'll settle for *Define these terms.* Pick five, starting with *What is a file's state?*

13-5 Interaction between types is the most confusing concept of all. Can you take one hundred integer values stored in a file, put them in an array, then put them back into the file in reverse order? Of course! Make up three questions that involve transferring data between files and other data types.

13-6 In most cases, a file-handling program is meant to process a stream of data. The simplest file program, Copy, does nothing to its data, per se; it just connects an input stream (reading a file) to an output stream (writing a file). The 'process' is just read and echo.

Make up three questions that could be solved with program Copy simply by adding a few statements to its process. For instance, *Write a program that copies every other value* would fall into this category, since it can be solved by adding a single extra read call.

13-7 There's another way to build from the basic Copy program—make its data stream more complicated. For example, *Three files contain judges' scores (one per line) for a competition. Create a file that holds the average of the first lines, second lines, etc.* Make up three questions that involve merging values from two or three files into a single output file.

13-8 Next, do the reverse. For example, *A file holds letters, digits, and spaces. Send each category to a separate file.* Make up three process questions that cause a single input file to split into three output files.

13-9 What are files good for? Like arrays and records, files are more useful for some tasks than for others. Make up six applications (e.g. sorting twenty numbers), then ask: *Which three of these need files for a reasonable solution?*

13-10 Secretly, deep down in her heart, every programmer wants to know just how big a file can be. How might you find out? Please, don't do this if you're sharing a disk with somebody else!

13-11 Most computer systems won't limit the number of files a user can have, but they will restrict the number of files that can be open during a single program. Find out your system's limits.

13-12 When they're input from a keyboard, output by a program, or stored in a file, numbers are usually sequences of digit characters. This is the most convenient way to do things, but it's not the most parsimonious. Write a program that generates a sequence of integer values, and compare the size of the files created when they're stored as text and as integer.

13-13 Suppose that a record has three fields: a string type, an integer, and a char value. Outline the process you'd follow to:

a)   store the data for twenty such records in an ordinary textfile;

b)   read the data from a textfile into an array of records;

c)   store the records *as records* in a new file;

d)   read the records back into the array from the new file;

e)   store the array of records' contents into a textfile;

f)   make sure that the first file and the last file are the same.

13-14 What happens on your system if a program that has been writing to a file doesn't call Close? Are all the file's contents there?

13-15 What's an easy way to count the number of different words in a file? Well, the way I do it is to rearrange the file into one-word lines, then sort the file, then get rid of any duplicated lines, and finally count the number of lines that are left. On UNIX or MS-DOS systems the command might look like this (although the exact command names will vary):

```
rearrange data.in | sort | unique | countlines > results.out
```

Write a program that can take care of the third job—finding unique lines. Give your program the following options:

a)   Print just one instance of each line that appears one or more times.

b)   Print just one instance of each line that is *not* repeated, and ignore lines that are repeated.

c)   Print one instance of each line that is repeated, and ignore lines that are not repeated.

d)   Print an error message and quit if the file is not sorted to begin with.

You can assume that each line is just one word long.

13-16 Restricting access to programs or computer systems by requiring passwords is very common. (After all, if it weren't common, we wouldn't be reading all the time about passwords being cracked, now would we?) Passwords are usually kept in a dedicated password file that holds the names and passwords of users. Any program that requires a password check can look up the user's name in the password file, then see if the password she supplies is correct.

Usually, the file is open to public access—anybody can read it—but the passwords are encrypted. Password-checking programs work by encrypting the password the user supplies, then checking it against the encrypted version that's already in the file. In theory (and in practice), such systems can be cracked by trying commonly used passwords—like the user's name—or default passwords like changeme.

Write a set of routines that could be used to maintain a password file. It should be able to check passwords, as well as changing and adding them. The method you use for encryption isn't important, but making your routines robust and bullet-proof is. Special question: How can you deal with the prospect that two programs may try to change the password file at the same time?

13-17 The song *Midnight Train to Georgia* is known not only for its moving lyrics by J. Weatherly and the intensity of the performance by Gladys Knight and the Pips, but also for the beautiful arrangement by T. Camillo. The background vocals are so effective that when the Pips appeared on *Saturday Night Live* they were able to perform a reasonable rendition of the song without Gladys to sing lead.

If you'd like an assignment that is highly suitable for an all-night project, try solving the problem of printing a lyric sheet for *Midnight Train to Georgia*. Assume that you have two files, one containing the lead vocal parts and the other holding the backup singers' words. Write a program that merges the two files, line by line, into a single output file. In other words, your output file should look like this:

```
Gladys (lead)                           Pips (backup)
LA proved too much for the man          Too much for the man
So he's leaving a life he's come to know   He couldn't make it
      . .                                      . .
```

Hint: If you don't know the words, you can get the recording on 45 from Buddah Records.

13-18 *Run-length encoding* is a data compression technique that exploits repetition to shorten overall length. Any series of identical characters:

```
aaaaabbccccdddefg. . .
```

can be replaced by a marker (so that the source text can contain digit characters) and count. Here the marker is a backslash:

```
\5abb\4c\3defg. . .
```

Note that the replacements for **a** and **c** saved room, while **d** had no real effect, and **b** and **e** through **g** were untouched, since compressing them would have actually wasted space. Write programs that use run-length encoding to compress, and uncompress, a file.

13-19 Natural phenomena are often difficult to analyze because a wide range of values may obscure an underlying pattern. For example, consider the measurement of ocean wave heights, which can range from a few centimeters to several meters—all within a single series of measurements. A human observer on the beach can estimate wave height fairly easily and accurately, though, because she ignores smaller waves. In formal terms, she focuses on the *significant wave height*—the height of, say, the tallest third of the waves. A computer, though, needs to have its data selectively filtered.

Write a program that analyzes the top third of the real values in a file. You may assume that all values fall between 0 and 5 meters, with 0.1 meter accuracy. However, the data file itself is of unknown length. Answer these questions:

a)   How many waves were in the 2.3—2.4 meter interval?

b)   What was the range of the top-third waves?

c)   What was the average height of the top-third waves?

13-20 A *macro* is a brief, uniquely identified sequence of characters that represents a longer text sequence. Macros are usually defined in a *macro file*; a brief macro name is followed by the macro's definition. A *macro preprocessor* spots macro names in input text, looks up their definitions in the macro file, then *expands* them as part of output.

Suppose that our macro file read:

```
\P
Whereas the party of the first part,
\.
\D
the party of the second part,
\.
```

Raw source text might be:

\P
an unnamed plaintiff, and
\D
defendant (the University of California, Berkeley) ...

Preprocessor output would be:

```
Whereas the party of the first part,
an unnamed plaintiff, and
the party of the second part,
defendant (the University of California, Berkeley) ...
```

Note that a macro call starts with a backslash and appears on a line by itself. The macro definition begins similarly and ends with a '\.' on a line by itself.

Write a program that allows the definition and use of one-letter macro names. Be sure to make your program relatively robust. It should at least be able to handle a macro that is called, but isn't defined. You need not allow macros that contain other macros, but your program should be able to recognize attempts to define them.

13-21 Many schools require a term or two of foreign-language study. Let's kill two birds with one stone by writing a drill program for verb conjugation.

Suppose that an unnamed foreign language (often used by the author on vacation) has three categories of regular verbs—those that end with *are*, those with *ere*, and those with *ire*. Their regular conjugations are:

infinitive	**compr*are***	**vend*ere***	**part*ire***
I	*-o*	*-o*	*-o*
you	*-i*	*-i*	*-i*
he, she, it	*-a*	*-e*	*-e*
we	*-iamo*	*-iamo*	*-iamo*
you (plural)	*-ate*	*-ete*	*-ite*
they	*-ano*	*-ono*	*-ono*

Create three files (one for each category) of English verbs and their foreign counterparts. Write a program that asks the user to conjugate a verb into a form chosen at random, e.g.:

```
to drink   (you, plural)     Type 'return' for answer.
```

then prints the correct answer on request. Note that the files contain only the English and foreign language verbs. The conjugation forms should be hardwired into your program.

13-22 Repetitive drill is an ideal problem for computer solution. The computer teacher—singleminded, purposeful, and utterly relentless—thinks nothing of asking questions, again and again, until you are as close to perfection as a mere human can be.

For simplicity, let's consider a drill problem with one-line questions and answers—say, states and their capital cities. A poor drill program simply travels through the entire list, then starts over again. A slightly more effective drill program will repeat only the questions that were answered incorrectly. The most effective drill program will return to incorrectly answered questions more frequently, but not exclusively, and not always in the same order.

One suggested algorithm for repetitive drill is:

a)   Take a question from the head of the list.

b) If it's answered incorrectly, reinsert the question among the first *n* questions.

c) If it's answered correctly, put the question on the end of the list.

Write a program that implements this algorithm. How might you propose to set the value of *n*? (Suggestion: when a question is answered correctly, mark it and reinsert it. When it's been answered correctly twice, put it on the end of the list, and decrement *n*.) For the purposes of this exercise, you can trust the user to confess if her answer was incorrect.

13-23 *Computer-aided instruction* is a classroom assistant whose imminent arrival has been heralded for some time now. Let's try to speed things up with a computer-aided multiple-choice question tester. Write a program that lets an instructor prepare, and a student take, multiple-choice tests. The instructor's options should be:

a) Add a question: she should be prompted for the question, the correct answer, then alternate wrong answers.

b) Print the test: print the test with questions numbered and answers labeled **a, b, c**, and so on. **a** is always the correct answer.

c) Delete a question: she should be prompted for the question's number.

The student's options are:

a) Take the test: the possible answers should be presented in random order, of course.

b) Confirm: the correct answer should be shown.

c) Review: as an alternative to immediate confirmation, missed questions should be repeated.

The student's name and score (correct answers/questions) should be added to a permanent file of scores.

Even high-level languages like Pascal generally provide some facilities for low-level work; fortunately, they usually come dressed up in formal attire. Dressed for ball. (p. 483)

14

The **set** Type

The **set** types define variables with an internal structure, just as **record** and **array** types do. The structure of a set is quite limited: it can hold a small number of simple values of just one type.

However, the primitive operations that are defined for sets make them very powerful. They allow unexpectedly easy access to some ideas of parallel programming. Sets let us store or remove many values at once, without having to get our hands dirty on nuts-and-bolts operations.

Section 14-1 describes the set operators and relations, then turns to some basic set applications. Section 14-2 works on longer examples. I'll also outline some more sophisticated applications.

Strictly Pascal

14-1

LET'S BEGIN WITH AN EXAMPLE of the set type in action. Program Groucho, below, is a feeble attempt at duplicating one feature of the Groucho Marx television show *You Bet Your Life*. On the show, accidentally stumbling upon the secret word of the day was worth $100, delivered by duck. In our program, typing in any character from a set of 'secret' characters causes some output.

a set example

```
program Groucho (input, output);
    {Spots values in a set of 'secret' letters.}
type Letterset = set of char;
var Secret:  Letterset;
    Ch:  char;
begin
    {Begin by initializing the Secret set variable.}
    Secret := ['g', 'r', 'o', 'u', 'c', 'h', 'o'];
    {Then, try to prompt some input.}
    writeln ('Try to guess the secret letters.  Start typing.');
    while not eoln do begin
        read (Ch);
        if Ch in Secret then begin
            write ('Beep!!  ')
        end
    end;
    writeln
end.  {Groucho}
```

```
Try to guess the secret letters.  Start typing.
This is a really dumb program.
Beep!! Beep!! Beep!! Beep!! Beep!! Beep!! Beep!!
```

As a means of data storage, plain and simple, the set's advantage is that it represents and allows access to many values without the need for subscripts or field names. Despite itself, Groucho manages to demonstrate a few set features:

— Sets hold values of one type, as Secret holds char values.

some set features

— Sets can represent more than one value at a time, as Secret represents six different letters.

— Sets hold just one instance of each value, as Secret holds just one 'o'.

— We can check if a value is included in a set, as we Beep!! if Ch is in the Secret set.

> The definition of a set type contains the set type's identifier, the reserved words **set of**, and the type of *elements* the set will contain (the set's *base type*).

set type definition

> type identifier ⟶ = **set of** ⟶ *base type identifier* ⟶ ;

The maximum *cardinality* of a set (the maximum number of elements it can have) varies among Pascal systems, but sets typically have up to 256 members (that makes **set of** char legal). The base type can be any ordinal type. It can be a named type, or it can be supplied as an enumerated type or subrange defined on the spot, as part of the definition. For example:

```
type CharSetTYPE = set of char;
     VitaminTYPE = (A, B1, B2, B3, B6, B12, C, D, E);    {an enumeration}
     VitaSetTYPE = set of VitaminTYPE;
     LowNumberTYPE = 1..12;                               {a subrange}
     LowSetTYPE = set of LowNumberTYPE;
     HighSetTYPE = set of 100 .. 150;

var InputCharacters, OutputCharacters: CharSetTYPE;
    FruitVitamins, VegetableVitamins: VitaSetTYPE;
    Responses: LowSetTYPE;
    HighNumbers: HighSetTYPE:
```

Self-Check Questions

Q. Which of these are illegal definitions. Why?

    a) TruthSetTYPE = **set of** boolean;
    b) IntegerSetTYPE = **set of** integer;
    c) VowelSetTYPE = **set of** [´a´, ´e´, ´i´, ´o´, ´u´];

A. Definition *a* is perfectly legal, since it creates a set of the boolean values TRUE and FALSE. Definition *b*, in contrast, is probably illegal because the range of integer is likely to overwhelm most system's legal range for set definitions. Definition *c* is definitely illegal because the group of vowels listed isn't a type or a subrange. Yes, the vowels are a group of values; no, they can't be a type in Pascal.

Q. A set's *powerset* is the collection of different sets that can be created from a given base type. Suppose that a set's base type contains the numbers 1, 2, and 3. How many sets (including the empty set or set of no values) are in its powerset? What are they?

A. As a rule, if the cardinality, or number of values, of a set's base type is n, its powerset has 2^n different values. This is because each element may, or may not, be represented. The three-element set described above has eight sets in its powerset:

[1]	[1, 2]	[1, 3]	[1, 2, 3]
[2]	[2, 3]	[3]	[] *which is the empty set*

Set Assignment

Set variables with the same type can be assigned to each other by name. However, assignments that involve individual elements are a bit more complicated.

Individually named elements of the set's base type must go between square brackets: [ ]. As usual, two dots (..) mean 'through and including':

set assignments

```
OutputCharacters := ['a'..'z', 'A'..'Z', '0'..'9'];
FruitVitamins := [A .. B3, B12, C, E];
VegetableVitamins := FruitVitamins;
InputCharacters := [SomeCharacterValue];
OutputCharacters := [chr(74)];
InputCharacters := OutputCharacters;
Responses := [];
```

The final assignment is unusual because it makes Responses an empty set that contains no values at all. Such assignments are as necessary to sets as initializing assignments to 0 might be for integer variables. Note that Responses = [] is a reasonable boolean expression. It's TRUE if Responses has no members and FALSE otherwise.

I don't want to dwell on details, but it's important to be able to distinguish between values that have a set type and values that (coincidentally, perhaps) share a set's base type. Suppose that InChars is a variable with set type CharSetTYPE, which was in turn defined as a **set of** char. In that case:

set type vs. base type

SomeLetter	*Assume this has type* char
'A'	*has type* char
[SomeLetter]	*has type* CharSetTYPE
['A']	*has type* CharSetTYPE
InChars	*has type* CharSetTYPE

A final point about set values is that they're unordered. Thus, these are equivalent representations of the same set:

set order

$$['A'..'E', 'X'] \qquad ['X', 'B'..'D', 'E', 'A']$$

Self-Check Questions

Q. Which of these sets have the same value? Are any of them illegal representations of sets? Assume that LowTYPE consists of the numbers 1 through 10.

a) [1..10]	*b)* [1..5, 6..9, 10]
c) [1..3, '4', 5..10]	*d)* [1..5, 3, 5..10]
e) [10..6, 5..1]	*f)* [10, 9, 8, 7, 6, 5, 4, 3, 2, 1]
g) [0..10]	*h)* [1..5, 1..9]

A. Expressions *a, b, d,* and *f* are all equivalent. Of the others, only *h* is legal.

Boolean Relations Between Sets

Sets can be inspected or compared in expressions that have boolean values. The most important of these relations involves the **in** operator. The expression:

value **in** *set expression*

is TRUE if a *value* is one of the elements of *set expression*, and FALSE otherwise.

Suppose, for example, that FirstCh, SecondCh, and ThirdCh are all values of type char, while Grades is of the CharSetTYPE (base type char) I defined earlier. These are all legal expressions that have boolean values TRUE or FALSE:

using in

'X' in [FirstCh .. SecondCh]
FirstCh in [SecondCh, ThirdCh]
SecondCh in ['a' .. FirstCh]
'A' in Grades

All of the regular relational operators can be given set operands. They're summarized below, along with a TRUE example expression.

set relations

Sign	Operation	A TRUE *Example*
=	set equality	[1..3] = [1, 2, 3]
<>	set inequality	[2..5] <> []
>=	set 'contains'	[1..10] >= [2..9]
<=	set 'is contained by'	[5] <= [5, 7..9]
in	set membership	7 in [3..11]

As an additional example, suppose that WordLetters has the set type CharSetTYPE defined earlier. The first expression below is TRUE if the WordLetters set includes all the vowels (a vexatious problem without sets), while the second is a barefaced lie unless WordLetters includes the letters 'a' through 'f'.

{*Can you think of any words for which these are TRUE?*}
WordLetters >= ['a','e','i','o','u']
['a'..'f'] <= WordLetters

Self-Check Questions ──────────────────────────────

Q. What words *do* contain all the vowels? How about the letters 'a' through 'f'?

A. It's obvious that 'vexatious' and 'barefaced' comply. But this is an ultraconservative, hardly authoritative list. More feedback?

Set Operators

New set-valued expressions can be constructed with the *set operators* for union, intersection, and difference.

union

The *union*, +, of two sets (or of two representations of Pascal sets) is a set that contains *all* the members of both sets: SetA + SetB.

For example, suppose that the variables below all have CharSetTYPE. Some legitimate set unions are:

IncludedLetters := IncludedLetters + OutputCharacters;
IncludedLetters := MissingLetters +
              OutputCharacters + ['D'..'T']

intersection

> The *intersection*, *, of two sets is a set that contains all values that belong to both sets: SetA * SetB.

If two sets don't contain any common values, their intersection is, of course, the empty set. For example, assume that we've defined the months as an ordinal type. This set expression:

[January .. June, August] * [May .. September]

yields a set expression of three elements—[May, June, August]. The intersection of [January .. May] and [July .. November] is the empty set [ ].

difference

> The *difference*, −, of two sets is a set that contains all the members of the first set that are not also members of the second set: SetA − SetB.

difference of empty sets

Can we try to remove a value that's not included in a set variable? Certainly. The second assignment below is fruitless, but legal:

MissingLettters := [ ];   {MissingLetters *is now an empty set.*}
MissingLetters := MissingLetters − ['A' .. Z']

symmetric difference

We can use the set operators to construct other relations. For example, the *symmetric difference* of two sets is the set of values in one set or the other, but not both. Symmetric set difference is, more or less, the inverse of set intersection. We can get the symmetric difference of two sets by finding their sum, then subtracting their intersection.

Suppose that, as above, we have enumerated the names of the months. To find the symmetric difference of:

[January .. June, August] *and* [May .. September]

we'd begin with their sum:

the sum

[January .. June, August] + [May .. September] *equals* [January .. September]

then find their intersection, which is:

minus the intersection

[January .. June, August] * [May .. September] *equals* [May, June, August]

and finally subtract the intersection from the sum:

equals the symmetric difference

[January .. September] − [May, June, August]
  equals [January .. April, July, September]

Since [January .. May] and [July .. November] have no overlapping membership, their symmetric difference equals their union: [January .. May, July .. November]. Thus, whereas intersection is useful for finding elements common to two sets (the golden months in which oysters may be eaten with blueberries, perhaps), symmetric set difference finds elements that aren't paired.

Remember that if part of an expression is made of individual set elements, the elements must go between square brackets.

elements go between brackets

Grades *is a set variable, so it's unadorned.*
['A'..'C'] *must include brackets.*
Grades * Grades *is an expression made from sets.*
Grades + ['E'] *is also an expression made from sets.*

Self-Check Questions

Q. Consider these definitions:

1. A *proper subset* of a set must contain fewer elements than the whole set.

2. Two *disjoint sets* cannot contain any elements in common.

Write expressions that are TRUE if *a*) SetOne is a proper subset of WholeSet and *b*) SetOne and SetTwo are disjoint.

A. Are these the only expressions that solve the problem?

    a) (SetOne <= WholeSet) **and** (SetOne <> WholeSet)
    b) (SetOne * SetTwo) = []

Q. A set's *complement* consists of the values that belong to the same base type, but aren't in a particular set. Thus, the complement of the empty set is a 'full' set and vice versa. In the set of [1 .. 10], [2 .. 5] is the complement of [1, 6 .. 10].

Suppose that Letters represents part or all of the set of lower-case letters (call it LowerSetTYPE). How could you change the value of Letters to its complement?

A. It's easy—just subtract the current value of Letters from the full set:

    Letters := ['a'..'z'] – Letters;

Standard Practices and Examples

14-2

LET'S LOOK AT SOME EXAMPLES OF the set operators for union, intersection, and so on. Union and difference register the appearance—but not the number of appearances—of a set's elements. For instance:

> Write a program that reads a text sample, then lets us know which lower-case letters *do* appear and which upper-case letters *don't* appear.

The notion of upper and lower cases comes from the shelves that were once used to store movable metal type; I've shown one below. It's hard to avoid recognizing that the data abstraction on which a solution to our counting problem will be based bears a suspicious resemblance to a set.

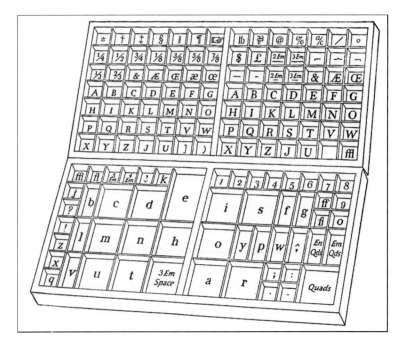

the upper and lower
parts of a printer's type
case

Let's begin with two sets: one holds the upper-case letters and the other is empty. The set type turns out to be convenient as an underlying type for this abstraction for a simple reason: we don't have to bother checking the character before adding to or deleting from a set. If a lower-case character has already been saved, saving it again won't hurt. Similarly, if an upper-case character has been removed, it can be removed again without error. A specification for the program's main loop might be:

> *Goal: Produce sets of used lower-case and unused upper-case letters.*
> *Bound: All the letters in the sample have been seen.*
> *Plan: Read a letter.*
>   *Add it to a set of used lower-case letters.*
>   *Delete it from a set of unused upper-case letters.*

Even though our abstraction relies on the properties and operations of a built-in type, we still require primitives:

— *Initialization:* the set variables are given meaningful initial values— IncludedLetters starts out as an empty set, while MissingLetters initially contains every capital letter.

— *Update:* the union and difference operators are used to update the set variables as values are read. As I mentioned, it's no error to remove (or add) a value more than once.

— *Inspection:* a **for** loop is needed to inspect the set variable element-by-element. Note that the same loops could be used to establish the final cardinality, or number of elements, of IncludedLetters and MissingLetters.

In pseudocode, we:

> *initialize the sets;*
> **while** *there are characters to be read* **do**
>   *read, then update the sets;*
> **for** *every lower-case letter* **do**
>   **if** *it's in the set, print it;*
> **for** *every upper-case letter* **do**
>   **if** *it's in the set, print it;*

The final Pascal program follows.

set union/difference program

```
program Tracker (input, output);
    {Uses sets to find which letters do and don't appear in a text sample.}
type CharSetTYPE = set of char;

var Current: char;
    IncludedLetters, MissingLetters: CharSetTYPE;

begin
    writeln ('Type in a line of your wide-ranging vocabulary.');
    {Initialization}
    IncludedLetters := [ ];
    MissingLetters := ['A' .. 'Z'];
    {Update}
    while not eoln do begin
        read (Current);
        IncludedLetters := IncludedLetters + [Current];
        MissingLetters := MissingLetters − [Current]
    end;
    {Inspection}
    writeln ('Lower-case letters included were:');
    for Current := 'a' to 'z' do begin
        if Current in IncludedLetters then begin
            write (Current)
        end
    end; {for}
    writeln;
    {Inspection}
    write ('Upper-case letters not included were:');   writeln;
    for Current := 'A' to 'Z' do begin
        if Current in MissingLetters then begin
            write (Current)
        end;
    end; {for}
    writeln
end.  {Tracker}
```

```
Type in a sample of your wide-ranging vocabulary.
Pack My Box With Five Dozen Quick Brown Foxes
Lower-case letters included were:
acehiknorstuvwxyz
Upper-case letters not included were:
ACEGHIJKLNORSTUVXYZ
```

Modification Problems ──────────────────────────

1. Although it isn't necessary, change Tracker so that it checks for each letter's current presence or absence before adding it to, or deleting it from, a set.

2. Create a procedure SetOut that prints the contents of its CharSetTYPE argument. Are any other arguments (like a particular range) useful?

3. Modify Tracker so that it asks you for, then reads, a small set of characters. Then, have it search through a file (an on-line dictionary would be great) for words that are (take your pick) *a superset, a subset, the same as* the small set you typed in.

QWERTY vs. Dvorak Keyboards

Let's use sets to compare the efficiency of two popular typewriter keyboards. The *QWERTY* keyboard (mine is shown below) is the current standard.

Unfortunately, few of the most frequently used letters (e, t, a, o, n, r, i, and s) appear on the center 'home' row—the row of keys that a typist's fingers normally rest on. It is said that the keyboard was intentionally designed this way in order to slow down typists and reduce the tendency of mechanical linkages to jam.

Many new keyboard designs have been proposed. The Linotype machine (patented in 1885, and until recently the standard device for setting type) had as its home row the phrase ETAOIN SHRDLU. The common letters were put up front (despite the inconvenience of using the left little finger for e, the commonest of all) in order to keep the machine's mechanical linkages short and secure.

A more modern keyboard, which some computers can be made to use, is the *Dvorak* system, patented in 1936 and shown below. Since the most common characters are in the home row, fewer jumps are required while typing.

```
P Y F G C R L
A O E U I D H T N S
Q J K X B M W V Z
```

Just how beneficial is the Dvorak keyboard? Suppose we write a program that compares the number of jumps a text sample would require from QWER-TY and Dvorak typists. The central loop will keep track of which categories each character falls into:

loop specification

> *Goal: Count the jumps a particular text sample will require.*
> *Bound: The end of the text sample.*
> *Plan: Read a character.*
> *Adjust the counts, as appropriate.*

Sets are the data type of choice because we do have to hold a collection of values, but don't have to individually count their exact numbers. If we define CharSetTYPE as a **set of** char, we can declare variables that represent the 'home' and 'others' characters of the keyboards above. A variable—call it Valid, of type CharSetTYPE—will help restrict the characters we consider, so that extraneous characters from the input file (like ends-of-line) don't affect our count.

why use sets?

What kind of conclusions should the program arrive at? Naturally we want to count the number of jumps that are made. However, this information isn't particularly helpful unless we know the total count of characters considered. The pseudocode below includes these refinements.

pseudocode refinement

> *get a file of input data ready;*
> *initialize the* Valid, *'home' row, and 'other' row set variables;*
> **while** *there are characters to read*
> *read a character;*
> **if** *it's in the* Valid *set of characters*
> *increment the* Total *count;*
> *count any jumps from the QWERTY or Dvorak home row*
> **end** *the* **if** *statement*
> **end** *of the loop;*
> *print the number of jumps for each keyboard and the size of the sample*

The completed program is shown below. I gave it the program source as input.

(program follows)

*typewriter keyboard
program*

```
program KeyTypes (input, output);
    {Compares the jumps required by QWERTY and Dvorak keyboards.}
type CharSetTYPE = set of char;
var QWERTYHome, DvorakHome, QWERTYOthers,
                    DvorakOthers, Valid:  CharSetTYPE;
    QWERTYJumps, DvorakJumps, Total:  integer;
    Current: char;
begin
    Valid := ['a'..'z', 'A'..'Z'];
    QWERTYHome := ['a','s','d','f','g','h','j','k','l','A',
                        'S','D','F','G','H','J','K','L'];
    DvorakHome := ['a','n','i','s','f','e','d','t','h','o','r',
                        'A','N','I','S','F','E','D','T','H','O','R'];
    QWERTYOthers := ['a'..'z', 'A'..'Z'] – QWERTYHome;
    DvorakOthers := ['a'..'z', 'A'..'Z'] – DvorakHome;
    QWERTYJumps := 0;
    DvorakJumps := 0;
    Total := 0;
    while not eof do begin
        read (Current);
        if Current in Valid then begin
            Total := Total + 1;
            if Current in QWERTYOthers then begin
                QWERTYJumps := QWERTYJumps + 1
            end;
            if Current in DvorakOthers then begin
                DvorakJumps := DvorakJumps + 1
            end  {counting the jumps}
        end   {counting the Valid characters}
    end;
    write ('Total input was:    ');
    writeln (Total : 1);
    write ('QWERTY jumps:    ');
    writeln (QWERTYJumps : 1);
    write ('Dvorak jumps:    ');
    writeln (DvorakJumps : 1)
end.   {KeyTypes}
```

Many tedious lines of input appear first. Then . . .

```
Total input was:    694
QWERTY jumps:    487
Dvorak jumps:    234
```

Modification Problems

1. Modify program KeyTypes so that it performs the same check for the home row (ETAOIN SHRDLU) of a Linotype machine.

Sets as Flag Variables

One standard application of sets is to use them as flag variables.

> State variables represent program conditions. A *flag variable* is a state variable that can represent more than one state at a time.

For example, consider these definitions:

```
type OptionTYPE = (ErrorRecovery, InputChecks,
                        OutputChecks, Testing, LongMessages);
     OptionSetTYPE = set of OptionTYPE;
var AllOptions, TestOptions: OptionSetTYPE;
```

A program might begin by initializing AllOptions and TestOptions:

```
AllOptions := [ErrorRecovery .. LongMessages];
TestOptions := [InputChecks, Testing];
```

After being initialized, AllOptions contains every value of the ordinal type OptionTYPE; every flag is set. We can reduce its membership by using the set difference operator:

```
AllOptions := AllOptions – TestOptions;
   {AllOptions is [ErrorRecovery, OutputChecks, LongMessages] }
AllOptions := AllOptions – [ErrorRecovery .. OutputChecks];
   {AllOptions is [LongMessages] }
```

Flag variables can be put to some unexpected tasks. For example, most of our programs so far are written expressly to move from state to state. Ordinary state variables suffice for such programs because they have to represent only one state at a time—usually, a clue to the next action we want to take.

But imagine using states to record where we've been or where we might go. Flags can provide a snapshot that records the states a program has gone through, or describes the legal states a program may attain. For example, the value of PlayerStatus, below, can limit the commands permitted a player, while FeaturesUsed can help with an end-of-game wrap up.

```
type FeatureTYPE = (WarpSpeed, Lasers, ... );
     FeatureSetTYPE = set of FeatureTYPE;
```

using flags

```
var EXPERT, AVERAGE, NOVICE,        {I'll initialize and use these like constants.}
    PlayerStatus,        {E.g. EXPERT or NOVICE, to limit the player.}
    FeaturesUsed: FeatureSetTYPE;
```

Sets as `Parallel´ Variables

Even high-level languages like Pascal generally provide some facilities for low-level work; fortunately, they usually come dressed up in formal attire. So far, we've relied on sets as a convenient alternative to other data types. But if we want, we can take a radically different view by focusing on the set operators.

Instead of seeing them as the primitives of the data abstraction we call a set, we can look at them as the primitives of an as yet unnamed abstraction for *parallel processing*, or performing different calculations simultaneously.

Now, thanks to the lingering remnants of New Math, basic set concepts have been drilled into you since the third or fourth grade. A set union or intersection probably doesn't strike you as remarkable. However, these are really abstract names for parallel operations. Since we have a language for working on sets as whole collections, rather than as individual elements, we're implicitly performing operations on elements in parallel.

Suppose we were to use an array of boolean values as a substitute for a set. Although we could still achieve the same effects—we could, say, determine the complement of such an array or find the common elements of two arrays—we'd have to program the operations component-by-component. In contrast, the set operators add, subtract, or compare elements wholesale *without more programming*.

Thus, sets let us think in terms of parallel operations. Not only does this lead to more easily written programs, but some kinds of problems turn out to have elegant solutions that we wouldn't ordinarily think of. Let's look very briefly at two examples: appointment scheduling and chessboard management.

How are sets useful in scheduling appointments? Consider these:

problem: scheduling appointments

```
const LIMIT = 25;  {number of employees}

type WorkHoursTYPE = 1..16;
     HourSetTYPE = set of WorkHoursTYPE;
     EmployeeTYPE = array [1 .. LIMIT] of HourSetTYPE;

var CEO, VIP,  {Chief executive officer, very important person.}
    FULL, EMPTY,  {I'll use these like constants.}
    Free, Booked, Possible: HourSetTYPE;
    Staff: EmployeeTYPE;
```

As hard-working power tools, CEO and VIP have their hours numbered (1 through 16, that is). We begin by assigning existing appointments:

initializing the calendars

```
FULL := [1..16];
EMPTY := [];
CEO := [1, 3..5];
VIP := [3, 6];
```

Recall that the complement of a set is the set of elements it *doesn't* contain. In Pascal, a set's complement is found by subtracting the set from a variable or constant that holds all the elements. We can use complements to determine CEO's unscheduled time, then arrange a meeting with VIP:

CEO meets VIP

```
{The complement of CEO yields her free hours.}
Free := FULL – CEO;
{When can CEO and VIP meet?  At the intersection.}
Possible := Free * (FULL – VIP);
```

All hours are checked at once.

The same technique applies to finding a time when none of the Staff are busy: complement their individual schedules, and see if the intersection that results is EMPTY or not. In pseudocode:

> *put every hour in* Possible;
> **for** *every staff person*
>   *remove her unavailable hours from the* Possible *pool;*
> *see if any hours are left*

As you read the Pascal version, below, don't forget that each component of the Staff array is a set that holds hours in which meetings are scheduled.

finding free Staff time

```
Possible := FULL;
for Hour := 1 to LIMIT do begin
    Possible := Possible * (FULL – Staff [Hour])
end;   {Possible holds the intersection of all the complements.}
if Possible = EMPTY
    then begin writeln ('A meeting is impossible.') end
    else begin write ('Potential meeting times are:    ');
            for Hour := 1 to 16 do begin
                if i in Possible then begin write(Hour : 3) end
            end; {for}
            writeln
end  {if}
```

Sets in Chess

A second group of examples that take advantage of parallel set operations are found on a chessboard. Set operations are crucial to the success of some computer chess programs, which may have to analyze millions of positions in a limited time. Suppose that we were to number the sixty-four squares of a board and define a set on the basis of this base type. A number of possibilities present themselves:

basing chess strategy on
sets

— Suppose we create a set of 'legal move' squares for each white piece. The union of the white-piece legal move sets is a set of squares that are potentially under attack.

— Suppose we create a set of positions occupied by black pieces. The intersection of the black 'occupied' set, and the 'legal move' union of white sets is the set of currently endangered black pieces.

— Suppose we create a set of 'legal move' positions for each of the black pieces. A set of safe moves for any black piece is the black legal move set minus the white legal move union.

— How might black spot a trap, e.g. white is willing to give up a small piece if it can take a larger piece in return? A potential trap exists if the intersection between one black piece's legal move set and the white 'occupied' set shares one or more elements with the white legal move union.

Note that the actual computer operations that underlie the set operators might, or might not, really execute in parallel. In fact, some of the fastest chess-playing machines require custom-built hardware for parallel execution. Nevertheless, we can use the set operators to describe the analysis of the board in terms of single operations. The abstract ideas of set relations, reified by a concrete package of set operators, let us discuss hard ideas in simple terms.

Syntax Summary

❏   set: the underlying type of a variable that can represent more than one value—the set's *elements*—of an ordinal type. The set's *base type* must be a subrange or enumerated type, and its *cardinality* (size) is often limited to 256.

```
type BaseTYPE = ´a´..´e´;
     SetTYPE = set of BaseTYPE;
     CharSetTYPE = set of char;
     LastCharsSetTYPE = ´v´..´z´;
var Few: BaseTYPE;
    Lots, Many: CharSetTYPE;
    Some: LastCharsSetTYPE;
```

❏   set values: can be constructed from set elements. They must go between square brackets.

```
Few := [´b´..´d´];
Lots := [´b´..´d´, ´t´, ´w´..´z´];
Many := Lots;   {a set variable doesn't need brackets}
```

❏   set operators: take set-valued operands and return set values. They are:

+	union — *the merger of two sets*
*	intersection — *the values common to two sets*
−	difference — *the 'subtraction' of set members*

❏   set relations: the boolean operators as applied to set operands. They are:

Sign	Operation	A TRUE Example
=	set equality	[1..3] = [1, 2, 3]
<>	set inequality	[2..5] <> []
>=	set 'contains'	[1..10] >= [2..9]
<=	set 'is contained by'	[5] <= [5, 7..9]
in	set membership	7 in [3..11]

Remember . . .

❏   A set's *cardinality* is the number of values in its base type—the maximum number of elements a set can have. Maximum set cardinality is often 256; this makes sets of char legal.

❏   A set's *powerset* is the group of different sets that can be formed from a given base type. It always includes the *empty set* of no values.

❏   A set variable's *complement* is the set of values the variable *doesn't* contain.

❏   *Flags* are state variables—they let us know something about a program's current condition. Because they can represent more than one value, sets are particularly useful for implementing flags.

Big Ideas

The Big Idea in this chapter is:

1. *Sets are useful because they take care of bookkeeping automatically.* Anything that can be done with a set of values can also be done with an array. However, the set operators manage in one step what might otherwise require a whole procedureful of code.

Begin by Writing the Exam . . .

14-1   In real-world programming practice, sets usually don't show up until fairly large programs are at hand. As a result, most of the set questions you encounter will be relatively technical. Begin to study by presenting a half-dozen set-type definitions and asking *Which of these are legal?* As an alternative, think up a half-dozen categories (like vegetables) for which you might reasonably be asked *Define these as set types.*

14-2   Set-valued expressions are also a good ground for *Which are legal?* or *Which expressions are the same?* questions. Try to confuse the issue by mixing up set-valued expressions with boolean expressions that use set operands.

14-3   Although Pascal provides a variety of operations on sets, output of set contents is not among them. However, if I were a student, I would certainly expect to be asked to write a procedure that takes a set and prints its contents. Take three of the sets defined in this chapter, and propose *Write an output primitive* questions.

14-4   A similar question would ask for a primitive that counts a set's elements. Again, pose the problem with three sets from the chapter.

14-5   Given the details of set syntax, *Where's the bug?* should be an easy problem to develop. But it's important to test understanding of set semantics, too. Make up three *Where's the bug?* test segments that err because they initialize sets improperly (or not at all), or because they use the wrong set operators or relations.

14-6   Certainly you can define the term *powerset*. But can you anticipate a question that asks you to list a set's powerset? By providing simple set-type definitions, pose two such questions. Just how complicated could such a set reasonably be?

14-7   Program Tracker presents a typical set application—tracking the appearance of letters. However, reading random amounts of input looking for upper- or lower-case letters doesn't require much imagination. Instead, why not see how many words must be read before each letter has been seen or how many characters can be read before a duplicate can be found? Make up three more questions of this ilk.

14-8   Can you define any other kinds of sets (like the set of digit characters or of punctuation marks) for a search? Ask two questions that ask you to *a)* count appearances of values in two categories, and *b)* print the category of values as they appear.

Warmups and Test Programs

14-9   A set of sixteen values can be thought of as the equivalent of an array of sixteen boolean components. Making every array component TRUE is, more or less, like putting every potential element into a set variable. How would you compare the amount of time the two kinds of assignments take? How does the set assignment compare to a 'complete array' assignment, i.e. initializing the array by assigning it another, already initialized array?

14-10   What error messages are caused by neglecting to specify a set's type in an expression? By using the wrong kind of brackets? By using the wrong type of values as elements (e.g. using single-digit integer values instead of the digit char values)?

14-11   Define an ordinal type that represents the months. Then, define a set that can hold MonthTYPE values. Show how to initialize a set variable to *a)* months that have 31 days, *b)* months that have 30 days, *c)* months that have 28 days, *d)* months that don't have the letter 'r' in them.

14-12   Let us imagine that Movers, Groovers, Quakers, Shakers, Lovers, and Fighters are all set variables that represent various constituencies of the base type PopulationTYPE. Write expressions that represent *a)* the entire group, *b)* the Movers and Groovers, *c)* the Lovers who are not Fighters, *d)* the Shakers who are Quakers but not Groovers, *e)* the Fighters who are not Movers, and Movers who aren't Fighters, and *f)* the Groovers and Lovers who are also Shakers.

14-13 Write procedures that take a set parameter of type **set of** char and let you know:

a)   the smallest value in the set;

b)   the largest value in the set;

c)   the cardinality of the set;

d)   the set's contents; and

e)   the set's complement.

14-14 Suppose that SingleSetTYPE variables can hold the single-digit numbers 0 through 9. On the assumption that you have two SingleSetTYPE variables, write boolean functions that let you know if:

a)   one set is a proper subset of the other;

b)   two sets, between them, have all the elements of the sets' base type; or if

c)   two sets, between them, have all the elements of the sets' base type without any duplication.

14-15 Suppose that sets were not part of Pascal. How would you go about duplicating the set abstraction with arrays of boolean components? Outline procedures that would allow the basic set operations (union, difference, and so on) on array-type operands.

Programming Problems

14-16 Write a program that reads a text sample and prints every word that contains all the vowels. If you have access to an on-line dictionary, use that as data. If not, try:

> If an authoritative argument for the augmentation of coeducational boardinghouses is to be communicated, dialogue to exhaustion is often necessary, since vexatious ultraconservatives take tenacious precautions against the refutation of their reputations. They consider sensible feedback to be simultaneously sacrilegious and revolutionary since, after all, barefaced oneupmanship is an ostentatious form of persuasion.

Can you modify your program to find two words (included) that contain the letters ´a´, ´b´, ´c´, ´d´, ´e´, and ´f´?

14-17 Write a program that reads three lines of text and prints:

a)   the vowels that appear on all three lines;

b)   the consonants that appear on the first two lines;

c)   the letters that appear on the first line.

14-18 A freshman programming student invents a simple way to shuffle a deck of cards—she defines a set of the integer values 1..52, then chooses a random number between 1 and 52. Each time she picks a number, she removes it from the set and adds it to an array. Should she ever pick a number that has already been chosen, she simply picks again.
How long will it take her to deal two ten-card hands using this method? How long do you think it will take her to shuffle 52 cards?

14-19 Pascal sets are useful because of the operators defined for set expressions. Sets in general, though, are limited by a basic concept—that a set contains only one instance of a given member. Suppose we correct this deficiency by defining a *bag* as a set that can hold up to five instances of each value.
Write a program that uses an array of sets to implement a bag of the integer subset 1..25. Write procedures that make use of the set operators to do bag addition, subtraction, and intersection.

14-20 For a text-oriented version of the bag problem, above, define a bag of characters. How many sets are required for the bag that contains this input sample (ignoring punctuation and capitalization)? What are the contents of each set?

```
Why jog exquisite bulk, fond crazy vamp,
Daft buxom jonquil, zephyr's gawky vice?
Guy fed by work, quiz Jove's xanthic lamp—
Zow!  Qualms by deja vu gyp fox-kin thrice.
```

14-21 Yet another text-oriented bag problem. Two anagrams contain the exact same bag of letters (ignoring spaces and punctuation). Write a program that checks anagrams. As sample input, try:

```
multiple-word anagrams / plague raw mortal minds
Donald Ervin Knuth / hunt, drink, and love / halt unkind vendor!
Ronald Wilson Reagan / No, darlings—no ERA law.
```

14-22 A group of twenty faculty members at an unnamed university has spent a year engaged in mutual backscratching. They have agreed that whenever one faculty member acknowledges (in print) the inspiration or encouragement of another, the second must return the favor.

Near the end of the year, the faculty gather to total up their accounts. Prof. A notes that she has thanked Profs. E, G, M, and N; Prof. B records that she has acknowledged Profs. A, G, and R, and so on. Clearly some accounts are unbalanced; although B has thanked A, A has not thanked B for something else.

Write a program that helps the faculty determine who owes whom. Assume that input consists of twenty sets (for Professors A through T) of names (A through T again). Hint: use an **array**[´A´.. T´] of appropriate sets.

14-23 Two engineers are comparing the merits of a number of building materials. They are having a difficult time of it because the tests are all equally important and cannot be rank-ordered in any way. Worse yet, in any given test, each material either passed or failed.

Write a program that reads the results of ten tests on five materials. Create, for each material, a set of the tests it has passed. Write primitives that determine:

a) if any material has passed every test *all the others* have;

b) if any material has passed all the tests that *any single other* has, plus at least one more;

c) if any materials have passed none of the same tests;

d) if any materials have identical test results.

14-24 *Wheel of Misfortune* is one of the many television shows that would be available if I were in charge. The rules are simple: an equation is shown, with blank lights taking the place of the factors of each term. The players take turns calling out digits; any correct numbers are lit up. The first player to guess the contents of the equation wins.

For example, the equation $27 + 23 = 2 * 25$ would initially be shown as:

□□ + □□ = □ * □□

After the guess '2' it would be:

2□ + 2□ = 2 * 2□

A guess of '5' would yield:

2□ + 2□ = 2 * 25

Unfortunately, a numerically oriented Vanna White is not available. Write a program that takes her place.

14-25 Write a program that plays Tic-Tac-Toe. Number the boxes, then use one set to hold X choices and another to hold the O's. Naturally, an array of sets should be used to hold, and check, winning positions.

A chain of pointers isn't like a ball of string. If the end gets lost, it's really gone. Hold on to those pointers! (p. 538)

15

The Pointer Types

In her autobiography, Helen Keller described a wonderful moment: the day that she, unable to hear, speak, or see, came to understand that every thing had a name. Suddenly she realized that she had a way to communicate; you could learn about things by learning their names.

Pointers will bring you a tool that's precisely the opposite, but is quite wonderful nonetheless: a way to work with things *without* names. We'll create anonymous variables on the fly, as we need them, and use pointers in place of identifiers.

In this chapter, we'll see how to build structures whose components can be put into any order that's convenient and meaningful. Our basic tool will be a *node*—a record that has some fields for information and one or more *pointer* fields that locate the node's neighbors. I won't kid you—pointers can be confusing at first. But they are the basis of all advanced programming, so don't give up.

Section 16–3 uses pointers with recursion and may follow this chapter.

Strictly Pascal

15-1

I HATE ROUNDABOUT INTRODUCTIONS, BUT I'M willing to make an exception for pointers. Life will be easier later if you have a feel for why pointers are necessary and why certain details of usage are an inevitable consequence of what pointers are used for.

Let's begin with an example that seems as though it can be solved with our old tools (arrays and records), but which winds up giving us the motivation we'll need to 'invent' pointers on our own. Suppose that we're working with this array of records:

```
type StringTYPE = packed array [1 .. 3] of char;
     ItemTYPE = record
                     Data: StringTYPE;
                     Next: integer
                end;
     ListTYPE = array [1..20] of ItemTYPE;

var List: ListTYPE;
    First, Last, CurrentPtr: integer;
```

We might use the array to hold a sequence of words in alphabetical order:

the words are alphabetized

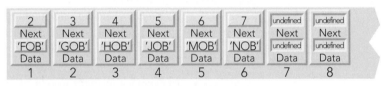

First = 1, Last = 6, CurrentPtr = 7

As you can see, the Next field of each component holds a subscript. If you follow the trail of Next fields, you'll read the words in alphabetical order. However, since the physical (subscript) order and logical (alphabetical) order of the components are the same, the Next field doesn't seem to serve any purpose.

physical and logical order

But Next is useful if we add new words to the end of our carefully ordered array. Depending on what arrives, physical and logical order may break down. Not every word causes problems, mind you. If a lucky word like 'Sob' arrives, it can be stored in the seventh record without messing up the array's order.

But what if 'Lob' shows up instead? Since it follows 'Job', components 'Mob' and 'Nob' have to move to the right to make room. A word like 'Bob' is much worse, since every word has to slide down.

problems with insertion

It's time to get smart and take advantage of the Next field. Even if we jumble the records stored in the array, as I have below, we can still use each record's Next field to keep track of alphabetical order:

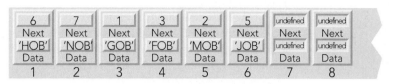

First = 4, Last = 2, CurrentPtr = 7

the array is jumbled, but
ordered

I'll show you how easy it is to store a new word at the end of the array (in List[CurrentPtr], which happens to be List[7] now) without messing up the ordered sequence of Next fields. Consider three (independent, not consecutive) cases:

New word	Changes	Inserts...
'Sob'	List[7].Data := 'Sob'; List[7].Next := 8; CurrentPtr := CurrentPtr + 1; Last := 7;	*a new 'highest' word*
'Bob'	List[7].Data := 'Bob'; List[7].Next := 4; CurrentPtr := CurrentPtr + 1; First := 7;	*a new 'lowest' word*
'Lob'	List[7].Data := 'Lob'; List[7].Next := 5; List[5].Next := 8; CurrentPtr := CurrentPtr + 1;	*a new word in the middle*

subscripts as links

Physical and logical order are independent now. Even though the physical ordering of the components is jumbled, we use the Next fields to keep the sequence alphabetized. The records are connected by their subscripts in a *linked* list of components.

the catch

Although it makes a very pretty picture, there is a major flaw in the method I've used to store words. It depends on an array declaration; but an array's size is fixed at compile time. If words keep arriving, we'll eventually run out of room to store them in the array. While we could try to avoid problems by the simple expedient of declaring enormous arrays, real-life limits on computer memory rule out this dodge out; we can't declare an array that's big enough for every eventuality.

We Invent Pointers!

What we would like, then, is to have records that can be tied together without being locked into an array. In some way, we'd like each record's Next field to hold the next record's name, instead of holding its subscript in an array.

But at the same time, we don't want to have to declare each record as a separate variable. How many records will we need? We can't tell, because we don't know how many words there will eventually be. As you might expect, pointers come to the rescue.

pointers represent
addresses

> Pointers let us *dynamically allocate* record variables—create them one at a time, as we need them, while a program is running. A pointer variable represents the 'subscript,' in computer memory, of a dynamically allocated variable. This 'subscript' is called an *address*.

Take something on faith: computer memory is nothing more than a big array, whose subscripts are called addresses. When we declare program variables, we're just grabbing little pieces of memory. Record and array variables are just slightly larger hunks of the big memory array.

A pointer's actual value is an address, or subscript in computer memory. When we dynamically allocate, say, a record variable with a pointer, two things happen:

— First, the computer sets aside enough storage in its memory to hold the record. This is a variable, but it's anonymous, since it doesn't have a fixed name. I'll usually refer to it as a *location*.

— Then, the address that marks this location, or particular piece of memory, is given to the pointer variable.

An ordinary variable represents the value stored in a location in memory.

A pointer variable represents the address of a location in memory.

Now, an ordinary variable *names* its piece of memory. An assignment to an ordinary variable changes the value stored there. For all intents and purposes, the name *is* the variable, and we can only make assignments *to* it.

A pointer variable, in contrast, *addresses* its piece of memory. There are two ways to make an assignment with a pointer—either *to* it or *through* it.

assigning to pointers

— An assignment *to* a pointer changes the address it represents, not the value stored at the address.

assigning through
pointers

— An assignment *through* a pointer changes the value stored at the location the pointer addresses. To go through a pointer, follow its name with a circumflex (ˆ).

In this text, I'll use an up-arrow (↑) instead, because it's much more legible.

Even though a pointer's value acts as a numerical subscript, we can't add to it, subtract from it, or use its value. However, there are a few interesting things that we can do:

— We can inspect the location that the pointer addresses (or its fields, if it's a record).

— We can change that location's value (or its field's values, if it's a record).

— We can see if two pointers have the same value—if they address the same location or stored variable.

— We can assign a pointer's value to another pointer variable (or to a pointer-type *field* in a record), so that they point to the same address.

The last point is the most useful for us now. If a record's Next field has a pointer type we can use it to store a pointer's value. Each record can have a Next field that holds the address of another record.

Most programs that employ pointers use them with records. The combination is powerful, but notation (the combination of arrows and dots) makes it a little confusing at first. Let's start with a simpler program that doesn't do anything practical, but will provide a very clear example of pointer declaration and allocation.

```
program Pointers (input, output);
    {Demonstrates pointer allocation and assignment.}
type CharPOINT = ↑ char;                                          {1}
var FirstPtr, SecondPtr, ThirdPtr:  CharPOINT;                    {2}
begin
    {Allocate a char-sized location for each pointer to address.}
    new (FirstPtr);                                               {3}
    new (SecondPtr);

    FirstPtr ↑ := 'A';       {Give the location a value.}         {4}
    SecondPtr ↑ := 'B';      {Store a different value here.}
    ThirdPtr := FirstPtr;    {Give the first location a second name.}  {5}
    write (FirstPtr ↑);
    write (SecondPtr ↑);
    write (ThirdPtr ↑);
    writeln
end.   {Pointers}
```

pointers to char variables

ABA

Here's what to look for in Pointers:

1. *Definition* sets the Pascal type of the location the pointer addresses.

2. *Declaration* creates the pointer variables.

3. *Allocation* gives the pointer the address of the location (i.e. the anonymous variable) it will name.

4. *Assignment to a location*, e.g. FirstPtr ↑ := 'A', stores a value in the variable the pointer addresses.

5. *Assignment to a pointer*, e.g. ThirdPtr := FirstPtr, gives the pointer a different address value.

We'll review each of these steps in detail over the next few pages. But why don't we run a test bed first? Program PointBed, below, is basically a copy of Pointers. I've show what you would see if you were to run it on a typical personal computer that did *not* pre-initialize pointers in any way. Note that I've put two kinds of variables in the variables window: the pointers themselves and the char values they point to.

I've intentionally left in a few of the details that you couldn't ordinarily see if you were just running a Standard Pascal program. First, my generic environment always shows actual pointer values as PTR(*location*). The value in parentheses is either two hexadecimal (base 16, indicated by a dollar sign) numbers that identify a particular location in memory, or **NIL**, which is the pointer equivalent of 'no value.' Right now, we're about to execute the very first program statement. All the values shown are garbage values that were lying around in memory before the program started.

before the first
procedure call

```
┌───────────── POINTBED.PAS ─────────────
│ program PointBed (input, output);
│   {A first test bed for pointers.}
│
│ type CharPOINT = ^ char;
│
│ var FirstPtr, SecondPtr, ThirdPtr:  CharPOINT;
│
│ begin                                      ┌───── Variables ─────
│   new (FirstPtr);            {Allocate}    │ FirstPtr: PTR($71,$0)
│   new (SecondPtr);                         │ SecondPtr: PTR($0,$9009)
│   FirstPtr^ := 'A';      {Assign through}  │ ThirdPtr: NIL
│   SecondPtr^ := 'B';                       │ FirstPtr^: 'è'
│   ThirdPtr := FirstPtr;     {Assign to}    │ SecondPtr^: 't'
│   write (FirstPtr^);                       │ ThirdPtr^: '■'
│   write (SecondPtr^);                      │
│   writeln (ThirdPtr^);                     │
│ end.   {PointBed}
```

At first, everything in the watch window is a junk value that happened to be in memory. But as soon as we step past the first new call and allocate a location for FirstPtr you'll see two changes. Since FirstPtr gets a new value, it addresses a new memory location. And, because FirstPtr ↑ represents the value stored *in* that location, FirstPtr ↑ will show a new junk value.

after the first new

```
┌───────────── POINTBED.PAS ─────────────
│ begin                                      ┌───── Variables ─────
│   new (FirstPtr);            {Allocate}    │ FirstPtr: PTR($675F,$0)
│   new (SecondPtr);                         │ SecondPtr: PTR($0,$9009)
│   FirstPtr^ := 'A';      {Assign through}  │ ThirdPtr: NIL
│   SecondPtr^ := 'B';                       │ FirstPtr^: '['
│   ThirdPtr := FirstPtr;     {Assign to}    │ SecondPtr^: 't'
│   write (FirstPtr^);                       │ ThirdPtr^: '■'
│   write (SecondPtr^);                      │
│   writeln (ThirdPtr^);                     │
│ end.   {PointBed}
```

We get the same pair of changes when we allocate SecondPtr, below. However, the memory location it points to is different. Compare the $0 to the $8; the actual numbers aren't important, but the fact that they differ is.

```
                   — POINTBED.PAS ———————
begin                                        —— Variables ——
  new (FirstPtr);              {Allocate}   FirstPtr: PTR($675F,$0)
  new (SecondPtr);                          SecondPtr: PTR($675F,$8)
  FirstPtr^ := 'A';        {Assign through} ThirdPtr: NIL
  SecondPtr^ := 'B';                         FirstPtr^: '['
  ThirdPtr := FirstPtr;       {Assign to}   SecondPtr^: 'z'
  write (FirstPtr^);                         ThirdPtr^: '■'
  write (SecondPtr^);
  writeln (ThirdPtr^);
end.   {PointBed}
```

after the second new

The next two statements make assignments through the pointers. First, we initialize FirstPtr↑:

```
                   — POINTBED.PAS ———————
begin                                        —— Variables ——
  new (FirstPtr);              {Allocate}   FirstPtr: PTR($675F,$0)
  new (SecondPtr);                          SecondPtr: PTR($675F,$8)
  FirstPtr^ := 'A';        {Assign through} ThirdPtr: NIL
  SecondPtr^ := 'B';                         FirstPtr^: 'A'
  ThirdPtr := FirstPtr;       {Assign to}   SecondPtr^: 'z'
  write (FirstPtr^);                         ThirdPtr^: '■'
  write (SecondPtr^);
  writeln (ThirdPtr^);
end.   {PointBed}
```

after initializing FirstPtr↑

Next comes SecondPtr↑:

```
                   — POINTBED.PAS ———————
begin                                        —— Variables ——
  new (FirstPtr);              {Allocate}   FirstPtr: PTR($675F,$0)
  new (SecondPtr);                          SecondPtr: PTR($675F,$8)
  FirstPtr^ := 'A';        {Assign through} ThirdPtr: NIL
  SecondPtr^ := 'B';                         FirstPtr^: 'A'
  ThirdPtr := FirstPtr;       {Assign to}   SecondPtr^: 'B'
  write (FirstPtr^);                         ThirdPtr^: '■'
  write (SecondPtr^);
  writeln (ThirdPtr^);
end.   {PointBed}
```

after initializing
SecondPtr↑

Finally, as we step past the assignment to ThirdPtr, you'll see two simultaneous changes once more:

```
                   — POINTBED.PAS ———————
begin                                        —— Variables ——
  new (FirstPtr);              {Allocate}   FirstPtr: PTR($675F,$0)
  new (SecondPtr);                          SecondPtr: PTR($675F,$8)
  FirstPtr^ := 'A';        {Assign through} ThirdPtr: PTR($675F,$0)
  SecondPtr^ := 'B';                         FirstPtr^: 'A'
  ThirdPtr := FirstPtr;       {Assign to}   SecondPtr^: 'B'
  write (FirstPtr^);                         ThirdPtr^: 'A'
  write (SecondPtr^);
  writeln (ThirdPtr^);
end.   {PointBed}
```

now two pointers are
identical

Since ThirdPtr now addresses a new location, ThirdPtr↑ represents the value stored there. It's the same location, and the same stored value, that FirstPtr refers to.

Modification Problems

1. Ready to modify Pointers (or PointBed)? Add whatever is needed to make all three pointers address the same location—say, the one that holds a 'B' now.
2. Change Pointers so that it uses pointers to integer values instead of char.

Definition, Declaration, Allocation

As you know, ordinary variables can hold values of only a specific type. In consequence, they can be assigned only values of that one type. Pointers have a similar restriction: they can *address* variables of only a particular type. A pointer's type definition says what that type is. A pointer can address either a simple variable (like a char) or one that's structured (like a record type). The syntax chart of a pointer type definition is:

pointer type definition

> *type identifier* ⟶ = ∧ ⟶ *type identifier* ⟶ ;

For example:

some typical definitions

```
type CharPOINT = ↑ char;  {from the example above}
     NodePOINT = ↑ NodeTYPE;  {a more practical definition}
     NodeTYPE = record
                     Letter: char;
                     Next: NodePOINT
                end;
var FirstCharPtr, SecondCharPtr: CharPOINT;
    FirstNodePtr, LastNodePtr: NodePOINT;
```

There are two differences between CharPOINT and NodePOINT:

— They *have* different types (even though they're both pointers).

— They *address* different types.

Although CharPOINT and NodePOINT are both pointer types, they aren't the same type, any more than two separately defined array types would be the same. Nor do FirstCharPtr and FirstNodePtr address the same type of variable; one addresses a char variable, while the other addresses a record.

an exception to define-before-you-use

> Note that the definition NodePOINT = ↑ NodeTYPE violates the define-before-you-use rule. This is a legal exception to the rule: a pointer type definition may precede the definition of the record it points to.

Because the NodeTYPE definition refers to NodePOINT, there's no way for Pascal to avoid having to make this exception.

Our next step is to allocate locations in memory—the 'anonymous' variables our pointers will address—with the standard procedure new. After we've defined and declared pointer variables to work with, these calls allocate storage for two of our pointers:

begin
    new (FirstCharPtr);
    new (FirstNodePtr);

allocation

The call new (FirstCharPtr) tells the computer to set aside a space big enough to hold a char variable and to have FirstCharPtr address that space. The second call allocates a space big enough for a NodeTYPE record and gives FirstNodePtr its address.

Procedure dispose frees space for reallocation. Most programs won't require deallocation (the applications we'll look at don't use all that much memory), but it's important to know how it's done:

deallocating pointers

    {Return locations to the computer.}
    dispose (FirstCharPtr);
    dispose (FirstNodePtr);

To summarize, we prepared to use pointers by:

1. Defining a new type as a pointer to variables of some type.

2. Declaring variables with the pointer type.

3. Allocating locations for the pointer variables to address.

Self-Check Questions

Q. Quick: what's wrong with this call?

    {an incorrect call}
    new (NodePOINT);

A. It makes a common mistake; it uses the name of a pointer *type* where it should use the name of a pointer *variable*, e.g.:

    new (FirstNodePtr);

Q. Is this sequence of calls legal? What does it do?

    new (FirstCharPtr);
    new (FirstCharPtr);

A. The sequence is legal, but I can't think of any reason you'd want to make it. The first call allocates a location and gives FirstCharPtr its address. The second call allocates a second location and reassigns FirstCharPtr. Thus, the address of the first location is lost; no pointer addresses it, and it can't be used for anything.

Assignment To and Through Pointers

A pointer variable can get a value in three different ways:

1. A call of new will give it the address of a new location in memory.

2. It can be assigned the value of another pointer variable, so that they both address the same location.

3.   It can be assigned a 'non-value' called nil. nil can be assigned to *any* pointer-type variable.

For example, let's allocate a location for FirstCharPtr, then give SecondCharPtr the same address, and finally make FirstCharPtr a nil-valued pointer.

assignments to pointers

```
new (FirstCharPtr);
SecondCharPtr := FirstCharPtr;
FirstCharPtr := nil;
```

Although FirstCharPtr and SecondCharPtr are both defined—they both have values—the content of the location that SecondCharPtr addresses is still undefined. We haven't assigned anything to it yet.

> The actual address values that pointers hold can be compared only for equality or to nil. They cannot be printed or used in any other kind of expression. Only pointers of the same type can be compared.

A pointer that equals nil doesn't address a location:

```
{Determine if FirstCharPtr addresses a storage location.}
if  FirstCharPtr = nil
     then write ('Warning!  Nil pointer.  No location to access.')
     else write ('A location has been allocated for this pointer.')
```

comparing pointers

If two pointers equal each other, it means that they address the same location *or* they're both nil.

```
{What does it mean that FirstCharPtr and SecondCharPtr have the same value?}
if  FirstCharPtr = SecondCharPtr
     then write ('They have the same address or are both nil.')
     else write ('The pointer values differ.')
```

So much for assignment to pointers. Assignment *through* a pointer stores a value in the location that the pointer addresses.

how pointers name variables

> A pointer identifier that is followed by a circumflex (ˆ) names a dynamically allocated variable. Without the arrow, the pointer identifier names an address in memory. With the arrow, the pointer identifier names the variable stored at that address.

As noted, I'll always use the up-arrow (↑) because it's more readable in this typeface, but your keyboard probably uses a circumflex. (*Don't* try to use the ↑ key by mistake, though.)

Allocating and assigning a value to a char location is pretty easy. After the lines below, both FirstCharPtr ↑ and SecondCharPtr ↑ equal 'T'.

allocating simple variables

```
new (FirstCharPtr);
FirstCharPtr ↑ := 'T';
SecondCharPtr := FirstCharPtr;
```

Working with a pointer to a record is more interesting. Recall that the basic definition is:

type NodePOINT = ↑ NodeTYPE; {a more practical definition}
    NodeTYPE = record
            Letter: char;
            Next: NodePOINT
      end;
  var FirstNodePtr, LastNodePtr: NodePOINT;

When a pointer addresses a record, the pointer identifier followed by a circumflex is the record's name. Dot notation will be needed to make an assignment to a single field of that record:

allocating structured variables

new (FirstNodePtr);
FirstNodePtr ↑.Letter := 'W';

Names are going to get a little more confusing:

FirstNodePtr *is a pointer that can represent an address or be* nil
FirstNodePtr ↑ *is the record at that address*
FirstNodePtr ↑.Letter *is one field of that record*

Now let's try a test question to see if you understand pointers. Suppose we've allocated and initialized FirstNodePtr. What's the difference between this assignment:

LastNodePtr := FirstNodePtr;

a test question

and this call and assignment?

new (LastNodePtr);
LastNodePtr ↑ := FirstNodePtr ↑;

The first assignment makes LastNodePtr address the same location (which holds a record) as FirstNodePtr. In effect, there's only one variable, but it has two names, FirstNodePtr ↑ and LastNodePtr ↑. In contrast, the second set of statements allocates a new location for LastNodePtr to address. Then, we make a record-to-record assignment between the two locations (since they're both records). The two records have the same values, but they're different variables.

Finally, let's get a little bit ahead of ourselves. Recall that the record that FirstNodePtr addresses has two fields. We've been working with the Letter field. Now let's try something with the Next field of FirstNodePtr ↑—the one that has type NodePOINT:

{We can initialize it . . .}
FirstNodePtr ↑.Next := nil;
{. . . or allocate it.}
new (FirstNodePtr ↑.Next);

FirstNodePtr is a pointer that addresses a record. One field of that record, Next, is also a pointer that addresses a record. By allocating a new record for that field to address, we've just invented the *linked list!* We'll spend most of the section 15–2 looking at links.

But first, how about another test bed? Program NodeBed, below, works with the same sort of node record and takes the first few steps of building a linked list. Once again, I'm showing memory location values that are typical for a personal computer. However, you should bear in mind that there's no way to display their actual values in Standard Pascal.

Note that I've arranged my generic environment so that the variables window shows both fields, in order of declaration, of the NodeTYPE record. As the program is about to execute its first statement, every variable has a garbage value.

about to allocate the
first pointer

```
————————— NODEBED.PAS —————————
program NodeBed (input, output);
  {A test bed for your basic node.}
type NodePTR = ^NodeTYPE;
     NodeTYPE = record
                    Letter:  char;
                    Next:   NodePTR
                end;
var FirstPtr, CurrentPtr:  NodePTR;
begin
    new (FirstPtr);
    CurrentPtr := FirstPtr;
    FirstPtr^.Letter := 'A';
    new (FirstPtr^.Next);              ——————— Watches ———————
    CurrentPtr := CurrentPtr^.Next;   FirstPtr: PTR($571E,$14DE)
    CurrentPtr^.Letter := 'B';        FirstPtr^: ('R',PTR($4441,$524F))
    CurrentPtr^.Next := NIL;          CurrentPtr: PTR($2308,$EC9A)
end.  {NodeBed}                       CurrentPtr^: ('&',PTR($B02,$31D2))
```

As we step through NodeBed you'll see a progression of updates like those in PointBed. As FirstPtr is allocated, FirstPtr ↑ changes as well:

after the first new call

```
————————— NODEBED.PAS —————————
var FirstPtr, CurrentPtr:  NodePTR;
begin
    new (FirstPtr);
    CurrentPtr := FirstPtr;
    FirstPtr^.Letter := 'A';           ——————— Watches ———————
    new (FirstPtr^.Next);             FirstPtr: PTR($6757,$0)
    CurrentPtr := CurrentPtr^.Next;   FirstPtr^: ('t',PTR($D800,$12))
    CurrentPtr^.Letter := 'B';        CurrentPtr: PTR($2308,$EC9A)
    CurrentPtr^.Next := NIL;          CurrentPtr^: ('&',PTR($B02,$31D2))
end.  {NodeBed}
```

Remember that the actual pointer values are totally irrelevant. What's interesting is whether or not two pointers have the *same* value—that means they point to the same location. After the assignment to CurrentPtr, pointers *and* the locations they point to are identical:

```
┌──────────────── NODEBED.PAS ────────────────┐
│ var FirstPtr, CurrentPtr: NodePTR;           │
│ begin                                        │
│     new (FirstPtr);                          │
│     CurrentPtr := FirstPtr;     ┌──── Watches ────────────┐
│     FirstPtr^.Letter := 'A';    │ FirstPtr: PTR($6757,$0)         │
│     new (FirstPtr^.Next);       │ FirstPtr^: ('t',PTR($D800,$12)) │
│     CurrentPtr := CurrentPtr^.Next; │ CurrentPtr: PTR($6757,$0)    │
│     CurrentPtr^.Letter := 'B';  │ CurrentPtr^: ('t',PTR($D800,$12)) │
│     CurrentPtr^.Next := NIL;    └─────────────────────────┘
│ end.  {NodeBed}                              │
└──────────────────────────────────────────────┘
```

after making the
pointers identical

There are two also simultaneous updates when I assign FirstPtr↑.Letter the letter ´A´:

```
┌──────────────── NODEBED.PAS ────────────────┐
│ var FirstPtr, CurrentPtr: NodePTR;           │
│ begin                                        │
│     new (FirstPtr);                          │
│     CurrentPtr := FirstPtr;     ┌──── Watches ────────────┐
│     FirstPtr^.Letter := 'A';    │ FirstPtr: PTR($6757,$0)         │
│     new (FirstPtr^.Next);       │ FirstPtr^: ('A',PTR($D800,$12)) │
│     CurrentPtr := CurrentPtr^.Next; │ CurrentPtr: PTR($6757,$0)    │
│     CurrentPtr^.Letter := 'B';  │ CurrentPtr^: ('A',PTR($D800,$12)) │
│     CurrentPtr^.Next := NIL;    └─────────────────────────┘
│ end.  {NodeBed}                              │
└──────────────────────────────────────────────┘
```

after changing the Letter
field

Suppose that I skip a couple of steps. In the shot below, notice that CurrentPtr has the same value as the Next field (the PTR part) of FirstPtr↑. CurrentPtr↑'s own Letter field holds the letter ´B´, and its Next field points to yet another location in memory.

```
┌──────────────── NODEBED.PAS ────────────────┐
│ var FirstPtr, CurrentPtr: NodePTR;           │
│ begin                                        │
│     new (FirstPtr);                          │
│     CurrentPtr := FirstPtr;     ┌──── Watches ────────────┐
│     FirstPtr^.Letter := 'A';    │ FirstPtr: PTR($6757,$0)        │
│     new (FirstPtr^.Next);       │ FirstPtr^: ('A',PTR($6757,$8)) │
│     CurrentPtr := CurrentPtr^.Next; │ CurrentPtr: PTR($6757,$8)   │
│     CurrentPtr^.Letter := 'B';  │ CurrentPtr^: ('B',PTR($2E00,$2)) │
│     CurrentPtr^.Next := NIL;    └─────────────────────────┘
│ end.  {NodeBed}                              │
└──────────────────────────────────────────────┘
```

after changing only the
new Letter field

After we make the final assignment, the Next field is nil.

```
┌──────────────── NODEBED.PAS ────────────────┐
│ var FirstPtr, CurrentPtr: NodePTR;           │
│ begin                                        │
│     new (FirstPtr);                          │
│     CurrentPtr := FirstPtr;     ┌──── Watches ────────────┐
│     FirstPtr^.Letter := 'A';    │ FirstPtr: PTR($6757,$0)        │
│     new (FirstPtr^.Next);       │ FirstPtr^: ('A',PTR($6757,$8)) │
│     CurrentPtr := CurrentPtr^.Next; │ CurrentPtr: PTR($6757,$8)   │
│     CurrentPtr^.Letter := 'B';  │ CurrentPtr^: ('B',NIL)         │
│     CurrentPtr^.Next := NIL;    └─────────────────────────┘
│ end.  {NodeBed}                              │
└──────────────────────────────────────────────┘
```

the program is done

Self-Check Questions

Q. Write a program segment that prints the value in the location that FirstCharPtr (a pointer to a char) addresses; but make it robust, just in case FirstCharPtr is **nil**.

A. Since a **nil** pointer doesn't address a location, it can't be followed by a circumflex. In other words, this would be illegal:

```
{An illegal example.}
FirstCharPtr := nil;
writeln (FirstCharPtr↑);
```

To avoid the mistake of trying to look at a location that hasn't been allocated, we have to see if FirstCharPtr is **nil** first:

```
if FirstCharPtr = nil
    then writeln ('Nil pointer.')
    else writeln (FirstCharPtr↑)
```

Some Practice with Names

Before we get to more link operations, it's absolutely essential to understand the distinction between pointers and the locations they address. If you've got it under control, skip this section.

If not, let's just look at a few examples of notation without introducing anything new. Note that even though using arrows is unusual, we have had to use extra characters to construct variable names before:

constructing variable
names

Kind of variable	Extra notation it requires
unstructured	none
array	square brackets: [ ]
record	period: .
pointer	circumflex: ↑

If the variable a pointer addresses is structured, things get more complicated. But with patience, you can put together every variable's name:

pointers to variables

Kind of pointer	Example
to an integer	NumberPtr ↑
to an array	RowPtr ↑[3]
to a record	FractionPtr ↑.Numerator

Now let's take another look at pointer assignments. I'll use these pointers:

```
type NumberPOINT = ↑ integer;
var OnePtr, TwoPtr, ThreePtr: NumberPOINT;
```

Suppose that I allocate two new variables:

```
new (OnePtr);
new (TwoPtr);
```

Although OnePtr and TwoPtr are pointers, OnePtr↑ and TwoPtr↑ are integer-type variables. The distinction is a little confusing at first, but you've got to learn it. This assignment changes OnePtr↑ the integer variable:

changing the location

OnePtr↑ := 17;

This assignment, in contrast, changes OnePtr the pointer:

changing the pointer

OnePtr := TwoPtr;

OnePtr and TwoPtr now have the same value—the same address. This means that OnePtr↑ and TwoPtr↑ both refer to the exact same anonymous integer variable in memory. Incidentally, what happened to the location that OnePtr used to address, the one that we stored 17 in? It's in limbo. We can't use it because we don't know where it is.

Sometimes, it's easier to understand what's right by looking at what's wrong. Consider these incorrect statements, and their corrected versions:

Wrong	*Right*
a) OnePtr := 5;	OnePtr↑ := 5;
b) TwoPtr↑ := nil;	TwoPtr := nil;
c) write (ThreePtr);	write (ThreePtr↑);
d) OnePtr↑ := TwoPtr + ThreePtr;	OnePtr↑ := TwoPtr↑ + ThreePtr↑;

some incorrect statements

a)   Tries to assign 5 to OnePtr instead of assigning it to the location OnePtr addresses.

b)   Errs because **nil** may be assigned only to a pointer—not to the location the pointer addresses (unless it too is a pointer).

c)   Attempts to print the value represented by Third—which is the unprintable address of a location within the computer—instead of printing the value stored in that location.

d)   Tries to add two addresses instead of adding the values stored at those addresses. Addresses may be compared only for equality and aren't used in arithmetic expressions.

Self-Check Questions ────────────────────────

Q. Try some harder examples. Consider this definition.

type RowPOINT = ↑ RowTYPE;
          RowTYPE = **array** [1..10] **of** char;
var RowPtr: RowPOINT;

What is the effect of each of the statements, below? Consider them independently, as though each one follows this allocation call:

new (RowPtr); *then, in turn . . .*
a) RowPtr := **nil**;
b) new (RowPtr);
c) RowPtr↑ := **nil**;

    d) RowPtr := ´X´;
    e) RowPtr↑ := ´Y´;
    f) RowPtr↑[1] := ´Z´;
    g) RowPOINT[2] := ´A´;

A. And, the answers are:

a, b) Both are legal. However, the effect of the original call to new is undone. The memory that was previously allocated is now unreachable.

c)   Illegal. Although RowPtr is a pointer variable, the location it addresses, RowPtr↑, is an array. An array can't be assigned the value **nil**.

d)   Also illegal. Since RowPtr is a pointer variable, it can be assigned only **nil** or the value of another pointer.

e)   Alas, illegal as well. As in statement *c*, RowPtr↑ is an entire array. It can't be assigned a single char value.

f)   Legal. It assigns ´Z´ to the first component of the array that RowPtr addresses.

g)   Illegal, because RowPOINT is an array type identifier, not the name of a variable (like RowPtr).

Standard Practices: Basic Link Operations

15-2

POINTERS TO SIMPLE VALUES LIKE CHAR ARE EASY to understand, and convenient for practice. In real programs, though, pointers just about always address records. The type definition we'll see most frequently is of a record that has some data fields and at least one pointer field. Why have the pointer field? So that it can address another record of the same type.

nodes and links

> A record that includes a pointer to another record of the same type is usually called a *node*. The pointer field that ties one record to the next is called a *link*.

The true beauty of pointers is expressed by the idea of a node. If each record can point to another record through one of its fields, then we can put together chains of records that are as long as we like. In this section we'll look at linked nodes, and write code for most of the basic operations we'll work with them.

    For example, suppose that FirstNodePtr is a pointer to a record that has one or more Data fields (their type doesn't really matter) and a Next field that is a pointer with the same type as FirstNodePtr. Now, FirstNodePtr might be **nil**:

        FirstNodePtr → **nil**

Or, if we allocate FirstNodePtr, it will point to a record. Most people draw pictures to help them follow what pointers are doing, so I will too.

Since the record's Next field is a pointer too, it gets an arrow as well. If we allocate FirstNodePtr ↑.Next, then allocate the Next field of *that* record, we'll wind up with a sequence like this:

I think you get the idea. A definition that could underlie the basic node is:

a basic node

```
type NodePOINT = ↑ NodeTYPE;
     NodeTYPE = record
                    Next: NodePOINT;
                    Data: DataTYPE  {This could even be another record.}
                end;
var FirstNodePtr: NodePOINT;
```

We can use FirstNodePtr and the Next field to allocate away to our hearts' content:

```
new (FirstNodePtr);
new (FirstNodePtr ↑.Next);
new (FirstNodePtr ↑.Next ↑.Next);
new (FirstNodePtr ↑.Next ↑.Next ↑.Next);
```

The series of allocations gives us this structure:

where:

checking the names

```
FirstNodePtr              {Represents an address.}
FirstNodePtr ↑            {The record at that address.}
FirstNodePtr ↑.Data         {One field of that record—a stored value.}
FirstNodePtr ↑.Next          {Represents an address.}
FirstNodePtr ↑.Next ↑         {The record at that address.}
FirstNodePtr ↑.Next ↑.Data    {One field of that record—a stored value.}
```

The illustrated list above shows one of the peculiarities of linked structures. Although the computer has allocated four different locations in memory for nodes, only a single identifier—FirstNodePtr—is associated with them. This is a source of convenience and confusion. For instance, we can access the entire list through FirstNodePtr to make the last record's Next field **nil** instead of merely undefined.

FirstNodePtr ↑.Next ↑.Next ↑.Next ↑.Next := **nil**;

At the same time, a misstep might cause us to lose contact with part of the list. The assignment below advances the pointer variable so that it addresses the second record in the list.

FirstNodePtr := FirstNodePtr ↑.Next;

Unfortunately, this leaves us with no way of accessing the very first list node. We'll see how to use auxiliary pointers to avoid this problem in a minute.

Self-Check Questions

Q. Given the situation in the illustration above, what are the effects of these assignments?

    a) FirstNodePtr ↑ := FirstNodePtr ↑.Next ↑;
    b) FirstNodePtr := FirstNodePtr ↑.Next;
    c) FirstNodePtr ↑.Next := FirstNodePtr;

A. I'm assuming that the assignments are entirely independent of each other; i.e. we revert to the starting situation after each assignment:

a)   Makes the first record's contents equal the second record's contents *and* cuts the second record out of the list (because the first record's Next field now points to the third record).

b)   Makes FirstNodePtr point to the second record *and* cuts the first record out of the list (because nothing points to it).

c)   Makes the Next field of the first record point to the first record *and* loses the rest of the list (because the first record's Next field points to the first record).

Q. The basic node definition on the last page includes the declaration of FirstNodePtr as a variable of type NodePOINT. Could you also declare a variable of type NodeTYPE?

A. Certainly, as I've done below. Note that since HeadOfList is a regular variable, a NodeTYPE record exists immediately. In contrast, CurrentNodePtr has to be dynamically allocated.

    type *definitions of* NodePOINT *and* NodeTYPE *from above*;
    var CurrentNodePtr: NodePOINT;   {*must be allocated*}
         HeadOfList: NodeTYPE;   {*is allocated automatically*}

Q. Suppose that I actually do declare a HeadOfList record along with a pointer to a record, as above. Is either of these assignments legal? Why or why not?

    a) CurrentNodePtr := HeadOfList;
    b) CurrentNodePtr ↑ := HeadOfList;

A. Assignment *a* is illegal. HeadOfList is a record, not a pointer like CurrentNodePtr, so the assignment violates the basic assignment compatibility rule. There's no way to use new to make CurrentNodePtr address the HeadOfList record.

We can, however, copy HeadOfList. Assignment *b* is perfectly all right as long as CurrentNodePtr points to a record (that is, as long as it has been allocated). The type of CurrentNodePtr ↑ is the record NodeTYPE—the same as the type of HeadOfList.

Abstractions That Use Linked Lists

The individual nodes of a linked structure may be attached to each other in a variety of patterns, as though they were Lego blocks or Tinkertoys. A *linked list* is a series of nodes that are connected by pointers into a more-or-less straight line. We created a linked list in the examples above.

The linked list is the chief building block of a variety of data abstractions. Recall that an abstract structure is defined in terms of its primitive operations—*what is it?* is answered by *what can you do with it?* We can come up with several different abstract structures simply by varying the rules that govern how a node is added or taken away:

Queues have new records added to one end and taken from the other end. Since all travel is in one direction, queues are FIFO—*first-in, first-out*—structures.

a few abstractions

Stacks have new records added to ('pushed on') or taken from ('popped off') just one end of the list (the 'top'). Stacks are LIFO—*last-in, first-out*—structures.

Trees can have more than one linked list attached to each node. Trees are useful when the order of storage depends on the values that are being stored. We'll pursue them in 16–4.

Each of these abstract structures can be defined in terms of primitives for initialization, assignment, inspection, and so on. We'll do that for stacks and queues in the next section, and for trees in 16–4. However, abstraction without the ability to implement is useless. Lest we take false pride in our talents, we'll have to master a few nitty-gritty operations:

— maintaining auxiliary pointers to various parts of a list, especially its first and last nodes;

— adding to the end of a linked list;

— traveling through an entire list;

basic link manipulations

— searching for a particular node;

— inserting into the middle of a linked list;

— merging two lists together or inserting one list into another;

— deleting individual nodes or sublists;

— disposing of lists.

Maintaining Pointers and Extending Lists

Our first concern will be the auxiliary pointers that allow list manipulation. Linked structures usually have several auxiliary pointers that maintain contact with the beginning of a list, its end, our current position, and so on.

> Auxiliary pointers are your only means of finding a list, so use them early and often.

For example, suppose that FirstNodePtr points to the beginning of a list of our generic NodeTYPE records. If we had an auxiliary pointer that was named CurrentNodePtr (with the same type as FirstNodePtr), the assignment:

CurrentNodePtr := FirstNodePtr ↑.Next ↑.Next ↑.Next

doesn't change the list, but it does *advance* a pointer through the list:

advancing the auxiliary pointer

The auxiliary pointer CurrentNodePtr makes assignments far from FirstNodePtr much easier to follow:

CurrentNodePtr ↑.Data := Value;
CurrentNodePtr ↑.Next := **nil**;

Extending a list is our second concern. What is the purpose and effect of these statements? Assume the situation of the illustration above.

list extension

new (CurrentNodePtr ↑.Next);
CurrentNodePtr := CurrentNodePtr ↑.Next;
CurrentNodePtr ↑.Next := **nil**;

These statements extend the chain, but keep CurrentNodePtr pointing to the very last link. The result looks like this:

Let's consider the three statements in turn. The first statement:

new (CurrentNodePtr ↑.Next);

allocates a new location. CurrentNodePtr ↑.Next now addresses an undefined record, and the **nil** value is lost. The second statement:

CurrentNodePtr := CurrentNodePtr ↑.Next;

is potentially the most confusing. It advances the current position pointer, moving it to the end of the list. The illustration below shows how the pointer is reconnected.

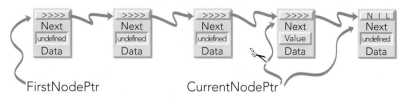

FirstNodePtr   CurrentNodePtr

The final statement of the list extension makes the new list end **nil**.

> CurrentNodePtr ↑.Next := **nil**;

using nil

> In general, **nil** should always be used to mark the end of linked structures. Every pointer, or pointer field, should either have an address or be **nil**.

Self-Check Questions

Q. Given the situation above, what would be the effect of making the assignment:

> CurrentNodePtr ↑.Next := FirstNodePtr;

A. Draw the pointer. It turns the sequence of nodes into a *circular* list that doesn't really have an end.

Q. How would you do the opposite of extending the list? In other words, instead of adding a new node to the end, get rid of the node at the beginning.

A. Doing the job requires an additional temporary pointer:

> TempNode := FirstNodePtr; {*Save a pointer to the head.*}
> FirstNodePtr := FirstNodePtr ↑.Next; {*Advance the head by one node.*}
> dispose (TempNode); {*Free the node's storage.*}
> TempNode := **nil**; {*Keep the pointer defined.*}

Searching for a Node

The precaution of making the last pointer in a linked list **nil** simplifies our third concern—traveling through a list. It's important to state the goals and bounds of list-traversal loops very carefully. Are you looking for an item or for the node before an item? Will you be bounded by the list's last node or by the **nil** value that ends the list?

Suppose that we want to find a list's end; we want a pointer to the last node in the list. A loop specification is:

a list search
specification

> *Goal: Have a pointer to the list's last node.*
> *Bound: The current node's Next field is **nil**.*
> *Plan: Advance a pointer to the next node in the list.*

In the code segment below, assume that CurrentNodePtr is pointing to a node in a linked list. We can advance it to the list's end by searching for the nil-valued Next pointer—the last node. Note that we check before advancing, because we might be at the last node already.

travel through a linked list

```
{Precondition: CurrentNodePtr addresses any node.}
while CurrentNodePtr ↑.Next <> nil do begin
    CurrentNodePtr := CurrentNodePtr ↑.Next
end
{Postcondition: CurrentNodePtr addresses the last node.}
```

finding a particular node

Our fourth concern is to find a particular node. We want to traverse the linked list, but we stay prepared to leave the loop early. As in an ordinary array search, a list-searching loop's basic action is to move to the next component. Its exit condition, if it is to be correct, must contain a double test: either we find the sentinel we want or we run out of data.

loop specification

Goal: Have a pointer to the node that has a particular Data field.
Intentional bound: The current node's Data field is the one we want.
Necessary bound: The current node's Next field is nil.
Plan: Advance a pointer to the next node in the list.

Since there are two reasons for leaving the loop, an additional check has to be made afterward. The appropriate code segment is:

searching for SoughtValue

```
{Precondition: FirstNodePtr addresses any node.}
CurrentNodePtr := FirstNodePtr;    {Start at the beginning.}
while (CurrentNodePtr ↑.Data <> SoughtValue) and
                  (CurrentNodePtr ↑.Next <> nil) do begin
    CurrentNodePtr := CurrentNodePtr ↑.Next
end;
{Postcondition: If SoughtValue is there, it's in the CurrentNodePtr.}
if CurrentNodePtr ↑.Data = SoughtValue
    then writeln ('Value found.')
    else writeln ('Value not found.')
```

Self-Check Questions

Q. Suppose that you wanted to put the searching code above into a procedure. What parameters would you need?

A. Well, if we were searching an array, we'd pass the array and the value we want to find. To search a linked list, we need a pointer to the head of the list, along with the value we're looking for. For the example above, we'd like to make a call along the lines of:

```
Find (CurrentNodePtr, SoughtValue);
```

This would correspond to a heading like:

```
procedure Find (CurrentPtr: NodeTYPE; Value: DataTYPE);
```

We'll look at more detailed examples of pointers as parameters later in this chapter.

An Example: Creating and Printing a List

Let's write a program that uses what we've learned so far—creating a list, adding to it, maintaining auxiliary pointers, and finally inspecting and printing the list. Our problem will be:

problem: making a linked list

Read and save a sequence of positive numbers that ends with a zero or negative sentinel. Print the sentinel that ends the sequence, then echo the sequence in order.

We could, if we wanted, decide to describe our solution as a data abstraction. As usual, the abstraction will be defined in terms of its primitives for initialization, assignment, and inspection:

the list primitives

> **type** NodeTYPE, NodePOINT *will underlie the list of numbers.*
> **procedure** Initialize *creates the list.*
> **procedure** Store *extends the list and adds a new value to it.*
> **procedure** Print *prints the list's contents, in order.*

Drafting a more formalized name layer is useful mainly because it makes us consider how auxiliary pointers will be used:

a more formal name layer

> **type** NodeTYPE, NodePOINT *don't have to be detailed yet.*
> **var** FirstNodePtr, CurrentNodePtr: NodePOINT;
> **procedure** Initialize (FirstNodePtr);
>   *{Returns a pointer to an empty, but allocated, node.}*
> **procedure** Store (CurrentNodePtr, TheNumber);
>   *{Extends the list by one node, and stores a new value there.}*
> **procedure** Print (FirstNodePtr);
>   *{Prints the numbers stored in the linked list.}*

However, I'm going to write this program without using primitive procedures because we're going to take a special look at pointers as parameters later on.

For now, we can assume that the linked list will consist of nodes. Each node will have a Data field that holds the number and a Next field that either points to the next node or is nil. The heart of a program that uses the linked list will have three parts—a few statements that initialize the list, one loop to read and store values, and a second loop that prints the list's contents.

Since input ends with a zero or negative number, the read-and-store loop has a sentinel bound:

read-and-store loop specification

> *Goal: Hold a series of non-negative numbers in the order they arrive.*
> *Bound: Reading a zero or negative number.*
> *Plan: Read a number.*
>   *Add a new node to the end of the list.*
>   *Advance* CurrentNodePtr *to the new node.*
>   *Make its* Next *field* nil.
>   *Make its* Data *field equal the number.*

Making the new node's Next field nil is quite important, because it marks the end of the list.

Let's start to pseudocode the list program. I can outline the first two steps, which initialize and create the list, as:

initialize the list by allocating its first node, via FirstNodePtr;
point an auxiliary pointer CurrentNodePtr *to the first node;*
read TheNumber;
while *it isn't the sentinel* **do begin**
    add a new node to the end of the list;
    advance the CurrentNodePtr *pointer to it;*
    make its Next *field* **nil**;
    save TheNumber *in it;*
    read the next TheNumber
end *of the loop;*
    {*Postcondition: The first stored value is in the node that follows* FirstNodePtr.
    The last stored value is in the node whose Next *field is* **nil**.}
echo the sentinel value;

reading the values

Note the specific mention, in the loop's postcondition, of the positions of the first and last values.

the postcondition

> Because there are no fixed recipes for creating linked lists, postconditions assume unusual importance. It isn't enough to say why the loop ended. Loops that generate linked lists should clearly document the structures they create.

In this case, the detail worth remembering is that the first node doesn't hold a value. Why not? Just because it was a bit easier to write the list-building loop that way.

Once we spot (and echo) the sentinel, it's time to print the list's contents.

printing loop specification

Goal: Print the numbers held in the list headed by FirstNodePtr.
Bound: The current node's Next *field is* **nil**.
Plan: Advance a CurrentNodePtr *pointer, if possible.*
    Print the current node's Data *field.*

In the pseudocode version of the specification, I've reused the CurrentNodePtr that helped create the list:

{*Remember that the first node's* Data *field is undefined.*}
point CurrentNodePtr *to the first node again;*
while *the current node's* Next *field isn't* **nil** **do begin**
    advance the CurrentNodePtr *pointer to the* Next *node;*
    print the current node's Data *field*
end *of the loop*
{*Postcondition: We've printed every defined* Data *field in the list.*}

printing the list

Note that we could have traversed the list with the FirstNodePtr pointer. However, that would leave us without a pointer to the head of the list—a colossal mistake in most applications.

The final Pascal code of LinkEcho is shown below. It illustrates some of the basic linked list methods, so you should be sure to understand it.

linked list program

```pascal
program LinkEcho (input, output);
    {Stores positive numbers in a linked list, then echoes the sentinel and list.}
type NodePOINT = ↑ NodeTYPE;
     NodeTYPE = record
                     Next: NodePOINT;
                     Data: integer
                end;
var FirstNodePtr, CurrentNodePtr: NodePOINT;
    TheNumber: integer;
begin
    new (FirstNodePtr);
    FirstNodePtr ↑.Next := nil;
    CurrentNodePtr := FirstNodePtr;
    {We've initialized the list by creating the first node.}
    writeln ('Please enter numbers to echo (negative sentinel).');
    read (TheNumber);
    while TheNumber >= 0 do begin
        {Since the number wasn't a sentinel, we have to add a node…}
        new (CurrentNodePtr ↑.Next);
            {…then advance the CurrentNodePtr pointer…}
        CurrentNodePtr := CurrentNodePtr ↑.Next;
            {…then initialize its Next field…}
        CurrentNodePtr ↑.Next := nil;
            {…then save the new number…}
        CurrentNodePtr ↑.Data := TheNumber;
            {…and finally get the next number.}
        read (TheNumber)
    end; {while}
    {Postcondition: FirstNodePtr ↑.Next and CurrentNodePtr hold the first and last
    stored values. CurrentNodePtr ↑.Next is nil, and we've read the sentinel.}
    readln;
    write (TheNumber : 4);          {Print the sentinel.}
    CurrentNodePtr := FirstNodePtr; {Its Data field is empty.}
    while CurrentNodePtr ↑.Next <> nil do begin
        CurrentNodePtr := CurrentNodePtr ↑.Next;
        write (CurrentNodePtr ↑.Data : 4)
    end; {while}
    {Postcondition: We've printed every defined Data field in the list.}
    writeln
end.  {LinkEcho}
```

```
Please enter numbers to echo (negative sentinel).
12  59  33  18  3  65  -82  111
-82  12  59  33  18  3  65
```

Inserting Nodes

We've seen how to maintain, search, travel, and add to the end of a list. Let's move on to inserting or deleting one or more nodes. For example, suppose that we wanted to save a list of values (like the list above), but keep them in numerical order. After reading in a new value, we'd search through the list for its proper position, then insert it between two nodes. Assume that CurrentPtr addresses the next lower number. A single new node, addressed by the pointer TempPtr, can be appended after CurrentPtr with:

inserting after the current pointer

```
new (TempPtr);
TempPtr ↑.Data := 3000;
TempPtr ↑.Next := CurrentPtr ↑.Next;    {This order is crucial.}
CurrentPtr ↑.Next := TempPtr;
```

Note that the order of the assignments is critical. We have to attach the new node before disconnecting CurrentPtr from its predecessor.

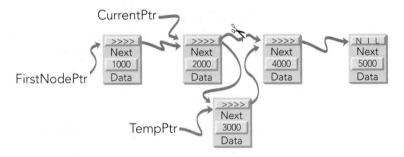

Although it seems impossible (think about it before you read the code), an existing node addressed by NewNode can be inserted *before* the current pointer position node with:

inserting before the current pointer

```
new (TempPtr);
TempPtr ↑ := CurrentPtr ↑;
CurrentPtr ↑.Next := TempPtr;
CurrentPtr ↑.Data := NewNode ↑.Data;
dispose (NewNode);
NewNode := CurrentPtr;
CurrentPtr := CurrentPtr ↑.Next;
```

As you can see, I engaged in sleight-of-hand and didn't really insert the node addressed by NewNode into the list. Instead, I created a new, blank node:

> new (TempPtr);

gave it the same Data and Next fields as CurrentPtr:

> TempPtr↑ := CurrentPtr↑;   {a record-to-record assignment}

inserted it after CurrentPtr:

> CurrentPtr↑.Next := TempPtr;

the most complicated pointer maneuver we'll see

and copied the new node's data in CurrentPtr:

> CurrentPtr↑.Data := NewNode↑.Data;

Since the new node's data have been stored in CurrentPtr↑.Data, the node itself is superfluous. We can deallocate it:

> dispose (NewNode);

arrange for the NewNode pointer to address the duplicate copy:

> NewNode := CurrentPtr;

and finally, advance CurrentPtr to the node that holds the data that CurrentPtr originally addressed:

> CurrentPtr := CurrentPtr↑.Next;

It will take a little effort to follow that sequence, but once you do, you shouldn't have any further trouble with pointers. Here's an outline of the nodes involved in the insertion, and a pair of scissors—try filling in the pointers. I'll leave it to you to figure out how to insert a node before the *first* node in a list.

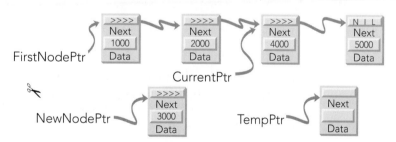

Self-Check Questions

Q. Ok, how *do* you make an insertion before the first node in a list?

A. It takes essentially the same code as above. But in the sequence above, we made sure to advance CurrentPtr so that it ended up pointing to the same stored values. If we were inserting a node before the FirstNodePtr, we wouldn't want to advance the pointer; its name says that it should always point to the first node in the list.

Deleting Nodes

Let's look at the final group of basic list manipulations. They involve inserting or deleting *sublists*, which may be one or more nodes long. As always, having plenty of auxiliary pointers makes the job easier.

sublist insertion

Suppose that we want to insert a new list between two nodes of a currently existing list. Two reconnections do the trick. The new list goes between the nodes addressed by CurrentNodePtr and CurrentNodePtr ↑.Next.

NewEndPtr ↑.Next := CurrentNodePtr ↑.Next;
CurrentNodePtr ↑.Next := NewHeadPtr;

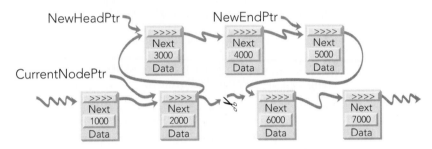

Auxiliary pointers are also useful for deleting one or more nodes from a list. However:

don't let go!

> Don't let go of the list! Don't mistake a firm grip on the deleted segment for a pointer to the list itself. If the list gets away, it is impossible to retrieve.

When done correctly, list deletions take only a reconnection or two. Suppose this is the situation.

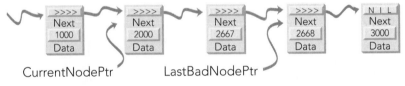

sublist deletion

We can delete all nodes from (not including) CurrentNodePtr ↑ through (and including) LastBadNodePtr ↑ with:

CurrentNodePtr ↑.Next := LastBadNodePtr ↑.Next;

LastBadNodePtr ↑ would be retained in the new list were we to make this assignment instead:

CurrentNodePtr ↑.Next := LastBadNodePtr;

Note that I haven't bothered to dispose of the nodes I cut out. In a program that does a great deal of pointer manipulation, though, a *list disposal* scheme is essential to ensure that we don't inadvertently run out of memory.

Q. Suppose that two pointers—CurrentNodePtr and PreviousNode—address the first node in a list. If the last node of the list is nil, what is the effect of this code?

```
while CurrentNodePtr <> nil do begin
    CurrentNodePtr := PreviousNode ↑.Next;
    dispose (PreviousNode);
    PreviousNode := CurrentNodePtr
end;
```

A. The code segment carries out a simple scheme for list disposal. It requires two pointers; one lags behind so that the record it addresses can be deallocated.

Pointers as Parameters

Pointers can be confusing, so I've deliberately kept examples simple and accompanied them with plenty of pictures. As we begin to write programs based on pointer types, though, we'll have to package the basic operations in procedures. It's obviously easier to draft programs using primitive procedure calls than with detailed pointer assignments.

It's important to understand how pointers are used as parameters. The problem is that we usually think of variable parameters as being changeable, while value parameters are 'safe,' in the sense that incorrectly changing a value parameter won't screw up a main-program variable.

But pointers play by a much looser set of rules. When a pointer is passed as a variable parameter, its address can be changed, as well as the contents of the location at that address. This is expected. When a pointer is passed as a value parameter, changing the address it contains is just a local assignment. This is expected too. But suppose I define a pointer type and make some declarations:

location contents can always be changed

```
type NodePOINT = ↑ NodeTYPE;
     NodeTYPE = record
                    Next: NodePOINT;
                    Data: char
                end;
var CurrentPtr: NodePOINT;
procedure VarExample (var VarPointer: NodePOINT);
    ·· .  {body of the procedure}
procedure ValueExample (ValuePointer: NodePOINT);
    ·· .  {body of the procedure}
begin   {main program}
    ·· .  {new and do things with CurrentPtr, then call . . .}
    VarExample (CurrentPtr);
    ValueExample (CurrentPtr);
```

some definitions to work with

> Even if a pointer has been passed as a value parameter, the contents of the
> location it addresses can be changed permanently.

After CurrentPtr has been allocated, assignments to or through CurrentPtr
change CurrentPtr, or the location it addresses, as expected. Within procedure
VarExample, assignments made either to, or through, VarPointer are just like assignments to or through CurrentPtr. Variable parameters are useful for traditional reasons: they let us write general-purpose procedures without having to
know the names of main-program variables.

It is procedure ValueExample that is of special interest. Within ValueExample, changes made to ValuePointer are local, no matter what argument initializes ValuePointer. Suppose, for example, that ValueExample is called with
CurrentPtr as its argument. These assignments:

. . . to value parameters

```
{Inside procedure ValueExample.}
ValuePointer := nil;
new (ValuePointer);
{These assignments are strictly local.}
```

make it impossible to access any of the locations addressed by CurrentPtr from
within the procedure. However, on return to the calling program, CurrentPtr
(and any list it heads) is in its original condition.

On the other hand, assignments *through* ValuePointer are permanent. For
instance:

. . . through value
parameters

```
{Inside ValueExample.}
ValuePointer ↑.Data := 'X';
new (ValuePointer ↑.Next);
{These assignments change globally accessible locations.}
```

On return to the main program, CurrentPtr ↑.Data will hold a new value, while
CurrentPtr ↑.Next points to a new location.

> If you really don't want to change the variable a pointer addresses, pass the
> variable—not the pointer to it—as a value parameter.

Even though we'll usually employ pointers to NodeTYPE variables, once in a
while we'll create a value parameter of type NodeTYPE—the record—as well.

Self-Check Questions

Q. What is the output of program Passage? What conclusions can you draw about
passing pointers as value parameters?

```
program Passage (input, output);
     {Demonstrates some effects of passing a pointer as a value parameter.}
type NodePOINT = ↑ NodeTYPE;
     NodeTYPE = record
                    Next: NodePOINT;
                    Data: char
               end;
var CurrentPtr: NodePOINT;
procedure Change (TempPtr: NodePOINT);
    begin
        TempPtr↑.Data := 'C';          {Which of these are}
        TempPtr := TempPtr↑.Next;      {local assignments?}
        TempPtr↑.Data := 'D'
    end; {Change}
begin
    new (CurrentPtr);
    CurrentPtr↑.Data := 'A';
    new (CurrentPtr↑.Next);
    CurrentPtr↑.Next↑.Data := 'B';
    write (CurrentPtr↑.Data);
    write (CurrentPtr↑.Next↑.Data);
    Change (CurrentPtr);
    write (CurrentPtr↑.Data);
    writeln (CurrentPtr↑.Next↑.Data)
end.   {Passage}
```

*value parameter pointer
program*

A. Passage demonstrates the hazards of passing pointers as parameters. Its output is:

ABCD

rather than the expected ABAB. Since TempPtr is a pointer, it addresses the same location in memory as its argument, CurrentPtr. Changes to TempPtr don't affect CurrentPtr, but any changes to the location TempPtr addresses do. After all, TempPtr↑ and CurrentPtr↑ are the exact same record. We could even have used TempPtr to extend—or remove—the entire list!

Example: List Disposal

Let's look at a concrete example. Procedure FreeList, below, disposes of locations that aren't needed anymore. Its argument points to the head of such a list; by convention, the list's last pointer will be **nil**.

As you read FreeList, ask yourself this important question: Why is it necessary to declare Head as a variable parameter? After all, calls of dispose *through* Head would have the desired effect even if Head were a value parameter. But what might go wrong if I used a value parameter?

```
procedure FreeList (var Head:  NodePOINT);
   var TempPtr:  NodePOINT;
   begin
      TempPtr := Head;           {Initialize TempPtr.}
      while Head <> nil do begin
         Head := Head↑.Next;        {Advance the list head.}
         dispose (TempPtr);
            {Dispose of the previous node.}
         TempPtr := Head;           {Reinitialize TempPtr.}
      end
   end;  {FreeList}
```

In FreeList, the local pointer variable TempPtr identifies locations that are slated for removal. The condition of TempPtr at the end of the procedure doesn't really matter. Head, on the other hand, must wind up with the value nil—not only because that provides the exit condition of the loop, but because it should be defined back in the main program. If Head had been declared as a value parameter, its argument would, technically, be undefined on return to the main program.

Extended Examples: Stacks and Queues

15-3

LET'S TURN TO A FEW LONGER PROGRAMS THAT rely on pointers. As will often be the case in advanced programming, we'll focus on tools as much as programs. In other words, as soon as we write the tools, we'll take credit for all the problems that could be solved using them.

The tools we'll create are *stacks* and *queues*, which I can describe as *structure* abstractions. This term serves as a reminder that the abstraction is defined in terms of the relationship between stored values, rather than by the kinds of values that it stores. The structure's primitive operations serve to order and rearrange the structure, rather than to calculate values.

Stacks

What does it mean to specify relations between values, while ignoring the values themselves? Well, consider the abstract structure known as a *stack*. A stack obeys two rules:

— A new value can be added to the stack.

— The newest of the remaining values can be retrieved from the stack.

These operations have common names: we save a value with a *push* and remove a value with a *pop*. Stacks get their name from a kind of stack we've all pushed and popped—a spring-loaded stack of trays in a cafeteria.

What's interesting is that the stack operations are totally independent of the sort of values that are being saved. Without knowing anything about the 'values' of stacked data, a stack can be defined in terms of the sequential relation of values: they may be saved in order and retrieved in reverse order.

underflow

In practice, push and pop aren't quite sufficient to define a stack. A stack might be *empty*, which would cause a pop to fail. Emptiness (which could lead to *stack underflow*) is a possibility for any stack, regardless of its implementation. Three operations, then, define an abstract stack no matter how it is programmed:

1. *Push* means 'save a value.'

primitive stack operations

2. *Pop* means 'get the remaining value that was saved most recently.'

3. *Empty* means 'there are no values to pop.'

We'll generally see two or three more operations added to the definition of computer stacks. These additional terms are more closely related to implementation. For instance, an array-based stack is more likely to run the risk of fullness (or *stack overflow*) than one based on pointers. On the other hand, 'remove' might be relevant only for a pointer-based stack, since only pointers can actually free unneeded memory. I'll just list them all:

4. *Initialize* means 'give a name to a new, empty stack.'

three additional stack primitives

5. *Remove* means 'remove the stack's contents.'

6. *Full* means 'there is no more room to push values onto the stack.'

primitives require implementation knowledge

> All six of these operations are primitive: we can't write them unless we know something about how the stack is actually implemented, e.g. as an array or linked list. It is possible to define other stack-related operations, of course, but they can be written using the primitives.

Let's settle on a name layer for a stack. I'll make a partial implementation commitment—we'll write it using pointers—but I'll still leave out as many details as I can. Although the list of headings below might seem suspiciously well-formed, it really didn't take very much insight to design it. All we need to know is what kind of information each primitive will require: at least, a pointer to the stack; at most, a pointer and an item to be put on or taken off:

the stack name layer

```
type StackPOINT doesn't have to be defined yet.
type DataTYPE, of stored items, doesn't have to be defined yet.
procedure Initialize (var TopPtr: StackPOINT);
    {Initialize a new stack.}
function Empty (TopPtr: StackPOINT) : boolean;
    {TRUE if there are no pushed values.}
procedure Push (var TopPtr: StackPOINT; Item: DataTYPE);
    {Add Item to the stack.}
procedure Pop (var TopPtr: StackPOINT; var Item: DataTYPE);
    {Remove the top item from the stack and return it as Item.}
procedure Remove (var TopPtr: StackPOINT);
    {dispose of any current stack contents.}
```

Q. Procedure Pop actually removes the top value from the stack. Using the primitives described above, show how you might program a new operation called Top—'get a copy of the value on top of the stack, but *don't* remove it.'

A. Let's assume that Stack has type StackPOINT and that Data and TopCopy have type DataTYPE. We pop the top value, copy it, then push it back on the stack.

```
{The heart of a non-primitive Top procedure that copies a stack's top value.}
if not Empty(Stack) then
      Pop (Stack, Data);        {Pop the top value…}
      TopCopy := Data;          {…copy it…}
      Push (Stack, Data)        {…then push it back on the stack.}
end
```

The Implementation Layer

As an abstraction, the stack is done. But as a practical matter (and it's the practical matters that will be causing problems for the next few weeks), we still have to implement the stack in Pascal.

Stacks are often built with pointers because a linked list can get longer and longer, while an array is limited to its defined size. A node that's suited for stack work differs from the nodes we've used for linked lists previously in the subtlest way possible. Can you spot it?

a stack's underlying data type

```
type DataTYPE = whatever we want to stack;
     StackPOINT = ↑ NodeTYPE;
     NodeTYPE = record
                     Last:  StackPOINT;
                     Data:  DataTYPE
                end;
var Item:  DataTYPE;
    StackPtr:  StackPOINT;
```

The difference between this node and the others is that the node's internal pointer is called Last, rather than Next. Why? Because it always points to an existing past node, rather than to some potential node we might add in the future. A picture of a stack might, when compared to our earlier lists, show its pointers in reverse:

bottom of the stack   *top of the stack*

Let's start implementing the primitives. The first question to ask is *what is an empty stack?* Suppose that I say it's a stack whose TopPtr is **nil**-valued. That means that procedure Initialize will be:

```
procedure Initialize (var TopPtr: StackPOINT);
    {Initialize a 'top-of-stack' pointer.}
    begin
        TopPtr := nil
    end;  {Initialize}
```

Sticking to the convention *empty means that* TopPtr *equals* nil makes function Empty easy to write:

```
function Empty (TopPtr: StackPOINT) : boolean;
    {TopPtr is nil if the stack is empty.}
    begin
        Empty := TopPtr = nil
    end;  {Empty}
```

The definitions of Push and Pop, in turn, are:

```
procedure Push (var TopPtr: StackPOINT;
                    Item: DataTYPE);
    {Add Item to the stack.}
    var TempPtr: StackPOINT;
    begin
        new (TempPtr);
        TempPtr ↑.Data := Item;      {Create and fill a new node...}
        TempPtr ↑.Last := TopPtr;    {...point it to the current top...}
        TopPtr := TempPtr            {...then 'advance' the top pointer.}
    end;  {Push}
```

```
procedure Pop (var TopPtr: StackPOINT;
                   var Item: DataTYPE);
    {Return the stack's top item, then remove its node.}
    var TempPtr: StackPOINT;
    begin
        if not Empty (TopPtr) then begin
            Item := TopPtr ↑.Data;
            TempPtr := TopPtr;           {Save a pointer to the old top node...}
            TopPtr := TopPtr ↑.Last;
            dispose (TempPtr)            {...so that it can be disposed of later.}
        end
    end;  {Pop}
```

The fifth and final procedure is Remove. It's a list-removal routine much like the earlier example FreeList:

procedure Remove (**var** TopPtr: StackPOINT);
   {*Remove the stack, leaving the TopPtr node* **nil**.}
  var TempPtr: StackPOINT;
begin
  while TopPtr <> **nil do begin**
    TempPtr := TopPtr;   {*Save a pointer to the old top node.*}
    TopPtr := TopPtr ↑.Last;   {*Move the top pointer down.*}
    dispose (TempPtr)   {*Dispose of the former top node.*}
  end {while}
end; {Remove}

Remove procedure

Stack Applications

What's a stack good for? A basic application is reversing input.

> Push *all incoming* Item *values onto stack*;
> Pop *the* Item *values from the stack until it's empty*;

If values are pushed onto a stack in order of receipt, they will be popped in reverse. The exact type definition of Item is important for a Pascal program, but it's really irrelevant to the design of our algorithm. The pseudocode below applies equally well to reversing digits in a number, characters in a string, words in a line, or lines in a file:

reversing input

```
Initialize (Stack);
while not eof do begin          {create the stack}
    read an Item;
    Push (Stack, Item)
end the stacking loop;
while not Empty(Stack) do begin      {print the stack}
    Pop (Stack, Item);
    print Item
end the unstacking loop;
```

Another standard stack application comes in evaluating expressions. You might already be familiar with a stack notation (called *postfix* or *reverse Polish notation*) commonly used for stating expressions. In postfix, operators follow their operands, rather than coming in between them as in ordinary *infix* notation.

infix vs. postfix

Infix	*Postfix*
(A + B) * C	A B + C *
(A − B) / (C * D)	A B − C D * /
((A * (B / C)) − (D * E))	A B C / * D E * −

Postfix gets rid of parentheses; operands are pushed onto a stack as they appear, then popped off, as needed, as operators arrive. Although it's tempting to write a program that translates infix into postfix, you'll be able to do it in your head with a few minutes' practice.

Suppose that we have a ready supply of postfix expressions. How can we evaluate such an expression in Pascal? Well, assuming we can read the input sequence of operands and binary (two-operand) operators one value at a time, there are just two basic rules:

evaluating postfix expressions

1.   If we read an operand value, push it onto the stack.

2.   If we read an operator, pop the top two values from the stack, perform the operation, then push the result back onto the stack.

In Pascal pseudocode, the evaluation rules become:

stack-oriented expression evaluation

> **while not** eof **do begin**
>   *read the next* Item;
>   **if** Item *was an operand*
>   **then begin** Push (Stack, Item) **end**
>   **else** *it's an operator, so* **begin**
>   Pop (Stack, Term1);
>   Pop (Stack, Term2);
>   *carry out the appropriate operation;*
>   Push (Stack, TheResult);
>   **end** *the* **if** *statement;*
>   **end** *of the loop;*
>   Pop (Stack, RemainingTerm);
>   *print* RemainingTerm

Note that the pseudocode doesn't contain any checks for incorrect input. Were input to arrive in infix form (say, as **A** ✳ **B**), a premature Pop could cause a program crash or incorrect output. You should figure out how checks for an empty stack could deal with this kind of problem.

In addition to simple applications like the reversals and arithmetic described above, the stack is an extremely important abstraction for many facets of computer and program operation, including:

— *Language translation.* When programming languages are translated into a form the computer understands, meaning may be unclear, particularly when statements or definitions are nested. Stacks are used to delay processing of 'outer' sequences until 'inner' sequences have been translated.

other stack applications

— *Subprogram calls.* Calling a procedure or function implies that another ongoing process (e.g. the main program) will have to be temporarily suspended. Stacks are used to preserve the current state of uncompleted processes, and to let them be reinvoked in the proper order.

— *Delayed evaluation.* Suppose that evaluating a function requires a call of the function itself. This special instance of stacked subprogram calls, called *recursion*, is a particularly exciting application of the computer's stack. We'll explore recursion in detail in Chapter 16.

— *Delimiter matching.* Checking that paired delimiters, like parentheses or comment brackets, are supplied in sufficient quantity and proper order requires stacking the delimiters. Whenever a closing delimiter is encountered, the top of the stack should contain its matching opener; if it doesn't, there's an error.

Because of their conceptual simplicity, stacks are also employed when order is unimportant. For example, a stack is often used to maintain a list of free storage space (e.g. the subscripts of unused array components). The order in which free space is retrieved is irrelevant. However, procedures we might name Save and Retrieve and function NoneAvailable can easily be seen as revisions of Push, Pop, and Empty.

Self-Check Questions

Q. How would you use the primitives we've written to reverse the order of a stack's contents?

A. Easily—just use the original stack's pops as the reversed stack's pushes:

```
Initialize (CopyStack);
while not Empty (OriginalStack) do begin
    Pop (OriginalStack, Item);
    Push (CopyStack, Item)
end;
{Postcondition:  OriginalStack is empty.}
```

Queues

The queue is the second of the classic abstract structures. It differs from the stack by a slight variation in its underlying rules: we can remove the oldest stored value, rather than the newest.

queue abstraction rules

— A new value can be added to the queue.

— The oldest remaining value can be removed from the queue.

We have all waited in queues at one time or another. Queues are lines; we enter at the rear and wait with more or less patience as earlier arrivals remove themselves from the front. If stacks bring cafeteria trays to mind, queues should make you think about PEZ dispensers—they fill from the bottom and empty from the top.

Queue primitives parallel those provided for stacks. Three basic operations are required:

1. *Enqueue* means 'save a value.'

basic queue operations

2. *Retrieve* means 'get the oldest value that remains.'

3. *Empty* means 'there are no values in the queue.'

Additional functions and procedures may be defined as well, as long as they don't contravene (break) the first-in, first-out basis of the queue:

4. *Initialize* means 'give a name to a new, empty queue.'

5. *Remove* means 'remove the queue's contents.'

6. *FullQ* means 'the queue can't hold any more values.'

As was the case with the stack abstraction, we can decide on a name layer for the queue without making too many choices about implementation. One important difference to bear in mind, though, is that a queue has two ends—the front and the rear—whereas a stack has only a top.

the queue name layer

```
type QueuePOINT doesn't have to be defined yet.
type DataTYPE, of stored items, doesn't have to be defined yet.
procedure Initialize (var FrontPtr, RearPtr: QueuePOINT);
    {Initialize a new queue.}
function Empty (FrontPtr, RearPtr: QueuePOINT) : boolean;
    {TRUE if the queue is empty.}
procedure Enqueue (var RearPtr: QueuePOINT; Item: DataTYPE);
    {Add Item to end of the queue.}
procedure Retrieve (var FrontPtr: QueuePOINT; var Item: DataTYPE);
    {Remove the oldest item from the queue and return it as Item.}
procedure Remove (var FrontPtr: QueuePOINT);
    {dispose any current queue contents.}
```

As before, I haven't bothered with a 'structure is full' procedure in this implementation.

Self-Check Questions

Q. Is it possible to use the primitives described above to write a NextItem procedure—a procedure that lets us inspect the item at the front of the queue without removing it?

A. Not easily. Once an item has been removed, it can only be returned to the end of the queue. Inspecting the front item would require copying the entire queue. If it's needed, NextItem is a good candidate for implementation as a primitive.

The Implementation Layer

The implementation of queues is aided immensely by the fact that we can steal most of our code from earlier examples. The basic node will be:

a queue's underlying data type

```
type DataTYPE = whatever we want to queue;
    QueuePOINT = ↑ NodeTYPE;
    NodeTYPE = record
                   Next: QueuePOINT;
                   Data: DataTYPE
               end;
var Item: DataTYPE;
    FrontPtr, RearPtr: QueuePOINT;
```

Let me ask a question, though. Which of these two possibilities—both based on NodeTYPE—will best serve our purposes? Which direction should the pointer go—this way:

first alternative

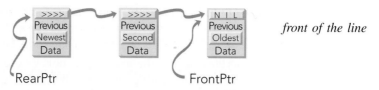

front of the line

or is this arrangement easier to deal with? In both cases, we add values to the rear, and remove them from the front.

second alternative

front of the line

Take a piece of scrap paper and draft the code you'll need to Enqueue and Retrieve in each case. The first alternative, which is a lot like the simple linked list we practiced with earlier, turns out to be deceptive. Although adding values to the rear is a piece of cake, keeping the FrontPtr pointer correctly positioned as items are retrieved would be quite tedious. The pointers go in only one direction; how can FrontPtr back up?

However, the simple change introduced in the second alternative makes life much easier. Why not have each component point to the component behind, rather than the one in front? It's easy to add a new node to RearPtr and to advance FrontPtr down the queue as nodes are removed.

In the code of the Initialize procedure below, notice that the queue contains a component even when it's empty. This design decision is invisible to the user, but it simplifies some aspects of implementing the data abstraction. Indeed, I could have gone even further and sandwiched all new components between permanently empty FrontPtr and RearPtr nodes.

Initialize procedure

```
procedure Initialize (var FrontPtr, RearPtr: QueuePOINT);
   {Do the initialization required to set up an empty queue.}
begin
   new (RearPtr);
   RearPtr↑.Next := nil;
   FrontPtr := RearPtr
end;  {Initialize}
```

In the queue I've initialized, FrontPtr and RearPtr both address the same empty node. If we stick with that rule, we can detect an empty queue with:

Empty function

```
function Empty (FrontPtr, RearPtr: QueuePOINT) : boolean;
   {TRUE if the queue is empty.}
begin
   Empty := FrontPtr = RearPtr
end;  {Empty}
```

Note that the node's contents, if it has any, are irrelevant. We're checking to see *where* the pointers go, not *what* they point to.

Having committed ourselves to this method of representing and detecting the empty queue, we are obligated to keep one end of the queue occupied by an empty node. I've kept it at the rear in procedure Enqueue, below:

Enqueue procedure

```
procedure Enqueue (var RearPtr: QueuePOINT; Item: DataTYPE);
    {Add an Item value to the queue.}
    begin
        RearPtr ↑.Data := Item;              {'Fill' the currently empty rear node.}
        new (RearPtr ↑.Next);                {Create and add a new empty node.}
        RearPtr := RearPtr ↑.Next;           {'Advance' the rear pointer.}
        RearPtr ↑.Next := nil                {The empty last node is nil.}
    end; {Enqueue}
```

The definition of Retrieve, in turn, is:

Retrieve procedure

```
procedure Retrieve (var FrontPtr: QueuePOINT;
                    var Item: DataTYPE);
    {Retrieve the front (i.e. oldest) value from the queue.}
    var TempPtr: QueuePOINT;
    begin
        TempPtr := FrontPtr;                 {Save a pointer to the old front node.}
        Item := FrontPtr ↑.Data;             {Get and save the oldest value.}
        FrontPtr := FrontPtr ↑.Next;         {Advance the front pointer.}
        dispose (TempPtr)                    {Remove the old front node.}
    end; {Retrieve}
```

Finally, as with the stack, a pointer-based implementation makes a FullQ function superfluous for our purposes. The fifth and last procedure is Remove.

Remove procedure

```
procedure Remove (var FrontPtr: QueuePOINT);
    {Return each node in the queue to computer memory.}
    var TempPtr: QueuePOINT;
    begin
        while FrontPtr ↑.Next <> nil do begin
            TempPtr := FrontPtr;             {Save a pointer to the old leading node}
            FrontPtr := FrontPtr ↑.Next;     {so that it can be disposed of later.}
            dispose (TempPtr)
        end {while}
    end; {Remove}
```

Self-Check Questions

Q. Procedure Remove gets only one argument—the FrontPtr pointer. What is the value of RearPtr after a Remove call?

A. As the code now stands, RearPtr points to the same empty node as FrontPtr. Thus, the list hasn't been entirely disposed of. The last node could be removed, and both pointers set to nil.

Q. Empty is TRUE if FrontPtr and RearPtr address the same node. Will Empty compare the same addresses each time it's called?

A. No. Every time an item is removed from the queue FrontPtr points to a different node. Eventually, when all the items are removed, FrontPtr has worked its way over to the same node that RearPtr addresses.

Queue Applications

In programs, as in real life, queues are found wherever supply and demand (in jargon, *servers* and *clients*) cannot be assured to stay in lockstep. Why does a queue form at the bank? Because demand for services, in the form of customers, sometimes exceeds the available supply of tellers. The queue serves as a *buffer*; it keeps the supply and demand processes at arm's length.

why do queues form?

Programs need queues because statement-by-statement program execution isn't always suited to problem solving. Although we usually think of program operation as a three-step waltz of input, process, and output, this model breaks down when input or processing is unpredictable. Data may come too quickly, or in irregular spurts, or might have to be held for additional processing later. A technical term that can be applied to such uncoordinated activity is *asynchronous processing*—the input, processing, and output steps are not synchronized and may even be running at the same time.

queue applications

For example, think about the operation of a time-shared computer system. Jobs that need the undivided attention of an unshareable resource (like a printer) can be queued until their turns arrive. Tasks (like users' programs) that can be interrupted without harm are more interesting. Here, the necessary resource of computer CPU power can be shared. The operating system maintains a *run queue* of unfinished jobs. Each job is given a small amount of processor time (its *time slice*), then returned to the run queue if it's still unfinished. If time slices are appropriately chosen, and the queue is not too long, each user has the illusion of having the computer's undivided attention.

A few word games will help illustrate the use of queues as buffers, or temporary holding places. Notice anything peculiar about these sentences?

> *Just a white shark.*
> *Space, time, and relativity with a ridiculous script.*
> *A nauseating nitwit ineffably embalmed.*

Suppose that we supply each sentence, in turn, as input to the following code segment. Naturally, I'll assume that the queue-oriented procedures have been written to hold char-type data items. What will the output be?

mystery code segment

```
NewWord := TRUE;
while not eoln do begin
    read (Ch);
    write (Ch);
    if NewWord          {TRUE when the first letter of a new word is read.}
        then begin Enqueue (Letters, Ch);
                    NewWord := FALSE
        end
        else NewWord := (Ch = ' ')
                {Assume there's just one space between words.}
end; {while}
{Postcondition: There's no more input . . . but what does the queue hold?}
```

```
write ('--');
while not Empty(Letters) do begin {until the queue is empty}
    Retrieve (Letters, Ch);
    write (Ch)
end; {while}
writeln
```

Within the first loop, every character is echoed but certain characters are queued. The second loop prints the queue's contents. Under what circumstances will a character be added to the queue? If it's the first letter of a new word. The segment's output (after three runs) is:

```
Just a white shark.--Jaws
Space, time, and relativity with a ridiculous script.--Starwars
A nauseating nitwit ineffably embalmed.--Annie
```

These self-describing phrases are called *mynorcas*. An *automynorcagram* is a more complex variation on the same theme. It's a phrase that is generated by its own letters; e.g. *This happy instance shows how a pleasing phrase yields its new sentence* and so on.

A second such example uses a stack as well as a queue to detect palindromes—sequences that are the same both backward and forward. The ground rules of text palindrome formation generally allow spaces and punctuation to be ignored. Letter-oriented examples are such a routine exercise that I'll try a word-oriented variation: palindromic sentences. How might we decide if these are palindromes?

detecting palindromes

> *So patient a doctor to doctor a patient so.*
> *Girl, bathing on Bikini, eyeing boy, finds boy eyeing bikini on bathing girl.*

We'd really like to be able to read each sentence forward and backward simultaneously. Well, since a stack of words effects a reversal, we can.

spotting a palindromic
sentence

```
while not eof do begin          {stack and queue the words}
    read a word, ignoring capitalization and punctuation;
    Push the word onto a stack;
    Enqueue the word in a queue
end;
repeat          {compare the stored values—assume non-empty lists}
    Pop a word from the stack;
    Retrieve a word from the queue;
until they don't match or Empty stack or queue;
decide why we left the loop, and report the results;
```

Each word is both stacked and queued. Then, since the stack is a LIFO (last-in, first-out) structure, while the queue is FIFO (first-in, first-out), we can compare the input sequence backward and forward simultaneously.

A Few Definition Exercises

When I learned to program pointers I found that understanding something in the book was a lot easier than recreating it when I had to pound terminal keys.

Even though our examples will involve abstract structures based on simple nodes as above, let's look at some more involved definitions. They'll help you see how pointers fit into the pantheon of types and give you some practice with their definition syntax. Don't worry—you won't have to write programs that solve the problems I'll pose. But you should feel up to defining an underlying type for any picture you'd care to draw.

problem: editor data type

Define a data type suited to building a text editor. Each line must hold up to 80 characters, but the total number of lines shouldn't be restricted. Common editing operations, like deleting and moving lines, and printing subsections of the text, should be convenient to perform.

a file?

What are the considerations to weigh in coming up with a definition? Well, an ordinary file of characters meets the 'unlimited overall size' criterion, but changing files by reading and writing them is extremely inconvenient— changing the order of a few lines requires a considerable amount of work.

an array?

How about a two-dimensional array of char or a one-dimensional array of eighty-character strings? Arrays let us access lines at random, and defining each line as a string makes it relatively easy to delete, move, and print lines. On the other hand, we face a sticky choice in defining the array—either we grab all available memory by declaring the largest array possible, or we limit the text editor's capacity in violation of the problem specification.

As you might expect, pointers allow a neat solution. Why not define a record that holds a full line of eighty characters, along with a field that points to another line? The definition is:

```
type StringTYPE = packed array [1 .. 80] of char;
     LinePOINT = ↑ LineTYPE;
     LineTYPE = record
                      Next: LinePOINT;
                      Data: StringTYPE;
                end;

var FirstPtr, CurrentPtr, Last, other auxiliary pointers: LinePOINT;
```

a linked list of lines

This is almost identical to the NodeTYPE definition from near the beginning of the chapter. Instead of characters, though, we'll store eighty-character lines. The illustration below shows a typical editing situation:

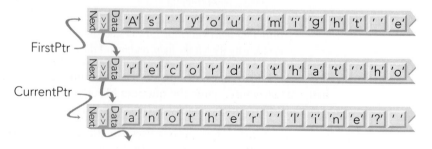

Auxiliary pointers won't always be simple variables, as our next problem shows:

<blockquote>
A manufacturer has labeled her product line with single letters, followed by specific product numbers. In other words, there is an 'A' line, a 'B' line, and so on through the 'Z' line. She wants a data type definition that will allow quick access to any particular line, but doesn't limit the number of products in each line. Assume that product information is stored in a variable of type InfoTYPE.
</blockquote>

problem: array with buckets

Once again, we will rely on using records (to hold each product's information) that also contain pointer fields (so that we can link a line of products together).

How can we separate the 'A', 'B', etc. lines, though? Quick access is the clue. An array subscripted by ['A'..'Z'] provides random access to each line—if the array's components are pointers.

an array of lists

```
type NodePOINT = ↑ NodeTYPE;
     NodeTYPE = record
                    Next: NodePOINT;
                    Data: DataTYPE
                end;
     InfoTYPE = array ['A'..'Z'] of NodePOINT;

var Info: InfoTYPE;
    CurrentPtr: NodePOINT;
```

This data structure is known, informally, as an *array with buckets*. There is an application called *hashing* in which the image of tossing information into empty buckets, which can be added as necessary, is especially vivid. Once again, I can draw a picture of Info's appearance after it's been initialized:

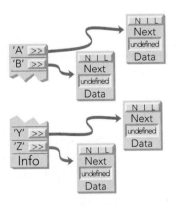

Each of the 26 array components is a pointer to the head of a linked list.

Now, the data types we've defined so far have kept pointers on an equal footing with data. Ignoring auxiliaries, every item of data has been associated with a single pointer, and just one path of pointers has described the way it's ordered. But suppose we want pointers to allow different logical descriptions of a single large data set? We've encountered a classic database problem:

<blockquote>
A company that keeps voluminously detailed records on its employees has a problem. For various reasons, different staff groups within the company want to keep the records in different kinds of order: the Layoff
</blockquote>

staff wants employees ordered by nearness to retirement or tenure, the Health staff wants them ordered by frequency of absence, the Payroll staff wants them ordered by social security number, and so on. Assuming that records are too large for duplicate sets to be kept, define a data type that will allow each division reasonable access to the database.*

Employee records are 'big,' in the sense that such records usually take a fair amount of space in memory. After all, they hold a lot of information. Pointers, in contrast, are small. What we'd like to do is have just one copy of the master list of employee records, but have differently ordered lists of pointers to the master.

Although the database problem sounds difficult, we can solve it with a very simple definition of a record that holds two pointers. One of the pointers will address another record of the same type; as before, we'll make a linked list. But instead of storing the employee data in our node records, we'll just store pointers *to* the data.

In the definition below, BaseNodeTYPE holds *only* pointers. It provides the skeleton of the database structure. A second record type, which does not include a pointer field, holds each employee's personal history.

```
type DataTYPE = record
                    whatever the employee records contain
             end;
     DataPOINT = ↑ DataTYPE;
     NodePOINT = ↑ BaseNodeTYPE;
     BaseNodeTYPE = record
                       NextNode: NodePOINT;
                       Employee: DataPOINT
                    end
var MainList, WatchList, HealthList,
    PayrollList, CurrentPtr: NodePOINT;
```

The list of records headed by MainList can be set up in any convenient order—say, in alphabetical order of one of the fields in the data record. It is paralleled by other lists that access the same data, but maintain different logical orderings.

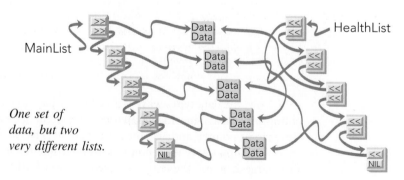

One set of data, but two very different lists.

---

* This problem brings to mind former Prime Minister Asquith's crack about the WWI British military command: 'They keep three sets of records—one to mislead the War Office, one to mislead the public, and one to mislead themselves.'

Background: Are There Limits to Linked Structures?

Thus I have heard.

The greatest mistake made in Computer/Human interfaces is the denial of the computer. Systems that are backfitted to previous conceptions of the universe are always limited by what has gone before. Computers should not simulate reality—they should transcend it.

From *The Zen of Programming*, by Geoffrey James, © 1988, InfoBooks, Santa Monica, Ca. 90406.

15-4 Program Engineering Notes

PROGRAM ENGINEERING WITH POINTERS REQUIRES LESS new knowledge and more conscious application of old knowledge. Take everything you know about the importance of 'seeing' data stored in arrays and records, and start to believe it.

The most important tool there is for working with pointers is a *print the structure* procedure. Unfortunately, any problems you have with pointers may show up sooner than you expected! Try to look at writing and debugging your Dump procedure as a shakedown cruise that takes place before the ship is built.

In time, you'll come to understand pointers via the same road that leads to Carnegie Hall—practice, practice, practice. Don't worry if you start out copying a lot of your code from the book. I did, too, when I first started.

One of the ideas that's hardest to follow at first is that pointer variables can be in many different states. A pointer variable can be:

— *Unallocated and undefined*—its start-of-program state. The pointer addresses nothing, and it has no value.

— *Defined as* nil. It can be compared to nil or to another pointer of the same type, but it still doesn't address anything.

— *Allocated, but addressing an uninitialized location*. Right after allocation, the variable it points to hasn't been initialized yet.

— *Allocated and pointing to an initialized variable*—ready to be used.

nil pointer bugs

A pointer that doesn't address a location can't be followed by a circumflex, even if it has been defined as nil. Attempting to do so *should* cause a program crash. However, since the many Pascal compilers don't detect nil references, this error will lead to incorrect results.

To avoid nil pointer references, be sure that the pointer has been allocated (with a call of new) or has been assigned the value of an existing pointer of the same type.

Nil pointer references can be caused by failing to allocate pointers. There is a corresponding bug that's the result of allocating too many. It's called a *heap overflow*. For example, suppose we use the same old node pointer we've relied on all along to allocate an endless linked list:

```
{Allocate the first node in a list.}
new (CurrentPtr);
{Then enter a buggy loop that never terminates.}
repeat
    {Allocate another link in the list.}
    new (CurrentPtr ↑.Next);
    {Advance the auxiliary pointer there.}
    CurrentPtr := CurrentPtr ↑.Next
until 1 = 2
```

Runtime Error: Heap overflow error.

As you can see, the loop allocates endlessly; the linked list gets longer and longer. The error message refers to a *heap overflow*. 'Heap' is a technical term that describes the computer's supply of as yet unallocated memory. When a pointer is allocated, the location it uses comes from the heap; when it's deallocated, the location is returned there. In any case, trying to allocate a location once the heap has been used up is called an overflow. Naturally, it causes a crash.

dispose can lead to a hard-to-debug problem. Suppose two pointers address the same location, then one is deallocated. What happens to the other pointer?

```
new (FirstPointer);
SecondPointer := FirstPointer;
dispose (FirstPointer);
FirstPointer := nil;
{What has happened to SecondPointer?}
```

In most compilers, *nothing* has happened to it—it still addresses the deallocated location. SecondPointer is said to be a *dangling* pointer—it's an auxiliary pointer that's still hanging around. It's generally a good programming practice to explicitly set pointers to nil whenever they're not being used.

set dangling pointers to nil

Linked Structure Bugs

A general problem of linked structures is the inadvertent loss of a pointer.

hold on tight

> It *is* possible to lose a location. And, once a location or chain of locations is gone, there's no way to recapture it.

A chain of pointers isn't like a ball of string. If the end gets lost, it's really gone. The best way to avoid this problem is to draw a picture that duplicates your code, and to check the order of program statements carefully.

Don't worry about using an extra auxiliary pointer or two, either. Programmers often read about overflows, then become needlessly stingy when it comes to declaring pointers. But there's no need to be chintzy; overflows occur

use auxiliary pointers

when you allocate variables in thousands or tens of thousands, not when you declare a handful of auxiliary pointers. When one pointer serves two purposes, bugs happen. Extra pointers are cheap, so use them.

Once a linked structure has been created, there are a few typical errors to watch out for. Most common is the attempt to boldly go where no one has gone before—past the end of a linked list. The problem is simply the pointer version of the classic search-loop bug: knowing why we *want* the loop to end doesn't guarantee that it will terminate before disaster strikes.

— When you search the input stream, check for **not** eof.

necessary bounds on searches

— When you search an array, watch for the last component.

— When you search a linked list, look out for **nil**-valued pointers.

The appearance of this necessary bound varies, but its purpose is always the same—look before you loop. An incorrect loop hopes for the best:

```
{A loop with a potential bug—Sought might not be there.}
CurrentPtr := HeadPtr;    {Start CurrentPtr at the head of the list.}
while (CurrentPtr ↑.Value <> Sought) do begin
    CurrentPtr := CurrentPtr ↑.Next
end
```

One correct version has a double bound condition and an extra check that follows the loop. Can you see why this won't always be correct, though? Try to figure out the loop's precondition, below.

one possible alternative

```
{A possibly correct, but probably buggy, version of the same loop.}
CurrentPtr := HeadPtr;    {Start CurrentPtr at the head of the list.}
{What precondition has to exist here, before the loop?}
while (CurrentPtr ↑.Value <> Sought) and
        (CurrentPtr ↑.Next <> nil) do begin
    CurrentPtr := CurrentPtr ↑.Next
end;
{Postcondition:  if Sought is there, CurrentPtr addresses it.}
if CurrentPtr ↑.Value = Sought
    then begin writeln ('Found the value.') end
    else begin writeln ('Didn''t find the value.') end
```

The missing precondition is that the list always contains at least one allocated node. If it doesn't, either of the checks in the **while** loop should cause a crash and will definitely be in error. Now, this isn't an unreasonable precondition, because in many instances, linked structures *will* always have at least one node. We used that approach in the queue abstraction we implemented.

But what if the HeadPtr pointer and, thus, the CurrentPtr pointer might be nil? We need this alternative version of the search loop:

{*A different version of the same loop.*}
Searching := TRUE;   {*Use an auxiliary boolean variable.*}
CurrentPtr := HeadPtr;   {*Start CurrentPtr at the head of the list.*}
{*Now, CurrentPtr might be nil.*}

a second alternative

while (CurrentPtr <> **nil**) **and** Searching **do begin**
    if (CurrentPtr ↑.Value = Sought)
        then Searching := FALSE   {*since we've found it*}
        else CurrentPtr := CurrentPtr ↑.Next
end;
{*Postcondition: if CurrentPtr isn't nil, it addresses Sought.*}
if CurrentPtr <> **nil**
    then begin writeln ('Found the value.') **end**
    else begin writeln ('Didn''t find the value.') **end**

> Neither implementation style is right or wrong. It's *your* abstraction; as long as the primitives perform, you can put it together any way you like. What is important is remembering your own implementation decisions!

As you might expect, there are a number of bugs that are associated with structures that may be based on linked lists, rather than with pointers per se. Look out for boundary conditions; ask yourself if your procedure will work:

boundary bugs

— at the beginning of the list?

— at the end of the list?

— if the list is empty?

For example, a common bug is attempting to pop a value from an empty stack. A call of Empty(Stack) avoids the issue.

In closing, let me stress the importance of data abstraction and the object-oriented design methods we've used. You may feel, at first, that it is your own weakness as a programmer that makes a page of assignments to and through pointers look complicated. It ain't so. In large quantities, pointers are confusing to everybody. Use procedures and functions to cut them down to size.

Syntax Summary

❏   pointer: a variable that holds the *address* of a record or other variable. Its type definition is:

    type NamePOINT = ↑ *the type it addresses;*

❏   A pointer can address any type, but it will usually address a record.

❏   node: the building block of a linked data structure. Typically, it's a record that has one or more fields that store data and at least one pointer-typed field that links it to the next node:

type NodePOINT = ↑ NodeTYPE;
NodeTYPE = **record**
                Data: integer;
                Link: NodePOINT
      end;
var HeadPtr, Tail: NodePOINT;

❑ dynamic allocation: creates a location for a pointer to address. The standard procedure new takes one argument: a pointer variable.

    new (HeadPtr);

❑ dynamic deallocation: returns the location that a pointer addresses to the computer for reallocation:

    dispose (HeadPtr);

❑ nil: a non-value that can be assigned to a pointer of any type. nil is used to initialize pointers that don't address locations:

    Tail := nil;

❑ circumflex: the '^' that's used to construct the name of the location a pointer addresses. I use the up-arrow here because it's easier to read.

    HeadPtr ↑ *is the entire* NodeTYPE *record*;
    HeadPtr ↑.Data *is one field of the record*;

Remember . . .

❑ 'Location,' 'anonymous variable,' and 'variable addressed through a pointer' are three different ways of describing the same thing—a dynamically allocated variable.

❑ An address can be changed by making an assignment *to* the pointer, but the variable at that address is changed by making the assignment *through* the pointer.

❑ The value—an address—that a pointer represents can't be inspected. It can be compared only for equality to nil, or to another pointer of the same type.

❑ Pointers can be assigned only nil or the value of another pointer of the same type.

❑ A linked list is a chain of nodes held together by pointers. Stacks and queues can be built with linked lists, but they're defined as abstractions in terms of their primitive operations: push, pop, and so on.

❑ A *stack* is a LIFO, or last-in, first-out, structure. The *queue*, in contrast, is FIFO, or first-in, first-out.

❑ Losing track of the end of a list is one of the most common pointer bugs. Use auxiliary pointers early and often.

❑ When you deal with linked structures, the first procedure you write should be a Dump procedure that prints the structure's contents.

The Big Ideas in this chapter are:

1. *All the elaborate rules for definition, creation, and access of pointers have just one purpose—to let a programmer work with variables that don't have permanent names.* Pointers separate variables from their identifiers, and vice versa. A single variable can have more than one name, or a single name can refer to different variables. In effect, a pointer is an identifier that isn't tied to just one variable.

2. *Pointers are prized because they can link records.* Most pointer applications involve lists or chains of records. Pointers make the lists easy to add to and easy to reconfigure. They let us mimic the structure of data, rather than having to force it into one of the basic types.

3. *Data structures are characterized by the rules they follow and the operations they allow—not by the way they are implemented or by the values they store.* A linked list is usually built with pointers, but it could be made from an array of records. The primitives define the structure, not its implementation.

15-1   The first idea that has to be nailed down is that a pointer can have *any* address type—it can point to an integer, a record, an array, etc. One way to make this point is to ask for a program that reads and adds two numbers, then prints their sum, but uses only pointer variables. Make up three other questions of this type.

15-2   The syntax of a legal pointer type definition is a detail, true, but it's one you have to know. Here's one that isn't legal:

```
type TestPOINT = ↑ record;
     RecordTYPE = record
                          Data: char;
                          Last: TestPOINT
                  end;
```

Why not? The pointer should be to RecordTYPE, not to **record**.
      Make up five definitions, of varying degrees of legality, as *Fix the bug* questions. Make them harder by venturing away from the vanilla *record-with-a-pointer-field* model.

15-3   Suppose that the definition above had been done correctly. You might declare a few variables:

```
var Test, Trial: TestPOINT;
    HeadPtr, Tail: RecordTYPE;
```

then go to town with them. For example:

a)   What can you new and dispose?

b)   What can be assigned to what?

Write a number of statements in each category, and ask *Which of these are legal?* For example, which of *these* are legal?

```
new (HeadPtr);
Test := Tail;
```

Neither, of course! For an interesting variation, try putting together potentially illegal sequences of two statements.

15-4 Refer back to the definition examples from the end of section 15-3. In each case, we pose a problem, define one or more data types, and draw a picture of the final structure. Make up three more questions of this sort. For instance:

> A computer science teacher who is seeking tenure has found that the best way to ensure high teaching ratings is to tell students that they are above average. Since she doesn't wish to lie, she organizes her records in several different ways: by homework scores, by quiz grades, by exam grades, and by class attendance. In this way, she's almost always able to find some way in which each student excels. Define a data type that might be used for the job.

15-5 What can you do in the course of traversing a simple linked list? Well, you might just have to locate the end. You might have to print every data value in the list. You might have to print every *other* value. You might have to find a particular value. You might even have to make up three more questions of this sort.

15-6 Usually, the last pointer in a linked list is **nil**. But for purposes of examination, it might point anywhere—back to the head of the list, perhaps, or to its third component. Make up two *Reattach the end of the list* questions. *For fun:* Which of these letter shapes can you duplicate with a linked list: D P B R? What about with two lists?

15-7 You know what the basic linked list operations are: traverse, find, insert, and so on. But how good would you be at attaching proper names to the Pascal code that does each job? Take appropriate code segments from the text, mix them up in a hat, then see how long it takes you to properly identify the first one you pull out.

15-8 Consider the following code segment. We can assume that FirstPtr points to the head of a linked list, and that CurrentPtr, FirstPtr, and NextPtr are all pointer variables of the same type.

```
CurrentPtr := FirstPtr;
while CurrentPtr <> nil do begin
    TempPtr := CurrentPtr;
    CurrentPtr := CurrentPtr↑.NextPtr;
    Temp↑.NextPtr := FirstPtr
end
```

What does it do? It causes every link in the list to point back to the very first node.

Make up three *What does it do?* questions by writing three variations on the code segment. You'll find that they don't have to be complicated!

15-9 Draw a straightforward, garden-variety, linked list. This will be your *before* picture. Then, draw three *after* pictures (a picture of the example above will be a good start). Then, ask yourself *Which of these three would be a good test question?*

15-10 Take one of the basic linked-list-handling code segments that appears in the text, and put it into a procedure. Make it into a test question by presenting the heading in as many variations of value and variable parameters as seems appropriate. The question, of course, is *Which heading is correct?*

Warmups and
Test Programs

15-11 What's the difference between a **nil** pointer and an uninitialized pointer?

15-12 Can a pointer point to a pointer? Can it point to itself? Can you think of any possible reason for doing so?

15-13 Write a program that determines if *a*) two pointers to integers refer to the same value and/or *b*) they refer to the same location.

15-14 All right—the moment we've all been waiting for. How many items can you allocate before your system runs out of gas? Hint: print the current count every thousand allocations or so, so that you can be sure your program is working.

15-15 What error message results from giving new a second argument that is the size of a pointer variable, rather than giving it the size of the item (e.g. the record) the pointer locates?

15-16 What error message results from attempting to print the value of a pointer? From trying to add 1 to it? From inspecting a **nil** pointer?

15-17 How would you reverse the contents of a stack? Using a queue? Using another stack?

15-18 Write a procedure that checks two linked lists to see if their contents are identical. Can you have your procedure check to see if they include any of the same locations as well?

15-19 Write a procedure that removes the first *n* nodes from a list. Can you remove the last *n* nodes as well?

Programming Problems

15-20 In section 15-3 I described a solution to the problem of spotting palindromic sentences. Implement the solution, using the method (simultaneously stacking and queueing the words) I described.

15-21 In a *doubly-linked list*, each node has pointers to the front and rear. Define, then implement, then test, a set of primitive operators for a doubly-linked list. At the very least, you should be able to add, delete, insert, and locate nodes at arbitrary positions in the list.

15-22 In a *circular* linked list, the first node is attached to the last. Thus, a single pointer can address both the head and tail.

We can use a circular linked list to solve an old problem about a ship caught in a terrible storm. Although there were thirty passengers plus the captain on board, there was room in the lifeboats for only fifteen of them. As the captain was reluctant to leave anybody behind, she resolved to throw half the passengers overboard before loading the boats.

As it happens, half of the passengers had slighted the captain by not dining at her table during the cruise. The captain, in revenge, arranged all the passengers in a circle and began to count. Every *n*th passenger went overboard; naturally, the captain's friends were never chosen. Here's how the passengers were originally arranged (I've shown the friends with **O** and the enemies with **X**):

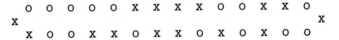

The question is *What number was n?* Start counting at the upper-left **O**.

15-23 An *automynorcagram* is a sentence whose words are determined by its letters:

Each additional character has a distinctly desirable idiosyncrasy that is . . .

Write a program that represents an automynorcagram as a linked list. In addition to linking the letters that form the sentence, you should link individual letters to the start of the words they generate. In the example above, the E of *each* would point to itself, the *a* to *additional*, the *c* to *character*, the *h* to *has*, and so on.

15-24 Some of the more athletic among you may be familiar with the exercise known as *running stadium steps*. Repeatedly running up and down steep flights of stairs has no practical application, of course, but it is believed to build character.

One programming equivalent of running stadium steps is to base a one-line text editing system on a linked list. Write a program that has primitives for adding, deleting, printing, measuring, and locating characters and substrings within a line.

15-25 'The only good stack is an empty stack' is an expression that is often heard in mathematical programming. This thought is especially applicable to parentheses and brackets; a solitary delimiter is invariably up to no good.

Write a program that reads an expression and stacks the delimiters {, [, and (. As their matching counterparts },], and) appear, they should be popped. Your program should detect two error conditions—unpaired delimiters (like {5/[3+7]) and misordered delimiters (like {5/[3+7]–2])—and announce which delimiter was expected. All operands and operators should be ignored.

15-26 Suppose that each of three linked lists is internally ordered from least to greatest. Write a procedure that merges them to form a fourth list that goes from greatest to least.

15-27 Most computer systems use various kinds of *buffers*, or temporary holding places, to minimize the amount of work required of the CPU. Buffers are like semi-autonomous worker bees; they can do simple tasks that do not require any appreciable computation.

In one common application, buffers do the grunt work of holding a line of characters until the user hits the return key. Suppose that a line is a maximum of 128 characters long. A buffer should:

a) let additional characters be added to the end of the line, up to the maximum;

b) let the user backspace to delete single characters;

c) let the user 'rubout' or delete the entire line;

d) let the user end the line with a carriage return or equivalent.

Implement a line buffer, using a doubly-linked list as the underlying data structure. This is sometimes called an *input-restricted dequeue* (short for *double-ended queue*), since values can be added only on the user's side and not on the system side.

15-28 Assignment of computer memory to running processes is the basic *dynamic storage allocation* problem. The problem is a bit like packing suitcases for somebody we don't know very well. Should we cram everything in as it arrives? Or perhaps it would be smarter to pack several suitcases at once, and put each new item in the smallest spot that can contain it.

Although in reality computer memory is very much like a long array, it is convenient to represent it as a linked list of 'free' and 'occupied' areas. Memory is initially a single element labeled 'free' with a very large *Size* field. As each new job arrives, an additional 'taken' element, with its size, is added to the list at the expense of the 'free' element.

The allocation problem becomes interesting when we let jobs release memory. Free space is no longer found only at the end of the list. Instead, the list holds interspersed segments of open memory and used memory. How do we decide where to place a new job? Two simple strategies, similar to those we might use in packing suitcases, are *first fit*—stick the new job in the first area that's big enough and *best fit*—put the new job in the smallest open area that will do.

Write procedures capable of modeling each strategy. They should be able to:

a) search a linked list for the first 'free' element with *Size* equal to or greater than some required n;

b) search for the 'free' element with *Size* closest to, but not less than, n;

c) recognize, and merge, contiguous 'free' elements.

Hint: you may want to consider keeping an auxiliary list of pointers to 'free' elements.

15-29 An interesting problem proposed by R. Hamming is to print a list, in numerical order and with no duplicates, of numbers that have no prime factors other than 2, 3, or 5. The appropriate sequence begins 2,3,4,5,6,8,9,10,12,15,16,18,20... Each term is a number of the form $2^i 3^j 5^k$, for all non-negative integer i, j, k values.

One approach to solving this problem involves the repeated creation and merger of lists. Suppose we start with a $List_{final}$, empty to begin with, of all the terms of the answer. A $List_{temp}$, initially 2, 3, 5, contains some, but not all, of the terms that go into a $List_{final}$. Finally, we can begin to generate a $List_{2terms}$, a $List_{3terms}$, and a $List_{5terms}$ by multiplying the current contents of $List_{temp}$ by 2, 3, and 5.

Now we have a *final* list, a *temp* list, and three *term* lists. The final list grows by being merged with the current temp list. The temp list, in turn, is replaced by the merger of the three term lists. New term lists are generated by multiplying the new temp list by 2, 3, and 5.

Write a program that carries out all this list generation and merging. How do you know how much of the final list can be safely printed at any point?

Additional exercises, problems, and projects accompany the discussion of recursion in 16–4.

The stack can, and usually, does, grow and shrink during the course of a program. Why recursion seems like a familiar concept to many readers. (p. 550)

16

Recursive Programming

'There's more than one way to skin a cat,' as the saying goes, and nowhere is this more true than in programming. Although we've spent many pages discussing multiple and overlapping uses of different control statements and the tradeoff between algorithms and data structures, there is still one unmentioned tool left in our bag of tricks—*recursion*.

A recursive subprogram calls itself. Now, this property alone might seem unremarkable. We will see, though, that recursion adds enormous power to Pascal. It is as much a technique for structuring ideas and thinking as it is for structuring programs.

I've split the discussion into four parts. Section 16-1 introduces the idea of the runtime stack, and deals strictly with recursion as a substitute for looping. It can probably be read with ease following Chapter 6. Section 16-2, in turn, adds the array type to the picture to allow the development of more elaborate algorithms. It can follow Chapter 9. Finally, section 16-3 presents recursion in the context of pointers and describes the definition of recursive data types; it should follow Chapter 15.

Recursive Procedures and Functions

16-1

HOW CAN YOU PRINT A SENTENCE IN REVERSE without using arrays or pointers? Think about it for a minute, then consider this deceptively simple program:

recursive sentence-reverse program

```
program Recur (input, output);
    {Uses recursion to read a line and echo it in reverse.}
procedure StackTheCharacters;
    var TheCharacter: char;
    begin
        read (TheCharacter);
        if not eoln then begin
            StackTheCharacters          {The recursive call.}
        end;
        write (TheCharacter)
    end;  {StackTheCharacters}
begin
    writeln ('Enter a sentence that is not a palindrome.');
    StackTheCharacters;          {The first call.}
    writeln
end.  {Recur}
```

Enter a sentence that is not a palindrome.
Was that a Toyota I saw?
?was I atoyoT a taht saW

Why didn't I want a palindrome? Because if I reversed it, how could I tell?

Program Recur takes an ordinary sentence of text as input, then prints it in reverse. It manages this magic with a procedure that calls itself.

recursion defined

> A procedure or function that calls itself is said to be *recursive*.

When procedure StackTheCharacters is first called, it reads a character value for its local variable TheCharacter. Then, unless the first character ended the line, StackTheCharacters is called again. However, the final statement of the first call, which is write (TheCharacter), is still pending while the next instance of the procedure call tries to read a character again.

Now, leaving uncompleted statements behind is nothing new. We do it every time we call any procedure or function, yet we still manage, somehow, to get back to the main program. Sooner or later we'll get back to StackTheCharacters' closing output statement and print the value of the first character.

What happens in the second call of StackTheCharacters? Well, it's déjà vu all over again. Once again, a new local variable (TheCharacter) is created. Once more, a letter is read so that TheCharacter can have a value. And, once recursive calls more, if we haven't reached the end of the input line, StackTheCharacters is called. As before, the very last write (TheCharacter) call is still waiting to be executed.

The Recursive Stack

Since it's hard to visualize what happens in a series of identical procedure calls, computer scientists use a metaphor to help explain recursion.

the stack

> The variables and pending statements of a partially executed program or subprogram go on a *stack* within the computer.

When we jump out of a subprogram (by calling another procedure or function) all currently active variables, along with any pending statements, are added to the stack. The number of times this can occur—the height of the stack—is limited only by the memory resources of the computer.

StackTheCharacters is a procedure, not a loop, but I can describe it in a way that's very much like a loop specification:

a recursive specification

> *Goal: Print a sentence in reverse.*
> *Stacking Plan: Read a character.*
> *Bound: We've reached the end of the line.*
> *Unstacking Plan: Print a character.*

Suppose that I 'unfold' program Recur and show every statement that actually does something. If we look only at the input statements—the stacking plan—executed during procedure StackTheCharacters, we'll see something like the series shown below. Although we keep creating local variables named TheCharacter, Pascal's scope rule (that the most local variable takes precedence) gives the current input value to the most recently created instance.

```
writeln ('Please enter a sentence. ');
```
building the stack
```
    read (TheCharacter);              {Reading in 'W'.}
        read (TheCharacter);          {Reading in 'a'.}
            read (TheCharacter);        {Reading in 's'.}
              ⋱    {Intermediate calls...}
                read (TheCharacter);    {Reading in 'a'.}
                  read (TheCharacter);  {Reading in 'w'.}
                    read (TheCharacter);  {Reading in '?', the last call.}
```

The chain of calls to StackTheCharacters continues until we read the question mark that ends the sentence. At last we'll get past the **if** statement! We can finally complete the last invocation of StackTheCharacters by printing the character we just read—the question mark. Then, the computer executes the statements of the unstacking plan:

```
                    write (TheCharacter);   {Printing the '?'.}
                  write (TheCharacter);     {Printing the 'w'.}
                write (TheCharacter);       {Printing the 'a'.}
              ⋱    {Intermediate calls...}
            write (TheCharacter);           {Printing the 's'.}
        write (TheCharacter);               {Printing the 'a'.}
    write (TheCharacter);                   {Printing the 'W'.}
writeln           {This is the last statement in the main program.}
```
undoing the stack

The program returns to where it was when the procedure call was made—to the calling procedure and eventually to the main program.

Recursion will call for a number of test beds. We'll start with a look at the Recur program itself. When I took this snapshot, the program had finally read the period that ends **ABCDE.** Notice that I've opened the *call stack* window. The original program 'call,' Recur, is on the bottom. Stacked above it are five calls of StackTheCharacter. We're just about to print the period and end the call that's on top of the stack. If you can tell me what the screen will look like as I continue to single step through the program, you're starting to understand recursion.

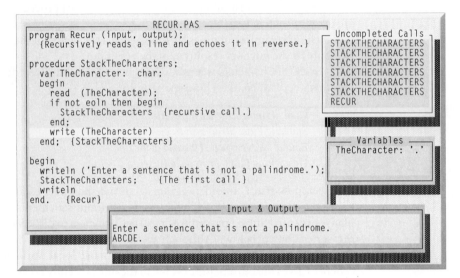

about to make the first write call

using the call stack

```
———————— RECUR.PAS ————————
program Recur (input, output);
  {Recursively reads a line and echoes it in reverse.}

procedure StackTheCharacters;
  var TheCharacter:  char;
  begin
    read  (TheCharacter);
    if not eoln then begin
      StackTheCharacters   {recursive call.}
    end;
    write (TheCharacter)
  end; {StackTheCharacters}

begin
  writeln ('Enter a sentence that is not a palindrome.');
  StackTheCharacters;    {The first call.}
  writeln
end.   {Recur}
```

```
— Uncompleted Calls —
  STACKTHECHARACTERS
  STACKTHECHARACTERS
  STACKTHECHARACTERS
  STACKTHECHARACTERS
  STACKTHECHARACTERS
  STACKTHECHARACTERS
  RECUR
```

```
———— Variables ————
  TheCharacter: '.'
```

```
——————— Input & Output ———————
Enter a sentence that is not a palindrome.
ABCDE.
```

Modification Problems

1. Modify Recur so that it reverses a number by reading it one digit character at a time. Spot the end of the number by spotting a space.

2. What would happen to program Recur if the output statement preceded the shaded recursive call, rather than following it?

Recursion with Parameters

Now, a stack is actually created in any series of procedure or function calls—the sequence need not be recursive. The stack can, and usually does, grow and shrink during the course of a program. However, it will always be empty when a program ends normally.*

Procedure StackTheCharacters is a good introduction to recursion because it uses the stack in an obvious way. Each time a recursive call is made in StackTheCharacters, local variables and uncompleted statements are left on the stack.

---

* This simplified explanation of stacks helps explain how the computer keeps track of scope within a program. *All* identifiers defined in a subprogram are put on the stack when the subprogram is invoked. Then, when an identifier is used, the computer looks down the stack for the identifier's most recent definition or declaration. Although the stack may contain several different usages of a single name, the most recent definition is the first one found.

However, recursive calls don't have to leave *anything* useful on the stack. For instance, program UnDigit, below, leaves almost no undone business. Its recursive procedure, ReverseDigits, prints a single digit and then calls itself:

> *Goal: Print a positive integer in reverse.*
> *Stacking Plan: Print the 'ones' digit.*
> *Bound: There are no more digits to print.*
> *Unstacking Plan: —*

But there's no 'unstacking' plan. When the very last call is made, all that's left is the **end** of each of the previous calls.

end recursion

> This kind of recursion is called *end* or *tail* recursion. When the procedure makes its recursive call, no unfinished statements are left on the stack.

recursive integer-reverse program

```
program UnDigit (input, output);
    {Recursively reverses the digits of a positive integer.}
var Data: integer;
procedure ReverseDigits (Number: integer);
    begin
        write (Number mod 10 : 1);   {Print the 'ones' digit.}
        {If there are more digits, divide away the 'ones' digit and pass the result.}
        if (Number div 10) <> 0 then begin
            ReverseDigits (Number div 10)
        end
    end;   {ReverseDigits}
begin
    writeln ('Please enter a positive integer.');
    readln (Data);
    ReverseDigits (Data);
    writeln
end.   {UnDigit}
```

```
Please enter a positive integer.
26407
70462
```

Procedures that use end recursion are usually easy to write iteratively (using a looping statement). For example:

iterative reversing procedure

```
procedure IterativeReverse (TheNumber: integer);
    begin
        repeat
            write (TheNumber mod 10 : 1);
            TheNumber := TheNumber div 10;
        until TheNumber = 0
    end;   {IterativeReverse}
```

Once again, seeing will be believing. In the screen shot below, I've stepped part of the way through UnDigit. The call stack is a bit more useful this time, because it shows the argument value along with the procedure name. As we join the program, ReverseDigits has just printed the digit 3 and is deciding if there should be another recursive call.

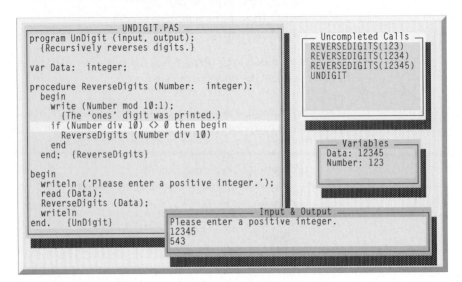

```
                 ─── UNDIGIT.PAS ───
  program UnDigit (input, output);
    {Recursively reverses digits.}

  var Data:  integer;

  procedure ReverseDigits (Number:  integer);
    begin
      write (Number mod 10:1);
        {The 'ones' digit was printed.}
      if (Number div 10) <> 0 then begin
        ReverseDigits (Number div 10)
      end
    end; {ReverseDigits}

  begin
    writeln ('Please enter a positive integer.');
    read (Data);
    ReverseDigits (Data);
    writeln
  end.   {UnDigit}
```

```
─── Uncompleted Calls ───
 REVERSEDIGITS(123)
 REVERSEDIGITS(1234)
 REVERSEDIGITS(12345)
 UNDIGIT
```

```
─── Variables ───
 Data: 12345
 Number: 123
```

```
──── Input & Output ────
 Please enter a positive integer.
 12345
 543
```

Modification Problems

1. Reversing a real value is harder than reversing an integer. Try to modify UnDigit so that it reverses the whole portion and fractional portion of a real separately, so that **123.456** is printed as 321.654.

2. I usually check addition by re-adding the figures in reverse. Turn Recur or UnDigit into a program that reads and stacks a line's worth of integer values. Add them before you put them on the stack, then add them as they come off. Are the sums the same?

Self-Check Questions

Q. Is the procedure in Print recursive? Should it be? What does it do?

```
program Print (input, output);
procedure Echo;
    var TheCharacter: char;
    begin
        read (TheCharacter);
        write (TheCharacter);
        if TheCharacter <> '.' then begin Echo end
    end; {Echo}
begin
    write ('Type in a sentence that ends with a period.');
    writeln;
    Echo;
    writeln
end. {Print}
```

A. Echo offers another demonstration of end recursion. The stack is created, but it doesn't hold any statements to execute. The series of TheCharacter local variables is saved, but gets thrown away when the recursive calls end. The stack is built, but not used. A **while** loop would also do the job, because the program just echoes an input line.

```
Enter a sentence that ends with a period.
They had a hot time in the Cretaceous.
They had a hot time in the Cretaceous.
```

Recursive Functions

Like procedures, functions can be written recursively. In program Summer, below, function Sum uses a series of recursive calls to add a series of numbers from 1 through its argument Limit.

recursive summing function

```
program Summer (input, output);
    {Uses a recursive function for addition.}
var Bound: integer;
function Sum (Limit: integer) : integer;
    {Recursively sums the positive numbers 1 through Limit.}
    begin
        if Limit = 1
            then Sum := Limit
            else Sum := Limit + Sum(Limit – 1)
    end;  {Sum}
begin
    write ('I add 1..n the hard way.  What''s n?   ');
    readln (Bound);
    write ('The sum is:   ');
    writeln (Sum (Bound) : 1 )
end.  {Summer}
```

```
I add 1..n the hard way.  What's n?  250
The sum is:  31375
```

The stack that function Sum produces is a bit peculiar when compared to our recursive procedure calls. Rather than variables or statements, it contains a series of partially evaluated expressions.

stacking recursive function calls

> The general outline of Sum is typical of recursive functions: the recursive call occurs while an expression is being calculated. Thus, the stack serves to delay the expression's evaluation.

Let's assume that Sum is called with 5 as its first Limit argument. Here's the stack of partial evaluations that's built during the sequence of calls:

$$Sum := 5 + \boxed{Sum\ (5\text{--}1)}\ \{\textit{first}\}$$
$$Sum := 4 + \boxed{Sum\ (4\text{--}1)}\ \{\textit{second}\}$$
$$Sum := 3 + \boxed{Sum\ (3\text{--}1)}\ \{\textit{third}\}$$
$$Sum := 2 + \boxed{Sum\ (2\text{--}1)}\ \{\textit{fourth}\}$$
$$Sum := \boxed{1}\ \{\textit{fifth}\}$$

None of the stacked expressions can be calculated until Sum gets a non-recursive value—the fifth call, which doesn't depend on calling Sum again. Let's follow the sequence of assignments as they're able to be made:

$$Sum := \boxed{1}\ \{\textit{fifth}\}$$
$$Sum := \boxed{2+1}\ \{\textit{fourth}\}$$
$$Sum := \boxed{3+3}\ \{\textit{third}\}$$
$$Sum := \boxed{4+6}\ \{\textit{second}\}$$
$$Sum := \boxed{5+10}\ \{\textit{first}\}$$

the bound call

> The last of a series of recursive calls is the *bound* call. The circumstances that give rise to the bound call form the exit condition of the recursion.

infinite recursion

By our definition of the function, Sum's bound call occurs when its argument is 1. An *infinite* recursion occurs if the exit condition can't be met, and the bound call is never made.

You should be getting the hang of recursion by now, so here's one last test bed. As before, we find ourselves in the midst of a series of recursive calls. We're trying to decide whether or not we've reached the bound condition. What will happen next?

```
 ───────── SUMMER.PAS ─────────
program Summer (input, output);
  {Uses a recursive function for addition.}

function Sum (Limit:  integer) : integer;
  {Recursively sums 1 through Limit.}
  begin
    if Limit = 1
      then Sum := Limit
      else Sum := Limit + Sum(Limit - 1)
  end;   {Sum}

begin
  writeln (Sum (5) : 1 );
end.   {Summer}
```

```
── Uncompleted Calls ──
SUM(2)
SUM(3)
SUM(4)
SUM(5)
SUMMER
```

```
──── Variables ────
Limit: 2
```

Modification Problems

1. Modify Summer so that it produces a table of sums, i.e. 1..1, 1..2, 1..3, and so on. How high can you go before you overstep the bounds of integer?

2. Modify Sum so that it calculates factorials, rather than powers. For instance, 5 factorial is 5×4×3×2×1.

Recursive Definitions

A recursive function is usually specified by calling the function as part of its own definition. This leads to a recursive definition, and takes some getting used to. The definition typically has two steps:

recursive definition

— Define the function for its bound case.

— Define the function in terms that bring it one step closer to the bound.

I can express the same idea in terms of bounds and plans as:

recursive specification

> *Goal: Evaluate a function call for some argument.*
> *Stacking plan: Call the function with a reduced argument.*
> *Bound: The argument can't be reduced any further.*
> *Unstacking plan: Evaluate the expression.*

Notice that the stacking plan *call the function with a reduced argument* really implies *take the smallest step you can toward the bound*. Usually, this requires subtracting 1 from the recursive function call's argument. As was the case with loop specifications, the recursion ends because we reach the bound.

For example, consider function Sum. Its bound is that the parameter Limit equals 1. In the bound case, Sum actually equals Limit, because the sum of the numbers from 1 through 1 is just 1.

But how can we define the function in a way that takes small steps toward the bound? By recognizing that if Limit is greater than 1, then Sum(Limit) can be expressed as Limit plus Sum(Limit−1).

> Sum(Limit) *equals* Limit + Sum(Limit − 1)

This restatement brings us one step closer to the ultimate recursive bound. If I put the two parts together, we have:

> If Limit equals 1, the sum of 1 to Limit is Limit.

the recursive definition

> If Limit exceeds 1, the sum of 1 to Limit equals Limit plus the sum of 1 to Limit less 1.

Or, stated as a recursive specification:

the recursive specification

> *Goal: Recursively evaluate the call* Sum(Limit).
> *Stacking plan: Add* Limit *to* Sum(Limit − 1).
> *Bound:* Limit *equals one.*
> *Unstacking plan: Evaluate the stacked calls.*

If you reconsider the **if** statement from function Sum, you'll see that it says exactly the same thing in Pascal.

```
if Limit = 1
    then Sum := Limit
    else Sum := Limit + Sum(Limit − 1)
```

problem: exponentiation

Once you get the hang of it, it's fun to make up recursive definitions of some of the basic functions. For example, how would you use recursion to raise a number X to the *n*th power, where *n* is a positive integer?

The plain English definition of a Power function is easy: 'multiply X by itself *n* times.' But that sounds like an invitation to a **for** loop. Getting a recursive definition starts by considering the bound case. What is X raised to the first power? Why, it's X, of course. And if *n* exceeds one, we can define the function in a way that brings us one step closer to the bound:

the recursive definition

If *n* equals 1, then X to the *n* equals X.

If *n* is greater than 1, then X to the *n* equals X times X to the *n*–1.

Restating this as a recursive specification gives us:

the recursive specification

Goal: Recursively evaluate the call Power(X, n).
Stacking plan: Multiply X *by* Power(X, n – 1).
Bound: n *equals one.*
Unstacking plan: Evaluate the stacked calls.

As you read function Power, below, note that it requires two value parameters. At each step of the recursive algorithm we must know the values of both X and n. However, as you can see from the algorithm we described above, X remains constant while n steadily declines.

recursive power function

```
function Power (X: real; n: integer) : real;
   {Recursively calculates Xⁿ. Assume n > 0.}
   begin
      if n = 1
         then Power := X
         else Power := X * Power (X, n – 1)
   end;   {Power}
```

Another definition that's easy to state recursively in English is that of the *n*th Fibonacci number. The Fibonacci sequence begins 1, 1, then each subsequent value is the sum of the previous two: 1, 1, 2, 3, 5, 8 and so on. The recursive definition is:

problem: recursive Fibonacci definition

If *n* is 1 or 2, the *n*th Fibonacci number is 1.

If *n* is 3 or more, the *n*th Fibonacci number is the sum of the previous two.

A specification that's a bit more like Pascal is:

the recursive specification

Goal: Recursively evaluate the call Fibonacci(Which).
Stacking plan: Add Fibonacci(Which – 1) *to* Fibonacci(Which – 2).
Bound: Which *equals* 1 *or* 2.
Unstacking plan: Evaluate the stacked calls.

Finally, the function itself is:

recursive Fibonacci numbers

```
function Fibonacci (Which: integer) : integer;
   begin
      if (Which=1) or (Which=2)
         then Fibonacci := 1
         else Fibonacci := Fibonacci(Which – 1) + Fibonacci(Which – 2)
   end;   {Fibonacci}
```

Although I won't show it here, both Power and Fibonacci can easily be implemented as iterative functions. However, recursive solutions can be much more elegant than their iterative counterparts. I'd hate to say that shortness is a virtue in itself, but recursive subprograms can often be written more briefly and clearly than iterative ones. When you become comfortable with recursion and start to recognize 'standard' recursive algorithms, you'll appreciate the ease with which such algorithms can be put into programs.

Modification Problems

1. Write test harnesses for functions Power and Fibonacci. What's the largest Fibonacci number you can calculate?

2. A Fibonacci-like sequence can actually begin with any two numbers. Modify Fibonacci so that it works properly for the sequence that starts 2, 2, 4, 6, 10 . . .

The Towers of Hanoi

Our first examples kept recursion simple by minimizing the numbers of statements and variables involved. The final introductory procedure will be the most complicated, even though it's just intended to help us play a game:

problem: towers of Hanoi

The *Towers of Hanoi* game is played with three pegs and a pile of disks of different sizes. We start with all the disks stacked on one peg, like this:

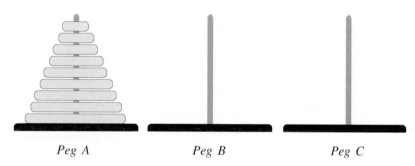

Peg A　　　　*Peg B*　　　　*Peg C*

The object of the game is to move the entire stack from peg A to peg C, while obeying two rules:

the rules

1. Only one disk can be moved at a time.

2. A larger disk can never go on top of a smaller one.

Write a program that gives step-by-step instructions for moving a stack of height *n* from peg A to C.

The original version of this game is said to have been played on a set of three diamond needles and sixty-four golden disks. The end of the game was supposed to mark the end of the world.

the 1- or 2-disk problem

Let's try to get a handle on how the moves are made for stacks of various heights. Clearly a height of 1 is trivial: we move the disk directly from A to C, which is empty. What about a height of 2? We put the smaller top disk out of the way—to B. Then the larger bottom disk goes to C, and the smaller disk from B to C.

the 3-disk problem

With a stack of height 3 it gets interesting. Let's suppose, though, that we restate the problem (as I'm liable to do when I'm up to something). Instead of moving 3 disks from A to C, let's move 2 disks from A to B—we already know how to move two disks from one peg to another. Next, move the third disk directly to C. Finally, make another two-disk move, from B to C. We've switched all three disks.

the 4-disk problem

How about starting with 4 disks? Once more, let's begin by restating the problem. Can we move 3 disks from A to B? Sure—it's essentially the same as moving them from A to C. Then we switch the fourth disk directly from A to C, and, finally, transfer 3 disks from B to C.

developing a recursive statement

As you can probably gather, I've insisted on restating the problem in a particular way each time so that we can develop a special insight. We begin to solve the Towers of Hanoi problem for a stack of height n by trying to solve it for a stack of height $n - 1$. This solution must wait until we solve for $(n-1) - 1$ and so on. Eventually we get to the trivial case of n equaling 1 and begin to work our way back up.

induction

Without realizing it, we've used a high-priced method of thinking called *induction*. We start by solving a simple case of the Towers of Hanoi problem—a height of one or two. Then, we show that even if we start with a larger number, we can always work our way down to a problem that we know how to solve.

This is the heart of what will become our recursive solution to the problem. We can move n disks from peg A to peg C by first moving $n - 1$ of them to peg B. The recursive statement of the solution is:

1. Move $n - 1$ disks from A to B.

the recursive Hanoi algorithm

2. Move 1 disk from A to C.

3. Move $n - 1$ disks from B to C.

In steps 1 and 3, of course, we will use the remaining peg as an auxiliary 'holding' peg. Since the empty peg changes, it might be easier to refer to FromPeg, ToPeg, and UsingPeg rather than A, B, and C. A recursive specification is:

> *Goal: Solve the Tower of Hanoi problem for height* N.
> *Stacking plan:* Move N − 1 *disks from* FromPeg *to* UsingPeg.
> *Bound: There's just one disk left (it goes from* FromPeg *to* ToPeg*).*
> *Unstacking plan:* Move N − 1 *disks from* UsingPeg *to* ToPeg.

In understanding program Hanoi, below, it may help to imagine that the three pegs are arranged in a circle rather than in a line. The particular pegs that FromPeg, ToPeg, and UsingPeg represent will change (they'll actually seem to rotate). However, we'll always eventually find ourselves fulfilling the second step of our algorithm and announcing a particular move.

Towers of Hanoi
program

program Hanoi (input, output);
    {*Recursively solves the Towers of Hanoi problem. Moves disks from A to C.*}
var Height: integer;
procedure Move (Height: integer; FromPeg, ToPeg, UsingPeg: char);
    {*Recursive procedure for determining moves. Keep this order—from,*
     to, using—in mind when you read the recursive calls.}
    begin
        if Height = 1
            then begin write ('Move a disk from ');
                        write (FromPeg);
                        write (' to ');
                        write (ToPeg);
                        writeln
            end
            else begin Move (Height – 1, FromPeg, UsingPeg, ToPeg);
                        write ('Move a disk from ');
                        write (FromPeg);
                        write (' to ');
                        write (ToPeg);
                        writeln;
                        Move (Height – 1, UsingPeg, ToPeg, FromPeg)
            end {if}
    end; {Move}
begin
    write ('How many disks are you going to start with? ');
    readln (Height);
    Move (Height, 'A', 'C', 'B')
end. {Hanoi}

```
How many disks are you going to start with? 4
Move a disk from A to B
Move a disk from A to C
Move a disk from B to C
Move a disk from A to B
Move a disk from C to A
Move a disk from C to B
Move a disk from A to B
Move a disk from A to C
Move a disk from B to C
Move a disk from B to A
Move a disk from C to A
Move a disk from B to C
Move a disk from A to B
Move a disk from A to C
Move a disk from B to C
```

1. Why will the world end when the sixty-four disk stack is moved? Modify Hanoi so that it simply counts steps, rather than printing them. For instance, moving four disks took fifteen steps. Have it list the number of steps required for stacks of height one, two, three, and so on, as high as you can go.

Recursive Array Programming

16-2

MANY INTERESTING PROGRAMMING PROBLEMS INVOLVE recursive array manipulation. Arrays are useful because they store large amounts of data, while recursion is handy for describing what we want done with them.

The recursion we'll see is different from our previous examples. Before, we used recursion to solve problems that were stated 'one-dimensionally,' so to speak. We would recursively progress along one particular path until we found the end of the sentence (or evaluated an expression, or reached the beginning or end of a series). Then, we'd tumble all the way back to the start of the sequence of recursive calls, and the program would be finished.

Now, though, we'll use recursion to allow algorithms that require movement in several 'dimensions,' some of which may be false starts, and others of which might help lead in the right direction.

backtracking algorithms

> *Backtracking* algorithms involve a series of trial and error solutions. We travel toward a solution until we know we're heading in the wrong direction, then backtrack to where we think we took the incorrect turn. Then, we try again.

The children's game of Hot and Cold uses a classic backtracking algorithm. One player takes guesses as to what the second player is thinking of. The second player tells the first if a guess is hot (close) or cold (far from the truth). Since in-between degrees of warmth are allowed (warmer, cooler, 'now you're boiling to death!'), the first player continually guesses and backtracks.

Backtracking algorithms are particularly suited to recursive programming methods. Each recursive call creates a context, or environment, associated with one step toward a solution. The sequence of steps that got us there is preserved in the series of recursive calls. Were we to look at the stack of recursive calls, we'd generally find it growing and shrinking repeatedly as we search toward—or back away from—potential solutions.

Generating Permutations

Let's start with a program that builds and backtracks as it finds many 'right' answers. The problem involves *permutations*.

A permutation is a rearrangement of a set of objects. For instance, the letters *abc* can be rearranged into six different permutations: *abc, acb, bac, bca, cab,* and *cba.* Write a program that reads a string of letters and prints every possible permutation.

As a rule, there will be N!, or N *factorial* different ways to go; for the example above, N! equals $3 \times 2 \times 1$.

Let's begin with a simple case: a string, *abcd*. I can say that to print each permutation, I must print every permutation that starts with *a*, then every permutation that starts with *b*, then *c*, and finally *d*. How can we give each letter its moment at the head of the string? By swapping it with the first. In other words:

> *To print the permutations of a string . . .*
>
> **for** *each component of the string*
>   *swap it with the first component;*
>   *print the permutations of a string*

You might imagine that we're building pile after pile of strings. Each pile, in effect, has the raw materials of a set of permutations: one pile starts with *a*, another with *b* and so on. Within each pile we can ignore the first letter or letters and build smaller piles with what remains.

A pile gets to be as high as it can when there are no letters further down to build new piles from. That can be our bound condition: we've reached the last component of the string:

the recursive specification

> *Goal: Print every permutation of a string.*
> *Stacking plan: Swap the current first component with one further down.*
> *Bound: The current component is the last component.*
> *Unstacking plan: Print the current string.*

The final version of program Permute is on the next page (its output and modification problems appear below). Don't worry if you find Permute easy to follow but hard to understand. With recursive programs, it's sometimes easier to know that the program will work than to have a good mental picture of why it does!

(*program follows*)

```
Give me a short string to permute:  abcd
abcd abdc acbd acdb
adbc adcb bacd badc
bcad bcda bdac bdca          Output is broken into rows.
cabd cadb cbad cbda
cdab cdba dabc dacb
dbac dbca dcab dcba
```

Modification Problems

1. Make Permute easier to follow by printing the strings that are saved as part of the stacking plan. In other words, print a string for each recursive call of PrintPermutations.

2. Permute builds its piles from front to back—all variations given the first letter, then all variations starting from the second, etc.—but prints its permutations from back to front—first all the last letter permutations, then all the next-to-last permutations, and so on. Reverse its operation.

3. Use Permute as the heart of a program that prints lettered mnemonics for telephone numbers. In other words, read a telephone number, then print all possible versions of the three letters that accompany every number but 1 and 0.

```
program Permute (input, output);
    {Prints every permutation of an input string.}
const MAX = 10;
type StringTYPE = packed array [1 .. MAX] of char;
var TheString: StringTYPE;
    Length: integer;
procedure PrintPermutations (TheString: StringTYPE; Current, Length:  integer);
    {The recursive procedure.}
    var i: integer;
        Ch: char;
    begin
        if Current < Length then begin
            for i := Current to Length do begin
                Ch := TheString[Current];    {Swap the current component.}
                TheString[Current] := TheString[i];
                TheString[i] := Ch;
                PrintPermutations (TheString, Current + 1, Length)
            end   {for}
        end   {if}
        else begin      {Only print the interesting part.}
            for i := 1 to Length do write (TheString[i]);
            writeln
        end   {else}
    end;  {PrintPermutations}
begin
    write ('Give me a short string to permute:    ');
    Length := 0;
    while not eoln and (Length < MAX) do begin
        Length := Length + 1;
        read (TheString [Length])
    end;
    readln;   {Dump any remaining characters.}
    PrintPermutations (TheString, 1, Length)
end. {Permute}
```

Maze Searching and Backtracking

Searching through a maze is an ideal problem for recursive solution. I'll state the problem like this:

> Imagine that you are trapped in the center of a maze. Find all paths to the outside world.

Let's assume that the maze is given to us as a pattern of characters that mark walls, and blanks that mark potential paths to the exit. We'll always start in position 6,6. For example, this is a 12-by-12 maze, with our starting position (at 6,6) marked with an **s**:

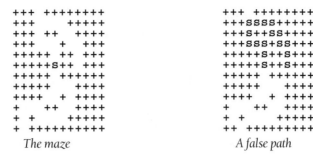

```
+++ ++++++++          +++ ++++++++
+++     +++++         +++SSSS+++++
+++ ++  ++++          +++S++SS++++
+++   +   +++         +++SSS+SS+++
+++++ ++ +++          +++++S++S+++
+++++S++ +++          +++++S++S+++
+++++ ++++++          +++++ ++++++
+++++    ++++         +++++    ++++
++++  +  ++++         ++++  +  ++++
+     ++ ++++         +     ++ ++++
+ +      +++++        + +      +++++
+ ++++++++++          ++ ++++++++++
```

The maze   *A false path*

First, let's agree on how we'll store the maze. An easy approach is to hold it in a two-dimensional array of char that goes from 1 to MAXCOL horizontally and from 1 to MAXROW vertically. When we initially read in our data, we'll put

data type definition a + in each wall location, and leave potential paths blank. As we search the maze, we'll mark each step with an **s**. We'll know that we're at an exit if we find ourselves on row 1 or MAXROW, or at column 1 or MAXCOL. The Pascal type definition is:

> **type** ArrayTYPE = **array** [1..MAXROW, 1..MAXCOL] **of** char;
> **var** Maze: ArrayTYPE;

Now, how does one get out of a maze? Well, if you're Theseus, you trail a string behind you on the way in, then trace it back out again. Even if you don't have any string, a simple rule—stick to one wall, and always turn right—will eventually get you out of the maze.

Working with a computer, though, imposes certain limitations. Perhaps there's no Minotaur chasing us, but there's no string, either. Moreover, the path may be too narrow for a 'stick to a wall' rule. We may not be able to turn right, and if we reach a dead end, we'll have to back out (as shown in the right-hand illustration, above). We're more in the position of the monster than the hero!

Fortunately, the phrase 'back out' gives us a hint. Recall that one effect of recursive procedure calls is to create a stack of partially executed subprograms.

using the recursive stack Each one can have variables and pending statements associated with it. If each step down a path involves a recursive procedure call—building the stack—we can also imagine that exiting the sequence of procedure calls will back us out along our original path.

How can we state a maze searching method recursively? Let's try some inductive thinking as a warmup exercise. Suppose that we're one step away from an exit. Can we get to the door? Sure—just take one step. It may take several tries (once in each direction) but we'll certainly find the way out.

Suppose that we're two steps away. Can we get to the spot that's only one step away? Yes. If we take one step in any direction, we have a one in four chance of landing in the one-step-away spot. Obviously, we can cover all the bases by stepping left, up, right, and down in turn.

using induction Now comes the clever step—our inductive leap. What if we're N steps away? Can we get to be one step away? Of course. No matter what N starts at, we can always get to N − 1. Since N keeps going down, it will eventually reach 2, and we'll be home free. No matter how many steps away we are, we can always get to a position we're sure we know how to solve.

Being clever was easy compared to stating the algorithm recursively:

first refinement

To search a maze (from the current spot) . . .
mark the current spot as part of the way out;
if *we're at the exit*
  then *print the maze*
  else *search a maze (from a new starting position)*

I've added a new step to the mental warmup we worked on. Each time we call the *search a maze* procedure we mark our present position. The maze itself is passed as a value parameter to each call of the procedure. Note that the path of positions we've marked grows one step longer on each call. You can think of it as a snapshot of our current state—where we are, and how we got there.

The key to the algorithm is finding the new starting position. If we can—if there's no wall there—we'll *search a maze* starting one step to the left. Then, if we can, we'll *search a maze* starting one step up. Then we'll search to the right, and finally down, each time making sure that we're not running into a wall. The shaded section below corresponds to the **else** part shaded above:

second refinement

To search a maze (from the current spot) . . .
mark the current spot as part of the way out;
if *we're at the exit*
  then *print the maze*
  else **if** *we can, search a maze (starting one step left);*
    if *we can, search a maze (starting one step up);*
    if *we can, search a maze (starting one step right);*
    if *we can, search a maze (starting one step down);*

Once more, the maze, with our current position marked on the pathway out, is passed as a value parameter to the *search a maze* procedure. In effect, we are always searching a maze that has already been partially searched. The computer maintains a stack of copies of the maze—one for each of the partially completed procedure calls. Each copy shows the path that led to that particular location. If we're at the exit, the current copy of the maze shows the way out.

If we don't get to an exit, nothing happens at all. Suppose we take a left turn into a dead end. Since we can't go left, forward, or right, that particular invocation of the procedure ends, and its copy of the maze (with an incorrect path out) is removed. The completed program is shown below.

maze searching program

```
program Threader (input, output);
    {Recursively finds and prints all exit paths from a maze.}
const MAXROW = 12;
    MAXCOL = 12;
    OPEN = ' ';
    THEWAYOUT = 's';
type ArrayTYPE = array [1..MAXROW, 1..MAXCOL] of char;
var Maze: ArrayTYPE;
```

```
procedure StoreTheMaze (var Maze: ArrayTYPE);
    {Reads in the maze.}
    var i,j: integer;
    begin
        for i := 1 to MAXROW do begin
            for j := 1 to MAXCOL do begin
                read ( Maze[i, j] )
            end;
            readln    {Get rid of the end-of-line.}
        end
    end; {StoreTheMaze}

procedure PrintTheMaze (Maze: ArrayTYPE);
    {Prints the maze contents, showing the exit path.}
    var i, j: integer;
    begin
        for i := 1 to MAXROW do begin
            for j := 1 to MAXCOL do begin
                write ( Maze[i, j] )
            end;
            writeln
        end;
        writeln   {Space between solutions.}
    end; {PrintTheMaze}

function AtAnExit (Row, Col: integer) : boolean;
    {Tells whether or not we are on the border of the maze.}
    begin
        AtAnExit := (Row = 1) or (Row = MAXROW)
            or (Col = 1) or (Col = MAXCOL)
    end; {AtAnExit}

procedure Explore (Maze: ArrayTYPE; Row, Col: integer);
    {Recursive procedure for searching the maze.}
    begin
        Maze [Row, Col] := THEWAYOUT;
        if AtAnExit (Row, Col)
            then PrintTheMaze (Maze)
            else begin   {inspect the possible pathways}
{up}        if Maze [Row – 1, Col] = OPEN then Explore (Maze, Row – 1, Col);
{right}     if Maze [Row, Col+1] = OPEN then Explore (Maze, Row, Col+1);
{down}      if Maze [Row+1, Col] = OPEN then Explore (Maze, Row+1, Col);
{left}      if Maze [Row, Col – 1] = OPEN then Explore (Maze, Row, Col – 1)
            end {else}
    end; {Explore}
begin
    writeln ('Reading the starting maze.');
    StoreTheMaze (Maze);
    writeln;
    writeln ('Solutions to the maze are:');
    Explore (Maze, 6, 6)   {Start searching from the center.}
end. {Threader}
```

                                    (output follows)

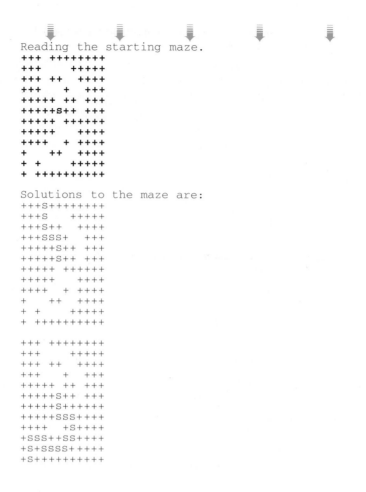

```
Reading the starting maze.
+++ ++++++++
+++     +++++
+++ ++  ++++
+++   +   +++
+++++ ++ +++
+++++S++ +++
+++++ ++++++
+++++    ++++
++++   +  ++++
+     ++  ++++
+ +      +++++
+ ++++++++++
```

```
Solutions to the maze are:
+++S++++++++
+++S     +++++
+++S++   ++++
+++SSS+   +++
+++++S++ +++
+++++S++ +++
+++++ ++++++
+++++    ++++
++++   +  ++++
+     ++  ++++
+ +      +++++
+ ++++++++++
```

```
+++ ++++++++
+++     +++++
+++ ++  ++++
+++   +   +++
+++++ ++ +++
+++++S++ +++
+++++S++++++
+++++SSS+++
++++   +S++++
+SSS++SS++++
+S+SSSS+++++
+S++++++++++
```

Modification Problems

1. It's not likely that you'll want to type in an entire maze each time you run Threader. Modify the program so that it reads its maze from an existing file.

2. How many dead ends does Threader encounter? Modify the program so that it prints dead-end paths, rather than successful ones.

3. Why search for a path to an exit? Why not reverse the problem: start at an exit, and search for a path to the center? Modify Threader to do it.

Recursive Sorting: Quicksort*

The sorting algorithms we saw in Chapter 10 were stated iteratively, which made them easy to understand. One of the best sorting algorithms is almost invariably given recursively. Called *Quicksort*, it was devised by C.A.R. Hoare, who also invented the **case** statement (a question that will probably never appear in *Trivial Pursuit*). At worst, Quicksort is also an O (n^2) algorithm, but in practice, its running time is usually proportional to n log_2 n. (If none of that

---

* This discussion is optional. It should follow the discussions of sorting and complexity in Chapter 10 if it's assigned.

made sense, go read about complexity in section 10-4.) Let's reinvent it, and see how and why it works.

The algorithms we've looked at so far have always concentrated on methodically working from one end of an array to the other. Let's try a different approach this time—*divide-and-conquer*. Suppose that we put all the 'big' values in one half of the array and all the 'small' values in the other half. Then, once we have the array neatly divided, we'll take each half and do the exact same thing. Eventually, we'll get down to subarrays of length one or two, and the array will be sorted.

divide-and-conquer

Sounds easy, doesn't it? Let's keep an eye on one of the stored values as we rearrange the array. Suppose that the very smallest value (let it be A) starts out at the far right end of the array—the place where the biggest value is supposed to be:

We'll take the small values and put them into the left-hand half of the array:

sorting by splitting

Were we to check the halves—and split *them* in two—we'd move the A again:

Eventually, the A will get to its proper position at the start of the array:

How long did it take the A to get to its final resting place? Each time we moved it halfway home. As a general rule about divide-and-conquer methods...

> In general, an algorithm that works by splitting the remainder in two will take about $log_2 n$ steps to complete.

Our rule is true because $log_2 n$ is the maximum number of times we can divide n by 2—$log_2 n$ of 4 is 2, $log_2 n$ of 8 is 3, $log_2 n$ of 32 is 5, etc.

Our algorithm requires that we repeatedly move the A into the proper half of the remainder of the array. If the original array is n components long, $log_2 n$ steps are required. Since the array has n components to begin with, we'll have to repeat our basic algorithm n times to sort the entire array. The running time of our algorithm, then, will be proportional to n times $log_2 n$, which is written as $O(n \, log_2 n)$.

complexity is discussed in detail in section 10-4

Now, our algorithm looks good on paper, but we've relied on magic too often to implement it as a program. How do we know what 'big' and 'small' values are? How do we know which half of the array to put any given value in? What do we do with the value that was already stored in the component we so cavalierly took over? This was the problem Hoare faced. Stop reading for a moment, and try to imagine how he solved it.

Hoare's solution was very clever. He began by picking a value at random from the array. This lucky value, he claimed, could be considered to be the dividing point between 'big' and 'small.' Then, he searched the left side of the array for a bigger or equal value and the right side of the array for a smaller value. These values, he said correctly, were in the wrong sides of the array, so he switched them. He started the searches from the ends, going toward the middle, so that eventually the two searches would meet.

One last insight remained. Where would the starting value be when the two searches finished? It would be in its final resting place in the sorted array. As a result, he could ignore this 'middle' value when he repeated the whole process on the left and right sides of the array.

Let's work on the array below. Our wild guess will be that a value taken from near the middle (N, here) divides the 'big' and 'small' values:

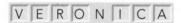

We exchange the first value greater than or equal to N (working from the left) with the first value less than N (working from the right):

Now we repeat the step. E can stay where it is, so we move on to R and swap it with C:

If we take a final step we'll be able to swap two more values:

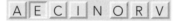

Our left and right searches meet at this point. Note that the N is in the correct position for the final sorted array. As it happens, the right-hand array is completely sorted as well. Were we to Quicksort it, we'd pick the R as the middle value, and realize that it was properly located right away. The left-hand array isn't sorted yet, but one more Quicksort pass will rearrange it correctly whether we choose E or I as the starting midpoint.

What are the differences between Hoare's Quicksort algorithm and the algorithm we started out with? Our original method relied on neatly dividing the array in half each time, so we know that it's an $n \log_2 n$ algorithm. We were able to do this because we assumed that we would magically know the median value stored in each array segment.

Since Hoare didn't rely on magic, Quicksort might pick a very non-median value to be the basis of the left/right separation of values. In fact, if we somehow pick the very worst value each time—the highest or lowest value in each segment—Quicksort turns out to be an n^2 Slowsort! Fortunately, this would require very bad luck indeed. On the average, we will pick a reasonably median number by chance (even though we were a little bit unlucky in our example, above). Since we'll be splitting the subarrays roughly in half each time, we can expect Quicksort to be an $n \log_2 n$ algorithm.

It's interesting to note that Hoare might have taken an entirely different tack. The Quicksort algorithm roughly organizes the array before splitting it in half. However, the opposite approach (splitting, then organizing) is also effective. Suppose that we divide the original array in half, then in half again, and so on, until we have an array of length two. This array can be sorted easily. Then, two ordered arrays of length two can be merged, then two arrays of length four, etc. This is the basis of the recursive algorithm called *merge sort*, which we won't get into.

merge sort

The final Quicksort algorithm can be described recursively like this:

> *to sort an array by Quicksort …*
> > *pick some starting component value from the array;*
> > *exchange equal or larger components (working from the left) with*
> > *equal or smaller components (working from the right);*
> > **if** *it's longer than one component,* *sort the left-hand array by Quicksort;*
> > **if** *it's longer than one component,* *sort the right-hand array by Quicksort;*

recursive refinement

Let's look at the shaded section more closely. I'll begin by picking some StarterValue as a starting component, then expand the pseudocode above to:

> **repeat**
> > *working from* Start *to* Finish, *try to find a component with*
> > > value >= *to* StarterValue;
> > *working from* Finish *to* Start, *try to find a component with*
> > > value <= *to* StarterValue;
> > *switch these two components;*
> > *move left one, and right one, so that we don't check*
> > > *the components we just exchanged*
> **until** *left and right pass;*

second refinement

After each sorting run, the component that holds StarterValue is in its final position—components to the left are smaller, while components to the right are larger.

Can you see why the algorithm is stated recursively? Our intention is to 'sort of sort' the array into two sections. Then, we'll sort of sort one of those sections, then one of the new subsections, etc. We can keep track of the Start and Finish that delimit each subsection by having them declared as value parameters associated with a particular instance of the recursive call.

How do we choose our starting value? As we've formulated the algorithm, we pick the value of the component in the middle of the array segment we're sorting, with:

> StarterValue := Data [((Start + Finish) **div** 2)] ;

What information does each call of the Quicksort procedure need? It must have the subscripts of the left and right ends of the array being sorted. The array itself is passed as a **var** parameter, which means that only a single copy of the array ever exists. The completed procedure is shown below:

quicksort procedure

```
procedure Quicksort (Start, Finish: integer;
                    var Data: TheArrayTYPE);
    {Recursively sort array Data, with bounds Start and Finish, using Quicksort}
    var StarterValue, Left, Right, Temp: integer;
    begin
        Left := Start;
        Right := Finish;
        StarterValue := Data [(Start+Finish) div 2];    {Pick a starter.}
        repeat
            while Data [ Left ] < StarterValue do begin
                Left := Left + 1
            end;
            {Postcondition: We've found a bigger value on the left.}
            while StarterValue < Data [ Right ] do begin
                Right := Right – 1
            end;
            {Postcondition: We've found a smaller value on the right.}
            if Left <= Right then begin    {If we haven't gone too far...}
                Temp := Data [ Left ];     {...switch them.}
                Data [ Left ] := Data [ Right ];
                Data [ Right ] := Temp;
                Left := Left + 1;          {Move the bounds.}
                Right := Right – 1
            end   {then}
        until Right <= Left;
        {Postcondition: The array is 'sort of sorted' about StarterValue.}
        if Start < Right then Quicksort (Start, Right, Data);
        if Left < Finish then Quicksort (Left, Finish, Data)
    end; {Quicksort}
```

The procedure's first call is:

Quicksort (1, ARRAYLIMIT, Data);

performance of algorithms

Earlier we mentioned that the worst-case performance of an algorithm was not the only measure of its suitability. Thinking only in terms of worst-case performance can be misleading, because a particular algorithm's worst case might be very unlikely to occur. A more Panglossian body of computer science research is devoted to calculating an algorithm's *expected* performance, or the behavior it is likely to exhibit most of the time.

When sorting algorithms are compared by expected performance, Quicksort dominates the field. Even though the algorithm's worst case makes it no better than the much-maligned bubble sort, it is the method of choice for most sorting jobs.

Modification Problems

1. Test the Quicksort procedure. What sort of test data are required for a thorough workout? Be sure to produce test data for both the best and worst starting cases.

Recursion and Pointers

16-3

IN MOST PEOPLE'S MINDS, RECURSION FOLLOWS a three-step progression. It starts as curiosity, moves on to convenience, and winds up as a necessity.

The final transition often takes place when recursion encounters the pointer. The reason is that pointers can be used to build recursively defined data structures. The best example of a recursively defined data structure is a *tree*. For example:

a general tree

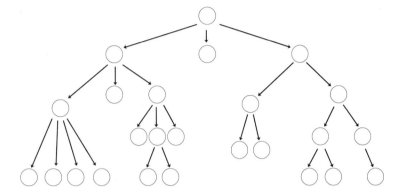

A recursive definition of a tree would describe it as a node that's linked to one or more trees, or to nothing. Like each twig in this real tree, every branch can lead to finer branches, but it never allows another path back to the root.

Now, the subtrees must be *distinct*; no two trees can share the same node. If you look carefully at the either of the pictures above, whole forests are visible. Any starting point leads to one or more subtrees.

tree terminology

> The *root* of a tree is its first (topmost) node. The nodes that each element points to are its *children*; it is the *parent*. Finally, a node that has no children is called a *leaf*.

binary trees

Limiting each node to a maximum of two children (i.e. to two potential subtrees) creates a *binary*, or two-part, tree. This is a structure we'll explore in detail. The basic node definition is:

```
type NodePOINT = ↑ NodeTYPE;
      NodeTYPE= record
                     Data: DataTYPE;
                     LeftPtr, RightPtr: NodePOINT
               end;
var CurrentPtr: NodePOINT;
```

> If you haven't read about pointers yet, go back one chapter! Arrows that appear in our code won't make any sense to you.

Recursive Tree Searching

Suppose that I start by describing the recursive steps of one tree-searching algorithm in English. Assume that CurrentPtr starts by addressing the root.

To Search a Tree . . .

recursive tree-searching
algorithm

1. If CurrentPtr ↑'s left child isn't **nil**, point CurrentPtr at the left child and search the tree.

2. If CurrentPtr ↑'s right child isn't **nil**, point CurrentPtr at the right child and search the tree.

3. Print the value stored in the current node.

In practice, each time we return to action 1 (the equivalent of making a recursive procedure call) the values associated with the current node will be saved, along with any pending actions.

> Using recursion allows backtracking without backward pointers.

I can rephrase the same algorithm in terms of its bound and plans:

recursive specification

> *Goal: Print every node's stored value.*
> *Stacking Plan: Visit the left subtree.*
> *Visit the right subtree.*
> *Bound: Reaching a leaf, or node that has no subtrees.*
> *Unstacking Plan: Print the current node's stored value.*

I've implemented the algorithm in the recursive procedure InspectTree, below. It assumes that char values are stored in the tree and that the tree isn't empty.

binary tree inspection
procedure

```
procedure InspectTree (CurrentPtr: NodePOINT);
    {Visits every node of a non-empty binary tree.}
    begin
        if CurrentPtr ↑.LeftPtr <> nil then begin
            InspectTree (CurrentPtr ↑.LeftPtr)
        end;
        if CurrentPtr ↑.RightPtr <> nil then begin
            InspectTree (CurrentPtr ↑.RightPtr)
        end;
        write (CurrentPtr ↑.Data)
    end;  {InspectTree}
```

The effect of InspectTree can be described as:

Go down the tree as far as possible, trying to go left, but going right if necessary. Print this node's value. Back up one node, then go down the tree again, following the same strategy—left if possible, right if necessary—until you come to a dead end or a node you've already visited. Inspect this node, then repeat the search process. When there are no more nodes to search—each child has been visited already—the root has been found, and the entire tree has been inspected.

If you have difficulty imagining the operation of a recursive procedure, stepping through an example on a small tree may help. Looking at the boundary cases of a large tree is also useful.

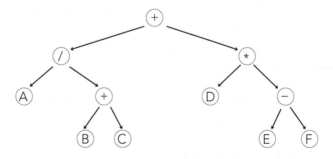

postorder (RPN) search

We can use InspectTree to search the binary tree above. Its nodes will be searched in the following order, called *postorder*. *Postfix* and *reverse Polish* (or *RPN*) are other names for this particular notation.

$$A \ B \ C \ + \ / \ D \ E \ F \ - \ * \ +$$

If you own a stack-type calculator you'll recognize this as an arithmetic expression, equivalent to A/(B+C)+D*(E−F). In postorder search, a node's subtrees are inspected before the node itself is. As a result, the root is seen last.

Self-Check Questions

Q. Suppose that I reorder the three statements of InspectTree like this:

{*First variation.*}
write (CurrentPtr↑.Data);
if CurrentPtr↑.LeftPtr <> **nil then** InspectTree (CurrentPtr↑.LeftPtr);
if CurrentPtr↑.RightPtr <> **nil then** InspectTree (CurrentPtr↑.RightPtr)

{*Second variation.*}
if CurrentPtr↑.LeftPtr <> **nil then** InspectTree (CurrentPtr↑.LeftPtr);
write (CurrentPtr↑.Data);
if CurrentPtr↑.RightPtr <> **nil then** InspectTree (CurrentPtr↑.RightPtr)

Are the variations legal? What do they do when applied to the example tree above?

A. Both variations work perfectly well. They change only the order values are printed in. The first yields a *preorder* search: first a node is inspected, and then its subtrees. Applying the preorder algorithm to the tree above will give us: + / A + B C * D − E F

The second modification produces an *inorder* search. The left subtree is searched, then the node, and finally the right subtree. The search path followed is: A / B + C + D * E − F

Programming Binary Trees

The applications of binary trees are unexpectedly diverse. Consider the tree below. Can you guess what it represents?

a mystery tree

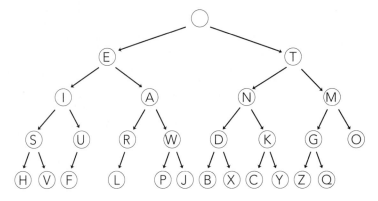

Perhaps the type definition of each node will help.

```
type NextNodePOINT = ↑ CodeNodeTYPE;
     CodeNodeTYPE = record
                        Letter: char;
                        Dot, Dash: NextNodePOINT
                    end;
var RootPtr: NextNodePOINT;
```

As you may guess, the tree represents Morse code. Procedure Decode, below, uses the code tree to translate a file of Morse into the letters it stands for. Its argument is RootPtr, which points to the root of the stored code-tree. Since we never backtrack (and don't need a stack) Decode wasn't written recursively. However, we do have to maintain a pointer to the root of the code tree, to start all over again for each new letter.

Morse code decoding procedure

```
procedure Decode (RootPtr: NextNodePOINT);
   {Decodes Morse code input. Each full letter must be followed by a blank.}
   var CurrentPtr: NextNodePOINT;
      InputCharacter: char;
   begin
      CurrentPtr := RootPtr;
      while not eof do begin
         read (InputCharacter);
         case InputCharacter of
         '.' : CurrentPtr := CurrentPtr ↑.Dot;
         '−' : CurrentPtr := CurrentPtr ↑.Dash;
         ' ' : begin
                  write (CurrentPtr ↑.Letter);
                  CurrentPtr := RootPtr
               end
         end {case}
      end; {while}
      writeln
   end;  {Decode}
```

```
.−− .− .−.   . −.−   −− −.−−   −... −−− −..−
.−− .. −   ..− .. −...−   −. −−− −−−.. . −.
.−.. .. −−−. ..−   −−− −−.   .−−− ..− −−. ...
```

PACK MY BOX WITH FIVE DOZEN LIQUOR JUGS

Morse can be stored in a binary tree because the dot/dash code is essentially a series of yes/no questions. Surprisingly, most data can be stored and retrieved using binary trees. Interactive computer guessing games are a good example. The computer plays by trying to guess something; say, the name of a singer the player is thinking of. Although singers may have many characteristics, considering only one at a time reduces the description to a string of binary (two-way) choices. For instance:

binary tree applications

```
Think of a singer.  Is the singer female?
yes
Is her hair blonde?
no
Is her hair brown?
yes
Is she Tiffany?
no                        etc.
```

The program relies on two kinds of stored data—characteristics and (ultimately) names. The most crucial set of facts—the relationship between characteristic and name—is contained in the binary tree that *holds* the information. The program begins at the tree's root and asks the question stored as a string in that node. Whether the left or right node is visited next depends on the answer: sometimes a further question is required (and the process starts again), and sometimes we reach a leaf or final node (and with it, a name).

Incidentally, such programs can learn as they play. For instance, the following interaction might take place if a leaf has supplied an incorrect guess. Internally, a new node is added to the stored data structure.

```
I guessed wrong.  What singer were you thinking of?
Ricky Lee Jones
Type in an additional question I should have asked.
Does she have any talent?
Is the correct answer yes or no?
yes                              etc.
```

Trees of Words

embedding information

A subtle aspect of understanding tree structures is recognizing the relation between the way data are stored and the way that they're retrieved again. This is especially true when a hand-drawn representation of a tree's stored data doesn't (at first glance) show its order or purpose. Consider this tree:

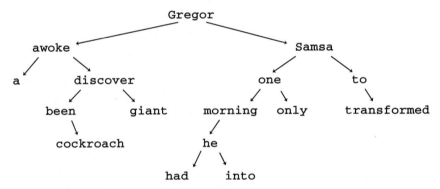

The tree stores the words of this sentence:

Gregor Samsa awoke one morning only to discover he had been transformed into a giant cockroach

in alphabetical order (disregarding capitalization). The first word, Gregor, goes to the root of the tree. The second word follows the first alphabetically, so it's stored in the right child. The third word precedes the first alphabetically, so it goes into the left-hand node. The fourth word, one, comes after the first, but before the second. It goes to the root's right child's left child. The final resting place of each word is determined by traveling down the tree, turning left or right, or making a new node as necessary.

As you may imagine, I can describe the ordering algorithm recursively.

To Build an Alphabetically Ordered Tree . . .

1. If the current node is nil, store the new word there and stop.

2. If the new word precedes the word in the current node, point to the left child and build an alphabetically ordered tree.

binary tree building

3. If the new word follows the word in the current node, point to the right child and build an alphabetically ordered tree.

4. If the new word is the same as the word in the current node, stop.

In procedure AddAWord, below, the final **else** (which represents step 4) isn't necessary and could be omitted. I've just included it to touch all the bases.

binary tree building procedure

```
type StringTYPE = packed array [1 .. 80] of char;
     WordPOINT = ↑WordStoreTYPE;
     WordStoreTYPE = record
                          Word: StringTYPE;
                          Before, After: WordPOINT
                     end;    {Other definitions and declarations.}
procedure AddAWord (var Current: WordPOINT; NewWord: StringTYPE);
     {Adds the string NewWord to an alphabetically ordered binary tree.}
     begin
         if Current=nil
            then begin
                new (Current);
                Current↑.Word := NewWord;
                Current↑.Before := nil;
                Current↑.After := nil
            end
            else if NewWord < Current↑.Word
                then AddAWord (Current↑.Before, NewWord)
                else if Current↑.Word < NewWord
                    then AddAWord (Current↑.After, NewWord)
                    else {The word is a duplicate—NewWord=Current↑.Word.}
     end;  {AddAWord}
```

AddAWord is probably the most complicated recursive procedure you will have to deal with. Note that AddAWord is an end recursion; the stack isn't used to store values or pending statements. It could easily be written iteratively.

It will come as a welcome surprise to find that a job that seems complicated, like printing the contents of a tree in alphabetical order, is really pretty easy. All it takes is an inorder traversal, which was one of the possible variations on procedure InspectTree, which we wrote a few pages back. The output of InOrder, below, assumes that CurrentWord currently addresses the root of the `Gregor Samsa awoke...` tree. (I put the output on two lines myself.)

binary tree inspection procedure

```
procedure InOrder (CurrentWord: WordPOINT);
     {Prints the nodes of a non-nil alphabetically ordered binary tree in order.}
     begin
         if CurrentWord↑.Before <> nil then begin
             InOrder (CurrentWord↑.Before)
         end;
         writeln (CurrentWord↑.Word);
         if CurrentWord↑.After <> nil then begin
             InOrder (CurrentWord↑.After)
         end
     end;  {InOrder}
```

```
a awoke been cockroach discover giant gregor had
he into morning one only samsa to transformed
```

Modification Problems ―――――――――――――――――――

1. Write a test harness for AddAWord. Use it to build a tree of words, and then modify procedure InOrder to print the tree's contents in reverse.

2. Modify AddAWord so that it counts appearances of words as well as organizing them.

Self-Check Questions ―――――――――――――――――――

Q. Will all structures produced by AddAWord look tree-like? Draw the trees that would be produced by these input sentences:

    a big cat did everything

    zesty young xylophones wed violins

A. A quick perusal reveals that the sample sentences are in alphabetical and reverse-alphabetical order. They produce *degenerate* trees—trees that can't be distinguished from ordinary lists.

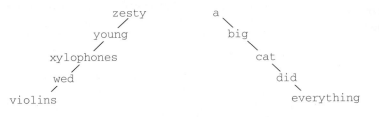

――――――――――
Remember . . .

❏   A recursive procedure or function calls itself. However, there must always be a check that can prevent the recursive call from occurring and allow the subprogram to end.

❏   Uncompleted recursive calls, and the variables that are associated with each call, are described as being *stacked*. A series of recursive calls that accidentally doesn't end eventually leads to stack overflow and a program crash.

❏   *End* or *tail* recursions don't use the stack to hold data, and they are often replaced by simpler iterative statements.

❏   Recursion is useful for *backtracking* algorithms because the stack can hold a snapshot of our data at each step of the search for a solution. If a trail fails to pan out, we can backtrack—end part of a sequence of recursive calls—until we reach the step that went astray.

❏   A *binary tree* is a linked structure that obeys two key restrictions. First, each node points to zero, one, or two additional nodes. Second, all of the nodes in any subtree are totally isolated from the rest of the tree; two trees can have a common root, but they can't share any nodes.

❏   Recursion is useful for tree-searching algorithms because it allows backtracking without backward pointers. The most common binary tree searches are *preorder*, *inorder*, and *postorder*. They differ in the order in which specific nodes are inspected.

The Big Ideas of Chapter 16 are:

1. *Many, many recursive subprograms follow a small handful of stereotypical models.* The best way to learn recursive programming is to focus on the similarity between problems, and to learn to state problems in a way that makes their similarities apparent.

2. *Recursion isn't necessary, but it's useful.* Recursive programs are a good example of trading design time for programming time, since we can take advantage of the computer's stack to support more sophisticated algorithms and implementations. Unfortunately, since we can't employ the primitives we're used to—there aren't any 'push' or 'pop' operators for the recursive stack—programs may be harder to design *at first*. In the long run, though, recursion will become one more tool in your bag of programming tricks.

16-1   Pick your favorite arithmetic operation (addition, say), then ask the basic recursive function question: *Use recursion to implement this operation.*

16-2   An indirect approach to testing students' understanding of recursion is to ask how deep the recursive stack will become for a particular call. For instance, calling our recursive function Sum(5) led to a stack that was four calls deep. Take three examples from the text, and ask *How deep will the stack of recursive calls be?* for each.

16-3   What is the last call in a series of recursive calls called? What kind of recursion doesn't use the stack? Make up three *What is . . .* questions.

16-4   Pick three recursive procedures or functions, then ask *Write these without using recursion.*

16-5   We've seen that if we supply the recursive definition of a procedure or function, then writing the subprogram is pretty easy. It's also not too hard to start with a recursive calculation, then rephrase it as a recursive definition. However, what is pleasantly difficult is to write a definition or subprogram that has a misstated bound condition (an off-by-one error works nicely), then ask *Where's the bug?* Try three.

16-6   Consider program Threader. If you look at its recursive procedure Explore, you'll see that four one-word comments (*up, right,* and so on) are invaluable for helping visualize what the program does. You can make up a rather interesting variation on *What's the output?* in three steps:

a)   get rid of the comments,

b)   rearrange the **if** statements,

c)   ask *Which of these solutions was printed first?*

Try it. Can you pry a similar question out of program Hanoi?

16-7   What's a convenient way to see if somebody understands the basic definition of a binary tree? By drawing three trees, then asking *Which of these is a binary tree?*

16-8   Crash alert—how many recursive calls can you make before you run into trouble? Does the size of the recursive procedure have any effect on the maximum number of calls? What about the size or number of its parameters or local variables?

16-9   Write a recursive procedure that, for no immediately obvious reason, reads a sequence of positive numbers, sums them in reverse, and returns the sum.

16-10   Write a recursive definition of integer division.

16-11   Write a procedure that uses recursion to print the contents of a linked list in reverse.

16-12 Write a recursive procedure that reverses the contents of a linked list without modifying any of its pointers.

Recursion that involves loop equivalents.

Programming
Problems

16-13 The basic stacking problems discussed in the text involved reading, and holding, a sequence of input characters. However, it's just as easy to recursively build a stack that holds the digits of a number. Write recursive procedures that:

a)   count the number of digits in an integer;

b)   print an integer with no leading blank spaces;

c)   print an integer with commas in appropriate places.

Hint: remember that (n **mod** 10) yields the rightmost digit of n, and (n **div** 10) effectively 'strips' the digit off.

16-14 The standard example of a recursive function (always, by law, accompanied by a note attesting to its impracticality), is the computation of factorials:

> *If n equals 0, then n! equals 1*

> *If n exceeds 0, then n! equals n×(n−1)!*

Implement a recursive Factorial function. Can you think of a way to prevent integer overflow, or at least to spot it in advance?

16-15 The second standard example of recursion is Euclid's algorithm for computing two numbers' greatest common divisor, discussed in section 6-3. The recursive statement of his algorithm is:

> *if q equals 0 then GCD(p, q) equals p*

> *if q≠0 then GCD(p, q) equals GCD(q, p **mod** q)*

Write a recursive version of Euclid's algorithm.

16-16 The third classic recursive function is *Ackermann's function*. It takes two integer arguments *m* and *n*. For initial *m* and *n* greater than zero, its definition is:

> if *m* = 0 then *Ackermann(m,n)* equals *n*+1

> if *n* = 0 then *Ackermann(m,n)* equals *Ackermann(m−1, 1)*

> if neither *n* nor *m* = 0 then *Ackermann(m,n)* is *Ackermann(m−1, Ackermann(m, n−1))*

Ackermann's function grows with amazing speed and takes an astonishing number of calls (*Ackermann(3,4)* requires over 10,000 calls to be evaluated!). Implement it, and find the largest *m* and *n* values you can reasonably use as arguments.

16-17 Two ordered lists of numbers are to be merged. Unfortunately, one list is sorted from least to greatest, while the other is supplied from greatest to least. Write a program that uses recursion to merge the lists:

a)   from the smallest value to the largest;

b)   from the largest value to the smallest.

16-18 When the order in which expressions are evaluated is controlled by parentheses, recursion lets subexpressions be stacked until they are required. For example, the expression below must be evaluated 'in parts' if it is to be evaluated correctly:

> (2 * ((3 * 4) + (6 − 5)))
> (2 * (12 + 1))
> (2 * 13)
> 26

An implicit requirement of a recursive program for evaluating such expressions is that *mutual recursion* be employed. A single procedure cannot handle the simultaneous tasks of matching parentheses and evaluating subexpressions. Instead, two procedures are required. One procedure does the work of skipping parentheses, reading operations, and performing calculations, while the second either reads a value *or* calls the first procedure again (if the upcoming character is another opening parenthesis instead of a value).

In words, I can describe the two procedures like this:

> *to evaluate an expression*
>> *skip a parenthesis;*
>> *read a value;*
>> *read the operator;*
>> *read a value;*
>> *skip a parenthesis;*
>> *perform the operation;*
>
> *to read a value*
>> **if** *the next character is an opening parenthesis*
>>> **then** *evaluate an expression*
>>> **else** *get the value*

Write a program that evaluates expressions in the form given above. Assume that all input is correct, contains no spaces, and is fully parenthesized.

Recursion that requires array types.

16-19 Write a function that recursively finds the product of the contents of a one-dimensional array of LIMIT components. The code itself is very easy the hard part is thinking up a recursive statement of the problem. Hint: the product equals the current component's value times the solution for the rest of the array.

16-20 Suppose you choose an arbitrary point on a two-dimensional grid. How many different paths lead to this point from the lower-left corner of the grid? Write a recursive program that finds out. Restrict travel to steps toward the upper or right-hand side of the grid. Hint: treat this as a maze-searching problem.

16-21 *Flood filling* is a technique used by graphics programmers to color an arbitrary shape—i.e. fill it with lit pixels. Suppose that we can rely on a function Inside(x,y) that lets us know if we are within the area we want to fill. The flood-filling algorithm is:

> *to flood fill an area*
> **if** Inside(x, y) **then**
>> *light the current pixel;*
>> *flood fill x, y+1;*
>> *flood fill x, y−1;*
>> *flood fill x+1, y;*
>> *flood fill x−1, y;*

The initial x, y point is chosen at random.

Define a two-dimensional array of on/off pixels, and an Inside function that determines if any particular pixel is inside a simple shape (a circle or rectangle) 'drawn' on the array. Then, write a recursive flood-fill procedure to turn all enclosed elements on.

16-22 A messy programmer eating a pizza pie at her terminal manages to splatter various ingredients over a two-dimensional array. Each spot covers one or more contiguous array elements. As penance, she resolves to write a program that can count the number of splotches she has created.

Help her out by writing a recursive spot-counting program. Assume that your program's input will be a two-dimensional array of integer, with spots marked by 1's, and empty areas filled by 0's. Hint: travel through the array with ordinary loops, but whenever you encounter a spot—an area of 1's—use a recursive procedure to search (and renumber) it.

Recursion that uses pointer types.

16-23 A *leaf* of a binary tree is a node that has no children. Are the leaves of a binary tree listed in the same relative order by preorder, postorder, and inorder searches? Write a program that searches a tree using each of the search paths, saves the 'output' of each search in a linked list, then compares the order of leaves in each list. (Hint: start by creating an ordered list of leaves only.)

16-24 The *internal path length* of a tree is defined to be the sum of the number of paths to each and every node. By definition, counting starts just above the root. The distance to the root is 1, the distance to each of the root's children is 2, each child's children have path lengths of 3, and so on.

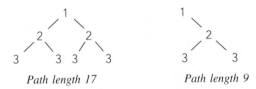

Path length 17   Path length 9

Write a subprogram that is passed a pointer to the root of a tree, and returns its internal path length.

16-25 Many chemical substances have more than one molecular form, although each form shares the same atomic formula. These *isomers* can have surprisingly different physical properties, due to geometrical rearrangement of chemical bonds. A simple example of this is found in *optical* isomerism. Two substances that have the same formula and internal bonds, but are mirror images of each other, are optical isomers. They are identical except in the manner they reflect polarized light.

As a problem simpler than writing an isomer-analysis problem, write a procedure that creates a mirror image of a binary tree. In the mirror image, left subtrees will become right subtrees, and so on. How difficult is it to show that two trees are identical except for being reflections?

Below, for your entertainment, is the output of the Xmaze demo program as run on a Sun workstation. The entrance is on the left, the exit is on the right. The program generates a random maze, then solves it recursively. The gray pathways are false tries; the black line solves the maze. Now, I can figure out how to solve the maze. But can somebody please tell me how it's generated in the first place?

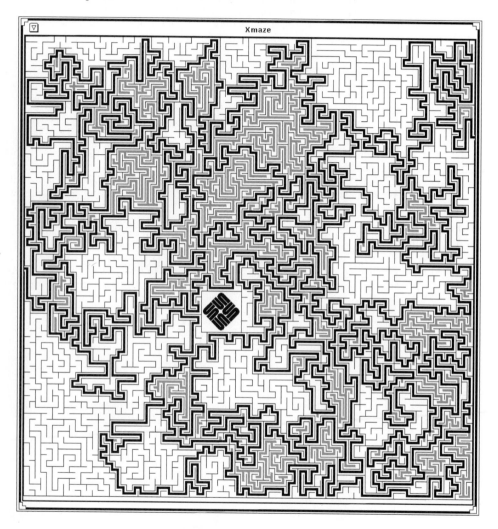

Programs with many goto*s are so tangled and difficult to trace through that they're often called* spaghetti *programs.* Above, *Jackson Pollack's Mother.* (p. A3)

A Few Details

The **goto** *Statement*
Shorthand Declarations of Anonymous Types
Records with Variants ✦ *Dynamically Allocating Variants*
pack *and* unpack
Procedures and Functions as Parameters ✦ page

IN THE INTEREST OF MAKING THE REST of the book flow a bit more smoothly, I've left out a few details. This appendix briefly explains the areas that were overlooked.

1. The **goto** statement.

2. A shorthand for type definitions and variable declarations.

3. The definition of record variants.

4. The standard procedures pack and unpack.

5. Procedures and functions as parameters.

6. Dynamic allocation of record variants.

7. The standard procedure page.

The goto Statement

All the programs we wrote moved from statement to statement in direct order, except where a procedure or function call caused a temporary detour. However, we can *label* any statement with a number and explicitly direct the program to *go to* that point. This is arranged by defining *labels* and using the **goto** statement.

There are three steps to take in using a **goto**. First, the labels used to mark statements must be defined.

labels

> A *label* is a number of one to four digits. The reserved word **label** marks the label definition part. It immediately follows the program (or subprogram) heading.

label declaration part

label ──────→ 1 to 4 digits ──────→ ;

There are ten thousand possible labels—0 through 9999. This segment designates 1, 2, and 3 as labels.

{*Program or subprogram heading.*}
label 1, 2, 3;   {*The label definition part.*}
{*Constant definition part.*}   *etc.*

The second step is to use the label by putting it, and a colon, in front of a statement.

{*How to label a statement.*}
1: writeln ('Abnormal program termination. ');

The label is ignored except as an identifying mark. Unless it is skipped over, every labeled statement is executed in the normal course of events. It need not be specifically gone to.

Finally, the **goto** statement tells the computer that program execution should continue from a particular labeled statement. For example:

{*Making a jump.*}
if DataIsBad **then goto** 1;

A **goto** can direct program control either forward or backward. Any actions between the **goto** and the labeled statement are skipped.

There are a few restrictions on where a **goto** can go to. Basically, a **goto** cannot access a relatively internal block or statement. We can't jump from the main program to a procedure, although the reverse is allowed. Likewise, we can't jump into the middle of a structured statement (although we can jump out of one or change our position within one).

In a sense, the **goto** is a historical anachronism in high-level programming languages. When the first languages were created, their designers (being hopelessly logical) saw that nearly everything a programmer wanted to do could be handled with just two control statements—**if . . . then** and **goto**. For example:

why have the goto?

{*A bad example of how to sum numbers.*}
Count := 1;
Sum := 0;
1: Sum := Sum + Count;
Count := Count + 1;
if Count <= 100 **then goto** 1;
write ('The sum of the numbers 1 through 100 is ');
writeln (Sum : 1);

We've come to know and love the shaded sequence by its semantic equivalent—the **repeat** statement.

However, Pascal has a much more sophisticated system of controlling program flow—its subprograms and control statements. In fact, we can claim quite correctly that Pascal lets the programmer do just about everything she wants *without* using **goto**s and that minimizing **goto**s is a virtue. For one thing, most control statement names (like subprogram identifiers) help document what's going on. Statement labels, in contrast, are nondocumenting, or even 'anti'-documenting. As arbitrary numbers, labels aren't the least mnemonic. Their appearance gives no hint of their effect.

structured programming

A more serious problem of using the **goto** is the way it can distort the patterns of a program. In recent years a lot of emphasis has been placed on *structured programming*. Procedures and functions give a program structure by breaking its action into cleanly defined parts, while Pascal's structured statements help clearly delineate cause and effect. I haven't made a big deal about structured programming because we haven't really had nonstructured tools—like the **goto**—to work with.

spaghetti programs

> Programs with many **goto**s are so tangled and difficult to trace through that they're often called *spaghetti* programs.

If the **goto** is so bad, why was it included in Pascal? Partly for sentimental reasons. Languages like FORTRAN depend heavily on the **goto**. People who learned to program in such languages find that **goto**s make it easier for them to work.

There are also extraordinary circumstances in which using **goto**s may be permissible. Most common is the 'I want to get out of here in a hurry' case. Suppose, for example, that program input is coming from punched cards or tape, and an input checking procedure spots incorrect data. Since we know that there's no point in continuing to process input, we can issue an error message and go to the very end of the program (because it's o.k. to label an empty statement just before the **end**).

```
    . . .        {Assume we're in an input-checking procedure.}
    if DatalsBad then begin
        writeln ('Abnormal program termination - - bad data.');
        goto 1        {Quit program.}
    end;
    . . .        {Rest of the program.}
  1: end.  {Main program.}
```

The **goto** is also properly used for beating a hasty retreat from a function whose arguments are determined to be inappropriate. In these cases the desirability of graceful degradation may outweigh the stigma attached to using **goto**s.

Self-Check Questions

Q. What will the output of this program segment be? Assume all labels are validly defined.

```
goto 2;
    ·.      {Other statements.}
1: writeln ('You have been eaten by a troll.  Game over.');
2: writeln ('You have turned into a vat of glue.  Game over.');
3: writeln ('A hobgoblin has munched you.  Game over.');
4: writeln ('Bats flew away with you.  Game over.')
end.   {Main program.}
```

A. As I mentioned earlier, the label is disregarded except as an identifying mark. Each statement from label 2 on is executed.

```
You have turned into a vat of glue.  Game over.
A hobgoblin has munched you.  Game over.
Bats flew away with you.  Game over.
```

Shorthand Declarations of Anonymous Types

As I've pointed out a few times, high-level languages are designed mainly for the benefit of people who use them in programming, rather than for the computers such programs ultimately direct. Thus, Wirth named Pascal's control statements **repeat**, **while**, **if**, etc., even though **a**, **b**, **c**, and so on are equally convenient from a computer's viewpoint. Although the semantics—the effect—of both meaningful and meaningless reserved words might be the same, their syntax—the actual words and the way they're used—are intended to inhibit errors and help programmers.

> human engineering

> Designing a system for the ease and convenience of the people who use it is called *human engineering*. A human-engineered product is created with sympathy for its users, and with an understanding of their problems and of errors they might make.

A subtle aspect of the human engineering of programming languages is the recognition that people are often in a hurry when they write programs. This is reflected in Pascal by an easing of certain syntax rules or, more accurately, by allowing a simpler alternative syntax in some situations.

> When a structured type is defined, the definition can include descriptions of subtypes.

In the past, we've built up complicated structures by using type identifiers that were already defined. To define an array of records, we'd first define the record type, then use its identifier in defining the array type. However, this step can be skipped. For example:

> a two-in-one definition

```
type BoardTYPE = array [ 1 .. 10 ] of record
                                Taken: boolean;
                                Marker: char
                        end;   {of the record}
```

This shorthand is appropriate in a program that doesn't include any variables (or parameters) of the record type I defined on the fly. The same principle extends to variable declarations.

anonymous types

> When a variable is declared, its type must be given. However, it can be given an *anonymous* type that is described on the spot. The type isn't named and thus doesn't have to be defined in advance.

We might even legally make the following variable declaration:

a shorthand declaration

```
var BoardTYPE = array [ 1 .. 10 ] of record
                              Taken: boolean;
                              Marker: char
                      end;   {of the record}
```

Board is now an array-type variable, just as though the array and record types used in its declaration had been defined separately. We can make normal assignments to it:

```
Board [3].Taken := TRUE;
Board [3].Marker := 'A';
```

Enumerated ordinal types can also be described rather than defined:

```
var Hue, Color:  (red, blue, green);
```

Hue and Color are variables of a type with no name.

Why didn't I mention these shortcuts earlier? Some of my reasons have to do with programming and teaching style. First of all, the syntax of individually defined types is easier to debug. Second, individually defined data types are easier to alter (and more likely to be improved) than monolithic definitions. Third, individually defined types are usually better documented than single large types.

why do things the long way?

There are also semantic reasons for doing things the long way. Recall that a variable parameter and its argument must be of identical types, as must the variables on both sides of many assignment statements (such as an assignment between two record or array-type variables). However . . .

restrictions on parameters

> Two variables (or a parameter and its argument) have an identical type only if they're defined with the exact same type identifier. They must have named types and can't have anonymous types.

This means that a type identifier—not a shorthand description of the type—must be used in many variable declarations and in *all* declarations of variable parameters. Other situations require that two variables be *type compatible*.

> Two variables (or a parameter and its argument) are type compatible if they both represent ranges of the same underlying type.

Again, this leads to a frequent requirement that a type be defined, rather than described. In the example below, Red, Blue, and Green are being locally redefined. The attempted assignment between noncompatible variables in this program segment is illegal:

```
program Trial (input, output);
var Color: (Red, Blue, Green);
procedure Show;
    var Hue: (Red, Blue, Green);
    begin
        Hue := Color;          {This assignment is a type clash.}
          ·.   etc.
```

Both variable declarations are fine, but the variable types are mismatched.

In summary, the shorthand form of type definition and variable declaration should be confined to small programs or procedures in which the issue of type will not arise. If a program is going to become large or use procedures, the types of its variables should be defined. This makes data structures easier to alter and debug and allows variables to be passed as parameters and used in assignments.

Records with Variants

Each of the records I've defined so far has had a fixed contingent of fields. However, Wirth enhanced Pascal records by allowing the definition of *record variants*. When we use record variants, the effective number and type of fields in a single record may change during the course of a program. This means that two variables can be of the same record type, yet have different numbers or types of fields.

I'll discuss record variants briefly. First I'll consider a record that has *only* a variant part, then I'll define a record with a fixed part *and* a variant part. Finally, I'll establish the syntax of record variants.

Let's begin with a data structuring problem that illustrates the need for record variants in the first place. Suppose that we're recording measurements that describe several four-sided figures. Each shape is defined by a different group of dimensions.

Shape	Required Dimensions
Square	*Side*
Rectangle	*Length, Width*
Rhomboid	*Side, AcuteAngle*
Trapezoid	*Top, Bottom, Height*
Parallelogram	*Top, Side, ObtuseAngle*

why do we need variants?

Now, we could easily define five different records—one for each shape. Or it might be more convenient to define a single record with enough fields to record the dimensions of *any* of the shapes. However, both solutions have shortcomings. The first makes it difficult to define general-purpose subprograms, because each record type requires its own procedures and functions.

shortcomings of records

The second solution is grossly inefficient, and a program that stored hundreds or thousands of such records might run into trouble.

Record variants come to the rescue. If you examine the list of shapes, it's easy to imagine a WhatShape field that could tell us which fields are actually required in the rest of the record and which are superfluous.

the tag field

> The idea that the value of one field could or should determine the rest of the structure is the basis of record variants. One field is designated to be a *tag* or marker field—a field whose value tags or marks the proper group of *variant* fields.

Dimensions is redefined below as a record with variants. WhatShape is the tag field, and the record contains five groups of variant fields.

a record with variants

```
type Shape = (Square, Rectangle, Rhomboid, Trapezoid, Parallelogram
      Dimensions = record
                        case WhatShape: Shape of        {The tag field}
                           Square: (Side1: real);
                           Rectangle: (Length, Width: real);
                           Rhomboid: (Side2: real; AcuteAngle: 0 .. 360);
                           Trapezoid: (Top1, Bottom, Height: real);
                           Parallelogram: (Top2, Side3: real; ObtuseAngle: 0 .. 360)
                     end;  {Dimensions}
var FourSidedObject: Dimensions;
```

> Each variant's fields must be unique. No field identifier can appear in more than one group. The tag field, in contrast, is shared by all of the variant groups.

Until the tag field has a value, the remainder of the record variant's structure is undefined. At this point, we can make an assignment only to the tag field, WhatShape.

> FourSidedObject.WhatShape := Rectangle;

activating variants

Once WhatShape has been given a value, the fields associated with that value (given in parentheses in the Dimension definition above) are created. The assignment above activates a certain group of fields—in this case, Length and Width. As long as the value of WhatShape is Rectangle, these are the only fields that FourSidedObject will contain. We can make the assignments:

> FourSidedObject.Length := 4.3;
> FourSidedObject.Width := 7.5;

but an attempted assignment to a field in one of the other variant groups (say, Top1 or ObtuseAngle) is an error.

What if the value of the tag field changes? If we now say that:

> FourSidedObject.WhatShape := Parallelogram;

we find ourselves able to access three new, but as yet undefined, fields—Top2, Side3, and ObtuseAngle. The former variant fields Length and Width simply don't exist any more; they've been deactivated and replaced. Thus, record variants act as an antibugging device by restricting the assignments that can be made to a record variable.

advantages of variants

A single record variant definition (like Dimensions) has other advantages over the five separate definitions we might have made. Suppose that we want to write a function that computes and represents the area of variable Four-SidedObject. In function Area, below, a single variable of type Dimensions is passed as a parameter, then dissected within the routine. If we were using five different records, we'd have to write five different subprograms. But since Dimensions is defined as a record variant, just one declaration suffices.

using the active variant

```
function Area (Object: Dimensions): real;
    {Computes an area that depends on an active variant.}
    begin
        with Object do
            case WhatShape of
                Square: Area := sqr (Side1);
                Rectangle: Area := Length * Width;
                Rhomboid: Area := sqr (Side2) * sin (AcuteAngle);
                Trapezoid: Area := (Top1 + Bottom) / 2 * Height;
                Parallelogram: Area := Top2 * Side3 * sin (ObtuseAngle)
            end {case}
    end; {Area}
```

Notice how the **case** statement in Area parallels the construction of the variant part of Dimensions. Using a tag field as the **case** expression is quite common and is why record variants are similar to **case** statements.

The variant parts of the Dimensions record were disjoint, which means that they shared only the tag field. However, Pascal lets us define records that share fields, and have variants as well.

fixed and variant parts

> A record definition may include a *fixed part* and a *variant part*. The fixed part *always* comes before the variant part, and only one variant part is allowed (although variants may be nested).

Below, the Year, Fee, and ExpirationDate fields form Registration's fixed part, and are shared (along with the tag field VehicleType) by every variant.

```
type Model = (Motorcycle, Car, Truck;
     Registration = record
                    Year: 1915 .. 1999;
                    Fee: real;
                    ExpirationDate: 1993 .. 1999;
                    case VehicleType: model of
                        Motorcycle: (EngineSize: 50 .. 1200);
                        Car: (Cylinders: 2 .. 8; SmogRequired: boolean);
                        Truck: (Axles: 2 .. 10; Weight, Tare: integer)
                    end; {Registration}
```

The current value of the tag field VehicleType determines which group of variant fields will be accessible. Other applications that require records with both fixed and variant fields include employment records, library records, medical records, and the like—any time some storage is specialized, and some is general.

The syntax of a record with a variant part is, without doubt, the toughest in Pascal. By using the reserved word **case** in a misplaced moment of economy, Wirth managed to confuse nearly everybody. The reason is that the **case** of a record variant is only superficially similar to the **case** of a **case** statement. A record type's syntax chart is:

record type

$$\textit{type identifier} \longrightarrow \textbf{=} \enspace \textbf{record} \longrightarrow \textit{field list} \longrightarrow \textbf{end}$$

The syntax of a field list is much harder to follow. If you read it carefully, you'll see that the field list is partially defined in terms of itself. Note that if a tag field selector value (or values) doesn't have any variant fields associated with it, an empty field list must be provided; *no* field names are put between the parentheses.

field list

Dynamically Allocating Variants

When a record with variant fields is dynamically allocated, enough space is set aside to store the largest of its variant groups. When each variant group requires about the same amount of storage, this method of storage allocation poses no disadvantages. However, programmers sometimes find themselves in the predicament of dynamically allocating many records of one type, but requiring only the smallest variant group of each. Fortunately, Pascal provides a mechanism for limiting the size of each location.

new can take additional arguments

> The dynamic allocation procedure new may be given additional arguments, corresponding to relatively nested tag field values. The location that is allocated has enough space to store the record's fixed fields, as well as those of the variant part specified by the stated tag field(s). It is, however, totally undefined.

Suppose that we have this type definition:

```
type LibraryItem = (Book, Magazine, Record);
     Card = ↑CardCatalog;
     CardCatalog = record
                      Available: boolean;
                      Name: packed array [1 .. 50] of char;
                      case Item: LibraryItem of
                         Book: (ISBNNumber: array [1 .. 10] of char);
                         Magazine: (Volume, Issue: integer);
                         LP: (DiscNumber: integer; ReRelease: boolean)
                   end;
     var CurrentCard: Card;
```

The statement:

```
new (CurrentCard);
```

allocates a complete record large enough to hold the fixed fields, plus any of the variant fields. If we know that we're going to store a magazine, however, the statement:

specifying the tag field

```
new (CurrentCard, Magazine);
```

allocates a record whose fields are Available, Name, Item, Volume, and Issue. Don't forget, though, that Item is still undefined.

> The deallocation procedure dispose must be given additional arguments (representing tag field values) when a record allocated in the manner described above is disposed of.

Disposing of the record we allocated earlier requires this call:

```
dispose (CurrentCard, Magazine);
```

pack and unpack

In Chapter 9, I mentioned the reserved word **packed** in connection with the definition of string types. However, the notion of packing a data structure to minimize the amount of storage it requires within the computer can be applied to any of Pascal's structured types (but usually just to arrays and records).

Although declaring a data structure to be packed saves space in the computer's memory, it generally slows down program execution. This is because the computer has to go through special manipulations to access the component values of packed data. In other words, the computer goes through the time-consuming process of unpacking the stored structure each time one of its fields or elements is altered or inspected.

Now, in the programs we've dealt with in this text, the trade-off between program execution speed and data storage space is not a big concern. However, efficiency is something that has to be considered when very large programs are created. Fortunately, Pascal includes some standard procedures that let the programmer take advantage of the space saving aspect of packing the largest common data structure—the array—without sacrificing execution time.

> The standard procedure unpack assigns the contents of a packed array to a regular array. Its syntax is:
>
> unpack (PackedArray, NotPackedArray, StartingSubscript);

PackedArray is a variable of a packed array type, NotPackedArray is a variable of a similar (except that it's not packed) array type, and StartingSubscript is the position in NotPackedArray where the assignment starts.

Let's suppose that we've made the following definitions.

    type PackedTYPE = packed array [Lower .. Upper] of Data;
         OrdinaryTYPE = array [Minimum .. Maximum] of Data;
    var PackedArray: PackedTYPE;
        NotPackedArray: OrdinaryTYPE;
        StartingSubscript: Minimum .. Maximum;

We'll also assume that:

    (Maximum − Minimum) >= (Upper − Lower)

In other words, PackedArray is the same size as, or smaller than, NotPackedArray. This restriction is necessary because the StartingSubscript argument lets us assign a small packed array to part of a larger array that isn't packed.

A call of unpack:

    unpack (PackedArray, NotPackedArray, StartingSubscript);

is equivalent to:

    for i := Lower to Upper do
        NotPackedArray [i − Lower + StartingSubscript] := PackedArray [i]

However, unpack is usually implemented in a manner that's faster to execute than this for statement.

> The standard procedure pack reverses the process. Its syntax is:
>
> pack (NotPackedArray, StartingSubscript, PackedArray);

Using the same variables as above, we find that this call:

    pack (NotPackedArray, StartingSubscript, PackedArray);

is equivalent to the statement:

    for i := Lower to Upper do
        PackedArray [i] := NotPackedArray [i − Lower + StartingSubscript]

Again, we can assume that the procedure is implemented in an optimum manner.

Note, incidentally, that when PackedArray and NotPackedArray both have the same number of stored components, StartingSubscript must equal the first legal subscript of NotPackedArray. This is true for both procedures.

Self-Check Questions

Q. Since we can assign their elements one at a time, why couldn't we just make a complete array assignment; i.e.:

> PackedArray := NotPackedArray;

What's the necessity of either pack or unpack?

A. Once more we've run into the subtle difference between identical and compatible types. For two arrays to be assignable to each other, they must be of an identical type—declared with exactly the same type identifier. Since one array is packed and the other is not, this is clearly impossible. Thus, pack and unpack are required to effect the assignment.

Procedures and Functions as Parameters

Procedures and functions may be passed as parameters to other subprograms. This feature is usually taken advantage of in more advanced applications programs, especially when nonstandard library routines are available. As a result, the syntax of procedure and function parameter declarations may be enhanced at your installation, and what I say may be misleading.

At any rate, the general syntax of subprograms as parameters is just about what we would expect—the reserved word **procedure** or **function**, the subprogram's name and parameter list, and its type (if it's a function). For example:

> **procedure** Graph (**function** Compute (Limit: real): real; OffSet: integer);

When two or more subprograms go in one parameter list, the word **procedure** or **function** must be repeated for each.

> **function** GreatestResult (**function** A (ItsArgument: real) : real;
> **function** B (AnotherArgument: real) : real;
> TheArgument: real) : real;

don't pass the arguments

Now, when a subprogram is passed as a parameter, its arguments should *not* be passed along with it. In other words, GreatestResult might be called like this:

> **if** GreatestResult (Sine, Cosine, pi/4) > Minimum **then**   *etc.*

In this call, functions Sine and Cosine are the arguments of A and B, while pi/4 is their eventual argument. Calls have to be arranged this way to avoid prematurely evaluating argument functions or procedures.

Within GreatestResult, A and B (now representing Sine and Cosine) are called normally.

```
function GreatestResult (function A (ItsArgument: real) : real;
                              function B (AnotherArgument: real) : real;
                              TheArgument : real): real;
{Represents the greater of A and B.}
var First, Second: real;
begin
    First := A (TheArgument);
    Second := B (TheArgument);
    if First > Second
        then GreatestResult := First;
        else GreatestResult := Second
end; {GreatestResult}
```

As you might imagine, a procedure or function parameter must be equivalent in type and parameter list to its argument. Because of this restriction, we can pass only real-type functions having one real argument apiece to GreatestResult.

page

page is similar to writeln. However, it's designed to be used with printers, rather than monitors. In addition to going to the next output line, page also moves ahead to the next physical page of output. page's exact effect depends on your system. Frankly, it's not often used.

B

Useful Procedures

A Random Number Generator
A Better Implementation
Screen Control Procedures

MOST REAL-WORLD PASCAL IMPLEMENTATIONS supply a variety of extended functions and procedures. Unfortunately, extensions vary from system to system. That's to be expected, since extensions may rely on implementation-specific details.

This appendix contains explanations of, and code for, a few useful subprograms you might not have:

1. A high-quality random number generator function, Random.

2. A small package of screen control procedures for any VT100- or ANSI.SYS-compatible system. This include DEC terminals and IBM PC-compatible micros.

A Random Number Generator

A *random number generator* produces numbers that, insofar as possible, appear to have been picked out of a hat. Numbers that are produced by computer can't really be random, of course—once you know the generation algorithm you can predict what number will appear next. Nevertheless, it is easy to generate *pseudorandom* numbers that have the general characteristics of truly random numbers. These include:

— A large number of values should be fairly, but not too precisely, distributed.

— The order in which values have appeared shouldn't help anybody predict what the next value will be.

In other words, if we could truly pick one thousand numbers that fell in the range 1 .. 10 at random, it wouldn't be plausible for there to be exactly one hundred of each—that's too uniform a distribution. Nor would it be realistic for the numbers to appear in order of increasing value, because that would help us predict what was coming up.

Until quite recently, it was common to use mechanical, as opposed to algorithmic, methods to generate random numbers. Once collected, they were sold in books and could be copied as needed. For example, Volume XV in the series *Tracts for Computers* (by which was meant 'people who compute'), published by Cambridge University Press and released in 1959, was titled *Random Sampling Numbers.* Where did the numbers come from? Some 40,000 numbers were picked from English census reports one digit at a time, then written out in longhand!

Most computerized random number generation is based on the *linear-congruential* method, which was first introduced by D. Lehmer some ten years earlier in 1949. In Lehmer's method, we take a starting number, called the *seed*, then perform a multiplication and division on it like this:

the linear congruential formula

```
{Producing a new pseudorandom integer from Seed.}
Seed := (MULTIPLIER*Seed) mod MODULUS;
```

Lehmer's method produces a stream of numbers that range from 0 through MODULUS less 1. What's interesting is that each number helps generate the next; every random number takes a turn as the seed for its successor. The sequence isn't entirely random because it eventually repeats.

In fact, it's a good idea to think of the numbers as forming a circle, and the first seed as being a starting point on it. If you begin with the same seed, you'll always get the same series of numbers. This is a lifesaver during debugging because you know what numbers to expect. However, most programs that use random numbers must find some other method for picking a starting seed. Typically, they will rely on a nonstandard function call, perhaps to a time-of-day function.

Now, the basic algorithm generates whole-number values for Seed. If we then divide the value of Seed by MODULUS, we wind up with a number that falls between 0.0 and 0.999 . . . .

```
{Getting a random decimal fraction.}
Random := Seed / MODULUS;
```

In practice, random number generators do this for us. They're written as functions that return a real-valued fraction. To go back to a whole number in the range 1 .. N, you should:

> *save the random fraction;*
> *multiply it by* N;
> *add* 1 *to the product;*

getting random whole numbers

In Pascal, the conversion is:

```
{Going from random integer to random real fraction.}
Temp := Random (Seed):
Temp := 1 + (Temp * N);
```

I've put the steps together in function Random, below. Note that Seed is passed as a variable parameter, because it must change on every call. Thus, Random actually returns two values—unusual in a function, but customary in this particular case.

The values Random uses for its modulus and multiplier were suggested by J. Stanley Warford (see *Good Pedagogical Random Number Generators*, Warford, SIGSCE Bulletin, March 1992, p. 142). He took the trouble of testing random number generators in various ranges:

Best generator in the range	Modulus	Multiplier
10 – 20	17	5
20 – 50	37	5
50 – 100	83	58
100 – 200	139	101
200 – 500	467	24
500 – 1000	797	30
1000 – 2000	1013	28
2000 – 4096	2027	15

You might want to try out some of the smaller ranges to get a feel for how Lehmer's algorithm works.

random number function

```
function Random (var Seed : integer) : real;
    {Returns a pseudorandom number such that 0.0 ≤ Random < 1.0.}
    const MODULUS = 2027;          {Values suggested by Warford.}
          MULTIPLIER = 15;
    begin
        Seed := (Seed * MULTIPLIER) mod MODULUS;
        Random := Seed / MODULUS
    end;  {Random}
```

Modification Problems

1. Modify Random so that it returns integer values rather than reals. Then put it in a program that tabluates its performance in one of the smaller ranges listed in the table above.

A Better Implementation

Choosing specific values for MULTIPLIER and MODULUS is a task fraught with peril, because not every pair leads to a long sequence before numbers start to repeat. Fortunately, an excellent survey of random number generation (see *Random Number Generators: Good Ones Are Hard to Find*, Park and Miller, Communications of the ACM, October 1988, p. 1192) suggests using a MULTIPLIER of 16807 and a MODULUS of 2147483647, or $2^{31} - 1$.[*]

Park and Miller's MODULUS value is quite large. In fact, on many microcomputer Pascal implementations, it may be too large to be used in ordinary integer arithmetic. If that's the case on your system, you will almost certainly

---

[*] To be honest, I have no choice, since they cited an earlier edition of this book as including a particularly lousy random number generator. Serves me right: I copied it from somebody else!

find an extended type called longint; use it instead of integer for the temporary variables in Random.

Not coincidentally, the MODULUS value equals the largest value that can be stored using longint values. The final algorithm of function Generate is complicated by the need to avoid arithmetic overflow.

Like Random, Generate is an unusual function because it has a variable parameter. There's no clean way to avoid this, since the Seed variable has to be changed with every call. Generate could be written as a procedure, of course, but it usually isn't.

a random number generator

```
function Generate (var Seed: integer) : real;
    {Algorithm 2 from CACM, pg. 1195, vol. 31, no. 10, (October, 1988).}
    const MODULUS = 2147483647;
          MULTIPLIER = 16807;
          QUOTIENT = 127773;      {MODULUS div MULTIPLIER}
          REMAINDER = 2836;       {MODULUS mod MULTIPLIER}
    var Low, Hi, Test: integer;
    begin
        {First, perform the calculation while avoiding overflow.}
        Hi := Seed div QUOTIENT;
        Low := Seed mod QUOTIENT;
        Test := (MULTIPLIER * Low) – (REMAINDER * Hi);
        {Second, update the seed for next time.}
        if Test > 0
            then Seed := Test
            else Seed := Test + MODULUS;
        {Third, return a value in the range 0.0 < Generate ≤ 1.0}
        Generate := Seed / MODULUS
    end;   {Generate}
```

Modification Problems

1. Modify Generate so that it takes a second integer argument named Limit, then returns an integer value in the range 1 .. Limit.

2. In their article, Park and Miller suggest that a good test for the generator is to use an initial seed of 1, and see if the 10,000th number it cranks out is 1,043,618,065. Modify Generate so that it tests the test (be careful about an off-by-one error).

Screen Control Procedures

Examples in the rest of the text have used only monitor and terminal screens for line-by-line character output. That's because under normal circumstance, a terminal 'listens' for characters sent by the computer and prints them as they arrive. Sending a character to the screen as part of ordinary output displays the character, then moves the cursor one space to the right.

However, the American National Standards Institute, or ANSI, has adopted a set of *escape sequences* that control screen printing.

escape sequences

> An *escape sequence* is a special character or two that directs a terminal to obey commands contained in the letters that follow, instead of simply printing them. In other words, the letters 'escape' normal processing so that they can be interpreted as commands.

The ANSI set was originally developed by the Digital Equipment Corporation for their VT100 terminal. It's simple to understand, easily extended, and widely used. Almost every PC will correctly interpret ANSI escape sequences, and almost every ordinary terminal is VT100-compatible.

The complete set of ANSI escape sequences is quite detailed. It includes controls for:

— going to an arbitrary screen location before printing,

— erasing various on-screen areas,

— controlling the foreground (printing) and background screen colors, and

— controlling the size and intensity of printed characters.

The actual escape sequences are entirely arbitrary and non-mnemonic, of course. They begin with the two-character sequence `Esc` [, followed by arguments if necessary. A Pascal program can produce the `Esc` character as chr (27).* For example, to clear the screen and leave the cursor in the upper-left corner, send the four-character escape sequence:

the clear-screen
sequence

chr (27) [2 J

Note that I say *send*, rather than *print*. Since it is an escape sequence, the terminal interprets the sequence as a command to be obeyed, rather than printed. In Pascal, I'd write a ClearScreen procedure as:

clearing the screen

```
procedure ClearScreen;
    {Clears the screen.  Terminal must obey ANSI/VT100 escape sequences.}
    const ESCAPE = 27;    {The ASCII position of the ESCAPE key.}
    begin
        write (chr(ESCAPE), '[2J')
    end; {ClearScreen}
```

The second basic procedure moves the cursor to a particular location. The upper-left corner of the screen is treated as position 1,1.

the cursor-positioning
sequence

chr (27) *Row* ; *Column* H

> By custom, the cursor-positioning procedure is called GotoXY. Note that the Y coordinate specifies the row (usually in the range 1 .. 25), while the X coordinate gives the column (usually in the range 1 .. 80).

---

* This is true in the ASCII set, which most computers employ. In the EBCDIC set, used on IBM mainframes, the ESC character has ordinal position 39.

Thus, the X,Y arguments of the procedure call are in reverse order of the *Row, Column* escape sequence. The Pascal procedure is:

going to an X, Y location

```
procedure GotoXY (Column, Row: integer);
    {Moves the cursor.  Terminal must obey ANSI/VT100 escape sequences.}
    const ESCAPE = 27;    {The ASCII position of the ESCAPE key.}
    begin
        {I've used 6 separate write statements to avoid confusion.}
        write (chr(ESCAPE));
        write ('[');
        write (Column : 1);    {The field width must be 1 to avoid extra blanks.}
        write (';');
        write (Row : 1);
        write ('H')
    end;  {GotoXY}
```

I think that you can manage to code the other escape sequences on your own. How will you know if your system supports the ANSI/VT100 escape sequences? Try them! The complete set follows.

ANSI / VT100 Escape Sequences
(Not all systems will support all escape sequences. In ASCII, ESC is chr (27).)

Escape sequence	Effect on the screen
ESC[X;YH	*move the cursor to screen coordinates X, Y*
ESC[NA	*move the cursor up by N lines*
ESC[NB	*move the cursor down by N lines*
ESC[NC	*move the cursor right by N spaces*
ESC[ND	*move the cursor left by N spaces*
ESC[2J	*erase the screen, then go to the upper left corner*
ESC[K	*erase from the current position to the end of the line*
ESC[s	*save the cursor position in a hidden variable (ESC7 on VT100)*
ESC[u	*go to the position saved by the call above (ESC8 on VT100)*

ESC[*val* m *or* ESC[*val;val; . . . ;val* m

    give the display one or more attributes. Legal values for 'val' are:

	General characteristics	Foreground color		Background color	
0	*reset to terminal defaults*	30	*Black*	40	
1	*high intensity characters*	31	*Red*	41	
2	*faint intensity*	32	*Green*	42	
3	*italic characters*	33	*Yellow*	43	
4	*underline characters*	34	*Blue*	44	
5	*blink on*	35	*Magenta*	45	
6	*blink rapidly*	36	*Cyan*	46	
7	*reverse video*	37	*White*	47	
8	*don't show letters printing*				

E.g., ESC [0;1;5;31;43m *sets bright, flashing, red letters on a yellow background.*

C

Real Arithmetic

Real Number Storage
We Invent Floating-Point Storage
The Fundamental Problem: Round-off Error
Convergence and Error

LET'S CONSIDER THE PROBLEM OF SUNTAN LOTION arithmetic. As you probably know, suntan lotion is rated with an *SPF* number—the higher the number, the better the protection. But have you ever wondered how different SPF numbers mix?

For instance, suppose that you cover yourself from head to toe with minimally protective SPF 4. But the day is hot, and you are pale, so you put on an additional layer of SPF 16. What level of protection have you achieved? Halfway between, at 10? The sum of the two, 20? The lower? The higher? Naturally, I couldn't rest until I spoke directly with the Coppertone people. According to the very patient woman I spoke with, the higher number takes precedence—the lower number is ignored. The sum of 4 and 16 is 16.

Doing arithmetic with real numbers on computers is not entirely unlike doing math with suntan lotion. What seems obvious may not always be correct. Let's take a closer look at the culprit—the way reals are stored—and then see how that affects the design of arithmetic algorithms.

Real Number Storage

When it comes to real numbers, programmers must usually work with approximations. This is a little counterintuitive, because we usually think of computers as being extremely precise.

But just because a number is precise doesn't mean that it's correct. For example, ½ equals 0.5 exactly, and ¼ equals 0.25. But does ⅓ exactly equal 0.3? Not at all. No matter how many digits I supply—3.333333333333—the decimal real will have a slight *round-off error*. It is precise, but it's still a slightly incorrect approximation of the value I really want.

Thus, blaming round-off error on the limited number of digits available for storing real numbers misstates the situation. The real problem is that numbers that are easy to express algebraically, like ⅓, don't have decimal equivalents. Size doesn't matter. Instead, the decision to store numbers, rather than expressions, is the culprit.

Why store numbers inexactly? Well, schemes for real computer arithmetic represent a series of compromises. We *could* store expressions; sometimes it would take more space and sometimes less. But it would exact a terrible price in speed. The goal is to:

ground rules for real arithmetic

— *minimize* the storage space required to hold individual numbers,

— *maximize* the speed of arithmetic calculations, and

— *maintain* the accuracy of arithmetic at a necessary level.

In practical terms, accurate doesn't mean correct or exact. Instead, a number is accurate if it's precise enough for its application. That precision is measured as the number of *significant digits* in the number.

We Invent Floating-Point Storage

You'll get a feel for the trade-offs of real arithmetic if we take a moment to revisit a few of the key moments in the history of real storage. I'll simplify matters considerably, of course, and work in decimal digits instead of the binary bits used by computers.

Let's imagine that we're at a conference given by the big computer manufacturers to describe their plans for arithmetic. We're joined by scientists of all persuasions—cosmologists, particle physicists, and so on. At first, all the computer manufacturers have agreed to set aside, say, six digits to represent numbers:

| A | A | A | A | A | A | *a simple six-digit storage scheme*

This scheme lets us write exactly every whole number from 0 through 999,999. The manufacturers are very happy with this method, since it will let them number their new products. Intel can have the 80686, Motorola can produce the 68050, etc.

inventing real storage

But the scientists in the audience are displeased: 'We want to use decimals,' they cry. The engineers huddle. 'No problem,' they eventually say. 'Just pretend that there's a decimal point in the middle:'

| A | A | A | . | B | B | B | *inventing fixed-point representation*

We've just invented *fixed-point* representation, which was actually used by early computers. Unfortunately, (even ignoring the lack of a plus or minus sign) this solution pleases almost nobody. The largest number, 999.999, barely measures the distance from Chicago to Boston. The smallest non-zero value, 0.001, isn't nearly precise enough for the laboratory. Overall, six-digit fixed-point seems more suited for calculating batting averages than anything else. We can imagine the debate raging, the decimal point moving left and right.

But how can we get a broader range of numbers without using more digits? By inventing *floating-point* notation. Suppose that we divide our six digits like this:

| A | A | | B | . | B | B | B | *inventing floating-point representation*

inventing floating-point
representation

Let the AA represent any number from 0 through 99. We'll use it as a *scale factor*—stored numbers will be multiplied by 10 raised to the AA power. The other four digits, called the *mantissa*, can range from 0.000 through 9.999. The smallest number we can show, 0.001×10^0, is still 0.001. The biggest, 9.999×10^{99}, is very, very big indeed.

'But wait a minute,' comes the shout. 'Who needs numbers that big? Are you cosmologists planning to count every proton in the universe? We physicists want more accuracy for the *small* numbers!' The solution is quite clever: subtract 50 from the scale factor, no matter what it is. That gives us a range of scale factors from −50 through +49, which is equivalent to these numbers:

Smallest number:	0.001×10^{-50}
Biggest number:	9.999×10^{49}
Exact contiguous integer *equivalents:*	0 *through* 10,000

We're still working with just six digits, mind you, but we're getting much more out of them. Everybody is reasonably happy: the cosmologists can count very large numbers, and the particle physicists can have extremely accurate small numbers.

In practice, computers use several such tricks to store positive and negative reals and to keep as many non-zero digits as possible within the mantissa. The digits are divided somewhat differently: we get a larger number of significant digits in exchange for a smaller range of numbers. There are also storage rules that minimize duplication. It's not obvious at first, but the simple scheme above wastes information by letting the same number be stored in more than one way (since 1.000×10^1 equals 0.100×10^2 equals 0.010×10^3 and so on).

single and double
precision

However, since no one storage scheme will satisfy everybody, most compilers will let the programmer choose one of several: *single precision* and *double precision* reals are almost always available. In effect, increased accuracy can almost always be obtained at the cost of increased storage and reduced speed of calculation.

The Fundamental Problem: Round-off Error

Let's move on to difficulties that arise from performing calculations with real numbers. There are two basic problems, collectively known as *round-off error*.

round-off error

— *Rounding* means that we introduce an error because we think that it gives us a closer approximation of what we want.

— *Chopping* means that we lose important digits because there isn't room to store them.

Rounding is nothing new. Suppose that we have four digits to work with. If we store ⅔ as 0.667, we've intentionally introduced a rounding error. 0.667 is less accurate than the five-digit number 0.6666 is, but it's better than 0.666 would be. We accept it as the lesser of two evils; it's the best we can do with the number of digits we have.

Chopping results from the deal we made a few moments ago when we invented floating-point representation. What deal? We agreed that a number could be either very large, or very small—never both. In other words, we can store the sum of these two fixed-point numbers exactly:

{Fixed-point is limited, but it's exact.}

100.000	*a relatively large number*
+ 0.001	*a relatively small number*
100.001	*the sum can be stored accurately*

But if we perform a similar calculation with floating-point numbers, the smaller value may be lost. In effect, instead of having three digits on either side of the decimal point, we have six digits to distribute as we please:

{Floating-point has a broader range, but in only one direction.}

chopping floating-point numbers

10000.0	*this number is large, but can be stored*
+ 0.00001	*this number is small, but can be stored*
10000.00001	*there aren't enough digits to store this number*
10000.0	*this is the number that will be saved instead*

Since we only have six digits, there isn't any way to store the answer accurately. As a rule, the *least significant* digits—those at the far right—are chopped off and lost.

Round-off errors are *the* important consideration in designing numerical algorithms. That's because for all intents and purposes, we must assume that every calculation has the potential of introducing a tiny error. Although one small error may be insignificant, repeating that error may lead to totally unreliable results.

Convergence and Error

In fact, it's convenient to imagine that every numerical algorithm is a race:

— How fast does the algorithm *converge* on an answer?

convergence vs. error propagation

— How fast does round-off error *propagate* or spread through the stored partial result?

Designing computer algorithms to be fast misses the point. Raw speed isn't this issue. Instead, the algorithm must add accuracy faster than the computer 'adds' error. For example, consider two ways to approach this simple arithmetic problem:

$$3.0 \times (1.0 / 3.0) \qquad \textit{do the division first}$$

Suppose that we do the division first. It introduces a round-off error instantly, because $\frac{1}{3}$ will be stored as $0.333\ldots$, no matter how many decimal digits are allowed. The result, $0.999\ldots$, is wrong. Try it on your calculator.

But what happens when we use a different algorithm that rearranges the expression first? Now the answer will be correct regardless of the underlying representation.

$$(3.0 \times 1.0) / 3.0 \qquad \textit{do the multiplication first}$$

To be honest, on my computer both approaches yield the expected answer for this single operation. That's because modern computers are very clever about analyzing potential round-off error and choosing results that avoid mistakes. But if you try the same exercise on most hand calculators, you'll see the mistakes start to grow instantly.

Here are some of the issues that programmers who work with numerical algorithms must bear in mind:

— *Avoid using small and large numbers in the same expression.*

don't mix large and small

Round-off error may keep the small numbers from being represented in the expression's result. Don't do this:

> {*This might not change the large number at all.*}
> **for** *each of many small numbers* **do**
>   *add each small number to a very large number;*

Instead, sum the small numbers first, then add their total:

> {*This has a better chance at working.*}
> Temp := 0.0;
> **for** *each of many small numbers* **do**
>   *add each small number to* Temp;
> *add* Temp *to the large number*

— *Avoid the expectation that a* real *will equal an* integer *or another* real.

don't expect exact comparisons

Again, round-off error may force two values that should be equal to be slightly unequal. Don't do this:

> {*This loop might not end.*}
> **repeat**
>   *perform a calculation on* Value;
> **until** Value = 0.0;

Instead, pick a value that's close enough to satisfy you:

> {*This bound is easier to meet.*}
> Epsilon := 0.00000001;
> **repeat**
>   *perform a calculation on* Value;
> **until** abs (Value) < Epsilon;

Put this way, Epsilon serves as an *absolute convergence test*, since we're using a fixed value to decide if we've calculated long enough. That's fine if we want to get close to zero.

absolute vs. relative tests

But think back to Newton's method for finding square roots, given in Chapter 6. That sort of algorithm terminates when two successive approximations are very close to each other. If the square root is very large, or is very close to zero, we may need to use Epsilon as a *relative* convergence test instead.

> {*Using a relative convergence test to set a safe bound.*}
> Epsilon := 0.00000001;
> **repeat**
>   Old := New;
>   *recalculate* New;
> **until** abs ((Old − New) / Old) < Epsilon;

—   *Be wary of division, since that's the most common source of inaccuracy.*

delay division
   Suppose that a division introduces a small rounding error. Following that division by multiplication compounds the error; it only gets worse. If you can, revise the order of operations, so that division is delayed. That's exactly what I did in the $3.0 \times (1.0 / 3.0)$ *vs.* $(3.0 \times 1.0) / 3.0$ example.

D

Pascal Pages

This appendix contains most of what there is to know about Pascal syntax, a little bit about semantics, and an abridged description of many standard procedures and functions. There's a quick reference for every syntactic entity, along with brief examples and some common bugs.

If you'd like a more formal and complete reference to Standard Pascal, check out my *Standard Pascal User Reference Manual* (1985, available from W.W. Norton). A reference manual for ANSI/IEEE Extended Pascal can be purchased from the IEEE, 345 East 47th Street, New York, NY, 10017.- Ask for ANSI/IEEE 770X3.160-1989

About Arrays

array type definition

identifier → = packed array [ordinal type identifier bound .. bound ,] of component type identifier ;

An array type definition includes a type name, its dimensions (given by one or more pairs of bounds), and the type of the components it will hold:

type *the array's name* = **array** [*bounds*] **of** *components*

For example:

type LetterCountTYPE = **array** [1 .. 10] **of** char;
    NumberTableTYPE = **array** [1 .. 20, 1 .. 10] **of** integer;
var Letters: LetterCountTYPE;
    Numbers, Values: NumberTableTYPE;

A string type is a **packed** one-dimensional array that has a lower bound of 1 and components of type char.

type StringTYPE = **packed array** [1 .. MAX] **of** char;

String types are granted privileges other arrays don't have:

— Strings may be compared if they have the same length.

— Strings may be assigned to one another if they have the same length, even if they're declared with different type identifiers.

— Strings may be output in their entirety.

— Constants may have string types.

Aside from strings, one array can be assigned to another in its entirety if they have the exact same type. Individual components are identified by subscript; naturally, the subscripts must have the proper order and type:

Letters [1] := 'a';
Numbers [1, 10] := 5;
Values := Numbers;

An array of arrays can use just one pair of brackets for all subscripts:

Complicated [1] [3] ['t'] *is the same as* Complicated [1, 3, 't']

The most common array loop traverses all or part of the structure:

for Count := 1 **to** 10 **do begin**
    Letters [Count] *gets modified*
end;

```
for Row := 1 to 20 do begin
    for Column := 1 to 10 do begin
        Numbers [ Row, Column ] gets modified
    end;
end;
```

The most common array bugs are:

— confusing the type of the array's subscript with the type of its components;

— attempting to inspect an *out-of-bounds* component that isn't in the array.

About Assignments

assignment statement

       variable identifier $\longrightarrow$:= $\longrightarrow$ *expression*

The assignment statement gives a value to a variable. The expression on the right is evaluated, then the result is stored in the variable on the left.

```
Old := 7;        {Initializing a variable.}
New := 2 * Old;
```

The expression and the variable must be *assignment compatible*. This means that:

— integer values can be assigned to real variables, but not vice versa;

— the variable can't be a file (but it can be the current file component);

— if the variable has a subrange type, the expression must fall into the subrange;

— if the variable has a string type, the expression must have the same number of components (but padding a short string with blanks is a common nonstandard).

Bugs commonly associated with assignment include:

— letting an uninitialized variable appear on the right-hand side; it may not have been initialized, but it has a value;

— assigning a value that is out of the legal range of the variable, but which isn't necessarily checked by the computer. This is usually a problem for out-of-range integer values.

About **case** Statements

case statement

case → *expression* → of

constant value : → *statement* → end

The **case** statement branches between two or more control paths. An expression, which must have an ordinal type (see *About Simple Types*), is evaluated. The result value is found in one of the lists of constants, and that action is taken. For example:

```
case Number of
    –1: ;   {An empty statement indicates a non-action.}
    2, 4, 6, 8:  Even := Even + 1;
    1, 3, 5, 7, 9:  Odd := Odd + 1;
    0:  Zero := Zero + 1;
    11, 12, 13, 14, 15: begin
                        writeln ('The value was in the range 11 .. 15.');
                        writeln ('Yes, this is an inconvenient way to show ranges.')
                    end
end; {case}
```

In standard Pascal, it is an error if the expression's value is not found. In addition:

— The constants must be either literal values or defined constants. They must have the same type as the expression.

— Every constant must be given individually (ranges aren't allowed, although this is a common extension).

— Each list of constants must be distinct.

The **case** statement's most common bugs arise from portability problems. Most Pascal implementations allow a missing **case** expression to 'fall though' the statement without harm, but this isn't always the case. And, although allowing ranges for constants is common, it isn't universal.

About Constant Definitions

constant definition part

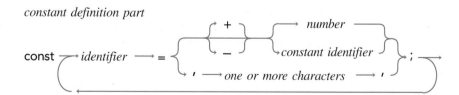

const → *identifier* → = { + / – } → *number* / *constant identifier* / ' → *one or more characters* → ' ;

Constant definitions give names to values. The values themselves must:

— have one of the standard types real, integer, char, or boolean; or

— be constants of an enumerated type; or

— be string values, given between single quotes.

As a matter of style, all or part of the constant's name is usually capitalized:

```
const STOREname = 'SocksRUs';
      PAIR = 2;
      SALEStax = 0.0825;
      WIDTH = 'E';
```

About Expressions

An expression represents a value. It can be a constant, variable, or literal value, or it may consist of operators and operands.

Operators expect to have operands of the proper type and produce results of a specific type.

real *operators:*	+ − * /
integer *operators:*	+ − * div mod
relational operators:	< <= = >= > <>
boolean *operators:*	not or and
set operators:	+ − * in

+ and − can also be used as *unary* (one-operand) operators with real or integer values.

The real operators take either real or integer operands. The expression's result is real if either *a)* any operand is real or *b)* the division operator / appears. The integer operator **div** returns the whole portion of a division, while **mod** returns the remainder.

Parentheses can and should be used to make the order of evaluation of expressions clear. The default order of operator precedence is:

not	*greatest*
div mod and * /	
or + −	
in < <= = >= > <>	*least*

Common problems that are associated with expressions are:

— type mismatches that are the result of missing parentheses, especially when the boolean operators are being used;

— an unexpected order of evaluation, because you relied on operator precedence instead of using parentheses;

— loops that won't terminate because the bound condition requires two real values to be exactly equal.

======   About Files

file type definition

$$\text{type identifier} \longrightarrow \;=\; \left\{ \begin{array}{c} \longrightarrow \text{text} \longrightarrow \\ \text{file of} \longrightarrow \text{component type} \end{array} \right\} \longrightarrow \;;$$

A file type definition names the file and specifies the type of its components. Files can have components of any type except another file type.

```
type RealFileTYPE = file of real;
     RecordFileTYPE = file of SomeRecordTYPE;
var TextFile: text;
    Readings, Data: RealFileTYPE;
    Information: RecordFileTYPE;
```

One file type, text, is predefined in Standard Pascal. The standard files input and output have type text. Textfiles are nominally the same as **file of** char. However, procedures readln and writeln and function eoln are defined only for textfiles.

The lifetime of a file depends on whether or not it appears in the program heading as a *program parameter*. If it does, the file is a permanent external file. If not, temporary storage will be set aside during program execution.

Unlike other variables, files must explicitly be set for inspection or assignment.

— reset (*file*) prepares a file to be read from its beginning.

— rewrite (*file*) removes any contents the file may currently have and prepares it to be written.

Every file variable has a buffer, called the *file window*, associated with it. The file window, shown as the file's name folowed by a circumflex, allows access to the current file component. Two procedures manipulate the file window, and a function checks for the end of the file:

— get (*file*) places the file's next component in the file window.

— put (*file*) adds the file window's current component to the file.

— eof (*file*) is RUE if the last componenent is in the file window.

```
rewrite (Readings);
Readings ↑ := 6.3;
put (Readings);
reset (Data);          {Performs the first get automatically.}
writeln (Data ↑ : 1 : 2);          {Note that the window has type real.}
get (Data);
```

Procedures read and write simplify the process, but require a variable with the same type as the file's components.

```
read(F, V) is equivalent to  begin V := F ↑; get(F) end;
write(F, V) is equivalent to  begin F ↑ := V; put(F) end;
```

As noted, textfiles have special privileges. They are considered to be divided into distinct lines:

— writeln generates an end-of-line marker.

— readlin discards input until an end-of-line marker has been passed.

— eoln is TRUE if the end-of-line marker is about to be read.

About **for** Statements

for statement

for ⟶ *counter variable* ⟶ := ⟶ *expression* ⟶ to / downto ⟶ *expression* ⟶ do ⟶ *statement*

The **for** statement repeats actions a predetermined number of times. That can be just once (if the initial and limit values are equal), or even not at all.

> for *counter variable* := *initial value* **to** (*or* **downto**) *limit* **do**
> *action*

The counter variable, initial value and limit must all have the same ordinal (counting) type. If the initial value and limit are given by variables, they're evaluated *before* the loop is entered, so changes within the loop have no effect.

> for Count := 1 **to** Finish **do begin**   *actions*   **end**;
> for Letter := 'A' **to** 'Z' **do begin**   *actions*   **end**;
> for Number := 0 **downto** –10 **do begin**   *actions*   **end**;

If the **for** statement is in a procedure, its counter variable should be locally declared. It is an error to assign to the counter from within the loop.

The counter variable can be inspected within the loop, so it's often used as a source of data. However, it is undefined when the loop ends.

About **forward** Declarations

When procedures or functions call each other, it may be necessary to sidestep Pascal's 'declare before you call' rule. A **forward** declaration makes a subprogram's name and parameters known to the compiler before its actual declaration. When the declaration is finished, the parameter list is not repeated.

> **procedure** First (*parameter list*); **forward**;
> **procedure** CallsFirst (*parameter list*);
>   **begin**
>   *its body, including a call of* First
>   **end**; {CallsFirst}
> **procedure** First;
>   **begin**
>   *the declaration is completed*
>   **end**; {First}

About Function Declarations

function heading

function ⟶ *identifier* ⟶ (⟶ *parameter list* ⟶) ⟶ : ⟶ *type identifier* ⟶ ;

Aside from its heading, a function declaration is like a procedure declaration.

A function call represents a simple value. Although evaluating a function usually requires executing statements within the function, the call appears as part of an expression—never as a statement on its own. Function and procedure declarations follow variable declarations; they go right before the statement part of a main program or subprogram.

```
function ExampleFunction (ValueParam: integer) : integer;
    const Start = 20;
    {Local types may be defined, too.}
    var Local:  char;
    {Procedure and function declarations may appear as well.}
    begin
        {Body of the function.}
        ExampleFunction := the value it will return
    end;  {ExampleFunction}
```

Since the intention of a function is to calculate and return a single value, functions almost never have variable parameters. See *About Parameters* for further discussion of parameters.

A function must be declared using an existing type name. And, although this isn't a syntactic requirement, a function invariably contains an assignment that gives the function the value it will return. See *About Procedures* for additional comments on identifier scope.

About Identifiers

identifier

letter ⟶ (digit / letter) ⟶

A Pascal identifier must begin with a letter, then can include any sequence of letters and digits. It's smart to use identifiers that give some clue as their purpose in the program. For example:

Counter — *ordinary variables are capitalized*
PAYscale — *the first full word of constants are capitalized*
NewTYPE — *the last word of a type definition is capitalized*

About **if** Statements

if statement

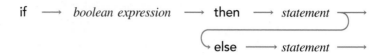

The **if** statement decides whether an action should take place. Its syntax doesn't require a compound statement's **begin** and **end**, but they're almost always used.

> if boolean *expression* **then begin**
>   *sequence of statements*
> **end**

With an **else** part, **if** selects one of two alternative control paths. A semicolon may not appear before the reserved word **else**.

> if boolean *expression*
>   **then begin**
>   *sequence of*
>   *statements*
>   **end**   {*no semicolon*}
>   **else begin**
>   *alternative sequence*
>   *of statements*
>   **end;**   {*semicolon is ok*}

Any **else** part is always the alternative of the most recent **then** it can be legally associated with. That rules out a **then** that *a)* already has an **else** part or *b)* is completely enclosed by a compound statement:

> if *condition 1*
>   **then if** *condition 2*
>   **then** *action 2*
>   **else** *alternative to action 2*
>   **else** *alternative action for condition 1*

> if *condition 1*
>   **then if** *condition 2* **then** *action 2* **end**
>   **else** *alterntive action for condition 1*

if's most common semantic bugs arise from misstated boolean conditions:

— *impossible conditions* are errors because they can't be met;

— *unavoidable conditions* are wrong because they will always be met;

— *boundary condition errors* hinge on the turning point between TRUE and FALSE.

About Parameters

parameter list

The parameter list, given between parentheses, is an optional part of every procedure and function heading.

Pascal has two kinds of parameters: value and variable.

— A value parameter is a local variable that is initialized by its argument. Changing the value parameter has no effect on the argument.

— A variable parameter is a local identifier that temporarily renames its argument. Changing the variable parameter is identical to changing the variable it represents.

There is always a one-to-one correspondence, by position, between parameters in the subprogram heading, and arguments in the subprogram call.

A value parameter's argument is assigned to the value parameter when the subprogram is called, so their types must be assignment compatible (see *About Assignments*). A variable parameter, in contrast, must have a type that is identical to its argument; in effect it must be declared with the same type identifier.

Parameter declarations are similar to variable declarations. However, a new **var** must appear whenever a new type of variable parameter is declared:

```
procedure GetValues (Testee, Day: char;          {value}
               var Raw, Percent: integer);        {variable}

procedure UseValues ( Testee: char;               {value}
                  var Changed, Out: integer;      {variable}
                  Used, Time: integer);           {value}

procedure ReviewResults ( Testee: char;           {value}
                     Raw: integer;                {value}
                     var Percent: real);          {variable}
```

A parameter must be declared with an existing type identifier.

A direct reference to a global variable is called a side effect and leads to hard-to-find bugs; use parameters instead. The main problems associated with parameters are:

— *Symptom*: the procedure seems to work, but nothing changes in the main program. *Diagnosis*: using a value parameter where you had intended to use a variable parameter; an assignment that should have been permanent becomes temporary.

— *Symptom*: the procedure works, but it breaks the main program. *Diagnosis*: using a variable parameter where you had intended to use a value parameter; a temporary assignment became permanent instead.

About Pointers

pointer type definition

> *type identifier* $\longrightarrow$ = ^ $\longrightarrow$ *type identifier* $\longrightarrow$;

A pointer type definition names the type and provides the type of the location the pointer variable will reference. A location may have any simple or structured type, but it can't be a file.

```
type IntegerPOINT = ↑ integer;
     NodePOINT = ↑ NodeTYPE;  {The most common definition.}
     NodeTYPE = record
                     Letter: char;
                     Next: NodePOINT
                end;
 var FirstNumPtr, SecondNumPtr: IntegerPOINT;
     FirstNodePtr, LastNodePtr: NodePOINT;
```

Note that a pointer definition can precede the definition of the type it points to.

— Any pointer can be assigned the value nil.

— Any pointer can be used as an argument to procedure new, which allocates a location for it to refer to.

— Any pointer can be used as an argument to procedure dispose, which deallocates the location.

— A pointer can be assigned the value of another pointer of the same type. It then refers to the same location.

— The value of a pointer cannot be inspected. It may only be compared for equality to nil or to another pointer of the same type.

For example:

```
new (FirstNumPtr);
SecondNumPtr := FirstNumPtr;
dispose (FirstNumPtr);        {But SecondNumPtr still points there.}
FirstNodePtr := nil;
```

A circumflex (I use an up-arrow because it's easier to read) can follow the name of any pointer that refers to a location:

```
new (FirstNumPtr);
FirstNumPtr ↑ := 3;
new (FirstNodePtr);
FirstNodePtr ↑.Letter := ´A´;
FirstNodePtr ↑.Next := nil;
```

It's an error to attempt to inspect the value of a nil pointer (except for equality, as noted), to refer to a location that hasn't been allocated.

Pointers are generally used in conjuction with records, as we saw in the partnership between NodePOINT and NodeTYPE, above. They build a linked data structure: one or more fields hold data, and one or more pointer fields refer to other records in the structure. Some structures that are commonly implemented using pointers are:

— *Linked list*: a chain of nodes that can be traversed in one (singly linked) or both (doubly linked) directions.

— *Binary tree*: each node points to zero, one, or two subnodes, but no node is referred to by more than one pointer.

The standard segment of list-traversal code is:

```
{Traveling through a linked list.}
while Current ↑.Next < > nil do begin
    Current := Current ↑.Next
end;
{Postcondition: Current refers to the last node.}
```

Searching through a linked list leads to the most common hazard: attempting to inspect a **nil** pointer. Don't check to see if the current node has the value you want or is **nil**, because if it *is* **nil**, you can't inspect any fields. Instead, stop the search when the current Data field has what you want or the Next field is **nil**. A post-loop test will be necessary to decide which of the loop bounds terminates the traversal.

About Procedure Declarations

procedure declaration

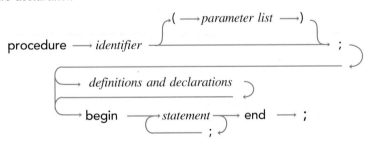

A procedure call, or invocation, is a statement that carries out a series of actions. Procedure and function declarations follow variable declarations; they go right before the statement part of a main program or subprogram.

```
procedure ExampleProcedure (ValueParam: integer; var VarParam: integer);
    const Start = 20;
    {Local types may be defined, too.}
    var Local: char;
    {Procedure and function declarations may appear as well.}
    begin
        {Body of the procedure.}
    end;  {ExampleProcedure}
```

Procedures can have their own local definitions and declarations, which exist only for the duration of the procedure call. The parameter mechanism (see *About Parameters*) lets a procedure be given arguments: value parameters bring values in from the calling program, and variable parameters let variables changed by the procedure return to the calling program.

A procedure declaration creates a new scope. Consequently:

— Identifiers that already have meaning in the main program can be reused without conflict, because the local definitions take precedence.

— Local identifiers, including parameters, aren't recognized outside of the procedure.

One procedure can't call or refer to another procedure's local identifiers.

Under normal circumstances, a procedure must be declared before it can be called. But, if necessary, a **forward** declaration allows out-of-order calls. See *About Forward Declarations*.

About Programs

program

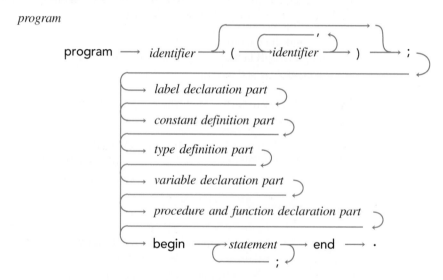

Although Pascal programs are free-format—their layout doesn't matter—definitions and declarations must take place in the order shown. See *About* **forward** *Declarations*, as well as other specific headings.

About Records

record type (with fixed-part only)

A record definition supplies the record's type name and the names and types of its fields. The fields can have any type, simple or structured.

```
type CoordinateTYPE = record
                          x, y: real;
                      end;
     ApartmentTYPE = record
                          Floor: integer;
                          Letter: char;
                          Wing: (north, south, east west)
                      end;
var Position, Location:  CoordinateTYPE;
    ToLet, ForLease:  ApartmentTYPE;
```

A record definition establishes a new scope. This means that identifiers created within the record don't conflict with identifiers that had been defined previously.

Individual fields are referred to by name. A fully qualified identifier consists of the record variable's name, a period, and the field's name. One record can be assigned to another if they have the exact same type. However, they can't be input, output, or compared as a whole.

```
Position.x := 3.1;
Position.y := 0.9;
Location := Position;
```

Typically, records appear as the components of arrays or files:

```
type        {continued from above}
    ReadingsTYPE = array [ 0 .. 23, 1 .. 31 ]
                               of CoordinateTYPE;
    BuildingTYPE = array [ 1 .. 50 ] of ApartmentTYPE;
var Readings:  ReadingsTYPE;
    Building:  BuildingTYPE;
```

The **with** statement establishes a reference to a particular record and lets its fields be inspected directly:

with statement

```
with    ──→ record variable ──→  do  ──→  statement  ──→
```

For example:

```
with ToLet do begin
    ToLet.Floor := 4;
    ToLet.Letter := 'C';
    ToLet.Wing := north
end;
ForLease := ToLet;
```

A common bug is to repeatedly refer to the same record when you think you're working through an array of records. The code below is correct:

```
for Current := 1 to 50 do begin
    with Building[ Current ] do begin
        Floor := 1;          etc.
```

If the **with** statement were outside the **for** loop, it would be syntactically correct, but it wouldn't do the right thing.

The records described above had a fixed contingent of fields. However, fields may also be defined in a manner that lets the compiler overlay (reuse storage) if possible:

record type

type identifier $\longrightarrow$ = record $\longrightarrow$ *field list* $\longrightarrow$ end

field list

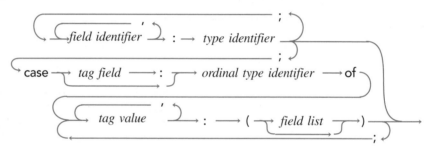

The set of available fields depends on the current value of the tag field. In the example below, Visible is a fixed field that's always available. The value of the tag field Figure controls the variants. Note that *a)* parentheses are required even if no fields are given, as in the case of point, and *b)* the variant fields must all have unique names.

```
type ShapeTYPE = (circle, square, triangle, point);
     DimensionTYPE = record
                    Visible:  boolean;
                    case Figure: ShapeTYPE of
                        circle : (Diameter: real);
                        square : (side: real);
                        point : ( );
                        triangle : (Side1: real; Angle1, Angle2: 0 .. 360);
                    end
```

About Sets

set type definition

type identifier $\longrightarrow$ = set of $\longrightarrow$ *base type identifier* $\longrightarrow$;

A set type definition names the type and specifies the type of components the set holds. Components must have an ordinal type, so **set of** real isn't allowed.

```
type SmallSET = set of 1 .. 10;
     SeasonTYPE = (spring, summer, fall, winter);
     SeasonSET = set of SeasonTYPE;
     CharSET = set of char;
var Numbers: SmallSET;
    Year: SeasonSET;
    Used, UnUsed: CharSET;
```

There's no fixed limit on the base type's size, but **set of** char is usually legal.

Set values are constructed by being listed between square brackets. Contiguous values are indicated with two dots, as we see below. Every set has the empty set, [ ] as a value.

```
Year := [ spring, winter ];
Numbers := [ 1 .. 3, 5, 7 .. 9 ];
Used := [ ];
UnUsed := Used;
```

Sets may be compared using the relational operators:

Sign	Operation	A TRUE Example
=	set equality	[1..3] = [1, 2, 3]
<>	set inequality	[2..5] <> []
>=	set 'contains'	[1..10] >= [2..9]
<=	set 'is contained by'	[5] <= [5, 7..9]
in	set membership	7 in [3..11]

Set operators take set-valued operands and return set-valued results:

+	*union — the merger of two sets*
*	*intersection — the values common to two sets*
−	*difference — the 'subtraction' of set members*

About Simple Types

The simple types contain unstructured values. Four simple types are predefined in Pascal:

— char: a collection of characters. The digit characters must be ordered (beginning with '0') and contiguous, while the letters must be in alphabetical order, but don't have to be next to each other.

— boolean: the values FALSE, TRUE, in that order.

— integer: whole numbers in the range −MAXINT .. MAXINT.

— real: decimals, which may include a scale factor, E, that means 'times 10 to the power that follows.'

real is the only simple type that is not an ordinal type too. The syntax chart of a real constant value is:

real number

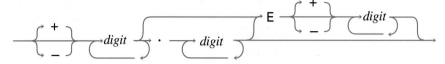

Many portability problems arise from assuming that a local implementation of one of these types is actually standard. For example, ASCII—the most commonly used character set—does have contiguous letters, but that isn't required. Similarly, most minicomputers and workstations will have an integer range of $-2147483648 .. 2147483647$, but on microcomputers, the actual range is often $-32768 .. 32767$.

New ordinal types can be enumerated, or listed and given a type name.

enumerated type definition

$$type\ identifier \longrightarrow\ =\ (\ \rightarrow constant\ identifier\ ,\ ) \longrightarrow ;$$

A subrange of any ordinal type may be given a unique type identifier as a subrange, as well:

subrange type definition

$$type\ identifier \longrightarrow\ = \longrightarrow lower\ bound \longrightarrow\ .. \longrightarrow upper\ bound \longrightarrow ;$$

```
type ColorTYPE = (red, green, blue, white, black);
     PrimaryTYPE = red .. blue;
     PositiveTYPE = 1 .. MAXINT;
     LowerCaseTYPE = 'a' .. 'z';
```

— Values of an ordinal type are numbered according to their place in the definition, beginning with the 'zeroth' value.

— A subrange must consist of contiguous values, so Vowels = 'a','e','i','0','u'; is illegal.

— real subranges are not legal.

Although values of an enumerated ordinal type can be assigned to variables and passed as parameters, they can't be input or output: they have no external character representation in Standard Pascal. Allowing I/O is a common extension and is a common cause of portability problems.

About Variable Declarations

variable declaration part

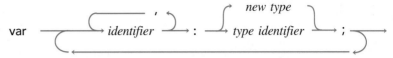

Variable declarations take two forms. Most commonly, a variable is given a named type: either one of the standard types char, integer, real, boolean, or text, or a new type you've defined (see *About Type Definitions*)

```
var Letter: char;
    Number, Counter: integer;
    DataFile, Results: text;
    Table: TableTYPE;
    Colors: ColorTYPE;
```

A type may also be described on the spot. However, this leads to problems with type compatibility and parameter declarations:

```
{variable declaration continues . . . }
    Small: 1 .. 10;
    Hue: record details of the definition end;
```

About while and repeat

while statement

while ⟶ *boolean expression* ⟶ do ⟶ *statement* ⟶

repeat statement

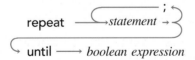

until ⟶ *boolean expression*

while and repeat are conditional loops. The repeat loop's action must take place at least once, but the while loop action can be skipped entirely. Some typical loop goals are:

while *a sentinel hasn't been spotted* do begin *get and process a value* end;
while *a count hasn't been reached* do begin *take and count an action* end;
while *a limit hasn't been achieved* do begin *iterate a calculation* end;
while *unknown data remain* do begin *reduce the solution space* end;

Although while does not syntactically require the begin and end of a compound statement, they're almost always used.

The boolean condition that sets the loop's bound invariably relies on a value that is changed within the loop. The chief hazard of a missed or mistaken update is an infinite loop. The most common errors that involve loops derive from:

— confusing the loop's goal—what you wanted, with its bound—why it ended;

— a bound that isn't sufficient to guarantee termination;

— an action that approaches the loop's goal properly, but arrives at the loop bound too early or late;

— a postcondition that misstates the actual reason the loop ended.

Index to Programs

E

About Software on the Diskette

Using pcpix
pcpix *Error Messages*
Hung Programs, Infinite Loops, and Rebooting DOS
pcpix *Standard Pascal Language Features*
pcpix *Compiler Directives*
pcpix *Extended Pascal Language Features*

The diskette that comes with this book includes software for preparing and running Pascal programs, along with all code from the text, various data samples, and other miscellaneous goodies and documentation. You'll find installation instructions inside the back cover. Two particularly useful programs are:

look inside the back cover and on the diskette for more information

— pcpix is a command-line Pascal interpreter for MS-DOS. It's based on the Dr. Pascal programming environment from Visible Software, and is similar in operation to the UNIX Pascal load-and-go interpreter pix. A variety of features (e.g. references to uninitialized variables and nil pointers are detected at runtime) make is especially suitable for student work. I've documented it below, and there's more material on the disk.

— elvis is a public-domain version of the traditional UNIX editor vi. It was written by Steve Kirkendall, ported to MS-DOS by Guntran Blohn and Martin Patzel, and will run on any IBM-compatible computer. Your teacher can copy and distribute my tutorial *Facts Every Teenager Should Know about* Vi from the Instructor's Manual, since there's not enough room for it here (sorry!). It's on the diskette as well.

As I write this, Visible Software is working on a third program for all you Macintosh users out there. MacPIX is like pcpix, but it runs on Apple computers. If you have a Mac diskette you'll find additional documentation on-line.

I've hunted for and supplied these tools because many schools make students use centralized computer systems. My own students have let me know just how frustrating it is to have to wait in line for a terminal when they have their own perfectly good computers at home. Unfortunately, most commercially available Pascal systems have so many extensions built into them that programs that worked fine at home won't run properly on the school's computer. pcpix and MacPIX, like the Dr. Pascal interpreter they're based on, are honest-to-goodness Standard Pascal systems. Your programs should move painlessly from home to school.

a plea for help

> I've tried to arrange the diskette so that it's easy to understand and use. However, whenever I have to choose between *a)* supplying as much free stuff as possible, and *b)* avoiding potential problems by providing the bare minimum, I usually go with the first option. PLEASE help each other out. And, a few years down the road, you should start thinking about putting some software in the public domain yourself!

Using pcpix

First, install pcpix according to the instructions inside the back cover. To test-run a Pascal program, go to the directory that contains **sample.pas** (there's a copy of it in the **book** directory) and type:

```
c:\book>  pcpix sample.pas
```

I've shown the DOS prompt as c:\book>, but yours might be different. After you hit Enter here's what you'll see:

running a short program

```
c:\book>  pcpix sample.pas
Translation begins...
Execution begins...
Guess what?  You just ran a Pascal program!
Execution ends.
```

program files must be
plain ASCII

Pascal programs must be plain ASCII files (like the ones that **elvis** produces). They can't contain the formatting commands that many word processors use. If you rely on a word processor to create programs, be sure to save them as plain ASCII text.

pcpix works in two steps.

— First, it prints Translation begins, and translates the Pascal program into a form the computer can *execute*, or run.

— Then, it prints Execution begins, and executes the translated program. When the program is done, pcpix prints Execution ends.

The first step is similar to the operation of the UNIX pi command, while the second is like the UNIX px. Like pi, pcpix is designed to find and diagnose program errors, if there are any, very quickly. Unlike pi, it doesn't save a permanent copy of the executable program.

pcpix has two command-line options. **/r** repeats program execution and is useful for program testing. When you use the **/r** option, the program is translated only once:

the **/r** option repeats
execution

```
c:\book>  pcpix sample.pas /r
Translation begins...
Execution begins...
Guess what?  You just ran a Pascal program!
Repeat execution? (Y/N) y
Guess what?  You just ran a Pascal program!
Repeat execution? (Y/N) n
Execution ends.
```

The second option, **/L** (or **/l**), translates the program, then echoes it with error messages (see below) as they would appear on-screen, but does not run it. This option is useful for getting a program *listing* (hard copy) with error messages in place.

the /L option produces a listing with error messages

```
c:\book>  pcpix sample.pas /L
```
  Print the program and errors on-screen.
```
c:\book>  pcpix sample.pas /L > prn
```
  Send the program, with error messages, to the printer.

pcpix Error Messages

A program can fail in three different ways:

syntax errors

— A *syntax* error is a mistake in Pascal's grammer. pcpix will spot the error during translation, and print a *syntax error diagnostic*. You have to fix the error before the program can be translated and run correctly. Syntax errors are very common, even for experienced programmers, so don't be discouraged if you get a few.

runtime errors

— A *runtime* error occurs when a program is executing. Typical causes are referring to an undefined variable, trying to divide a number by zero, or typing in a word when the program expected a number. The consequence is a *crash* (the program stops) and a *postmortem diagnostic* that explains what went wrong.

semantic errors

— A *semantic* error is a mistake in a program's results. The only way to find semantic errors is by program testing.

Many times pcpix is able to figure out what the syntax error is by looking at the context it was spotted in. For example, if the reserved word **program** doesn't appear at the beginning of a program, it's obvious to pcpix what the fix should be:

a syntax error diagnostic

```
c:\book>  pcpix headbug.pas
Translation begins...
   3  var Counter: integer;
E274    ^ Program heading:  'program' expected
Continue listing errors? (Y/N)              etc.
```

pcpix prints the line number the error was spotted on (3, above), as well as an internal error number (E274 here) that has no official Pascal meaning. Note that pcpix can't always tell exactly what the error was—it just recognizes that the current word or line seems out of place.

If it can, pcpix will temporarily apply the fix it thinks is correct, then go looking for more errors. *All errors must be fixed before the program can be run.*

pcpix describes just one line's errors at a time. That's because an error early in a program can cause a slew of spurious, nonexistent errors to be diagnosed later on. It's a good idea to have a listing, or hard-copy printout, of your program on hand as you debug it. Don't try to fix more than a few errors at a time—mark and fix the ones you're sure of first.

Here's what a runtime error looks like. Assume that this program tries to divide the first number by the second:

a runtime error
postmortem

```
c:\book>  pcpix realbug.pas
Translation begins...
Execution begins...
Give me two numbers to divide:  1   0
Runtime error in realbug at line 10:
Integer divide by zero
```

There is extensive documentation of the pcpix runtime errors on the diskette.

Hung Programs, Infinite Loops, and Rebooting DOS

It is possible for a Pascal program to fail in a way that either *a*) doesn't cause a runtime error, or *b*) causes a runtime error that *hangs*, or locks up, a PC. pcpix can't report on such errors, of course.

killing a program

You'll know if you're in this predicament if a program takes far longer than you expect to produce output, or if the computer stops responding to keyboard input. To kill a DOS program, press and hold the keys Ctrl C at the same time. If that doesn't work, try Ctrl Break instead.

If the DOS prompt doesn't reappear, you may have to reboot your computer. First, make sure there aren't any diskettes inserted in the diskette drive (unless you need to boot from one, of course). Press the three-key combination Ctrl Alt Delete and wait a moment. If nothing happens, you'll have to press the computer's reset button or turn the power off and on again.

pcpix Standard Pascal Language Features

Identifiers: Lower- and upper-case letters are equivalent, and any length is allowed. The underscore character is allowed only if Extended Pascal is enabled (see below).

Ranges: integer values fall into the range $-32767 .. 32767$. real values use IEEE double-precision format; exponents from $-308 .. 308$ are permitted, and roughly fifteen digits of decimal accuracy are provided.

Field widths: Defaults are seven spaces for integer values, twenty-three for real. The first character in floating point output is either a space or a minus sign.

Comments: Comments may not appear within comments, even if the alternative brackets (* and *) are used.

Sets: Sets may have 256 members, so **set of** char is legal.

Strings: An array declared as a **packed array** [1 .. *n*] **of** char is a string type, as described in Chapter 9. Any string constant assigned to such an array must have the same length—pcpix will not pad the string with blanks if it's too short (unless Extended Pascal is enabled, below).

pcpix Compiler Directives

By default, pcpix processes programs written in Standard Pascal. However, instructions to the compiler can be embedded within a program to enable certain features. The comment must appear before the start of the program, like this:

enabling Extended
Pascal

```
{%E+}
program UseExtensions (input, output);    etc.
```

The rest of the program proceeds normally. Multiple directives may be merged in a single comment, e.g. {*%E+,O+*}.

{*%E+*} enables the Extended Pascal features described in detail below.

{*%O+*} enables nonstandard file-handling procedures. In Standard Pascal, a disk file's actual name must appear in the program heading. In effect, this requires file names to be hard-wired into programs, and makes it impossible to supply a file name when the program actually runs. pcpix provides two-argument forms of reset and rewrite as found in Berkeley Pascal and THINK Pascal:

using real file names

```
program Testing (input, output, F, G);
        {Demonstrates extended file procedures.}
var F, G: text;  {Files must appear in the heading and be declared as usual.}
begin
    reset (F, 'File.In');    {Opens File.In for reading.}
    rewrite (G, 'File.Out');    {Opens File.Out for reading.}
    {F and G now refer to actual files.}
    ...  etc.
```

There are also two-argument forms of assign and open; e.g. assign (F, *'name'*). These are identical in effect, and must be followed by Standard Pascal calls of reset or rewrite.

{*%T+*} prohibits legal Standard Pascal constructs that are not implemented in Turbo Pascal. This option does *not* let pcpix run any Turbo Pascal program. Instead, it helps verify that a program developed using a Standard Pascal system will also run on a Turbo Pascal system.

pcpix Extended Pascal Language Features

pcpix makes various features of Extended Pascal available. I've described these features *very* briefly, since pcpix isn't exactly the right tool to use to write industrial strength Extended Pascal programs! To enable the Extended Pascal features, your program must begin with the compiler directive {*%E+*} as described above. The new features include:

Underscore: The underscore character may appear in identifiers, but not as the first or last character; nor may two underscores appear in a row.

Extended numbers: A whole number can start with a base (or radix) followed by the # character and the rest of the number. For example, 16#FF represents 255 in base 16, and 2#101 represents 5 in base 2. Such numbers can be used as constants only, and they may not be written or read.

Termination: Procedure HALT terminates program execution immediately.

String padding: When strings with unequal lengths are compared, the shorter one is automatically padded with blanks to make the comparison legal. Similarly, a short string is automatically padded with blanks so that it may be assigned to a longer string-type array.

Extended string type: The type STRING is predefined. A STRING definition must specify the string's maximum length, given between parentheses:

```
{Two Extended Pascal string definitions.}
type Short = STRING (5);
     Long = STRING (255);
```

Extended string operations: There are a number of ways to work with both standard (fixed-length) string types, and the Extended Pascal variable-length string types. Note that the functions described here return structured types, also permitted by Standard Pascal.

— length(S) is a function call that returns the length of the string S.

— index(S1, S2) is a function call that decides if S2 is a substring of (is found within) S1. If it is, index returns the starting position of the first occurence. If it isn't found, index returns zero.

— substr(S1, i, j) is a function call that returns the substring, within S1, that begins in position i and has j characters.

— trim(S) is a function that returns the value of its argument, but with all trailing (ending) blanks removed.

— + serves as a concatenation operator, so ´ab´ + ´cde´ equals ´abcde´.

— S[$i .. j$] represents a string that consists of the ith through jth components of string S. This form may appear on the left-hand side of an assignment.

Date and time: A type TimeSTAMP is predefined:

```
type TimeSTAMP = packed record
                DateValid, TimeValid: boolean;
                year: 1 .. MAXINT;
                month: 1 .. 12;
                day: 1 .. 31;
                hour: 0 .. 23;
                minute: 0 .. 59;
                second: 0 .. 59;
                millisecond: 0 .. 999;  {This is a pcpix extension.}
            end;
```

A procedure and two functions use TimeSTAMP variables. Assume that Store has type TimeSTAMP:

— Procedure GetTimeStamp (Store) assigns values to all the Store fields.

— Function Time (Store) returns a string that represents the saved time.

— Function Date (Store) returns a string that represents the saved date.

Ordinal functions: succ and pred may be given a second integer argument that indicates how much to increment or decrement the first argument by.

A few additional features of Extended Pascal are too complicated to explain in the space available here. They include:

Functions: Functions may return structured types, except for files. Aliases, called *result variable specifications*, may be used to refer to the function without call int.

File binding: A variety of extensions that permit runtime file binding are implemented.

Index

Dr. Pascal from Visible Software

✓ *Dr. Pascal* is a system for writing, running, and debugging Pascal programs. It lets users look inside their programs as they run — a capability that facilitates the discovery and understanding of errors. Dr. Pascal has many features that make writing, testing, and modifying Pascal programs easier. In this course, Dr. Pascal would be used in place of the PCPIX interpreter and a text editor. Why buy Dr. Pascal for $39 when PCPIX is free? Because...

✓ *Dr. Pascal will help you do well in this course.* Although PCPIX can run all the programs in the text, an integrated environment like Dr. Pascal will make it much easier to do the course's programming problems. Dr. Pascal's visible execution will also make it easier for you to learn Pascal. Also...

✓ *Dr. Pascal will save you time and frustration.* Dr. Pascal is much faster to use than PCPIX and other Pascal systems. You can see exactly what your program is doing and instantly move from editing to running to debugging, while the 'Pascal Keys' let you type whole Pascal structures with a single keystroke. With the visible capability and Dr. Pascal's extensive error checking, people find their errors more quickly and get their programs finished and working correctly.

A complete Pascal system Dr. Pascal edits and runs your programs — no other software is required. Programs are automatically indented and formatted.

Visible execution Each line is highlighted as it executes, allowing you literally to watch your program as it runs. Experienced programmers find bugs more quickly, and novices learn to program more easily.

Error checks Dr. Pascal extensively error checks programs as they run, and indicates the exact location and cause of errors. This makes it easy to find errors — like 'undefined values' — that are hard to identify in other Pascal systems.

Screen editor Dr. Pascal's integrated editor can be used to write and edit programs. Instantly switch from debugging to editing and back.

Procedure editor The procedure editor recognizes procedures as syntactic units. It lets you inspect, edit, or move procedures independently.

ISO Standard Pascal Dr. Pascal fully implements the nationally (IEEE, ANSI) and internationally (ISO, BSI) recognized Pascal standard. Programs written with Dr. Pascal will almost always run correctly on other Pascal systems, even on different types of computers.

Extended/Turbo features Dr. Pascal makes additional features of Extended Pascal available. In addition, a *Turbo* option disables Standard Pascal features that are not available in Turbo Pascal.

Dr. Pascal is supplied on a single diskette and comes complete with extensive documentation and single-user license. Normal retail price is $89, but purchasers of *Oh! Pascal!* qualify to receive the full Dr. Pascal environment for just $39, plus $4 shipping/handling (mention order code N-1).

Also Available from Visible Software

✓ *Professional Extended Pascal Compiler:* If your interest in programming goes beyond class exercises, Visible Software provides an Extended Pascal compiler for MS-DOS. This compiler will produce executable files (.EXE) from Pascal programs developed ith Dr. Pascal or PCPIX.

Features   Optimize code for smallest space or fastest execution; target 8088, 80286, 80386 or higher Intel processors with or without math coprocessors; link to Intel standard format object files; trap errors; many features for low-level programming of memory locations, interrupts, BIOS, DOS, etc. Default 32-bit integer and 64-bit IEEE real types. No 64K limit on programs, modules, or global data. Includes excellent separate compilation features derived from Modula-2.

Language   Provides four switch-selectable levels of standard compatibility: 0) ISO/ANSI Standard Pascal, 1) Level 1 Pascal with conformant arrays, 2) a large subset of ANSI/IEEE/ISO Extended Pascal, and 3) all of the preceding with platform-specific extensions.

Portability   ANSI/IEEE/ISO Extended Pascal is an international standard — not a loose collection of operating-system dependent features. Programs developed on DOS can be ported to larger machines that support the new standard.

✓ *Public Domain Programming Tools:* A suite of tools for programming projects, including *Compare* for file comparison, *Version* to maintain several versions of a single program, *Crossref* to cross reference programs, and *Analyze* for execution timing and analysis. The tools are supplied with both Pascal source (requires extended Pascal compiler) and precompiled executables.

✓ *Public Domain Pascal-S:* Complete Standard Pascal source code for a Pascal subset compiler. This is an excellent example of how a language compiler works. Comes with documentation by Niklaus Wirth.

To order, or for more information, photocopy (or handwrite) and mail the order form below, or call Visible Software directly. Phone orders can be made at any time of day or night on the answering machine, but remember to mention order code N-1.

Visible Software / Box 949 / Newark, DE. 19715-0949 / Phone: (302) 455-9400

Using the Diskette

The diskette opposite contains all program code from *Oh! Pascal!*, as well as a PC or Macintosh-based Standard Pascal interpreter based on Visible Software's *Dr. Pascal* (see their special offer, below), a PC-based text editor, and a variety of useful data files. Since the book (and this page) goes into production long before the diskette does, you'll find additional information in the diskette itself. Type **readme** (or click on the appropriate icon) to get started.

If you're familiar with the terms used below, please help somebody who isn't.

PC Notes

To help keep things as simple as possible on the PC side, I've used a high-capacity diskette and avoided elaborate compression. Two DOS batch files, **to360.bat** and **to720.bat**, are supplied to split the diskette into lower-capacity diskettes. Type **to360** or **to720** for instructions.

Installing software and other files is a two-step process. You should keep the original diskette, but you can remove compressed files from your main drive after uncompressing.

— First, copy files from the diskette to your hard drive or to another diskette.

— Second, and only if necessary, uncompress the files on your hard disk.

The diskette has three main *directories* of files:

code holds **pcpix** (a Pascal interpreter), **elvis** (a text editor), and associated files and documentation.

book contains additional subdirectories. They hold all of the book's example Pascal programs, organized by chapter.

data holds files of data that may be useful for programming assignments or trying out ideas.

Where should files from the diskette go?

code files — **pcpix.exe**, **elvis.exe**, and **dperrors** — can go anywhere. There are two ways to make sure that DOS will be able to find them:

— Install them in a directory DOS already searches. You can find out the names of these directories by typing **path** as a DOS command. DOS will print a list of drive and directory names, separated by semicolons.

— Install the files in a new directory, and add its name to your existing search path. The current path name is set in your **autoexec.bat** file — you'll find a call of the DOS **path** command there.

If you have a ramdisk, improve **elvis**'s performance by by identifying it with an environment variable named **TMP**. Add the DOS **set** command (e.g. **set TMP=e:**) to your **autoexec.bat** file.

book subdirectories and files should go into their own directory. Keeping each chapter's programs in a separate directory seems wasteful at first, but it's much easier to keep things straight in the long run.

`mkdir c:\book`	*Make a directory called **book***
`xcopy a:\book /s c:\book`	*Copy all files, including subdirectories, from the **book** directory on drive **a** to the **book** directory on drive **c**.*

data files should go where they're needed — usually into the directory that contains the program that will use the data.

Macintosh Notes

Put the diskette in the drive and double-click on the icon to unstuff and install all software. (Yes, this looks awfully like one of those Macintosh vs. Windows advertisements, but the Mac really is easier to deal with!)

Special Offer on Dr. Pascal — Turn the Page!

The pcpix or MacPIX software is based on the Dr. Pascal visible programming environment — a high-quality learning tool from Visible Software that lets you watch programs as they run. Dr. Pascal is available at reduced cost to readers of *Oh! Pascal!* Turn the page for product and ordering information.